SSAT/ISEE
SUCCESS

2005

SSAT/ISEE SUCCESS

2005

Reading: Elaine Bender, Jeffrey E. Levitsky
Mathematics: Christi Heuer, Mark Weinfeld
Verbal Analysis: Dominic Marullo, Patricia Burgess
Writing: Jo Norris Palmore

Includes a vocabulary-building chapter
by Merriam-Webster—with Greek and
Latin roots, quizzes, and a practice exam

Merriam-Webster®

THOMSON

PETERSON'S

Australia • Canada • Mexico • Singapore • Spain • United Kingdom • United St...

About Thomson Peterson's

Thomson Peterson's (www.petersons.com) is a leading provider of education information and advice, with books and online resources focusing on education search, test preparation, and financial aid. Its Web site offers searchable databases and interactive tools for contacting educational institutions, online practice tests and instruction, and planning tools for securing financial aid. Thomson Peterson's serves 110 million education consumers annually.

Editorial Development: American BookWorks Corporation

Special thanks to Joan Marie Rosebush and Amy Kierce

Petersons.com/publishing

Check out our Web site at www.petersons.com/publishing to see if there is any new information regarding the test and any revisions or corrections to the content of this book. We've made sure the information in this book is accurate and up-to-date; however, the test format or content may have changed since the time of publication.

For more information, contact Thomson Peterson's, 2000 Lenox Drive, Lawrenceville, NJ 08648; 800-338-3282; or find us on the World Wide Web at www.petersons.com/about.

Editor: Joe Ziegler; Production Editor: Teresina Jonkoski; Manufacturing Manager: Ray Golaszewski; Composition Manager: Gary Rozmierski; Interior and Cover Design: Allison Sullivan.

ISBN 0-7689-1612-7

Printed in the United States of America

10 9 8 7 6 5 4 3 2 1   06 05 04

Fifth Edition

CONTENTS

INTRODUCTION

ABOUT THIS BOOK

If you're reading this book now, it's likely you're planning to take a very important test—either the Secondary School Admission Test (SSAT) or the Independent School Entrance Examination (ISEE). The results of these tests can well determine whether you'll be accepted to your first-choice private high school. This book is part of our popular "Success" series and is designed to help you prepare for these tests. It is an accepted fact that the more you practice, the better you will do on the test. Therefore, we have provided plenty of practice material for you.

The book is set up to take you step-by-step through each test. The first part of the book contains two diagnostic tests, one for the SSAT and one for the ISEE. Use the results of these diagnostics to evaluate your strengths and weaknesses. While it is important to study and review everything that will appear on the test, the diagnostic test will help you focus on those subjects that need additional work.

After the diagnostics, you will find review material for the four major areas covered on both exams: Verbal Analysis, Mathematics, Reading Comprehension, and Writing an Essay. Read through and study these chapters, answer the practice questions, and take notes on anything you don't understand. You should then ask one of your teachers to help you. You will also find "Merriam-Webster's Roots to Word Mastery," a special vocabulary-building chapter. Written by the staff at Merriam-Webster exclusively for Peterson's test-prep students, this chapter will help you prepare for your exam by building your vocabulary through Greek and Latin word roots.

The third section of the book presents two full-length sample tests for both the SSAT and ISEE tests. Take the tests under conditions that are similar to the actual exam. For example, the actual SSAT consists of five sections, and you are given 25 minutes to complete the writing section and 30 minutes to complete each of the four multiple-choice sections. However, one section is experimental and does not count toward your final score. Therefore, you will have only four sections on the SSAT tests in this book, so allocate about 2 hours for each test. The actual ISEE contains five sections and takes almost 3 hours, so give yourself enough time to take the sample tests at the end of this book.

We suggest that you take each test, and after a break, check your answers. If you don't understand why you got something wrong, go back and look at the questions again. Then look in the review sections for clarification, and if you still don't understand the answer, go to one of your teachers for help.

ABOUT THE TESTS

THE SSAT

Let's look closely at each exam, starting with the SSAT. As we said, the actual exam consists of five sections. The questions are multiple choice, with five choices each. (The ISEE questions have only four choices.) The questions cover the following topics:

Writing Sample
Verbal
Quantitative
Reading Comprehension

The following chart will give you an idea of what to expect.

Writing Sample	1 topic	25 minutes
Verbal	30 synonyms 30 analogies	30 minutes
Quantitative	2 sections 25 questions each	60 minutes
Reading Comprehension	7 reading passages 40 questions	30 minutes

All questions are equal in value, and there is no penalty for unanswered questions. However, you will lose ¼ point for incorrect answers. It is therefore suggested that if you have a pretty good idea of the answer, perhaps narrowed down to two choices out of five, you should take a chance and guess. If you're truly in the dark, leave that question unanswered.

THE ISEE

The Upper Level ISEE (candidates for grades 9–12) consists of five sections. Except for the essay portion, all questions are multiple choice. The five sections are:

Verbal Reasoning
Quantitative Reasoning
Reading Comprehension
Math Achievement
Essay

Did you notice that there are two math sections? However, the Quantitative Reasoning section is somewhat different than the Math Achievement questions. One half of the questions are regular mathematics, and the other half are called "quantitative comparisons." You are asked to compare two unknowns and make a determination between these as to which is the greater, if they are equal, or if the answer cannot be determined from the given information. You can find greater detail later in this book.

Here is how the sections appear:

Verbal Reasoning	20 synonyms 20 sentence completions	20 minutes
Quantitative Reasoning	35 questions	35 minutes
Reading Comprehension	9 reading passages 40 questions	40 minutes
Math Achievement	45 mathematical ability	40 minutes
Essay	1 topic	30 minutes

The scoring for the ISEE is different than that of the SSAT, since you are not penalized for incorrect answers. It's important to try to make educated guesses using the process of elimination, but NEVER leave an unanswered question on this examination. Since there are only four choices, you have at least a 25 percent chance of getting the answer right—and even if you get it wrong, there's no penalty.

ABOUT YOUR SCORES

Both tests are scored on a scale, and you are ranked against other students. Both the SSAT and ISEE scores are sent to you (or your parents), and you will receive diagnostic information. This report also goes out to the schools (at your request) to which you are applying, and they can use those scores to develop an instructional plan for you.

AN IMPORTANT NOTE FOR EIGHTH AND NINTH GRADERS

You may find that some of the test questions that appear on the SSAT or ISEE are extremely difficult or cover material that you have not yet been exposed to. This is intentional. Keep in mind that the same upper-level exam is administered to students in grades 8, 9, 10, and 11. However, your final score will only be compared to the scores of other students in your grade. When the Secondary School Admission Test Board and the Educational Records Bureau send admissions officers your scores, they'll include the average test scores of all students your age who have taken the test. No one expects you to compete against older students, so don't worry if you encounter vocabulary questions that seem too advanced or math concepts that you haven't mastered in school yet. It won't be held against you. Besides, because you're working with this book, you'll be better prepared to deal with those tough questions when you take the real test!

ADDITIONAL INFORMATION

To get an application booklet and additional information, you can call or write to the following:

SSAT

Secondary School Admission Test Board
CN 5339
Princeton, New Jersey 08543
Telephone: 609-683-4440
Fax: 800-442-7728 (toll-free)
E-mail: ssatics@ssatb.com
World Wide Web: http://www.ssat.org

ISEE

ISEE Operations Office	or	Educational Records Bureau
423 Morris Street		220 East 42nd Street, Suite 100
Durham, North Carolina 27701		New York, New York 10017
Telephone: 800-446-0320		Telephone: 800-989-3721
(toll-free)		(toll-free)
Fax: 919-682-5775		
E-mail: isee@erbtest.com		
World Wide Web:		
http://www.erbtest.org		

One final reminder: Although these tests are important, they are not the entire picture that will be looked at by the school to which you apply. They will take into account your academic performance, extracurricular activities, and so on. Keep in mind that these tests do not measure how smart you are. Like most standardized tests, they measure your ability to take these types of tests. And to do well, you must practice, practice, practice.

Good Luck!

PETERSON'S PRIVATE SCHOOL RESOURCES

PRIVATE SCHOOL SNAPSHOTS

In the following pages you will find valuable data on private secondary schools from *Peterson's Guide to Private Secondary Schools 2005*. These snapshots will guide your search, whether you're focused on a specific geographic region or across the country. We've provided quick answers to key questions about each school, such as:

- Are its students boarding, day, or both?
- Is it coeducational?
- What grades are offered at the school?
- How many students are enrolled?
- What is the student/faculty ratio?

The chart also provides information about Advanced Placement subject areas and sports.

PETERSON'S GUIDE TO PRIVATE SECONDARY SCHOOLS 2005

Once you've used the following chart to help you identify prospective schools, be sure to check out *Peterson's Guide to Private Secondary Schools 2005*, the only comprehensive private school guide available. You'll find detailed profiles on approximately 1,500 accredited private schools worldwide, as well as valuable advice on planning your search and financing a private school education.

	STUDENTS ACCEPTED				GRADES			STUDENT/FACULTY			SCHOOL OFFERINGS (number)	
	Boarding		Day									
	Boys	Girls	Boys	Girls	Lower	Middle	Upper	Total	Upper	Student/ Faculty Ratio	Advanced Placement Subject Areas	Sports
Alabama												
Alabama Christian Academy, Montgomery			X	X	K4–5	6–8	9–12	955	325	22:1		14
The Altamont School, Birmingham			X	X	5–8		9–12	416	204	5:1	17	14
American Christian Academy, Tuscaloosa			X	X	K–6	7–9	10–12	595	123	12:1	2	32
Bayside Academy, Daphne			X	X	PS–6	7–8	9–12	660	230	8:1	11	23
Houston Academy, Dothan			X	X	PK–6		7–12	620	274	12:1	8	8
Indian Springs School, Indian Springs	X	X	X	X			8–PG	264	264	9:1	18	14
Lee-Scott Academy, Auburn			X	X	PK–6		7–12	642	278	12:1	4	10
Lyman Ward Military Academy, Camp Hill	X				6–8		9–12	240	105	12:1	3	30
Madison Academy, Madison			X	X	PS–6		7–12	845	390	15:1		3
Marion Military Institute, Marion	X	X	X	X			9–12	115	115	12:1		40
Mars Hill Bible School, Florence			X	X	K–4	5–8	9–12	568	192	12:1	5	31
McGill Toolen Catholic High School, Mobile			X	X			9–12	1,052	1,052	13:1	6	18
The Montgomery Academy, Montgomery			X	X	K–4	5–8	9–12	827	249	7:1	18	14
Randolph School, Huntsville			X	X	K–6	7–8	9–12	757	252	12:1	16	16
St. Bernard Preparatory School, Inc., Cullman	X	X	X	X			9–12	116	116	7:1	2	11
Saint James School, Montgomery			X	X	PK–5	6–8	9–12	1,167	360	22:1	13	18
St. Paul's Episcopal School, Mobile			X	X	PK–5	6–8	9–12	1,610	564	16:1	6	15
Shades Mountain Christian School, Hoover			X	X	K4–6	7–8	9–12	462	147	22:1	2	14
Three Springs, Huntsville	X	X								10:1		14
Tuscaloosa Academy, Tuscaloosa			X	X	PK–4	5–8	9–12	518	161	16:1	8	11
Westminster Christian Academy, Huntsville			X	X	K4–6	7–8	9–12	746	223	12:1	5	13
Alaska												
Grace Christian School, Anchorage			X	X	K–6		7–12	701	374	21:1	6	8
Heritage Christian High School, Anchorage			X	X	K–6	7–8	9–12	364	172	13:1	2	8
Pacific Northern Academy, Anchorage			X	X	K–5	6–8	9–12	205	33			
Arizona												
Alpha Omega Academy, Chandler			X	X				2,300		100:1		
Arizona's Children Association Zemsky-Covert School, Tucson	X	X	X	X	K–6	7–8	9–12	60	12	12:1		
Brophy College Preparatory, Phoenix			X				9–12	1,210	1,210	15:1	14	40
Desert Christian High School, Tucson			X	X		6–8	9–12	355	218	13:1		10
The Fenster School of Southern Arizona, Tucson	X	X	X	X			9–12	120	120	8:1	1	16
Green Fields Country Day School, Tucson			X	X	3–5	6–8	9–12	186	98	4:1	6	13
New Way Learning Academy, Scottsdale			X	X	K–5	6–8	9–12	130	40	8:1		
Northwest Community Christian School, Phoenix			X	X	PK–6	7–8	9–12	1,288	325	14:1	1	9
Oak Creek Ranch School, West Sedona	X	X				6–8	9–12	83	72	8:1		55
The Orme School, Mayer	X	X	X	X		7–8	9–PG	130	114	6:1	5	45
Phoenix Christian High School, Phoenix			X	X		7–8	9–12	529	406	17:1	5	15
Phoenix Country Day School, Paradise Valley			X	X	PK–4	5–8	9–12	736	258	9:1	15	12
St. Gregory College Preparatory School, Tucson			X	X		6–8	9–PG	406	229	16:1	12	23
St. Paul's Preparatory Academy, Phoenix	X		X				9–12	75	75	10:1		5

| | STUDENTS ACCEPTED | | | | GRADES | | | STUDENT/FACULTY | | | SCHOOL OFFERINGS (number) | |
| | Boarding | | Day | | | | | | | | | |
	Boys	Girls	Boys	Girls	Lower	Middle	Upper	Total	Upper	Student/ Faculty Ratio	Advanced Placement Subject Areas	Sports
Arizona—continued												
Salpointe Catholic High School, Tucson			X	X			9–12	1,314	1,314	25:1	12	18
Verde Valley School, Sedona	X	X	X	X			9–PG	88	88	5:1	6	44
Xavier College Preparatory, Phoenix				X			9–12	1,143	1,143	22:1	18	21
Arkansas												
Pulaski Academy, Little Rock			X	X	PK–4	5–8	9–12	1,270	381	13:1	16	21
Subiaco Academy, Subiaco	X		X				9–12	190	190	6:1	10	57
California												
Academy of Our Lady of Peace, San Diego				X			9–12	760	760	15:1	9	9
Anacapa School, Santa Barbara			X	X	7–8		9–12	56	34	12:1	1	12
The Archer School for Girls, Los Angeles				X		6–8	9–12	450	230	6:1	12	13
Army and Navy Academy, Carlsbad	X		X			7–8	9–12	311	262	9:1	9	36
Arrowhead Christian Academy, Redlands			X	X		6–8	9–12	584	370	15:1		13
Arrowsmith Academy, Berkeley			X	X			9–12	120	120	10:1	2	8
The Athenian School, Danville	X	X	X	X		6–8	9–12	447	292	9:1	11	14
Balboa City School, San Diego			X	X				100				3
Bentley School, Oakland			X	X	K–5	6–8	9–12	600	248	8:1	15	14
Bishop Alemany High School, Mission Hills			X	X			9–12	1,519	1,519	18:1	11	16
Bishop Conaty-Our Lady of Loretto High School, Los Angeles				X			9–12	472	472	17:1	5	5
Bishop Montgomery High School, Torrance			X	X			9–12	1,132	1,132	17:1	11	15
The Bishop's School, La Jolla			X	X		7–8	9–12	660	472	8:1	19	17
The Branson School, Ross			X	X			9–12	320		15:1	13	15
Brentwood School, Los Angeles			X	X	K–6	7–8	9–12	988	463	10:1	19	19
Bridgemont High School, San Francisco			X	X		6–8	9–12	89	52	7:1	3	8
Bridges Academy, Sherman Oaks			X	X		6–8	9–12	83	57	9:1		2
The Buckley School, Sherman Oaks			X	X	K–5	6–8	9–12	761	293	7:1	17	9
Calvary Chapel High School, Downey			X	X	K–6	7–8	9–12	1,168	385		6	18
Calvin Christian High School, Escondido			X	X	PK–5	6–8	9–12	638	229	15:1	5	10
Campbell Hall (Episcopal), North Hollywood			X	X	K–6	7–8	9–12	800	300	8:1	17	18
Capistrano Valley Christian Schools, San Juan Capistrano			X	X	PS–6	7–8	9–12	745	220	9:1	7	12
Cardinal Newman High School, Santa Rosa			X				9–12	419	419	15:1	8	17
Castilleja School, Palo Alto				X		6–8	9–12	416	236	6:1	18	12
Cate School, Carpinteria	X	X	X	X			9–12	265	265	5:1	19	28
CEDU Schools, Running Springs	X	X						145	90			12
Central Catholic High School, Modesto			X	X			9–12	448	448	23:1	8	14
Chadwick School, Palos Verdes Peninsula			X	X	K–6	7–8	9–12	764	307	6:1	13	18
Chaminade College Preparatory, West Hills			X	X			9–12	1,079	1,079	18:1	18	31
Christian Junior-Senior High School, El Cajon			X	X		7–8	9–12	624	391	11:1	5	12
The College Preparatory School, Oakland			X	X			9–12	328	328	8:1	11	13
Convent of the Sacred Heart High School, San Francisco				X			9–12	204	204	6:1	19	11
Cornelia Connelly School, Anaheim				X			9–12	233	233	16:1	12	9
Crespi Carmelite High School, Encino			X				9–12	533	533	13:1	11	13

	STUDENTS ACCEPTED				GRADES			STUDENT/FACULTY			SCHOOL OFFERINGS (number)	
	Boarding		Day									
	Boys	Girls	Boys	Girls	Lower	Middle	Upper	Total	Upper	Student/ Faculty Ratio	Advanced Placement Subject Areas	Sports
California—*continued*												
Crossroads School for Arts & Sciences, Santa Monica			X	X	K-5	6-8	9-12	1,139	491	17:1	13	10
Crystal Springs Uplands School, Hillsborough			X	X		6-8	9-12	357	251	10:1	15	9
Damien High School, La Verne			X				9-12	1,170	1,170	22:1	19	24
De La Salle High School, Concord			X				9-12	1,035	1,035	28:1	9	20
Delphi Academy of Los Angeles, Lake View Terrace			X	X	K-3	4-8	9-12	260	88	18:1		19
Don Bosco High School, Rosemead			X				9-12	900	900	30:1		16
Drew College Preparatory School, San Francisco			X	X			9-12	233	233	10:1	8	21
Dunn School, Los Olivos	X	X	X	X		6-8	9-12	234	176	7:1	11	31
Emerson Honors High Schools, Orange	X		X	X	K-6		7-12	183	83	20:1	4	9
Fairmont Private Schools and Preparatory Academy, Anaheim			X	X	PK-6	7-8	9-12	2,231	328	15:1	15	12
Flintridge Sacred Heart Academy, La Canada Flintridge		X		X			9-12	400	400	10:1	12	21
Fresno Christian Schools, Fresno			X	X	K-6	7-8	9-12	762	281	20:1	4	12
The Frostig School, Pasadena			X	X	1-5	6-8	9-12	120	48	6:1		4
Futures High School, Oceanside, Oceanside			X	X		7-8	9-12	30	27	1:1		
Futures High School—San Diego, San Diego			X	X			7-12	125	125	8:1	8	
Garces Memorial High School, Bakersfield			X	X			9-12	662	662	19:1	5	15
The Grauer School, Encinitas			X	X		6-8	9-12	92	56	7:1	2	28
Happy Valley School, Ojai	X	X	X	X			9-12	88	88	7:1	3	31
The Harker School, San Jose			X	X	K-6	7-8	9-12	1,584	564	11:1	18	14
Harvard-Westlake School, North Hollywood			X	X		7-9	10-12	1,551	819	8:1	19	20
The Head-Royce School, Oakland			X	X	K-5	6-8	9-12	750	315	9:1	19	20
Highland Hall, A Waldorf School, Northridge			X	X	N-6	7-8	9-12	386	107	6:1		7
Hillcrest Christian School, Granada Hills			X	X	K-5	6-8	9-12	820	170	10:1	4	8
Holy Names High School, Oakland				X			9-12	309	309	21:1	6	8
Idyllwild Arts Academy, Idyllwild	X	X	X	X		8	9-PG	246	240	12:1	4	19
International High School of FAIS, San Francisco			X	X			9-12	310	310	6:1	14	24
Jesuit High School, Carmichael			X				9-12	1,000	1,000	18:1	12	15
Junipero Serra High School, San Mateo			X				9-12	975	975	27:1	4	22
Justin-Siena High School, Napa			X	X			9-12	657	657	18:1	5	15
Kings Christian School, Lemoore			X	X	PK-6	7-8	9-12	355	124	14:1	1	17
La Cheim School, Pleasant Hill			X	X	1-5	6-8	9-12	42	24	4:1		7
Laguna Blanca School, Santa Barbara			X	X	K-4	5-8	9-12	380	180	12:1	19	19
La Jolla Country Day School, La Jolla			X	X	N-4	5-8	9-12	1,028	378	17:1	18	29
La Monte Academie, Laguna Hills			X	X	1-6	7-8	9-12	40	25	12:1		
Laurel Springs School, Ojai			X	X	1-4	5-8	9-12	3,655	1,473	1:1		20
Lick-Wilmerding High School, San Francisco			X	X			9-12	396	396	9:1	17	10
Linfield Christian School, Temecula			X	X	K-5	6-8	9-12	779	310	17:1	5	12
Loretto High School, Sacramento				X			9-12	535	535	13:1	6	19
Los Angeles Baptist Junior/Senior High School, North Hills			X	X		7-8	9-12	983	645	22:1	9	11

| | STUDENTS ACCEPTED | | | | GRADES | | | STUDENT/FACULTY | | | SCHOOL OFFERINGS (number) | |
| | Boarding | | Day | | | | | | | | | |
	Boys	Girls	Boys	Girls	Lower	Middle	Upper	Total	Upper	Student/Faculty Ratio	Advanced Placement Subject Areas	Sports
California—*continued*												
Los Angeles Lutheran High School, Sylmar			X	X		7-8	9-12	275	171	16:1		10
Louisville High School, Woodland Hills				X			9-12	507	507	15:1	15	11
Loyola High School, Jesuit College Preparatory, Los Angeles			X				9-12	1,210	1,210	14:1	19	13
Lutheran High School, La Verne			X	X			9-12	112	112	12:1	4	13
Lycee International de Los Angeles, Los Angeles			X	X	PK-5	6-8	9-12	384	62	8:1	3	11
Maranatha High School, Pasadena			X	X			9-12	418	418	11:1	11	13
Marin Academy, San Rafael			X	X			9-12	402	402	9:1	17	29
Marin Catholic High School College Preparatory, Kentfield			X	X			9-12	725	725	12:1	12	25
Marlborough School, Los Angeles				X		7-9	10-12	530	245	6:1	19	14
Marymount High School, Los Angeles				X			9-12	397	397	8:1	16	19
Mater Dei High School, Santa Ana			X	X			9-12	2,210	2,210	27:1	18	18
Mayfield Senior School, Pasadena				X			9-12	305	305	8:1	12	21
Menlo School, Atherton			X	X		6-8	9-12	755	539	11:1	19	16
Mercy High School College Preparatory, San Francisco				X			9-12	576	576	15:1	9	8
Mesa Grande Seventh-Day Academy, Calimesa			X	X	K-6	7-8	9-12	323	112	10:1		6
Midland School, Los Olivos	X	X					9-12	77	77	5:1		21
Milken Community High School of Stephen Wise Temple, Los Angeles			X	X		7-8	9-12	834	590	7:1	19	18
Modesto Adventist Academy, Ceres			X	X	K-5	6-8	9-12	290	110	11:1		11
Montclair College Preparatory School, Van Nuys	X	X	X	X	6-8		9-12	439	319	20:1	14	4
Monterey Bay Academy, La Selva Beach	X	X	X	X			9-12	236	236	14:1	1	4
Monte Vista Christian School, Watsonville	X	X	X	X		6-8	9-12	1,080	759	16:1	7	20
Moreau Catholic High School, Hayward			X	X			9-12	1,054	1,054	21:1	13	21
Mountain View Academy, Mountain View			X	X			9-12	162	162	14:1	2	5
NAWA Academy, French Gulch	X	X				7-8	9-12	34	30	8:1		77
North Hills Preparatory School, North Hills			X	X		7-8	9-12	109	101	12:1	4	4
Notre Dame Academy, Los Angeles				X			9-12	470	470	12:1	8	8
Notre Dame High School, Belmont				X			9-12	733	733	17:1	10	28
Oak Grove School, Ojai	X	X	X	X	PK-6	7-8	9-12	132	41	5:1	3	25
Oakwood School, North Hollywood			X	X	K-6		7-12	756	471	10:1	17	39
Ojai Valley School, Ojai	X	X	X	X	PK-5	6-8	9-12	355	118	5:1	7	37
Orinda Academy, Orinda			X	X		7-8	9-12	113	100	9:1		10
Oxford School, Rowland Heights			X	X		7-8	9-12	60	53	14:1	1	2
Pacific Academy, Encinitas			X	X				35	35	5:1		
Pacific Christian on the Hill, Los Angeles			X	X		7-8	9-12	103	66	16:1	6	14
Pacific Hills School, West Hollywood			X	X		6-8	9-12	290	187	15:1		8
Palma High School, Salinas			X			7-8	9-12	632	471	20:1	11	5
Paraclete High School, Lancaster			X	X			9-12	755	755	19:1	5	12
Providence High School, Burbank			X	X			9-12	550	550	24:1	11	12
Ramona Convent Secondary School, Alhambra				X		7-8	9-12	549	467	12:1	12	7
Ribet Academy, Los Angeles			X	X	1-5	6-8	9-12	504	220	15:1	13	24
Rio Hondo Preparatory School, Arcadia			X	X		6-8	9-12	166	71	4:1	7	6
Rio Lindo Adventist Academy, Healdsburg	X	X	X	X			9-12	170	170	8:1		15
Ripon Christian Schools, Ripon			X	X	K-5	6-8	9-12	735	260	20:1	1	14

	STUDENTS ACCEPTED				GRADES			STUDENT/FACULTY			SCHOOL OFFERINGS (number)	
	Boarding		Day									
	Boys	Girls	Boys	Girls	Lower	Middle	Upper	Total	Upper	Student/ Faculty Ratio	Advanced Placement Subject Areas	Sports
California—*continued*												
Rolling Hills Preparatory School, Palos Verdes Estates			X	X		6–8	9–12	260	152	9:1	8	18
Rosary High School, Fullerton				X					652	17:1	8	10
Sacramento Adventist Academy, Carmichael			X	X	K–6	7–8	9–12	384	154	12:1		5
Sacramento Country Day School, Sacramento			X	X	PK–5	6–8	9–12	544	141	10:1	11	8
Sacred Heart Cathedral Preparatory, San Francisco			X	X			9–12	1,254	1,254			16
Sacred Heart Preparatory, Atherton			X	X			9–12	466	466	8:1	13	16
Sage Hill School, Newport Coast			X	X			9–12	390	390	15:1	6	16
St. Catherine's Military School, Anaheim	X		X		K–6	7–8		180	80	12:1		16
Saint Elizabeth High School, Oakland			X	X			9–12	287	287	15:1	3	7
Saint Francis High School, La Canada Flintridge			X				9–12	610	610	15:1	13	9
Saint Francis High School, Mountain View			X	X			9–12	1,485	1,485	28:1	16	30
St. Ignatius College Preparatory, San Francisco			X	X			9–12	1,416	1,416	12:1	14	21
Saint John Bosco High School, Bellflower			X				9–12	1,123	1,123	16:1	11	14
St. Margaret's Episcopal School, San Juan Capistrano			X	X	N–5	6–8	9–12	1,211	380	12:1	19	24
Saint Mary's College High School, Berkeley			X	X			9–12	630	630	17:1	7	16
Saint Monica's High School, Santa Monica			X	X			9–12	621	621	15:1	5	13
Saint Patrick—Saint Vincent High School, Vallejo			X	X			9–12	645	645	30:1	7	13
Salesian High School, Richmond			X	X			9–12	570	570	25:1	7	10
San Domenico School, San Anselmo		X	X	X	PK–5	6–8	9–12	550	142	9:1	9	34
San Francisco University High School, San Francisco			X	X			9–12	414	414	8:1	18	22
Santa Catalina School, Monterey		X	X	X	PK–5	6–8	9–12	556	294	7:1	19	41
Servite High School, Anaheim			X				9–12	779	779	19:1	14	11
Southwestern Academy, San Marino	X	X	X	X	6–8		9–PG	222	174	4:1	11	32
Squaw Valley Academy, Olympic Valley	X	X	X	X		6–8	9–12	51	45	5:1	4	40
Stanbridge Academy, San Mateo			X	X				72	45	7:1		
Sterne School, San Francisco			X	X		6–8	9–12	54	26	12:1		6
Stevenson School, Pebble Beach	X	X	X	X	PK–5	6–8	9–12	742	526	10:1	18	35
The Thacher School, Ojai	X	X	X	X			9–12	242	242	5:1	17	35
Tri-City Christian Schools, Vista			X	X	PK–6	7–8	9–12	1,127	257	12:1	4	16
University of San Diego High School, San Diego			X	X			9–12	1,450	1,450	19:1	13	20
The Urban School of San Francisco, San Francisco			X	X			9–12	253	253	8:1	8	38
Ursuline High School, Santa Rosa				X			9–12	367	367	11:1	4	11
Victor Valley Christian School, Victorville			X	X	K–6	7–8	9–12	360	100	12:1	5	10
Viewpoint School, Calabasas			X	X	K–5	6–8	9–12	1,135	399	10:1	19	23
Village Christian Schools, Sun Valley			X	X	K–5	6–8	9–12	1,800	580	17:1	8	16
Villanova Preparatory School, Ojai	X	X	X	X			9–12	290	290	8:1	8	16
The Waverly School, Pasadena			X	X	PK–6	7–8	9–12	258	66	7:1	10	7
The Webb Schools, Claremont	X	X	X	X			9–12	353	353	7:1	19	32
Westridge School, Pasadena				X	4–6	7–8	9–12	513	266	9:1	14	
Westview School, Los Angeles			X	X		6–8	9–12	90	64	8:1		3

| | Boarding | | Day | | GRADES | | | STUDENT/FACULTY | | | SCHOOL OFFERINGS (number) | |
	Boys	Girls	Boys	Girls	Lower	Middle	Upper	Total	Upper	Student/Faculty Ratio	Advanced Placement Subject Areas	Sports
California—continued												
Whittier Christian High School, La Habra ...			X	X			9-12	519	519	10:1	5	13
Windward School, Los Angeles			X	X		7-8	9-12	474	325	7:1	10	6
Woodside International School, San Francisco			X	X		6-8	9-12	100	90	10:1	4	2
Woodside Priory School, Portola Valley....	X	X	X	X		6-8	9-12	339	232	10:1	18	16
Colorado												
Accelerated Schools, Denver.............	X	X	X	X	K-5	6-8	9-12	100	70	7:1	4	3
Alexander Dawson School, Lafayette			X	X	K-4	5-8	9-12	398	176	6:1	12	37
Bridge School, Boulder..................			X	X		6-8	9-12	105	46	6:1		4
Colorado Academy, Denver..............			X	X	PK-5	6-8	9-12	855	314	12:1	16	19
The Colorado Rocky Mountain School, Carbondale......................	X	X	X	X			9-12	165	165	5:1	8	30
The Colorado Springs School, Colorado Springs			X	X	PS-5	6-8	9-12	461	130	17:1	8	18
Colorado Timberline Academy, Durango...	X	X	X	X			9-12	30	30			12
Crested Butte Academy, Crested Butte	X	X	X	X			9-PG	52	52	4:1	5	1
Denver Academy, Denver			X	X	1-6	7-8	9-12	420	236	6:1		32
Denver Christian High School, Denver			X	X	K-5	6-8	9-12	1,078	355	18:1		
Denver Lutheran High School, Denver			X	X			9-12	228	228	17:1	3	16
Forest Heights Lodge, Evergreen	X				K-5	6-8	9-12	24	3	5:1		36
Fountain Valley School of Colorado, Colorado Springs....................	X	X	X	X			9-12	219	219	5:1	15	35
J. K. Mullen High School, Denver........			X	X			9-12	1,010	1,010	17:1	7	21
Kent Denver School, Englewood			X	X		6-8	9-12	639	418	7:1	15	27
The Lowell Whiteman School, Steamboat Springs	X	X	X	X			9-12	92	92	7:1	5	65
Regis Jesuit High School, Aurora			X	X					835	16:1	8	23
St. Mary's Academy, Englewood..........			X	X	K-5	6-8	9-12	785	302	10:1	9	13
University of Denver High School, Denver .			X	X			9-12	116	116	8:1	8	5
Vail Mountain School, Vail..............			X	X	K-5	6-8	9-12	262	77	10:1	6	41
Connecticut												
Academy of the Holy Family, Baltic		X		X			9-12	55	55	8:1		3
Avon Old Farms School, Avon...........	X		X				9-PG	369	369	6:1	15	50
Brunswick School, Greenwich			X		PK-4	5-8	9-12	844	309	8:1	19	13
Canterbury School, New Milford	X	X	X	X			9-PG	357	357	6:1	17	27
Cheshire Academy, Cheshire.............	X	X	X	X		6-8	9-PG	376	319	7:1	12	24
Choate Rosemary Hall, Wallingford	X	X	X	X			9-12	850	850	8:1	19	58
Christian Heritage School, Trumbull			X	X	K-6	7-8	9-12	560	193	9:1	5	11
Convent of the Sacred Heart, Greenwich ..				X	PS-4	5-8	9-12	652	211	7:1	14	18
Eagle Hill School, Greenwich	X	X	X	X				210	105	4:1		30
Eagle Hill-Southport, Southport...........			X	X				101	29	4:1		6
East Catholic High School, Manchester			X	X			9-12	674	674	13:1	5	18
The Ethel Walker School, Simsbury		X		X		6-8	9-PG	184	157	6:1	15	27
Fairfield College Preparatory School, Fairfield........................			X				9-12	894	894	15:1	11	29
The Forman School, Litchfield	X	X	X	X			9-12	162	162	3:1	2	20
The Glenholme School, Washington	X	X	X	X				100	70	12:1		20
Greens Farms Academy, Greens Farms			X	X	K-5	6-8	9-12	580	244	7:1	15	24
Greenwich Academy, Greenwich........				X	PK-4	5-8	9-12	755	279	15:1	19	39
Grove School, Madison..................	X	X	X	X		7-8	9-13	103	87	5:1		67

| | STUDENTS ACCEPTED | | | | GRADES | | | STUDENT/FACULTY | | | SCHOOL OFFERINGS (number) | |
| | Boarding | | Day | | | | | | | | | |
	Boys	Girls	Boys	Girls	Lower	Middle	Upper	Total	Upper	Student/ Faculty Ratio	Advanced Placement Subject Areas	Sports
Connecticut—*continued*												
The Gunnery, Washington	X	X	X	X			9-PG	275	275	8:1	8	14
Hamden Hall Country Day School, Hamden			X	X	PK-6	7-8	9-12	580	255	8:1		13
Hopkins School, New Haven			X	X		7-8	9-12	661	501	6:1	15	35
The Hotchkiss School, Lakeville	X	X	X	X			9-PG	563	563	5:1	18	65
Hyde School, Woodstock	X	X	X	X			9-12	210	210	8:1		12
Indian Mountain School, Lakeville	X	X	X	X	PK-4	5-6	7-9	255	146	4:1		15
Kent School, Kent	X	X	X	X			9-PG	546	546	7:1	19	38
King & Low-Heywood Thomas School, Stamford			X	X	PK-5	6-8	9-12	650	242	6:1	10	23
Kingswood-Oxford School, West Hartford			X	X		6-8	9-12	589	382	8:1	16	20
The Loomis Chaffee School, Windsor	X	X	X	X			9-PG	726	726	5:1	13	37
Marianapolis Preparatory School, Thompson	X	X	X	X			9-PG	230	230	9:1	9	35
The Marvelwood School, Kent	X	X	X	X			9-12	144	144	4:1		36
The Master's School, West Simsbury			X	X	N-6	7-8	9-12	459	145	10:1	5	25
Mercy High School, Middletown				X			9-12	674	674	14:1	11	21
Miss Porter's School, Farmington		X		X			9-12	321	321	7:1	18	39
Northwest Catholic High School, West Hartford			X	X			9-12	615	615	12:1	13	34
Notre Dame High School, West Haven			X				9-12	707	707	12:1		17
The Oxford Academy, Westbrook	X						9-13	38	38	2:1	8	10
Pomfret School, Pomfret	X	X	X	X			9-PG	347	347	5:1	19	22
The Rectory School, Pomfret	X		X	X		5-9		171	136	3:1		43
Rumsey Hall School, Washington Depot	X	X	X	X	K-5	6-9		300	189	8:1		51
Sacred Heart Academy, Stamford				X			9-12	130	130	10:1	5	6
St. Luke's School, New Canaan			X	X		5-8	9-12	450	215	8:1	6	16
St. Margaret's-McTernan School, Waterbury			X	X	PK-5	6-8	9-12	448	148	5:1	14	17
Saint Thomas More School, Oakdale	X					8	9-PG	211	195	9:1		23
Salisbury School, Salisbury	X		X				9-PG	259	259	4:1	10	23
South Kent School, South Kent	X		X				9-PG	125	125	4:1	5	24
Suffield Academy, Suffield	X	X	X	X			9-PG	400	400	6:1	11	28
The Taft School, Watertown	X	X	X	X			9-PG	572	572	6:1	19	46
Trinity Catholic High School, Stamford			X	X			9-12	405	405	14:1	8	19
Watkinson School, Hartford			X	X		6-8	9-PG	277	194	5:1		26
Wellspring Foundation, Bethlehem	X	X	X	X				52				
Westminster School, Simsbury	X	X	X	X			9-PG	372	372	5:1	19	22
Westover School, Middlebury		X		X			9-12	208	208	5:1	17	43
The Williams School, New London			X	X		7-8	9-12	329	247	8:1	7	14
The Woodhall School, Bethlehem	X		X				9-PG	42	42	3:1	7	41
Wooster School, Danbury			X	X	K-5	6-8	9-12	416	144	6:1	12	15
Delaware												
Archmere Academy, Claymont			X	X			9-12	496	496	9:1	18	19
The Cedars Academy, Bridgeville	X	X					6-12	40	40	8:1		3
Padua Academy, Wilmington				X			9-12	629	629	14:1	10	12
St. Andrew's School, Middletown	X	X					9-12	278	278	7:1	11	29
St. Mark's High School, Wilmington			X	X			9-12	1,568	1,568	15:1	18	18
Sanford School, Hockessin			X	X	PK-3	4-8	9-12	700	246	8:1	16	12
The Tatnall School, Wilmington			X	X	N-4	5-8	9-12	721	252	8:1	15	15

	Boarding		Day		Grades			Student/Faculty			School Offerings (number)	
	Boys	Girls	Boys	Girls	Lower	Middle	Upper	Total	Upper	Student/Faculty Ratio	Advanced Placement Subject Areas	Sports
Delaware—continued												
Tower Hill School, Wilmington..........			X	X	PK–4	5–8	9–12	742	229	7:1	17	21
Ursuline Academy, Wilmington..........			X	X	PK–6	7–8	9–12	653	224	7:1	11	15
Wilmington Christian School, Hockessin ...			X	X	PK–6		7–12	631	324	11:1	3	9
Wilmington Friends School, Wilmington ...			X	X	PK–5	6–8	9–12	815	247	10:1	7	13
District of Columbia												
The Field School, Washington............			X	X		7–8	9–12	280	210	6:1	5	13
Georgetown Day School, Washington			X	X	PK–5	6–8	9–12	1,025	450	7:1	19	16
Georgetown Visitation Preparatory School, Washington				X			9–12	450	450	10:1	10	15
Gonzaga College High School, Washington.			X				9–12	890		10:1	14	23
Maret School, Washington..............			X	X	K–4	5–8	9–12	600	291	7:1	15	19
National Cathedral School, Washington....				X	4–6	7–8	9–12	560	301	7:1	17	36
St. Albans School, Washington	X		X		4–8		9–12	564	313	7:1	13	24
St. Anselm's Abbey School, Washington ...			X			6–8	9–12	254	149	4:1	17	14
St. John's College High School, Washington			X	X			9–12	1,050	1,050	13:1	12	32
Florida												
Admiral Farragut Academy, St. Petersburg..	X	X	X	X	PK–5	6–8	9–12	448	267	10:1		28
Allison Academy, North Miami Beach			X	X		6–8	9–12	120	85	15:1	3	16
American Academy, Plantation			X	X	1–6	7–8	9–12	478	202	12:1		19
American Heritage School, Plantation			X	X	PK–6		7–12	1,924	1,077	13:1	7	16
Argo Academy, Sarasota	X	X					12	24	24	4:1		10
Belen Jesuit Preparatory School, Miami			X			6–8	9–12	1,130	622	13:1	13	18
The Benjamin School, North Palm Beach ..			X	X	PK–5	6–8	9–12	1,163	351	16:1	17	18
Berkeley Preparatory School, Tampa			X	X	PK–5	6–8	9–12	1,172	475	8:1	16	23
Bishop Verot High School, Fort Myers.....			X	X			9–12	778	778	17:1	10	16
The Bolles School, Jacksonville...........	X	X	X	X	PK–5	6–8	9–12	1,711	761	10:1	19	20
Canterbury School, Fort Myers			X	X	PK–5	6–8	9–12	633	211	10:1	14	15
The Canterbury School of Florida, St. Petersburg			X	X	PK–5	6–8	9–12	400	91	8:1	12	22
Cardinal Gibbons High School, Fort Lauderdale			X	X			9–12	1,200	1,200	18:1	12	17
Cardinal Newman High School, West Palm Beach			X	X			9–12	805	805	25:1	5	17
Carrollton School of the Sacred Heart, Miami				X	PK–3	4–6	7–12	680	350	9:1	7	14
Chaminade-Madonna College Preparatory, Hollywood			X	X			9–12	872	872	19:1	10	21
Christian Home and Bible School, Mount Dara....................			X	X	K–5	6–8	9–12	683	202	13:1	2	11
The Community School of Naples, Naples .			X	X	PK–5	6–8	9–12	752	241	8:1	19	16
Eckerd Youth Alternatives, Clearwater	X	X			4–5	6–8	9–12	782	319	10:1		5
Episcopal High School of Jacksonville, Jacksonville			X	X		6–8	9–12	891	561	11:1	13	19
Father Lopez High School, Daytona Beach .			X	X			9–12	289	289	20:1	8	16
The First Academy, Orlando			X	X	K–4	5–8	9–12	736	206	22:1	7	19
Florida Air Academy, Melbourne..........	X		X			6–8	9–12	375	280	16:1	6	47
Forest Lake Academy, Apopka	X	X	X	X			9–12	501	501	27:1	5	12
The Geneva School, Winter Park			X	X	K4–6		7–12	274	68	4:1	4	7
Glades Day School, Belle Glade..........			X	X	PK–6	7–8	9–12	540	237	10:1	1	12

www.petersons.com

	STUDENTS ACCEPTED				GRADES			STUDENT/FACULTY			SCHOOL OFFERINGS (number)	
	Boarding		Day									
	Boys	Girls	Boys	Girls	Lower	Middle	Upper	Total	Upper	Student/ Faculty Ratio	Advanced Placement Subject Areas	Sports
Florida—continued												
Gulliver Preparatory School, Miami			X	X	PK-4	5-8	9-12	1,792	685	8:1	19	25
Jesuit High School of Tampa, Tampa			X				9-12	627	627	13:1	7	16
John Carroll High School, Fort Peirce			X	X			9-12	520	520	18:1	6	18
Lake Highland Preparatory School, Orlando			X	X	PK-6	7-8	9-12	1,848	607	13:1	19	22
Miami Country Day School, Miami			X	X	PK-5	6-8	9-12	1,000	351	9:1	17	22
Montverde Academy, Montverde	X	X	X	X	PK-6		7-PG	273	161	10:1	3	31
The North Broward Preparatory Upper School, Coconut Creek	X	X	X	X	PK-5	6-8	9-12	1,913	750	8:1	14	24
Northside Christian School, St. Petersburg			X	X	PS-5	6-8	9-12	877	221	11:1	5	15
Oak Hall School, Gainesville			X	X	PK-5	6-8	9-12	744	231	11:1	14	17
Out-Of-Door-Academy, Sarasota			X	X	PK-6	7-8	9-12	615	190	8:1	12	11
Palmer Trinity School, Miami			X	X		6-8	9-12	600	341	14:1	16	28
Pine Crest School, Fort Lauderdale			X	X	PK-5	6-8	9-12	1,638	749	11:1	19	24
Pope John Paul II High School, Boca Raton			X	X			9-12	925	925	28:1	6	18
Rabbi Alexander S. Gross Hebrew Academy of Greater Miami, Miami Beach			X	X	N-5	6-8	9-12	589	143	4:1	8	4
Ransom Everglades School, Miami			X	X		6-8	9-12	938	568	14:1	19	21
Saint Andrew's School, Boca Raton	X	X	X	X	K-5	6-8	9-12	1,073	554	10:1	17	17
St. Johns Country Day School, Orange Park			X	X	PK-5	6-8	9-12	700	216	10:1	17	53
Saint Stephen's Episcopal School, Bradenton			X	X	PK-5	6-8	9-12	758	264	11:1	14	27
Shorecrest Preparatory School, Saint Petersburg			X	X	PK-4	5-8	9-12	968	222	6:1	19	14
Tampa Preparatory School, Tampa			X	X		6-8	9-12	604	419	10:1	18	25
Trinity Preparatory School, Winter Park			X	X		6-8	9-12	802	483	10:1	16	15
University School of Nova Southeastern University, Fort Lauderdale			X	X	PK-5	6-8	9-12	1,535	457	15:1	18	16
The Vanguard School, Lake Wales	X	X	X	X		5-8	9-PG	131	103	10:1		19
Westminster Christian School, Miami			X	X	PK-5	6-8	9-12	1,162	438	11:1	10	13
Georgia												
Arlington Christian School, Fairburn			X	X	K-6	7-8	9-12	480		16:1	3	10
Athens Academy, Athens			X	X	N-4	5-8	9-12	814	312	8:1	8	11
Atlanta International School, Atlanta			X	X	PK-5	6-8	9-12	848	246	8:1		12
Augusta Preparatory Day School, Martinez			X	X	PS-4	5-8	9-12	520	174	9:1	13	9
Benedictine Military School, Savannah			X				9-12	371	371	10:1	5	24
Ben Franklin Academy, Atlanta			X	X			9-12	130	130	3:1		4
Brandon Hall School, Atlanta	X		X	X	4-5	6-8	9-PG	150	116	3:1	2	17
Brenau Academy, Gainesville		X		X			9-PG	80	80	8:1		13
Brookstone School, Columbus			X	X	K4-4	5-8	9-12	825	250	7:1	14	16
Brookwood School, Thomasville			X	X	PK-5	6-8	9-12	436	119	10:1	6	13
Bulloch Academy, Statesboro			X	X	PK-5	6-8	9-12	555	114	16:1		14
Calvary Baptist Day School, Savannah			X	X	PK-5	6-8	9-12	871	273	16:1	2	10
Chatham Academy, Savannah			X	X	1-5	6-8	9-12	90	30	9:1		15
The Cottage School, Roswell			X	X		6-8	9-12	159	113	10:1		26
Darlington School, Rome	X	X	X	X	PK-5	6-8	9-PG	907	462	9:1	17	33
The Edge, Stone Mountain	X					7-8	9-12	3	2	4:1		37
First Presbyterian Day School, Macon			X	X	PK-5	6-8	9-12	939	314	15:1	11	15

	STUDENTS ACCEPTED				GRADES			STUDENT/FACULTY			SCHOOL OFFERINGS (number)	
	Boarding		Day									
	Boys	Girls	Boys	Girls	Lower	Middle	Upper	Total	Upper	Student/ Faculty Ratio	Advanced Placement Subject Areas	Sports
Georgia—continued												
Flint River Academy, Woodbury.........			X	X	N-5	6-8	9-12	307	113	13:1	2	14
Frederica Academy, St. Simons Island			X	X	PK-5	6-8	9-12	320	78	5:1	4	10
The Galloway School, Atlanta			X	X	PK-4	5-8	9-12	737	241	10:1	11	12
Greater Atlanta Christian Schools, Norcross.........................			X	X	P4-5	6-8	9-12	1,811	613	19:1	17	17
The Heritage School, Newnan...........			X	X	PK-4	5-8	9-12	360	83	7:1	13	19
Hidden Lake Academy, Dahlonega	X	X					8-PG	150	150	9:1		38
Holy Innocents' Episcopal School, Atlanta .			X	X	PS-5	6-8	9-12	1,304	391	10:1	10	13
Horizons School, Atlanta	X	X	X	X	K-5	6-7	8-PG	135	85	10:1		3
La Grange Academy, La Grange			X	X	K-5	6-8	9-12	297	67	15:1	5	11
Lakeview Academy, Gainesville..........			X	X	PK-5	6-8	9-12	548	122	12:1	9	14
The Lovett School, Atlanta..............			X	X	K-5	6-8	9-12	1,517	589	9:1	16	48
Marist School, Atlanta..................			X	X			7-12	1,032	1,032	10:1	19	18
North Cobb Christian School, Kennesaw ..			X	X	PK-6	7-8	9-12	911	221	9:1		21
Pace Academy, Atlanta..................			X	X	K-6		7-12	842	532	10:1	17	17
Pacelli Catholic High School, Columbus ...			X	X			9-12	181	181	20:1	7	11
The Paideia School, Atlanta.............			X	X	N-6	7-8	9-12	876	382	12:1	8	12
Piedmont Academy, Monticello..........			X	X	K4-5	6-8	9-12	293	88	17:1		13
Rabun Gap-Nacoochee School, Rabun Gap.	X	X	X	X		6-8	9-12	274	189	12:1	8	41
Riverside Military Academy, Gainesville....	X					7-8	9-12	382	342	12:1	6	46
St. Andrew's on the Marsh School, Savannah.........................			X	X	PK-4	5-8	9-12	457	135	9:1	7	14
St. Francis School, Alpharetta...........			X	X	K-5	6-8	9-12	821	297	14:1		16
St. Pius X Catholic High School, Atlanta ...			X	X			9-12	1,000	1,000	15:1	19	20
Savannah Christian Preparatory School, Savannah.........................			X	X	PK-5	6-8	9-12	1,488	455	23:1	5	13
The Savannah Country Day School, Savannah.........................			X	X	PK-5	6-8	9-12	985	310	10:1	16	26
Stratford Academy, Macon..............			X	X	PK-5	6-8	9-12	951	293	13:1	16	17
Tallulah Falls School, Tallulah Falls........	X	X	X	X		7-8	9-12	143	114	8:1	6	55
Trinity Christian School, Dublin			X	X	K4-5	6-8	9-12	293	94	6:1		12
Valwood School, Valdosta			X	X	PK-5	6-8	9-12	394	114	11:1	3	10
The Walker School, Marietta.............			X	X	PK-5	6-8	9-12	1,040	355	14:1		25
Wesleyan School, Norcross			X	X	K-4	5-8	9-12	1,057	403		16	15
The Westfield Schools, Perry............			X	X	PK-6		7-12	637	288	12:1	6	15
The Westminster Schools, Atlanta			X	X	K-5	6-8	9-12	1,751	766	14:1	17	30
Whitefield Academy, Mableton...........			X	X	K-5	6-8	9-12	522	177	5:1		11
Woodward Academy, College Park........			X	X	PK-6	7-8	9-12	2,858	1,049		19	22
Yeshiva Atlanta, Atlanta			X	X			9-12	108	108	4:1	6	6
Hawaii												
ASSETS School, Honolulu...............			X	X	K-8		9-12	405	104	7:1	2	33
Hanalani Schools, Mililani			X	X	PK-6		7-12	674	232	9:1	4	14
Hawaii Baptist Academy, Honolulu.......			X	X	K-6		7-12	1,027	632	11:1	8	24
Hawaii Preparatory Academy, Kamuela....	X	X	X	X	K-5	6-8	9-12	603	347	8:1	15	41
Iolani School, Honolulu			X	X	K-6	7-8	9-12	1,831	940	12:1	19	26
Island School, Lihue...................			X	X	PK-5	6-8	9-12	294	81	15:1		13
Kauai Christian Academy, Kilauea			X	X	PS-3	4-6	7-12	76	14	5:1		
La Pietra-Hawaii School for Girls, Honolulu.........................				X		6-8	9-12	242	134	10:1	5	25
Maryknoll School, Honolulu			X	X	PK-5	6-8	9-12	1,398	568	11:1	12	32

	STUDENTS ACCEPTED				GRADES			STUDENT/FACULTY			SCHOOL OFFERINGS (number)	
	Boarding		Day									
	Boys	Girls	Boys	Girls	Lower	Middle	Upper	Total	Upper	Student/ Faculty Ratio	Advanced Placement Subject Areas	Sports
Hawaii—continued												
Mid-Pacific Institute, Honolulu	X	X	X	X		6–8	9–12	1,126	736	19:1	7	31
Molokai Christian Academy, Hoolehua			X	X	PK–5	6–8	9–12	59	18	10:1		4
The Parker School, Kamuela			X	X		6–8	9–12	130	97	6:1	2	8
Punahou School, Honolulu			X	X	K–8		9–12	3,752	1,729	13:1	14	23
St. Andrew's Priory School, Honolulu				X	K–4	5–8	9–12	480	160	7:1	8	28
St. Anthony's Junior-Senior High School, Wailuku			X	X		7–8	9–12	288	176	10:1	3	13
Saint Francis School, Honolulu				X		6–8	9–12	405	318	20:1	7	21
Saint Joseph Junior-Senior High School, Hilo			X	X		7–8	9–12	225	162	12:1	5	13
Idaho												
Bishop Kelly High School, Boise			X	X			9–12	621	621	14:1		6
Boulder Creek Academy, Bonners Ferry	X	X						60	60	8:1		38
The Community School, Sun Valley			X	X	PK–5	6–8	9–12	315	115	8:1	4	29
Gem State Adventist Academy, Caldwell	X	X	X	X			9–12	132	132	13:1	1	7
Greenleaf Academy, Greenleaf			X	X	K–6	7–8	9–12	235	88			11
Nampa Christian Schools, Inc., Nampa			X	X	PK–5	6–8	9–12	631	215	20:1		8
Northwest Academy, Naples	X	X						60				26
Rocky Mountain Academy, Bonners Ferry	X	X							150			24
Illinois												
Aquin Central Catholic High School, Freeport			X	X		7–8	9–12	175	120	10:1	4	5
Benet Academy, Lisle			X	X			9–12	1,290	1,290	18:1	12	17
Bishop McNamara High School, Kankakee			X	X			9–12	428	428	21:1	8	22
Boylan Central Catholic High School, Rockford			X	X			9–12	1,286	1,286	15:1	7	27
Brehm Preparatory School, Carbondale	X	X	X	X		6–8	9–12	80	75	4:1		10
Broadview Academy, La Fox	X	X	X	X			9–12	82	82	8:1		6
The Chicago Academy for the Arts, Chicago			X	X			9–12	150	150	16:1	7	
Elgin Academy, Elgin			X	X	PS–4	5–8	9–12	409	102	5:1	7	9
Fox River Country Day School, Elgin	X	X	X	X	PK–4	5–8		203	28	16:1		15
Fox Valley Lutheran Academy, Elgin			X	X			9–12	33	33	6:1		6
Francis W. Parker School, Chicago			X	X	PK–5	6–8	9–12	902	314	8:1		14
The Governor French Academy, Belleville	X	X	X	X	1–8		9–12	225	60	6:1	5	23
Hales Franciscan High School, Chicago			X				9–12	241	241	18:1		10
Holy Cross High School, River Grove			X				9–12	400	400	14:1		16
Holy Trinity High School, Chicago			X	X			9–12	400	400	14:1		10
Illiana Christian High School, Lansing			X	X			9–12	671	671	18:1	6	10
Immaculate Conception School, Elmhurst			X	X			9–12	225	225		4	10
Immaculate Heart of Mary High School, Westchester				X			9–12	445	445	16:1	5	9
Keith Country Day School, Rockford			X	X	PK–5	6–8	9–12	318	99	9:1	7	6
Lake Forest Academy, Lake Forest	X	X	X	X			9–12	350	350	8:1	19	22
The Latin School of Chicago, Chicago			X	X	JK–5	6–8	9–12	1,088	429	8:1	14	36
Loyola Academy, Wilmette			X	X			9–12	2,000	2,000	17:1	18	44
Luther High School North, Chicago			X	X			9–12	270	270	16:1	3	13
Luther High School South, Chicago			X	X		7–8	9–12	249	202	11:1	2	11
Marist High School, Chicago			X	X			9–12	1,382	1,382	19:1		17
Marmion Academy, Aurora			X				9–12	462	462	11:1	8	20

	Boarding		Day		GRADES			STUDENT/FACULTY			SCHOOL OFFERINGS (number)	
	Boys	Girls	Boys	Girls	Lower	Middle	Upper	Total	Upper	Student/Faculty Ratio	Advanced Placement Subject Areas	Sports
Illinois—*continued*												
Montini Catholic High School, Lombard . . .			X	X			9–12	634	634	20:1	10	18
Morgan Park Academy, Chicago			X	X	PK–5	6–8	9–12	538	181	5:1	11	18
Mother McAuley High School, Chicago				X			9–12	1,703	1,703	18:1	12	14
Mount Carmel High School, Chicago			X				9–12	755	755	15:1	10	17
Nazareth Academy, LaGrange Park			X	X			9–12	763	763	19:1	11	13
The North Shore Country Day School, Winnetka			X	X	PK–5	6–8	9–12	454	171	7:1	10	14
Quincy Notre Dame High School, Quincy . .			X	X			9–12	507	507	23:1	2	16
Resurrection High School, Chicago				X			9–12	901	901	14:1	9	13
Roycemore School, Evanston			X	X	PK–4	5–8	9–12	245	69	9:1	12	4
Sacred Heart/Griffin High School, Springfield			X	X				780		17:1		15
Saint Edward Central Catholic High School, Elgin			X	X			9–12	450	450	15:1	4	15
Saint Francis De Sales High School, Chicago.			X	X			9–12	340	340	15:1	4	8
Saint Patrick High School, Chicago.			X				9–12	990	990	20:1	8	14
St. Scholastica Academy, Chicago				X			9–12	250	250	9:1	5	10
Timothy Christian High School, Elmhurst . .			X	X	K–6	7–8	9–12	1,074	440	14:1	7	12
Trinity High School, River Forest				X			9–12	511	511	16:1		10
University of Chicago Laboratory Schools, Chicago.			X	X	N–4	5–8	9–12	1,679	465	10:1	16	13
Wheaton Academy, West Chicago			X	X			9–12	524	524	13:1	9	32
The Willows Academy, Des Plaines				X		6–8	9–12	208	108	10:1	7	1
Woodlands Academy of the Sacred Heart, Lake Forest.		X		X			9–12	200	200	9:1	6	8
Yeshiva High School, Skokie	X		X				9–12	155	155	13:1	5	7
Indiana												
Bishop Luers High School, Fort Wayne			X	X			9–12	547	547	18:1	4	21
Canterbury High School, Fort Wayne.			X	X	K–4	5–8	9–12	734	268	16:1	14	10
The Culver Academies, Culver	X	X	X	X			9–PG	766	766	9:1	14	34
Evansville Day School, Evansville			X	X	PK–4	5–8	9–12	319	69	10:1	10	9
Howe Military School, Howe.	X	X			5–8		9–12	160	106	9:1		22
La Lumiere School, La Porte	X	X	X	X			9–12	110	110	6:1	3	20
Lutheran High School, Indianapolis			X	X			9–12	251	251	13:1	3	14
Marian High School, Mishawaka			X	X			9–12	769	769	21:1	2	25
Marquette High School, Michigan City.			X	X					222	10:1	5	10
New Horizon Youth Ministries, Marion	X	X				7–8	9–12	26	24	3:1		
Park Tudor School, Indianapolis.			X	X	PK–5	6–8	9–12	976	402	9:1	14	15
Reitz Memorial High School, Evansville			X	X			9–12	825	825	16:1		
Iowa												
Des Moines Christian School, Des Moines . .			X	X	PK–6	7–8	9–12	679	162	18:1	4	9
Maharishi School of the Age, Fairfield	X	X	X	X	PS–6	7–9	10–12	339	124	8:1		6
Rivermont Collegiate, Bettendorf			X	X	PS–5	6–8	9–12	258	49	5:1	8	13
Scattergood Friends School, West Branch . .	X	X	X	X			9–PG	56	56	3:1		20
Kansas												
Bishop Ward High School, Kansas City			X	X			9–12	450	450	18:1	4	15
Hayden High School, Topeka			X	X			9–12	500	500	15:1	6	19
Independent School, Wichita			X	X	1–5	6–8	9–12	750	206	8:1	10	15

| | STUDENTS ACCEPTED | | | | GRADES | | | STUDENT/FACULTY | | | SCHOOL OFFERINGS (number) | |
| | Boarding | | Day | | | | | | | | | |
	Boys	Girls	Boys	Girls	Lower	Middle	Upper	Total	Upper	Student/ Faculty Ratio	Advanced Placement Subject Areas	Sports
Kansas—continued												
Maur Hill Prep School, Atchison..........	X	X	X	X			9-12	238	238	8:1		34
Sacred Heart High School, Salina.........			X	X								14
St. John's Military School, Salina..........	X					6-8	9-12	184	157	12:1		20
Saint Thomas Aquinas High School, Overland Park.....................			X	X			9-12	1,265	1,265	16:1		15
Wichita Collegiate School, Wichita.......			X	X	PS-4	5-8	9-12	973	295	15:1	17	12
Kentucky												
Assumption High School, Louisville.......				X			9-12	975	975	11:1	16	18
Beth Haven Christian School, Louisville....			X	X	K4-5	6-8	9-12	320	86	11:1		6
Calvary Christian Academy, Covington			X	X	K4-6	7-8	9-12	675	208	16:1	10	13
Community Christian Academy, Independence			X	X	PS-6	7-8	9-12	205	45	12:1		3
Kentucky Country Day School, Louisville ..			X	X	JK-4	5-8	9-12	779	202	9:1	12	18
Lexington Catholic High School, Lexington..........................			X	X			9-12	870	870	14:1	12	21
Louisville Collegiate School, Louisville.....			X	X	K-5	6-8	9-12	633	157	8:1	18	18
Millersburg Military Institute, Millersburg ..	X		X			6-8	9-12	55	50	9:1		22
Oneida Baptist Institute, Oneida..........	X	X	X	X		6-8	9-12	375	250	11:1	5	14
St. Francis High School, Louisville			X	X			9-12	126	126	8:1	11	23
Saint Patrick's School, Maysville			X	X	1-8		9-12	269	88	13:1		10
Shedd Academy, Mayfield	X	X	X	X	1-5	6-8	9-12	30	15	4:1		22
Trinity High School, Louisville			X				9-12	1,381	1,381	13:1		38
Woodbridge Academy, Lexington.........			X	X				22	12	8:1		
Louisiana												
Academy of the Sacred Heart, Grand Coteau		X		X	PK-4	5-8	9-12	353	140	8:1	5	14
Archbishop Blenk Girls High School, Gretna...........................				X		8-12		633	633	16:1	4	15
Archbishop Shaw High School, Marrero ...			X			8-9	10-12	528	367	24:1	4	15
Central Catholic Diocesan High School, Morgan City.......................			X	X		7-8	9-12	216	151	15:1		16
Episcopal High School, Baton Rouge			X	X	K-5	6-8	9-12	1,065	404	11:1	17	18
The Episcopal School of Acadiana, Cade...			X	X		6-8	9-12	352	187	8:1	10	14
Isidore Newman School, New Orleans			X	X	PK-5	6-8	9-12	1,158	445	18:1	18	13
Jesuit High School of New Orleans, New Orleans..........................			X			8	9-12	1,401	1,157	13:1	12	20
The Louise S. McGehee School, New Orleans..........................				X	PK-4	5-8	9-12	453	127	8:1	6	22
Metairie Park Country Day School, Metairie..........................			X	X	K-5	6-8	9-12	725	239	7:1	12	12
Redeemer-Seton High School, New Orleans..........................			X	X			9-12	341	341	15:1		12
St. Joseph's Academy, Baton Rouge				X			9-12	778	778	15:1	7	12
St. Martin's Episcopal School, Metairie.....			X	X	PK-5	6-8	9-12	787	277	10:1	11	14
Saint Thomas More Catholic High School, Lafayette.........................			X	X			9-12	1,069	1,069	21:1	7	17
Teurlings Catholic High School, Lafayette..			X	X			9-12	591	591	26:1	3	20
Vandebilt Catholic High School, Houma ...			X	X			8-12	915	915	25:1		13
Westminster Christian Academy, Opelousas.........................			X	X	PK-6	7-8	9-12	920	228	10:1	4	12

	STUDENTS ACCEPTED				GRADES			STUDENT/FACULTY			SCHOOL OFFERINGS (number)	
	Boarding		Day									
	Boys	Girls	Boys	Girls	Lower	Middle	Upper	Total	Upper	Student/ Faculty Ratio	Advanced Placement Subject Areas	Sports
Maine												
Berwick Academy, South Berwick			X	X	K-4	5-8	9-12	574	246	12:1	12	10
Bridgton Academy, North Bridgton	X		X				PG	185	185	10:1		26
Carrabassett Valley Academy, Carrabassett Valley	X	X	X	X		8-9	10-PG	100	72	6:1		38
Dirigo Day School, Lewiston	X	X						2	2	7:1		
Elan School, Poland	X	X				7-8	9-12	120	119	9:1		46
Fryeburg Academy, Fryeburg.............	X	X	X	X			9-PG	670	670	16:1	9	61
Gould Academy, Bethel	X	X	X	X			9-PG	206	206	5:1	5	32
Hebron Academy, Hebron...............	X	X	X	X		6-8	9-PG	247	200	7:1	9	21
Hyde School, Bath.....................	X	X	X	X			9-12	221	221	6:1		13
Kents Hill School, Kents Hill............	X	X	X	X			9-PG	215	215	6:1	11	24
Liberty School, Inc., Blue Hill			X	X			9-12	55	55	8:1	4	46
Maine Central Institute, Pittsfield	X	X	X	X			9-PG	513	513	15:1	4	22
North Yarmouth Academy, Yarmouth			X	X		6-8	9-12	302	174	8:1	13	17
Saint Dominic Regional High School, Auburn			X	X			9-12	360	360		5	2
Washington Academy, East Machias.......	X	X	X	X			9-12	344	344	11:1	5	10
Maryland												
Academy of the Holy Cross, Kensington ...				X			9-12	563	563	14:1	12	16
Archbishop Curley High School, Baltimore .			X				9-12	561	561	13:1	6	20
Archbishop Spalding High School, Severn..			X	X			9-12	973	973	14:1	11	25
Baltimore Lutheran Middle and Upper School, Towson....................			X	X		6-8	9-12	517	319	12:1	3	12
The Boys' Latin School of Maryland, Baltimore			X		K-5	6-8	9-12	623	263	8:1	7	17
The Bryn Mawr School for Girls, Baltimore			X	X	K-5	6-8	9-12	802	330	7:1	18	42
The Bullis School, Potomac.............			X	X	3-5	6-8	9-12	604	350	15:1	17	20
Calvert Hall College High School, Towson .			X				9-12	1,110	1,110	13:1	18	25
The Calverton School, Huntingtown			X	X	PK-5	6-8	9-12	406	120	11:1		8
The Catholic High School of Baltimore, Baltimore				X			9-12	299	299	14:1	6	11
Connelly School of the Holy Child, Potomac.........................				X		6-8	9-12	443	306	12:1	9	49
Elizabeth Seton High School, Bladensburg .				X			9-12	536	536	13:1	10	18
Friends School of Baltimore, Baltimore			X	X	PK-5	6-8	9-12	979	351	15:1	14	16
Garrison Forest School, Owings Mills		X	X	X	N-5	6-8	9-12	633	209	8:1	13	20
Georgetown Preparatory School, North Bethesda........................	X		X				9-12	420	420	8:1	19	45
Gilman School, Baltimore..............			X		P1-5	6-8	9-12	975	436	7:1	19	28
Glenelg Country School, Glenelg			X	X	PK-5	6-8	9-12	737	194	6:1	14	23
Gunston Day School, Centreville			X	X			9-12	123	123	7:1	7	12
The Holton-Arms School, Bethesda.......				X	3-6	7-8	9-12	645	307	8:1	10	19
Home Study International, Silver Spring ...			X	X	PK-6	7-8	9-PG	1,582	991	21:1		
Institute of Notre Dame, Baltimore				X			9-12	435	435	13:1	5	20
The Key School, Annapolis			X	X	PK-4	5-8	9-12	720	206	10:1	12	29
Landon School, Bethesda..............			X		3-5	6-8	9-12	660	325	10:1	12	20
Loyola-Blakefield, Baltimore............			X			6-8	9-12	959	708	10:1	16	21
Maryvale Preparatory School, Brooklandville				X		6-8	9-12	366	267	9:1	5	13

	Boarding		Day		GRADES			STUDENT/FACULTY			SCHOOL OFFERINGS (number)	
	Boys	Girls	Boys	Girls	Lower	Middle	Upper	Total	Upper	Student/ Faculty Ratio	Advanced Placement Subject Areas	Sports
Maryland—continued												
McDonogh School, Owings Mills	X	X	X	X	K–4	5–8	9–12	1,270	569	9:1	16	26
Mount De Sales Academy, Catonsville				X			9–12	464	464	12:1		11
New Dominion School, Oldtown	X					7–8	9–12	62	38	6:1		11
The Newport School, Kensington			X	X	N–4	5–8	9–12	105	15	9:1	4	3
The Nora School, Silver Spring			X	X			9–12	60	60	6:1		25
Notre Dame Preparatory School, Towson				X		6–8	9–12	702	539	9:1	14	16
Oldfields School, Glencoe		X		X			8–12	182	182	4:1	8	19
Our Lady of Good Counsel High School, Wheaton			X	X			9–12	1,070	1,070	14:1	11	21
The Park School, Brooklandville			X	X	PK–5	6–8	9–12	889	327	8:1	6	9
Queen Anne School, Upper Marlboro			X	X		6–8	9–12	279	156	8:1	7	17
Roland Park Country School, Baltimore			X	X	K–5	6–8	9–12	712	289	7:1	19	17
St. Andrew's Episcopal School, Potomac			X	X		6–8	9–12	450	327	8:1	8	16
Saint James School, St. James	X	X	X	X		8	9–12	215	189	7:1	11	23
St. John's Literary Institution at Prospect Hall, Frederick			X	X			9–12	325	325	10:1		21
Saint Mary's High School, Annapolis			X	X			9–12	585	585	17:1	4	16
St. Mary's-Ryken High School, Leonardtown			X	X			9–12	638	638	13:1		15
St. Paul's School, Brooklandville			X	X	P1–4	5–8	9–12	858	317	9:1	12	26
St. Paul's School for Girls, Brooklandville				X		5–8	9–12	468	250	7:1	14	15
Saints Peter and Paul High School, Easton			X	X			9–12	194	194	8:1	7	8
St. Timothy's School, Stevenson		X		X			9–PG	100	100	4:1	9	23
Sandy Spring Friends School, Sandy Spring	X	X	X	X	PK–4	5–8	9–12	507	208	7:1	8	18
Severn School, Severna Park			X	X		6–8	9–12	572	376	12:1	11	15
Stone Ridge School of the Sacred Heart, Bethesda			X	X	JK–4	5–8	9–12	793	337	9:1	16	24
Thornton Friends School, Silver Spring			X	X		6–8	9–12	88	55	6:1		11
Washington Waldorf School, Bethesda			X	X	PS–4	5–8	9–12	307	69	8:1	1	6
West Nottingham Academy, Colora	X	X	X	X		6–8	9–PG	190	165	6:1	9	23
Worcester Preparatory School, Berlin			X	X	PK–5	6–8	9–12	540	154	10:1	9	8
Massachusetts												
The Academy at Charlemont, Charlemont	X	X	X	X		7–8	9–PG	95	59	7:1		10
Academy at Swift River, Cummington	X	X					9–12	140	140	9:1		39
Academy of Notre Dame, Tyngsboro			X	X	K–5	6–8	9–12	691	216	13:1		14
Bancroft School, Worcester			X	X	K–5	6–8	9–12	598	237	7:1	14	13
Beacon High School, Brookline			X	X				51	51	3:1		6
Beaver Country Day School, Chestnut Hill			X	X		6–8	9–12	396	277	8:1	10	23
Belmont Hill School, Belmont	X		X			7–9	10–12	420		8:1	10	22
The Bement School, Deerfield	X	X	X	X	K–5		6–9	228	109	7:1		33
Berkshire Country Day School, Lenox			X	X	PK–3	4–6	7–12	356	141	6:1		15
Berkshire School, Sheffield	X	X	X	X			9–PG	383	383	8:1	19	31
Bishop Feehan High School, Attleboro			X	X			9–12	996	996	13:1	8	18
Bishop Stang High School, North Dartmouth			X	X			9–12	750	750	12:1	14	37
Boston College High School, Boston			X				9–12	1,299	1,299	13:1	19	19
Boston University Academy, Boston			X	X		8	9–12	156	141	7:1		28
Brimmer and May School, Chestnut Hill			X	X	N–5	6–8	9–12	384	114	7:1	6	20
Brooks School, North Andover	X	X	X	X			9–12	355	355	5:1	14	18

	Boarding Boys	Boarding Girls	Day Boys	Day Girls	Grades Lower	Grades Middle	Grades Upper	Total	Upper	Student/Faculty Ratio	Advanced Placement Subject Areas	Sports
Massachusetts—*continued*												
Buckingham Browne & Nichols School, Cambridge			X	X	PK-6	7-8	9-12	961	466	8:1	19	27
Buxton School, Williamstown	X	X	X	X			9-12	90	90	5:1		25
The Cambridge School of Weston, Weston	X	X	X	X			9-PG	320	320	7:1	10	41
Cape Cod Academy, Osterville			X	X	K-5	6-8	9-12	400	172	8:1	6	6
Catholic Memorial, West Roxbury			X			7-8	9-12	851	650	13:1	6	15
Chapel Hill-Chauncy Hall School, Waltham	X	X	X	X			9-12	161	161	5:1	2	17
Commonwealth School, Boston			X	X			9-12	145	145	5:1	13	18
Concord Academy, Concord	X	X	X	X			9-12	348	348	7:1	14	32
Cushing Academy, Ashburnham	X	X	X	X			9-PG	425	425	8:1	14	25
Dana Hall School, Wellesley		X		X		6-8	9-12	450	330	7:1	12	29
Deerfield Academy, Deerfield	X	X	X	X			9-PG	598	598	5:1	19	40
The DeSisto School, Stockbridge	X	X						75	75	5:1		45
Eaglebrook School, Deerfield	X		X			6-9		255	232	4:1		66
Eagle Hill School, Hardwick	X	X	X	X		8-8	9-12	135	127	4:1		30
Falmouth Academy, Falmouth			X	X		7-8	9-12	219	140	4:1	4	4
Fay School, Southborough	X	X	X	X	1-5	6-9		380	212	6:1		32
The Fessenden School, West Newton	X		X		K-4	5-6	7-9	472	193	7:1		24
F. L. Chamberlain School, Middleborough	X	X	X	X		7-8	9-12	104	64	4:1		14
Fontbonne Academy, Milton				X			9-12	646	646	13:1	6	20
Governor Dummer Academy, Byfield	X	X	X	X			9-12	365	365	8:1	14	18
Groton School, Groton	X	X	X	X		8	9-12	355	328	5:1	13	25
Hillside School, Marlborough	X		X		5-6	7-9		110	85	4:1		38
Holyoke Catholic High School, Granby			X	X			9-12	446	446	13:1	4	16
The John Dewey Academy, Great Barrington	X	X					10-PG	30	30	3:1		
Landmark School, Prides Crossing	X	X	X	X	2-4	5-8	9-12	415	290	3:1		27
Lawrence Academy, Groton	X	X	X	X			9-12	391	391	8:1	8	25
Lexington Christian Academy, Lexington			X	X		6-8	9-12	349	233	10:1	9	26
Linden Hill School, Northfield	X							15		3:1		10
The MacDuffie School, Springfield	X	X	X	X		6-8	9-12	198	142	7:1	6	9
Malden Catholic High School, Malden			X				9-12	740	740	14:1	9	25
Middlesex School, Concord	X	X	X	X			9-12	334	334	6:1	19	21
Milton Academy, Milton	X	X	X	X	K-6	7-8	9-12	999	669	6:1	11	28
Miss Hall's School, Pittsfield		X		X			9-12	162	162	5:1	19	29
Montrose School, Natick				X		6-8	9-12	108	49	10:1	2	4
The Newman School, Boston			X	X			9-PG	230	230	10:1	6	16
Newton Country Day School of the Sacred Heart, Newton				X		5-8	9-12	373	224	7:1	16	24
Noble and Greenough School, Dedham	X	X	X	X		7-8	9-12	543	433	7:1	16	18
Northfield Mount Hermon School, Northfield	X	X	X	X			9-PG	1,030	1,030	6:1	19	51
Phillips Academy (Andover), Andover	X	X	X	X			9-PG	1,087	1,087	6:1	14	44
The Pingree School, South Hamilton			X	X			9-12	296	296	7:1	10	19
Pioneer Valley Christian School, Springfield			X	X	PS-5	6-8	9-12	320	110	19:1		6
Pope John XXIII Central High School, Everett			X	X			9-12	462	462	15:1		14
Presentation of Mary Academy, Methuen				X			9-12	300	300	15:1		14
The Rivers School, Weston			X	X		7-8	9-12	390	307	7:1	13	18

| | STUDENTS ACCEPTED | | | | GRADES | | | STUDENT/FACULTY | | | SCHOOL OFFERINGS (number) | |
| | Boarding | | Day | | | | | | | | | |
	Boys	Girls	Boys	Girls	Lower	Middle	Upper	Total	Upper	Student/Faculty Ratio	Advanced Placement Subject Areas	Sports
Massachusetts—*continued*												
Riverview School, East Sandwich	X	X				6-8	9-PG	117	108	4:1		19
The Roxbury Latin School, West Roxbury			X				7-12	287	287	8:1	11	10
St. John's Preparatory School, Danvers			X				9-12	1,154	1,154	12:1	16	34
Saint Mark's School, Southborough	X	X	X	X			9-12	328	328	5:1	14	22
St. Sebastian's School, Needham			X			7-8	9-12	341	241	7:1	15	13
Stoneleigh-Burnham School, Greenfield		X		X			9-PG	151	151	5:1	8	18
Tabor Academy, Marion	X	X	X	X			9-12	480	480	7:1	19	21
Thayer Academy, Braintree			X	X		6-8	9-12	651	433	7:1	13	48
Trinity Catholic High School, Newton			X	X			9-12	241	241	15:1		14
Ursuline Academy, Dedham				X			7-12	398	398	11:1	4	11
Valley View School, North Brookfield	X					5-8	9-12	54	29	5:1		40
The Waldorf High School of Massachusetts Bay, Lexington			X	X			9-12	51	51	5:1		3
Walnut Hill School, Natick	X	X	X	X			9-12	280	280	5:1	6	4
Waring School, Beverly			X	X		6-8	9-12	148	98	8:1	5	8
Wilbraham & Monson Academy, Wilbraham	X	X	X	X		6-8	9-PG	334	274	7:1	11	40
The Williston Northampton School, Easthampton	X	X	X	X		7-8	9-PG	544	453	7:1	12	30
Willow Hill School, Sudbury			X	X		6-8	9-12	57	41	3:1		11
The Winchendon School, Winchendon	X	X	X	X			8-PG	174	174	6:1	4	29
The Winsor School, Boston				X		5-8	9-12	421	228	7:1	8	14
The Woodward School, Quincy				X		6-8	9-12	172	111	8:1	4	4
Worcester Academy, Worcester	X	X	X	X		6-8	9-PG	623	460	7:1	14	20
Xaverian Brothers High School, Westwood			X				9-12	1,045	1,045	13:1	14	12
Michigan												
Academy of the Sacred Heart, Bloomfield Hills			X	X	N-4	5-8	9-12	499	113	14:1	5	7
Brother Rice High School, Bloomfield Hills			X				9-12	642	642	15:1	18	14
Catholic Central High School, Redford			X				9-12	961	961	15:1	11	16
Christian High School, Grand Rapids			X	X			9-12	1,080	1,080	17:1	3	18
Cranbrook Schools, Bloomfield Hills	X	X	X	X	PK-5	6-8	9-12	1,608	770	8:1	14	40
Detroit Country Day School, Beverly Hills	X	X	X	X	PK-5	6-8	9-12	1,564	617	8:1	17	28
Divine Child High School, Dearborn			X	X			9-12	893	893	13:1	7	19
Eton Academy, Birmingham			X	X	1-5	6-8	9-12	188	49	8:1		6
Greenhills School, Ann Arbor			X	X		6-8	9-12	496	287	14:1	8	13
Hackett Catholic Central High School, Kalamazoo			X	X			9-12	465	465	17:1	6	19
Holland Christian High School, Holland			X	X				2,246			6	2
Interlochen Arts Academy, Interlochen	X	X	X	X			9-PG	455	455	6:1	3	41
Ladywood High School, Livonia				X			9-12	469	469	14:1		22
Lansing Christian School, Lansing			X	X	PK-5	6-8	9-12	618	191	12:1	2	3
The Leelanau School, Glen Arbor	X	X	X	X			9-12	60	60	10:1	3	40
Lutheran High School East, Harper Woods			X	X			9-12	103	103	11:1	3	10
Lutheran High School Northwest, Rochester Hills			X	X			9-12	258	258	15:1	3	19
Marian High School, Bloomfield Hills				X			9-12	554	554	14:1	10	14
Montcalm School, Albion	X					6-8	9-12	14				53
Powers Catholic High School, Flint			X	X			9-12	723	723		8	
The Roeper School, Bloomfield Hills			X	X	PK-5	6-8	9-12	625	189	9:1	14	10

	STUDENTS ACCEPTED				GRADES			STUDENT/FACULTY			SCHOOL OFFERINGS (number)	
	Boarding		Day									
	Boys	Girls	Boys	Girls	Lower	Middle	Upper	Total	Upper	Student/ Faculty Ratio	Advanced Placement Subject Areas	Sports
Michigan—_continued_												
St. Mary's Preparatory School, Orchard Lake.	X		X				9–12	450	450	5:1	8	30
Southfield Christian High School, Southfield			X	X	K–6	7–8	9–12	817	286	20:1	7	18
University Liggett School, Grosse Pointe Woods.			X	X	PK–5	6–8	9–12	703	241	9:1	14	16
University of Detroit Jesuit High School and Academy, Detroit.			X			7–8	9–12	943	806	16:1	7	14
Valley Lutheran High School, Saginaw			X	X			9–12	344	344	17:1	2	6
The Valley School, Flint			X	X	PK–4	5–8	9–12	111	33	12:1	2	4
West Catholic High School, Grand Rapids.			X	X			9–12	615	615	21:1	6	25
Minnesota												
Academy of Holy Angels, Richfield.			X	X			9–12	840	840	13:1	7	14
Benilde–St. Margaret's School, St. Louis Park.			X	X		7–8	9–12	1,121	860	12:1	10	25
The Blake School, Hopkins			X	X	PK–5	6–8	9–12	1,316	487	8:1	11	18
Breck School, Minneapolis.			X	X	PK–4	5–8	9–12	1,196	395	11:1	7	19
Concordia Academy, St. Paul.			X	X			9–12	505	505	14:1	4	16
Cotter High School, Winona	X	X	X	X		7–8	9–12	467	345	16:1	17	18
Cretin-Derham Hall, Saint Paul			X	X			9–12	1,300	1,300	16:1	7	22
International Academy of Minnesota, St. Paul.	X	X	X	X			7–9	23	23	5:1		7
International School of Minnesota, Eden Prairie.			X	X	PS–5	6–8	9–12	530	93	4:1	18	29
Lutheran High School, Bloomington.			X	X			9–12	124	124	15:1	3	10
Marshall School, Duluth.			X	X		5–8	9–12	554	350	10:1	9	18
Minnehaha Academy, Minneapolis			X	X	PK–5	6–8	9–12	1,202	518	14:1	16	26
Mounds Park Academy, St. Paul			X	X	K–4	5–8	9–12	701	260	5:1	3	14
Nacel International School, Saint Paul	X	X	X	X			9–12	26	26	15:1		
St. Croix Lutheran High School, West St. Paul.	X	X	X	X			9–12	387	387	15:1	3	15
Saint John's Preparatory School, Collegeville.	X	X	X	X		7–8	9–PG	320	260	12:1	6	31
St. Paul Academy and Summit School, St. Paul.			X	X	K–5	6–8	9–12	924	390	10:1		19
St. Thomas Academy, Mendota Heights.			X			7–8	9–12	655	492	12:1	7	23
Shattuck-St. Mary's School, Faribault	X	X	X	X		6–8	9–PG	308		7:1	14	28
Mississippi												
Brookhaven Academy, Brookhaven			X	X	PK–6	7–8	9–12	484	133	20:1		10
Copiah Academy, Gallman.			X	X	1–3	4–6	7–12	496	250	17:1		12
Jackson Academy, Jackson.			X	X	PK–6	7–9	10–12	1,483	289	15:1	10	13
Jackson Preparatory School, Jackson			X	X		7–9	10–12	872	411	11:1	9	15
Madison-Ridgeland Academy, Madison.			X	X	K–5	6–8	9–12	805	186	13:1	12	13
New Summit School, Jackson			X	X	K–6	7–8	9–12	55	40	5:1		
Our Lady Academy, Bay St. Louis				X		7–8	9–12	297	187	13:1	5	11
Parklane Academy, McComb.			X	X	PK–3	4–6	7–12	853	418	27:1	3	9
St. Andrew's Episcopal School, Ridgeland.			X	X	PK–4	5–8	9–12	1,128	290	14:1	15	19
St. Stanislaus College Prep, Bay St. Louis.	X		X			6–8	9–12	550	380	12:1	3	21
Vicksburg Catholic School, Vicksburg			X	X	PK–6	7–8	9–12	654	162	12:1	1	14

| | STUDENTS ACCEPTED | | | | GRADES | | | STUDENT/FACULTY | | | SCHOOL OFFERINGS (number) | |
| | Boarding | | Day | | | | | | | | | |
	Boys	Girls	Boys	Girls	Lower	Middle	Upper	Total	Upper	Student/ Faculty Ratio	Advanced Placement Subject Areas	Sports
Mississippi—*continued*												
Washington County Day School, Greenville			X	X	PK-5	6-8	9-12	825		20:1		11
Missouri												
The Barstow School, Kansas City			X	X	PS-5	6-8	9-12	609	168	9:1	16	10
Chaminade College Preparatory School, St. Louis	X		X			6-8	9-12	950	600	11:1	18	10
Cor Jesu Academy, St. Louis				X			9-12	538	538	12:1	12	10
Crossroads School, St. Louis			X	X		7-8	9-12	204	140	9:1	6	19
John Burroughs School, St. Louis			X	X					595	8:1	7	18
Kansas City Academy of Learning, Kansas City			X	X		6-8	9-12	62	40	6:1		
Logos School, St. Louis			X	X		7-8	9-12	144	122	6:1		4
Lutheran High School North, St. Louis			X	X			9-12	380	380	14:1	3	12
Lutheran High School South, St. Louis			X	X			9-12	617	617	13:1	5	18
Mary Institute and St. Louis Country Day School (MICDS), St. Louis			X	X	JK-4	5-8	9-12	1,222	581	8:1	18	32
Missouri Military Academy, Mexico	X				5	6-8	9-PG	248	198	9:1	5	41
Notre Dame High School, St. Louis				X			9-12	450	450	10:1	6	9
The Pembroke Hill School, Kansas City			X	X	PS-5	6-8	9-12	1,187	407	8:1	15	20
Rockhurst High School, Kansas City			X				9-12	1,032	1,032	13:1	8	23
Saint Elizabeth Academy, St. Louis				X					200	10:1		17
Saint Louis Priory School, St. Louis			X			7-8	9-12	394	255	8:1	14	15
Saint Paul Lutheran High School, Concordia	X	X	X	X			9-12	171	171	12:1		17
Saint Teresa's Academy, Kansas City				X			9-12	528	528	13:1		25
Springfield Catholic High School, Springfield			X	X			9-12	327	327	12:1	10	11
Thomas Jefferson School, St. Louis	X	X	X	X		7-8	9-PG	69	52	6:1	12	10
University of Missouri—Columbia High School, Columbia			X	X							1	
Valle Catholic High School, Ste. Genevieve			X	X			9-12	150	150	8:1	1	12
Visitation Academy of St. Louis County, St. Louis			X	X	PK-6		7-12	696	455	10:1	11	9
Wentworth Military Academy and Junior College, Lexington	X	X	X	X		7-8	9-12	104	91	5:1		27
Whitfield School, St. Louis			X	X			6-12	471	471	8:1	5	15
Montana												
Loyola-Sacred Heart High School, Missoula			X	X			9-12	182	182	17:1	5	11
Lustre Christian High School, Lustre	X	X	X	X			9-12	22	22			3
Manhattan Christian High School, Manhattan			X	X	PK-5	6-8	9-12	354	146	12:1	2	7
Montana Academy, Marion	X	X						60	60	2:1	1	40
Nebraska												
Brownell-Talbot School, Omaha			X	X	PK-4	5-8	9-12	461	120	11:1	11	19
Creighton Preparatory School, Omaha			X				9-12	1,015	1,015	14:1	14	20
Father Flanagan's Boys' Home, Boys Town	X	X				4-8	9-12	450	350			9
Kearney Catholic High School, Kearny			X	X	6	7-8	9-12	307	182	13:1		11
Mount Michael Benedictine High School, Elkhorn	X		X				9-12	168	168	7:1	7	7
Nebraska Christian Schools, Central City	X	X	X	X	K-6	7-8	9-12	207	126	10:1		6

| | STUDENTS ACCEPTED | | | | GRADES | | | STUDENT/FACULTY | | | SCHOOL OFFERINGS (number) | |
| | Boarding | | Day | | | | | | | | | |
	Boys	Girls	Boys	Girls	Lower	Middle	Upper	Total	Upper	Student/ Faculty Ratio	Advanced Placement Subject Areas	Sports
Nebraska—continued												
Pius X High School, Lincoln			X	X			9–12	960	960	16:1	5	15
Nevada												
Bishop Gorman High School, Las Vegas . . .			X	X			9–12	856	856	19:1	14	14
Faith Lutheran High School, Las Vegas			X	X		6–8	9–12	1,048	522	17:1	7	12
The Meadows School, Las Vegas			X	X	PK–5	6–8	9–12	870	240	11:1	8	9
Mountain View Christian High School, Las Vegas			X	X	K–6	7–8	9–12	571	117	8:1		10
Sage Ridge School, Reno			X	X		6–8	9–12	153	47	5:1	6	13
New Hampshire												
Bishop Brady High School, Concord			X	X			9–12	446	446	15:1	7	25
Bishop Guertin High School, Nashua			X	X			9–12	889	889	27:1	14	28
Brewster Academy, Wolfeboro	X	X	X	X			9–PG	351	351	6:1	10	29
Cardigan Mountain School, Canaan	X		X			6–9		184	170	4:1		34
The Derryfield School, Manchester			X	X		6–8	9–12	378	240	7:1	10	23
Dublin Christian Academy, Dublin	X	X	X	X	K–6	7–8	9–12	136	62	8:1		6
Dublin School, Dublin	X	X	X	X			9–12	127	127	5:1	4	45
Hampshire Country School, Rindge	X				3–6		7–12	20	16	4:1		24
High Mowing School, Wilton	X	X	X	X			9–12	111	111	4:1		40
Holderness School, Plymouth	X	X	X	X			9–12	283	283	7:1	11	41
Kimball Union Academy, Meriden	X	X	X	X			9–PG	313	313	6:1	15	29
The Meeting School, Rindge	X	X	X	X			9–12	31	31	2:1		25
New Hampton School, New Hampton	X	X	X	X			9–PG	330	330	5:1	5	45
Phillips Exeter Academy, Exeter	X	X	X	X			9–PG	1,048	1,048	5:1	19	37
Portsmouth Christian Academy, Dover			X	X	PK–5	6–8	9–12	766	253	18:1	4	10
Proctor Academy, Andover	X	X	X	X			9–PG	336	336	4:1	11	56
St. Paul's School, Concord	X	X					9–12	526	526	5:1	19	31
St. Thomas Aquinas High School, Dover . . .			X	X			9–12	700	700	15:1	8	19
Tilton School, Tilton	X	X	X	X			9–PG	195	195	5:1	8	28
Trinity High School, Manchester			X	X			9–12	519	519	18:1	4	21
Wediko School Program, Windsor	X		X					40	12	2:1		16
The White Mountain School, Bethlehem . . .	X	X	X	X			9–PG	100	100	4:1		39
New Jersey												
The American Boychoir School, Princeton .	X		X			6–8		60	43	6:1		13
Baptist High School, Haddon Heights			X	X			9–12	236	236	10:1	4	9
Barnstable Academy, Oakland			X	X		5–8	9–12	150	110	8:1	5	13
Benedictine Academy, Elizabeth				X			9–12	190	190	15:1	6	14
Bishop Eustace Preparatory School, Pennsauken			X	X			9–12	783	783	14:1	9	20
Blair Academy, Blairstown	X	X	X	X			9–PG	430	430	7:1	17	29
Christian Brothers Academy, Lincroft			X				9–12	927	927	14:1	16	16
Collegiate School, Passaic Park			X	X	PK–6		7–12	167	54	9:1		
Delbarton School, Morristown			X			7–8	9–12	540	455	7:1	19	29
Dwight-Englewood School, Englewood			X	X	PK–5	6–8	9–12	940	412	9:1		7
Eastern Christian High School, North Haledon			X	X	PK–4	5–8	9–12	1,022	387	10:1	6	31
Gill St. Bernard's School, Gladstone			X	X	PS–4	5–8	9–12	599	163	8:1	6	10
Hawthorne Christian Academy, Hawthorne			X	X				465				
The Hudson School, Hoboken			X	X		5–8	9–12	202	82	10:1		9

| | STUDENTS ACCEPTED | | | | GRADES | | | STUDENT/FACULTY | | | SCHOOL OFFERINGS (number) | |
| | Boarding | | Day | | | | | | | | | |
	Boys	Girls	Boys	Girls	Lower	Middle	Upper	Total	Upper	Student/ Faculty Ratio	Advanced Placement Subject Areas	Sports
New Jersey—continued												
The Hun School of Princeton, Princeton...	X	X	X	X		6-8	9-PG	580	480	8:1	14	36
Immaculata High School, Somerville			X	X			9-12	884	884	15:1	5	11
Immaculate Conception High School, Lodi.				X			9-12	196	196	11:1	3	15
Immaculate Conception High School, Montclair			X	X			9-12	317	317	10:1		13
Kent Place School, Summit			X	X	N-5	6-8	9-12	624	236	6:1	18	12
The Lawrenceville School, Lawrenceville ..	X	X	X	X			9-PG	805	805	8:1	11	41
Mary Help of Christians Academy, North Haledon				X			9-12	244	244	12:1	3	9
Marylawn of the Oranges, South Orange...				X			9-12	194	194	9:1	2	10
Montclair Kimberley Academy, Montclair ..			X	X	PK-3	4-8	9-12	1,048	426	7:1	14	18
Moorestown Friends School, Moorestown .			X	X	PS-4	5-8	9-12	688	255	9:1	12	17
Morristown-Beard School, Morristown.....			X	X		6-8	9-12	450	328	7:1	10	24
Mount Saint Mary Academy, Watchung....				X			9-12	363	363	9:1	9	14
Newark Academy, Livingston			X	X		6-8	9-12	551	412	9:1	19	30
The Newgrange School, Hamilton			X	X				69	16	3:1		3
Notre Dame High School, Lawrenceville...			X	X			9-12	1,272	1,272	24:1	11	30
Oak Knoll School of the Holy Child, Summit			X	X	K-6		7-12	543	300	8:1	11	11
Oratory Preparatory School, Summit			X			7-8	9-12	255	205	10:1	13	16
Our Lady of Mercy Academy, Newfield....				X			9-12	223	223	18:1	1	12
Paul VI High School, Haddonfield........			X	X			9-12	993	993	17:1	7	10
The Peddie School, Hightstown	X	X	X	X			8-PG	524	524	6:1	10	22
The Pennington School, Pennington	X	X	X	X		6-8	9-12	442	356	9:1	12	21
The Pingry School, Martinsville..........			X	X	K-6	7-8	9-12	1,011	511	8:1	17	22
Princeton Day School, Princeton			X	X	JK-4	5-8	9-12	892	375	8:1	13	20
Purnell School, Pottersville		X		X			9-12	81	81	5:1		27
Queen of Peace High School, North Arlington			X	X			9-12	722	722	15:1	3	13
Ranney School, Tinton Falls.............			X	X	N-5	6-8	9-12	725	202		17	16
Rutgers Preparatory School, Somerset			X	X	PK-4	5-8	9-12	712	299	7:1	19	11
Saddle River Day School, Saddle River.....			X	X	K-5	6-8	9-12	318	135	8:1	13	14
Saint Augustine Preparatory School, Richland			X				9-12	469	469	13:1	12	17
St. Benedict's Preparatory School, Newark .			X			7-8	9-12	578	497	10:1		21
Saint Dominic Academy, Jersey City.......				X			9-12	491	491	12:1	8	12
Saint Joseph's High School, Metuchen.....			X				9-12	845	845	15:1	8	18
St. Mary's Hall, Burlington			X	X	PK-6		7-12	183	96	9:1	8	7
Seton Hall Preparatory School, West Orange			X				9-12	950	950	11:1	16	19
Stuart Country Day School of the Sacred Heart, Princeton			X	X	PS-5	6-8	9-12	546	140	12:1	18	13
Villa Victoria Academy, Ewing			X	X	PK-6		7-12	266	147	6:1	6	8
Villa Walsh Academy, Morristown				X		7-8	9-12	236	203	8:1	11	10
The Wardlaw-Hartridge School, Edison			X	X	PK-5	6-8	9-12	417	144	9:1	17	13
Woodcliff Academy, Wall................			X	X	2-6	7-8	9-12	78	30	3:1		10
New Mexico												
Albuquerque Academy, Albuquerque......			X	X		6-8	9-12	1,033	611	8:1	18	15
Bosque School, Albuquerque.............			X	X		6-8	9-12	408	184	9:1		10
Brush Ranch School, Terrero.............	X	X						30	30	5:1		60
Desert Academy, Santa Fe			X	X		7-8	9-12	136	91	7:1		8

| | STUDENTS ACCEPTED | | | | GRADES | | | STUDENT/FACULTY | | | SCHOOL OFFERINGS (number) | |
| | Boarding | | Day | | | | | | | | | |
	Boys	Girls	Boys	Girls	Lower	Middle	Upper	Total	Upper	Student/ Faculty Ratio	Advanced Placement Subject Areas	Sports
New Mexico—*continued*												
Menaul School, Albuquerque			X	X		6–8	9–12	259	174	10:1	5	11
Navajo Preparatory School, Inc., Farmington	X	X	X	X					200	15:1		8
St. Pius X High School, Albuquerque			X	X			9–12	1,049	1,049	16:1	8	13
Sandia Preparatory School, Albuquerque			X	X		6–8	9–12	627	364	9:1		27
Santa Fe Preparatory School, Santa Fe			X	X		7–8	9–12	343	172	7:1	8	14
The United World College—USA, Montezuma	X	X					11–12	200	200	8:1		51
New York												
Academy of Mount Saint Ursula, Bronx				X			9–12	455	455	15:1	6	8
Adelphi Academy, Brooklyn			X	X	PK–4	5–8	9–12	175	85	8:1		16
The Albany Academy, Albany	X		X	X	PK–4	5–8	9–PG	362	186	15:1	15	16
Albany Academy for Girls, Albany				X	PK–4	5–8	9–12	327	152	12:1	19	13
Allendale Columbia School, Rochester			X	X	N–5	6–8	9–12	484	141	9:1	12	11
The Beekman School, New York			X	X			9–PG	80	80	8:1	19	
Berkeley Carroll School, Brooklyn			X	X	N–4	5–8	9–12	764	211	8:1	9	11
The Birch Wathen Lenox School, New York			X	X	K–5	6–8	9–12	445	145	12:1	10	21
Bishop Grimes High School, East Syracuse			X	X		7–8	9–12	607	360	14:1	7	12
Bishop Kearney High School, Brooklyn				X			9–12	1,052	1,052	10:1		21
Bishop Loughlin Memorial High School, Brooklyn			X	X			9–12	870	870		2	22
Brooklyn Friends School, Brooklyn			X	X				586		7:1		4
The Browning School, New York			X		K–4	5–8	9–12	371	106	18:1	14	8
Buffalo Academy of the Sacred Heart, Buffalo				X			9–12	378	378	10:1	9	12
The Buffalo Seminary, Buffalo				X			9–12	158	158	12:1	12	38
The Calhoun School, New York			X	X	N–4	5–8	9–12	645	176	5:1	6	17
Cascadilla School, Ithaca	X	X	X	X			9–PG	55	55	6:1	10	30
Catholic Central High School, Troy			X	X		7–8	9–12	497	395	13:1		14
The Chapin School, New York				X	K–3	4–7	8–12	650	232	4:1	17	63
Charles Finney School, Penfield			X	X	PK–5	6–8	9–12	388	213	10:1		
Christian Brothers Academy, Albany			X			6–8	9–12	513	369	13:1	8	15
Christian Brothers Academy, Syracuse			X	X			7–12	740	740		8	17
Christian Central Academy, Williamsville			X	X	K–6	7–8	9–12	300	78	4:1	3	5
Collegiate School, New York			X		K–4	5–8	9–12	631	212	4:1		9
Columbia Grammar and Preparatory School, New York			X	X	PK–6		7–12	987	487	7:1	14	24
Convent of the Sacred Heart, New York				X	PK–4	5–7	8–12	655	235	5:1	18	18
The Dalton School, New York			X	X	K–3	4–8	9–12	1,286	452	7:1	11	5
Darrow School, New Lebanon	X	X	X	X			9–PG	124	124	4:1		28
Doane Stuart School, Albany			X	X	N–4	5–8	9–12	276	95	5:1	15	12
The Dominican Academy of the City of New York, New York				X			9–12	252	252	10:1	11	6
The Dwight School, New York			X	X	K–4	5–8	9–12	429	243	6:1	6	22
Emma Willard School, Troy		X		X			9–PG	307	307	5:1	16	34
The Ethical Culture Fieldston School, Bronx			X	X	PK–6	7–8	9–12	1,610	525	10:1	14	47
The Family Foundation School, Hancock	X	X					7–12	248	248	15:1		11
Fontbonne Hall Academy, Brooklyn				X			9–12	514	514	12:1		9
Fordham Preparatory School, Bronx			X				9–12	901	901	11:1	14	17

	STUDENTS ACCEPTED				GRADES			STUDENT/FACULTY			SCHOOL OFFERINGS (number)	
	Boarding		Day									
	Boys	Girls	Boys	Girls	Lower	Middle	Upper	Total	Upper	Student/Faculty Ratio	Advanced Placement Subject Areas	Sports
New York—continued												
French-American School of New York, Larchmont			X	X	N–5		6–10	601	171	6:1		8
Friends Academy, Locust Valley			X	X	N–5	6–8	9–12	748	356	6:1	19	16
Friends Seminary, New York			X	X	K–4	5–8	9–12	645	260	8:1	13	19
Garden School, Jackson Heights			X	X	N–6		7–12	350		11:1	6	6
The Gow School, South Wales	X					7–9	10–PG	129	87	4:1		57
Green Meadow Waldorf School, Chestnut Ridge			X	X	N–8		9–12	385	90			7
Hackley School, Tarrytown	X	X	X	X	K–5	6–8	9–12	789	372	4:1	19	19
The Harley School, Rochester			X	X	N–4	5–8	9–12	512	157	8:1	15	9
The Harvey School, Katonah	X	X	X			6–8	9–12	300	200	7:1	10	20
The Hewitt School, New York				X	K–3	4–7	8–12	458	145	6:1	8	14
Holy Angels Academy, Buffalo				X			9–12	330	330	10:1	1	21
Hoosac School, Hoosick	X	X	X	X			8–PG	118	118	5:1	3	32
The Horace Mann School, Riverdale			X	X	N–5	6–8	9–12	1,745	708	9:1	19	33
Houghton Academy, Houghton	X	X	X	X	K–6	7–8	9–PG	230	136	17:1		18
Immaculata Academy, Hamburg				X			9–12	167	167	7:1		9
Iona Preparatory School, New Rochelle			X				9–12	730	730	13:1	12	17
The Karafin School, Mount Kisco			X	X		7–8	9–12	80	74	6:1		36
Keio Academy of New York, Purchase	X	X	X	X			9–12	316	316		1	20
Kildonan School, Amenia	X	X	X	X	2–6	7–9	10–PG	142	53	6:1		9
The Knox School, St. James	X	X	X	X		6–8	9–12	109	78	3:1	6	24
Little Red School House and Elisabeth Irwin High School, New York			X	X	N–4	5–8	9–12	519	135	5:1	5	13
Long Island Lutheran Middle and High School, Brookville			X	X		6–8	9–12	595	389	11:1	10	18
Loyola School, New York			X	X			9–12	210	210	7:1	6	13
Lycee Français de New York, New York			X	X	PK–5	6–9	10–12	1,047	174	3:1	4	14
Manlius Pebble Hill School, DeWitt	X	X	X	X	PK–5	6–8	9–12	587	264	8:1	19	20
Maplebrook School, Amenia	X	X	X	X				77	64	8:1		38
Martin Luther High School, Maspeth			X	X			9–12	420	420	13:1	7	19
The Mary Louis Academy, Jamaica Estates				X			9–12	1,039	1,039	14:1	7	11
Marymount School, New York			X	X	N–3	4–7	8–12	517	215	16:1	18	25
The Masters School, Dobbs Ferry	X	X	X	X		5–8	9–12	465	345	7:1	15	26
McQuaid Jesuit High School, Rochester			X			7–8	9–12	872	680	14:1	15	37
Millbrook School, Millbrook	X	X	X	X			9–12	243	243	8:1	11	14
Mount Mercy Academy, Buffalo				X			9–12	453	453	20:1		10
National Sports Academy at Lake Placid, Lake Placid	X	X	X	X		8	9–PG	77	73	6:1	3	26
New York Military Academy, Cornwall-on-Hudson	X	X	X	X		7–8	9–12	317	274	15:1	2	32
The Nightingale-Bamford School, New York				X	K–4	5–8	9–12	533	161	6:1	12	14
North Country School, Lake Placid	X	X	X	X		4–9		75	57	3:1		39
Northwood School, Lake Placid	X	X	X	X			9–12	153	153	8:1	2	47
Notre Dame- Bishop Gibbons School, Schenectady			X	X		6–8	9–12	392	176	11:1	6	13
Notre Dame High School, Batavia			X	X			9–12	208	208	10:1		17
Oakwood Friends School, Poughkeepsie	X	X	X	X		6–8	9–12	170	136	8:1	8	17
Our Lady of Mercy Academy, Syosset				X			9–12	451	451			27
Our Lady of Victory Academy, Dobbs Ferry				X			9–12	413	413	13:1	6	7

| | STUDENTS ACCEPTED | | | | GRADES | | | STUDENT/FACULTY | | | SCHOOL OFFERINGS (number) | |
| | Boarding | | Day | | | | | | | | | |
	Boys	Girls	Boys	Girls	Lower	Middle	Upper	Total	Upper	Student/ Faculty Ratio	Advanced Placement Subject Areas	Sports
New York—continued												
The Packer Collegiate Institute, Brooklyn Heights			X	X	PK–4	5–8	9–12	940	305	7:1	16	5
The Park School of Buffalo, Snyder			X	X	N–4	5–8	9–12	291	112	9:1	11	12
Polytechnic Preparatory Country Day School, Brooklyn			X	X	N–4	5–8	9–12	940	450	8:1	13	19
Portledge School, Locust Valley			X	X	N–5	6–8	9–12	407	132	6:1	10	9
Poughkeepsie Day School, Poughkeepsie			X	X	PK–4	5–8	9–12	350	115	8:1	3	26
Preston High School, Bronx				X			9–12	551	551	15:1	6	6
Professional Children's School, New York			X	X		4–8	9–12	190	149	8:1	1	
Redemption Christian Academy, Troy	X	X	X	X	K–6	7–8	9–PG	83	41	10:1		3
Regis High School, New York			X				9–12	516	516	10:1		11
Riverdale Country School, Riverdale			X	X	PK–6		7–12	1,046	617	8:1	8	19
Robert Louis Stevenson School, New York			X	X			7–PG	75	75	6:1		26
The Rockland Country Day School, Congers			X	X	K–4	5–8	9–12	173	45	2:1	14	16
Rye Country Day School, Rye			X	X	PK–4	5–8	9–12	828	354	7:1	15	20
Sacred Heart High School, Yonkers			X	X			9–12	386	386	15:1	5	9
Saint Agnes Boys High School, New York			X				9–12	400	400	16:1	3	5
Saint Joseph's Collegiate Institute, Buffalo			X				9–12	852	852	14:1		15
St. Thomas Choir School, New York	X				4–6		7–8	32	15	3:1		24
Saint Vincent Ferrer High School, New York				X			9–12	440	440	16:1		9
School for Young Performers, New York			X	X	K–5	6–8	9–12	12	10	1:1	19	
School of the Holy Child, Rye				X		5–8	9–12	306	202	9:1	14	17
Smith School, New York			X	X			8–12	60	60	4:1	9	1
Soundview Preparatory School, Mount Kisco			X	X		6–8	9–PG	67	49	8:1	4	3
The Spence School, New York				X	K–4	5–8	9–12	621	185	7:1	3	20
Staten Island Academy, Staten Island			X	X	PK–4	5–8	9–12	408	126	5:1	12	10
Stella Maris High School and the Maura Clarke Junior High Program, Rockaway Park			X	X		6–8	9–12	476	411	11:1	2	11
The Stony Brook School, Stony Brook	X	X	X	X		7–8	9–12	361	283	9:1	15	17
Storm King School, Cornwall-on-Hudson	X	X	X	X			9–PG	120	120	6:1	2	49
Trevor Day School, New York			X	X	N–5	6–8	9–12	775	236	6:1	6	13
Trinity-Pawling School, Pawling	X		X			7–8	9–PG	306	281	7:1	14	20
United Nations International School, New York			X	X	K–4	5–8	9–12	1,511	429	10:1		49
The Ursuline School, New Rochelle				X		6–8	9–12	805	646	15:1	10	13
The Waldorf School of Garden City, Garden City			X	X	N–5	6–8	9–12	348	85	7:1		12
The Windsor School, Flushing			X	X		6–8	9–13	103	87	14:1	7	11
Winston Preparatory School, New York			X	X		6–8	9–12	139	79	3:1		5
York Preparatory School, New York			X	X		6–8	9–12	298	214	8:1	3	27
North Carolina												
The Achievement School, Inc., Raleigh			X	X	1–5	6–8	9–12	120	39	5:1		1
Asheville School, Asheville	X	X	X	X			9–12	242	242	4:1	15	58
Auldern Academy, Siler City		X					9–12	40	40	6:1		19
Camelot Academy, Durham			X	X	K–6		7–12	85	45	10:1	6	3
Cannon School, Concord			X	X	PK–4	5–8	9–12	707	158	7:1	9	14
Cape Fear Academy, Wilmington			X	X	PK–5	6–8	9–12	513	164	8:1	11	11

	STUDENTS ACCEPTED				GRADES			STUDENT/FACULTY			SCHOOL OFFERINGS (number)	
	Boarding		Day									
	Boys	Girls	Boys	Girls	Lower	Middle	Upper	Total	Upper	Student/Faculty Ratio	Advanced Placement Subject Areas	Sports
Carolina—continued												
...a Day School, Asheville			X	X	PK-5	6-8	9-12	651	206	9:1	16	11
...Academy, Cary			X	X		6-8	9-12	671	371	11:1		45
...arlotte Catholic High School, Charlotte			X	X			9-12	1,019	1,019		14	23
Charlotte Christian School, Charlotte			X	X	JK-5	6-8	9-12	975	362	9:1	18	18
Charlotte Country Day School, Charlotte			X	X	PK-4	5-8	9-12	1,604	453	12:1	14	20
Charlotte Latin School, Charlotte			X	X	K-5	6-8	9-12	1,339	448	9:1	14	25
Christ School, Arden	X		X				8-12	170	170	5:1	5	49
Cresset Christian Academy, Durham			X	X	PS-5	6-8	9-12	317	89	8:1	5	10
Fayetteville Academy, Fayetteville			X	X	PK-5	6-8	9-12	374	133	15:1	8	14
Forsyth Country Day School, Lewisville			X	X	PK-4	5-8	9-12	951	358	6:1	8	15
Gaston Day School, Gastonia			X	X	PK-4	5-8	9-12	395	95	9:1	9	11
Greenfield School, Wilson			X	X	PS-4	5-8	9-12	320	67	3:1	3	7
Greensboro Day School, Greensboro			X	X	K-5	6-8	9-12	871	318	10:1	17	18
Guilford Day School, Greensboro			X	X	1-5	6-8	9-12	123	62	8:1		5
Harrells Christian Academy, Harrells			X	X	K-5	6-8	9-12	386	96	18:1	11	8
The Hill Center, Durham Academy, Durham			X	X	K-5	6-8	9-12	169	72	4:1		
Oak Ridge Military Academy, Oak Ridge	X	X	X	X		7-8	9-12	250	200	8:1	12	27
The O'Neal School, Southern Pines			X	X	PK-4	5-8	9-12	411	143	9:1	8	9
The Patterson School, Patterson	X	X	X	X		7-8	9-12	30	28	3:1		40
Providence Day School, Charlotte			X	X	PK-5	6-8	9-12	1,470	443	10:1	19	22
Ravenscroft School, Raleigh			X	X	PK-5	6-8	9-12	1,101	365	6:1	17	19
Ridgecroft School, Ahoskie			X	X	PK-5	6-8	9-12	333	93	15:1		11
Rocky Mount Academy, Rocky Mount			X	X	PK-5	6-8	9-12	415	119	7:1	8	8
St. David's School, Raleigh			X	X	PK-4	5-8	9-12	460	181	10:1	15	16
Saint Mary's School, Raleigh		X		X			9-12	230	230	9:1	9	16
Salem Academy, Winston-Salem		X		X			9-12	194	194	9:1	10	20
Stone Mountain School, Black Mountain	X					6-8	9-12	58	30	4:1		41
Wayne Country Day School, Goldsboro			X	X	PK-6		7-12	239	102	15:1	5	9
Westchester Academy, High Point			X	X	K-5	6-8	9-12	460	166	9:1	14	10
Ohio												
The Andrews School, Willoughby		X		X		6-8	9-12	170	112	5:1	7	32
Archbishop Alter High School, Kettering			X	X			9-12	713	713	14:1	7	16
Catholic Central High School, Springfield			X	X			9-12	201	201	11:1	4	14
Central Christian High School, Kidron			X	X	K-5	6-8	9-12	350	223	13:1		11
Chaminade-Julienne High School, Dayton			X	X			9-12	974	974	14:1	7	13
Cincinnati Country Day School, Cincinnati			X	X	PK-5	6-8	9-12	860	318	9:1	11	13
The Columbus Academy, Gahanna			X	X	PK-4	5-8	9-12	944	312	8:1	17	14
Columbus School for Girls, Columbus				X	PK-5	6-8	9-12	655	243	12:1	13	46
Delphos Saint John's High School, Delphos			X	X			9-12	354	354	14:1		12
Elyria Catholic High School, Elyria			X	X			9-12	492	492	14:1	5	15
Gilmour Academy, Gates Mills	X	X	X	X	PK-6	7-8	9-12	758	422	9:1	15	39
The Grand River Academy, Austinburg	X						9-12	104	104	7:1	3	50
Hathaway Brown School, Shaker Heights			X	X	PS-4	5-8	9-12	823	286	6:1	13	12
Hawken School, Gates Mills			X	X	PK-5	6-8	9-12	946	435	9:1	15	14
Laurel School, Shaker Heights			X	X	PS-4	5-8	9-12	639	195	8:1	15	11
Lawrence School, Broadview Heights			X	X	1-6		7-11	220	120	11:1		9
Magnificat High School, Rocky River				X			9-12	833	833	12:1		13

	STUDENTS ACCEPTED				GRADES			STUDENT/FACULTY			SCHOOL OFFERINGS (number)	
	Boarding		Day									
	Boys	Girls	Boys	Girls	Lower	Middle	Upper	Total	Upper	Student/ Faculty Ratio	Advanced Placement Subject Areas	Sports
Ohio—*continued*												
Maumee Valley Country Day School, Toledo			X	X	N-6	7-8	9-12	456	168	10:1	8	14
The Miami Valley School, Dayton			X	X	PK-5	6-8	9-12	480	172	7:1	12	11
Olney Friends School, Barnesville	X	X	X	X			9-12	66	66	4:1	3	14
Padua Franciscan High School, Parma			X	X			9-12	1,067	1,067	18:1	5	33
Purcell Marian High School, Cincinnati			X	X			9-12	600	600	11:1	6	20
Saint Augustine Academy, Lakewood				X			9-12	225	225	10:1	2	16
St. Francis de Sales High School, Toledo			X				9-12	678	678	16:1	18	15
Saint Ignatius High School, Cleveland			X				9-12	1,379	1,379	16:1	13	31
Saint Joseph Central Catholic High School, Fremont			X	X			9-12	282	282	13:1	2	13
Saint Xavier High School, Cincinnati			X				9-12	1,451	1,451	15:1	19	16
The Seven Hills School, Cincinnati			X	X	PK-5	6-8	9-12	1,062	310	15:1	13	13
Stephen T. Badin High School, Hamilton			X	X			9-12	676	676	18:1	3	2
The Summit Country Day School, Cincinnati			X	X	PK-3	4-8	9-12	1,100	314	9:1	19	18
University School, Hunting Valley			X		K-5	6-8	9-12	868	395	15:1	13	14
Ursuline Academy School, Cincinnati				X			9-12	650	650			15
The Wellington School, Columbus			X	X	PK-4	5-8	9-12	586	172	12:1	13	13
Western Reserve Academy, Hudson	X	X	X	X			9-12	386	386	6:1	19	43
Oklahoma												
Bishop McGuinness Catholic High School, Oklahoma City			X	X	9-10		11-12	662	333	20:1	4	15
Casady School, Oklahoma City			X	X	PK-4	5-8	9-12	918	334	9:1	17	29
Cascia Hall Preparatory School, Tulsa			X	X		6-8	9-12	587	371	12:1	13	18
Heritage Hall, Oklahoma City			X	X	PS-4	5-8	9-12	843	316	18:1	6	16
Holland Hall School, Tulsa			X	X	PK-3	4-8	9-12	1,025	350	10:1	18	17
Victory Christian School, Tulsa			X	X	K-5	6-8	9-12	1,385	415	20:1	4	11
Oregon												
The Academy for Global Exploration, Eugene	X	X								3:1		43
Canyonville Christian Academy, Canyonville	X	X	X	X		6-8	9-12	149	135	12:1	4	5
The Catlin Gabel School, Portland			X	X	PS-5	6-8	9-12	688	252	7:1	4	25
The Delphian School, Sheridan	X	X	X	X	K-4	5-7	8-12	250				10
East Linn Christian Academy, Lebanon			X	X	PK-6	7-8	9-12	281	119	13:1		6
Hosanna Christian School, Kamath Falls			X	X	PK-6	7-8	9-12	265	51	8:1		7
J Bar J Learning Center, Bend				X		7-8	9-12	25	22	12:1		31
Mount Bachelor Academy, Prineville	X	X						84		4:1		34
The Northwest Academy, Portland			X	X		6-8	9-12	88	61	15:1		
Oak Hill School, Eugene			X	X	K-5	6-8	9-12	99	29	2:1	18	13
Oregon Episcopal School, Portland	X	X	X	X	PK-5	6-8	9-12	747	246	7:1	8	9
Portland Lutheran School, Portland	X	X	X	X	PK-5	6-8	9-12	293	95	6:1		12
Regis High School, Stayton			X	X			9-12	190	190	15:1	1	15
St. Mary's School, Medford			X	X		6-8	9-12	322	194	10:1	16	28
Salem Academy, Salem			X	X	K-6	7-8	9-12	438	194	17:1	2	11
Santiam Christian School, Corvallis			X	X	PS-6	7-8	9-12	778	288	17:1		11
Wellsprings Friends School, Eugene			X	X			9-12	47	47	6:1		7
Western Mennonite School, Salem	X	X	X	X		6-8	9-12	187	130	13:1	1	8

| | STUDENTS ACCEPTED | | | | GRADES | | | STUDENT/FACULTY | | | SCHOOL OFFERINGS (number) | |
| | Boarding | | Day | | | | | | | | | |
	Boys	Girls	Boys	Girls	Lower	Middle	Upper	Total	Upper	Student/ Faculty Ratio	Advanced Placement Subject Areas	Sports
sylvania												
...gton Friends School, Jenkintown			X	X	PK-5	6-8	9-12	679	299	8:1	7	11
...Agnes Irwin School, Rosemont				X	K-4	5-8	9-12	653	237	7:1	12	25
...kiba Hebrew Academy, Merion Station			X	X		6-8	9-12	335	260	7:1	8	9
The Baldwin School, Bryn Mawr				X	PK-5	6-8	9-12	635	194	8:1	11	20
Bishop Carroll High School, Ebensburg			X	X			9-12	294	294	12:1		11
Bishop McDevitt High School, Wyncote			X	X			9-12	810	810	20:1	5	20
Carson Long Military Institute, New Bloomfield	X					6-8	9-12	182	142	11:1		19
Central Catholic High School, Pittsburgh			X				9-12	868	868	15:1	9	19
CFS, The School at Church Farm, Paoli	X		X			7-8	9-12	195	150	8:1	4	16
Chestnut Hill Academy, Philadelphia			X		PK-5	6-8	9-12	551	188	7:1	14	16
Christopher Dock Mennonite High School, Lansdale			X	X			9-12	427	427	14:1	1	10
The Concept School, Westtown			X	X		5-8	9-12	43	30	4:1		16
Country Day School of the Sacred Heart, Bryn Mawr				X	PK-4	5-8	9-12	371	191	10:1	5	7
Delaware County Christian School, Newtown Square			X	X	K-5	6-8	9-12	948	389	12:1	8	12
Delaware Valley Friends School, Paoli			X	X		7-8	9-12	166	131	5:1		12
Devon Preparatory School, Devon			X			6-8	9-12	279	192	10:1	13	14
The Ellis School, Pittsburgh				X	K-4	5-8	9-12	496	185	7:1	12	9
The Episcopal Academy, Merion			X	X	PK-5	6-8	9-12	1,119	428	7:1	12	25
Friends' Central School, Wynnewood			X	X	PK-4	5-8	9-12	1,002	377	9:1		25
Friends Select School, Philadelphia			X	X	PK-4	5-8	9-12	508	219	8:1	3	10
George School, Newtown	X	X	X	X			9-12	542	542	7:1	9	34
Germantown Friends School, Philadelphia			X	X	K-5	6-8	9-12	898	363	9:1		17
Girard College, Philadelphia	X	X			1-5	6-8	9-12	623	181	14:1	2	17
The Grier School, Tyrone		X				7-8	9-PG	192	168	6:1	5	31
The Harrisburg Academy, Wormleysburg			X	X	N-4	5-8	9-12	464	109	8:1	11	9
The Haverford School, Haverford			X		PK-5	6-8	9-12	951	331	8:1	19	25
The Hill School, Pottstown	X	X	X	X			9-PG	482	482	6:1	14	24
The Hill Top Preparatory School, Rosemont			X	X		6-8	9-12	85	59	3:1		37
Holy Ghost Preparatory School, Bensalem			X				9-12	508	508	11:1	14	18
The Janus School, Mount Joy			X	X	1-7		8-12	72	27	3:1		
Keystone National High School, Bloomsburg			X	X			9-12	8,700	8,700			
Kimberton Waldorf School, Kimberton			X	X	PK-8		9-12	382	102	7:1		13
The Kiski School, Saltsburg	X						9-PG	196	196	5:1	14	28
Lancaster Country Day School, Lancaster			X	X	K-5	6-8	9-12	520	171	5:1	11	15
Lansdale Catholic High School, Lansdale			X	X			9-12	848	848		5	21
La Salle College High School, Wyndmoor			X				9-12	1,034	1,034	11:1	17	25
Lehigh Valley Christian High School, Allentown			X	X			9-12	170	170	12:1	3	7
Linden Hall School for Girls, Lititz		X		X		6-8	9-PG	125	81	4:1	4	13
Living Word Academy, Lancaster			X	X	K-5	6-8	9-12	363	160	14:1	3	9
Malvern Preparatory School, Malvern			X			6-8	9-12	595	434	9:1	15	17
Mercersburg Academy, Mercersburg	X	X	X	X			9-PG	444	444	5:1	17	35
Mercyhurst Preparatory School, Erie			X	X			9-12	762	762	15:1		22
Milton Hershey School, Hershey	X	X			K-5	6-8	9-12	1,285	568	15:1	5	12

	STUDENTS ACCEPTED				GRADES			STUDENT/FACULTY			SCHOOL OFFERINGS (number)	
	Boarding		Day									
	Boys	Girls	Boys	Girls	Lower	Middle	Upper	Total	Upper	Student/ Faculty Ratio	Advanced Placement Subject Areas	Sports
Pennsylvania—*continued*												
MMI Preparatory School, Freeland			X	X		6–8	9–12	177	114	10:1	10	12
Moravian Academy, Bethlehem			X	X	PK–5	6–8	9–12	790	276	7:1	9	8
Mount Saint Joseph Academy, Flourtown				X			9–12	558	558	15:1	14	15
The Oakland School, Pittsburgh			X	X			8–12	60	60	6:1	3	32
Our Lady of the Sacred Heart, Coraopolis			X	X			9–12	318	318	12:1		13
The Pathway School, Norristown	X	X	X	X				158	92	6:1		5
Perkiomen School, Pennsburg	X	X	X	X		5–8	9–PG	243	198	7:1	12	18
The Phelps School, Malvern	X		X		7–8		9–12	143	129	8:1		25
Philadelphia-Montgomery Christian Academy, Erdenheim			X	X	K–5	6–8	9–12	418	172	10:1	2	8
Pine Forge Academy, Pine Forge	X	X	X	X			9–12	183	183	15:1		6
Quigley Catholic High School, Baden			X	X			9–12	192	192	12:1	3	18
Saint Basil Academy, Jenkintown				X			9–12	378	378	9:1	9	11
St. Joseph's Preparatory School, Philadelphia			X				9–12	985	985	23:1	14	18
Sewickley Academy, Sewickley			X	X	PK–5	6–8	9–12	795	308	6:1	14	24
Shady Side Academy, Pittsburgh	X	X	X	X	K–5	6–8	9–12	954	502	8:1	6	23
The Shipley School, Bryn Mawr			X	X	PK–5	6–8	9–12	844	322	8:1	17	23
Solebury School, New Hope	X	X	X	X		7–8	9–PG	220	191	5:1	7	29
Springside School, Philadelphia				X	PK–4	5–8	9–12	628	175	10:1	18	26
Valley Forge Military Academy and College, Wayne	X					7–8	9–PG	451	411	12:1	4	35
Villa Joseph Marie High School, Holland				X			9–12	340	340	13:1	6	7
Villa Maria Academy, Erie			X	X			9–12	455	455		4	14
Villa Maria Academy, Malvern				X			9–12	441	441	9:1	14	15
Westtown School, Westtown	X	X	X	X	PK–5	6–8	9–12	782	403	8:1	10	29
William Penn Charter School, Philadelphia			X	X	K–5	6–8	9–12	877	406	15:1	13	16
Winchester Thurston School, Pittsburgh			X	X	PK–5	6–8	9–12	602	173	7:1	17	23
The Woodlynde School, Strafford			X	X	1–5	6–8	9–12	323	123	6:1		12
Wyoming Seminary, Kingston	X	X	X	X	PK–8		9–PG	822	444	8:1	19	17
York Country Day School, York			X	X	PS–5	6–8	9–12	210	60		8	6
Rhode Island												
La Salle Academy, Providence			X	X		7–8	9–12	1,315	1,226	13:1	10	24
Lincoln School, Providence				X	N–5	6–8	9–12	421	160	6:1	15	25
Mount Saint Charles Academy, Woonsocket			X	X			7–12	971	971	14:1	10	20
Portsmouth Abbey School, Portsmouth	X	X	X	X			9–12	306	306	7:1	14	18
Prout School, Wakefield			X	X			9–12	476	476	12:1		21
Providence Country Day School, East Providence			X	X		5–8	9–12	295	196	6:1	11	18
Rocky Hill School, East Greenwich			X	X	PS–5	6–8	9–12	333	148	6:1	8	14
St. Andrew's School, Barrington	X	X	X	X		6–8	9–12	185	152	5:1		11
St. George's School, Middletown	X	X	X	X			9–12	340	340	5:1	19	21
The Wheeler School, Providence			X	X	N–5	6–8	9–12	781	310	13:1	11	14
South Carolina												
Aiken Preparatory School, Aiken			X	X	PK–5	6–8	9–12	157	20	5:1		12
Ashley Hall, Charleston			X	X	PS–5	6–8	9–12	615	173	13:1	18	28
Beaufort Academy, Beaufort			X	X	PK–4	5–8	9–12	334	87	11:1	5	15
Ben Lippen Schools, Columbia	X	X	X	X	K–5	6–8	9–12	869	345	15:1	7	15
Camden Military Academy, Camden	X					7–8	9–12	305	236	12:1	5	11

	Boarding		Day		GRADES			STUDENT/FACULTY			SCHOOL OFFERINGS (number)	
	Boys	Girls	Boys	Girls	Lower	Middle	Upper	Total	Upper	Student/Faculty Ratio	Advanced Placement Subject Areas	Sports
South Carolina—*continued*												
Cardinal Newman School, Columbia			X	X		7–8	9–12	380	229	10:1	3	14
Christ Church Episcopal School, Greenville			X	X	K–4	5–8	9–12	951	286	10:1	16	14
Hammond School, Columbia			X	X	PS–4	5–8	9–12	907	231	9:1	14	20
Hilton Head Preparatory School, Hilton Head Island			X	X	1–5	6–8	9–12	393	130	12:1	19	15
Porter-Gaud School, Charleston			X	X	1–5	6–8	9–12	878	328	15:1	13	16
Spartanburg Day School, Spartanburg			X	X	PK–4	5–8	9–12	464	129	11:1	16	11
Trident Academy, Mt. Pleasant			X	X	K–6	7–8	9–12	145	48	4:1		8
Wilson Hall, Sumter			X	X	PS–5	6–8	9–12	750	180	12:1	14	19
South Dakota												
Dakota Christian High School, New Holland			X	X			9–12	54	54	8:1		15
Freeman Academy, Freeman	X	X	X	X	5–8		9–12	77	37	8:1		6
Sioux Falls Christian High School, Sioux Falls			X	X	K–5	6–8	9–12	602	182	17:1	3	7
Sunshine Bible Academy, Miller	X	X	X	X	K–5	6–8	9–12	80	55	6:1		10
Tennessee												
Battle Ground Academy, Franklin			X	X	K–4	5–8	9–12	919	387	11:1	12	15
Baylor School, Chattanooga	X	X	X	X	6–8		9–12	1,026	696	8:1	17	49
Boyd-Buchanan School, Chattanooga			X	X	K4–5	6–8	9–12	963	322	14:1	7	10
Brentwood Academy, Brentwood			X	X		6–8	9–12	731	425	10:1	5	22
Chattanooga Christian School, Chattanooga			X	X	K–5	6–8	9–12	1,052	387	18:1	4	35
David Lipscomb High School, Nashville			X	X	PK–4	5–8	9–12	1,477	519	16:1	4	14
Davidson Academy, Nashville			X	X	PK–6	7–8	9–12	910	289	10:1	4	15
Donelson Christian Academy, Nashville			X	X	K–5	6–8	9–12	884	292	15:1	6	13
Evangelical Christian School, Cordova			X	X	K–5	6–8	9–12	1,430	488	11:1	5	15
Father Ryan High School, Nashville			X	X			9–12	952	952	13:1	11	25
First Assembly Christian School, Cordova			X	X	PK–6		7–12	550	267	12:1	2	5
Franklin Road Academy, Nashville			X	X	PK–4	5–8	9–12	953	313	9:1	10	20
Friendship Christian School, Lebanon			X	X	PK–4	5–8	9–12	513	186	15:1	2	17
Girls Preparatory School, Chattanooga				X		6–8	9–12	767	438	8:1	12	42
Harding Academy, Memphis			X	X				620		13:1	6	14
The Harpeth Hall School, Nashville				X		5–8	9–12	567	356	8:1	13	35
Hutchison School, Memphis				X	PK–4	5–8	9–12	826	256	16:1	13	10
The King's Academy, Seymour	X	X	X	X	K–5	6–8	9–12	359	110	20:1	3	25
Knoxville Catholic High School, Knoxville			X	X			9–12	506	506	14:1	9	19
Lausanne Collegiate School, Memphis			X	X	PK–4	5–8	9–12	715	200	9:1	13	43
The McCallie School, Chattanooga	X		X			6–8	9–12	890	631	8:1	19	52
Memphis University School, Memphis			X			7–8	9–12	617	423	17:1	19	11
Middle Tennessee Christian School, Murfreesboro			X	X	PK–6	7–8	9–12	590	156	12:1	3	12
Montgomery Bell Academy, Nashville			X			7–8	9–12	665	473	9:1	16	34
Nashville Christian School, Nashville			X	X	K4–5	6–8	9–12	486	163	20:1	5	21
Saint Agnes Academy, Memphis				X			9–12	357	357	8:1	8	11
St. Andrew's–Sewanee School, Sewanee	X	X	X	X		7–8	9–12	259	195	7:1	6	31
St. Benedict at Auburndale, Cordova			X	X	PK–6	7–8	9–12	1,196	498	15:1	4	15
St. Cecilia Academy, Nashville				X			9–12	272	272	9:1	10	17
St. Mary's Episcopal School, Memphis				X	PK–4	5–8	9–12	828	239	10:1	14	14

| | STUDENTS ACCEPTED | | | | GRADES | | | STUDENT/FACULTY | | | SCHOOL OFFERINGS (number) | |
| | Boarding | | Day | | | | | | | | | |
	Boys	Girls	Boys	Girls	Lower	Middle	Upper	Total	Upper	Student/ Faculty Ratio	Advanced Placement Subject Areas	Sports
Tennessee—continued												
University School of Jackson, Jackson			X	X	PK–4	5–8	9–12	1,291	334	13:1	10	15
University School of Nashville, Nashville			X	X	K–4	5–8	9–12	995	347	12:1	19	19
The Webb School, Bell Buckle	X	X	X	X		6–8	9–PG	292	218	8:1	6	62
Webb School of Knoxville, Knoxville			X	X	K–5	6–8	9–12	1,051	435	10:1	19	24
Texas												
Alexander Smith Academy, Houston			X	X			9–12	70	70	7:1	4	11
Allen Academy, Bryan	X		X	X	PK–6		7–12	346	121	10:1	4	13
All Saints' Episcopal School of Fort Worth, Fort Worth			X	X	K–6	7–8	9–12	775	234	9:1	9	24
Bishop Dunne High School, Dallas			X	X		7–8	9–12	584	499	11:1	11	14
Bishop Lynch Catholic High School, Dallas			X	X			9–12	1,161	1,161	14:1	13	31
The Briarwood School, Houston			X	X	K–6	7–8	9–12	233	72	8:1		6
The Brook Hill School, Bullard	X	X	X	X		5–8	9–12	184	109	7:1		11
Central Catholic High School, San Antonio			X				9–12	514	514	12:1	8	21
Cistercian Preparatory School, Irving			X			5–8	9–12	344	170	9:1	19	8
Cliffwood School, Houston			X	X	K–5	6–8	9–12	60	17	12:1		
Dallas Academy, Dallas			X	X		7–8	9–12	133	107	8:1		12
Dallas Christian School, Mesquite			X	X	PK–5	6–8	9–12	774	261	15:1		11
Duchesne Academy of the Sacred Heart, Houston				X	PK–4	5–8	9–12	647	241	7:1	11	11
The Emery Weiner School, Houston			X	X		6–8	9–11	327	108	6:1		13
Episcopal High School, Bellaire			X	X			9–12	611	611	9:1	9	19
The Episcopal School of Dallas, Dallas			X	X	PK–4	5–8	9–12	1,118	381	8:1	15	18
Fairhill School, Dallas			X	X	1–5	6–8	9–12	220	88			8
First Baptist Academy, Dallas			X	X	K–4	5–8	9–12	785	248	11:1	4	16
Fort Worth Christian School, Fort Worth			X	X	PK–5	6–8	9–12	788	259	12:1	6	15
Fort Worth Country Day School, Fort Worth			X	X	K–4	5–8	9–12	1,105	375	10:1	17	15
Gateway School, Arlington			X	X		7–8	9–12	31	23	10:1		4
Greenhill School, Addison			X	X	PK–4	5–8	9–12	1,250	428	18:1	13	32
The Hockaday School, Dallas		X		X	PK–4	5–8	9–12	1,018	438	12:1	19	51
Houston Learning Academy-Central Campus, Houston			X	X			9–12	54	54	15:1		
Huntington-Surrey School, Austin			X	X			9–12	70	70	4:1	6	
Hyde Park Baptist School, Austin			X	X	K–6	7–8	9–12	779	189	7:1	15	34
Jesuit College Preparatory School, Dallas			X				9–12	999	999	11:1	10	24
The John Cooper School, The Woodlands			X	X	K–5	6–8	9–12	853	278	12:1	12	12
Keystone School, San Antonio			X	X	K–5	6–8	9–12	389	113	10:1	9	7
Lakehill Preparatory School, Dallas			X	X	K–4	5–8	9–12	385	107	8:1	10	11
Loretto Academy, El Paso			X	X	PK–5	6–8	9–12	662	366	18:1	6	12
Lutheran High School of Dallas, Dallas			X	X		7–8	9–12	314	221	14:1	5	13
Lydia Patterson Institute, El Paso			X	X		8	9–12	470	276	20:1		4
Marine Military Academy, Harlingen	X						8–12	402	402	12:1	6	27
The Monarch School, Houston			X	X				69	22	8:1		
Northland Christian, Houston			X	X	K–5	6–8	9–12	719	220	11:1	4	16
The Oakridge School, Arlington			X	X	PS–4	5–8	9–12	744	228	9:1	15	15
Saint Agnes Academy, Houston				X			9–12	785	785	15:1	11	17
St. Anthony Catholic High School, San Antonio	X	X	X	X			9–12	314	314	20:1		14
St. Augustine High School, Laredo			X	X		6–8	9–12	643	442	25:1	2	9

	STUDENTS ACCEPTED				GRADES			STUDENT/FACULTY			SCHOOL OFFERINGS (number)	
	Boarding		Day									
	Boys	Girls	Boys	Girls	Lower	Middle	Upper	Total	Upper	Student/Faculty Ratio	Advanced Placement Subject Areas	Sports
Texas—continued												
St. John's School, Houston			X	X	K–5	6–8	9–12	1,218	527	7:1	16	18
St. Mark's School of Texas, Dallas			X		1–4	5–8	9–12	817	355	8:1	19	23
Saint Mary's Hall, San Antonio			X	X	PK–5	6–8	9–PG	879	311	8:1	19	18
St. Pius X High School, Houston			X	X			9–12	620	620	14:1	6	14
St. Stephen's Episcopal School, Austin	X	X	X	X		6–8	9–12	645	443	8:1	12	15
St. Thomas High School, Houston			X				9–12	638	638	15:1	9	15
San Marcos Baptist Academy, San Marcos	X	X	X	X		6–8	9–12	211	166	10:1	5	26
Second Baptist School, Houston			X	X	PK–5	6–8	9–12	1,000	325	7:1	17	18
Southwest Christian School, Inc., Fort Worth			X	X	PK–6	7–8	9–12	635	179	16:1		9
Still Creek Christian School, Bryan			X	X		6–8	9–12	25	8	2:1		
Texas Military Institute, San Antonio	X	X	X	X		6–8	9–12	325	227	7:1	14	17
Trinity Christian Academy, Addison			X	X	K–4	5–8	9–12	1,457	466	10:1	14	19
Trinity School of Midland, Midland			X	X	PK–5	6–8	9–12	460	155	8:1	13	16
Trinity School of Texas, Longview			X	X	K–5	6–8	9–12	216	66	4:1	10	10
Trinity Valley School, Fort Worth			X	X	K–4	5–8	9–12	950	319	10:1	15	11
Tyler Street Christian Academy, Dallas			X	X	P3–6	7–8	9–12	216	70	10:1		7
Valley Grande Academy, Weslaco	X	X	X	X			9–12	100	100	5:1		3
Walden Preparatory School, Dallas			X	X			9–12	50	50	6:1		
Westbury Christian School, Houston			X	X	K–6	7–8	9–12	470	228	10:1	7	13
The Winston School, Dallas			X	X	1–6	7–8	9–12	219	114	5:1		12
The Winston School San Antonio, San Antonio			X	X	K–6	7–8	9–12	171	72	12:1		12
Utah												
The Academy at Cedar Mountain, Cedar City	X	X				7–8	9–12	30	26	4:1		13
Aspen Ranch, Loa	X	X				7–8	9–12	72	66	8:1		24
A City for Children and Teens, Springville			X	X	K–5		6–12	40	23	10:1		
Cross Creek Programs, LaVerkin	X	X				7–8	9–12	385	365	17:1		37
Intermountain Christian School, Salt Lake City			X	X	PK–5	6–8	9–12	287	62		4	3
Oakley School, Oakley	X	X					9–PG	100	100			16
Pine Ridge Academy, Draper	X	X	X	X		7–9	10–12	42	24	4:1		
Provo Canyon School, Provo	X	X				7–8	9–12	207	191	10:1		20
Realms of Inquiry, Salt Lake City			X	X	PK–6	7–8	9–12	96	28	6:1	5	53
Rowland Hall-St. Mark's School, Salt Lake City			X	X	PK–5	6–8	9–12	955	289	14:1	15	26
Salt Lake Lutheran High School, Salt Lake City			X	X			9–12	98	98	15:1		7
Sorenson's Ranch School, Koosharem	X	X					7–12	120	120	10:1		34
Wasatch Academy, Mt. Pleasant	X	X	X	X			9–12	133	133	6:1	6	48
The Waterford School, Sandy			X	X	PK–5	6–8	9–12	991	274	5:1	14	26
Vermont												
Burke Mountain Academy, East Burke	X	X	X	X			8–PG	61	61	7:1	2	7
Burr and Burton Academy, Manchester	X	X	X	X			9–12	551	551		6	21
The Greenwood School, Putney	X							40		3:1		17
King George School, Sutton	X	X						65		3:1	8	19
Long Trail School, Dorset	X	X	X	X		6–8	9–12	157	80	6:1	9	37
Lyndon Institute, Lyndon Center	X	X	X	X			9–12	619	619	14:1	3	22
Pine Ridge School, Williston	X	X	X	X				98	98	2:1		23

| | STUDENTS ACCEPTED | | | | GRADES | | | STUDENT/FACULTY | | | SCHOOL OFFERINGS (number) | |
| | Boarding | | Day | | | | | | | | | |
	Boys	Girls	Boys	Girls	Lower	Middle	Upper	Total	Upper	Student/ Faculty Ratio	Advanced Placement Subject Areas	Sports
Vermont—*continued*												
The Putney School, Putney	X	X	X	X			9–PG	214	214	5:1	2	53
Rock Point School, Burlington	X	X	X	X			9–12	40	40	5:1		27
St. Johnsbury Academy, St. Johnsbury	X	X	X	X			9–PG	959	959	9:1	19	35
Stratton Mountain School, Stratton Mountain	X	X	X	X		7–8	9–PG	113	92	6:1		11
Vermont Academy, Saxtons River.	X	X	X	X			9–PG	263	263	7:1	8	72
Virginia												
Bishop Ireton High School, Alexandria			X	X			9–12	811	811	14:1	11	23
The Blue Ridge School, St. George.	X						9–12	170	170	6:1		37
Broadwater Academy, Exmore			X	X	PK–5	6–8	9–12	457	91	13:1	7	11
Cape Henry Collegiate School, Virginia Beach			X	X	PK–5	6–8	9–12	1,015	339	10:1	12	31
Chatham Hall, Chatham		X		X			9–12	134	134	4:1	18	17
Christchurch School, Christchurch.	X		X	X			8–PG	231	231	7:1	13	19
The Collegiate School, Richmond.			X	X	K–4	5–8	9–12	1,524	463	15:1	11	24
Crawford Day School, Portsmouth			X	X				60		2:1		
Eastern Mennonite High School, Harrisonburg			X	X		6–8	9–12	336	222	10:1		10
Episcopal High School, Alexandria	X	X					9–12	423	423	6:1	19	44
Fishburne Military School, Waynesboro. . . .	X		X			8	9–12	180	160	8:1	3	25
Flint Hill School, Oakton			X	X	JK–4	5–8	9–12	921	337	10:1	18	31
Fork Union Military Academy, Fork Union .	X		X			6–8	9–PG	650	544	17:1	5	37
Foxcroft School, Middleburg.		X		X			9–12	186	186	6:1	12	23
Fuqua School, Farmville.			X	X	PK–5	6–8	9–12	500	151	16:1	5	11
Hampton Roads Academy, Newport News .			X	X		6–8	9–12	502	311		18	15
Hargrave Military Academy, Chatham	X		X	X		7–8	9–PG	425	387	11:1	3	50
Highland School, Warrenton			X	X	PK–5	6–8	9–12	495	192	5:1	16	31
Isle of Wight Academy, Isle of Wight.			X	X	PK–7		8–12	521	176	13:1	4	7
Little Keswick School, Keswick	X							30	10	4:1		14
The Madeira School, McLean.		X		X			9–12	302	302	6:1	15	17
Massanutten Military Academy, Woodstock.	X	X	X	X		6–8	9–PG	190	158	12:1	1	64
Miller School, Charlottesville.	X	X	X	X		6–8	9–12	141	98	6:1	10	38
New Dominion School, Dillwyn	X	X					6–12	106	106	6:1		6
Norfolk Academy, Norfolk.			X	X	1–6	7–9	10–12	1,212	335	9:1	17	25
Norfolk Collegiate School, Norfolk.			X	X	K–5	6–8	9–12	861	303	7:1	18	15
Notre Dame Academy, Middleburg.			X	X			9–12	285	285	9:1	11	25
Oak Hill Academy, Mouth of Wilson	X	X	X	X		8	9–12	114	112	9:1	2	22
Oakland School, Keswick.	X	X	X	X				86	86	5:1		34
The Potomac School, McLean			X	X	K–3	4–8	9–12	875	315	6:1	14	22
Randolph-Macon Academy, Front Royal. . . .	X	X	X	X		6–8	9–PG	363	292	8:1	7	28
Roanoke Catholic School, Roanoke			X	X	PK–7		8–12	595				
St. Anne's–Belfield School, Charlottesville. .	X	X	X	X	PK–4	5–8	9–12	843	311	12:1	11	14
St. Catherine's School, Richmond.		X		X	PK–5	6–8	9–12	834	326	6:1	17	30
St. Christopher's School, Richmond.		X			JK–5	6–8	9–12	911	287	6:1	18	23
Saint Gertrude High School, Richmond				X			9–12	265	265	9:1	6	12
St. Margaret's School, Tappahannock.		X		X			8–12	152	152	6:1	5	19
St. Stephen's & St. Agnes School, Alexandria			X	X	JK–5	6–8	9–12	1,155	445	7:1	19	22
Stuart Hall, Staunton.		X	X	X		5–8	9–12	166	99	7:1	4	11

| | STUDENTS ACCEPTED | | | | GRADES | | | STUDENT/FACULTY | | | SCHOOL OFFERINGS (number) | |
| | Boarding | | Day | | | | | | | | | |
	Boys	Girls	Boys	Girls	Lower	Middle	Upper	Total	Upper	Student/Faculty Ratio	Advanced Placement Subject Areas	Sports
Virginia—*continued*												
Tandem Friends School, Charlottesville....			X	X		5-8	9-12	231	133	8:1	5	6
Thornton Friends School/N.V.A., Alexandria			X	X			9-12	33	33	5:1		12
Timber Ridge School, Cross Junction......	X					6-8	9-12	80	68	9:1		10
Virginia Episcopal School, Lynchburg	X	X	X	X			9-12	244	244	6:1	16	24
Wakefield School, The Plains			X	X	PK-5	6-8	9-12	434	114	9:1	19	12
Woodberry Forest School, Woodberry Forest	X						9-12	386	386	8:1	19	30
Washington												
The Academic Institute, Inc., Bellevue.....			X	X		7-8	9-13	37	36	4:1		
Annie Wright School, Tacoma...........		X	X	X	PK-5	6-8	9-12	411	95	8:1	8	8
Auburn Adventist Academy, Auburn	X	X	X	X			9-12	260	260	15:1		17
Bellarmine Preparatory School, Tacoma....			X	X			9-12	1,018	1,018	23:1	8	16
Bellevue Christian School, Clyde Hill......			X	X	PK-6	7-8	9-12	1,300	360	21:1		18
Bishop Blanchet High School, Seattle......			X	X			9-12	1,069	1,069	17:1	4	18
The Bush School, Seattle			X	X	K-5	6-8	9-12	538	204	7:1	8	27
Cascade Christian Academy, Wenatchee ...			X	X	K-5	6-8	9-12	172	53	9:1		13
Charles Wright Academy, Tacoma			X	X	PK-5	6-8	9-12	672	278	8:1	12	16
Christa McAuliffe Academy, Yakima......			X	X	K-6	7-8	9-12	347	244	23:1	2	
Chrysalis School, Woodinville			X	X	3-6	7-8	9-12	230	160			
DeSales Catholic Middle/High School, Walla Walla			X	X		6-8	9-12	254	121	14:1	4	8
Eastside Catholic High School, Bellevue ...			X	X			9-12	460	460	13:1	6	21
Explorations Academy, Bellingham........			X	X				20	17	5:1	1	
Gonzaga Preparatory School, Spokane.....			X	X			9-12	878	878	19:1	11	20
John F. Kennedy Memorial High School, Burien................................	X	X	X	X			9-12	854	854	18:1	13	19
Lakeside School, Seattle			X	X		5-8	9-12	740	486	9:1		14
The Northwest School, Seattle	X	X	X	X		6-8	9-12	437	322	9:1		15
Northwest Yeshiva High School, Mercer Island			X	X			9-12	120	120	4:1		6
O'Dea High School, Seattle			X				9-12	485	485	13:1	2	17
The Overlake School, Redmond			X	X		5-8	9-12	465	252	9:1	14	23
Saint George's School, Spokane			X	X	K-5	6-8	9-12	361	119	9:1	9	9
Seattle Academy of Arts and Sciences, Seattle..............................			X	X		6-8	9-12	523	307	9:1		13
Seattle Christian Schools, Seattle..........			X	X	K-6	7-8	9-12	719	254	12:1	5	20
Shoreline Christian, Shoreline			X	X	PS-6	7-8	9-12	310	111	10:1		8
University Prep, Seattle			X	X		6-8	9-12	443	243	9:1	7	10
West Virginia												
The Linsly School, Wheeling.............	X	X	X	X	5-8		9-12	380	262	13:1	7	51
Mount de Chantal Visitation Academy, Wheeling			X	X	PK-6		7-12	204	81	6:1	19	11
Notre Dame High School, Clarksburg			X	X		7-8	9-12	150	104	8:1	2	14
Wisconsin												
Conserve School, Land O' Lakes..........	X	X					9-12	135	135	8:1	5	67
Dominican High School, Whitefish Bay....			X	X			9-12	349	349	13:1	5	18
Edgewood High School, Madison			X	X			9-12	615	615	12:1	8	19

| | STUDENTS ACCEPTED | | | | GRADES | | | STUDENT/FACULTY | | | SCHOOL OFFERINGS (number) | |
| | Boarding | | Day | | | | | | | | | |
	Boys	Girls	Boys	Girls	Lower	Middle	Upper	Total	Upper	Student/ Faculty Ratio	Advanced Placement Subject Areas	Sports
Wisconsin—continued												
Fox Valley Lutheran High School, Appleton			X	X			9–12	612	612	14:1	4	11
Marquette University High School, Milwaukee			X				9–12	1,032	1,032	15:1	18	16
Notre Dame de la Baie Academy, Green Bay			X	X			9–12	741	741	15:1	14	16
Pius XI High School, Milwaukee			X	X			9–12	1,390	1,390	14:1	8	22
The Prairie School, Racine			X	X	PK–4	5–8	9–12	646	211	13:1	11	9
St. John's Northwestern Military Academy, Delafield	X		X			7–8	9–12	300	253	12:1		30
Saint Joseph High School, Kenosha			X	X		7–8	9–12	485	320	20:1	4	12
St. Lawrence Seminary, Mt. Calvary	X						9–12	224	224	15:1		22
University Lake School, Hartland			X	X	JK–5	6–8	9–12	339	92	9:1	5	9
University School of Milwaukee, Milwaukee			X	X	PK–4	5–8	9–12	1,051	335	10:1	19	27
Wayland Academy, Beaver Dam	X	X	X	X			9–12	154	154	6:1	11	36
Wisconsin Academy, Columbus	X	X	X	X			9–12	126	126	13:1		5
Northern Mariana Islands												
Mount Carmel School, Saipan			X	X	1–5	6–8	9–12	609	177	15:1	3	10
Puerto Rico												
Baldwin School of Puerto Rico, Inc., Bayamon			X	X	PK–6	7–8	9–12	800	180	15:1	7	12
Caribbean Preparatory School, San Juan			X	X	PK–6	7–8	9–12	802	157	10:1	5	36
Colegio Ponceno, Coto Laurel			X	X	PK–6	7–8	9–12	1,150		10:1		2
Escuela Superior Catolica de Bayamon, Bayamon			X	X				650				9
Fowlers Academy, Guaynabo			X	X		7–8	9–12	87	65	8:1		4
Robinson School, San Juan			X	X	PK–6		7–12	580	253	18:1	8	40
Virgin Islands												
The Antilles School, Charlotte Amalie			X	X	N–5	6–8	9–12	511	162	12:1	10	15
St. Croix Country Day School, Kingshill			X	X	N–6	7–8	9–12	492	164	12:1	8	8
Aruba												
International School of Aruba, San Nicolas			X	X	PK–5	6–8	9–12	163	52	8:1	5	7
Australia												
The Southport School, Southport, Queensland	X		X		K–7		8–12	1,300	800	11:1		22
Austria												
The American International School, Vienna			X	X	PK–5	6–8	9–PG	746	255	7:1	9	18
American International School Salzburg, A-5020 Salzburg	X	X	X	X		7–8	9–PG	84	76	7:1	13	20
Bahrain												
Naseem International School, Riffa			X	X	N–6	7–9	10–12	790	230	15:1		13
Belgium												
Antwerp International School, Ekeren			X	X	PS–5	6–8	9–12	590	218	8:1		2
International School of Brussels, Brussels			X	X	N–6	7–9	10–13	1,397	394	10:1	7	16

| | STUDENTS ACCEPTED | | | | GRADES | | | STUDENT/FACULTY | | | SCHOOL OFFERINGS (number) | |
| | Boarding | | Day | | | | | | | | | |
	Boys	Girls	Boys	Girls	Lower	Middle	Upper	Total	Upper	Student/Faculty Ratio	Advanced Placement Subject Areas	Sports
Bermuda												
The Bermuda High School for Girls, Pembroke HM 08				X	1–6	7–9	10–13	665	135	7:1		30
Bolivia												
American Cooperative School, La Paz			X	X	PK–5	6–8	9–12	492	131	10:1	7	15
Brazil												
Chapel School, Sao Paulo			X	X	PK–6		7–12	700	285	9:1		
Escola Americana de Campinas, Campinas-SP			X	X	PK–5	6–8	9–12	422	102		5	27
Escola Americana do Rio de Janeiro, Rio de Janeiro			X	X	N–5	6–8	9–12	975	246	14:1		28
Canada												
Academie Sainte Cecile Private School, Windsor, ON	X	X	X	X	1–8		9–12	245	112	10:1		18
The Academy for Gifted Children (PACE), Richmond Hill, ON			X	X	1–3	4–7	8–12	294	126	15:1		27
Albert College, Belleville, ON	X	X	X	X	1–6	7–8	9–PG	269	164	8:1	5	60
Appleby College, Oakville, ON	X	X	X	X		7–8	9–12	626	498	7:1	10	28
Armbrae Academy, Halifax, NS			X	X	K–6		7–12	228	104	9:1	5	11
Ashbury College, Ottawa, ON	X	X	X	X	4–8		9–13	634	468	15:1		36
Austin Christian Academy, Austin, MB			X	X	K–3	4–8	9–12	39	8	8:1		
Balmoral Hall School, Winnipeg, MB		X	X	X	N–5	6–8	9–12	534	153	6:1	12	58
Banff Mountain Academy, Banff, AB	X	X	X	X			9–12	22	22	5:1		35
Bearspaw Christian School, Calgary, AB			X	X	1–6	7–9	10–12	394	54	20:1		8
The Bethany Hills School, Bethany, ON		X	X	X	1–6	7–8	9–13	94	46	7:1		47
Bishop's College School, Lennoxville, QC	X	X	X	X		7–9	10–12	264	169	8:1	13	18
The Bishop Strachan School, Toronto, ON		X		X	PK–6		7–12	850	610	10:1	15	41
Brentwood College School, Mill Bay, BC	X	X	X	X			8–12	425	425	8:1		67
British Columbia Christian Academy, Port Coquitlam, BC			X	X	K–3	4–7	8–12	263	103	15:1		8
Columbia International College of Canada, Hamilton, ON	X	X	X	X	9–10	11	12	1,100	700	20:1	5	28
Concordia High School, Edmonton, AB	X	X	X	X				133		10:1		5
Covenant Canadian Reformed School, Neerlandia, AB			X	X	K–6	7–9	10–12	159	35	10:1		15
Crawford Adventist Academy, Willowdale, ON			X	X	JK–6	7–8	9–12	513	163	16:1		6
Crescent School, Willowdale, ON			X		3–6	7–8	9–12	660	354	12:1	8	21
Crofton House School, Vancouver, BC				X	1–6		7–12	673	445	11:1	6	25
De La Salle College, Toronto, ON			X	X	5–6	7–8	9–13	565	405	15:1	8	16
Eastside Christian Academy, Calgary, AB			X	X	K–6	7–9	10–12	88	10	6:1		5
Edison School, Okotoks, AB			X	X	PK–6		7–12	172	72	12:1	7	7
Equilibrium International Education Institute, Calgary, AB			X	X			10–12	100	100	15:1		13
Fraser Academy, Vancouver, BC			X	X	1–7		8–12	183	113	5:1		15
Glenlyon-Norfolk School, Victoria, BC			X	X	JK–5	6	9–12	668	247	10:1		26
Grace Christian School, Charlottetown, PE			X	X	K–6	7–9	10–12	154	23	10:1		5
Grande Prairie Christian School, Grande Prairie, AB			X	X	K–6	7–9	10–12	95	14	12:1		3

	STUDENTS ACCEPTED				GRADES			STUDENT/FACULTY			SCHOOL OFFERINGS (number)	
	Boarding		Day									
	Boys	Girls	Boys	Girls	Lower	Middle	Upper	Total	Upper	Student/ Faculty Ratio	Advanced Placement Subject Areas	Sports
Canada—*continued*												
Greater Victoria Christian Academy, Victoria, BC			X	X	PK–6	7–9	10–12	157	15	17:1		1
Grenville Christian College, Brockville, ON	X	X	X	X	PK–5	6–8	9–12	258	126	6:1		23
Halifax Grammar School, Halifax, NS			X	X	K–4	5–9	10–12	520	188	10:1		15
Hamilton District Christian School, Ancaster, ON			X	X			9–12	576	576	17:1		20
Hamilton Learning Centre, Hamilton, ON			X	X	3–6	7–8	9–13	55	25	5:1		29
Havergal College, Toronto, ON		X		X	JK–6	7–8	9–12	911	472	10:1	4	72
Heritage Christian Academy, Calgary, AB			X	X	K–6	7–9	10–12	377	78	7:1		48
Heritage Christian School, Jordan Station, ON			X	X	K–8		9–12	530	160	15:1		5
Hillcrest Christian School, Grande Prairie, AB			X	X	K–6	7–9	10–12	47	9	6:1		3
Hillfield Strathallan College, Hamilton, ON			X	X	PK–4	5–8	9–12	1,116	356	13:1	3	18
Immanuel Christian High School, Lethbridge, AB			X	X		7–9	10–12	298	166	18:1		8
Imperial College of Toronto, Etobicoke, ON	X	X					12–13	175	175	19:1		
Kelowna Christian, Kelowna, BC			X	X	K–5	6–8	9–12	779	228	15:1		
Kingsway College, Oshawa, ON	X	X	X	X			9–12	175	175	12:1		11
Lakefield College School, Lakefield, ON	X	X	X	X			7–12	360	360	7:1	5	31
Lakeland Christian Academy, Cold Lake, AB			X	X	1–6	7–9	10–12	30	5	8:1		
Landmark East School, Wolfville, NS	X	X	X	X		6–9	10–12	70	35	2:1		34
The Laureate Academy, Winnipeg, MB			X	X	1–6	7–8	9–12	95	45	5:1		27
Lower Canada College, Montreal, QC			X	X	K–6	7–8	9–12	745	315	22:1	13	53
Luther College High School, Regina, SK	X	X	X	X			9–12	413	413	16:1		12
Malaspina International High School, Nanaimo, BC	X	X	X	X			10–12	125	125	8:1	5	39
Maxwell International Baha'i School, Shawnigan Lake, BC	X	X	X	X		7–9	10–12	150	113	10:1	2	18
Meadowridge Senior School, Maple Ridge, BC			X	X	JK–7		8–12	453	161	9:1		10
Mentor College, Mississauga, ON			X	X	JK–4	5–8	9–12	1,715	600	14:1		43
Metropolitan Preparatory Academy, Toronto, ON			X	X		6–8	9–12	435	335	18:1		15
Miss Edgar's and Miss Cramp's School, Montreal, QC				X	K–5	6–8	9–11	339	114	9:1	2	16
Mississauga Private School, Toronto, ON			X	X	JK–6	7–8	9–12	360	140	13:1		
Neworld Academy, Toronto, ON			X	X			11–12	80	80	8:1		3
Peoples Christian Academy, Toronto, ON			X	X	JK–6		7–13	800	355	12:1		9
Pickering College, Newmarket, ON	X	X	X	X	JK–8		9–13	397	215	9:1		12
Providence Christian School, Monarch, AB			X	X	K–6	7–9	10–12	92	24	12:1		
Queen Margaret's School, Duncan, BC		X	X	X	K–7		8–12	250	140	7:1	7	37
Quinte Christian High School, Belleville, ON			X	X			9–12	126	126	15:1		8
Richmond International High School/ College, Richmond, BC			X	X			10–12	90	90	10:1	4	6
Ridley College, St. Catharines, ON	X	X	X	X		5–8	9–PG	606	491	9:1	10	62
Robert Land Academy, Wellandport, ON	X				6–9	10	11–12	146	56	15:1		68
Rocklyn Academy, Meaford, ON		X					9–12	27	27	3:1		25

	STUDENTS ACCEPTED				GRADES			STUDENT/FACULTY			SCHOOL OFFERINGS (number)	
	Boarding		Day									
	Boys	Girls	Boys	Girls	Lower	Middle	Upper	Total	Upper	Student/ Faculty Ratio	Advanced Placement Subject Areas	Sports
Canada—continued												
Rockway Mennonite Collegiate, Kitchener, ON.	X	X	X	X		6-8	9-12	455	335	10:1		30
Rosseau Lake College, Rosseau, ON	X	X	X	X		7-8	9-12	158	139	6:1		75
Rothesay Netherwood School, Rothesay, NB.	X	X	X	X		6-8	9-12	232	181	7:1	11	48
Royal Canadian College, Vancouver, BC			X	X		8-10	11-12	92	72	15:1		4
Sacred Heart School of Halifax, Halifax, NS			X	X	K-6		7-12	479	231	18:1	5	14
St. Andrew's College, Aurora, ON	X		X			6-8	9-12	530	393	10:1	5	61
St. Clement School, Ottawa, ON.			X	X		7-8	9-12	38	23	12:1		27
St. George's School of Montreal, Montreal, QC.			X	X	PK-6		7-11	543	351	18:1	6	17
St. John's-Ravenscourt School, Winnipeg, MB.	X	X	X	X	1-5	6-8	9-12	728	331	8:1	10	41
Saint John's School of Alberta, Stony Plain, AB.	X					7-9	10-12	127	63	10:1		9
St. Margaret's School, Victoria, BC.		X		X	K-6		7-12	433	254	8:1	5	65
St. Michaels University School, Victoria, BC.	X	X	X	X	K-5	6-8	9-12	870	502	10:1	16	54
St. Paul's High School, Winnipeg, MB			X				9-12	570	570	14:1	3	15
Sedbergh, Montebello, QC.	X	X	X	X	5-6	7-9	10-12	79	47	4:1		53
Selwyn House School, Westmount, QC.			X		K-6	7-8	9-11	570	173	15:1		32
Shawnigan Lake School, Shawnigan Lake, BC.	X	X	X	X			8-12	413	413	10:1	9	45
Sheila Morrison School, Utopia, ON.	X	X	X	X	4-6	7-8	9-12	39	21	3:1		54
Southridge Senior Secondary, Surrey, BC.			X	X	K-3	4-7	8-12	673	321	10:1	9	27
Spruce Ridge Christian School, Cermona, AB.			X	X	3-5	6-9	10-12	10	4	5:1		
Stanstead College, Stanstead, QC	X	X	X	X	7-9		10-12	223	145	8:1	13	38
Strathcona-Tweedsmuir School, Okotoks, AB.			X	X	1-6	7-9	10-12	714	236			12
The Study School, Westmount, QC				X	K-3	4-6	7-11	433	192	8:1		27
Toronto District Christian High School, Woodbridge, ON.			X	X			9-12	444	444	13:1		7
Traditional Learning Academy, Coquitlam, BC.			X	X	K-3	4-7	8-12	171	51	15:1		
Trafalgar Castle School, Whitby, ON		X		X				244	228	10:1	2	29
Trinity College School, Port Hope, ON	X	X	X	X		5-8	9-12	595	494	8:1	9	38
Upper Canada College, Toronto, ON	X		X		1-7		9-13	1,123	697	11:1		48
Venta Preparatory School, Ottawa, ON	X	X	X	X	1-7		8-10	79	26	6:1		
Victory Christian School, Edmonton, AB			X	X	1-6	7-9	10-12	210	40	15:1		13
Webber Academy, Calgary, AB			X	X	K-6	7-9	10-11	633	53	18:1	5	24
Westgate Mennonite Collegiate, Winnipeg, MB.			X	X		7-9	10-12	312	154	15:1	5	31
West Island College, Calgary, AB			X	X		7-9	10-12	378	181	12:1	9	39
Westpark School, Portage la Prairie, MB			X	X	K-4	5-8	9-12	226	68	13:1		6
Willow Wood School, Don Mills, ON.			X	X	1-6	7-8	9-12	240	110	7:1		13
Windsor Christian Fellowship Academy, Windsor, ON			X	X	K-3	4-7	8-12	80	23	11:1		7
York House School, Vancouver, BC.				X	K-6		7-12	611	319	8:1	9	12
The Yorkland School, Willowdale, ON			X	X		7-8	9-12	351	229	15:1		15
The York School, Toronto, ON.			X	X	1-6	7-8	9-13	520	180	12:1		41

	STUDENTS ACCEPTED				GRADES			STUDENT/FACULTY			SCHOOL OFFERINGS (number)	
	Boarding		Day									
	Boys	Girls	Boys	Girls	Lower	Middle	Upper	Total	Upper	Student/ Faculty Ratio	Advanced Placement Subject Areas	Sports
China												
Shanghai American School, Shanghai......			X	X	PK–5	6–8	9–12	1,905	520	8:1	16	22
Colombia												
Colegio Bolivar, Cali....................			X	X	PK–5	6–8	9–12	1,185	270	10:1	1	10
Colegio Nueva Granada, Bogota			X	X	PK–5	6–8	9–12	1,590	354	15:1	7	14
Costa Rica												
American International School of Costa Rica, San Jose.....................			X	X	PK–6	7–8	9–12	172	52	7:1	3	7
Marian Baker School, San Jose...........			X	X				210				3
Denmark												
Copenhagen International School, 2900 Hellerup			X	X	K–5		6–12	531	264	7:1		4
Ecuador												
Academia Cotopaxi, Quito...............			X	X	PK–5	6–8	9–PG	453	127	7:1		4
Alliance Academy, Quito	X	X	X	X	PK–6	7–8	9–12	448	186	6:1	10	14
Egypt												
Schutz American School, Alexandria			X	X	PK–4	5–8	9–12	198	70	4:1	6	8
France												
American School of Paris, Saint Cloud.....			X	X	PK–5	6–8	9–13	738	312	8:1	10	11
CIV International School of Sophia Antipolis, 06902 Sophia Antipolis Cedex............................	X	X	X	X	1–5	6–9	10–12	920	385	17:1		26
Germany												
Black Forest Academy, 79396 Kandern	X	X	X	X	1–6	7–8	9–12	336	228	8:1	12	5
The Frankfurt International School, 61440 Oberursel.........................			X	X	PK–5	6–8	9–12	1,402	531	10:1		38
International School Hamburg, Hamburg ..			X	X	PK–5	6–8	9–12	669	187	7:1		8
Munich International School, Starnberg....			X	X	PK–4	5–8	9–12	1,203	368	6:1		22
Schule Schloss Salem, Salem	X	X	X	X	5–7	8–11	12–13	675	315	5:1		51
Greece												
American Community Schools of Athens, Athens................................			X	X	JK–5	6–8	9–12	639	299	17:1	12	10
Campion School, Athens, Athens			X	X	PK–6	7–9	10–13	559	201	18:1		19
TASIS Hellenic International School, Kifissia—Athens.....................	X	X	X	X	PK–5	6–9	10–12	254	91	9:1	3	9
Honduras												
Mazapan School, La Ceiba			X	X	1–6	7–8	9–12	294	97	12:1		10
India												
India International School, Jaipur			X	X	1–3	4–8	9–12	2,264	700	20:1		4
Woodstock School, Uttaranchal	X	X	X	X	K–5	6–8	9–12	475	287	7:1	17	16
Indonesia												
Hope International School, Tangerang.....			X	X	N–6		7–12	992	468	11:1		11
Jakarta International School, Jakarta-Selatan			X	X	PK–5	6–8	9–12	2,370	856	16:1	14	30

	Students Accepted				Grades			Student/Faculty			School Offerings (number)	
	Boarding		Day									
	Boys	Girls	Boys	Girls	Lower	Middle	Upper	Total	Upper	Student/ Faculty Ratio	Advanced Placement Subject Areas	Sports
Ireland												
St. Andrew's College, Dublin, County Dublin			X	X			8–12	924	924			29
Italy												
American Overseas School of Rome, Rome	X	X	X	X	PK–5	6–8	9–13	599	199	18:1	10	7
American School of Milan, Noverasco di Opera, Milan			X	X	N–5	6–8	9–12	449	123	8:1		14
CCI The Renaissance School, Lanciano	X	X	X	X			10–12	120	120	7:1	9	35
Marymount International School, Rome			X	X	PK–5	6–8	9–12	840	232	15:1	1	8
St. Stephen's School, Rome, Rome	X	X	X	X			9–PG	201	201	6:1	10	6
Japan												
Columbia International School, Tokorozawa, Saitama	X	X	X	X	1–6	7–9	10–12	219	129	16:1		11
Hokkaido International School, Sapporo	X	X	X	X	PK–6	7–9	10–12	182	38	10:1	6	7
St. Mary's International School, Tokyo			X		K–6	7–8	9–12	916	257	10:1		19
St. Maur International School, Yokohama			X	X	PK–5	6–8	9–12	423	132	4:1	8	8
Seisen International School, Tokyo			X	X	K–6	7–8	9–12	688	159	6:1	2	15
Yokohama International School, Yokohama			X	X	N–5	6–8	9–12	608	160	12:1	10	15
Kuwait												
The English School, Kuwait, Safat			X	X				400	50			9
Fawzia Sultan International School, Safat			X	X				146	37	8:1		3
New English School, Hawalli			X	X	K–2	5–6	7–13	1,991	856	7:1		20
Latvia												
International School of Latvia, Jurmala			X	X	PK–5		6–12	143	70	10:1	2	9
Luxembourg												
International School of Luxembourg, L-1430 Luxembourg			X	X	PS–5	6–8	9–12	593	153	8:1		5
Malaysia												
Alice Smith School, Kuala Lumpur			X	X	7–9	10–11	12–13	468	89	9:1		28
The International School of Kuala Lumpur, Ampang			X	X	PK–5	6–8	9–13	1,179	465	9:1	14	29
Mexico												
The American School Foundation, Mexico City, D.F.			X	X	PK–5	6–8	9–12	2,500	667	10:1	18	14
American School Foundation of Monterrey, Monterrey			X	X	N–5	6–8	9–12	2,183	438	12:1	12	20
Westhill Institute, DF			X	X	PK–6	7–9	10–12	568	85	12:1	6	5
Myanmar												
International School Yangon, Yangon			X	X	PK–5	6–8	9–12	371	111		10	2
Netherlands												
The American School of The Hague, 2241 BX Wassenaar			X	X	K–4	5–8	9–13	1,040	360	7:1	16	12
International School of Amsterdam, Amstelveen			X	X	PS–5	6–8	9–13	904	201	11:1		14

| | STUDENTS ACCEPTED | | | | GRADES | | | STUDENT/FACULTY | | | SCHOOL OFFERINGS (number) | |
| | Boarding | | Day | | | | | | | | | |
	Boys	Girls	Boys	Girls	Lower	Middle	Upper	Total	Upper	Student/ Faculty Ratio	Advanced Placement Subject Areas	Sports
Netherlands—*continued*												
Rotterdam International Secondary School, Wolfert van Borselen, Rotterdam			X	X				144		10:1		7
Oman												
The British School, Muscat, Ruwi.........			X	X				700	50	11:1		15
Peru												
Colegio Franklin D. Roosevelt, Lima 12....			X	X	N-5	6-8	9-12	1,219	377	11:1		45
Portugal												
American International School of Lisbon, Linho, Sintra.....................			X	X	N-5	6-8	9-12	451	123	8:1	6	4
Qatar												
American School of Doha, Doha..........			X	X	PK-5	6-8	9-12	609	190	20:1	9	11
Republic of Korea												
Seoul Foreign School, Seoul..............			X	X	PK-5	6-8	9-12	1,244	331	10:1	2	8
Seoul International School, Seoul			X	X	PK-5	6-8	9-12	1,095	330	13:1	11	7
Romania												
American International School of Bucharest, Judeti Ilfov			X	X	PK-5	6-8	9-12	465	134	7:1		12
Russian Federation												
Anglo-American School of Moscow, Moscow			X	X	PK-5	6-8	9-12	1,063	224	6:1		19
Moscow Economic School, Moscow			X	X	K-4	5-9	10-12	670	103	3:1		9
Saudi Arabia												
The British International School, Jeddah, Jeddah............................			X	X	6-8	9-10	11-12	608	94	10:1		9
Singapore												
Overseas Family School, Singapore 238515.			X	X	PK-5	6-8	9-12	1,950		8:1		6
Spain												
The American School of Madrid, Madrid ...			X	X	PK-5	6-8	9-12	719	220	10:1		7
British Council School of Madrid, Madrid ..			X	X				1,887		13:1		
International College Spain, Madrid			X	X	PK-5	6-8	9-12	598	194	10:1		17
Switzerland												
College du Leman International School, Versoix......................	X	X	X	X	K-5	6-8	9-13	1,794	602	11:1	15	47
Ecole d'Humanite, CH 6085 Hasliberg-Goldern.....................	X	X	X	X				143	119	5:1		22
Gstaad International School, Gstaad.......	X	X	X	X		8-9	10-12	23	10	5:1	5	25
Institut auf dem Rosenberg, Anglo-American Section, CH-9000 St. Gallen ..	X	X	X	X	2-6	7-8	9-13	146	128	5:1	10	22
International School of Basel, Reinach BL 2			X	X	PK-5	6-10	11-12	859	88	10:1	5	24
The International School of Geneva, Geneva.....................			X	X	6-6		7-13	3,400			7	14
International School of Lausanne, Pully....			X	X	PK-5	6-8	9-12	450	80	8:1		22

	STUDENTS ACCEPTED				GRADES			STUDENT/FACULTY			SCHOOL OFFERINGS (number)	
	Boarding		Day									
	Boys	Girls	Boys	Girls	Lower	Middle	Upper	Total	Upper	Student/ Faculty Ratio	Advanced Placement Subject Areas	Sports
Switzerland—*continued*												
Leysin American School in Switzerland, Leysin	X	X					9-PG	317	317	6:1	12	58
Riverside School, Zug			X	X				87	39	6:1	16	29
St. George's School in Switzerland, 1815 Clarens/Montreux		X	X	X	K-5	6-8	9-12	324	91	7:1		18
TASIS, The American School in Switzerland, CH-6926 Montagnola-Lugano	X	X	X	X		7-8	9-PG	328	298	6:1	16	17
Zurich International School, 8802 Kilchberg			X	X	PS-6	7-8	9-13	955	276	7:1	17	15
Taiwan												
Taipei American School, Taipei			X	X	PK-5	6-8	9-12	2,187	826	10:1	17	12
Thailand												
Dulwich International College, Phuket	X	X	X	X	1-6	7-11	12-13	769	67	6:1		56
New International School of Thailand, Bangkok			X	X	N-5		6-12	1,282	616			10
Ruamrudee International School, Bangkok			X	X	K-5	6-8	9-12	1,749	698	10:1	12	9
Turkey												
Dogus High School, Istanbul			X	X	1-5	6-8	9-11	1,135	420	5:1		16
United Arab Emirates												
Al-Worood School, Abu Dhabi			X	X	K-6	7-9	10-12	2,074	361	17:1		3
United Kingdom												
American Community School-Egham Campus, Surrey			X	X	3-5	6-8	9-12	550	107	6:1		9
The American Community School–Middlesex Campus, Hillingdon			X	X	PK-4	5-8	9-13	573	211	8:1	12	11
The American Community School–Surrey Campus, Cobham, Surrey	X	X	X	X	PK-4	5-8	9-12	1,250	361	9:1	10	14
The American School in London, London			X	X	PK-4	5-8	9-12	1,278	428	10:1	17	16
Brockwood Park School, Bramdean, Hampshire	X	X						48	48	6:1		
Marymount International School, Surrey		X		X		6-8	9-12	209	150	8:1		17
Queenswood, Hatfield, Hertfordshire		X		X	6-8	9-10	11-12	403	246	7:1		43
St. Clare's, Oxford, Oxford	X	X	X	X			10-13	360	360	7:1		26
TASIS The American School in England, Thorpe, Surrey	X	X	X	X	N-5	6-8	9-13	651	316	8:1	19	46
Zimbabwe												
Harare International School, Harare			X	X	1-5	6-8	9-12	378	113	10:1	10	25

SSAT Diagnostic Test

Part I

WRITING THE ESSAY

WRITING SAMPLE	**TIME: 25 MINUTES**

Directions: Using two sheets of lined theme paper, plan and write an essay on the topic assigned below. DO NOT WRITE ON ANOTHER TOPIC. AN ESSAY ON ANOTHER TOPIC IS NOT ACCEPTABLE.

Topic: Winter comes fast on the lazy.

Assignment: Do you agree or disagree with the topic statement? Support your position with one or two specific examples from personal experience, the experience of others, current events, history, or literature.

Name: _____

Write your essay here.

_____

_____

_____

_____

_____

_____

_____

_____

_____

_____

_____

_____

_____

_____

_____

_____

_____

_____

_____

_____

_____

(Continue, if necessary.)

Part II

MULTIPLE CHOICE

VERBAL	30 QUESTIONS

Directions: Each of the following questions consists of one word followed by five words or phrases. You are to select the one word or phrase whose meaning is closest to the word in capital letters.

1. DISCOVER
   - (A) detect
   - (B) botch
   - (C) verify
   - (D) falsify
   - (E) assure

2. FIDELITY
   - (A) pleasantness
   - (B) purity
   - (C) faithlessness
   - (D) sympathy
   - (E) loyalty

3. HOSTILE
   - (A) kind
   - (B) friendly
   - (C) sorry
   - (D) antagonistic
   - (E) generous

4. PROMPT
   - (A) organized
   - (B) timely
   - (C) distant
   - (D) tardy
   - (E) tidy

5. AFFIRMATIVE
   - (A) unwise
   - (B) relevant
   - (C) ancient
   - (D) positive
   - (E) negative

6. POTENT
   - (A) powerful
   - (B) disorderly
   - (C) resentful
   - (D) brave
   - (E) clumsy

7. STEADFAST
   - (A) faithful
   - (B) slow
   - (C) disloyal
   - (D) immovable
   - (E) arrogant

8. PASSIVE
   - (A) unfriendly
   - (B) doubtful
   - (C) narrow
   - (D) participate
   - (E) active

9. HAPHAZARD
   - (A) lucky
   - (B) clever
   - (C) aimless
   - (D) planned
   - (E) instant

10. LUSTROUS

    (A) dull

    (B) wicked

    (C) inaccurate

    (D) candid

    (E) glossy

11. ASSESSMENT

    (A) total

    (B) tax

    (C) evaluation

    (D) bill

    (E) due

12. CHANGE

    (A) alter

    (B) church

    (C) complete

    (D) decide

    (E) agree

13. BOUNTIFUL

    (A) miserly

    (B) considerate

    (C) faulty

    (D) lovely

    (E) generous

14. DREAM

    (A) hope

    (B) vision

    (C) demand

    (D) wealth

    (E) scared

15. VIRTUE

    (A) relationship

    (B) marriage

    (C) prosperity

    (D) happiness

    (E) goodness

Directions: The following questions ask you to find relationships between words. For each question, select the answer that best completes the meaning of the sentence.

16. Song is to recital as episode is to

    (A) bibliography.

    (B) series.

    (C) team.

    (D) agile.

    (E) prose.

17. Bald is to hirsute as anemic is to

    (A) tiny.

    (B) fat.

    (C) robust.

    (D) loud.

    (E) redundant.

18. Remove is to out as

    (A) abbreviate is to in.

    (B) annotate is to out.

    (C) interpolate is to in.

    (D) duplicate is to out.

    (E) emulate is to in.

19. Oblivious is to awareness as

    (A) comatose is to consciousness.

    (B) serene is to composure.

    (C) erudite is to knowledge.

    (D) adroit is to skill.

    (E) palpitate is to ignorance.

20. Explain is to clarity as

    (A) illuminate is to light.

    (B) deracinate is to precision.

    (C) invigorate is to energy.

    (D) refine is to purity.

    (E) coagulate is to gel.

21. Poltroon is to pusillanimous as

    (A) jester is to lachrymose.
    (B) dynamo is to supine.
    (C) optimist is to sanguine.
    (D) progressive is to hidebound.
    (E) cower is to coward.

22. Gold is to Midas as wisdom is to

    (A) eagle.
    (B) Satan.
    (C) conquest.
    (D) Athena.
    (E) Shakespeare.

23. Tone is to deaf as

    (A) arm is to lift.
    (B) touch is to smell.
    (C) paint is to brush.
    (D) sight is to sound.
    (E) color is to blind.

24. Radius is to diameter as

    (A) 3 is to 8.
    (B) 4 is to 6.
    (C) 12 is to 15.
    (D) 5 is to 10.
    (E) 9 is to 13.

25. Oak is to acorn as

    (A) stable is to barn.
    (B) tree is to branch.
    (C) tulip is to bulb.
    (D) library is to book.
    (E) ruler is to line.

26. $12\frac{1}{2}\%$ is to $\frac{1}{8}$ as

    (A) decade is to century.
    (B) 100% is to 1.
    (C) $\frac{6}{10}$ is to $\frac{1}{2}$.
    (D) $66\frac{2}{3}\%$ is to $\frac{2}{3}$.
    (E) second is to minute.

27. Bibliophile is to library as

    (A) dog is to biscuit.
    (B) neutron is to scientist.
    (C) philatelist is to post office.
    (D) machinist is to repair.
    (E) infant is to adult.

28. Galley is to kitchen as

    (A) fabric is to yarn.
    (B) teeth is to stomach.
    (C) ship is to house.
    (D) box is to package.
    (E) roof is to walls.

29. Retina is to eye as

    (A) wagon is to car.
    (B) chair is to leg.
    (C) sun is to earth.
    (D) piston is to engine.
    (E) spur is to horse.

30. Ballet is to choreographer as

    (A) paper is to ream.
    (B) people is to elect.
    (C) pistol is to trigger.
    (D) play is to director.
    (E) dove is to peace.

QUANTITATIVE (MATH)

25 QUESTIONS

Directions: Following each problem in this section, there are five suggested answers. Work each problem in your head or in the space provided (there will be space for scratchwork in your test booklet). Then look at the five suggested answers and decide which is best.

1. The average of three numbers is 15. What is two times the sum of the three numbers?

    (A) 6
    (B) 15
    (C) 30
    (D) 45
    (E) 90

2. How many factors does the number 12 have?

    (A) 2
    (B) 3
    (C) 4
    (D) 6
    (E) 8

3. John owns $\frac{1}{3}$ of the CDs in the collection. If there are a total of 120 CDs, how many does John own?

    (A) 20
    (B) 40
    (C) 60
    (D) 120
    (E) 360

4. What is the perimeter of an equilateral triangle, one side of which measures 6 inches?

    (A) 18 inches
    (B) 12 inches
    (C) 6 inches
    (D) 3 inches
    (E) It cannot be determined.

5. Tyler, Sharice, and James want to put their money together in order to buy a $270 radio. If Sharice agrees to pay twice as much as James, and Tyler agrees to pay three times as much as Sharice, how much will Sharice contribute?

    (A) $30
    (B) $60
    (C) $90
    (D) $150
    (E) $180

    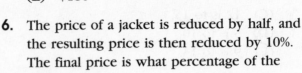

6. The price of a jacket is reduced by half, and the resulting price is then reduced by 10%. The final price is what percentage of the original price?

    (A) 10%
    (B) 40%
    (C) 45%
    (D) 55%
    (E) 60%

7. In a jar of gumdrops, the ratio of green gumdrops to red gumdrops is 5:3. If only green and red gumdrops are in the jar and the total number of gumdrops is 56, how many green gumdrops are in the jar?

    (A) 5
    (B) 8
    (C) 15
    (D) 28
    (E) 35

8. A stop sign has eight equal sides and a perimeter of 64. What is the length of each individual side?

   (A) 2
   (B) 4
   (C) 8
   (D) 12
   (E) It cannot be determined.

9. Two cardboard boxes have equal volume. The dimensions of one box are $3 \times 8 \times 10$. If the length of the other box is 4 and the width is 6, what is the height of the second box?

   (A) 2
   (B) 5
   (C) 10
   (D) 12
   (E) 16

10. At a fund-raiser, 300 people each donated y dollars. In terms of y, what was the total number of dollars donated?

    (A) 300
    (B) $300y$
    (C) $\dfrac{y}{300}$
    (D) $\dfrac{300}{y}$
    (E) $300 + y$

    300y

11. If a harvest yields 120 bushels of corn, 40 bushels of wheat, and 80 bushels of soybeans, what percent of the total harvest is corn?

    (A) 25%
    (B) 30%
    (C) 33%
    (D) 40%
    (E) 50%

12. Which of the following is a multiple of 6?

    (A) 1
    (B) 2
    (C) 3
    (D) 9
    (E) 12

13. A 3-foot, 2-inch board is how many times bigger than a 2-foot board?

    (A) 1.5
    (B) 1.6
    (C) 1.7
    (D) $\dfrac{19}{12}$
    (E) $\dfrac{17}{12}$

14. What is the distance between $(-14, -11)$ and $(-20, -7)$ along the line connecting them?

    (A) 5
    (B) 10
    (C) $2\sqrt{13}$
    (D) $4\sqrt{13}$
    (E) 13

15. What is the perimeter of a regular pentagon whose sides measure three units?

    (A) 7.5
    (B) 9
    (C) 12
    (D) 15
    (E) 18

16. What is 60 expressed as the product of its prime factors?

    (A) (15)(6)
    (B) (5)(12)
    (C) (5)(3)(3)(2)
    (D) (4)(5)(3)
    (E) (2)(5)(3)(2)

    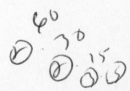

17. Mike bought 25 shares of Zooko stock at the closing price on Tuesday and sold them at the closing price on Friday. How much money did Mike lose on his investment?

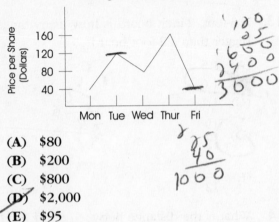

Zooko Manufacturing Company
Closing Price per Share

(A) $80
(B) $200
(C) $800
(D) $2,000
(E) $95

18. The hypotenuse of a right triangle is 10 and one leg is 6. Find the length of the other leg of the triangle.

(A) 16
(B) 10
(C) 8
(D) 12
(E) 4

19. Calculate the area of the hexagon.

$OP = 4\sqrt{3}, AB = 8$

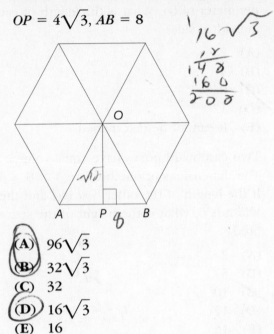

(A) $96\sqrt{3}$
(B) $32\sqrt{3}$
(C) 32
(D) $16\sqrt{3}$
(E) 16

20. If $|3a - 1| = 5$, which of the following is a possible value for a?

(A) -2
(B) -1
(C) 0
(D) 1
(E) 2

21. A coat is on sale for $128 after a discount of 20%. Find the original price.

(A) $102.40
(B) $153.60
(C) $160
(D) $180
(E) $148

22. Rachel worked one Saturday from 7:30 A.M. until 3 P.M. at the rate of $4.65 per hour. How much did she receive?

(A) $19.88
(B) $22.53
(C) $19.00
(D) $22.00
(E) $34.88

23.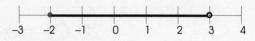

The graph shown above is of which inequality?

(A) $-2 < x < 3$

(B) $-2 \le x < 3$

(C) $-2 \le x \le 3$

(D) $-2 < x \le 3$

(E) $-2 < x$

24. How many socks would you need to remove from a drawer containing 10 blue socks, 15 black socks, and 5 red socks, to insure that you have at least 2 matching socks?

(A) 3

(B) 4

(C) 16

(D) 17

(E) 28

25. What is the sum of $\dfrac{a}{b}$ and $\dfrac{b}{a}$?

(A) $\dfrac{a+b}{ab}$

(B) $\dfrac{a^2 + b^2}{ab}$

(C) $\dfrac{(a+b)^2}{ab}$

(D) $\dfrac{a^2 + b^2}{2ab}$

(E) 1

READING COMPREHENSION   20 QUESTIONS

Directions: Read each passage carefully and then answer the questions about it. For each question, decide on the basis of the passage which one of the choices best answers the question.

Passage 1

Line   Although the special coloring of moths will hide them from most other insects and birds that want to eat them, it will not protect them from bats, since bats locate their prey
5   by hearing rather than by sight. Bats continually make high-pitched noises that reflect off a moth's body as echoes. These echoes inform the bats of their prey's location, and hunting bats follow these
10   echoes until they find the moth. To protect themselves from bats, some species of moths have developed defenses based on sound. These moths have ears that allow them to hear the sounds the bat makes. If the bat is
15   far enough away, the moth will hear it, but the bat is too far from it to receive the echo from the moth. The moth can then simply swerve out of the bat's path. But if the bat is closer to the moth, the moth is in immediate
20   danger. In order to avoid the bat, it flies wildly, moving in many directions and avoiding any ordered pattern. This tactic tends to confuse the bat. Other species of moths use sound to avoid the bats by
25   producing high-pitched sounds of their own. The many echoes from these sounds make it difficult for the bats to find the moths.

1. According to the passage, some moths escape from bats by

   (A) secreting a substance with a distracting odor.
   (B) making their own high-pitched sounds.
   (C) hiding in small crevices.
   (D) gathering under bright lights.
   (E) flying in circles.

2. Which of the following can be inferred from the passage about insects and birds that eat moths?

   (A) They hunt by sight rather than sound.
   (B) They are confused by the moths' sounds.
   (C) They have no need to protect themselves.
   (D) They fly in circles to find the moths.
   (E) They are often colorful.

3. The sounds bats hear when hunting are

   (A) made by the flapping of the moths' wings.
   (B) echoes of the sounds they make themselves.
   (C) echoes of the sounds made by the moths.
   (D) echoes of the sounds of other bats.
   (E) created by the movement of the air and wind.

4. Moths trying to escape from bats

   (A) always fly in the same direction.
   (B) may not know in which direction to fly.
   (C) do not always use the same strategy.
   (D) fly in an orderly pattern.
   (E) get as far from the bat as they can.

5. According to the passage, bats and some moths are alike because they rely on which of the following to help them survive?

- **(A)** Sight
- **(B)** Color
- **(C)** Odor
- **(D)** Sound
- **(E)** Taste

Passage 2

Line   One day, a thirsty fox fell into a well as she
was getting a drink of water. She could not
find a way to climb back up. After a short
time, a thirsty goat came to the edge of the
5   well, and seeing the fox below him, he
asked if the water was safe to drink.
Thinking quickly, the fox said the water was
pure and delicious and suggested that the
goat come down to have a drink. The goat
10   immediately jumped into the well. After he
had enough to drink, he asked the fox how
he could get back up and out of the well.
The fox replied, "I have a plan. Put your
front legs against the wall, and hold your
15   horns up. I will climb up your back, onto
your horns, and then I will jump out of the
well. Once I'm out, I'll help you get out."
The goat agreed, and the fox quickly got out
of the well. The goat called out to her: "Oh,
20   Ms. Fox, you said you would help me get
out of the well." The fox called down to the
goat, "Friend, if you had half as many brains
as you have hairs on your chin, you would
not have jumped into the well without first
25   thinking about how you would get out."

6. The fox told the goat the water was pure and delicious because

- **(A)** she had tasted it and knew that it was good.
- **(B)** she wanted to be kind to the goat.
- **(C)** she was lonely and wanted company.
- **(D)** she was afraid the goat would not drink it if she said it was bad.
- **(E)** she had thought of a plan to get out of the well.

7. The fox's last words suggest that she thinks the goat is

- **(A)** angry.
- **(B)** amused.
- **(C)** unintelligent.
- **(D)** clumsy.
- **(E)** uncomfortable.

8. All of the following describe the fox EXCEPT which word?

- **(A)** Clever
- **(B)** Helpful
- **(C)** Lying
- **(D)** Inconsiderate
- **(E)** Selfish

9. The fox gets out of the well by

- **(A)** climbing up the walls.
- **(B)** jumping out.
- **(C)** using the goat as a ladder.
- **(D)** calling for help until someone comes.
- **(E)** using a rope.

10. The best way to state the lesson the fox's last words suggest is

- **(A)** think before you act.
- **(B)** take advantage of opportunities.
- **(C)** drink before you get too thirsty.
- **(D)** never trust a fox.
- **(E)** all goats are foolish.

Passage 3

Line The wealthy hunting societies of Europe at
the end of the age of the glaciers did not
have their future under their own control.
The environment would determine their
5   fate, as it would the fate of the animals. But
the humans had an advantage the animals
did not. Although people did not notice it,
the climate had changed. Summers grew
longer and warmer, ice sheets shrank, and
10   glaciers retreated. Because of the changes in
climate, plant and animal life changed. The
mammoth, rhinoceros, and reindeer disappeared from western Europe, their going
perhaps hastened by the human hunters
15   themselves. On what had been open
grassland or tundra with dwarf birch and
willow trees, great forests spread, stocked
with the appropriate forest animals—red
deer, aurochs, and wild pigs. Because the
20   great herds of beasts on which they had
preyed disappeared, the economic basis of
the hunting societies was cut away. But this
provided a moment when early humans
were able to prove their advantage over the
25   biological specialization of animals: the
reindeer found his coat too hot to wear and
had to leave; humans merely took their coats
off and readjusted their habits.

11. The title that best expresses the idea of this
passage is

(A) "Humans Conflict With Their
Environment."
(B) "Human Adaptation to Climate
Change."
(C) "Changes in Plant and Animal Life."
(D) "Primitive Hunting Tribes."
(E) "Extinct Prehistoric Animals."

12. From the context of the passage, "auroch"
(line 19) most likely refers to

(A) the name of one of the hunting
societies.
(B) a type of bird.
(C) an animal that left Europe.
(D) an animal that became extinct.
(E) an animal that survived in Europe.

13. The disappearance of certain animals from
western Europe was

(A) caused mostly by human hunting.
(B) disastrous to primitive humans.
(C) the direct result of humans'
equipment.
(D) the immediate result of a more
advanced culture.
(E) a result of changes in climate.

14. The writer apparently believes that a
society's future course may be determined
by

(A) economic abundance.
(B) adapting to changes.
(C) the ambitions of the people.
(D) cultural enrichment.
(E) the clothing worn.

15. In the passage's last sentence, the word
"coat" means

(A) the same thing both times it is used.
(B) different things to different readers.
(C) something different each time it is
used.
(D) to cover with a substance.
(E) a thick layer of fur or hair.

Passage 4

Line   Although eating too much fat has been
shown to be harmful, some fat is essential in
the human diet. Fat helps in the absorption
of some vitamins, provides our bodies with
5   insulation, and is a source of energy. And
eating some fat in a meal helps people to
feel full for a longer period of time, so they
will not want to snack between meals. But
not all fat is healthy. There are two kinds of
10   fat, saturated and unsaturated. Saturated fat
is the kind of fat that is usually solid at room
temperature. It is found in meat and dairy
products. This kind of fat is very high in
calories, and it raises the blood cholesterol
15   level. High blood cholesterol can clog the
arteries, which may lead to heart attacks.
There are two types of unsaturated fat. One
type, called polyunsaturated, or "essential
fatty acid," is found in fish, sunflower seeds,
20   corn oil, and walnuts. Some research
suggests that essential fatty acids help to
prevent heart disease and aid in healthy
brain function and vision. Monounsaturated
fat is found in foods like olives, avocados,
25   and peanuts. Diets high in monounsaturated
fat can lower cholesterol levels. However,
even though some fat is needed, dietary
guidelines suggest that no more than 30% of
calories in a person's diet should come
30   from fat.

16. According to the passage, essential fatty
    acids

    (A) can be eaten in unrestricted amounts.
    (B) raise the level of cholesterol in the
        blood.
    (C) may aid in having good vision.
    (D) lower cholesterol levels.
    (E) are found in peanuts.

17. The best title for this passage is

    (A) "The Role of Fat."
    (B) "Types of Fat."
    (C) "Foods High in Saturated Fat."
    (D) "Why Fat Is Harmful."
    (E) "Benefits of Eating Fat."

18. Saturated fats could be found in all of the
    following EXCEPT

    (A) a grilled cheese sandwich.
    (B) tuna fish salad.
    (C) hamburgers and butter.
    (D) a pepperoni pizza.
    (E) sausages and bacon.

19. Monounsaturated fat

    (A) is an essential fatty acid.
    (B) helps to prevent heart disease.
    (C) is found in sunflower seeds and
        walnuts.
    (D) can lower cholesterol levels.
    (E) is solid at room temperature.

20. According to the passage,

    (A) all fats contain the same amount of
        calories.
    (B) monounsaturated fat has the smallest
        number of calories.
    (C) saturated fats are very high in calories.
    (D) calories from fat are always harmful.
    (E) counting calories is not important.

EXPLANATORY ANSWERS TO THE SSAT DIAGNOSTIC TEST

VERBAL

1. **The correct answer is (A).**

2. **The correct answer is (E).**

3. **The correct answer is (D).**

4. **The correct answer is (B).**

5. **The correct answer is (D).**

6. **The correct answer is (A).**

7. **The correct answer is (A).**

8. **The correct answer is (B).**

9. **The correct answer is (C).**

10. **The correct answer is (E).**

11. **The correct answer is (C).**

12. **The correct answer is (A).**

13. **The correct answer is (E).**

14. **The correct answer is (B).**

15. **The correct answer is (E).**

16. **The correct answer is (B).** A song is performed as part of a recital. The relationship is part to whole. An episode is part of a series. Choice (A) is incorrect because an author is not part of a bibliography. The relationship of author to bibliography is item to category. Choice (C) is incorrect because the relationship is leader to group. Choice (D) is incorrect because the relationship of dancer to agile is type to characteristic. Choice (E) is incorrect because the relationship of poetry to prose is similar to item to category. Both are genres of literature.

17. **The correct answer is (C).** Bald and hirsute are antonyms. Anemic and robust are antonyms. Choices (A) and (E) are incorrect because the words are synonyms. Choices (B) and (D) are incorrect because the words are not specifically related.

18. **The correct answer is (C).** The relationship is object to its function. When you remove something, you take material out. The same relationship is in choice (C): when you interpolate something, you put the material in.

19. **The correct answer is (A).** Someone who is oblivious lacks awareness. The relationship is word to antonym or opposites. The same relationship is in choice (A): someone who is comatose lacks consciousness.

20. **The correct answer is (D).** The relationship is word to antonym: when you explain something, you clarify it. The same relationship is in choice (D). When you refine something, you increase its purity.

21. **The correct answer is (C).** The relationship is object to its function. A poltroon (coward) is by definition pusillanimous (cowardly). An optimist is by definition sanguine (confident).

22. **The correct answer is (D).** Gold was important to Midas; wisdom was important to Athena. The relationship is worker and creation. Choices (A) and (C) are incorrect because the relationship is item to category. Choice (B) is incorrect because the relationship is synonymous. Choice (E) is incorrect because the relationship is type to characteristic.

23. **The correct answer is (E).** One who is deaf cannot perceive tone; one who is blind cannot perceive color. This is the analogy of action of object. The other answers cannot be correct: choice (B) is incorrect because touch and smell are both senses and equal; therefore, they cannot parallel "tone is to deaf." By the same token, choice (C) is incorrect because one uses a brush to paint is close to the proper answer; however, the relationship is object to its function. A brush is used to paint.

24. **The correct answer is (D).** The radius is half the diameter of a given circle. Similarly, 5 is half of 10. This is the analogy of part to whole. There appears to be no relationship with choices (A) and (E). Choices (B) and (C) do have a relationship of sorts, but it is not one half of the question.

25. **The correct answer is (C).** An oak grows from an acorn; a tulip grows from a bulb. This is the cause-to-effect relationship. Notice that in choice (A), the relationship is word to synonym. Both a stable and a barn are shelters for animals. Choice (B) is whole to part. Part of a tree is a branch. Choice (D) also has the relationship of part to whole. Part of a library is the books. Choice (E) has the relationship of object to its function. A ruler will allow you to make a line.

26. **The correct answer is (D).** $12\frac{1}{2}\%$ is equal to $\frac{1}{8}$ as $66\frac{2}{3}\%$ is equal to $\frac{2}{3}$. Both are fractions. The relationship is one of equals or synonyms. Choice (A) indicates a relationship of part to whole; a decade is one tenth of a century and is therefore incorrect for the relationship being sought; the same is true for choice (E). A second is part of a minute. Choice (B) is incorrect because there is not the relationship of equality that we need for the question. Choice (C) is incorrect because $\frac{6}{10}$ does NOT equal $\frac{1}{2}$. The premise is incorrect.

27. **The correct answer is (C).** A bibliophile, one who loves books, will spend time in the library. A philatelist, one who collects stamps, will spend time in the post office. The relationship is worker to workplace. Choice (A) is incorrect because the relationship is object to its function. A dog should eat a biscuit. Choices (B) and (D) are both the worker and creation relationship. None of these other choices have the worker to workplace relationship of the question.

28. **The correct answer is (C).** A galley is a kitchen, but on a ship, not in a house. The relationship is synonymous. Choice (A) is incorrect because it is part to whole. Yarn makes fabric. Choice (B) has no relationship that can fit with the question. Both items are part of the human body, but without the relationship of the question. Choice (D) has the relationship of object to its function: a box makes a package. Choice (E) is incorrect because a roof holds up the walls and is the relationship of object to function.

29. **The correct answer is (D).** The retina helps the eye function. A piston helps an engine to work. The relationship is cause to effect. Choice (A) is not correct because while both a wagon and a car are modes of transportation, their actual function is totally different. The relationship is item to category. Choice (B) has the relationship of part to whole. A leg is part of the chair. Choice (C) names two celestial objects: the relationship would be item to category. Choice (E) has the relationship of object to its function. One uses a spur to manipulate a horse.

30. **The correct answer is (D).** A choreographer directs a ballet as a director directs a play. The relationship is worker and creation. Choice (A) is not correct because the relationship is part to whole: 500 pages equal a ream. Choice (B) is worker and creation: the people elect. Choice (C) is part to whole: a trigger is part of a piston. Choice (E) is symbolic: a dove is the sign of peace.

QUANTITATIVE (MATH)

1. **The correct answer is (E).** If the average of three numbers is 15, then the SUM ÷ 3 = 15. Therefore, the SUM of the three numbers is 15 × 3 = 45. Two times the SUM of 45 is 90.

2. **The correct answer is (D).** Factors are all the numbers that divide a number evenly.

The factors of 12 are:

1 and 12

2 and 6

3 and 4

which result in a total of 6 factors in all.

3.   **The correct answer is (B).** This is a problem of multiplication by fractions. To find the number of CDs owned by John, multiply the total number by the fraction he owns.

$$\frac{1}{3} \times 120 = 40$$

4.   **The correct answer is (A).** An equilateral triangle is made up of three congruent, or equal, sides. To determine the perimeter of a triangle, sum the measure of all three sides.

$$6 + 6 + 6 = 18$$

5.   **The correct answer is (B).** There are three unknown pieces in this question. The contribution made by Tyler (T), the contribution made by Sharice (S), and the contribution made by James (J).

The total of all contributions is $270, so $T + S + J = 270$.

Sharice pays twice as much as James: $S = 2J$

Tyler pays three times what Sharice does: $T = 3S = 6J$ (from previous statement).

In terms of J, $6J + 2J + J = 270$. Solving for J, $9J = 270$ so $J = 30$ (amount paid by James). Since James pays $30, Sharice pays twice that, or $60.

6.   **The correct answer is (C).** If the jacket originally costs x dollars, when it is reduced by half, it costs $x - .5x$ dollars or simply $.5x$ dollars (original price minus discounted amount). If the new price of $.5x$ is then discounted another 10%, the resulting price is $.5x - .1(.5x)$, which equals $.45x$, or 45% of the original price.

7.   **The correct answer is (E).** Since the ratio of green to red gumdrops is 5:3, there are $5x$ green gumdrops and $3x$ red ones.

$$3x + 5x = 56$$
$$8x = 56$$
$$x = 7$$

so there are $5(7) = 35$ green gumdrops.

8.   **The correct answer is (C).** The perimeter is equal to the sum of each of the sides. Since all the sides are equal, to determine the length of one side, divide the perimeter by the total number of sides.

$$64 \div 8 = 8$$

9.   **The correct answer is (C).** Volume = length $\times$ width $\times$ height. The volume of both boxes is $3 \times 8 \times 10 = 240$. The volume of the second box is $4 \times 6 \times$ height $= 240$; therefore, the height of the box is $\frac{240}{4 \times 6}$ $= \frac{240}{24} = 10$.

10.   **The correct answer is (B).** Since each of the 300 attendees donated the same dollar amount, the total amount donated is the product of 300 and y.

11. **The correct answer is (E).** First, determine the total number of bushels in the harvest. $120 + 40 + 80 = 240$

To find the percentage of corn, divide the bushels of corn by the total number of bushels.

$$\frac{120}{240} = \frac{1}{2} = 50\%$$

12. **The correct answer is (E).** Multiples result when you multiply a number by an integer. Multiples are always greater than or equal to the original number. 12 is the multiple of 6 in this case because $6 \times 2 = 12$.

13. **The correct answer is (D).** Convert to common units. Inches are a good choice. The ratio then becomes 38:24, which is 19:12.

14. **The correct answer is (C).** Use the distance formula (the Pythagorean theorem in disguise).

The difference in x coordinates is $(-20) - (-14) = -6$. The difference in y coordinates is $(-7) - (-11) = 4$.

You can use the Pythagorean Theorem:

Distance =

$$\sqrt{(-6)^2+(4)^2} = \sqrt{36+16} = \sqrt{52} = \sqrt{2\times2\times13} = 2\sqrt{13}$$

15. **The correct answer is (D).** A pentagon has five sides. A regular pentagon has five congruent sides. To get the perimeter, multiply the length of each side by the number of sides.

$3 \times 5 = 15$

16. **The correct answer is (E).** To break a number into its prime factors, break it into factors, and break those factors into factors, until you cannot go any further. It doesn't matter what factors you begin with; you will reach the same prime factors. $60 = 10 \times 6 = 2 \times 5 \times 3 \times 2$. 5, 3, and 2 are prime numbers (they have exactly two factors, namely 1 and themselves).

Another way to approach this problem is to rule out the answers that have composite (non-prime) numbers. This rules out choices (A), (B), and (D). Test the remaining answers by multiplying them out. Only choice (E) comes to 60.

17. **The correct answer is (D).** First find the amount Mike paid for the shares.

$120 \times 25 = 3,000$

Then find the amount Mike sold the shares for.

$40 \times 25 = 1,000$

Then subtract. $3,000 - 1,000 = 2,000$

18. **The correct answer is (C).** By the Pythagorean Theorem:

$$a^2 + b^2 = c^2$$
$$a^2 + 6^2 = 10^2$$
$$a^2 + 36 = 100$$
$$\sqrt{a^2} = \sqrt{64}$$
$$a = 8$$

19. **The correct answer is (A).**

$$A = \frac{1}{2}(8)(4\sqrt{3}) = 16\sqrt{3} = \text{area of one triangle.}$$

There are six triangles in a hexagon.

$$6(16\sqrt{3}) = 96\sqrt{3}$$

20. **The correct answer is (E).**

$$|3a - 1| = 5$$
$$3a - 1 = 5$$
$$3a = 6$$
$$a = 2$$

OR

$$3a - 1 = -5$$
$$3a = -4$$
$$a = -\frac{4}{3}$$

a can equal 2 or $-\dfrac{4}{3}$

21. **The correct answer is (C).** Since \$128 is 80% of the original price, the base price is

$$B = \frac{P}{R} = \frac{128}{.80} = \$160$$

22. **The correct answer is (E).** The number of hours from 7:30 A.M. to 3 P.M. totals $7\frac{1}{2}$ hours.

Multiply $7\frac{1}{2}$ or $7.5 \times 4.65 = 34.875 = \$34.88$

23. **The correct answer is (B).** The line graph with a dark circle on -2 includes -2 and all numbers greater than -2. The open circle on 3 indicates all numbers less than 3. Put together: all numbers greater than or equal to -2 and less than 3:

$$-2 \leq x < 3$$

24. **The correct answer is (B).** It is possible to draw one of each color before getting a match. Three socks can be drawn without getting a matched pair. But if you've gone this far, the fourth sock drawn must match, as there are only three colors.

You *might* have drawn a pair before this, but you are not assured of having done so.

25. **The correct answer is (B).** Get common denominators to add fractions. Multiply $\frac{a}{b}$ by $\frac{a}{a}$ getting $\frac{a^2}{ab}$.

Multiply $\frac{b}{a}$ by $\frac{b}{b}$ getting $\frac{b^2}{ab}$. Then add the fractions by adding the numerators.

READING COMPREHENSION

Passage 1

1. **The correct answer is (B).** Choices (A), (C), and (D) provide information not mentioned in the passage. Choice (E) is incorrect because the passage says moths swerve away or fly wildly; it does not say they fly in circles.

2. **The correct answer is (A).** Choice (B) is incorrect because the passage does not say that insects and birds hear the moths' sounds. Choices (C) and (D) are not stated in the passage, and nothing in the passage implies them. The insects and birds are not described, so choice (E) is incorrect.

3. **The correct answer is (B).** While moths may flap their wings, that is not what the bats hear, and while some moths make sounds, it is the echoes, not the sounds, that bats hear. So choices (A) and (D) are incorrect. Choice (C) is wrong because the passage states specifically that the bats hear the echoes of their own high-pitched noises. The passage does not mention air or wind sounds, so choice (E) is incorrect.

4. **The correct answer is (C).** The passage describes two ways that moths fly away from bats: they swerve or they fly in many directions. Each of the other answers names only one way in which the moths try to escape.

5. **The correct answer is (D).** Choices (A) and (B) refer to how some moths are protected from insects and birds. Nothing in the passage discusses how scent or taste is used by bats or moths, so choices (C) and (E) are incorrect.

Passage 2

6. **The correct answer is (E).** While choice (A) may be a true statement, it is not the reason she tells this to the goat. Choices (B), (C), and (D) are not suggested by the content of the passage.

7. **The correct answer is (C).** While the goat may be angry, choice (A), clumsy, choice (D), or uncomfortable, choice (E), the fox's words are about her opinion of the goat, not the goat's feelings. Choice (B) is not consistent with the goat's situation or the fox's opinion of him.

8. **The correct answer is (B).** While the fox may seem to be helping the goat, she only does this to trick him so that she can get out of the well.

9. **The correct answer is (C).** Nothing in the passage suggests choices (D) or (E). And while the fox does climb, choice (A), she climbs up the goat's back, not up the walls. Choice (B) is incorrect because the fox could not have jumped out without using the goat as a ladder.

10. **The correct answer is (A).** Choices (D) and (E) are incorrect because while they may be inferred from the story, they are not the lessons implied by the fox's words. Choice (C) is incorrect because it is too specific. The problem was not thirst, but acting without thinking. Choice (B) is wrong because it implies the opposite of what the goat did when he jumped into the well.

Passage 3

11. **The correct answer is (B).** The passage states humans adapted to the climate change. Choices (C), (D), and (E) describe only part of the content of the passage. Choice (A) is incorrect because the passage is not about a conflict.

12. **The correct answer is (E).** Because "auroch" is included in a list of "appropriate forest animals" that "stocked" the forest, it is a surviving animal. The other answers ignore this information.

13. **The correct answer is (E).** Although the passage states the animals' disappearance was "perhaps hastened" by hunting, hunting is not given as the major cause, so choice (A) is incorrect. The conclusion of the passage contradicts choice (B). The contents of choices (C) and (D) do not appear in the passage.

14. **The correct answer is (B).** While choices (A), (C), and (D) may determine what happens to a society, these are not discussed in the passage. Choice (E) is incorrect because the reference to coats in the passage's last sentence is an adaptation, not a cause.

15. **The correct answer is (C).** The first time it is used, "coat" refers to an animal's fur or hide; the second time it is used, it refers to an article of clothing worn by a person. Thus, choices (A) and (E) are incorrect. Choice (D) is incorrect because it refers to an action, not an object. Choice (B) is incorrect because the sentence does not require individual interpretation.

Passage 4

16. **The correct answer is (C).** Choice (A) is contradicted by the last sentence in the passage. Choice (B) is about saturated fat. Choices (D) and (E) apply to monounsaturated fat according to the passage.

17. **The correct answer is (A).** The other answers describe only part of the passage's content. Choice (A) is the most general, and it describes all of the content of the passage.

18. **The correct answer is (B).** The passage says saturated fat is found in meat and dairy products. All of the answers except choice (B) mention a meat or a dairy product.

19. **The correct answer is (D).** According to the passages, choices (A), (B), and (C) are true of polyunsaturated fat, and choice (E) is true of saturated fat.

20. **The correct answer is (C).** The passage contradicts choice (A). The passage does not state whether choice (B) is a fact. Choice (D) is contradicted by the first three sentences of the passage, and choice (E) is contradicted by the last sentence of the passage.

ISEE Diagnostic Test

Directions: Each question is made up of a word in capital letters followed by four choices. You are to circle the one word that is most nearly the same in meaning as the word in capital letters.

1. DISCREDIT

   (A) disengage
   (B) flaunt
   (C) disbelieve
   (D) please

2. SUCCULENT

   (A) crucial
   (B) tasty
   (C) clear
   (D) wicked

3. EXPLICIT

   (A) definite
   (B) rational
   (C) vital
   (D) inventive

4. DELETE

   (A) display
   (B) descend
   (C) invest
   (D) remove

5. INTEGRATE

   (A) merge into a whole
   (B) repeat endlessly
   (C) prove false
   (D) remain untouched

6. AMNESTY

   (A) loss of memory
   (B) comprehensive pardon
   (C) long angry speech
   (D) shortage of supplies

7. ASSET

   (A) insult
   (B) loss
   (C) agreement
   (D) benefit

8. SERENITY

   (A) sympathy
   (B) self-confidence
   (C) peacefulness
   (D) sweetness

9. CONFOUND

   (A) confuse
   (B) contain
   (C) eliminate
   (D) reproduce

10. BLIGHT

    (A) satisfy
    (B) strengthen
    (C) subtract
    (D) damage

11. No one anticipated that if the king should _____ his throne there would be such _____ results throughout the country.

   (A) dovetail..adventurous
   (B) abdicate..calamitous
   (C) inverse..venerable
   (D) abut..incredulous

12. The surgeon was well-respected for her _____, unlike her colleague who was known for his clumsiness.

   (A) philanthropy
   (B) arrogance
   (C) dexterity
   (D) pallor

13. Although she pleaded that she loved him, his _____ made him doubt her _____.

   (A) skepticism..verity
   (B) flippancy..enmity
   (C) stoicism..trepidation
   (D) drudgery..fabrication

14. The judge stopped the trial when he declared that, "Since the petition has been filed _____, it is _____."

   (A) belatedly..repugnant
   (B) erroneously..fallacious
   (C) despicably..sprightly
   (D) respectively..insightful

15. The principal told the parents that their son was _____, and, therefore, he behaved in a _____ manner.

   (A) incognito..pert
   (B) tractable..vigilant
   (C) curt..adept
   (D) pugnacious..belligerent

16. After the legal _____, the loser of the case was required to pay _____.

   (A) precursor..gallantry
   (B) confrontation..reparation
   (C) parable..prospectus
   (D) affray..jurisdiction

17. Upset by the treachery of his general, the king planned his _____ with great rancor.

   (A) accord
   (B) foreboding
   (C) vengeance
   (D) repercussion

18. During the performance of the play, the audience cheered, applauded, and gave several standing ovations, a true _____ of _____.

   (A) embargo..plunder
   (B) fiasco..negation
   (C) sequel..tedium
   (D) potpourri..acclamation

19. After reading his student's research paper, the teacher was shocked that his student had no scruples about _____ from his resources.

   (A) terminating
   (B) pilfering
   (C) defraying
   (D) embezzling

20. After being convicted of shoplifting, the _____ pleaded with the judge to be _____.

   (A) rubble..disarming
   (B) loiterer..churlish
   (C) envoy..brazen
   (D) brigand..lenient

QUANTITATIVE REASONING
20 QUESTIONS

Directions: Any figures that accompany questions in this section may be assumed to be drawn as accurately as possible EXCEPT when it is stated that a particular figure is not drawn to scale. Letters such as *x, y,* and *n* stand for real numbers.

For Questions 1–10, work each in your head or on the space available on these pages. Then select the correct answer.

1. Rounded to the nearest tenth, what would 46.97 equal?

    (A) 46.0
    (B) 46.10
    (C) 46.9
    (D) 47.0

2. $2^3 + 5^2 =$

    (A) 16
    (B) 29
    (C) 33
    (D) 200

3. From a work force of 500,000 employed last year, 8% of the employees had to be fired. How many were dismissed at that time?

    (A) 100,000
    (B) 40,000
    (C) 30,000
    (D) 8,000

4. If $3a - 5 = 7$, then $a =$

    (A) -4
    (B) 4
    (C) $-\dfrac{2}{3}$
    (D) $\dfrac{2}{3}$

5. What is .03 expressed as a percent?

    (A) .0003%
    (B) 3%
    (C) .3%
    (D) .03%

6.

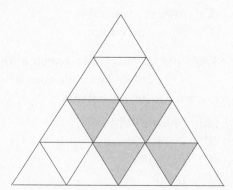

What percent of the entire figure is shaded?

    (A) $\dfrac{1}{4}$%
    (B) 40%
    (C) 25%
    (D) 50%

7. If the fractions $\dfrac{x+y}{3}$ and $\dfrac{x-y}{4}$ are added, what is the result?

    (A) $\dfrac{7x + y}{12}$
    (B) $\dfrac{2x}{7}$
    (C) $\dfrac{7x - y}{12}$
    (D) $\dfrac{5x + 4y}{12}$

8. If 35% of a number is 70, what is the number?

    (A) 24.5

    (B) 200

    (C) 50

    (D) 65

9. The solution set of the inequality $3x - 4 > 8$ is

    (A) $x > 4$

    (B) $x < 4$

    (C) $x > \dfrac{4}{3}$

    (D) $x < -\dfrac{4}{3}$

10. The circumference of a circle whose diameter is 7 inches is approximately

    (A) 22 inches.

    (B) 28 inches.

    (C) 38 inches.

    (D) 154 inches.

Directions: For Questions 11–20, note the given information, if any, and then compare the quantity in Column A to the quantity in Column B. Next to the number of each question, write

  A if the quantity in Column A is greater.

  B if the quantity in Column B is greater.

  C if the two quantities are equal.

  D if the relationship cannot be determined from the information given.

	Column A	Column B
11.	$.025 \times 1{,}000$	250
12.	$\dfrac{4}{9}$	44%
13.	$\sqrt{106}$	11

14.

$\angle H$	$\angle L$

| **15.** | $(12 + 8) \div 4$ | $12 + 8 \div 4$ |

Column A	**Column B**		**Column A**	**Column B**

16. Average of 0.3, −0.8, −0.2, +0.2, and 0.0 — Column B: 0.1

19.
$$10b - 17 = 13$$
$$9z - 27 = 0$$

Column A: b Column B: z

17. 54 sq. ft. — Column B: 648 sq. in.

20. The radius of a circle when the circumference is 9π — Column B: The radius of a circle when the area is 25π

18. $p < 0, q > 0$

Column A: pq   Column B: 0

Directions: Each passage below is followed by questions based on its content. Answer the questions following a passage on the basis of what is *stated* or *implied* in that passage.

Passage 1

Line Although most people go through life
without ever discovering that there is a
subject called "aesthetics," few would find
life bearable without some sort of primitive
5   aesthetic enjoyment—the sight of a loved
face, the taste of a good meal, or the feel of
a comfortable resting place. As civilized
beings, we might find it equally unbearable
to live in a world, such as that described in
10   George Orwell's *1984,* devoid of the
aesthetic pleasures derivable from art.
Fortunately, our world still contains an
almost infinite variety of natural and created
phenomena from which we can derive
15   aesthetic pleasure. Most people usually take
these phenomena and the pleasures associated with them for granted. Those who do
not take them for granted, but who seek to
understand their nature and value, are
20   engaged in the task (whether they know it
or not) that was initiated by Socrates and
Plato more than two thousand years ago and
that has kept aesthetics ever since an
ongoing concern.
25   But is the task really meaningful? Is it
worth the effort? Can its goal ever be
attained? There are critics of aesthetics who
would without hesitation answer "No!"
Some of these critics hold that aesthetic
30   experience is ineffable, completely beyond
the reach of rational description and
analysis, and that consequently aesthetics as
the theoretical study of this experience is
impossible. Others claim that aesthetics must

35   be by its nature such an abstract form of
speculation that it can have little or nothing
to do with real art and with "the blood and
guts" of creative endeavor. Still others are
afraid to study aesthetics for fear that it
40   might "clog up the springs of creativity"
with its obscure ideas about art and beauty.
Among these are some artists who would as
soon have a lobotomy as take a course in
aesthetics, and even a book on the subject is
45   to them, in William James's phrase, an
"abomination of desolation." Aesthetics has
also been criticized by poets for being too
unfeeling and critical; by art critics for being
too general and ill-informed; by psycholo-
50   gists for being immoral; by economists for
being useless; by politicians for being
undemocratic; by philosophers for being
dreary, desolate, and dull; and by students
for being "anesthetics in disguise."

1. In the context of the passage, the word
    ineffable (line 30) most likely means

    (A) indescribable.
    (B) intellectual.
    (C) ineffective.
    (D) inescapable.

2. According to the passage, the study of
    aesthetics was begun by

    (A) psychologists.
    (B) William James.
    (C) Socrates and Plato.
    (D) Dr. Samuel Jackson.

3. The primary purpose of the second para-
    graph is to

    (A) specifically criticize aesthetics.
    (B) describe the criticisms of aesthetics.
    (C) argue that aesthetics is unimportant.
    (D) discuss the value of aesthetics.

77

4. According to the passage, poets criticize aesthetics for being

    (A) immoral.
    (B) unfeeling.
    (C) scientific.
    (D) useless.

Passage 2

Line We lived in a small town in Monmouthshire, at the head of one of the coal valleys. Unemployment was endemic there, and enforced leisure gave rise to protracted
5 bouts of philosophy and politics. Most men leaned toward politics, since it gave an appearance of energy and deceived some people into believing they possessed power and influence. It was, if you like, political
10 theory, imaginative and vituperative. The hills about our town were full of men giving their views an airing; eloquence was commonplace.

    True power lay in the hands of a small
15 group—the aldermen and councilors of the town. To a man, they sold insurance and were prosperous. This was because they ran the municipal transport, the public parks and gardens, the collection of taxes, the
20 whole organization of local government in the town and its surrounding villages. They hired and fired, dispensed and took away. They were so corrupt that the Mafia never got a toehold among us. Those Italian boys
25 would have starved.

    In order to get anywhere in our town, you had to buy insurance. When teachers, for example, got their salaries at the end of the month, most of them paid heavy
30 insurance. The remainder of the teachers were the sons and daughters of councilors.

5. In the context of the passage, the word *protracted* (line 4) means

    (A) circular.
    (B) lengthy.
    (C) complicated.
    (D) unintelligible.

6. In the context of the passage, the statement "those Italian boys would have starved" (lines 24–25) means

    (A) the townspeople were prejudiced against other ethnic groups.
    (B) there was no work in town for the Italians either.
    (C) the Italians were not corrupt like the town councilors.
    (D) organized crime would not have been able to prosper in the town.

7. The discussion of "political theory" in paragraph 1

    (A) serves as a contrast to the "true power" described in paragraph 2.
    (B) provides the setting for the confrontation that occurs later.
    (C) prepares the reader for the eloquent political discussion that follows.
    (D) explains the townspeople's fascination with the town hall.

8. According to the passage, the powerful people in town all

    (A) sell insurance.
    (B) smoke cigars.
    (C) teach school.
    (D) own antiques.

Passage 3

Line   A colloid is larger than a molecule but small enough to be "suspended" in a solvent. It is a particle having dimensions between 1 micron and 1 millimicron. A micron is one
5   millionth of a meter. A millimicron, or nanometer, is one billionth of a meter. Such a particle cannot be seen with a microscope, but when carried in a solution, it will not diffuse through a membrane made from
10   parchment paper. In contrast, salt molecules or sugar molecules will diffuse. A colloid may consist of grains of a solid, bubbles of a gas, or droplets of a liquid dispersed in three kinds of mediums: (1) sols: solid colloids in a
15   liquid or a gas in a liquid; (2) gels: oblong shaped colloids forming a branched structure in a liquid; (3) emulsions: minute droplets of a liquid dispersed in a second liquid.
20   Colloids have a random motion (they zigzag) because of collisions with other molecules. They are stable while carrying the same electrical charge, which causes them to repel each other and literally
25   disperse themselves in a solvent or gaseous medium. (This phenomenon is known as Brownian motion.) Colloids will provide a path for a sharp beam of light, but may otherwise reflect normal light as a color.
30   (This is known as the Tyndell effect.) They are capable of absorbing themselves on solid surfaces.

9. A nanometer is

   (A) larger than a millimicron.
   (B) smaller than a millimicron.
   (C) larger than a micron.
   (D) smaller than a micron.

10. A salt molecule is

   (A) larger than a colloid.
   (B) smaller than a colloid.
   (C) heavier than a colloid.
   (D) lighter than a colloid.

11. Colloids are stable when they

   (A) have the same electrical charge.
   (B) are sols.
   (C) are gels.
   (D) zigzag.

12. The Tyndell effect deals with colloid

   (A) size.
   (B) reflection of light.
   (C) motion.
   (D) shape.

Passage 4

Ride a wild horse
with purple wings
striped yellow and black
except his head
Which must be red.

Ride a wild horse
against the sky
hold tight to his wings . . .
Before you die
Whatever else you leave undone,
Once, ride a wild horse
Into the sun.

13. This poem best expresses the power of

   (A) the imagination.
   (B) wild horses.
   (C) mythological creatures.
   (D) nature.

14. This poem primarily uses which one of the following literary techniques?

   (A) Rhythm
   (B) Assonance
   (C) Irony
   (D) Hyperbole

15. The poet's use of diction suggests the poem is aimed at

   (A) old people.
   (B) young people.
   (C) women.
   (D) cowboys.

16. The best title of the poem is

   (A) "Ride a Wild Horse."
   (B) "Horses of the Sun."
   (C) "A Horse of a Different Color."
   (D) "The Last Round-up."

MATH ACHIEVEMENT   25 QUESTIONS

Directions: Each question is followed by four suggested answers. Read each question and then decide which of the four suggested answers is best.

1. How many factors does the number 20 have?

   (A) 6
   (B) 4
   (C) 3
   (D) 2

2. $2^3 + 5^2 =$

   (A) 16,807
   (B) 200
   (C) 33
   (D) 16

3. Mary's investment of $3,500 increased over the course of a year to $5,075. What was the percent of increase?

   (A) 31%
   (B) 131%
   (C) 69%
   (D) 45%

4. What is the area of an equilateral triangle, one side of which measures 4 units?

   (A) 16
   (B) $4\sqrt{5}$
   (C) $4\sqrt{3}$
   (D) 12

5. What is the perimeter of an equilateral triangle, one side of which measures 15 inches?

   (A) 15 inches
   (B) 35 inches
   (C) 45 inches
   (D) 225 inches

6. The price of a dining room set is reduced by 10% and then goes on clearance for half of the resulting price. The final price is what percentage of the original price?

   (A) 40
   (B) 45
   (C) 55
   (D) 60

7. In a jar of beads, the ratio of green beads to red beads is 5:3. If only green and red beads are in the jar and the total number of beads is 56, how many red beads are in the jar?

   (A) 28
   (B) 21
   (C) 15
   (D) 8

8. Evaluate $3x^2 - 2x - 1$ when x is equal to -2.

   (A) 15
   (B) -15
   (C) -17
   (D) -7

9. On the following graph, what is the percent increase from the lowest point to the highest point?

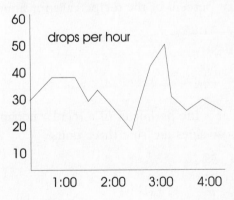

   (A) 60%
   (B) 150%
   (C) 250%
   (D) 300%

10. Which line is parallel to the line $y = 4x - 3$?

   (A) $y = 3x - 4$
   (B) $y + 4x = 3$
   (C) $2y - 8x = -1$
   (D) $x = 4y - 3$

11. Two cardboard boxes have equal volume. The dimensions of one box are $6 \times 8 \times 10$. If the length of the other box is 4 and the width is 6, what is the height of the second box?

   (A) 20
   (B) 3
   (C) 10
   (D) 24

12. At The Wee Little Clubhouse, each of the 12 members donated d dollars to the dues fund. In terms of d, what was the total number of dollars donated?

   (A) 12
   (B) $12d$
   (C) $\dfrac{d}{12}$
   (D) $\dfrac{12}{d}$

13. If a cake mix calls for 2.5 cups of sugar, 4 cups of flour, and 1.5 cups of melted butter, what percent of the recipe calls for flour?

   (A) 31.25%
   (B) 40%
   (C) 50%
   (D) 57%

14. What is the perimeter of a regular nonagon whose sides measure three units?

   (A) 39
   (B) 9
   (C) 12
   (D) 27

15. The hypotenuse of a right triangle is 13 and one leg is 12. Find the length of the other leg of the triangle.

   (A) 1
   (B) 5
   (C) 12
   (D) 25

16. Which number is not a factor of $6 \times 7 \times 12 \times 13 \times 2$?

   (A) 30
   (B) 21
   (C) 39
   (D) 48

17. $(-3)^2 - 4(-3) =$

   (A) 3
   (B) -15
   (C) 108
   (D) 21

18. If $\dfrac{2}{c} = \dfrac{6}{9}$, find the value of c.

   (A) 3
   (B) 2
   (C) 9
   (D) 18

19. If $|2a - 1| = 5$, which of the following is a possible value for a?

   (A) -2
   (B) -1
   (C) 0
   (D) None of the above.

20. Solve for x: $.02x + .12 = .20$

   (A) 3
   (B) -1
   (C) 4
   (D) 2

21. $|5x - 3| > 7$ is equivalent to

(A) $-\dfrac{4}{5} < x < 2$

(B) $-2 < x < \dfrac{4}{5}$

(C) $\dfrac{4}{5} < x < 2$

(D) $x > 2$ or $x < -\dfrac{4}{5}$

22.

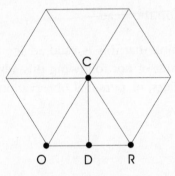

Calculate the area of the hexagon.
$OR = 8\sqrt{3}$, $CD = 4$

(A) $96\sqrt{3}$

(B) $32\sqrt{3}$

(C) 32

(D) $16\sqrt{3}$

23. A microwave is on sale for $158 after a discount of 30%. Find the approximate original price.

(A) $205.40

(B) $110.60

(C) $225.70

(D) $268.60

24. Rachel worked one weekend from 9:00 A.M. until 4:30 P.M. at the rate of $9.25 per hour. How much did she receive for both days?

(A) $69.38

(B) $104.06

(C) $138.75

(D) $277.52

25. If $|3a + 1| = 25$, which of the following is a possible value for a?

(A) -8

(B) $-\dfrac{26}{3}$

(C) $\dfrac{13}{3}$

(D) 9

$\sqrt{24} \cdot 6$

WRITING SAMPLE	TIME: 30 MINUTES

Directions: Using two sheets of lined theme paper, plan and write an essay on the topic assigned below. DO NOT WRITE ON ANOTHER TOPIC. AN ESSAY ON ANOTHER TOPIC IS NOT ACCEPTABLE.

Topic: There is a saying in Japan that "the nail that sticks out gets hit on the head."

Assignment: Write an essay giving your view of this saying. Do you think that this is valid advice for people? Is it safer to keep a low profile in life? What would be the result of not following this advice? Support your opinion with specific examples from history, current affairs, or personal observations.

Name: _____

Write your essay here.

_____
_____
_____
_____
_____
_____
_____
_____
_____
_____
_____
_____
_____
_____
_____
_____
_____
_____
_____
_____
_____
_____

(Continue, if necessary.)

www.petersons.com

EXPLANATORY ANSWERS TO THE ISEE DIAGNOSTIC TEST

VERBAL REASONING

1. The correct answer is (C).

2. The correct answer is (B).

3. The correct answer is (A).

4. The correct answer is (D).

5. The correct answer is (A).

6. The correct answer is (B).

7. The correct answer is (D).

8. The correct answer is (C).

9. The correct answer is (A).

10. The correct answer is (D).

11. The correct answer is (B). The clue is that *one action resulted in the other.* The word *king* is your trigger. The first word would be "something that a king would do regarding his throne." That eliminates choices (C) and (D). The second word is the "reaction of his subjects to his action." This would eliminate choice (A).

12. The correct answer is (C). The clue is the word *unlike;* it tells you that the words will be opposites. The trigger word is *surgeon.* The missing word is a "quality for which a surgeon would be admired." This eliminates choices (B) and (D). The opposite of *clumsiness* is *dexterity,* which eliminates choice (A).

13. The correct answer is (A). The clue is the word *although;* it tells you that the words will be opposites. The trigger word is *doubt.* He had one quality that made him doubt her love. That eliminates choices (B), (C), and (D). The clue for the second word is that it is "what he doubts about her."

14. The correct answer is (B). The clue is that *one action resulted in the other.* The trigger word is *judge.* The first word would be a "procedural error that would come before a judge." That eliminates choices (C) and (D). The second word would be the "determination the judge would make regarding that error." That would eliminate choice (A).

15. **The correct answer is (D).** The clue is in the words *principal* and *the parents;* the trigger word is *told.* The principal most likely would be having a conference with the parents to "tell them something negative about their son." That is the meaning of the first word. This would eliminate choices (A) and (B). The meaning of the second word is that the "son's behavior is a result of this negative quality; therefore, it is a negative behavior." This would eliminate choice (C).

16. **The correct answer is (B).** The clue for the first word is in the word *loser.* A word that reflects the notion of winning and losing is "contest." This eliminates choices (A) and (C). The trigger for the second word is *pay.* In court "contests," the loser often has to pay "damages" to the winner, as in the word *reparation.* This would eliminate choice (D).

17. **The correct answer is (C).** The clue word is *treachery,* and the trigger word is *planned.* The missing word will be a "reaction, on the part of the king, to treachery." This eliminates choices (A) and (B). The word *repercussion* in choice (D) implies a consequence of an action, but in the context of this sentence, it is just poor grammar. This eliminates choice (D).

18. **The correct answer is (D).** The clue for the first word is the series of words, "cheered, applauded, and gave several standing ovations." The first word would be a "mixture" or "group." The clue for the second word is "kinds of commendation" or "adulation." This eliminates all but choice (D).

19. **The correct answer is (B).** The clue is in the words "after reading his student's research paper." A teacher would look to see if a student "plagiarized" any of the resources. This would eliminate choices (A) and (C). The word *embezzling* in choice (D) is related to stealing. However, the clue from the word *scruples* would be that the student has "no conscience" about using someone else's work as his or her own. That would eliminate choice (D).

20. **The correct answer is (D).** The clue is *shoplifting.* The first word would describe someone who is "criminal." This eliminates choices (A) and (C). The trigger for the second word is *pleaded.* The second word would describe what a criminal would beg for from a judge, a quality like "mercy." This would eliminate choice (B).

QUANTITATIVE REASONING

1. **The correct answer is (D).** Begin by writing down as many digits of the given decimal number as required and drop the other digits. Then, starting from the left and going to the right, if the first digit dropped is 4 or less, the number obtained is correct as is. If the first digit dropped is 5 or more, increase by one the last digit in the number as written. Thus,

46.97 is 46.9 to the nearest tenth. Since we dropped a 7, and 7 > 5, increase the tenths digits by 1.

46.9 + .1 = 47.0

2. **The correct answer is (C).** First calculate powers, then add.

$$2^3 = 2 \times 2 \times 2 = 8$$
$$5^2 = 5 \times 5 = 25$$
$$8 + 25 = 33$$

3. **The correct answer is (B).** The word "of" typically indicates multiplication in a percent problem. $8\% = .08$.

$$500,000 \times .08 = 40,000 \text{ dismissed}$$

4. **The correct answer is (B).** Begin by adding 5 to both sides of the equation.

$$3a - 5 = 7$$
$$\underline{+5 \qquad +5}$$
$$3a \qquad = 12$$

Then, divide both sides by 3.

$$\frac{3a}{3} = \frac{12}{3}$$
$$a = 4$$

5. **The correct answer is (B).** To rename a decimal as a percent, multiply the decimal by 100.

$$.03 \times 100 = 3.00 = 3\%$$

6. **The correct answer is (C).** The total number of triangles is 16; the total number of shaded triangles is 4.

$$\text{Ratio of } \frac{\text{shaded}}{\text{total}} = \frac{4}{16} = \frac{1}{4} = 25\%.$$

7. **The correct answer is (A).** The least common denominator of the two fractions is 12.

$$\frac{x + y}{3} = \frac{4x + 4y}{12} \qquad \frac{x - y}{4} = \frac{3x - 3y}{12}$$

Now, combine like terms in the numerator:

$$\frac{4x + 4y + 3x - 3y}{12} = \frac{7x + y}{12}$$

8. **The correct answer is (B).** 35% of $N = 70$. Rewrite 35% as .35.

$$.35 \times N = 70$$

Divide both sides by .35.

$$N = 70 \div .35 = 200$$

9. **The correct answer is (A).** $3x - 4 > 8$

$$3x > 8 + 4$$
$$3x > 12$$
$$x > 4$$

10. **The correct answer is (A).** The formula for the circumference of a circle is C = πD.

Thus, C = π(7) ≈ (3.14)(7) = 21.98, which is almost 22.

11. **The correct answer is (B).** .025 × 1,000 = 25, which is less than 250.

12. **The correct answer is (A).** Begin by renaming $\frac{4}{9}$ as a decimal by dividing 4 by 9. The result of this division is .444444. . . . To write this decimal as a percent, move the decimal point two places to the right to obtain 44.4444. . . %. This percent is clearly larger than 44%.

13. **The correct answer is (B).** $\sqrt{106}$ is between the integers 10 and 11.

That is, $10 < \sqrt{106} < 11$, since $\sqrt{100} < \sqrt{106} < \sqrt{121}$

14. **The correct answer is (C).** The sum of the angles in a triangle is equal to 180°. Therefore,

$$m\angle H + 50° + 50° = 180°$$
$$m\angle H + 100° = 180°, \quad \text{which means that}$$
$$m\angle H = 80°. \quad \text{Similarly,}$$
$$m\angle L + 40° + 60° = 180°$$
$$m\angle L + 100° = 180°, \quad \text{so that}$$
$$m\angle L = 80°.$$

15. **The correct answer is (B).** In Column A, according to the order of operations, simplify within parentheses first:

$$(12 + 8) \div 4 = 20 \div 4 = 5$$

In Column B, according to the order of operations, divide before adding:

$$12 + 8 \div 4 = 12 + 2 = 14$$

16. **The correct answer is (B).** To find the average, we begin by finding the sum of the five numbers in Column A. The easiest way to do this is to add the positive numbers, then the negative numbers, then find the sum of the results.

$$(+0.3) + (0.2) + (0.0) = +0.5$$
$$(-0.2) + (-0.8) = -1.0$$

Thus, the total of the five numbers is
$$(+0.5) + (-1.0) = -0.5$$

To find the average, we divide this number by 5.
$$-0.5 \div 5 = -0.1.$$

Thus, the entry in Column B is greater.

17. **The correct answer is (A).** Since 1 sq. ft. is 12 in. × 12 in. = 144 sq. in., 54 sq. ft. is 54 × 144 = 7776 sq. in.

18. **The correct answer is (B).** Since *p* is negative and *q* is positive, the product *pq* is negative. The number 0 is greater than any negative number.

19. **The correct answer is (C).** We must use the given information to solve for b and z.

$$10b - 17 = 13 \quad \text{Add 17 to both sides.}$$
$$10b = 30 \quad \text{Divide by 10.}$$
$$b = 3 \quad \text{Similarly,}$$
$$9z - 27 = 0 \quad \text{Add 27 to both sides.}$$
$$9z = 27 \quad \text{Divide by 9.}$$
$$z = 3$$

20. **The correct answer is (B).** The formula for the circumference of a circle is $C = \pi D$. Thus, if the circumference of a circle is 9π, the diameter is 9 and the radius is 4.5.

The formula for the area of a circle is $A = \pi r^2$. Thus, if the area is 25π, the radius is 5.

READING COMPREHENSION

Passage 1

1. **The correct answer is (A).** Choice (B) is an unlikely answer, since the fact that something is intellectual would not make "the theoretical study of (aesthetic pleasure) . . . impossible" (paragraph 2). Choices (C) and (D) are unlikely for the same reason. Note that right after the author first uses the word *ineffable,* he includes an explanation of what it means: *completely beyond the reach of rational description and analysis;* thus, *indescribable* is the correct answer.

2. **The correct answer is (C).** Although choices (A), (B), and (D) are all people listed in the passage, the last sentence of paragraph 1 notes that those who study aesthetics "are engaged in the task . . . initiated by Socrates and Plato more than two thousand years ago."

3. **The correct answer is (B).** Choice (D) is unlikely since the fourth sentence of paragraph 2 begins, "There are critics of aesthetics who . . ." and then lists the complaints of critics. Although (C) is a more likely answer, the author is careful to note that these negative opinions about aesthetics are other people's opinions rather than his own opinion. Choice (A), though another likely possibility, is also incorrect—again, because the author is not criticizing aesthetics but describing the criticisms of other people, the correct answer is (B).

4. **The correct answer is (B).** Choices (A), (C), and (D) are all listed as criticisms of aesthetics in the passage, but the last sentence of paragraph 2 notes that "poets (criticize aesthetics) for being . . . unfeeling."

Passage 2

5. **The correct answer is (B).** Choice (A) may seem like a possibility because of the word *protracted;* however, it is a less likely answer based on the context. Choices (C) and (D), similarly, are less likely based on context. Men who are unemployed, with nothing to fill their time, are most likely to engage in lengthy discussions to pass the time.

6. **The correct answer is (D).** Choice (A) is incorrect because there is no suggestion of prejudice in the passage. In choices (B) and (C), since paragraph 2 mentions the Mafia, the implication is that the Italians being discussed are also corrupt and that they would not be seeking regular employment. The line suggests that since the town councilors are so corrupt, no other corrupt group would be able to operate in the town. Thus, the correct answer is (D).

7. **The correct answer is (A).** Choices (C) and (D) do not relate to the passage: the discussion that follows is not a political discussion, and the passage does not suggest that the townspeople are fascinated with the town hall. Although choice (B) is accurate, it is too general a description of the usual function of opening paragraphs in fiction. Note that sentence 3 in paragraph 1 states that the discussions of political theory "deceived some people into believing they possessed power and influence"; paragraph 2, in contrast, opens with the words "True power," line 14.

8. **The correct answer is (A).** Although many of the powerful people may have smoked cigars, choice (B), and owned antiques, choice (D), the passage does not mention this as a characteristic of all the powerful people in the town. Choice (C) is incorrect because teachers are hired by the powerful people; they are not powerful people themselves. Choice (A) is correct because paragraph 2 states that the powerful people in town "sold insurance."

Passage 3

9. **The correct answer is (D).** A nanometer is equal to a millimicron, which is one billionth of a meter. A micron is one millionth of a meter. Therefore, a nanometer is smaller than a micron.

10. **The correct answer is (B).** The reading contrasts the fact that a colloid cannot be seen with a microscope but cannot diffuse through a membrane made from parchment paper. The use of the phrase "but despite its size" following the statement that a colloid is too small to see implies that the colloid is too big to diffuse through the membrane. Therefore, the salt molecule is smaller than the colloid, and choice (B) is the correct answer. Nothing was mentioned about weight; therefore choices (C) and (D) are incorrect.

11. **The correct answer is (A).** Paragraph 2 states "they are stable while carrying the same electrical charge."

12. **The correct answer is (B).** Paragraph 2 states that the Tyndell effect is the property of colloids that provides a path for a sharp beam of light, but otherwise reflect normal light as color.

Passage 4

13. **The correct answer is (A).** One needs imagination to create the vehicle that will take you to unknown places. Choice (B) is a literal response, and choices (C) and (D) are too one-dimensional.

14. **The correct answer is (D).** This word means exaggeration. The poem uses choice (A), rhythm, but it is not a primary tool. Choices (B) and (C) are inappropriate.

15. **The correct answer is (B).** The words chosen, diction, are simple and direct and are aimed at young people. The poet, of course, wants all people to read the poem, but choice (A) is not the primary audience. Choices (C) and (D) are both inappropriate.

16. **The correct answer is (A).** This is based on the repetition of the line. Choice (C) is close but is not as central as choice (A). Choices (B) and (D) are inappropriate.

MATH ACHIEVEMENT

1. **The correct answer is (A).** Factors are all the numbers that divide a number evenly.

   The factors of 20 are:

   1 and 20

   2 and 10

   4 and 5

   which result in a total of 6 factors.

2. **The correct answer is (C).**

   First calculate powers, then add.

   $$2^3 = 2 \times 2 \times 2 = 8$$
   $$5^2 = 5 \times 5 = \underline{+25}$$
   $$33$$

3. **The correct answer is (D).**

   $$\frac{\$5,075}{\$3,500} = 1.45$$

   This represents a 45% increase (while retaining 100% of the original investment).

   You could also subtract the original investment of $3,500 from the present value of $5,075 (getting the amount of increase, which is $1,575). Then, the percent increase is $1,575 over the original investment of $3,500.

   $$\frac{\$1,575}{\$3,500} = .45, \text{ which is } 45\%$$

4. **The correct answer is (C).** An equilateral triangle can be divided into two congruent right triangles by bisecting any vertex.

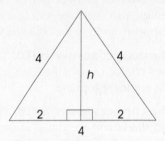

By the Pythagorean Theorem,

$$4^2 = h^2 + 2^2$$
$$16 = h^2 + 4$$
$$12 = h^2$$
$$h = \sqrt{12} = 2\sqrt{3}$$

You can also get this result by realizing that this forms a 30-60-90 triangle, whose sides are in the ratio $1:\sqrt{3}:2$

Area = one half base times height, so

$$A = (2)(2\sqrt{3}) = 4\sqrt{3}$$

5. **The correct answer is (C).** An equilateral triangle is made up of three congruent, or equal, sides. To determine the perimeter of a triangle, sum the measure of all three sides.

$$15 + 15 + 15 = 45$$

6. **The correct answer is (B).** If the dining room set originally costs x dollars, when it is reduced by 10%, it costs $x - .1x$ dollars or simply $.9x$ dollars (original price minus discounted amount). If the new price of $.9x$ is then discounted in half, the resulting price is $.9x - .5(.9x)$, which equals $.45x$, or 45% of the original price.

7. **The correct answer is (B).** Since the ratio of green to red beads is 5:3, there are $5x$ green beads and $3x$ red ones.

$$3x + 5x = 56$$
$$8x = 56$$
$$x = 7,$$

so there are $3(7) = 21$ red beads.

8. **The correct answer is (A).**

$$3x^2 - 2x - 1 =$$
$$3(-2)^2 - 2(-2) - 1 =$$
$$3(4) - (-4) - 1 =$$
$$12 + 4 - 1 = 15$$

9. **The correct answer is (B).** The lowest point is around 2:30 and has about 20 drops per hour. The highest point is around 3:00 with 50 drops per hour.

    The increase is 30 drops per hour. The base is at the lowest point (20 drops per hour) since we are looking for the percent increase from that point.

    $$\frac{30}{20} = 1.5 = 150\%$$

10. **The correct answer is (C).** Parallel lines have the same slope. The given line has a slope of 4. The slopes of the other answers are easiest to see if the equations are rewritten as slope-intercept form:

    $$y = mx + b$$
    $$2y - 8x = -1$$
    $$2y = 8x - 1$$
    $$y = 4x - \frac{1}{2}, \quad \text{which has a slope of 4}$$

    The other answers all have different slopes.

11. **The correct answer is (A).** Volume = length $\times$ width $\times$ height.

    The volume of both boxes is $6 \times 8 \times 10 = 480$.

    The volume of the second box is $4 \times 6 \times$ height $= 480$; therefore, the height of the box is $\frac{480}{4 \times 6} = \frac{480}{24} = 20$.

12. **The correct answer is (B).** Since each of the 12 members donated the same dollar amount, the total amount donated is the product of 12 and d.

13. **The correct answer is (C).** First, determine the total number of cups in the recipe.

    $$2.5 + 4 + 1.5 = 8$$

    To find the percentage of flour, divide the cups of flour by the total number of cups. $\frac{4}{8} = \frac{1}{2} = 50\%$

14. **The correct answer is (D).** A nonagon has nine sides. A regular nonagon has nine congruent sides. To get the perimeter, multiply the length of each side by the number of sides.

    $$3 \times 9 = 27$$

15. **The correct answer is (B).**

    By the Pythagorean Theorem:

    $$a^2 + b^2 = c^2$$
    $$a^2 + 12^2 = 13^2$$
    $$a^2 + 144 = 169$$
    $$\sqrt{a^2} = \sqrt{25}$$
    $$a = 5$$

16. **The correct answer is (A).** 30 has a factor of 5. (It is 6×5.) The given number does not have a factor of 5 anywhere. (None of the prime factors is 5 and none of the composite numbers contains a factor of 5.) The other answers can be made from factors contained in the given number. For example, 39 is 13×3, both of which are found in the given number (3 is a factor of 12).

17. **The correct answer is (D).**

Follow the correct order of operations.

$$(-3)^2 - 4(-3) = 9 - (-12)$$
$$= 9 + (+12)$$
$$= 21$$

18. **The correct answer is (A).**

Simplify $\dfrac{6}{9}$ as the equivalent of $\dfrac{2}{3}$.

Hence, $c = 3$.

19. **The correct answer is (A).**

$$|2a - 1| = 5$$
$$2a - 1 = 5$$
$$2a = 6$$
$$a = 3$$

OR

$$2a - 1 = -5$$
$$2a = -4$$
$$a = -2$$

a can equal 3 or -2

20. **The correct answer is (C).**

$$.02x + .12 = .20$$
$$\underline{-.12 = -.12}$$
$$.02x = .08$$
$$2x = 8$$
$$x = 4$$

21. **The correct answer is (D).**

$$5x - 3 > 7 \qquad\qquad -5x + 3 > 7$$
$$5x > 10 \qquad\qquad -5x > 4$$
$$x > 2 \qquad\qquad x < -\frac{4}{5}$$

Thus, x must be less than $-\dfrac{4}{5}$ or greater than 2.

22. **The correct answer is (A).**

$$A = \frac{1}{2}(4)\left(8\sqrt{3}\right) = 16\sqrt{3} = \text{area of one triangle.}$$

There are six triangles in a hexagon.

$$6\left(16\sqrt{3}\right) = 96\sqrt{3}$$

23. **The correct answer is (C).** Since $158 is 70% of the original price, the base price is

$$B = \frac{P}{R} = \frac{158}{.70} = \$225.70$$

24. **The correct answer is (C).**

The number of hours from 9:00 A.M. to 4:30 P.M. totals $7\frac{1}{2}$ hours.

Multiply: $7\frac{1}{2}$ or $7.5 \times 9.25 = 69.375$

Since a total of two days were spent working, the total will be $2 \times 69.375 = \$138.75$.

25. **The correct answer is (B).**

$$|3a + 1| = 25$$
$$3a + 1 = 25$$
$$3a = 24$$
$$a = 8$$

OR

$$3a + 1 = -25$$
$$3a = -26$$
$$a = -\frac{26}{3}$$

a can equal 8 or $-\frac{26}{3}$

Subject Reviews

STRATEGIES FOR VERBAL ANALYSIS/REASONING

One of the most important skills you must have in order to do well on either the SSAT or ISEE Verbal Analysis/Reasoning section is a strong vocabulary. At this point you already have some level of skill in order to have gone this far in school. However, you can always improve, and there are several steps that you can take in order to do so.

DEVELOPING YOUR VOCABULARY

READING

The single best way to improve your vocabulary skills is to read as much as you can, and take note of the words that you don't know or are unsure of their meaning. Read your local or national newspapers. Read magazines; whether you read *People* magazine or *Scientific American,* you're sure to encounter unfamiliar words. Write them down on an index card and then look them up.

INDEX CARDS

This is step two in the vocabulary development process. Once you have written down the words you don't know, look them up. Then write the definitions on the back of the card. Essentially, you will create a set of vocabulary flash cards. Now, you can review the words yourself, or have someone test you. Once you feel comfortable with the word, you can discard the card. Continue to review the words you don't know, even as you add to your pile of flash cards.

STUDY

The staff at Merriam-Webster gives you a head start with "Roots to Word Mastery," on pages 339–399. Here, you will find 100 Greek and Latin roots, which will help you master hundreds of new vocabulary words. Study the roots and put your new knowledge to work with the quizzes and practice test that appear in the chapter.

PRACTICE

It is an accepted fact that the more you practice, the better you will do on an actual exam. Therefore, you should answer the questions on the practice exams in this book, and if you missed any of the verbal questions, take extra time to read the answers so that you fully understand *why* you answered them incorrectly. And, of course, if you don't know some of the words, make flash cards.

READ AND LEARN THE DIRECTIONS

Almost all of the written tests that you will take in your lifetime will be timed. It is to your advantage to spend as much time as possible on answering the questions, rather than trying to figure out *how* to answer the questions. If you have to read and reread the directions in order to understand what is being asked of you, you will lose time from the overall test. Thus, take the time to understand what is required of you on the SSAT or ISEE before you take the test.

Q&A TECHNIQUES

There are several techniques or tricks to help you do well on these tests. If you combine these techniques with your vocabulary knowledge, you should do well on the exam.

ANSWERING MULTIPLE-CHOICE QUESTIONS

The first technique in answering a multiple-choice question is to guess at the answer. We don't mean a pie-in-the-sky guess but an educated one. If you are being asked to find a word that means almost the same as a given word, try to define the word yourself before reading the answers. If you can do that, you are more than halfway to the correct answer. Then read the answers. Which of the answers is the same or similar to your own definition? You'll quickly find that if you can define the word yourself (or fill in the blanks in a sentence-completion question), you will have very little trouble with that question.

The second technique is the process of elimination. Start by finding the word or words that you are fairly sure have no relationship to the given word. Eliminate them and that will reduce the number of choices. If you can eliminate two or three choices from the list, you've then got about a 50-50 chance of getting the correct answer.

The third technique is to use context clues. If you are given a sentence, try to find the description of the action that takes place, or the hidden definition within the sentence, or even a synonym that will give you a clue as to what the correct answer might be. You may find words that express positive or negative actions, happy or sad feelings, and so on. Use those clues to eliminate choices that don't fit with the action.

Check your answers. You may not have a lot of time when you go through the test, but that doesn't mean you should be careless. If you have extra time after finishing that section, go back and double-check your answers. However, keep in mind that your first answer is usually your correct answer.

Finally, make sure that you put your marks in the right place on the answer sheet. If you omit an answer, please be careful to answer the next question in the appropriate space. Once you fill in the wrong answer grid, all the rest of your answers will be incorrect. Check the answer number against the question you are answering to make sure you get it right.

Once again, remember that the key to success in answering synonym, sentence-completion, and analogy questions is to have a strong vocabulary. Building your vocabulary requires a day-by-day effort but will be well worth it in the end—when you take the actual SSAT or ISEE examination.

VERBAL ANALYSIS/REASONING REVIEW

A good way to prepare for the SSAT or ISEE examination is to familiarize yourself with the types of questions that these tests contain. These include vocabulary questions dealing with synonyms, sentence completion, and analogies. The review that follows is designed to further your understanding of the material covered on these two examinations.

SYNONYMS

The questions appear on both the SSAT and the ISEE. The only difference is that the SSAT questions have five answers, while the ISEE questions have four answers. In both, there is a capitalized word given, followed by answers. One of those answers is most nearly the same in meaning as the word in capital letters.

The most important way to study for this section is to read as much as you can, in all types of books, magazines, newspapers, and even this book. Always look up words that you don't know. Then write down the definition. You may never look at the paper again, but just the act of writing the word and definition will help it to stay in your mind. Of course, it's not possible to predict what words will be given on the exams, but the greater your vocabulary, the better your chance of getting the right answer.

One technique that's helpful is to look at the word and try to give your own definition of it, before you look at the answers. That's your own measure of whether or not you know the meaning of the word. Then look at the answers given and determine whether your definition is among them, or even close. Remember that the directions on the ISEE say "most nearly the same in meaning" and the directions on the SSAT say "whose meaning is closest to the word." Those phrases—"most nearly" and "is closest"—are key to answering synonym questions. It's not likely you will get an exact definition, but there is one that is fairly close.

Another technique that is important in any kind of multiple-choice question is using the process of elimination. What this means is that you should eliminate—cross off—any words that you know are incorrect. If you can cross off enough answers, you may narrow down your choices to only a few. In the ISEE, where there are only four choices, it makes it much easier.

Let's try some practice questions.

1. DAWDLE
    (A) hang loosely
    (B) waste time
    (C) fondle
    (D) splash
    (E) paint

2. ANGUISH
    (A) torment
    (B) boredom
    (C) resentment
    (D) stubbornness
    (E) clumsiness

3. IMPARTIAL
    (A) unlawful
    (B) incomplete
    (C) unprejudiced
    (D) unfaithful
    (E) unimportant

4. EMBROIL
    (A) explain
    (B) entangle
    (C) swindle
    (D) greet
    (E) imitate

5. INCANDESCENT
    (A) insincere
    (B) melodious
    (C) electrical
    (D) magical
    (E) glowing

ANSWERS

1. The correct answer is (B).
2. The correct answer is (A).
3. The correct answer is (C).
4. The correct answer is (B).
5. The correct answer is (E).

How did you do? How many did you get right? Here's a suggestion if you got more than one wrong. Learn the meaning of the following words:

anguish	incomplete
boredom	insincere
clumsiness	magical
dawdle	melodious
electrical	paint
embroil	resentment
entangle	splash
explain	stubbornness
fondle	swindle
glowing	torment
greet	unfaithful
imitate	unimportant
impartial	unlawful
incandescent	unprejudiced

If they look familiar, they should. These are words that were given in the previous five questions. If you had known the meaning of all of these words, you would have gotten all of the correct answers.

SENTENCE COMPLETION

These questions appear only on the ISEE. In a sentence-completion question, one or more words has been removed. You are required to supply a missing word or words that will best complete a sentence. These questions demand skill in figuring out meanings from context. Choose words that *best* fit the meaning of the sentence. In order to handle this type of question, you should first read the sentence as you see it without trying to fill in the word or words. After reading, consider the *main idea* of the sentence and *then* read the choices. Remember, *both* words must fit into the meaning of the sentence; therefore, read your choice into the sentence by supplying and evaluating *both* words.

Example

Choose words that best fit the meaning of the sentence:

> The zoology students sat quietly in their observation post; they were pleasantly surprised to observe, over the course of two days, a band of gorillas build a _____ camp each night. This always followed a day of _____ for the berries and leaves that constitute their diet.

(A) solid..trading

(B) sturdy..roaming

(C) interesting..seeking

(D) makeshift..foraging

(E) circular..farming

The correct answer is (D). Your knowledge of the meanings of words and the ability to use those words appropriately within a given context will help you answer sentence-completion questions. In addition, each sentence provides key words, specific examples, or an overall logic that helps direct you to the correct answer, regardless of your knowledge of the subject. The rules listed below are also useful:

1. As you read the sentence, note key words that show relationships. For example, *but, although, however,* and *on the other hand* indicate contrasting ideas. *And, another,* and *the same as* denote similarity. *Therefore, as a result, consequently, since,* and *because* signify a cause-effect relationship. In the example, the word *followed* indicates a time relationship.

2. Eliminate any answers that make no sense or that are grammatically incorrect. Choice (C) cannot be correct because the first blank requires a word beginning with a consonant. Choice (E) cannot be correct, because farming does not apply to gorillas or their food.

3. Do not be misled by answers that contain only one word that fits well into the sentence. *Both* words must make sense. For example, in choice (A), *solid* could be logically used to fill the first blank; however, *trading* is a human activity and does not fit logically into the context of the sentence.

4. Be guided by the logic and the meaning of the passage when two answers could be used to create a sensible thought. Choices (B) and (D) both list words that could be used to complete the sentence. However, since the camp is remade each night, it is probably *makeshift* rather than *sturdy*. Also, while the gorillas may be said to be *roaming* for food, *foraging* is a more specific and suitable word, because it means "searching for food."

Example

I attend the local college games, especially the one with our arch rival, State College. The game this year was extremely tough for us. State led throughout the game; but, after the _____ of a strong rally late in the ball game, we really thought we had a great chance of winning. Therefore, we were doubly _____ when our team lost.

- **(A)** lack..surprised
- **(B)** threat..amused
- **(C)** dispute..annoyed
- **(D)** excitement..disappointed
- **(E)** skill..doubtful

The correct answer is (D). Using the aforementioned clues and procedures, select the answer you think is best. The key words in the sentence that help you determine this answer are *strong, rally,* and *lost.* You can determine that by looking at the entire selection to see what its intent is.

Rule 2 indicates that choice (A) is not possible because it would make sense ONLY if the team had won.

Rule 3 indicates that choice (B) cannot be correct. While the word *threat* seems reasonable, the word *amused* does not.

Rule 4 applies to choice (D) and tells you that in the context of *strong, rally,* and *lost,* logically this is the correct answer.

In choices (C) and (E), the meanings are incorrect in the context; therefore, rule 4 would fit.

Example

Traditionally, countries with _____ borders requiring _____ must maintain a large army and support it by imposing taxes.

- **(A)** historic..markers
- **(B)** vulnerable..defense
- **(C)** vague..exploration
- **(D)** unwanted..elimination
- **(E)** contested..estimation

The correct answer is (B). Now, employing the four rules again, did you choose (B)?

Rule 3 fits here. While *historic* will work in the sentence, *markers* does not work because it makes no sense. A country does NOT employ an army to maintain its markers.

Rule 4 shows us that choice (B) is correct. Logic tells us that vulnerable borders need an army for defense.

Rule 4 also applies to choices (C) and (D) because they are NOT logical. A vague border would not require exploring. An unwanted border does not require an army to eliminate the border.

Rule 2 applies to choice (E), which makes no sense.

ANALOGIES

These questions only appear on the SSAT. An analogy question presents two words that are related in some way, and it requires you to first discover the relationship, then find another pair of words that is related in the same way.

Example

Advertising is to selling as

(A) reporting is to informing.
(B) training is to helping.
(C) discovering is to exploring.
(D) marketing is to research.
(E) creating is to destroying.

The correct answer is (A). To answer analogy questions, use the following strategies:

1. First, determine the relationship between the first pair of words and state that relationship in sentence form: "Advertising is a means of selling products to an audience."

2. Then, find the pair of words in the answers that can be substituted for the original pair: "Reporting is a means of informing an audience." None of the other answers expresses quite the same relationship. Although you can say, "Training is a means of helping an audience," the context is much more general. Choice (A) is the best answer.

The following table illustrates some of the most common types of relationships you will encounter in analogy questions:

Type of Analogy	Example
Action of Object	PLAY is to CLARINET as incise is to knife.
Cause to Effect	SUN is to SUNBURN as overeating is to indigestion.
Item to Category	IGUANA is to REPTILE as cat is to mammal.
Object to Its Function	PENCIL is to WRITING as tractor is to plowing.
Object to Its Material	CURTAINS is to CLOTH as windows is to glass.
Part to Whole	PAGE is to BOOK as limb is to tree.
Time Sequence	RECENT is to CURRENT as antique is to obsolete.
Word to Antonym	ASSIST is to HINDER as enthrall is to bore.
Word to Synonym	PROVISIONS is to SUPPLIES as portent is to omen.
Worker and Creation	ARTIST is to SKETCH as composer is to etude.
Worker and Work-place	CHEF is to KITCHEN as judge is to courtroom.
Word and Word Derived From	ACT is to ACTION as image is to imagine.

Now, using the two previously described procedures and the preceding table, look at the following examples:

Example

Mnemonic is to memory as

(A) trousers is to speech.
(B) glasses is to vision.
(C) earmuffs is to movement.
(D) blinders is to hearing.
(E) glove is to hand.

The correct answer is (B). Consider the relationship between the words MNEMONIC and MEMORY. A mnemonic device helps one to remember; therefore, a mnemonic device is designed to produce memory or to help one to remember.

Choices (A), (C), and (D) could not fit because each defies the relationship. Speech has no relationship to trousers. Earmuffs have no relationship to movement, and blinders have no relationship to hearing. Choice (E) does not work because, while a glove covers a hand, it does not help to produce a hand.

Choice (B) is correct because glasses are designed to aid vision or to help one to see. The relationship is identical. It is a Cause-to-Effect relationship.

Example

Waggish is to laughs as

(A) risible is to yawns.
(B) bilious is to smiles.
(C) lachrymose is to tears.
(D) ribald is to moans.
(E) frown is to grin.

The correct answer is (C). Again, using the previously described procedures, one can determine that a remark that is waggish is designed to produce laughs.

Looking at choices (A), (B), (D), and (E), you can see that they are incorrect because they do not produce the same relationship. Choices (A) and (E) are incorrect because the relationship is Word to Antonym. Choices (B) and (D) are incorrect because the relationship is not Cause to Effect. Therefore, the correct answer is (C).

Example

Act is to action as

(A) therapy is to thermometer.
(B) oblivion is to obvious.
(C) liturgy is to literature.
(D) image is to imagine.
(E) bowl is to bowdlerize.

The correct answer is (D). The relationship is word and word derived from. The word "action" derives from the word "act." Choice (A) is incorrect: thermometer (temperature measure) does not derive from the word "therapy." There is no relationship. Choice (B) is incorrect: the relationship is antonyms or opposites. Oblivion means forgotten; obvious means apparent. The relationship is different. Choice (C) is incorrect: liturgy (ritual) does not provide the root for the word "literature," which means a body of work. Choice (E) is incorrect: bowl (goblet) does not form the root for bowdlerize, which means to modify. There is no relationship.

www.petersons.com

110

Here's a slightly different version of an analogy question. These have three stem words in the question and only one word to find.

Example

Race is to fatigue as fast is to

(A) track.
(B) hunger.
(C) run.
(D) obesity.
(E) diet.

The correct answer is (B). Like the earlier examples, the first step to take is to determine the relationship between the first pair of words and state that relationship in sentence form. Running a race may cause the runner to fatigue. A fast may cause hunger.

These three sections are the basis of the Verbal Analysis section on both the SSAT and ISEE examinations. Once you have mastered this material, go back to the diagnostic tests and check your answers again. Then, go to the English Grammar Review section on page 299 to give yourself an overview of basic grammatical principles. These will help you with many of the questions you will encounter on these exams, since more than vocabulary is involved with these tests. A strong grounding in the basics of proper grammar and usage will make your work a lot easier.

STRATEGIES FOR TAKING THE MATH TEST

GENERAL SUGGESTIONS

Much of the success in test taking comes from being comfortable both physically and mentally with the test you are taking. Physical comfort is very easy to achieve. Just remember a few important points:

1. **Be on time.** Actually, being a few minutes early doesn't hurt. No one is helped by feeling rushed when beginning a test.

2. **Have a supply of #2 pencils with good erasers.** There will be no time for borrowing or sharpening a pencil once the test begins.

3. **Wear comfortable clothing.** Layers of clothing are the best since they can be removed or put on, depending on the temperature of the room. Don't wear shoes that pinch or a belt that is too tight.

4. **Avoid cramming.** Finish your preparation ahead of time, and relax the night before the test. Cramming just before the test begins is not helpful and often leads to panic and confusion. Be sure to get a good night's sleep before taking the test.

5. **Calculators are not permitted** for the test, so there is no need to bring one with you. Be sure that you remember how to perform all mathematical computations by hand!

Mental comfort is a little more difficult to achieve. *Preparation* is the key and comes with study and practice in the weeks and months before the test. Mental comfort is gained by becoming familiar with the test format, instructions, and the types of problems that will appear.

KNOW THE TEST FORMAT AND INSTRUCTIONS

Although the math topics that will be tested on the ISEE and the SSAT are essentially the same, the format and strategy for the math sections on these tests are somewhat different. Be certain that you are familiar with the structure of the test that you are going to take before you take it.

THE ISEE

On the ISEE there are two math sections, *Quantitative Reasoning* and *Math Achievement.* The Math Achievement section contains 45 questions, and you will have 40 minutes to answer them. The Quantitative Reasoning section contains 35 questions, and you will have 35 minutes to answer them.

All 45 of the questions in the Math Achievement section will be in the standard multiple-choice format, with four possible answers. On the other hand, only about half of the questions in the Quantitative Reasoning section are standard multiple choice; the remaining questions are in the special *Quantitative Comparison* format. The format and strategies for these special questions are discussed later in this section. In general, the Math Achievement section of the ISEE tests your knowledge of the various subject areas in mathematics, while the Quantitative Reasoning section measures general mathematical aptitude.

It is extremely important to remember that on the ISEE there is no penalty for an incorrect answer. You will receive one point for a correct answer and nothing for an incorrect answer or a question left blank. Clearly, then, it is to your advantage to answer every question. If you are not certain of the correct answer, try to eliminate as many of the incorrect answers as possible and make a guess from the remaining answers. Even if you cannot eliminate any answers, you might as well guess. Do not leave any questions blank on the ISEE.

The subject areas covered on the test include basic arithmetic skills (computations with fractions, decimals, and percents; ratios and proportions; and set of numbers), beginning algebra (algebraic representation, numerical evaluation, and solving equations and inequalities), geometry (lines and angles, geometric figures, areas and perimeters, and coordinate geometry), and some miscellaneous topics, such as set theory, the metric system, and graph reading. All of these topics are covered in detail, with many solved examples, later in this book.

THE SSAT

On the SSAT, there are also two math sections, but each section contains only 25 questions. You will be allotted 30 minutes for each of these two sections. Unlike the ISEE, all of the questions on the SSAT are in the standard multiple-choice format. Thus, there are no quantitative comparison questions on this test. Also note that on the SSAT, every question will have five possible answers. As on the ISEE, the math questions test your knowledge of mathematical subject areas as well as general mathematical aptitude.

Note that the SSAT does have an incorrect answer penalty. While you will receive one point for each correct answer, you will lose ¼ point for each incorrect answer. There is no penalty for leaving an answer blank. Students taking the SSAT often ask if they should guess on questions that they are not sure of. The general strategy is this: if you guess randomly on a series of questions, you are as likely to hurt as to help your score. However, on any question for which you are able to eliminate *one or more* answers as incorrect, the odds of guessing the correct answer tip in your favor, and you should guess.

The subject areas on the SSAT are the same as those listed previously for the ISEE and will be covered in detail later in this book.

Whether you are taking the ISEE or the SSAT, be sure that you have taken enough sample tests to be thoroughly familiar with the instructions. The instructions are a part of the timed test. DO NOT spend valuable time reading them as if you have never seen them before. Simply skim them to refresh your memory each time you start a new section of the test.

PACE YOURSELF

Before you begin any specific section on the exam, remind yourself how long you have to finish the section, and pace yourself accordingly. If you spend too much time on each question, you will not complete enough questions to receive a good score. Many very intelligent students work too slowly and spend too much time on details or neatness. As a result, they end up with a lower score than they should. As you work, put a mark next to the problems that would take too long and a different mark next to those that you don't know how to solve, so that you can go back to them later if you have time.

Bring a watch to the test and thus eliminate worry about how much time is left. When time is almost up, you should look over the rest of the problems and do those you know you can do most quickly.

All questions count the same. Allot your time accordingly. Remember that hard questions count the same as easy ones. Don't miss out on one that might be easy for you by stubbornly sticking to one that might be more difficult.

USE THE TEST BOOKLET SCRATCH AREA

For many problems, a simple sketch on the scratch area of the test booklet will make the solution readily apparent and will thus save time. Also, do not attempt to do all computation work in your head. Remember to use the scratch area of the test booklet; mark only answers on the answer sheet.

SPECIFIC SUGGESTIONS

All of the general suggestions will not help you if you are not prepared to solve the problems and arrive at the correct answers.

As we have seen, the exam requires the knowledge of arithmetic, algebra, and plane and coordinate geometry. Many of the problems require some insight and originality—that is, you will need to know not only *how* to perform certain operations but also *when* to perform them.

Vocabulary is very important. A problem that asks you to find a *quotient* will be hard to do if you do not know the meaning of this term. Some basic terms you should know:

sum:	the answer to an addition problem
difference:	the answer to a subtraction problem
product:	the answer to a multiplication problem
quotient:	the answer to a division problem
integer:	a whole number, either positive or negative or 0
prime number:	a number with exactly two factors, namely 1 and itself
even integers:	2, 4, 6, 8, etc.
odd integers:	1, 3, 5, 7, etc.
consecutive integers:	numbers in order, 1, 2, 3 or 7, 8, 9, etc.

Different types of problems call for different attacks. Of course, the most desirable situation is to know how to do all problems, work them out, and then fill in the letter space for the correct answer. But what if the answer you get is not among the choices, or you don't know how to do the problem in the first place? Then perhaps the following suggestions will help. However, remember that these are only suggested methods for problem solving. Always do a problem your way if you are more comfortable with it and if it will solve the problem just as quickly.

LOOK FOR SHORTCUTS

Rarely will a problem on your test involve a long, cumbersome computation. If you find yourself caught up in a maze of large numbers, you have probably missed a shortcut.

Example

Which is greater?

$$\frac{5}{23} \times \frac{7}{33} \quad \text{or} \quad \frac{7}{23} \times \frac{5}{31}$$

Solution: Examination of the problem will let you see that after multiplying, in each case the numerators of the resulting fractions will be the same (5×7 and 7×5). When the numerators of two fractions are the same, the fraction with the lesser denominator will be the greater fraction. In this case, the denominators are 23×33 and 23×31. It is not necessary to do the actual multiplication to see that 23×31 will be the lesser product (or denominator), making the greater fraction.

Example

If $6 \times 6 \times (x) = 12 \times 12 \times 12$, then $x =$

(A) 12
(B) 18
(C) 24
(D) 48

The correct answer is (D). Use factoring and division to eliminate the need to cube 12 and then divide by 36 (6×6). Factor and divide:

$$x = \frac{\overset{2}{\cancel{12}} \cdot \overset{2}{\cancel{12}} \cdot 12}{\underset{1}{\cancel{6}} \cdot \underset{1}{\cancel{6}}} = 48$$

ESTIMATE

On any timed competitive examination, it is necessary that you be able to estimate. Sometimes it is helpful to round off all numbers to a convenient power of 10 and estimate the answer. This will often enable you to pick the correct answer quickly without performing a lot of time-consuming computations. In some cases it will eliminate one or more of the answers right away, thus improving your chances if you have to guess.

Example

Which of the following is closest to the value of

$$\frac{3654 \times 248}{1756}?$$

(A) 50
(B) 500
(C) 5,000
(D) 5

The correct answer is (B). 3,654 is about 4,000. 248 is about 200 (or 300) and 1,756 is about 2,000. The problem then becomes:

$$\frac{\overset{2}{\cancel{4000}} \cdot 200}{\underset{1}{\cancel{2000}}} \cong 400$$

SUBSTITUTE

Change confusing problems to more meaningful ones by substituting simple numbers for letters. Many students get confused by problems containing letters in place of numbers. These letters are called *variables*. Just remember that the letters stand for numbers; therefore, the same operations can be performed on them. Just think of how you would do the problem if there were numbers, and then perform the same operations on the letters.

Example

If John's allowance is x a week and he saves m a week, what part of his allowance does he spend?

Solution: Substituting some numbers for the letters in the problem, we get: If John's allowance is \$5 a week and he saves \$1 a week, then he spends \$5 − \$1, or \$4 a week. This represents \$4 (part) out of \$5 (whole) or $\frac{4}{5}$ of his allowance. Transferring the number computation to the original problem, we get:

$$\frac{5-1}{5} \text{ or } \frac{x-m}{x} \text{ for the correct answer.}$$

Example

If a man was x years old y years ago, how many years old will he be z years from now?

Solution: Substitute small numbers for the letters. If a man was 20 years old 5 years ago, how many years old will he be 8 years from now? The man is now 25 years old (20 + 5). Eight years from now he will be 20 + 5 + 8, or 33 years old. Back in the original problem, substitute letters for numbers in your solution:

$$20 + 5 + 8 = x + y + z$$

WORK BACKWARD

Some experts advise against this, but in some cases it can be advantageous for you to look at the answers first. You can save valuable time by knowing that all the answers are in common fractional or decimal form. Then you will want to work only in the form in which the answers are given.

Are all the answers the same except for one digit or placement of a decimal? Knowing this can save you time.

Example

The square root of 106.09 is exactly

(A) .103
(B) 1.03
(C) 10.3
(D) 103

The correct answer is (C). Don't use your time to find the square root of 106.09. Work backward from the answers, which are all the same except for the placement of the decimal. Using the definition of square root (the number that when multiplied by itself will produce a given number), you can see that choice (C) is the only one that will give an answer of 106.09 when multiplied by itself.

Another type of problem in which it is helpful to work backward is the problem that contains an equation to solve. Trying each answer in the equation to see which one fits will help, especially if you are unsure of how to solve the equation.

Example

$x\sqrt{.16} = 4$. Find the value of x:

(A) 1
(B) .4
(C) .64
(D) 10

The correct answer is (D). Examination of the equation reveals that it is really $.4x = 4$ ($\sqrt{.16} = .4$). Checking each answer will reveal that $10 \times .4 = 4$; therefore, choice (D) is the correct answer.

ANSWER THE QUESTION

Always check to see if you have answered the question asked. You can be sure, for instance, that if you are doing a problem involving two angles, the values for both angles will be among the answers listed. Be sure that you have found the right value.

Example

If $3x + 2 = 12$, find $x - \dfrac{1}{3}$.

(A) $3\dfrac{1}{3}$
(B) 3
(C) 10
(D) 4

The correct answer is (B). Solve the equation:

Add -2 to both sides.

$$3x + 2 = 12$$
$$\underline{-2 = -2}$$
$$3x = 10$$

Divide by 3.

$$x = \frac{10}{3} = 3\frac{1}{3}$$

Notice that $x = 3\dfrac{1}{3}$ and that this answer is (A). However, the problem asked us to find $x - \dfrac{1}{3}$.

SPECIAL HELP FOR PROBLEM AREAS

FRACTIONS

Comparing Fractions

Many problems will require that you know how to compare fractions. A few simple steps will ensure that you can do this.

1. If the *denominators* of two fractions are the *same*, the fraction with the *greater numerator* will be the fraction with the *greater* value.

   Example

   Compare $\dfrac{3}{5}$ and $\dfrac{2}{5}$

   $3 > 2$, therefore $\dfrac{3}{5} > \dfrac{2}{5}$

2. If the *numerators* of two fractions are the *same*, the fraction with the *greater denominator* will be the *lesser* fraction.

   Example

   Compare $\dfrac{2}{13}$ and $\dfrac{2}{15}$

   $13 < 15$, therefore $\dfrac{2}{13} > \dfrac{2}{15}$

3. If the numerators and denominators are different, the fractions can be compared by cross-multiplying. Cross-multiplying eliminates the need to find a common denominator in order to use method 1.

   Example

   Compare $\dfrac{9}{13}$ and $\dfrac{11}{15}$

   Cross-multiply, putting the products above the numerators used in the products.

   $$\overset{\textstyle\boxed{135}\qquad\boxed{143}}{\dfrac{9}{13}\times\dfrac{11}{15}}$$

   $135 < 143$, therefore $\dfrac{9}{13} < \dfrac{11}{15}$

Complex Fractions

If complex fractions (a fraction within a fraction) cause your mind to go blank, try this little routine. Whenever you have a complex fraction, find the least common denominator for all the denominators within the fraction and multiply all *terms* by this denominator. This will simplify the complex fraction and make it easier to handle.

Example

$$\frac{\frac{2}{3} + \frac{3}{4}}{1 - \frac{1}{3}}$$

The least common denominator is 12. Multiply all terms by 12.

$$\frac{12\left(\frac{2}{3}\right) + \left(\frac{3}{4}\right)12}{12(1) - \frac{1}{3}(12)} = \frac{8 + 9}{12 - 4} = \frac{17}{8} = 2\frac{1}{8}$$

This routine can also be of use if the complex fraction contains letters or variables.

Example

Simplify

$$\frac{1 - \frac{1}{x}}{1 + \frac{1}{x}}$$

The least common denominator is x. Multiply all terms by x.

$$\frac{x(1) - \frac{1}{x}(x)}{x(1) + \frac{1}{x}(x)} = \frac{x - 1}{x + 1}$$

Percent

Percent problems are another source of trouble for many students. First, you should be sure you know how to rename a decimal as a percent (multiply by 100) and to rename a percent as a decimal or common fraction (divide by 100).

Examples

$$.35 = 35\% \ (.35 \times 100)$$

$$6\frac{1}{2}\% = 6.5\% = .065$$

$$(6\frac{1}{2}\% \div 100 = .065) \text{ or } (6.5\% \div 100 = .065)$$

It is also a good idea to memorize the equivalent fractions for certain percents. This will save you time, as they will typically come up several times on your test.

$$\frac{1}{2} = .50 = 50\% \qquad \frac{1}{6} = .1\overline{6} = 16\frac{2}{3}\%$$

$$\frac{1}{4} = .25 = 25\% \qquad \frac{5}{6} = .8\overline{3} = 83\frac{1}{3}\%$$

$$\frac{3}{4} = .75 = 75\% \qquad \frac{1}{8} = .125 = 12\frac{1}{2}\%$$

$$\frac{1}{5} = .20 = 20\% \qquad \frac{3}{8} = .375 = 37\frac{1}{2}\%$$

$$\frac{2}{5} = .40 = 40\% \qquad \frac{5}{8} = .625 = 62\frac{1}{2}\%$$

$$\frac{3}{5} = .60 = 60\% \qquad \frac{7}{8} = .875 = 87\frac{1}{2}\%$$

$$\frac{4}{5} = .80 = 80\% \qquad \frac{1}{10} = .10 = 10\%$$

$$\frac{1}{3} = .\overline{33} = 33\frac{1}{3}\% \qquad \frac{3}{10} = .30 = 30\%$$

$$\frac{2}{3} = .\overline{66} = 66\frac{2}{3}\% \qquad \frac{7}{10} = .70 = 70\%$$

$$1 = 100\% \qquad \frac{9}{10} = .90 = 90\%$$

Remembering that *of* in a mathematical problem usually means that you have to multiply. Algebraic equations can then be set up to solve the three types of percent problems.

Example

What is 15% of 32?

$$x = 15\% \times 32$$

$$x = (.15)(32) \text{ (rename 15\% as a decimal)}$$

$$x = 4.80$$

Example

9 is 30% of what number?

$$9 = 30\% \times x$$

$$9 = (.30)x \qquad \text{(rename 30\% as a decimal)}$$

$$\text{OR} \quad 9 = \left(\frac{3}{10}\right)x \qquad \text{(rename 30\% as a common fraction)}$$

$$30 = x \qquad \text{(divide by .3)}$$

$$\text{OR} \quad 30 = x \qquad \text{(multiply by } \frac{10}{3}\text{)}$$

Example

12 is what percent of 72?

$$12 = x\% \times 72$$

$$12 = \left(\frac{x}{100}\right)72 \qquad \text{(rewrite } x\% \text{ as a fraction)}$$

$$\frac{12}{72} = \frac{x}{100} \qquad \text{(divide by 72)}$$

$$\frac{1}{6} = \frac{x}{100} \qquad \text{(simplify } \frac{12}{72} \text{ to } \frac{1}{6}\text{)}$$

$$100 = 6x \qquad \text{(cross-multiply)}$$

$$16\frac{2}{3} = x \qquad \text{(divide by 6)}$$

If you have memorized your fractional equivalent chart, you will know that $16\frac{2}{3}\% = \frac{1}{6}$.

GEOMETRY

Many of the questions in the geometry area of your test will require recall of the numerical relationships learned in an informal geometry course. You will not be asked to do a formal proof! If you are thoroughly familiar with these relationships, you should not find the geometry questions difficult.

Be very careful with units, especially when finding area, perimeter, or volume. Change all dimensions to a common unit before doing the calculations.

IMPORTANT PROPERTIES AND FORMULAS

Memorize the following geometric properties to help speed your ability to solve the problems.

Properties of a Triangle

The sum of the measures of the angles of a triangle equals 180°.

The measure of an exterior angle of a triangle is equal to the sum of the measures of the remote interior angles.

An equilateral triangle has congruent sides and all angles measure to 60°.

An isosceles triangle has two congruent sides. The angles opposite these sides are also congruent.

In a right triangle, $a^2 + b^2 = c^2$, where a and b are the legs and c is the hypotenuse (Pythagorean Theorem).

Properties of Parallel Lines

Pairs of alternate interior angles are congruent.

Pairs of corresponding angles are congruent.

Pairs of interior angles on the same side of the transversal are supplementary (their measures' sum is 180°).

Properties of a Parallelogram

Opposite sides are parallel.

Opposite sides are congruent.

Opposite angles are congruent.

Diagonals bisect each other.

Properties of a Rectangle

The same properties as a parallelogram, plus:

All angles are right angles.

The diagonals are congruent.

Properties of a Rhombus

The same properties as a parallelogram, plus:

All sides are congruent.

The diagonals are perpendicular to each other.

The diagonals bisect the angles.

Properties of a Square

The same properties as a parallelogram, plus those of a rectangle, plus those of a rhombus.

IMPORTANT AREA FORMULAS

Area of a triangle: $A = \frac{1}{2}bh$ (b is the base, h is the height)

Area of a parallelogram: $A = bh$ (b is the base, h is the height)

Area of a square: $A = s^2$ (s is a side of the square)

Area of a circle: $A = \pi r^2$ (r is the radius of the circle)

Area of a rectangle: $A = lw$ (l is the length, w is the width)

or $A = bh$ (since a rectangle is a parallelogram)

Area of a trapezoid: $A = \frac{1}{2}h(b_1 + b_2)$ (h is the height, b_1 and b_2 are the bases)

VOLUME

The volume of most solids is found by finding the area of the base and multiplying by the height.

Volume of a rectangular solid: $V = lwh$ (base is a rectangle)

Volume of a cube: $V = s^3$ (base is a square)

Volume of a cylinder: $V = \pi r^2 h$ (base is a circle)

If you learn to recognize the relationships and formulas given above and the cases in which they apply, you will have the key to doing most of the problems involving geometry on the test.

QUANTITATIVE COMPARISON STRATEGIES FOR THE ISEE

Recall that on the ISEE, there are two math sections, *Quantitative Reasoning* and *Math Achievement*. While all 45 of the questions in the Math Achievement section will be in the standard multiple-choice format, only about half the questions in the Quantitative Reasoning section are standard multiple choice. The remaining questions are in the special Quantitative Comparison format. *Note that there are no Quantitative Comparison sections on the SSAT, so if you are taking that test, you may skip this section of the book.*

Quantitative Comparison questions are the only questions on the entire test that are not arranged in the standard multiple-choice format. Instead, in each of these questions, you are given two quantities, one in Column A and one in Column B. Your job, simply put, is to determine which of these two quantities is greater.

The answer scheme is simple. If the quantity in Column A is greater, you should choose (A). If the quantity in Column B is larger, you should choose (B). If the two quantities are of identical size, the answer is (C). Finally, if it is not possible to tell which quantity is greater, the answer is (D).

Occasionally, there will be some additional information given to help you determine the relative size of the two quantities. This information, when given, will be centered just above the Column A and Column B entries.

Following are the directions as they appear on the ISEE. They should be memorized so that you do not waste time reading them when you take the actual test.

> Directions: For the following questions note the given information, if any, and then compare the quantity in Column A to the quantity in Column B. Next to the number of each question, write:
>
> A   if the quantity in Column A is greater.
> B   if the quantity in Column B is greater.
> C   if the two quantities are equal.
> D   if the relationship cannot be determined from the information given.

To gain a better understanding of the choices (A) through (D), we will now look at four examples. These examples have been selected so that the answer to the first one is (A), the answer to the second is (B), and so on.

Column A	**Column B**

1.

$$\frac{1}{x} = 4$$

1   x

The correct answer is (A). The equation given in the common information can be solved to determine that $x = \frac{1}{4}$. Since $1 > \frac{1}{4}$, the correct choice is (A).

2. $\sqrt{26} - \sqrt{10}$ $\sqrt{26 - 10}$

The correct answer is (B). The entry in Column B is equal to 4. While we cannot exactly determine the value of Column A, if we estimate $\sqrt{26}$ and $\sqrt{10}$, we can see that its value is close to 2.

3.

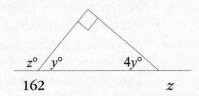

The correct answer is (C). Since a triangle contains 180°, $y° + 4y° + 90° = 180°$. Thus, $5y° = 90°$ and $y° = 18°$. Since $z° + y° = 180°$, z must be 162, choice (C).

4. $x^6 = 64$

2   x

The correct answer is (D). Solving the equation given as common information, we can determine that x is either 2 or -2. Thus, x is either less than or equal to 2.

HINTS AND STRATEGIES FOR QUANTITATIVE COMPARISON QUESTIONS

Before we look at some specific problem-solving strategies for Quantitative Comparison questions, let's examine some general strategies.

GENERAL STRATEGIES

1. Remember that your goal is to do as little work as possible to answer the question. You frequently don't need to determine the actual size of the quantities in Columns A and B to know which one is greater. As a simple example, if you have enough information to determine that the quantity in Column A is positive and the quantity in Column B is negative, then the quantity in Column A is greater, regardless of its actual value.

2. Be sure that you understand the meaning of the answers. For example, an answer of (A) indicates that the quantity in Column A is always greater than the quantity in Column B. If A is sometimes, but not always, greater, the answer is (D). Similarly, choice (C) is the answer only if the quantities are always equal.

3. Be sure that you only do as much math as is absolutely necessary to determine which quantity is greater. Estimate and approximate as much as possible. You can often answer a question correctly by doing very little actual mathematical computation.

4. While you are asked to answer 35 questions in 35 minutes in the Quantitative Reasoning section, it is not a good idea to figure that you should average slightly less than a minute a question. The Quantitative Comparison questions can generally be answered much more quickly than the other multiple-choice questions. A good guideline is that you should average about 30 seconds for each of these questions, which will allow you to average about a minute and a half for the more time-consuming multiple-choice questions.

5. Whenever both of the given quantities are purely numerical (contain only numbers, no letters), then both quantities have a definite size, and the answer cannot be choice (D). If you are not sure how to answer a problem with two purely numerical entities, be sure to guess either choices (A), (B), or (C).

SPECIFIC MATHEMATICAL STRATEGIES FOR QUANTITATIVE COMPARISON QUESTIONS

Whenever you can, eliminate common factors and terms from Column A and Column B. Then simply compare the remaining quantities. Often, sums and products can be combined term by term, or factor by factor.

Column A	Column B
1. $(108)^2 - (13)^2$	$(108 - 13)^2$

The correct answer is (A). The quantity in Column A, when factored, becomes $(108 - 13)(108 + 13)$. The quantity in Column B is equal to $(180 - 13)(180 - 13)$. Upon dividing the common factor of $(180 - 13)$, we see that we are comparing $(108 + 13)$ in Column A to $(108 - 13)$ in Column B.

2. $\dfrac{5}{6} + \dfrac{6}{7} + \dfrac{7}{8}$	$\dfrac{5}{7} + \dfrac{6}{8} + \dfrac{7}{9}$

The correct answer is (A). Simply note that each term in Column A is greater than the corresponding term in Column B.

3. $6(125)4$	$2(125)12$

The correct answer is (C). Divide the common factor of 125 from both sides. Then, both sides become equal to 24.

Remember that you can often determine which quantity is greater by simply estimating sizes.

4. $\dfrac{221}{333}$	$\dfrac{667}{999}$

The correct answer is (B). Note that the quantity in Column A is less than $\dfrac{2}{3}$ and that the quantity in Column B is greater than $\dfrac{2}{3}$.

A Quantitative Comparison question can be treated as if it were an algebraic inequality, with your job being to position the correct inequality sign ($=$, $<$, $>$) between entries. As such, you may perform any operation to both columns of the question that you can perform on both sides of an inequality. This means, whenever you wish, you can add or subtract the same number to Column A and Column B, multiply or divide both columns by the same positive number, or square both numbers (if both entries are positive). This strategy can be used to change the operations of subtraction and division to the relatively less confusing operations of addition and multiplication.

Column A	Column B

5. $\sqrt{89,905}$ 300

The correct answer is (B). Square both sides. Column A becomes 89,905 and Column B becomes 90,000.

6. $\sqrt{3}$ $\dfrac{4}{\sqrt{3}}$

The correct answer is (B). Do not waste any time estimating the values of the quantities. Simply multiply both entries by $\sqrt{3}$. Column A is then equal to $\sqrt{3} \times \sqrt{3} = 3$, while Column B is equal to $\dfrac{4}{\sqrt{3}} \times \sqrt{3} = 4$. Since $4 > 3$, the correct choice is (B).

7. $9\dfrac{5}{6} + \dfrac{1}{7}$ $10\dfrac{5}{6} - \dfrac{6}{7}$

The correct answer is (C). Eliminate the subtraction in Column B by adding $\dfrac{6}{7}$ to both entries. Column A then becomes

$$9\dfrac{5}{6} + \dfrac{1}{7} + \dfrac{6}{7} = 9\dfrac{5}{6} + 1 = 10\dfrac{5}{6}.$$

Column B becomes

$$10\dfrac{5}{6} - \dfrac{6}{7} + \dfrac{6}{7} = 10\dfrac{5}{6}.$$

Whenever you are comparing quantities containing variables, remember to consider both positive and negative values of the variables. Similarly, remember that the variables could have fractional values.

8.
$$3 < x < 5$$
$$4 < y < 6$$
x y

The correct answer is (D). Many people might answer (B) for this, assuming that $x = 4$ and $y = 5$. However, remember that x and y could also be fractional. For example, x could be 4.5, while y is 4.1.

If the column entries contain algebraic operations, it frequently helps to begin by performing these operations.

Column A	Column B
	$a = -2, c = 5$
$3a(2b + 5c)$	$2a(3b + 5c)$

9.

The correct answer is (B). To begin, expand both expressions. The entry in Column A becomes $6ab + 15ac$. Column B becomes $6ab + 10ac$. Subtract the common factor of $6ab$ and you'll see that we are actually comparing $15ac$ in Column A to $10ac$ in Column B. We know that $a = -2$ and $c = 5$. Thus, the entry in Column A becomes -150, while Column B becomes -100.

See if the common information can be manipulated to a form that is similar in appearance to the entry in one of the columns.

10.

	$5p + 7q = 13$
40	$15p + 21q$

The correct answer is (A). If you multiply both sides of the equation given as common information by 3, you will obtain $15p + 21q = 39$. Thus, the value of the expression in Column B is 39.

When either of the column entries contains variables, it is often very helpful to substitute numerical values for these variables and observe what happens. Any substitution you make will enable you to eliminate two of the possible answers. Suppose, for example, that you plug a value into the quantities, and for this particular value the quantity in Column A turns out to be greater. This means that the answer cannot be choices (B) or (C). Either Column A is always greater, choice (A), or sometimes greater, choice (D).

Column A	Column B
	$s \neq 1$
	$s \neq 0$
$\dfrac{r}{s}$	$\dfrac{r - 1}{s - 1}$

11.

The correct answer is (D). Try to substitute values for r and s. If, for example, $r = s = 2$, $\dfrac{r}{s} = \dfrac{r - 1}{s - 1}$. Thus, we know that the answer is either (C) or (D). Now let $r = 0$ and $s = 2$. Then, the value in Column A becomes 0, and the value in Column B becomes $-\dfrac{1}{2}$.

Remember that the powers of, roots of, and divisions by numbers between 0 and 1 behave differently than those with numbers greater than 1. For example, if you square a number greater than 1, the resulting number is greater than the original; yet, if you square a number less than 1, the resulting number is less than the original. Also, remember that powers of even and odd numbers behave differently. The following examples illustrate some of these variations.

12.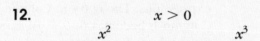
$$x > 0$$
$$x^2 \qquad\qquad x^3$$

The correct answer is (D). While intuition tells us that cubing a positive number yields a greater result than squaring the number, this result is actually true only for numbers greater than 1. In fact, $x^2 = x^3$ if $x = 1$, and if $x < 1$, $x^2 > x^3$. For example, if $x = \dfrac{1}{2}$, then $x^2 = \dfrac{1}{4}$ and $x^3 = \dfrac{1}{8}$. Thus, there is no way to tell if x^2 or x^3 is greater.

13.
$$x > 1$$
$$x^2 \qquad\qquad x^3$$

The correct answer is (B). As long as we know that $x > 1$, we have $x^3 > x^2$.

14.
$$0 < z < 1$$
$$\frac{12}{z} \qquad\qquad 12z$$

The correct answer is (A). When 12 is divided by z, $0 < z < 1$ will yield a number *greater* than 12, and when 12 is multiplied by z, $0 < z < 1$ will yield a number *less* than 1.

Remember the above strategies and guidelines as you try your hand at the quantitative comparison questions in the upcoming practice tests.

MATH REVIEW

NUMBERS AND SETS

PROPERTIES OF NUMBERS

Systems of Numbers

All of the numbers that are used in the math sections of the SSAT/ISEE are *real numbers*. In order to understand the real number system, it is easiest to begin by looking at some familiar systems of numbers that lie within the real number system.

The numbers that are used for counting

1, 2, 3, 4, 5, . . .

are called the *natural numbers*, the *counting numbers*, or, most commonly, the *positive integers*. The positive integers, together with the number 0, are called the set of *whole numbers*. Then, the positive integers, together with 0 and the *negative integers*

−1, −2, −3, −4, −5, . . .

make up the set of *integers*.

A real number is said to be a *rational number* if it can be written as the ratio of two integers, where the denominator is not 0. Thus, for example, numbers such as

$$-16\frac{2}{3}, \frac{-5}{6}, 0, 25, 12\frac{5}{8}$$

are rational numbers. Clearly, then, all integers and fractions are rational numbers. Percents and decimal numbers are rational as well, since they can also be written as the ratio of two integers. For example,

$$25\% = \frac{1}{4}, \text{ and } 9.125 = 9\frac{1}{8}.$$

Any real number that cannot be expressed as the ratio of two integers is called an *irrational number*. The most common irrational numbers that you will see on your test are square roots, such as $\sqrt{3}$ or $-\sqrt{5}$, and the number π, which represents the ratio of the circumference of a circle to its diameter.

Finally, the set of rational numbers, together with the set of irrational numbers, is called the set of *real numbers*.

Example

The number -257 is an integer. It is also rational since it can be written as $\frac{-257}{1}$, and is, of course, real.

The number $\frac{5}{8}$ is rational and real, and the number $\sqrt{7}$ is irrational and real.

Rounding of Numbers

From time to time, a test question will ask you to round an answer to a specific decimal place. The rules for the rounding of numbers are very simple. In the case of whole numbers, begin by locating the digit to which the number is being rounded. Then, if the digit just to the right is 0, 1, 2, 3, or 4, leave the located digit alone. Otherwise, increase the located digit by 1. In either case, replace all digits to the right of the one located with 0's.

When rounding decimal numbers, the rules are similar. Again, begin by locating the digit to which the number is being rounded. As before, if the digit just to the right is 0, 1, 2, 3, or 4, leave the located digit alone. Otherwise, increase the located digit by 1. Finally, drop all the digits to the right of the one located.

Example

Round the following numbers as indicated.

6,342 to the nearest 10

Begin by locating the ten's digit, which is a 4. The number to the right of the 4 is a 2. Thus, drop the 2 and replace it with a 0, yielding 6,340.

392.461 to the nearest tenth

The tenth's digit is 4. The digit just to the right of it is 6, so increase the tenth's digit by 1, making it a 5. Drop the two digits to the right of this. The answer is 392.5.

.0472 to the nearest thousandth

Following the rules above, we obtain .047.

Properties of Numbers Problems

1. Classify each of the following numbers as whole, integer, rational, irrational, and real.

 a. -7

 b. $\dfrac{1}{7}$

 c. $5\dfrac{2}{3}$

 d. 0

 e. $\sqrt{13}$

2. Round each of the numbers below to the indicated number of decimal places.

 a. 57,380 to the nearest hundred
 b. 1,574,584 to the nearest hundred thousand
 c. 847.235 to the nearest hundredth
 d. 9.00872 to the nearest thousandth

Solutions

1. a. -7 is real, rational, and an integer.

 b. $\dfrac{1}{7}$ is real and rational.

 c. $5\dfrac{2}{3}$ can be written as $\dfrac{17}{3}$ and is thus real and rational.

 d. 0 is real, rational, an integer, and a whole number.

 e. $\sqrt{13}$ is real and irrational.

2. a. Begin by locating the hundred's digit, which is 3. The digit to the right of it is 8, so increase the hundred's digit by 1, and replace all digits to the right with 0's. The answer is 57,400.

 b. The hundred thousand's digit is 5. The digit to the right of it is 7, so increase the 5 by 1, and replace all digits to the right with 0's. The answer is 1,600,000.

 c. The hundredth's digit is 3. The digit just to the right of it is 5, so increase the hundredth's digit by 1, making it a 4. Drop the digit to the right of this. The answer is 847.24.

 d. The thousandth's digit is 8. The digit just to the right of it is 7, so increase the thousandth's digit by 1, making it a 9. Drop the digits to the right of this. The answer is 9.009.

Set Theory and Venn Diagrams

Definitions

A *set* is any collection of objects. The objects in a particular set are called the *members* or the *elements* of the set. In mathematics, sets are usually represented by capital letters, and their members are represented by lowercase letters. Braces, { and }, are usually used to enclose the members of a set. Thus, the set *A*, which has members *a, b, c, d,* and *e* and no other members, can be written as $A = \{a, b, c, d, e\}$. Note that the order in which the elements of a set are listed is not important; thus, the set {1, 2, 3} and the set {2, 3, 1} represent identical sets.

The symbol used to indicate that an element belongs to a particular set is $\in$, and the symbol that indicates an element does not belong to a set is $\notin$. Thus, if $B = \{2, 4, 6, 8\}$, we can say $6 \in B$ and $7 \notin B$. If a set is defined so that it does not contain any elements, it is called the *empty* set, or the *null* set, and can be written as { }, or $\varnothing$.

There are several different notational techniques that can be used to represent a set. The simplest one is called *numeration*, in which all of the elements of the set are listed within braces. For example, if *C* is the set of all odd integers between 10 and 20, we can use numeration to represent the set as $C = \{11, 13, 15, 17, 19\}$. The other is called *set-builder notation.* In this notation, a short vertical bar is used to stand for the phrase "such that." For example, the set of all integers less than 15 can be written as

$$\{\chi \mid \chi < 15, \chi \text{ is an integer}\}$$

and is read, "The set of all χ such that χ is less than 15, and χ is an integer."

A set that contains a finite number of elements is called a *finite* set. A set that is neither finite nor empty is called an *infinite* set. When using the method of numeration to describe a set, we can use three dots to indicate "and so on." Thus, the infinite set containing all positive integers can be written as {1, 2, 3, 4, . . .}. The finite set containing all of the even integers between 2 and 200 can be numerated as {2, 4, 6, . . . , 200}.

Examples

1. Use numeration to express the set of whole numbers.

    {0, 1, 2, 3, 4, 5, . . .}

2. Use set-builder notation to express the set of integers that are greater than or equal to 200.

    $$\{\chi \mid \chi \geq 200, \chi \text{ is an integer}\}$$

Subsets and the Universal Set

Suppose that J is the set containing everyone who lives in New Jersey, and K is the set of all people living in New Jersey who are older that 65. Then, clearly, all members of K are also members of J, and we say "K is a subset of J." This relationship is written symbolically as $K \subseteq J$. In general, A is a *subset* of B if every element of A is also an element of B. For example, the set $A = \{2, 4, 6\}$ is a subset of the set $B = \{0, 2, 4, 6, 8, 10\}$. By convention, we agree that the null set is a subset of every other set. Thus, we can write $\varnothing \subseteq A$, where A is any set. Also note that if A and B contain exactly the same elements, then $A \supseteq B$ and $B \supseteq A$. In such a case, we write $A = B$. If $A \subseteq B$ but $A \neq B$, we call A a *proper subset* of B. This is written $A \subset B$. Thus, if A is a subset of B, and B contains at least one element that is not in A, then A is a proper subset of B and we write $A \subset B$.

In a particular discussion, the *universal set* represents the greatest possible set, that is, it is the set that contains all of the possible elements under consideration. All other sets in the discussion must therefore be subsets of the universal set, which is usually represented by the letter U. If N is a subset of U, then N', which is called the *complement* of N, is the set of all elements from the universal set that are not in N. For example, if, in a particular problem, U is the set of all integers and N is the set of negative integers, then N' is the set of all nonnegative integers.

Examples

1. List all of the subsets of $\{2, 4, 6\}$.

    $\{2\}, \{4\}, \{6\}, \{2, 4\}, \{2, 6\} \{4, 6\}, \{2, 4, 6\}, \varnothing$

2. If $U = \{7, 8, 9, 10, 11\}$, and $N = \{9, 11\}$, find N'.

    N' contains all of the elements of U that are not in N. Thus, $N' = \{7, 8, 10\}$.

Venn Diagrams, Union, and Intersection

Let U be a universal set, and N a subset of U. Then, the drawing below, called a *Venn diagram*, illustrates the relationship between U, N, and N'.

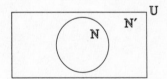

The *union* of two sets A and B, indicated $A \cup B$, is the set of all elements that are in either A or B. The *intersection* of two sets, indicated $A \cap B$, is the set of all elements that are in both A and B. Thus, if $A = \{2, 4, 6, 8, 10\}$ and $B = \{1, 2, 3, 4\}$, we have $A \cup B = \{1, 2, 3, 4, 6, 8, 10\}$ and $A \cap B = \{2, 4\}$. If $A \cap B = \varnothing$, then A and B are said to be *disjoint*.

The Venn diagrams below represent the operations of union and intersection.

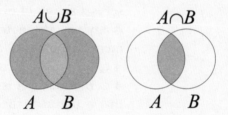

Set Problems

1. Use set-builder notation to describe the set of all integers greater than 12 and less than 48.

2. Use numeration to describe the set of negative integers.

3. List all of the subsets of the set $\{a, b, c, d\}$.

4. If $A = \{2, 4, 6\}$, $B = \{1, 3, 5\}$, and $C = \{2, 3, 4\}$, find $A \cup B, A \cup C, A \cap C, A \cap B$, and $A \cap (B \cup C)$.

5. If $U = \{2, 4, 6, 8, 10, 12, 14, 16, 18, 20\}$ and $W = \{2, 6, 12, 18\}$, find W'.

In problems 6–9, describe the sets listed in terms of D, E, and F and intersections, unions, and complements.

6. $\{\chi \mid \chi \in D \text{ and } \chi \notin E\}$

7. $\{\chi \mid \chi \in F \text{ or } \chi \in E\}$

8. $\{\chi \mid \chi \in D \text{ and } \chi \in E\}$

9. $\{\chi \mid \chi \in D \text{ and } \chi \text{ is not an element of either } E \text{ or } F\}$

10. Draw a Venn diagram to represent the set $(A \cap B) \cap C$.

Solutions

1. $\{\chi \mid 12 < \chi < 48, \chi \text{ is an integer}\}$

2. $\{\ldots, -4, -3, -2, -1\}$

3. $\varnothing, \{a\}, \{b\}, \{c\}, \{d\}, \{a, b\}, \{a, c\}, \{a, d\}, \{b, c\}, \{b, d\}, \{c, d\},$
    $\{a, b, c\}, \{a, b, d\}, \{a, c, d\}, \{b, c, d\}, \{a, b, c, d\}.$

4. $A \cup B = \{1, 2, 3, 4, 5, 6\}, A \cup C = \{2, 3, 4, 6\}, A \cap C = \{2, 4\},$
    $A \cap B = \varnothing, A \cap (B \cup C) = \{2, 4\}.$

5. $W' = \{4, 8, 10, 14, 16, 20\}$

6. $D \cap E'$

7. $F \cup E$

8. $D \cap E$

9. $D \cap (E \cup F)'$

10.

ARITHMETIC

WHOLE NUMBERS

Definitions

As we have already seen, the set of positive integers (natural numbers, counting numbers) can be written as the set $\{1, 2, 3, 4, 5, \ldots\}$. The set of positive integers, together with the number 0, are called the set of *whole numbers*, and can be written as $\{0, 1, 2, 3, 4, \ldots\}$.

Place Value

Whole numbers are expressed in a system of tens, called the *decimal* system. Ten *digits*—0, 1, 2, 3, 4, 5, 6, 7, 8, and 9—are used. Each digit differs not only in *face* value but also in *place* value, depending on where it stands in the number.

Examples

1. 237 means:

    $$(2 \cdot 100) + (3 \cdot 10) + (7 \cdot 1)$$

    The digit 2 has a face value of 2 but a place value of 200.

2. 35,412 can be written as:

$$(3 \cdot 10{,}000) + (5 \cdot 1{,}000) + (4 \cdot 100) + (1 \cdot 10) + (2 \cdot 1)$$

The digit in the last place on the right is said to be in the units or ones place, the digit to the left of that in the tens place, the next digit to the left of that in the hundreds place, and so on.

When we take a whole number and write it out as in the two examples above, it is said to be written in *expanded form*.

Odd and Even Numbers

A whole number is *even* if it is divisible by 2; it is *odd* if it is not divisible by 2. Zero is thus an even number.

Example

2, 4, 6, 8, and 320 are even numbers; 3, 7, 9, 21, and 45 are odd numbers.

Prime Numbers

The positive integer p is said to be a prime number (or simply *a prime*) if $p \neq 1$ and the only positive divisors of p are itself and 1. The first ten primes are 2, 3, 5, 7, 11, 13, 17, 19, 23, and 29. All other positive integers that are neither 1 nor prime are *composite numbers*. Composite numbers can be *factored*, that is, expressed as products of their divisors or factors; for example, $56 = 7 \cdot 8 = 7 \cdot 4 \cdot 2$. In particular, composite numbers can be expressed as products of their *prime* factors in just one way (except for order).

To factor a composite number into its prime factors, proceed as follows. First try to divide the number by the prime number 2. If this is successful, continue to divide by 2 until an odd number is obtained. Then attempt to divide the last quotient by the prime number 3 and by 3 again, as many times as possible. Then move on to dividing by the prime number 5, and other successive primes until a prime quotient is obtained. Express the original number as a product of all its prime divisors.

Example
Find the prime factors of 210.

$$2 \overline{)210}$$
$$3 \overline{)105}$$
$$5 \overline{)\ 35}$$
$$7$$

Therefore:

$$210 = 2 \cdot 3 \cdot 5 \cdot 7 \text{ (written in any order)}$$

and 210 is an integer multiple of 2, of 3, of 5, and of 7.

Consecutive Whole Numbers

Numbers are consecutive if each number is the successor of the number that precedes it. In a consecutive series of whole numbers, an odd number is always followed by an even number, and an even number by an odd. If three consecutive whole numbers are given, either two of them are odd and one is even or two are even and one is odd.

Examples

1. 7, 8, 9, 10, and 11 are consecutive whole numbers.

2. 8, 10, 12, and 14 are consecutive even numbers.

3. 21, 23, 25, and 27 are consecutive odd numbers.

4. 21, 23, and 27 are *not* consecutive odd numbers because 25 is missing.

The Number Line

A useful method of representing numbers geometrically makes it easier to understand numbers. It is called the *number line*. Draw a horizontal line, considered to extend without end in both directions. Select some point on the line and label it with the number 0. This point is called the *origin*. Choose some convenient distance as a unit of length. Take the point on the number line that lies one unit to the right of the origin and label it with the number 1. The point on the number line that is one unit to the right of 1 is labeled 2, and so on. In this way, every whole number is associated with one point on the line, but it is not true that every point on the line represents a whole number.

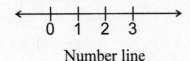

Number line

Ordering of Whole Numbers

On the number line, the point representing 8 lies to the right of the point representing 5, and we say $8 > 5$ (read "8 is greater than 5"). One can also say $5 < 8$ ("5 is less than 8"). For any two whole numbers a and b, there are always three possibilities:

$$a < b, \quad a = b, \quad \text{or} \quad a > b.$$

If $a = b$, the points representing the numbers a and b coincide on the number line.

Operations with Whole Numbers

The basic operations on whole numbers are addition (+), subtraction (−), multiplication (· or ×), and division (÷). These are all *binary* operations—that is, one works with two numbers at a time in order to get a unique answer. The operations of addition and multiplication on whole numbers are said to be *closed* because the answer in each case is also a whole number. The operations of subtraction and division on whole numbers are not closed because the unique answer is not necessarily a member of the set of whole numbers.

Examples

1. $3 + 4 = 7$ (a whole number)

2. $4 \cdot 3 = 12$ (a whole number)

3. $2 - 5 = -3$ (not a whole number)

4. $3 \div 8 = \dfrac{3}{8}$ (not a whole number)

Addition

If addition is a binary operation, how are three numbers—say, 3, 4, and 8—added? One way is to write:

$$(3 + 4) + 8 = 7 + 8 = 15$$

Another way is to write:

$$3 + (4 + 8) = 3 + 12 = 15$$

The parentheses merely group the numbers together. The fact that the same answer, 15, is obtained either way illustrates the *associative property* of addition:

$$(r + s) + t = r + (s + t)$$

The order in which whole numbers are added is immaterial—that is, $3 + 4 = 4 + 3$. This principle is called the *commutative property* of addition. Most people use this property without realizing it when they add a column of numbers from the top down and then check their result by beginning over again from the bottom. (Even though there may be a long column of numbers, only two numbers are added at a time.)

If 0 is added to any whole number, the whole number is unchanged. Zero is called the *identity element* for addition.

Subtraction

Subtraction is the inverse of addition. The order in which the numbers are written is important; there is no commutative property for subtraction.

$$4 - 3 \neq 3 - 4$$

The $\neq$ is read "not equal."

Multiplication

Multiplication is a commutative operation:

$$43 \cdot 73 = 73 \cdot 43$$

The result or answer in a multiplication problem is called the *product*.

If a number is multiplied by 1, the number is unchanged; the *identity element* for multiplication is 1.

Zero times any number is 0:

$$42 \cdot 0 = 0$$

Multiplication can be expressed with several different symbols:

$$9 \cdot 7 \cdot 3 = 9 \times 7 \times 3 = 9(7)(3)$$

Besides being commutative, multiplication is *associative:*

$$(9 \cdot 7) \cdot 3 = 63 \cdot 3 = 189$$

and

$$9 \cdot (7 \cdot 3) = 9 \cdot 21 = 189$$

A number can be quickly multiplied by 10 by adding a zero at the right of the number. Similarly, a number can be multiplied by 100 by adding two zeros at the right:

$$38 \cdot 10 = 380$$

and

$$100 \cdot 76 = 7,600$$

Division

Division is the inverse of multiplication. It is not commutative:

$$8 \div 4 \neq 4 \div 8$$

The parts of a division example are named as follows:

$$\text{divisor}\overline{)\,\text{dividend}}^{\text{quotient}}$$

If a number is divided by 1, the quotient is the original number.

Division by 0 is not defined (has no meaning). Zero divided by any number other than 0 is 0:

$$0 \div 56 = 0$$

Divisors and Multiples

The whole number b *divides* the whole number a if there exists a whole number k such that $a = bk$. The whole number a is then said to be an integer *multiple* of b, and b is called a *divisor* (or *factor*) of a.

Examples

1. 3 divides 15 because $15 = 3 \cdot 5$. Thus, 3 is a divisor of 15 (and so is 5), and 15 is an integer multiple of 3 (and of 5).

2. 3 does not divide 8 because $8 \neq 3k$ for a whole number k.

3. Divisors of 28 are 1, 2, 4, 7, 14, and 28.

4. Multiples of 3 are 3, 6, 9, 12, 15, . . .

Whole Number Problems

1. What is the prime factorization of 78?

2. What are the divisors of 56?

3. Which property is illustrated by the following statement?

    $(3 + 5) + 8 = 3 + (5 + 8)$

4. Which property is illustrated by the following statement?

    $(5 \cdot 7) \cdot 3 = (7 \cdot 5) \cdot 3$

5. Find the first five multiples of 7.

6. Find all of the common prime factors of 30 and 105.

7. Give an example to show that subtraction on the set of whole numbers is not commutative.

8. List all of the prime numbers between 50 and 90.

9. Write the number 786,534 in expanded notation.

10. In each of the statements below, replace the # with either $<$, $>$, or $=$ to make a true statement.

    a. $-12 \,\#\, 13$

    b. $\dfrac{1}{16} \,\#\, 0.0625$

    c. $3\dfrac{1}{2} \,\#\, 3\dfrac{2}{5}$

Solutions

1. $78 = 2 \cdot 39 = 2 \cdot 3 \cdot 13$

2. The divisors of 56 are 1, 2, 4, 7, 8, 14, 28, 56.

3. The Associative Property of Addition

4. The Commutative Property of Multiplication

5. 7, 14, 21, 28, 35

6. 30 can be factored as $2 \times 3 \times 5$. 105 can be factored as $3 \times 5 \times 7$. Thus, the common factors are 3 and 5.

7. $4 - 5 \neq 5 - 4$

8. The prime numbers between 50 and 90 are 53, 59, 61, 67, 71, 73, 79, 83, 87, and 89.

9. $786{,}534 = 7(100{,}000) + 8(10{,}000) + 6(1{,}000) + 5(100) + 3(10) + 4$

10. **a.** $-12 < 13$

    b. $\dfrac{1}{16} = 0.0625$

    c. $3\dfrac{1}{2} > 3\dfrac{2}{5}$

FRACTIONS

Definitions

If a and b are whole numbers and $b \neq 0$, the symbol $\dfrac{a}{b}$ (or a/b) is called a fraction. The upper part, a, is called the *numerator,* and the lower part, b, is called the *denominator.* The denominator indicates into how many parts something is divided, and the numerator tells how many of these parts are taken. A fraction indicates division:

$$\frac{7}{8} = 8\overline{)7}$$

If the numerator of a fraction is 0, the value of the fraction is 0. If the denominator of a fraction is 0, the fraction is not defined (has no meaning):

$$\frac{0}{17} = 0 \qquad \frac{17}{0} \text{ not defined (has no meaning)}$$

If the denominator of a fraction is 1, the value of the fraction is the same as the numerator:

$$\frac{18}{1} = 18$$

If the numerator and denominator are the same number, the value of the fraction is 1:

$$\frac{7}{7} = 1$$

Equivalent Fractions

Fractions that represent the same number are said to be *equivalent*. If m is a counting number and $\frac{a}{b}$ is a fraction, then: $\frac{m \times a}{m \times b} = \frac{a}{b}$ because $\frac{m}{m} = 1$ and $1 \times \frac{a}{b} = \frac{a}{b}$.

Example

$$\frac{2}{3} = \frac{4}{6} = \frac{6}{9} = \frac{8}{12}$$

These fractions are all equivalent.

Inequality of Fractions

If two fractions are not equivalent, one is less than the other. The ideas of "less than" and "greater than" were previously defined and used for whole numbers.

For the fractions $\frac{a}{b}$ and $\frac{c}{b}$: $\quad \frac{a}{b} < \frac{c}{b}$ if $a < c$

That is, if two fractions have the same denominator, the one with the lesser numerator has the lesser value.

If two fractions have different denominators, find a common denominator by multiplying one denominator by the other. Then use the common denominator to compare numerators.

Examples

1. Which is less, $\frac{5}{8}$ or $\frac{4}{7}$?

$$8 \cdot 7 = 56 = \text{common denominator}$$

$$\frac{5}{8} \times \frac{7}{7} = \frac{35}{56} \qquad \frac{4}{7} \times \frac{8}{8} = \frac{32}{56}$$

Since $32 < 35$,

$$\frac{32}{56} < \frac{35}{56} \text{ and } \frac{4}{7} < \frac{5}{8}$$

2. Which of the fractions, $\frac{2}{5}$, $\frac{3}{7}$, or $\frac{4}{11}$, is the greatest?

We begin by comparing the first two fractions. Since $\frac{2}{5} = \frac{14}{35}$ and $\frac{3}{7} = \frac{15}{35}$, we can see that $\frac{3}{7}$ is greater. Now, we compare $\frac{3}{7}$ to $\frac{4}{11}$. Since $\frac{3}{7} = \frac{33}{77}$ and $\frac{4}{11} = \frac{28}{77}$, we can see that $\frac{3}{7}$ is the greatest of the three fractions.

Simplifying to Simplest Form

The principle that

$$\frac{m \times a}{m \times b} = \frac{a}{b}$$

can be particularly useful in simplifying fractions to simplest form. Fractions are expressed in *simplest form* when the numerator and denominator have no common factor except 1. To simplify a fraction to an equivalent fraction in simplest form, express the numerator and denominator as products of their prime factors. Each time a prime appears in the numerator and the same prime appears in the denominator, $\frac{p}{p}$, substitute its equal value, 1.

Examples

1. Simplify $\frac{30}{42}$ to an equivalent fraction in simplest form:

$$\frac{30}{42} = \frac{2 \cdot 3 \cdot 5}{2 \cdot 3 \cdot 7} = 1 \cdot 1 \cdot \frac{5}{7} = \frac{5}{7}$$

In practice, this can be done even more quickly by dividing numerator and denominator by any number, prime or not, that will divide both evenly. Repeat this process until there is no prime factor remaining that is common to both numerator and denominator:

$$\frac{30}{42} = \frac{15}{21} = \frac{5}{7}$$

2. Simplify $\dfrac{77}{197}$ to an equivalent fraction in simplest form:

$$\frac{77}{197} = \frac{7 \times 11}{3 \times 5 \times 13}$$

Since the numerator and the denominator have no common factors, the fraction is already in simplest form.

PROPER FRACTIONS, IMPROPER FRACTIONS, AND MIXED NUMBERS

Definitions

A *proper fraction* is a fraction whose numerator is less than its denominator. Proper fractions always have a value less than 1:

$$\frac{3}{4} \qquad \frac{5}{8} \qquad \frac{121}{132} \qquad \frac{0}{1}$$

An *improper fraction* is a fraction with numerator equal to or greater than the denominator. Improper fractions always have a value equal to or greater than 1:

$$\frac{3}{2} \qquad \frac{17}{17} \qquad \frac{9}{1} \qquad \frac{15}{14}$$

A *mixed number* is a number composed of a whole number and a proper fraction. It is always greater than 1 in value:

$$3\frac{7}{8} \qquad 5\frac{1}{4} \qquad 11\frac{3}{14}$$

The symbol $3\frac{7}{8}$ means $3 + \dfrac{7}{8}$ and is read "three and seven eighths."

To Rename a Mixed Number as an Improper Fraction

Multiply the denominator by the whole number and add this product to the numerator. Use the sum so obtained as the new numerator, and keep the original denominator.

Example

Write $9\dfrac{4}{11}$ as an improper fraction.

$$9\frac{4}{11} = \frac{(11 \times 9) + 4}{11} = \frac{99 + 4}{11} = \frac{103}{11}$$

Note: In any calculations with mixed numbers, first rename the mixed numbers as improper fractions.

To Rename an Improper Fraction as a Mixed Number

Divide the numerator by the denominator. The result is the whole-number part of the mixed number. If there is a remainder in the division process because the division does not come out evenly, put the remainder over the denominator (divisor). This gives the fractional part of the mixed number:

$$\frac{20}{3} = 3\overline{)20} \;\; \begin{array}{c} 6 \\ \underline{18} \\ 2 \text{ remainder} \end{array} = 6\frac{2}{3}$$

Multiplication

Proper and Improper Fractions

Multiply the two numerators and then multiply the two denominators. If the numerator obtained is greater than the denominator, divide the numerator of the resulting fraction by its denominator:

$$\frac{3}{8} \times \frac{15}{11} = \frac{45}{88} \qquad \frac{3}{8} \times \frac{22}{7} = \frac{66}{56} = 1\frac{10}{56}$$

Multiplication of fractions is commutative.

Three or more fractions are multiplied in the same way; two numerators are done at a time, and the result is multiplied by the next numerator.

The product in the multiplication of fractions is usually expressed in simplest form.

Dividing Common Factors

In multiplying fractions, if any of the numerators and denominators have a common divisor (factor), divide each of them by this common factor and the value of the fraction remains the same. This process is called *dividing common factors.*

Example

$$\frac{27}{18} \times \frac{90}{300} = ?$$

$$\frac{27}{18} \times \frac{90}{300} = \frac{27}{18} \times \frac{9}{30} \qquad \text{Divide the numerator and denominator of the second fraction by 10.}$$

$$= \frac{\overset{9}{\cancel{27}}}{\underset{2}{\cancel{18}}} \times \frac{\overset{1}{\cancel{9}}}{\underset{10}{\cancel{30}}} \qquad \text{Divide: 18 and 9 each divisible by 9; 27 and 30 each divisible by 3.}$$

$$= \frac{9 \times 1}{2 \times 10} = \frac{9}{20} \qquad \text{Multiply numerators; multiply denominators}$$

Another method:

$$\frac{\overset{3}{\cancel{27}}}{\underset{2}{\cancel{18}}} \times \frac{\overset{3}{\cancel{9}}}{\underset{10}{\cancel{30}}} = \frac{3 \times 3}{2 \times 10} = \frac{9}{20}$$

Divide: 27 and 18 have common factor 9; 9 and 30 have common factor 3.

Note: Dividing can take place only between a numerator and a denominator in the same or a different fraction, never between two numerators or between two denominators.

Mixed Numbers

Mixed numbers should be renamed as improper fractions before multiplying. Then multiply as described above.

Example

To multiply

$$\frac{4}{7} \times 3\frac{5}{8},$$

rename $3\frac{5}{8}$ as an improper fraction.

$$3\frac{5}{8} = \frac{(8 \times 3) + 5}{8} = \frac{24 + 5}{8} = \frac{29}{8}$$

Then multiply.

$$\frac{\overset{1}{\cancel{4}}}{7} \times \frac{29}{\underset{2}{\cancel{8}}} = \frac{29}{14}$$

The answer can be left as $\frac{29}{14}$ or renamed as a mixed number:

$$2\frac{1}{14}$$

Fractions with Whole Numbers

Write the whole number as a fraction with a denominator of 1 and then multiply.

$$\frac{3}{4} \times 7 = \frac{3}{4} \times \frac{7}{1} = \frac{21}{4} = 5\frac{1}{4}$$

Note: When any fraction is multiplied by 1, its value remains unchanged. When any fraction is multiplied by 0, the product is 0.

Division

Reciprocals

Division of fractions involves reciprocals. One fraction is the *reciprocal* of another if the product of the fractions is 1.

Examples

1. $\dfrac{3}{4}$ and $\dfrac{4}{3}$ are reciprocals since

$$\overset{1}{\underset{1}{\cancel{\dfrac{3}{4}}}} \times \overset{1}{\underset{1}{\cancel{\dfrac{4}{3}}}} = \dfrac{1 \times 1}{1 \times 1} = 1$$

2. $\dfrac{1}{3}$ and 3 are reciprocals since

$$\underset{1}{\cancel{\dfrac{1}{3}}} \times \overset{1}{\cancel{\dfrac{3}{1}}} = 1$$

To find the reciprocal of a fraction, interchange the numerator and denominator—that is, "invert" the fraction, or "turn it upside down."

Proper and Improper Fractions

Multiply the first fraction (dividend) by the reciprocal of the second fraction (divisor). Simplify by division if possible. If you wish to, rename the answer as a mixed number when possible.

Example

$$\dfrac{9}{2} \div \dfrac{4}{7} = \dfrac{9}{2} \times \dfrac{7}{4} \quad \text{The reciprocal of } \dfrac{4}{7} \text{ is } \dfrac{7}{4} \text{ because } \dfrac{4}{7} \times \dfrac{7}{4} = 1.$$

$$= \dfrac{63}{8}$$

$$= 7\dfrac{7}{8}$$

Mixed Numbers and/or Whole Numbers

Both mixed numbers and whole numbers must first be renamed as equivalent improper fractions. Then proceed as described on the previous page.

Note: If a fraction or a mixed number is divided by 1, its value is unchanged. Division of a fraction or a mixed number by 0 is not defined. If a fraction is divided by itself or an equivalent fraction, the quotient is 1:

$$\frac{19}{7} \div \frac{19}{7} = \frac{19}{7} \times \frac{7}{19} \qquad \text{Reciprocal of } \frac{19}{7} \text{ is } \frac{7}{19}.$$

$$= 1 \times 1 = 1$$

Addition

Fractions can be added only if their denominators are the same (called the *common denominator*). Add the numerators; the denominator remains the same. Simplify the sum to the simplest form.

$$\frac{3}{8} + \frac{2}{8} + \frac{1}{8} = \frac{3 + 2 + 1}{8} = \frac{6}{8} = \frac{3}{4}$$

When the fractions have different denominators, you must find a common denominator. One way of doing this is to find the product of the different denominators.

Example

$$\frac{5}{6} + \frac{1}{4} = ?$$

A common denominator is $6 \cdot 4 = 24$.

$$\frac{5}{6} \times \frac{4}{4} = \frac{20}{24} \quad \text{and} \quad \frac{1}{4} \times \frac{6}{6} = \frac{6}{24}$$

$$\frac{5}{6} + \frac{1}{4} = \frac{20}{24} + \frac{6}{24}$$

$$= \frac{20 + 6}{24}$$

$$= \frac{26}{24}$$

$$= \frac{13}{12}$$

$$= 1\frac{1}{12}$$

Least Common Denominator

A denominator can often be found that is less than the product of the different denominators. If the denominator of each fraction will divide such a number evenly and it is the *least* such number, it is called the *least common denominator,* abbreviated as LCD. Finding a least common denominator may make it unnecessary to simplify the answer and enables one to work with lesser numbers. There are two common methods.

First Method: By Inspection

$$\frac{5}{6} + \frac{1}{4} = ?$$

LCD = 12 because 12 is the least number into which 6 and 4 divide evenly. Therefore:

$$12 \div 6 = 2 \qquad \text{multiply } \frac{5}{6} \times \frac{2}{2} = \frac{10}{12}$$

$$12 \div 4 = 3 \qquad \text{multiply } \frac{1}{4} \times \frac{3}{3} = \frac{3}{12}$$

Then:

$$\frac{5}{6} + \frac{1}{4} = \frac{10}{12} + \frac{3}{12}$$

$$= \frac{13}{12}$$

$$= 1\frac{1}{12}$$

Second Method: By Factoring

This method can be used when the LCD is not recognized by inspection. Factor each denominator into its prime factors. The LCD is the product of the greatest power of each separate factor, where *power* refers to the number of times a factor occurs.

Example

$$\frac{5}{6} + \frac{1}{4} = ?$$

Factoring denominators gives:

$$6 = 2 \cdot 3 \quad \text{and} \quad 4 = 2 \cdot 2$$
$$\text{LCD} = 2 \cdot 2 \cdot 3$$
$$= 12$$

Rename with LCD:

$$\frac{5}{6} \times \frac{2}{2} = \frac{10}{12} \qquad \frac{1}{4} \times \frac{3}{3} = \frac{3}{12}$$

$$\frac{5}{6} + \frac{1}{4} = \frac{10}{12} + \frac{3}{12}$$

$$= \frac{13}{12}$$

$$= 1\frac{1}{12}$$

The denominators 4 and 6 factor into $2 \cdot 2$ and $2 \cdot 3$, respectively. Although the factor 2 *appears* three times, its power is 2^2 from factoring 4. The factor 3 appears once, so its power is 3^1. Therefore, the LCD as a *product* of the *greatest power of each separate factor* is $2 \times 2 \times 3$.

The factoring method of adding fractions can be extended to three or more fractions.

Example

$$\frac{1}{4} + \frac{3}{8} + \frac{1}{12} = ?$$

Factoring denominators gives:

$$4 = 2 \cdot 2 \qquad 8 = 2 \cdot 2 \cdot 2 \qquad 12 = 2 \cdot 2 \cdot 3$$

$$\text{LCD} = 2 \cdot 2 \cdot 2 \cdot 3$$

$$= 24$$

Rename with LCD:

$$\frac{1}{4} \times \frac{6}{6} = \frac{6}{24} \qquad \frac{3}{8} \times \frac{3}{3} = \frac{9}{24}$$

$$\frac{1}{12} \times \frac{2}{2} = \frac{2}{24}$$

$$\frac{1}{4} + \frac{3}{8} + \frac{1}{12} = \frac{6}{24} + \frac{9}{24} + \frac{2}{24}$$

$$= \frac{6 + 9 + 2}{24}$$

$$= \frac{17}{24}$$

Addition of Mixed Numbers

Rename any mixed numbers as improper fractions. If the fractions have the same denominator, add the numerators. If the fractions have different denominators, find the LCD of the several denominators and then add numerators. Simplify the answer if possible. Write the answer as a mixed number if you wish.

Example

$$2\frac{2}{3} + 5\frac{1}{2} + 1\frac{2}{9} = ?$$

Factoring denominators gives:

$$3 = 3 \qquad 2 = 2 \qquad 9 = 3 \cdot 3$$
$$LCD = 2 \cdot 3 \cdot 3$$
$$= 18$$

Rename with LCD:

$$\frac{8}{3} \times \frac{6}{6} = \frac{48}{18} \qquad \frac{11}{2} \times \frac{9}{9} = \frac{99}{18} \qquad \frac{11}{9} \times \frac{2}{2} = \frac{22}{18}$$

$$2\frac{2}{3} + 5\frac{1}{2} + 1\frac{2}{9} = \frac{8}{3} + \frac{11}{2} + \frac{11}{9}$$

$$= \frac{48}{18} + \frac{99}{18} + \frac{22}{18}$$

$$= \frac{48 + 99 + 22}{18}$$

$$= \frac{169}{18} = 9\frac{7}{18}$$

Subtraction

Fractions can be subtracted only if the denominators are the same. If the denominators are the same, find the difference between the numerators. The denominator remains unchanged.

Example

$$\frac{19}{3} - \frac{2}{3} = ?$$

$$= \frac{19 - 2}{3}$$

$$= \frac{17}{3}$$

$$= 5\frac{2}{3}$$

When fractions have different denominators, find equivalent fractions with a common denominator and then subtract numerators.

Example

$$\frac{7}{8} - \frac{3}{4} = ?$$

Factoring denominators gives:

$$8 = 2 \cdot 2 \cdot 2 \qquad 4 = 2 \cdot 2$$

$$LCD = 2 \cdot 2 \cdot 2$$

$$= 8$$

Rename with LCD:

$$\frac{7}{8} = \frac{7}{8} \qquad \frac{3}{4} \times \frac{2}{2} = \frac{6}{8}$$

$$\frac{7}{8} - \frac{3}{4} = \frac{7}{8} - \frac{6}{8}$$

$$= \frac{7 - 6}{8}$$

$$= \frac{1}{8}$$

Mixed Numbers

To subtract mixed numbers, rename each mixed number as an improper fraction. Find the LCD for the fractions. Write each fraction as an equivalent fraction whose denominator is the common denominator. Find the difference between the numerators.

Example

$$3\frac{3}{8} - 2\frac{5}{6} = ?$$

$$LCD = 24$$

$$3\frac{3}{8} - 2\frac{5}{6} = \frac{27}{8} - \frac{17}{6}$$

$$= \frac{81}{24} - \frac{68}{24}$$

$$= \frac{13}{24}$$

If zero is subtracted from a fraction, the result is the original fraction:

$$\frac{3}{4} - 0 = \frac{3}{4} - \frac{0}{4} = \frac{3}{4}$$

Fraction Problems

In the following problems, perform the indicated operations and simplify the answers to simplest form.

1. $\dfrac{5}{12} \times \dfrac{4}{15}$

2. $\dfrac{1}{2} \div \dfrac{3}{8}$

3. $\dfrac{5}{12} + \dfrac{2}{3}$

4. $\dfrac{2}{3} - \dfrac{5}{11}$

5. $3\dfrac{1}{3} \times \dfrac{4}{5}$

6. $7\dfrac{4}{5} - 2\dfrac{1}{3}$

7. $2\dfrac{3}{5} + 7\dfrac{3}{5}$

8. $\dfrac{6}{7} \times \dfrac{3}{4} \times \dfrac{2}{3}$

9. $6 \times \dfrac{2}{3} \times 2\dfrac{5}{6}$

10. $2\dfrac{2}{3} \div 1\dfrac{7}{9}$

Solutions

1. $\dfrac{5}{12} \times \dfrac{4}{15} = \dfrac{\cancel{5}^{1}}{\cancel{12}_{3}} \times \dfrac{\cancel{4}^{1}}{\cancel{15}_{3}} = \dfrac{1}{9}$

2. $\dfrac{1}{2} \div \dfrac{3}{8} = \dfrac{1}{2} \times \dfrac{8}{3} = \dfrac{1}{\cancel{2}_{1}} \times \dfrac{\cancel{8}^{4}}{3} = \dfrac{4}{3}$

3. $\dfrac{5}{12} + \dfrac{2}{3} = \dfrac{5}{12} + \dfrac{8}{12} = \dfrac{13}{12} = 1\dfrac{1}{12}$

4. $\dfrac{2}{3} - \dfrac{5}{11} = \dfrac{22}{33} - \dfrac{15}{33} = \dfrac{7}{33}$

5. $3\dfrac{1}{3} \times \dfrac{4}{5} = \dfrac{10}{3} \times \dfrac{4}{5} = \dfrac{\overset{2}{\cancel{10}}}{3} \times \dfrac{4}{\underset{1}{\cancel{5}}} = \dfrac{8}{3} = 2\dfrac{2}{3}$

6. $7\dfrac{4}{5} - 2\dfrac{1}{3} = \dfrac{39}{5} - \dfrac{7}{3} = \dfrac{117}{15} - \dfrac{35}{15} = \dfrac{82}{15} = 5\dfrac{7}{15}$

7. $2\dfrac{3}{5} + 7\dfrac{3}{5} = \dfrac{13}{5} + \dfrac{38}{5} = \dfrac{51}{5} = 10\dfrac{1}{5}$

8. $\dfrac{6}{7} \times \dfrac{3}{4} \times \dfrac{2}{3} = \dfrac{6}{7} \times \dfrac{2}{4} \times \dfrac{3}{3} = \dfrac{6}{7} \times \dfrac{1}{2} \times \dfrac{1}{1} = \dfrac{3}{7} \times \dfrac{1}{1} \times \dfrac{1}{1} = \dfrac{3}{7}$

9. $6 \times \dfrac{2}{3} \times 2\dfrac{5}{6} = \dfrac{6}{1} \times \dfrac{2}{3} \times \dfrac{17}{6} = \dfrac{34}{3} = 11\dfrac{1}{3}$

10. $2\dfrac{2}{3} \div 1\dfrac{7}{9} = \dfrac{8}{3} \div \dfrac{16}{9} = \dfrac{8}{3} \times \dfrac{9}{16} = \dfrac{9}{3} \times \dfrac{8}{16} = \dfrac{3}{1} \times \dfrac{1}{2} = \dfrac{3}{2}$

DECIMALS

Earlier, we stated that whole numbers are expressed in a system of tens, or the decimal system, using the digits from 0 to 9. This system can be extended to fractions by using a period called a *decimal point*. The digits after a decimal point form a *decimal fraction*. Decimal fractions are less than 1—for example, .3, .37, .372, and .105. The first position to the right of the decimal point is called the *tenths' place*, since the digit in that position tells how many tenths there are. The second digit to the right of the decimal point is in the *hundredths' place*. The third digit to the right of the decimal point is in the *thousandths' place*, and so on.

Examples
1. .3 is a decimal fraction that means

$$3 \times \dfrac{1}{10} = \dfrac{3}{10}$$

read "three tenths."

2. The decimal fraction of .37 means

$$3 \times \frac{1}{10} + 7 \times \frac{1}{100} = 3 \times \frac{10}{100} + 7 \times \frac{1}{100}$$

$$= \frac{30}{100} + \frac{7}{100} = \frac{37}{100}$$

read "thirty-seven hundredths."

3. The decimal fraction .372 means

$$\frac{300}{1,000} + \frac{70}{1,000} + \frac{2}{1,000} = \frac{372}{1,000}$$

read "three hundred seventy-two thousandths."

Whole numbers have an understood (unwritten) decimal point to the right of the last digit (i.e., 4 = 4.0). Decimal fractions can be combined with whole numbers to make *decimals*—for example, 3.246, 10.85, and 4.7.

Note: Adding zeros to the right of a decimal after the last digit does not change the value of the decimal.

DECIMALS AND FRACTIONS

Renaming a Decimal as a Fraction

Place the digits to the right of the decimal point over the value of the place in which the last digit appears and simplify if possible. The whole number remains the same.

Example

Rename 2.14 as a fraction or mixed number. Observe that 4 is the last digit and is in the hundredths' place.

$$.14 = \frac{14}{100} = \frac{7}{50}$$

Therefore:

$$2.14 = 2\frac{7}{50}$$

Renaming a Fraction as a Decimal

Divide the numerator of the fraction by the denominator. First put a decimal point followed by zeros to the right of the number in the numerator. Add and divide until there is no remainder. The decimal point in the quotient is aligned directly above the decimal point in the dividend.

Example

Rename $\frac{3}{8}$ as a decimal.

Divide

$$
\begin{array}{r}
.375 \\
8\overline{)3.000} \\
\underline{24} \\
60 \\
\underline{56} \\
40 \\
\underline{40} \\
\end{array}
$$

When the division does not terminate with a 0 remainder, follow this procedure.

$$
\begin{array}{r}
.833 \\
6\overline{)5.000} \\
\underline{48} \\
20 \\
\underline{18} \\
20 \\
\underline{18} \\
2 \\
\end{array}
$$

The 3 in the quotient will be repeated indefinitely. It is called an *infinite decimal* and is written .833 . . . . = $.8\overline{3}$.

Addition

Addition of decimals is both commutative and associative. Decimals are simpler to add than fractions. Place the decimals in a column with the decimal points aligned under each other. Add in the usual way. The decimal point of the answer is also aligned under the other decimal points.

Example

43 + 2.73 + .9 + 3.01 = ?

$$
\begin{array}{r}
43. \\
2.73 \\
.9 \\
3.01 \\
\hline
49.64 \\
\end{array}
$$

Subtraction

For subtraction, the decimal points must be aligned under each other. Add zeros to the right of the decimal point if desired. Subtract as with whole numbers.

Examples

$$\begin{array}{r} 21.567 \\ -9.4 \\ \hline 12.167 \end{array} \qquad \begin{array}{r} 21.567 \\ -9.48 \\ \hline 12.087 \end{array} \qquad \begin{array}{r} 39.00 \\ -17.48 \\ \hline 21.52 \end{array}$$

Multiplication

Multiplication of decimals is commutative and associative:

$$5.39 \times .04 = .04 \times 5.39$$
$$(.7 \times .02) \times .1 = .7 \cdot (.02 \times .1)$$

Multiply the decimals as if they were whole numbers. The total number of decimal places in the product is the sum of the number of places (to the right of the decimal point) in all of the numbers multiplied.

Example

$8.64 \times .003 = ?$

$$\begin{array}{r} 8.64 \\ \times .003 \\ \hline .02592 \end{array} \qquad \begin{array}{r} 2 \\ +3 \\ \hline 5 \end{array} \qquad \begin{array}{l} \text{places to right of decimal point} \\ \text{places to right of decimal point} \\ \text{places to right of decimal point} \end{array}$$

A zero had to be added to the left of the product before writing the decimal point to ensure that there would be five decimal places in the product.

Note: To multiply a decimal by 10, simply move the decimal point one place to the right; to multiply by 100, move the decimal point two places to the right.

Division

To divide one decimal (the dividend) by another (the divisor), move the decimal point in the divisor as many places as necessary to the right to make the divisor a whole number. Then move the decimal point in the dividend (expressed or understood) a corresponding number of places, adding zeros if necessary. Then divide as with whole numbers. The decimal point in the quotient is placed above the decimal point in the dividend after the decimal point has been moved.

Example

Divide 7.6 by .32.

$$
.32\overline{)7.60} = 32\overline{)760.00}
$$

$$
\begin{array}{r}
23.75 \\
\hline
64 \\
\hline
120 \\
96 \\
\hline
240 \\
224 \\
\hline
160 \\
160 \\
\hline
\end{array}
$$

Note: "Divide 7.6 by .32" can be written as $\dfrac{7.6}{.32}$. If this fraction is multiplied by $\dfrac{100}{100}$, an equivalent fraction is obtained with a whole number in the denominator:

$$
\frac{7.6}{.32} \times \frac{100}{100} = \frac{760}{32}
$$

Moving the decimal point two places to the right in both divisor and dividend is equivalent to multiplying each number by 100.

Special Cases

If the dividend has a decimal point and the divisor does not, divide as with whole numbers and place the decimal point of the quotient above the decimal point in the divisor.

If both dividend and divisor are whole numbers but the quotient is a decimal, place a decimal point after the last digit of the dividend and add zeros as necessary to get the required degree of accuracy. (*See* Renaming a Fraction as a Decimal, page 159.)

Note: To divide any number by 10, simply move its decimal point (understood to be after the last digit for a whole number) one place to the left; to divide by 100, move the decimal point two places to the left; and so on.

Decimal Problems

1. Rename the following decimals as fractions and simplify.

 a. 1.16

 b. 15.05

2. Rename the following fractions as decimals.

 a. $\dfrac{3}{8}$

 b. $\dfrac{2}{3}$

In the following problems, perform the indicated operations.

3. $3.762 + 23.43$

4. $1.368 - .559$

5. $8.7 \times .8$

6. $.045 \div .5$

7. $73 - .46$

8. $5.43 + .154 + 17$

9. $7.2 \times .002$

10. $2.2 \div 8$

11. Which of the three decimals is the least: .09, .769, or .8?

Solutions

1. a. $1.16 = 1\dfrac{16}{100} = 1\dfrac{8}{50} = 1\dfrac{4}{25}$

 b. $15.05 = 15\dfrac{5}{100} = 15\dfrac{1}{20}$

2. a. $\dfrac{3}{8} = 8\overline{)3.000}$ $\quad.375$

 $\qquad \dfrac{24}{}$

 $\qquad 60$

 $\qquad \dfrac{-56}{}$

 $\qquad 40$

 b. $\dfrac{2}{3} = 3\overline{)2.00}$ $\quad.666...$

 $\qquad \dfrac{18}{}$

 $\qquad 20$

 $\qquad \dfrac{-18}{}$

 $\qquad 20$

3. $\quad$ 3.762
$\qquad\underline{+23.43}$
$\qquad$ 27.192

4. $\quad$ 1.368
$\qquad\underline{-.559}$
$\qquad$ .809

5. $\quad$ 8.7
$\qquad\underline{\times\ .8}$
$\qquad$ 6.96

6. $\qquad\quad$ 0.09
$\qquad$ .5.$\overline{)0.0.45}$
$\qquad\quad$ ↳ $\quad$ ↳

7. $\quad$ 73.00
$\qquad\underline{-\ .46}$
$\qquad$ 72.54

8. $\quad\ $ 5.43
$\qquad\ $ .154
$\qquad\underline{+17.000}$
$\qquad$ 22.584

9. $\quad$ 7.2 $\qquad$ (One digit to the right of the decimal point)
$\qquad\underline{\times .002}$ $\qquad$ (Three digits to the right of the decimal point)
$\qquad$ .0144 $\qquad$ (Four digits to the right of the decimal point)

10. $\qquad\ $ 0.275
$\qquad$ 8$\overline{)2.2}$

11. The easiest way to determine the least decimal number is to append 0's to the end of each of the numbers until they all have the same number of digits. Then, ignore the decimal points and see which number is the least. Thus, .09 = .090, .769 = .769, .8 = .800. Clearly, the least number is .09

PERCENTS

Percents, like fractions and decimals, are ways of expressing parts of whole numbers, as 93%, 50%, and 22.4%. Percents are expressions of hundredths—that is, of fractions whose denominator is 100. The symbol for percent is "%".

Example

$$25\% = \text{twenty-five hundredths} = \frac{25}{100} = \frac{1}{4}$$

The word *percent* means *per hundred*. Its main use is in comparing fractions with equal denominators of 100.

Relationship with Fractions and Decimals

Renaming a Percent as a Decimal

Divide the percent by 100 and drop the symbol for percent. Add zeros to the left when necessary.

$$30\% = .30 \qquad 1\% = .01$$

Remember that the short method of dividing by 100 is to move the decimal point two places to the left.

Renaming a Decimal as a Percent

Multiply the decimal by 100 by moving the decimal point two places to the right, and add the symbol for percent.

$$.375 = 37.5\% \qquad .001 = .1\%$$

Renaming a Percent as a Fraction

Drop the percent sign. Write the number as a numerator over a denominator of 100. If the numerator has a decimal point, move the decimal point to the right the necessary number of places to make the numerator a whole number. Add the same number of zeros to the right of the denominator as you moved places to the right in the numerator. Simplify where possible.

Examples

$$20\% = \frac{20}{100} = \frac{2}{10} = \frac{1}{5}$$

$$36.5\% = \frac{36.5}{100} = \frac{365}{1,000} = \frac{73}{200}$$

Renaming a Fraction as a Percent

Use either of two methods.

First Method

Rename the fraction as an equivalent fraction with a denominator of 100. Drop the denominator (equivalent to multiplying by 100) and add the % sign.

Example

Express $\frac{6}{20}$ as a percent.

$$\frac{6}{20} \times \frac{5}{5} = \frac{30}{100} = 30\%$$

Second Method

Divide the numerator by the denominator to get a decimal with two places (express the remainder as a fraction if necessary). Rename the decimal as a percent.

Example

Express $\dfrac{6}{20}$ as a percent.

$$\dfrac{6}{20} = 20\overline{\smash{)}6.00}\ \overset{.30}{} = 30\%$$
$$\underline{60}$$

Percent Problems

1. Rename the following percents as decimals:

   a. 37.5%

   b. 0.5%

2. Rename the following decimals as percents:

   a. 0.625

   b. 3.75

3. Rename the following fractions as percents:

   a. $\dfrac{7}{8}$

   b. $\dfrac{73}{200}$

4. Rename the following percents as fractions:

   a. 87.5%

   b. 0.02%

5. Rename $12\dfrac{1}{4}\%$ as a decimal.

6. Write .07% as both a decimal and a fraction.

7. Write $\dfrac{11}{16}$ as both a decimal and a percent.

8. Write 1.25 as both a percent and a fraction.

9. Which of the following is the greatest: $\dfrac{5}{8}$, 62%, or .628?

Solutions

1. **a.** $37.5\% = 0.375$

   b. $00.5\% = 0.005$

2. **a.** $0.625 = 62.5\%$

   b. $3.75 = 375\%$

3. **a.** $\dfrac{7}{8} = 8\overline{)7.000}^{\,0.875} = 87.5\%$

   b. $\dfrac{73}{200} = 200\overline{)73.000}^{\,0.365} = 36.5\%$

4. **a.** $87.5\% = 0.875 = \dfrac{875}{1,000} = \dfrac{35}{40} = \dfrac{7}{8}$

   b. $0.02\% = 0.0002 = \dfrac{2}{10,000} = \dfrac{1}{5,000}$

5. $12\dfrac{1}{4}\% = 12.25\% = 0.1225$

6. $.07\% = 0.0007 = \dfrac{7}{10,000}$

7. $\dfrac{11}{16} = 16\overline{)11.0000}^{\,.6875} = 68.75\%$

8. $1.25 = 125\% = \dfrac{125}{100} = \dfrac{5}{4}$

9. In order to determine the greatest number, we must write them all in the same form. Writing $\dfrac{5}{8}$ as a decimal, we obtain .625. If we write 62% as a decimal, we get .62. Thus, .628 is the greatest of the three numbers.

Solving Percent Problems

There are several different types of word problems involving percents that might appear on your test. In addition to generic percent problems, other applications you might be asked to solve involve taxation, commission, profit and loss, discount, and interest. All of these problems are solved in essentially the same way, as the examples that follow illustrate.

Note that when solving percent problems, it is often easier to rename the percent as a decimal or a fraction before computing. When we take a percent of a certain number, that number is called

167

the *base*, the percent we take is called the *rate*, and the result is called the *part*. If we let B represent the base, R represent the rate, and P represent the part, the relationship between these three quantities can be expressed by the following formula

$$P = R \times B$$

All percent problems can be solved with the help of this formula.

The first four examples below show how to solve all types of generic percent problems. The remaining examples involve specific financial applications.

Examples

1. In a class of 24 students, 25% received an A. How many students received an A?

   The number of students (24) is the base, and 25% is the rate. Rename the rate as a fraction for ease of handling and apply the formula.

   $$25\% = \frac{25}{100} = \frac{1}{4}$$

   $$P = R \times B$$

   $$= \frac{1}{\cancel{4}} \times \frac{\cancel{24}^{\,6}}{1}$$

   $$= 6 \text{ students}$$

   To choose between renaming the percent (rate) as a decimal or a fraction, simply decide which would be easier to work with. In Example 1, the fraction is easier to work with because division is possible. In Example 2, the situation is the same except for a different rate. This time, the decimal form is easier.

2. In a class of 24 students, 29.17% received an A. How many students received an A?

   Renaming the rate as a fraction yields:

   $$\frac{29.17}{100} = \frac{2917}{10,000}$$

   You can quickly see that the decimal is the better choice.

   $$29.17\% = .2917$$
   $$P = R \times B$$
   $$= .2917 \times 24$$
   $$= 7 \text{ students}$$

   $$\begin{array}{r} .2917 \\ \times \quad 24 \\ \hline 1.1668 \\ 5.834 \\ \hline 7.0008 \end{array}$$

3. What percent of a 40-hour week is a 16-hour schedule?

40 hours is the base and 16 hours is the part. $P = R \times B$

$$16 = R \times 40$$

Divide each side of the equation by 40.

$$\frac{16}{40} = R$$

$$\frac{2}{5} = R$$

$$40\% = R$$

4. A woman paid $15,000 as a down payment on a house. If this amount was 20% of the price, what did the house cost?

The part (or percentage) is $15,000, the rate is 20%, and we must find the base. Rename the rate as a fraction.

$$20\% = \frac{1}{5}$$

$$P = R \times B$$

$$\$15,000 = \frac{1}{5} \times B$$

Multiply each side of the equation by 5.

$$\$75,000 = B = \text{cost of house}$$

5. A salesperson sells a new car for $24,800 and receives a 5% commission. How much commission does he receive?

The cost of the car ($24,800) is the base, and the rate is 5%. We are looking for the amount of commission, which is the part.

$$P = 5\% \times \$24,800 = .05 \times \$24,800 = \$1,240$$

Thus, the salesperson receives a commission of $1,240.

6. Janet buys a laptop computer for $1,199 and has to pay 7% sales tax. What is the amount of sales tax she owes, and what is the total price of the computer?

The cost of the computer ($1,199) is the base, and the rate is 7%. We are looking for the amount of sales tax, which is the part.

$$P = 7\% \times \$1,199 = .07 \times \$1,199 = \$83.93$$

Thus, the sales tax is $83.93, and the total cost of the computer is $1,199 + $83.93 = $1,282.93.

Discount

The amount of discount is the difference between the original price and the sale, or discount, price. The rate of discount is usually given as a fraction or as a percent. Use the formula of the percent problems $P = R \times B$, but now P stands for the part or discount, R is the rate, and B, the base, is the original price.

Examples

1. A table listed at $160 is marked 20% off. What is the sale price?

$$P = R \times B$$
$$= .20 \times \$160 = \$32$$

This is the amount of discount, or how much must be subtracted from the original price. Then:

$$\$160 - \$32 = \$128 \text{ sale price}$$

2. A car priced at $9,000 was sold for $7,200. What was the rate of discount?

$$\text{Amount of discount} = \$9,000 - \$7,200$$
$$= \$1,800$$

Discount = rate × original price

$$\$1,800 = R \times \$9,000$$

Divide each side of the equation by $9,000:

$$\frac{\overset{20}{\cancel{1,800}}}{\underset{100}{\cancel{9,000}}} = \frac{20}{100} = R = 20\%$$

Successive Discounting

When an item is discounted more than once, it is called successive discounting.

Examples

1. In one store, a dress tagged at $40 was discounted 15%. When it did not sell at the lower price, it was discounted an additional 10%. What was the final selling price?

Discount = R × original price

First discount = .15 × $40 = $6

$40 − $6 = $34 selling price after first discount

Second discount = .10 × $34 = $3.40

$34 − $3.40 = $30.60 final selling price

2. In another store, an identical dress was also tagged at $40. When it did not sell, it was discounted 25% all at once. Is the final selling price lower or higher than in Example 9?

$$\text{Discount} = R \times \text{original price}$$
$$= .25 \times \$40$$
$$= \$10$$
$$\$40 - \$10 = \$30 \text{ final selling price}$$

This is a lower selling price than in Example 9, where two successive discounts were taken. Although the two discounts from Example 9 add up to the discount of Example 10, the final selling price is not the same.

Interest

Interest problems are similar to discount and percent problems. If money is left in the bank for a year and the interest is calculated at the end of the year, the usual formula $P = R \times B$ can be used, where P is the *interest*, R is the *rate*, and B is the *principal* (original amount of money borrowed or loaned).

Examples

1. A certain bank pays interest on savings accounts at the rate of 4% per year. If a man has $6,700 on deposit, find the interest earned after 1 year.

$$P = R \times B$$

Interest = rate · principal

$$P = .04 \times \$6,700 = \$268 \text{ interest}$$

Interest problems frequently involve more or less time than 1 year. Then the formula becomes:

$$\text{Interest} = \text{rate} \times \text{principal} \times \text{time}$$

2. If the money is left in the bank for 3 years at simple interest (the kind we are discussing), the interest is:

$$3 \times \$268 = \$804$$

3. Suppose $6,700 is deposited in the bank at 4% interest for 3 months. How much interest is earned?

Interest = rate $\times$ principal $\times$ time

Here the 4% rate is for 1 year. Since 3 months is $\dfrac{3}{12} = \dfrac{1}{4}$,

$$\text{Interest} = .04 \times \$6,700 \times \frac{1}{4} = \$67.$$

Percent-of-Change Problems

The percent-of-change problem is a special, yet very common, type of percent problem. In such a problem, there is a quantity that has a certain starting value (usually called the "original value"). This original value changes by a certain amount (either an increase or a decrease), leading to what is called the "new value." The problem is to express this increase or decrease as a percent.

Percent-of-change problems are solved by using a method analogous to that used in the problems above. First calculate the *amount* of the increase or decrease. This amount plays the role of the part, P, in the formula $P = R \times B$. The base, B, is the original amount regardless of whether there was a gain or a loss.

Examples

1. By what percent does Mary's salary increase if her present salary is $20,000 and she accepts a new job at a salary of $28,000?

   Amount of increase is:

   $28,000 - $20,000 = $8,000

   $$P = R \times B$$

   $$\$8,000 = R \times \$20,000$$

   Divide each side of the equation by $20,000. Then:

   $$\frac{\overset{40}{\cancel{8,000}}}{\underset{100}{\cancel{20,000}}} = \frac{40}{100} = R = 40\% \text{ increase}$$

2. On Tuesday, the price of Alpha stock closed at $56 a share. On Wednesday, the stock closed at a price that was $14 higher than the closing price on Tuesday. What was the percent of increase in the closing price of the stock?

   In this problem, we are given the amount of increase of $14. Thus,

   $$P = R \times B$$

   $14 = R \times 56$. Thus,

   $$R = \frac{14}{56} = \frac{1}{4} = 25\%.$$

   The percent of increase in the closing price of the stock is 25%.

Percent Word Problems

1. Janet received a rent increase of 15%. If her rent was $785 monthly before the increase, what is her new monthly rent?

2. School bus fares rose from $25 per month to $30 per month. Find the percent of increase.

3. A dress originally priced at $90 is marked down 35%, then discounted a further 10%. What is the new, reduced price?

4. Dave delivers flowers for a salary of $45 a day, plus a 12% commission on all sales. One day his sales amounted to $220. How much money did he earn that day?

5. A certain bank pays interest on money market accounts at a rate of 6% a year. If Brett deposits $7,200, find the interest earned after one year.

6. A small business office bought a used copy machine for 75% of the original price. If the original price was $3,500, how much did they pay for the copy machine?

7. A lawyer who is currently earning $42,380 annually receives a 6.5% raise. What is his new annual salary?

8. An industrial plant reduces its number of employees, which was originally 3,760, by 5%. How many employees now work at the plant?

9. The value of a mutual fund investment of $3,750 increased $500. What is the percent of increase in the price of the mutual fund?

10. Due to a decrease in demand for a particular computer printer, a computer supply store reduces the number of orders for the printer from 35 per month to 20 per month. What percent of decrease does this represent? Round your answer to the nearest whole number percent.

Solutions

1. Amount of increase = $785 × 15% = $785 × .15 = $117.75

   New monthly rent = $902.75

2. Amount of increase = $30 − $25 = $5

   Percent of increase = $\dfrac{5}{25} = \dfrac{1}{5} = 20\%$

3. Amount of first markdown = $90 × 35% = $90 × .35 = $31.50

    Reduced price = $90 − $31.50 = $58.50

    Amount of second markdown = $58.50 × 10%
    $$= \$58.50 \times .1$$
    $$= \$5.85$$

    Final price = $58.50 − $5.85 = $52.65

4. Commission = $220 × 12% = $220 × .12 = $26.40

    Money earned = $45 + $26.40 = $71.40

5. Interest = $7,200 × 6% = $7,200 × .06 = $432

6. Cost = $3,500 × 75% = $2,625

7. Amount of raise = $42,380 × 6.5% = $2,754.70

    New salary = $42,380 + $2,754.70 = $45,134.70

8. Number of employees who lost their jobs = 3,760 × 5% = 188

    Number of employees who now work at the plant
    = 3,760 − 188 = 3,572

9. Percent of increase = change/original value = $\dfrac{500}{3750}$ = 13.33%

10. The amount of the decrease is 35 − 20 = 15.

    The percent of decrease is $\dfrac{15}{35}$ = 42.857%, which rounds to 43%.

Signed Numbers

In describing subtraction of whole numbers, we said that the operation was not closed—that is, 4 − 6 will yield a number that is not a member of the set of counting numbers and zero. The set of *integers* was developed to give meaning to such expressions as 4 − 6. The set of integers is the set of all *positive and negative* whole numbers and zero. It is the set {..., −4, −3, −2, −1, 0, 1, 2, 3, 4, ...}.

The first three dots symbolize the fact that the negative integers go on indefinitely, just as the positive integers do. Integers preceded by a negative sign (called *negative integers*) appear to the left of 0 on a number line.

Decimals, fractions, and mixed numbers can also have negative signs. Together with positive fractions and decimals, they appear on the number line in this fashion:

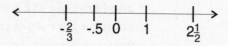

All numbers to the right of 0 are called *positive numbers*. They have the sign +, whether it is actually written or not. Business gains or losses, feet above or below sea level, and temperature above and below zero can all be expressed by means of signed numbers.

Addition

If the numbers to be added have the same sign, add the numbers (integers, fractions, decimals) as usual and use their common sign in the answer:

$$+9 + (+8) + (+2) = +19 \text{ or } 19$$
$$-4 + (-11) + (-7) + (-1) = -23$$

If the numbers to be added have different signs, add the positive numbers and then the negative numbers. Ignore the signs and subtract the lesser total from the greater total. If the greater total is positive, the answer will be positive; if the greater total is negative, the answer will be negative. The answer may be zero. Zero is neither positive nor negative and has no sign.

Example

$$+3 + (-5) + (-8) + (+2) = ?$$
$$+3 + (+2) = +5$$
$$-5 + (-8) = -13$$
$$13 - 5 = 8$$

Since the greater total (13) has a negative sign, the answer is −8.

Subtraction

The second number in a subtraction problem is called the *subtrahend*. In order to subtract, change the sign of the subtrahend and then continue as if you were *adding* signed numbers. If there is no sign in front of the subtrahend, it is assumed to be positive.

Examples

Subtract the subtrahend (bottom number) from the top number.

15	5	−35	−35	42
5	15	−42	42	35
10	−10	7	−77	7

Multiplication

If two and only two signed numbers are to be multiplied, multiply the numbers as you would if they were not signed. Then, if the two numbers have the *same sign,* the product is *positive.* If the two numbers have *different signs,* the product is *negative.* If more than two numbers are being multiplied, proceed two at a time in the same way as before, finding the signed product of the first two numbers, then multiplying that product by the next number, and so on. The product has a positive sign if all the factors are positive or there is an even number of negative factors. The product has a negative sign if there is an odd number of negative factors.

Example

$$-3 \cdot (+5) \cdot (-11) \cdot (-2) = -330$$

The answer is negative because there is an odd number (three) of negative factors.

The product of a signed number and zero is zero. The product of a signed number and 1 is the original number. The product of a signed number and -1 is the original number with its sign changed.

Examples

1. $-5 \cdot 0 = 0$

2. $-5 \cdot 1 = -5$

3. $-5 \cdot (-1) = +5$

Division

If the divisor and the dividend have the same sign, the answer is positive. Divide the numbers as you normally would. If the divisor and the dividend have different signs, the answer is negative. Divide the numbers as you normally would.

Examples

1. $-3 \div (-2) = \dfrac{3}{2} = 1\dfrac{1}{2}$

2. $8 \div (-.2) = -40$

If zero is divided by a signed number, the answer is zero. If a signed number is divided by zero, the answer is undefined. If a signed number is divided by 1, the number remains the same. If a signed number is divided by -1, the quotient is the original number with its sign changed.

Examples

1. $0 \div (-2) = 0$

2. $-\dfrac{4}{3} \div 0$ not defined

3. $\dfrac{2}{3} \div 1 = \dfrac{2}{3}$

4. $4 \div -1 = -4$

Signed Numbers Problems

Perform the indicated operations.

1. $+6 + (-5) + (+2) + (-8)$

2. $-5 - (-4) + (-2) - (+6)$

3. $-3 \cdot (+5) \cdot (-7) \cdot (-2)$

4. $9 \div (-.3)$

5. $(-3) + (-12) + 7 + (-13)$

6. $(-8) - (-5) + (-1) - (+3)$

7. $(3)(2)(1)(0)(-1)(-2)(-3)$

8. $\dfrac{(-8)(+3)}{(-6)(-2)(5)}$

9. $\dfrac{6}{15} \div \left(\dfrac{-12}{5} \right)$

10. $\dfrac{(+5) - (-13)}{(-4) + (-5)}$

Solutions

1. $+6 + (-5) = +1$
   $+1 + (+2) = +3$
   $+3 + (-8) = -5$

2. $-5 - (-4) = -5 + 4 = -1$
   $-1 + (-2) = -3$
   $-3 - (+6) = -9$

3. $-3 \cdot (+5) = -15$
   $-15 \cdot (-7) = +105$
   $+105 \cdot (-2) = -210$

4. $9 \div (-.3) = -30$

5. $(-3) + (-12) = -15$

    $-15 + 7 = -8$

    $-8 + (-13) = -21$

6. $(-8) - (-5) = -8 + 5 = -3$

    $-3 + -1 = -4$

    $-4 - (+3) = -7$

7. $(3)\,(2)\,(1)\,(0)\,(-1)\,(-2)\,(-3) = 0$, since, if 0 is a factor in any multiplication, the result is 0.

8. $\dfrac{(-8)\,(+3)}{(-6)\,(-2)\,(5)} = \dfrac{-24}{60} = -\dfrac{2}{5}$

9. $\dfrac{6}{15} \div \left(\dfrac{-12}{5}\right) = \dfrac{6}{15} \times \dfrac{5}{-12} = -\dfrac{1}{6}$

10. $\dfrac{(+5) - (-13)}{(-4) + (-5)} = \dfrac{5 + 13}{-9} = \dfrac{18}{-9} = -2$

POWERS, EXPONENTS, AND ROOTS

Exponents

The product $10 \times 10 \times 10$ can be written 10^3. We say 10 is raised to the *third power*. In general, $a \times a \times a \ldots \times a$ n times is written a^n. The *base* a is raised to the nth power, and n is called the *exponent*.

Examples

1. $3^2 = 3 \times 3$ read "3 squared"

2. $2^3 = 2 \times 2 \times 2$ read "2 cubed"

3. $5^4 = 5 \times 5 \times 5 \times 5$ read "5 to the fourth power"

If the exponent is 1, it is usually understood and not written; thus, $a^1 = a$.

Since

$$a^2 = a \times a \qquad \text{and} \qquad a^3 = a \times a \times a,$$

then

$$a^2 \times a^3 = (a \times a)(a \times a \times a) = a^5.$$

There are three rules for exponents. In general, if k and m are any numbers, and a is any number not equal to zero:

Rule 1: $a^k \times a^m = a^{k+m}$

Rule 2: $a^m \times b^m = (ab)^m$

Rule 3: $(a^k)^n = a^{kn}$

Examples

1. Rule 1: $2^2 \times 2^3 = 4 \times 8 = 32$

   and

   $2^2 \times 2^3 = 2^5 = 32$

2. Rule 2: $3^2 \times 4^2 = 9 \times 16 = 144$

   and

   $3^2 \times 4^2 = (3 \times 4)^2 = 12^2 = 144$

3. Rule 3: $(3^2)^3 = 9^3 = 729$

   and

   $(3^2)^3 = 3^6 = 729$

Roots

The definition of roots is based on exponents. If $a^n = c$, where a is the base and n the exponent, a is called the nth *root* of c. This is written $a = \sqrt[n]{c}$. The symbol $\sqrt{}$ is called a *radical sign*. Since $5^4 = 625$, $\sqrt[4]{625} = 5$ and 5 is the fourth root of 625. The most frequently used roots are the second (called the **square**) root and the third (called the **cube**) root. The square root is written $\sqrt{}$ and the cube root is written $\sqrt[3]{}$.

Square Roots

If c is a positive number, there are two values, one negative and one positive, which when multiplied together will produce c.

Example

$+4 \times (+4) = 16$ and $-4 \times (-4) = 16$

The positive square root of a positive number c is called the *principal* square root of c (briefly, the *square root* of c) and is denoted by $\sqrt{c}$:

$\sqrt{144} = 12$

If $c = 0$, there is only one square root, 0. If c is a negative number, there is no real number that is the square root of c:

$\sqrt{-4}$ is not a real number

Cube Roots

Both positive and negative numbers have real cube roots. The cube root of 0 is 0. The cube root of a positive number is positive; that of a negative number is negative.

Example

$2 \times 2 \times 2 = 8$

Therefore $\sqrt[3]{8} = 2$.

$-3 \times (-3) \times (-3) = -27$

Therefore $\sqrt[3]{-27} = -3$.

Each number has only one real cube root.

Expanded Form

We previously have seen how to write whole numbers in expanded form. Recall, for example, that the number 1,987 can be written as

$$1,987 = 1(1,000) + 9(100) + 8(10) + 7$$

Thus, 1,987 represents a number containing 7 "ones," 8 "tens," 9 "hundreds," and 1 "thousand." Using exponential notation, 1,987 can be written somewhat more compactly as

$$1,987 = 1(10^3) + 9(10^2) + 8(10^1) + 7$$

Examples

1. Write the number 50,127 in expanded form using exponential notation.

$$50,127 = 5(10^4) + 0(10^3) + 1(10^2) + 2(10^1) + 7$$

2. What number is represented by the expanded form $7(10^5) + 3(10^3) + 2(10^2) + 5(10^1) + 4$?

Note that there is no term corresponding to 10^4. Thus, the answer is 703,254.

Simplification of Square Roots

Certain square roots can be written in a "simplified" form. Just as all fractions should be simplified if possible, all square roots should also be simplified if possible. To simplify a square root means to remove any perfect square factors from under the square root sign.

The simplification of square roots is based on the *Product Rule for Square Roots:*

$$\sqrt{a \times b} = \sqrt{a} \times \sqrt{b}.$$

To illustrate the technique, let us simplify $\sqrt{12}$. Begin by writing 12 as 4×3, thus transforming the number under the square root sign into a product containing the perfect square factor 4.

$$\sqrt{12} = \sqrt{4 \times 3}$$

Then, using the Product Rule, write the square root of the product as the product of the square root.

$$\sqrt{12} = \sqrt{4 \times 3} = \sqrt{4} \times \sqrt{3}$$

Finally, compute $\sqrt{4}$ to obtain the simplified form.

$$\sqrt{12} = \sqrt{4 \times 3} = \sqrt{4} \times \sqrt{3} = 2\sqrt{3}$$

Examples

1. Simplify $\sqrt{98}$.

$$\sqrt{98} = \sqrt{2 \times 49}$$
$$= \sqrt{2} \times \sqrt{49} \quad \text{where 49 is a square number}$$
$$= \sqrt{2} \times 7$$

Therefore, $\sqrt{98} = 7\sqrt{2}$ and the process terminates because there is no whole number whose square is 2. $7\sqrt{2}$ is called a radical expression or simply a *radical*.

2. Which is greater, $\left(\sqrt{96}\right)^2$ or $\sqrt{2^{14}}$?

$$\left(\sqrt{96}\right)^2 = \sqrt{96} \times \sqrt{96} = \sqrt{96 \times 96} = 96$$

$$\sqrt{2^{14}} = 2^7 = 128 \text{ because } 2^{14} = 2^7 \times 2^7 \text{ by Rule 1}$$

or because $\sqrt{2^{14}} = \left(2^{14}\right)^{\frac{1}{2}} = 2^7$ by Rule 3.

Since $128 > 96$, $\sqrt{2^{14}} > \left(\sqrt{96}\right)^2$.

3. Which is greater, $2\sqrt{75}$ or $6\sqrt{12}$?

These numbers can be compared if the same number appears under the radical sign. Then the greater number is the one with the greater number in front of the radical sign.

$$\sqrt{75} = \sqrt{25 \times 3} = \sqrt{25} \times \sqrt{3} = 5\sqrt{3}$$

Therefore:

$$2\sqrt{75} = 2\left(5\sqrt{3}\right) = 10\sqrt{3}$$
$$\sqrt{12} = \sqrt{4 \times 3} = \sqrt{4} \times \sqrt{3} = 2\sqrt{3}$$

Therefore:

$$6\sqrt{12} = 6\left(2\sqrt{3}\right) = 12\sqrt{3}$$

Since $12\sqrt{3} > 10\sqrt{3}$, $6\sqrt{12} > 2\sqrt{75}$

Radicals can be added and subtracted only if they have the same number under the radical sign. Otherwise, they must be simplified to expressions having the same number under the radical sign.

4. Add $2\sqrt{18} + 4\sqrt{8} - \sqrt{2}$.

$$\sqrt{18} = \sqrt{9 \times 2} = \sqrt{9} \times \sqrt{2} = 3\sqrt{2}$$

Therefore:

$$2\sqrt{18} = 2\left(3\sqrt{2}\right) = 6\sqrt{2}$$

and

$$\sqrt{8} = \sqrt{4 \times 2} = \sqrt{4} \times \sqrt{2} = 2\sqrt{2}$$

Therefore:

$$4\sqrt{8} = 4\left(2\sqrt{2}\right) = 8\sqrt{2}$$

giving

$$2\sqrt{18} + 4\sqrt{8} - \sqrt{2} = 6\sqrt{2} + 8\sqrt{2} - \sqrt{2} = 13\sqrt{2}$$

Radicals are multiplied using the rule that

$$\sqrt[k]{a \times b} = \sqrt[k]{a} \times \sqrt[k]{b}$$

5. $\sqrt{2}\left(\sqrt{2} - 5\sqrt{3}\right) = \sqrt{4} - 5\sqrt{6} = 2 - 5\sqrt{6}$

A quotient rule for radicals similar to the Product Rule is:

$$\sqrt[k]{\frac{a}{b}} = \frac{\sqrt[k]{a}}{\sqrt[k]{b}}$$

6. $\sqrt{\dfrac{9}{4}} = \dfrac{\sqrt{9}}{\sqrt{4}} = \dfrac{3}{2}$

Exponents, Powers, and Roots Problems

1. Simplify $\sqrt{162}$.

2. Find the sum of $\sqrt{75}$ and $\sqrt{12}$.

3. Combine $\sqrt{80} + \sqrt{45} - \sqrt{20}$.

4. Simplify $\sqrt{5}\left(2\sqrt{2} - 3\sqrt{5}\right)$.

5. Divide and simplify $\dfrac{15\sqrt{96}}{5\sqrt{2}}$.

6. Calculate $5^2 \times 2^3$.

7. Simplify $\left(\sqrt{15}\right)^2$.

8. Simplify $\sqrt{216}$.

9. Combine $5\sqrt{18} + 7\sqrt{27}$.

10. Simplify $\sqrt{6}\,\sqrt{3}\,\sqrt{2}$.

Solutions

1. $\sqrt{162} = \sqrt{2 \times 81} = \sqrt{2} \times \sqrt{81} = 9\sqrt{2}$

2. $\sqrt{75} + \sqrt{12} = 5\sqrt{3} + 2\sqrt{3} = 7\sqrt{3}$

3. $\sqrt{80} + \sqrt{45} - \sqrt{20} = 4\sqrt{5} + 3\sqrt{5} - 2\sqrt{5} = 5\sqrt{5}$

4. $\sqrt{5}\left(2\sqrt{2} - 3\sqrt{5}\right) = 2\sqrt{10} - 3\sqrt{25}$

    $\qquad\qquad\qquad = 2\sqrt{10} - 3(5)$

    $\qquad\qquad\qquad = 2\sqrt{10} - 15$

5. $\dfrac{15\sqrt{96}}{5\sqrt{2}} = \dfrac{15(4\sqrt{6})}{5\sqrt{2}} = \dfrac{60\sqrt{6}}{5\sqrt{2}} = 12\sqrt{3}$

6. $5^2 \times 2^3 = 25 \times 8 = 200$

7. $\left(\sqrt{15}\right)^2 = 15$, since squares and roots are inverse operations.

8. $\sqrt{216} = \sqrt{2 \times 2 \times 2 \times 3 \times 3 \times 3}$

$\quad\quad = \sqrt{4 \times 9 \times 6}$

$\quad\quad = \sqrt{4}\sqrt{9}\sqrt{6}$

$\quad\quad = 2 \times 3\sqrt{6}$

$\quad\quad = 6\sqrt{6}$

9. $5\sqrt{18} + 7\sqrt{27} = 5\sqrt{9 \times 2} + 7\sqrt{9 \times 3}$

$\quad\quad\quad\quad\quad = 5\sqrt{9}\sqrt{2} + 7\sqrt{9}\sqrt{3}$

$\quad\quad\quad\quad\quad = 15\sqrt{2} + 21\sqrt{3}$

10. $\sqrt{6}\sqrt{3}\sqrt{2} = \sqrt{6 \times 3 \times 2} = \sqrt{36} = 6$

SYSTEMS OF MEASUREMENTS

The English System

When taking the SSAT/ISEE, you will need to be able to compute using both the English system of measurement and the metric system. It may also be necessary for you to convert measurements from one system to the other, but in such cases, you will be given the appropriate conversion factors.

Make sure you have the following relationships within the English system memorized:

Conversion Factors for Length

36 inches = 3 feet = 1 yard

12 inches = 1 foot

5,280 feet = 1,760 yards = 1 mile

Conversion Factors for Volume

2 pints = 1 quart

16 fluid ounces = 1 pint

8 pints = 4 quarts = 1 gallon

Conversion Factors for Weight

16 ounces = 1 pound

2,000 pounds = 1 ton

These conversion factors enable you to change units within the English system.

Examples

1. How many feet are in 5 miles?

    5 miles $\times$ (5,280 feet/1 mile) = 26,400 feet

    Notice how the unit of "miles" divides out of the numerator and denominator.

2. How many ounces are in 2 tons?

    2 tons $\times$ (2,000 pounds/1 ton) $\times$ (16 ounces/1 pound) = 64,000 ounces

    Notice how the units of "tons" and "pounds" divide out of the numerator and denominator.

The Metric System

In the metric system, distance or length is measured in meters. Similarly, volume is measured in liters, and mass is measured in grams. The prefixes below are appended to the beginning of these basic units to indicate other units of measure with sizes equal to each basic unit multiplied or divided by powers of 10.

$$giga = 10^9$$
$$mega = 10^6$$
$$kilo = 10^3$$
$$hecto = 10^2$$
$$deka = 10^1$$
$$deci = 10^{-1}$$
$$centi = 10^{-2}$$
$$milli = 10^{-3}$$
$$micro = 10^{-6}$$
$$nano = 10^{-9}$$
$$pico = 10^{-12}$$

From the preceding table, we can see, for example, that a kilometer is 1,000 times as long as a meter, 100,000 times as long as a centimeter, and 1,000,000 times as a long as a millimeter. Similarly, a centigram is $\frac{1}{100}$ the size of a gram.

Conversions among metric units can be made quickly by moving decimal points.

Examples

1. Convert 9.43 kilometers to meters.

    Since meters are smaller than kilometers, our answer will be greater than 9.43. There are 1,000 meters in a kilometer, so we move the decimal point three places to the right. 9.43 kilometers are equal to 9,430 meters.

2. Convert 512 grams to kilograms.

    Since kilograms are more massive than grams, our answer must be less than 512. There are 10^{-3} kilograms in a gram, so we move the decimal point three places to the left. 512 grams are equal to .512 kilograms.

Conversions between the English and the Metric Systems

Conversions between the English and metric systems are accomplished in the same way as conversions within the English system. Recall that any problem that requires you to make such a conversion will include the necessary conversion factors.

Examples

1. If 1 meter is equivalent to 1.09 yards, how many yards are in 10 meters?

    10 meters $\times$ (1.09 yards/1 meter) = 10.9 yards

2. If 1 yard is equivalent to .914 meters, how many meters are there in 24 yards?

    24 yards $\times$ (.914 meters/1 yard) = 21.936 meters

Systems of Measurement Problems

1. Express 38 meters in millimeters.

2. Express 871 millimeters in centimeters.

3. Which measurement is greater, 8,000 millimeters or 7 meters?

4. Arrange the following from least to greatest: 6,700 meters, 672,000 centimeters, and 6.6 kilometers.

5. Express 49 milligrams in centigrams.

6. 4.6 liters are how many milliliters?

7. A package weighing 32.5 kilograms is shipped to the United States. What is its weight in pounds? There are 2.2 pounds in a kilogram.

8. A line drawn on a blueprint measures 1.5 yards. What is its length in meters? There are .914 meters in a yard.

9. If the distance between two exits on a highway is 40 kilometers, what is the distance in miles? There are .62 miles in a kilometer.

10. A particular brand of bottled water is available in two different bottle sizes—a 2.25 quart bottle and a 2.1 liter bottle. Which bottle contains more water? There are 1.06 quarts in a liter.

Solutions

1. Since meters are larger than millimeters, our answer will be greater than 38. There are 1,000 millimeters in a meter, so we move the decimal point three places to the right. 38 meters are equal to 38,000 millimeters.

2. Since millimeters are smaller than centimeters, our answer will be less than 871. There are 10 millimeters in a centimeter, so we move the decimal point one place to the left. 871 millimeters are equal to 87.1 centimeters.

3. In order to answer this question, we must express both measures in the same units. Since, for example, 8,000 millimeters are equal to 8 meters, we can see that 8,000 millimeters are greater than 7 meters.

4. Let's start by expressing all measurements in meters.

    672,000 centimeters = 6,720 meters

    6.6 kilometers = 6,600 meters

    6,700 meters = 6,700 meters

    Thus, from least to greatest, we have 6.6 kilometers, 6,700 meters, and 672,000 centimeters.

5. Since there are 10 milligrams in a centigram, 49 milligrams are equal to 4.9 centigrams.

6. Since there are 1,000 milliliters in a liter, there are 4,600 milliliters in 4.6 liters.

7. 32.5 kgs = 32.5 kgs × (2.2 lbs/1 kg) = 71.5 lbs

8. 1.5 yards = 1.5 yards × (.914 meters/1 yard) = 1.371 meters

9. 40 kilometers = 40 kilometers × (.62 miles/1 kilometer) = 24.8 miles

10. Express 2.1 liters as quarts.

    2.1 liters = 2.1 liters × (1.06 quarts/1 liter) = 2.226 quarts. Thus, the quart bottle holds more.

ALGEBRA

Algebra is a generalization of arithmetic. It provides methods for solving problems that cannot be done by arithmetic alone or that can be done by arithmetic only after long computations. Algebra provides a shorthand way of simplifying long verbal statements to brief formulas, expressions, or equations. After the verbal statements have been simplified, the resulting algebraic expressions can be simplified. Suppose that a room is 12 feet wide and 20 feet long. Its perimeter (measurement around the outside) can be expressed as:

$$12 + 20 + 12 + 20 \text{ or } 2(12 + 20)$$

If the width of the room remains 12 feet but the letter l is used to symbolize length, the perimeter is:

$$12 + l + 12 + l \text{ or } 2(12 + l)$$

Further, if w is used for width, the perimeter of *any* rectangular room can be written as $2(w + l)$. This same room has an area of 12 feet by 20 feet, or 12×20. If l is substituted for 20, any room of width 12 has area equal to $12l$. If w is substituted for the number 12, the area of any rectangular room is given by wl or lw. Expressions such as wl and $2(w + l)$ are called *algebraic expressions*. An *equation* is a statement that two algebraic expressions are equal. A *formula* is a special type of equation.

EVALUATING FORMULAS

If we are given an expression and numerical values to be assigned to each letter, the expression can be evaluated.

Examples

1. Evaluate $2x + 3y - 7$ if $x = 2$ and $y = -4$.

    Substitute given values.

    $$2(2) + 3(-4) - 7 = ?$$

    Multiply numbers using rules for signed numbers.

    $$4 + -12 - 7 = ?$$

    Collect numbers.

    $$4 - 19 = -15$$

    We have already evaluated formulas in arithmetic when solving percent, discount, and interest problems.

2. Evaluate each of the following expressions if $a = 3$, b $= -2$, and $c = 0$.

    a. $-a^2$

    b. $3b - 4b^2$

    c. $ab + 4c$

Solutions

    a. $-a^2 = -(3)^2 = -(9) = -9$

    b. $3b - 4b^2 = 3(-2) - 4(-2)^2 = -6 - 4\,(4)$
          $= -6 - 16 = -22$

    c. $ab + 4c = (3)\,(-2) + 4(0) = -6 + 0 = -6$

3. If $x = 1$ and $y = -2$, find the value of $-x^2y^2$.

$$-x^2y^2 = -\,(1)^2\,(-2)^2 = -(1)\,(4) = -(4) = -4$$

4. The formula for temperature conversion is:

$$F = \frac{9}{5}\,C + 32$$

where C stands for the temperature in degrees Celsius and F for degrees Fahrenheit. Find the Fahrenheit temperature that is equivalent to 20°C.

$$F = \frac{9}{5}\,(20°C) + 32 = 36 + 32 = 68°F$$

5. The formula for the area of a triangle is $A = \dfrac{bh}{2}$. Find A if $b = 12$ and $h = 7$.

$$A = \frac{bh}{2} = \frac{12 \times 7}{2} = 42$$

ALGEBRAIC EXPRESSIONS

Formulation

A more difficult problem than evaluating an expression or formula is translating from a verbal expression to an algebraic one:

Verbal	Algebraic
Thirteen more than x	$x + 13$
Six less than twice x	$2x - 6$
The square of the sum of x and 5	$(x + 5)^2$
The sum of the square of x and the square of 5	$x^2 + 5^2$
The distance traveled by a car going 50 miles an hour for x hours	$50x$
The average of 70, 80, 85, and x	$\dfrac{70 + 80 + 85 + x}{4}$

Simplification

After algebraic expressions have been formulated, they can usually be simplified by means of the laws of exponents and the common operations of addition, subtraction, multiplication, and division. These techniques will be described in the next section. Algebraic expressions and equations frequently contain parentheses, which are removed in the process of simplifying. If an expression contains more than one set of parentheses, remove the inner set first and then the outer set. Brackets, [ ], which are often used instead of parentheses, are treated the same way. Parentheses are used to indicate multiplication. Thus, $3(x + y)$ means that 3 is to be multiplied by the sum of x and y. The *distributive law* is used to accomplish this:

$$a(b + c) = ab + ac$$

The expression in front of the parentheses is multiplied by each term inside. Rules for signed numbers apply.

Example

Simplify $3[4(2 - 8) - 5(4 + 2)]$.

This can be done in two ways.

Method 1

Combine the numbers inside the parentheses first:

$$
\begin{aligned}
3[4(2 - 8) - 5(4 + 2)] &= 3[4(-6) - 5(6)] \\
&= 3[-24 - 30] \\
&= 3[-54] = -162
\end{aligned}
$$

Method 2

Use the distributive law:

$$3[4(2 - 8) - 5(4 + 2)] = 3[8 - 32 - 20 - 10]$$
$$= 3[8 - 62]$$
$$= 3[-54] = -162$$

If there is a (+) before the parentheses, the signs of the terms inside the parentheses remain the same when the parentheses are removed. If there is a (−) before the parentheses, the sign of each term inside the parentheses changes when the parentheses are removed.

Once parentheses have been removed, the order of operations is multiplication and division from left to right, then addition and subtraction from left to right.

Example

$$(-15 + 17) \times 3 - [(4 \times 9) \div 6] = ?$$

Work inside the parentheses first: $(2) \times 3 - [36 \div 6] = ?$

Then work inside the brackets: $2 \times 3 - [6] = ?$

Multiply first, then subtract, proceeding from left to right: $6 - 6 = 0$

The placement of parentheses and brackets is important. Using the same numbers as above with the parentheses and brackets placed in different positions can give many different answers.

Example

$$-15 + [(17 \times 3) - (4 \times 9)] \div 6 = ?$$

Work inside the parentheses first:

$$-15 + [(51) - (36)] \div 6 = ?$$

Then work inside the brackets:

$$-15 + [15] \div 6 = ?$$

Since there are no more parentheses or brackets, proceed from left to right, dividing before adding:

$$-15 + 2\frac{1}{2} = -12\frac{1}{2}$$

Operations

When letter symbols and numbers are combined with the operations of arithmetic ($+$, $-$, $\times$, $\div$) and with certain other mathematical operations, we have an *algebraic expression*. Algebraic expressions are made up of several parts connected by an addition or a subtraction sign; each part is called a *term*. Terms with the same variable part are called *like terms*. Since algebraic expressions represent numbers, they can be added, subtracted, multiplied, and divided.

When we defined the commutative law of addition in arithmetic by writing $a + b = b + a$, we meant that a and b could represent any number. The expression $a + b = b + a$ is an *identity* because it is true for all numbers. The expression $n + 5 = 14$ is not an identity because it is not true for all numbers; it becomes true only when the number 9 is substituted for n. Letters used to represent numbers are called *variables*. If a number stands alone (the 5 or 14 in $n + 5 = 14$), it is called a *constant* because its value is constant or unchanging. If a number appears in front of a variable, it is called a *coefficient*. Because the letter x is frequently used to represent a variable, or *unknown*, the times sign $\times$, which can be confused with it in handwriting, is rarely used to express multiplication in algebra. Other expressions used for multiplication are a dot, parentheses, or simply writing a number and letter together:

$5 \cdot 4$ or $5(4)$ or $5a$

Of course, 54 still means fifty-four.

Addition and Subtraction

Only like terms can be combined. Add or subtract the coefficients of like terms, using the rules for signed numbers.

Example 1

1. Add $x + 2y - 2x + 3y$.

   $x - 2x + 2y + 3y = -x + 5y$

2. Perform the subtraction:

   $$-30a - 15b + 4c$$
   $$-(-5a + 3b - c + d)$$

   Change the sign of each term in the subtrahend and then add, using the rules for signed numbers:

   $$\begin{array}{r} -30a - 15b + 4c \\ 5a - 3b + c - d \\ \hline -25a - 18b + 5c - d \end{array}$$

3. Perform the following subtraction:

$$(b^2 + 6bk - 7k^2) - (3b^2 + 6bk - 10k^2)$$

Once again, change the sign of each term in the subtrahend and then add.

$$(b^2 + 6bk - 7k^2) - (3b^2 + 6bk - 10k^2)$$
$$= (b^2 + 6bk - 7k^2) + (3b^2 - 6bk + 10k^2)$$
$$= -2b^2 + 3k^2$$

Multiplication

Multiplication is accomplished by using the *distributive property*. If the multiplier has only one term, then

$$a(b + c) = ab + bc$$

Example

$$9x(5m + 9q) = (9x)(5m) + (9x)(9q)$$
$$= 45mx + 81qx$$

When the multiplier contains more than one term and you are multiplying two expressions, multiply each term of the first expression by each term of the second and then add like terms. Follow the rules for signed numbers and exponents at all times.

Examples

1. $(2x - 1)(x + 6)$

   $$= 2x(x + 6) - 1(x + 6)$$
   $$= 2x^2 + 12x - x - 6$$
   $$= 2x^2 + 11x - 6$$

2. $(3x + 8)(4x^2 + 2x + 1)$

   $$= 3x(4x^2 + 2x + 1) + 8(4x^2 + 2x + 1)$$
   $$= 12x^3 + 6x^2 + 3x + 32x^2 + 16x + 8$$
   $$= 12x^3 + 38x^2 + 19x + 8$$

If more than two expressions are to be multiplied, multiply the first two, then multiply the product by the third factor, and so on, until all factors have been used.

Algebraic expressions can be multiplied by themselves (squared) or raised to any power.

Examples

1. $(a + b)^2 = (a + b)(a + b)$

$$= a(a + b) + b(a + b)$$

$$= a^2 + ab + ba + b^2$$

$$= a^2 + 2ab + b^2$$

since $ab = ba$ by the commutative law.

2. $(a + b)(a - b) = a(a - b) + b(a - b)$

$$= a^2 - ab + ba - b^2$$

$$= a^2 - b^2$$

Factoring

When two or more algebraic expressions are multiplied, each is called a factor and the result is the *product*. The reverse process of finding the factors when given the product is called *factoring*. A product can often be factored in more than one way. Factoring is useful in multiplication, division, and solving equations.

One way to factor an expression is to remove any single-term factor that is common to each of the terms and write it outside the parentheses. It is the distributive law that permits this.

Examples

1. $3x + 12 = 3(x + 4)$

The result can be checked by multiplication.

2. $3x^3 + 6x^2 + 9x = 3x(x^2 + 2x + 3)$

The result can be checked by multiplication.

Expressions containing squares can sometimes be factored into expressions containing variables raised to the first power only, called *linear factors*. We have seen that

$$(a + b)(a - b) = a^2 - b^2$$

Therefore, if we have an expression in the form of a difference of two squares, it can be factored as:

$$a^2 - b^2 = (a + b)(a - b)$$

Examples

1. Factor $x^2 - 16$.

$$x^2 - 16 = (x)^2 - (4)^2 = (x - 4)(x + 4)$$

2. Factor $4x^2 - 9$.

$$4x^2 - 9 = (2x)^2 - (3)^2 = (2x + 3)(2x - 3)$$

Again, the result can be checked by multiplication.

A third type of expression that can be factored is one containing three terms, such as $x^2 + 5x + 6$. Since

$$\begin{aligned}(x + a)(x + b) &= x(x + b) + a(x + b)\\ &= x^2 + xb + ax + ab\\ &= x^2 + (a + b)x + ab\end{aligned}$$

An expression in the form $x^2 + (a + b)x + ab$ can be factored into two factors of the form $(x + a)$ and $(x + b)$. We must find two numbers whose product is the constant in the given expression and whose sum is the coefficient of the term containing x.

Examples

1. Find factors of $x^2 + 5x + 6$.

First find two numbers that, when multiplied, have $+6$ as a product. Possibilities are 2 and 3, -2 and -3, 1 and 6, and -1 and -6. From these select the one pair whose sum is 5. The pair 2 and 3 is the only possible selection, and so:

$$x^2 + 5x + 6 = (x + 2)(x + 3) \quad \text{written in either order}$$

2. Factor $x^2 - 5x - 6$.

Possible factors of -6 are -1 and 6, 1 and -6, 2 and -3, and -2 and 3. We must select the pair whose sum is -5. The only pair whose sum is -5 is $+1$ and -6, and so:

$$x^2 - 5x - 6 = (x + 1)(x - 6)$$

In factoring expressions of this type, notice that if the last sign is positive, both a and b have the same sign and it is the same as the sign of the middle term. If the last sign is negative, the numbers have opposite signs.

Many expressions cannot be factored.

3. Factor $2x^3 - 8x^2 + 8x$.

In expressions of this type, begin by factoring out the greatest common monomial factor, then try to factor the resulting trinomial.

$$\begin{aligned}2x^3 - 8x^2 + 8x &= 2x(x^2 - 4x + 4)\\ &= 2x(x - 2)(x - 2)\\ &= 2x(x - 2)^2\end{aligned}$$

Division

Method 1

$$\frac{36mx^2}{9m^2x} = 4m^1x^2m^{-2}x^{-1}$$

$$= 4m^{-1}x^1 = \frac{4x}{m}$$

Method 2

Division of common factors:

$$\frac{36mx^2}{9m^2x} = \frac{\overset{4}{\cancel{36}mx x}}{\cancel{9}mxm} = \frac{4x}{m}$$

This is acceptable because

$$\frac{ac}{bc} = \frac{a}{b}\left(\frac{c}{c}\right) \text{ and } \frac{c}{c} = 1$$

so that $\frac{ac}{bc} = \frac{a}{b}$.

Examples

1. If the divisor contains only one term and the dividend is a sum, divide each term in the dividend by the divisor and simplify as you did in Method 2.

$$\frac{9x^3 + 3x^2 + 6x}{3x} = \frac{\overset{3x^2}{\cancel{9x^3}}}{\cancel{3x}} + \frac{\overset{x}{\cancel{3x^2}}}{\cancel{3x}} + \frac{\overset{2}{\cancel{6x}}}{\cancel{3x}}$$

$$= 3x^2 + x + 2$$

This method cannot be followed if there are two or more terms in the denominator since:

$$\frac{a}{b + c} \neq \frac{a}{b} + \frac{a}{c}$$

In this case, write the example as a fraction. Factor the numerator and denominator if possible. Then use laws of exponents or divide common factors.

2. Divide $x^3 - 9x$ by $x^3 + 6x^2 + 9x$.

    Write as:

    $$\frac{x^3 - 9x}{x^3 + 6x^2 + 9x}$$

    Both numerator and denominator can be factored to give:

    $$\frac{x(x^2 - 9)}{x(x^2 + 6x + 9)} = \frac{\cancel{(x+3)}(x - 3)}{\cancel{(x+3)}(x + 3)} = \frac{x - 3}{x + 3}$$

Algebra Problems

1. Simplify: $4[2(3-7) - 4(2+6)]$

2. Subtract: $(-25x + 4y - 12z) - (4x - 8y - 13z)$

3. Multiply: $(5x + 2)(3x^2 - 2x + 1)$

4. Factor completely: $2x^3 + 8x^2 - 90x$

5. Factor completely: $32x^2 - 98$

6. Divide: $\dfrac{x^2 + 2x - 8}{x^2 - x - 20}$

7. Simplify: $6x - 2(3 - 3x)$

8. Add: $(a - b - c) + (a - b - c) - (a - b - c)$

9. Multiply: $(9a - 12)(9a + 12)$

10. Factor completely: $4a^2b + 12ab - 72b$

Solutions

1. $4[2(3-7) - 4(2+6)] = 4[2(-4)-4(8)] = 4[-8 - 32]$
    $= 4(-40) = -160$

2. $(-25x + 4y - 12z) - (4x - 8y - 13z)$
    $= -25x + 4y - 12z - 4x + 8y + 13z$
    $= -29x + 12y + z$

3. $(5x + 2)(3x^2 - 2x + 1)$
    $= 5x(3x^2 - 2x + 1) + 2(3x^2 - 2x + 1)$
    $= 15x^3 - 10x^2 + 5x + 6x^2 - 4x + 2$
    $= 15x^3 - 4x^2 + x + 2$

4. $2x^3 + 8x^2 - 90x = 2x(x^2 + 4x - 45) = 2x(x + 9)(x - 5)$

5. $32x^2 - 98 = 2(16x^2 - 49) = 2(4x - 7)(4x + 7)$

6. $\dfrac{x^2 + 2x - 8}{x^2 - x - 20} = \dfrac{(x + 4)(x - 2)}{(x - 5)(x + 4)}$

$$= \dfrac{\overset{1}{\cancel{(x + 4)}}(x - 2)}{(x - 5)\underset{1}{\cancel{(x + 4)}}} = \dfrac{x - 2}{x - 5}$$

7. $6x - 2(3 - 3x) = 6x - 6 + 6x = 12x - 6$

8. $(a - b - c) + (a - b - c) - (a - b - c)$
$= a - b - c + a - b - c - a + b + c$
$= a - b - c$

9. $(9a - 12)(9a + 12) = 81a^2 + 108a - 108a - 144 = 81a^2 - 144$

10. $4a^2b + 12ab - 72b = 4b(a^2 + 3a - 18) = 4b(a + 6)(a - 3)$

Equations

Solving equations is one of the major objectives in algebra. If a variable x in an equation is replaced by a value or expression that makes the equation a true statement, the value or expression is called a *solution* of the equation. (Remember that an equation is a mathematical statement that one algebraic expression is equal to another.)

An equation may contain one or more variables. We begin with one variable. Certain rules apply to equations whether there are one or more variables. The following rules are applied to give equivalent equations that are simpler than the original:

Addition: If $s = t$, then $s + c = t + c$.

Subtraction: If $s + c = t + c$, then $s = t$.

Multiplication: If $s = t$, then $cs = ct$.

Division: If $cs = ct$ and $c \neq 0$, then $s = t$.

To solve for x in an equation in the form $ax = b$ with $a \neq 0$, divide each side of the equation by a:

$$\dfrac{ax}{a} = \dfrac{b}{a} \quad \text{yielding} \quad x = \dfrac{b}{a}$$

Then, $\dfrac{b}{a}$ is the solution to the equation.

Examples

1. Solve $x + 5 = 12$.

   Subtract 5 from both sides.

   $$\begin{array}{rr} x + 5 = & 12 \\ -5 & -5 \\ \hline x = & 7 \end{array}$$

2. Solve $4x = 8$.

   Write $\dfrac{4x}{4} = \dfrac{8}{4}$.

   $x = 2$

3. Solve $\dfrac{x}{4} = 9$.

   Write $4 \times \dfrac{x}{4} = 9 \times 4$.

   Thus, $x = 36$.

4. Solve $3x + 7 = 19$.

   Subtract 7 from both sides.

   $3x = 12$

   Divide each side by 3.

   $x = 4$

5. Solve $2x - (x - 4) = 5(x + 2)$ for x.

$$2x - (x - 4) = 5(x + 2)$$

$\quad 2x - x + 4 = 5x + 10 \quad$ Remove parentheses by distributive law.

$\qquad\quad x + 4 = 5x + 10 \quad$ Combine like terms.

$\qquad\qquad\; x = 5x + 6 \quad$ Subtract 4 from each side.

$\qquad\quad -4x = 6 \qquad\quad$ Subtract $5x$ from each side.

$\qquad\qquad\; x = \dfrac{6}{-4} \qquad$ Divide each side by -4.

$\qquad\qquad\quad = -\dfrac{3}{2} \qquad$ Simplify fraction to simplest form. Negative sign now applies to the entire fraction.

Check the solution for accuracy by substituting in the original equation:

$$2\left(-\dfrac{3}{2}\right) - \left(-\dfrac{3}{2} - 4\right) \overset{?}{=} 5\left(-\dfrac{3}{2} + 2\right)$$

$$-3 - \left(-\dfrac{11}{2}\right) \overset{?}{=} 5\left(\dfrac{1}{2}\right)$$

$$-3 + \dfrac{11}{2} \overset{?}{=} \dfrac{5}{2}$$

$$-\dfrac{6}{2} + \dfrac{11}{2} \overset{?}{=} \dfrac{5}{2} \quad \text{check}$$

Equations Problems

Solve the following equations for x:

1. $3x - 5 = 3 + 2x$

2. $3(2x - 2) = 12$

3. $4(x - 2) = 2x + 10$

4. $7 - 4(2x - 1) = 3 + 4(4 - x)$

5. $7x + 6 = 4x + 6$

6. $3(x - 2) - 4(x - 3) = 8$

7. $\dfrac{2x + 3}{5} - 10 = \dfrac{4 - 3x}{2}$

8. $3(2x + 1) + 2(3x + 1) = 17$

9. $(w + 6) - (5 - 2w) = -2$

10. $(x - 5)^2 = 4 + (x + 5)^2$

Solutions

1. $3x - 5 = 3 + 2x$

   $\underline{-2x \qquad\qquad -2x}$

   $x - 5 = 3$

   $\underline{+5 \quad +5}$

   $x = 8$

2. $3(2x - 2) = 12$

   $6x - 6 = 12$

   $6x = 18$

   $x = 3$

3. $4(x - 2) = 2x + 10$

   $4x - 8 = 2x + 10$

   $4x = 2x + 18$

   $2x = 18$

   $x = 9$

4. $7 - 4(2x - 1) = 3 + 4(4 - x)$

   $7 - 8x + 4 = 3 + 16 - 4x$

   $11 - 8x = 19 - 4x$

   $11 = 19 + 4x$

   $-8 = 4x$

   $x = -2$

5. $7x + 6 = 4x + 6$

$\qquad 7x = 4x$

$\qquad 3x = 0$

$\qquad x = 0.$

6. $3(x - 2) - 4(x - 3) = 8$

$\qquad 3x - 6 - 4x + 12 = 8$

$\qquad -x + 6 = 8$

$\qquad -x = 2$

$\qquad x = -2$

7. $\dfrac{2x + 3}{5} - 10 = \dfrac{4 - 3x}{2}$

$$\left(10 \times \dfrac{2x + 3}{5}\right) - (10 \times 10) = \left(\dfrac{4 - 3x}{2} \times 10\right)$$

$\qquad 2(2x + 3) - 100 = 5(4 - 3x)$

$\qquad 4x + 6 - 100 = 20 - 15x$

$\qquad 4x - 94 = 20 - 15x$

$\qquad 4x = 114 - 15x$

$\qquad 19x = 114$

$\qquad x = 6$

8. $3(2x + 1) + 2(3x + 1) = 17$

$\qquad 6x + 3 + 6x + 2 = 17$

$\qquad 12x + 5 = 17$

$\qquad 12x = 12$

$\qquad x = 1$

9. $(w + 6) - (5 - 2w) = -2$

$\qquad w + 6 - 5 + 2w = -2$

$\qquad 3w + 1 = -2$

$\qquad 3w = -3$

$\qquad w = -1$

10. $(x - 5)^2 = 4 + (x + 5)^2$

$\qquad x^2 - 10x + 25 = 4 + x^2 + 10x + 25$ Subtract x^2 from both sides and combine terms.

$\qquad -10x + 25 = 10x + 29$

$\qquad 20x = -4$

$\qquad x = \dfrac{-1}{5}$

Word Problems Involving One Unknown

In many cases, if you read a word problem carefully, assign a letter to the quantity to be found, and understand the relationships between known and unknown quantities, you can formulate an equation with one unknown.

Number Problems and Age Problems

These two kinds of problems are similar to each other.

Examples

1. One number is 3 times another, and their sum is 48. Find the two numbers.

   Let x = second number. Then the first is $3x$. Since their sum is 48,

   $$3x + x = 48$$
   $$4x = 48$$
   $$x = 12$$

   Therefore, the first number is $3x = 36$.

   $36 + 12 = 48$ check

2. Art is now three times as old as Ryan. Four years ago, Art was five times as old as Ryan was then. How old is Art now?

   Let R = Ryan's age

   Then $3R$ = Art's age

   Four years ago, Ryan's age was $R - 4$, and Art's age was $3R - 4$.

   Since at that time Art was five times as old as Ryan, we have:

   $$5(R - 4) = 3R - 4$$
   $$5R - 20 = 3R - 4$$
   $$2R = 16$$
   $$R = 8, 3R = 24$$

   Art is 24 years old now.

Distance Problems

The basic concept is:

Distance = rate · time

Examples

1. In a mileage test, a man drives a truck at a fixed rate of speed for 1 hour. Then he increases the speed by 20 miles per hour and drives at that rate for 2 hours. He then reduces that speed by 5 miles per hour and drives at that rate for 3 hours. If the distance traveled was 295 miles, what are the rates of speed over each part of the test?

    Let x be the first speed, $x + 20$ the second, and $x + (20 - 5) = x + 15$ the third. Because distance = rate · time, multiply these rates by the time and formulate the equation by separating the two equal expressions for distance by an equals sign:

$$1x + 2(x + 20) + 3(x + 15) = 295$$
$$x + 2x + 3x + 40 + 45 = 295$$
$$6x = 210$$
$$x = 35$$

The speeds are 35, 55, and 50 miles per hour.

2. Two trains leave the Newark station at the same time traveling in opposite directions. One travels at a rate of 60 mph, and the other travels at a rate of 50 mph. In how many hours will the trains be 880 miles apart?

    The two trains will be 880 miles apart when the sum of the distances that they both have traveled is 880 miles.

    Let r_1 = the rate of the first train; r_2 = the rate of the second train.

    Let t_1 = the time of the first train; t_2 = the time of the second train.

    Then, the distance the first train travels is $r_1 t_1$, and the distance the second train travels is $r_2 t_2$. Our equation will be $r_1 t_1 + r_2 t_2 = 880$. Since $r_1 = 60$, $r_2 = 50$, and $t_1 = t_2$, we can rewrite the equation as:

$$60t + 50t = 880$$
$$110t = 880$$
$$t = 8$$

It will take 8 hours for the trains to get 880 miles apart.

Consecutive Number Problems

This type usually involves only one unknown. Two numbers are consecutive if one is the successor of the other. Three consecutive numbers are of the form x, $x + 1$, and $x + 2$. Since an even number is divisible by 2, consecutive even numbers are of the form $2x$, $2x + 2$, and $2x + 4$. An odd number is of the form $2x + 1$.

Examples

1. Find three consecutive whole numbers whose sum is 75.

    Let the first number be x, the second $x + 1$, and the third $x + 2$. Then:

    $$x + (x + 1) + (x + 2) = 75$$
    $$3x + 3 = 75$$
    $$3x = 72$$
    $$x = 24$$

    The numbers whose sum is 75 are 24, 25, and 26. Many versions of this problem have no solution. For example, no three consecutive whole numbers have a sum of 74.

2. Find three consecutive even integers whose sum is 48.

    We can express three consecutive even integers as x, $x + 2$, and $x + 4$. Thus, we have:

    $$x + (x + 2) + (x + 4) = 48$$
    $$3x + 6 = 48$$
    $$3x = 42$$
    $$x = 14$$

    The integers are 14, 16, and 18.

Work Problems

These problems concern the speed with which work can be accomplished and the time necessary to perform a task if the size of the work force is changed.

Examples

1. If Joe can type a chapter alone in 6 days and Ann can type the same chapter in 8 days, how long will it take them to type the chapter if they both work on it?

We let x = number of days required if they work together and then put our information into tabular form:

	Joe	Ann	Together
Days to type chapter	6	8	x
Part typed in 1 day	$\frac{1}{6}$	$\frac{1}{8}$	$\frac{1}{x}$

Since the part done by Joe in 1 day plus the part done by Ann in 1 day equals the part done by both in 1 day, we have:

$$\frac{1}{6} + \frac{1}{8} = \frac{1}{x}$$

Next we multiply each member by $48x$ to clear the fractions, giving:

$$8x + 6x = 48$$
$$14x = 48$$
$$x = 3\frac{3}{7} \text{ days}$$

2. Working alone, one pipe can fill a pool in 8 hours, a second pipe can fill the pool in 12 hours, and a third can fill it in 24 hours. How long would it take all three pipes, working at the same time, to fill the pool?

Using the same logic as in the previous problem, we obtain the equation:

$$\frac{1}{8} + \frac{1}{12} + \frac{1}{24} = \frac{1}{x}$$

To clear the fractions, we multiply each side by $24x$, giving:

$$3x + 2x + x = 24$$
$$6x = 24$$
$$x = 4$$

It would take the pipes 4 hours to fill the pool.

Word Problems with One Unknown

1. If 18 is subtracted from six times a certain number, the result is 96. Find the number.

2. A 63-foot rope is cut into two pieces. If one piece is twice as long as the other, how long is each piece?

3. Peter is now three times as old as Jillian. In six years, he will be twice as old as she will be then. How old is Peter now?

4. Lauren can clean the kitchen in 30 minutes. It takes Kathleen 20 minutes to complete the same job. How long would it take to clean the kitchen if they both worked together?

5. A train travels 120 miles at an average rate of 40 mph, and it returns along the same route at an average rate of 60 mph. What is the average rate of speed for the entire trip?

6. The sum of two consecutive odd integers is 68. Find the integers.

7. On election day, the winning candidate received 100 votes more than his opponent. If there were 8,574 votes cast in total, how many votes did the winning candidate get?

8. Ten less than four times a number is equal to the difference between the number and 1. What is the number?

9. Tony is now three years older than Karen. If seven years from now the sum of their ages is 79, how old is Karen now?

10. A freight train and a passenger train leave the same station at noon and travel in opposite directions. If the freight train travels at 52 mph and the passenger train travels at 84 mph, at what time are they 680 miles apart?

Solutions

1. Let x = the number.

   Then, $6x - 18 = 96$

   $$6x = 114$$
   $$x = 19$$

   The number is 19.

2. Let x = the length of the short piece.

   Then, $2x$ = the length of the longer piece.

   And $x + 2x = 63$

   $$3x = 63$$
   $$x = 21$$
   $$2x = 42$$

   The pieces are 21 feet and 42 feet.

3. Let J = Jillian's age now;

$3J$ = Peter's age now;

$J + 6$ = Jillian's age in 6 years;

$3J + 6$ = Peter's age in 6 years.

Then,

$3J + 6 = 2 (J + 6)$

$3J + 6 = 2J + 12$

$3J = 2J + 6$

$J = 6$

$3J = 18$

Peter is currently 18 years old.

4. Let x = the number of minutes to do the job working together.

Lauren does $\dfrac{x}{30}$ of the job.

Kathleen does $\dfrac{x}{20}$ of the job.

$\dfrac{x}{30} + \dfrac{x}{20} = 1$ (Multiply by 60)

$2x + 3x = 60$

$5x = 60$

$x = 12$

It would take 12 minutes to do the job together.

5. The train takes $\dfrac{120}{40} = 3$ hours out, and the train takes $\dfrac{120}{60} = 2$ hours back. The total trip takes 5 hours. The total distance traveled is 240 miles. Then,

$$\text{Rate} = \frac{\text{Distance}}{\text{Time}} = \frac{240}{5} = 48$$

The average rate is 48 mph.

6. Let x = the first odd integer.

Then, $x + 2$ = the second odd integer, and:

$$x + x + 2 = 68$$
$$2x + 2 = 68$$
$$2x = 66$$
$$x = 33$$
$$x + 2 = 35$$

The numbers are 33 and 35.

7. Let x = the number of votes the winning candidate got. Then, $x - 100$ = the number of votes the losing candidate got, and $x + x - 100 = 8,574$.

$$2x - 100 = 8,574$$
$$2x = 8,674$$
$$x = 4,337$$

The winning candidate got 4,337 votes.

8. Let x = the number. Then,

$$4x - 10 = x - 1$$
$$3x = 9$$
$$x = 3$$

The number is 3.

9. Let K = Karen's age.

Then, $K + 3$ = Tony's age.

In seven years, Karen's age will be $K + 7$, and Tony's will be $K + 10$.

Therefore, in 7 years, we will have:

$$(K + 7) + (K + 10) = 79$$
$$2K + 17 = 79$$
$$2K = 62$$
$$K = 31$$

Karen is 31 now.

10. Let t = the amount of time each train travels. Then, the distance the freight train travels is $52t$, and the distance the passenger train travels is $84t$. Thus,

$$52t + 84t = 680$$
$$136t = 680$$
$$t = 5$$

The trains each travel for 5 hours, so they will be 680 miles apart at 5 P.M.

Literal Equations

An equation may have other letters in it besides the variable (or variables). Such an equation is called a *literal equation*. An illustration is $x + b = a$, with x being the variable. The solution of such an equation will not be a specific number but will involve letter symbols. Literal equations are solved by exactly the same methods as those involving numbers, but we must know which of the letters in the equation is to be considered the variable. Then the other letters are treated as constants.

Examples

1. Solve $ax - 2bc = d$ for x.

$$ax = d + 2bc$$

$$x = \frac{d + 2bc}{a} \text{ if } a \neq 0$$

2. Solve $ay - by = a^2 - b^2$ for y.

$y(a - b) = a^2 - b^2$	Factor out common term.
$y(a - b) = (a + b)(a - b)$	Factor expression on right side.
$y = a + b$	Divide each side by $a - b$ if $a \neq b$.

3. Solve for S in this equation.

$$\frac{1}{R} = \frac{1}{S} + \frac{1}{T}$$

Multiply every term by RST, the LCD:

$$ST = RT + RS$$
$$ST - RS = RT$$
$$S(T - R) = RT$$
$$S = \frac{RT}{T - R} \qquad \text{If } T \neq R$$

Quadratic Equations

An equation containing the square of an unknown quantity is called a *quadratic* equation. One way of solving such an equation is by factoring. If the product of two expressions is zero, at least one of the expressions must be zero.

Examples

1. Solve $y^2 + 2y = 0$.

    $$y(y + 2) = 0 \quad \text{Factor out common factor.}$$

    $y = 0 \text{ or } y + 2 = 0 \quad$ Since product is 0, at least one of the
    factors must be 0.

    $$y = 0 \text{ or } y = -2$$

    Check by substituting both values in the original equation:

    $$(0)^2 + 2(0) = 0$$
    $$(-2)^2 + 2(-2) = 4 - 4 = 0$$

    In this case there are two solutions.

2. Solve $x^2 + 7x + 10 = 0$.

    $$x^2 + 7x + 10 = (x + 5)(x + 2) = 0$$
    $$x + 5 = 0 \quad \text{or} \quad x + 2 = 0$$
    $$x = -5 \text{ or} \quad x = -2$$

    Check:

    $$(-5)^2 + 7(-5) + 10 = 25 - 35 + 10 = 0$$
    $$(-2)^2 + 7(-2) + 10 = 4 - 14 + 10 = 0$$

Not all quadratic equations can be factored using only integers, but solutions can usually be found by means of a formula. A quadratic equation may have two real solutions, one real solution, or occasionally no real solutions. If the quadratic equation is in the form $Ax^2 + Bx + C = 0$, x can be found from the following formula:

$$x = \frac{-B \pm \sqrt{B^2 - 4AC}}{2A}$$

3. Solve $2y^2 + 5y + 2 = 0$ by formula. Assume $A = 2$, $B = 5$, and $C = 2$.

$$x = \frac{-5 \pm \sqrt{5^2 - 4(2)(2)}}{2(2)}$$

$$= \frac{-5 \pm \sqrt{25 - 16}}{4}$$

$$= \frac{-5 \pm \sqrt{9}}{4}$$

$$= \frac{-5 \pm 3}{4}$$

This yields two solutions:

$$x = \frac{-5 + 3}{4} = \frac{-2}{4} = \frac{-1}{2} \quad \text{and} \quad x = \frac{-5 - 3}{4} = \frac{-8}{4} = -2$$

So far, each quadratic we have solved has had two distinct answers, but an equation may have a single choice (repeated), as in:

$$x^2 + 4x + 4 = 0$$

$$(x + 2)(x + 2) = 0$$

$$x + 2 = 0 \text{ and } x + 2 = 0$$

$$x = -2 \text{ and } x = -2$$

The only solution is -2.

It is also possible for a quadratic equation to have no real solution at all.

4. If we attempt to solve $x^2 + x + 1 = 0$ by formula, we get:

$$x = \frac{-1 \pm \sqrt{1 - 4(1)(1)}}{2} = \frac{-1 \pm \sqrt{-3}}{2}$$

Since $\sqrt{-3}$ is real, this quadratic has no real answer.

Rewriting Equations

Certain equations written with a variable in the denominator can be rewritten as quadratics.

Example

Solve $-\dfrac{4}{x} + 5 = x$.

$-4 + 5x = x^2$	Multiply both sides by $x \neq 0$.
$-x^2 + 5x - 4 = 0$	Collect terms on one side of equals and set sum equal to 0.
$x^2 - 5x + 4 = 0$	Multiply both sides by -1.
$(x - 4)(x - 1) = 0$	Factor
$x - 4 = 0 \quad$ or $\quad x - 1 = 0$	
$x = 4 \quad$ or $\quad x = 1$	

Check the result by substitution:

$$-\dfrac{4}{4} + 5 \stackrel{?}{=} 4 \text{ and } -\dfrac{4}{1} + 5 \stackrel{?}{=} 1$$

$$-1 + 5 = 4 \qquad\qquad -4 + 5 = 1$$

Some equations containing a radical sign can also be converted into a quadratic equation. The solution of this type of problem depends on the principle that:

$$\text{If } A = B \text{ then } A^2 = B^2$$
$$\text{and if } A^2 = B^2 \text{ then } A = B \text{ or } A = -B$$

Equations Involving Square Roots

To solve equations in which the variable appears under a square root sign, begin by manipulating the equation so that the square root is alone on one side. Then square both sides of the equation. Since squares and square roots are inverses, the square root will be eliminated from the equation.

Examples

1. Solve $\sqrt{12x + 4} + 2 = 6$.

    Rewrite the equation as $\sqrt{12x + 4} = 4$. Now square both sides.

    $$(\sqrt{12x + 4})^2 = 4^2$$
    $$12x + 4 = 16$$
    $$12x = 12$$
    $$x = 1$$

It is easy to check that 1 is a solution to the equation by plugging the 1 into the original equation. However, sometimes when we use this procedure, the solution obtained will not solve the original equation. Thus, it is crucial to check your answer to all square root equations.

2. Solve $y = \sqrt{3y + 4}$.

$$y = \sqrt{3y + 4}$$
$$y^2 = 3y + 4$$
$$y^2 - 3y - 4 = 0$$
$$(y - 4)(y + 1) = 0$$
$$y = 4 \text{ or } y = -1$$

Check by substituting values into the original equation:

$$4 \overset{?}{=} \sqrt{3(4) + 4} \text{ and}$$
$$-1 = \sqrt{3(-1) + 4}$$
$$4 \overset{?}{=} \sqrt{16} \qquad -1 \overset{?}{=} \sqrt{1}$$
$$4 = 4 \qquad\quad -1 \neq 1$$

The single solution is $y = 4$; the false root $y = -1$ was introduced when the original equation was squared.

Equation Solving Problems

Solve the following equations for the variable indicated:

1. Solve for W: $P = 2L + 2W$

2. Solve for x: $ax + b = cx + d$

3. Solve for x: $8x^2 - 4x = 0$

4. Solve for x: $x^2 - 4x = 21$

5. Solve for y: $\sqrt{y + 1} - 3 = 7$

6. Solve for x: $4\sqrt{\dfrac{2x}{3}} = 48$

7. Solve $A = P + Prt$ for r

8. Solve for x: $3x^2 - x - 4 = 0$

9. Solve $\dfrac{q}{x} + \dfrac{p}{x} = 1$ for x

10. Solve for x: $3x^2 - 5 = 0$

Solutions

1. $P = 2L + 2W$

$$2W = P - 2L$$

$$W = \frac{P - 2L}{2}$$

2. $ax + b = cx + d$

$$ax = cx + d - b$$

$$ax - cx = d - b$$

$$x(a - c) = d - b$$

$$x = \frac{d - b}{a - c}$$

3. $8x^2 - 4x = 0$

$$4x(x - 2) = 0$$

$$x = 0, 2$$

4. $x^2 - 4x = 21$

$$x^2 - 4x - 21 = 0$$

$$(x - 7)(x + 3) = 0$$

$$x = 7, -3$$

5. $\sqrt{y + 1} - 3 = 7$

$$\sqrt{y + 1} = 10$$

$$\left(\sqrt{y + 1}\right)^2 = 10^2$$

$$y + 1 = 100$$

$$y = 99$$

6. Begin by dividing both sides by 4 to get $\sqrt{\frac{2x}{3}} = 12$. Then, square both sides.

$$\left(\sqrt{\frac{2x}{3}}\right)^2 = 12^2$$

$$\frac{2x}{3} = 144 \quad \text{Now, multiply both sides by 3.}$$

$$2x = 432$$

$$x = 216$$

7. $A = P + Prt$

$A - P = Prt$

$$\frac{A - P}{Pt} = r$$

8. $3x^2 - x - 4 = 0$. Here, $A = 3$, $B = -1$, and $C = -4$. Using the quadratic formula, we get:

$$x = \frac{-B \pm \sqrt{B^2 - 4AC}}{2A} = \frac{1 \pm \sqrt{1 - 4(3)(-4)}}{6}$$

$$= \frac{1 \pm \sqrt{1 + 48}}{6} = \frac{1 \pm \sqrt{49}}{6} = \frac{1 \pm 7}{6} = \frac{8}{6}, \frac{-6}{6}$$

Thus, $x = \frac{4}{3}$ or -1. Note that this equation could have been solved by factoring as well. The quadratic formula, however, can be used to solve all quadratic equations, including those that cannot be factored.

9. $\frac{q}{x} + \frac{p}{x} = 1$. Multiply both sides by x to clear the fraction, and obtain:

$q + p = x$

10. $3x^2 - 5 = 0$

This equation can easily be solved for x by first solving for x^2 and then taking the square root of both sides.

$$3x^2 = 5$$

$$x^2 = \frac{5}{3}$$

$$\sqrt{x^2} = \pm \sqrt{\frac{5}{3}}$$

Since $\sqrt{x^2} = x$, we have $x = \pm \sqrt{\frac{5}{3}}$.

Linear Inequalities

For each of the sets of numbers we have considered, we have established an ordering of the members of the set by defining what it means to say that one number is greater than the other. Every number we have considered can be represented by a point on a number line.

An *algebraic inequality* is a statement that one algebraic expression is greater than (or less than) another algebraic expression. If all the variables in the inequality are raised to the first power, the inequality is said to be a *linear inequality*. We solve the inequality by simplifying it to a simpler inequality whose solution is apparent. The answer is not unique, as it is in an equation, since a great number of values may satisfy the inequality.

There are three rules for producing equivalent inequalities:

1. The same quantity can be added or subtracted from each side of an inequality.

2. Each side of an inequality can be multiplied or divided by the same *positive* quantity.

3. If each side of an inequality is multiplied or divided by the same *negative* quantity, the sign of the inequality must be reversed so that the new inequality is equivalent to the first.

Examples

1. Solve $5x - 5 > -9 + 3x$.

   $5x > -4 + 3x$ Add 5 to each side.
   $2x > -4$ Subtract $3x$ from each side.
   $x > -2$ Divide by $+2$.

   Any number greater than -2 is a solution to this inequality.

2. Solve $2x - 12 < 5x - 3$.

   $2x < 5x + 9$ Add 12 to each side.
   $-3x < 9$ Subtract $5x$ from each side.
   $x > -3$ Divide each side by -3, changing sign of inequality.

   Any number greater than -3—for example, $-2\frac{1}{2}$, 0, 1, or 4—is a solution to this inequality.

3. $\dfrac{x}{3} - \dfrac{x}{2} > 1$

Begin by multiplying both sides by 6 to clear the fractions. We then obtain:

$$2x - 3x > 6$$
$$-x > 6$$

Now, divide both sides by -1, and reverse the inequality.

$$x < -6$$

Linear Equations with Two Unknowns

Graphing Equations

The number line is useful in picturing the values of one variable. When two variables are involved, a coordinate system is effective. The Cartesian coordinate system is constructed by placing a vertical number line and a horizontal number line on a plane so that the lines intersect at their zero points. This meeting place is called the *origin*. The horizontal number line is called the *x*-axis, and the vertical number line (with positive numbers above the *x*-axis) is called the *y*-axis. Points in the plane correspond to ordered pairs of real numbers.

Example

The points in this example are:

x	y
0	0
1	1
3	-1
-2	-2
-2	1

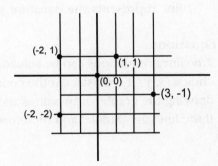

A first-degree equation in two variables is an equation that can be written in the form $ax + by = c$, where a, b, and c are constants. *First-degree* means that x and y appear to the first power. *Linear* refers to the graph of the solutions (x, y) of the equation, which is a straight line. We have already discussed linear equations of one variable.

Example

Graph the line $y = 2x - 4$.

First make a table and select small integral values of x. Find the value of each corresponding y and write it in the table:

x	y
0	-4
1	-2
2	0
3	2

If $x = 1$, for example, $y = 2(1) - 4 = -2$. Then plot the four points on a coordinate system. It is not necessary to have four points; two would do, since two points determine a line, but plotting three or more points reduces the possibility of error.

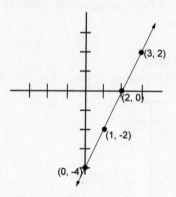

After the points have been plotted (placed on the graph), draw a line through the points and extend it in both directions. This line represents the equation $y = 2x - 4$.

Solving Simultaneous Linear Equations

Two linear equations can be solved together (simultaneously) to yield a choice (x, y) if it exists. On the coordinate system, this amounts to drawing the graphs of two lines and finding their point of intersection. If the lines are parallel and therefore never meet, no solution exists.

Simultaneous linear equations can be solved in the following manner without drawing graphs. From the first equation, find the value of one variable in terms of the other; substitute this value into the second equation. The second equation is now a linear equation in one variable and can be solved. After the numerical value of the one variable has been found, substitute that value into the first equation to find the value of the second variable. Check the results by substituting both values into the second equation.

Examples

1. Solve the system:

$$2x + y = 3$$
$$4x - y = 0$$

From the first equation, $y = 3 - 2x$. Substitute this value of y into the second equation to get:

$$4x - (3 - 2x) = 0$$
$$4x - 3 + 2x = 0$$
$$6x = 3$$
$$x = \frac{1}{2}$$

Substitute $x = \frac{1}{2}$ into the first of the original equations:

$$2\left(\frac{1}{2}\right) + y = 3$$
$$1 + y = 3$$
$$y = 2$$

Check by substituting both x and y values into the second equation:

$$4\left(\frac{1}{2}\right) - 2 = 0$$
$$2 - 2 = 0$$

2. The sum of two numbers is 87 and their difference is 13. What are the numbers?

Let x = the greater of the two numbers and y the lesser. Then,

$x + y = 87$
$x - y = 13$

Rewrite the second equation as $x = y + 13$ and substitute it into the first equation.

$(y + 13) + y = 87$
$2y + 13 = 87$
$2y = 74$
$y = 37$

Then, $x = 13 + 37 = 50$.

The numbers are 50 and 37.

3. A change-making machine contains $30 in dimes and quarters. There are 150 coins in the machine. Find the number of each type of coin.

Let x = number of dimes and y = number of quarters. Then:

$x + y = 150$

Since $.25y$ is the product of a quarter of a dollar and the number of quarters and $.10x$ is the amount of money in dimes:

$.10x + .25y = 30$

Multiply the last equation by 100 to eliminate the decimal points:

$10x + 25y = 3,000$

From the first equation, $y = 150 - x$. Substitute this value into the equivalent form of the second equation.

$10x + 25(150 - x) = 3,000$
$-15x = -750$
$x = 50$

This is the number of dimes. Substitute this value into $x + y = 150$ to find the number of quarters, $y = 100$.

Check:

$.10(50) + .25(100) = 30$
$\$5 + \$25 = \$30$

Linear Inequalities and Equations Problems

1. Solve for x: $12x < 5(2x + 4)$

2. Solve for y: $6y + 2 < 8y + 14$

3. Find the common solution:

   $x - 3y = 3$
   $2x + 9y = 11$

4. A coin collection consisting of quarters and nickels has a value of $4.50. The total number of coins is 26. Find the number of quarters and the number of nickels in the collection.

5. Mr. Linnell bought 3 cans of corn and 5 cans of tomatoes for $3.75. The next week, he bought 4 cans of corn and 2 cans of tomatoes for $2.90. Find the cost of a can of corn.

6. Solve for z: $6z + 1 \leq 3(z - 2)$

7. Find the common solution:

   $y = 3x + 1$
   $x + y = 9$

8. Find the common solution:

   $2x + y = 8$
   $x - y = 1$

9. A 20-foot piece of wood is cut into 2 pieces, one of which is 4 feet longer than the other. How long is each piece of wood?

10. A printer and monitor together cost $356. The monitor costs $20 more than two times the printer. How much do the printer and monitor cost separately?

Solutions

1. $12x < 5(2x + 4)$

   $12x < 10x + 20$

   $2x < 20$

   $x < 10$

2. $6y + 2 < 8y + 14$

   $6y < 8y + 12$

   $-2y < 12$

   $y > -6$

3. $x - 3y = 3$

$2x + 9y = 11$

Multiply the first equation by 3.

$3(x - 3y) = 3(3)$

$2x + 9y = 11$

$3x - 9y = 9$

$\underline{2x + 9y = 11}$

$5x = 20$

$x = 4$

Now substitute this answer for x in the second equation.

$2(4) + 9y = 11$

$8 + 9y = 11$

$9y = 3$

$y = \dfrac{1}{3}$

4. Let Q = the number of quarters in the collection.

Let N = the number of nickels in the collection.

Then: $.25Q + .05N = 4.50$

$Q + N = 26$

Multiply the first equation by 100 to clear the decimals:

$25Q + 5N = 450$

$Q + N = 26$

Multiply the second equation by -5 and add:

$25Q + 5N = 450$

$\underline{-5Q - 5N = -130}$

$20Q = 320$

$Q = 16$

$N = 10$

There are 16 quarters and 10 nickels.

5. Let c = the cost of a can of corn and

t = the cost of a can of tomatoes.

Then:

$3c + 5t = 3.75$
$4c + 2t = 2.90$

Multiply the first equation by 2, the second one by -5, and add:

$6c + 10t = 7.50$
$-20c - 10t = -14.50$
$-14c = -7.00$
$c = .50$

A can of corn costs 50¢.

6. $6z + 1 \leq 3(z - 2)$

$6z + 1 \leq 3z - 6$
$3z \leq -7$
$z \leq -\dfrac{7}{3}$

Note that even though the answer is negative, we do not reverse the inequality sign since we never multiplied or divided by a negative number.

7. $y = 3x + 1 \qquad x + y = 9$

Begin by substituting $y = 3x + 1$ into the second equation:

$x + (3x + 1) = 9$
$4x + 1 = 9$
$4x = 8$
$x = 2$

If $x = 2$, $y = 3(2) + 1 = 6 + 1 = 7$.

8. $2x + y = 8 \qquad x - y = 1$

From the second equation, we can see $x = y + 1$. Then, substituting into the first equation:

$2(y + 1) + y = 8$
$3y + 2 = 8$
$3y = 6$
$y = 2$

If $y = 2$, then $x = y + 1 = 2 + 1 = 3$.

9. Let L = the length of the longer piece of wood.

    Let S = the length of the shorter piece of wood. Then the equations are:

    $L + S = 20$

    $L - S = 4$

    From the second equation, we obtain $L = S + 4$. Substituting into the first equation, we get:

    $(S + 4) + S = 20$

    $\quad 2S + 4 = 20$

    $\qquad 2S = 16$

    $\qquad\; S = 8$

    The shorter piece of wood is 8 feet, so the longer piece is 12 feet.

10. The printer and monitor together cost $356. The monitor cost $20 more than two times the printer.

    Let P = the cost of the printer.

    Let M = the cost of the monitor. Then:

    $P + M = 356$

    $\quad M = 20 + 2P$

    Substituting for M in the first equation, we get:

    $P + (20 + 2P) = 356$

    $\qquad 3P + 20 = 356$

    $\qquad\quad 3P = 336$

    $\qquad\quad\; P = 112$

    Then $M = 20 + 2(112) = 244$.

    The printer costs $112, and the monitor costs $244.

RATIO AND PROPORTION

Many problems in arithmetic and algebra can be solved using the concept of *ratio* to compare numbers. The ratio of a to b is the fraction $\frac{a}{b}$. If the two ratios $\frac{a}{b}$ and $\frac{c}{d}$ represent the same comparison, we write:

$$\frac{a}{b} = \frac{c}{d}$$

This equation (statement of equality) is called a *proportion*. A proportion states the equivalence of two different expressions for the same ratio.

Examples

1. In a class of 39 students, 17 are men. Find the ratio of men to women.

   39 students − 17 men = 22 women

   Ratio of men to women is 17/22, also written 17:22.

2. The scale on a map is $\frac{3}{4}$ inch = 12 miles. If the distance between City A and City B on the map is $4\frac{1}{2}$ inches, how far apart are the two cities actually?

   Let x = the distance between the two cities in miles.

   Begin by writing a proportion that compares inches to miles.

   $$\frac{Inches \rightarrow}{Miles \rightarrow}\ \frac{\frac{3}{4}}{12} = \frac{\frac{9}{2}}{x}$$ Cross-multiply to solve the equation.

   $$\left(\frac{3}{4}\right)x = 12\left(\frac{9}{2}\right)$$

   $$\left(\frac{3}{4}\right)x = 54 \quad \text{Multiply by 4.}$$

   $$3x = 216$$

   $$x = 72$$

   The two cities are 72 miles apart.

3. A fertilizer contains 3 parts nitrogen, 2 parts potash, and 2 parts phosphate by weight. How many pounds of fertilizer will contain 60 pounds of nitrogen?

   The ratio of pounds of nitrogen to pounds of fertilizer is

   3 to 3 + 2 + 2 = $\frac{3}{7}$. Let x be the number of pounds of mixture. Then:

   $$\frac{3}{7} = \frac{60}{x}$$

   Multiply both sides of the equation by $7x$ to get:

   $$3x = 420$$

   $$x = 140 \text{ pounds}$$

COMPUTING AVERAGES AND MEDIANS

Mean

Several statistical measures are used frequently. One of them is the *average* or *arithmetic mean*. To find the average of N numbers, add the numbers and divide their sum by N.

Examples

1. Seven students attained test scores of 62, 80, 60, 30, 50, 90, and 20. What was the average test score for the group?

   $$62 + 80 + 60 + 30 + 50 + 90 + 20 = 392$$

   Since there are 7 scores, the average score is:

   $$\frac{392}{7} = 56$$

2. Brian has scores of 88, 87, and 92 on his first three tests. What grade must he get on his next test to have an overall average of 90?

   Let x = the grade that he needs to get. Then we have:

   $$\frac{88 + 87 + 92 + x}{4} = 90 \quad \text{Multiply by 4 to clear the fraction.}$$
   $$88 + 87 + 92 + x = 360$$
   $$267 + x = 360$$
   $$x = 93$$

   Brian needs to get a 93 on his next test.

3. Joan allotted herself a budget of $50 a week, on the average, for expenses. One week she spent $35, the next $60, and the third $40. How much can she spend in the fourth week without exceeding her budget?

   Let x be the amount spent in the fourth week. Then:

   $$\frac{35 + 60 + 40 + x}{4} = 50$$
   $$35 + 60 + 40 + x = 200$$
   $$135 + x = 200$$
   $$x = 65$$

   She can spend $65 in the fourth week.

Median

If a set of numbers is arranged in order, the number in the middle is called the *median.*

Example

Find the median test score of 62, 80, 60, 30, 50, 90, and 20. Arrange the numbers in increasing (or decreasing) order:

20, 30, 50, 60, 62, 80, 90

Since 60 is the number in the middle, it is the median. It is not the same as the arithmetic mean, which is 56.

If the number of scores is an even number, the median is the arithmetic mean of the middle two scores.

COORDINATE GEOMETRY

We have already seen that a coordinate system is an effective way to picture relationships involving two variables. In this section, we will learn more about the study of geometry using coordinate methods.

LINES

Recall that the general equation of a line has the following form:

$$Ax + By + C = 0$$

where A and B are constants and are not both 0. This means that if you were to find all of the points (x, y) that satisfy the above equation, they would all lie on the same line as graphed on a coordinate axis.

If the value of B is not 0, a little algebra can be used to rewrite the equation in the form

$$y = mx + b$$

where m and b are two constants. Since the two numbers m and b determine this line, let's see what their geometric meaning is. First of all, note that the point $(0, b)$ satisfies the above equation. This means that the point $(0, b)$ is one of the points on the line; in other words, the line crosses the y-axis at the point b. For this reason, the number b is called the *y-intercept* of the line.

To interpret the meaning of m, choose any two points on the line. Let us call these points (x_1, y_1) and (x_2, y_2). Both of these points must satisfy the equation of the line above, and so:

$$y_1 = mx_1 + b \text{ and } y_2 = mx_2 + b.$$

If we subtract the first equation from the second, we obtain

$$y_2 - y_1 = m(x_2 - x_1)$$

and solving for m, we find

$$m = (y_2 - y_1)/(x_2 - x_1).$$

The preceding equation tells us that the number m in the equation $y = mx + b$ is the ratio of the difference of the y-coordinates to the difference of the x-coordinates. This number is called the *slope* of the line. Therefore, the ratio $m = (y_2 - y_1)/(x_2 - x_1)$ is a measure of the number of units the line rises (or falls) in the y-direction for each unit moved in the x-direction. Another way to say this is that the slope of a line is a measure of the rate at which the line rises (or falls). Intuitively, a line with a positive slope rises from left to right; one with a negative slope falls from left to right.

Because the equation $y = mx + b$ contains both the slope and the y-intercept, it is called the *slope-intercept* form of the equation of the line.

Example

Write the equation $2x - 3y = 6$ in slope-intercept form.

To write the equation in slope-intercept form, we begin by solving for y.

$$-3y = 6 - 2x$$
$$3y = 2x - 6$$
$$y = \frac{2x}{3} - \frac{6}{3} \text{ or}$$
$$y = \frac{2x}{3} - 2$$

Thus, the slope of the line is $\frac{2}{3}$, and the y-intercept is -2.

This, however, is not the only form in which the equation of the line can be written.

If the line contains the point (x_1, y_1), its equation can also be written as:

$$y - y_1 = m(x - x_1)$$

This form of the equation of a line is called the *point-slope* form of the equation of a line, since it contains the slope and the coordinates of one of the points on the line.

Example

Write the equation of the line that passes through the point (2, 3) with slope 8 in point-slope form.

In this problem, $m = 8$, and $(x_1, y_1) = (2, 3)$. Substituting into the point-slope form of the equation, we obtain:

$$y - 3 = 8(x - 2)$$

Two lines are parallel if and only if they have the same slope. Two lines are perpendicular if and only if their slopes are negative reciprocals of each other. This means that if a line has a slope m, any line perpendicular to this line must have a slope of $\dfrac{-1}{m}$. Also note that a horizontal line has a slope of 0. For such a line, the slope-intercept form of the equation reduces to $y = b$.

Finally, note that if $B = 0$ in the equation $Ax + By + C = 0$, the equation simplifies to

$$Ax + C = 0$$

and represents a vertical line (a line parallel to the y-axis) that crosses the x-axis at $\dfrac{-C}{A}$. Such a line is said to have no slope.

Examples

1. Find the slope and the y-intercept of the following lines:

   a. $y = 5x - 7$

   b. $3x + 4y = 5$

Solutions

a. $y = 5x - 7$ is already in slope-intercept form. The slope is 5, and the y-intercept is -7.

b. Write $3x + 4y = 5$ in slope-intercept form:

$$4y = -3x + 5$$

$$y = \left(-\frac{3}{4}\right)x + \left(\frac{5}{4}\right)$$

The slope is $\dfrac{-3}{4}$, and the y-intercept is $\dfrac{5}{4}$. This means that the line crosses the y-axis at the point $\dfrac{5}{4}$, and for every 3 units moved in the x-direction, the line falls 4 units in the y-direction.

2. Find the equations of the following lines:

    a. The line containing the points (4, 5) and (7,11)

    b. The line containing the point (6, 3) and having slope 2

    c. The line containing the point (5, 2) and parallel to $y = 4x + 7$

    d. The line containing the point $(-2, 8)$ and perpendicular to $y = -2x + 9$

Solutions

    a. First, we need to determine the slope of the line.

$$m = \frac{(11 - 5)}{(7 - 4)} = \frac{6}{3} = 2.$$

Now, using the point-slope form:

$$y - 5 = 2(x - 4).$$

If desired, you can change this to the slope-intercept form: $y = 2x - 3$.

    b. Since we know the slope and a point on the line, we can simply plug into the point-slope form:

$$y - 3 = m(x - 6) \text{ to obtain}$$

$$y - 3 = 2(x - 6).$$

    c. The line $y = 4x + 7$ has a slope of 4. Thus, the desired line can be written as $y - 2 = 4(x - 5)$.

    d. The line $y = -2x + 9$ has a slope of -2. The line perpendicular to this one has a slope of $\frac{1}{2}$. The desired line can be written as $y - 8 = \left(\frac{1}{2}\right)(x + 2)$.

CIRCLES

From a geometric point of view, a circle is the set of points in a plane, each of whose members is the same distance from a particular point called the center of the circle. We can determine the equation of a circle by manipulating the distance formula.

Suppose that we have a circle whose radius is a given positive number r and whose center lies at the point (h, k). If (x, y) is a point on the circle, then its distance from the center of the circle would be

$$\sqrt{(x - h)^2 + (y - k)^2}$$

and since this distance is r, we can say

$$\sqrt{(x - h)^2 + (y - k)^2} = r.$$

Squaring both sides, we get the following result: the equation of a circle whose center is at (h, k) and whose radius r is given by:

$$(x - h)^2 + (y - k)^2 = r^2$$

Examples

1. Find the equation of the circle with radius 7, and center at $(0, -5)$.

    Substituting into the formula above, we obtain $x^2 + (y + 5)^2 = 49$.

2. Describe the set of points (x, y) with the property that $x^2 + y^2 > 25$.

    The equation $x^2 + y^2 = 25$ describes a circle, centered at the origin, with radius 5. The given set contains all of the points that are *outside* this circle.

Coordinate Geometry Problems

1. Find the y-intercept of the line $3x - 5y = 15$.

2. Find the equation of the line whose slope is -2 and whose y-intercept is 5.

3. Find the slope of the line $2x + 3y = 8$.

4. Find the equation of the line containing the points $(2, 4)$ and $(10, 9)$.

5. Find the equation of the line containing the point $(6, 3)$ and parallel to $y = 6x - 8$.

6. Find the equation of the line containing the point $(2, 3)$ and perpendicular to $y = -\frac{1}{3}x + 7$.

7. Find the equation of the circle centered at $(-2, 3)$ with radius 7.

8. Write the equation $4x - 5y = 12$ in slope-intercept form.

9. Find the equation of the line parallel to $x = 7$ and containing the point $(3, 4)$.

10. Write an inequality that represents all of the points inside the circle centered at $(4, 5)$ with radius 4.

11. Find the equation of the line perpendicular to $x = -3$, containing the point $(-3, -6)$.

12. Find the slope of the line containing the points $(-4, 6)$ and $(2, 6)$.

Solutions

1. A line crosses the y-axis at the point where $x = 0$.

$$3(0) - 5y = 15$$
$$-5y = 15$$
$$y = -3$$

The y-intercept is $(0, -3)$.

2. Using the slope-intercept formula for the equation of a line:

$$y = -2x + 5.$$

3. Put the equation in slope-intercept form:

$$2x + 3y = 8$$
$$3y = -2x + 8$$
$$y = -\frac{2}{3}x + \frac{8}{3}$$

The slope is $-\frac{2}{3}$.

4. The slope of the line would be $\dfrac{9 - 4}{10 - 2} = \dfrac{5}{8}$. Using the point-slope form:

$$(y - 4) = \frac{5}{8}(x - 2)$$

$$8(y - 4) = 5(x - 2)$$
$$8y - 32 = 5x - 10$$
$$5x - 8y = -22$$

5. The slope of $y = 6x - 8$ is 6. Using the point-slope form:

$$y - 3 = 6(x - 6)$$
$$y - 3 = 6x - 36$$
$$6x - y = 33$$

6. The slope of $y = -\frac{1}{3}x + 7$ is $-\frac{1}{3}$.

    The slope of the perpendicular line would be 3. Using the point-slope formula:

$$y - 3 = 3(x - 2)$$
$$y - 3 = 3x - 6$$
$$3x - y = 3$$

7. Using the general formula for the equation of a circle:

$$(x - (-2))^2 + (y - 3)^2 = 7^2 \quad \text{or} \quad (x + 2)^2 + (y - 3)^2 = 49$$

8. To write the equation in slope-intercept form, we begin by solving for y:

$$4x - 5y = 12$$
$$-5y = -4x + 12$$
$$y = \frac{-4x}{-5} + \frac{12}{-5} = \frac{4x}{5} - \frac{12}{5}$$

    Thus, the equation in slope-intercept form is:

    $y = \frac{4x}{5} - \frac{12}{5}$. The slope is $\frac{4}{5}$, and the y-intercept is $\frac{-12}{5}$.

9. Since $x = 7$ is vertical, any line parallel to $x = 7$ will be vertical also. The line parallel to $x = 7$ through $(3, 4)$ is $x = 3$.

10. The equation of the circle with center at $(4, 5)$ with radius 4 is $(x - 4)^2 + (y - 5)^2 = 4^2 = 16$.

    The points inside this circle are given by the inequality:

    $(x - 4)^2 + (y - 5)^2 < 16$.

11. The line $x = -3$ is vertical, so any line perpendicular to it is horizontal. The horizontal line through the point $(-3, -6)$ is $y = -6$.

12. The slope of the line containing the points $(-4, 6)$ and $(2, 6)$ is

    $m = \frac{6 - 6}{2 - (-4)} = \frac{0}{6} = 0$. Thus, the line is horizontal.

PLANE GEOMETRY

Plane geometry is the science of measurement. Certain assumptions are made about undefined quantities called points, lines, and planes, and then logical deductions about relationships between figures composed of lines, angles, and portions of planes are made based on these assumptions. The process of making the logical deductions is called a *proof*. In this summary, we are not making any proofs but are giving the definitions frequently used in geometry and stating relationships that are the results of proofs.

ANGLES

A line in geometry is always a straight line. When two straight lines meet at a point, they form an *angle*. The lines are called *sides* or *rays* of the angle, and the point is called the *vertex*. The symbol for angle is $\angle$. When no other angle shares the same vertex, the name of the angle is the name given to the vertex, as in angle *A*:

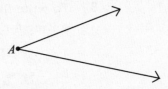

An angle may be named with three letters. In the following example, *B* is a point on one side and *C* is a point on the other. In this case, the name of the vertex must be the middle letter, and we have angle *BAC*.

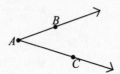

Occasionally, an angle is named by a number or small letter placed in the angle.

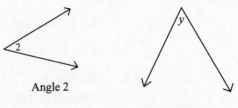

Angle 2   Angle *y*

Angles are usually measured in degrees. An angle of 30 degrees, written 30°, is an angle whose measure is 30 degrees. Degrees are divided into minutes; 60′ (read "minutes") = 1°. Minutes are further divided into seconds; 60″ (read "seconds") = 1′.

Vertical Angles

When two lines intersect, four angles are formed. The angles opposite each other are called *vertical angles* and are equal to each other.

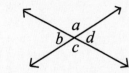

a and *c* are vertical angles.
$$m\angle a = m\angle c$$
b and *d* are vertical angles.
$$m\angle b = m\angle d$$

Straight Angle

A *straight angle* has its sides lying along a straight line. It is always equal to 180°.

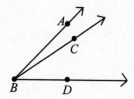

$$m\angle ABC = m\angle B = 180°$$
$\angle B$ is a straight angle.

Adjacent Angles

Two angles are *adjacent* if they share the same vertex and a common side but no angle is inside another angle. $\angle ABC$ and $\angle CBD$ are adjacent angles. Even though they share a common vertex *B* and a common side *AB*, $\angle ABD$ and $\angle ABC$ are not adjacent angles because one angle is inside the other.

Supplementary Angles

If the sum of two angles is a straight angle (180°), the two angles are *supplementary* and each angle is the supplement of the other.

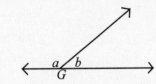

$\angle G$ is a straight angle and measures 180°.

$m\angle a + m\angle b = 180°$

$\angle a$ and $\angle b$ are supplementary angles.

Right Angles

If two supplementary angles are equal, they are both *right angles*. A right angle is one half a straight angle. Its measure is 90°. A right angle is symbolized by ⌐.

$\angle G$ is a straight angle.

$m\angle b + m\angle a = m\angle G$, and $m\angle a = m\angle b$

$\angle a$ and $\angle b$ are right angles.

Complementary Angles

Complementary angles are two angles whose sum is a right angle (90°).

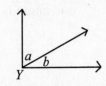

$\angle Y$ is a right angle.

$m\angle a + m\angle b = m\angle Y = 90°$.

$\angle a$ and $\angle b$ are complementary angles.

Acute Angles

Acute angles are angles whose measure is less than 90°. No two acute angles can be supplementary angles. Two acute angles can be complementary angles.

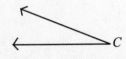

$\angle C$ is an acute angle.

Obtuse Angles

Obtuse angles are angles that are greater than 90° and less than 180°.

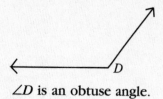

∠D is an obtuse angle.

Examples

1. In the figure, what is the value of *x*?

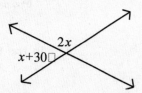

Since the two labeled angles are supplementary angles, their sum is 180°.

$$(x + 30°) + 2x = 180°$$
$$3x = 150°$$
$$x = 50°$$

2. Find the value of *x* in the figure.

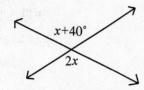

Since the two labeled angles are vertical angles, they are equal.

$$x + 40° = 2x$$
$$40° = x$$

3. If angle Y is a right angle and angle b measures $30°15'$, what does angle a measure?

Since angle Y is a right angle, angles a and b are complementary angles and their sum is $90°$.

$$m\angle a + m\angle b = 90°$$
$$m\angle a + 30°15' = 90°$$
$$m\angle a = 59°45'$$

4. In the figure below, what is the value of x?

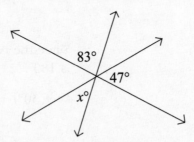

The angle that is vertical to the angle labeled $x°$ also has a measure of $x°$. This angle, along with those labeled $83°$ and $47°$, form a straight line and are thus supplementary. Therefore,

$$83° + 47° + x = 180°$$
$$130° + x = 180°$$
$$x = 50°$$

The value of x is $50°$.

LINES

A *line* in geometry is always assumed to be a straight line. It extends infinitely far in both directions. It can be determined if two of its points are known. It can be expressed in terms of the two points, which are written as capital letters. The following line is called $\overline{AB}$.

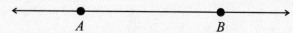

Or a line may be given one name with a small letter. The following line is called line *k*.

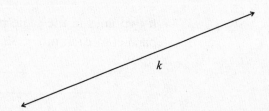

A *line segment* is a part of a line between two *endpoints*. It is named by its endpoints, for example, *A* and *B*.

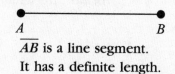

$\overline{AB}$ is a line segment.
It has a definite length.

If point *P* is on the line and is the same distance from *A* as from *B*, then *P* is the *midpoint* of segment $\overline{AB}$. When we say $AP = PB$, we mean that the two line segments have the same length.

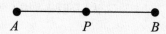

A part of a line with one endpoint is called a *ray*. $\overrightarrow{AC}$ is a ray, of which *A* is an endpoint. The ray extends infinitely far in the direction away from the endpoint.

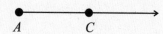

Parallel Lines

Two lines meet or intersect if there is one point that is on both lines. Two different lines may either intersect in one point or never meet, but they can never meet in more than one point.

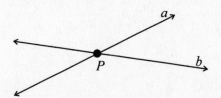

Two lines in the same plane that never meet no matter how far they are extended are said to be *parallel,* for which the symbol is ∥. In the following diagram, *a* ∥ *b*.

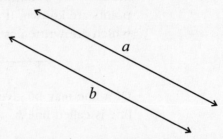

If two lines in the same plane are parallel to a third line, they are parallel to each other. Since *a* ∥ *b* and *b* ∥ *c*, we know that *a* ∥ *c*.

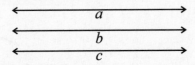

Two lines that meet each other at right angles are said to be *perpendicular,* for which the symbol is ⊥. Line *a* is perpendicular to line *b*.

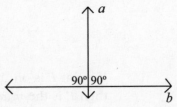

Two lines in the same plane that are perpendicular to the same line are parallel to each other.

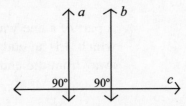

Line *a* ⊥ line *c* and line *b* ⊥ line *c*.
Therefore, *a* ∥ *b*.

A line intersecting two other lines is called a *transversal*. Line *c* is a transversal intersecting lines *a* and *b*.

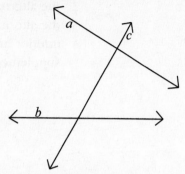

The transversal and the two given lines form eight angles. The four angles between the given lines are called *interior angles;* the four angles outside the given lines are called *exterior angles.* If two angles are on opposite sides of the transversal, they are called *alternate angles.*

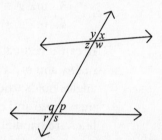

∠*z*, ∠*w*, ∠*q*, and ∠*p* are interior angles.
∠*y*, ∠*x*, ∠*s*, and ∠*r* are exterior angles.
∠*z* and ∠*p* are alternate interior angles; so are ∠*w* and ∠*q*.
∠*y* and ∠*s* are alternate exterior angles; so are ∠*x* and ∠*r*.

Pairs of *corresponding angles* are ∠*y* and ∠*q*, ∠*z* and ∠*r*, ∠*x* and ∠*p*, and ∠*w* and ∠*s*. Corresponding angles are sometimes called exterior-interior angles.

When the two given lines cut by a transversal are parallel lines:

1. the corresponding angles are congruent.
2. the alternate interior angles are congruent.
3. the alternate exterior angles are congruent.
4. interior angles on the same side of the transversal are supplementary.

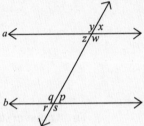

If line a is parallel to line b:

1. $m\angle y = m\angle q$, $m\angle z = m\angle r$, $m\angle x = m\angle p$, and $m\angle w = m\angle s$.
2. $m\angle z = m\angle p$ and $m\angle w = m\angle q$.
3. $m\angle y = m\angle s$ and $m\angle x = m\angle r$.
4. $m\angle z + m\angle q = 180°$ and $m\angle p + m\angle w = 180°$.

Because vertical angles are equal, $m\angle p = m\angle r$, $m\angle q = m\angle s$, $m\angle y = m\angle w$, and $m\angle x = m\angle z$. If any one of the four conditions for equality of angles holds true, the lines are parallel; that is, if two lines are cut by a transversal and one pair of the corresponding angles is congruent, the lines are parallel. If a pair of alternate interior angles or a pair of alternate exterior angles is congruent, the lines are parallel. If interior angles on the same side of the transversal are supplementary, the lines are parallel.

Examples

1. In the figure, two parallel lines are cut by a transversal. Find the measure of angle y.

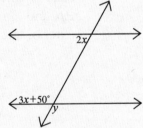

The two labeled angles are supplementary.

$$2x + (3x + 50°) = 180°$$
$$5x = 130°$$
$$x = 26°$$

Since $\angle y$ is vertical to the angle whose measure is $3x + 50°$, it has the same measure.

$$y = 3x + 50° = 3(26°) + 50° = 128°$$

2. In the figure, two parallel lines are cut by a transversal. Find x.

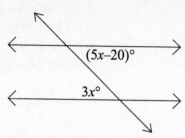

The two labeled angles are alternate interior angles, and thus are congruent. Therefore,

$$(5x - 20)° = 3x°$$
$$2x = 20°$$
$$x = 10°$$

x is 10°.

POLYGONS

A *polygon* is a closed plane figure composed of line segments joined together at points called *vertices* (singular, *vertex*). A polygon is usually named by giving its vertices in order.

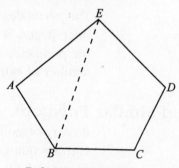

Polygon *ABCDE*

In the figure, points *A, B, C, D,* and *E* are the vertices, and the sides are $\overline{AB}$, $\overline{BC}$, $\overline{CD}$, $\overline{DE}$, and $\overline{EA}$. $\overline{AB}$ and $\overline{BC}$ are *adjacent* sides, and *A* and *B* are adjacent vertices. A *diagonal* of a polygon is a line segment joining any two nonadjacent vertices. $\overline{EB}$ is a diagonal.

Polygons are named according to the number of sides or angles. A *triangle* is a polygon with three sides, a *quadrilateral* a polygon with four sides, a *pentagon* a polygon with five sides, and a *hexagon* a polygon with six sides. The number of sides is always equal to the number of angles.

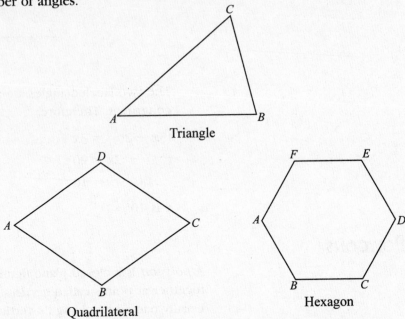

Triangle

Quadrilateral

Hexagon

The *perimeter* of a polygon is the sum of the lengths of its sides. If the polygon is regular (all sides congruent and all angles congruent), the perimeter is the product of the length of *one* side and the number of sides.

Congruent and Similar Polygons

If two polygons have congruent corresponding angles and congruent corresponding sides, they are said to be *congruent*. Congruent polygons have the same size and shape. They are the same in all respects except possibly position. The symbol for congruence is ≅.

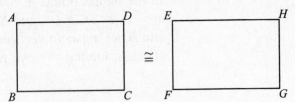

When two sides of congruent or different polygons are congruent, we indicate the fact by drawing the same number of short lines through the congruent sides.

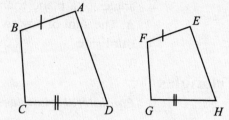

This indicates that *AB* = *EF* and *CD* = *GH*.

Two polygons with congruent corresponding angles and corresponding sides in proportion are said to be *similar*. The symbol for similar is ∼.

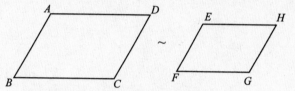

Similar figures have the same shape
but not necessarily the same size.

A *regular polygon* is a polygon whose sides are congruent and whose angles are congruent.

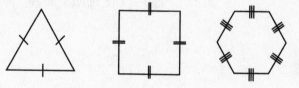

TRIANGLES

A *triangle* is a polygon of three sides. Triangles are classified by measuring their sides and angles. The sum of the measures of the angles of a plane triangle is always 180°. The symbol for a triangle is Δ. The sum of any two sides of a triangle is always greater than the third side.

Equilateral Triangles

Equilateral triangles have congruent sides and congruent angles. Each angle measures 60° because $\frac{1}{3}(180°) = 60°$.

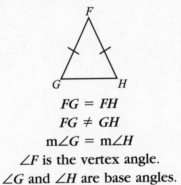

$$AB = AC = BC$$
$$m\angle A = m\angle B = m\angle C = 60°$$

Isosceles Triangles

Isosceles triangles have at least two congruent sides. The angles opposite the congruent sides are congruent. The two congruent angles are sometimes called the *base* angles and the third angle is called the *vertex* angle. Note that an equilateral triangle is isosceles.

$$FG = FH$$
$$FG \neq GH$$
$$m\angle G = m\angle H$$

∠F is the vertex angle.
∠G and ∠H are base angles.

Scalene Triangles

Scalene triangles have all three sides of different length and all angles of different measure. In scalene triangles, the shortest side is opposite the angle of smallest measure, and the longest side is opposite the angle of greatest measure.

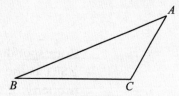

$AB > BC > CA$; therefore m$\angle C$ > m$\angle A$ > m$\angle B$.

Examples

1. In triangle *XYZ*, m$\angle Y$ is twice m$\angle X$, and m$\angle Z$ is 40° more than m$\angle Y$. How many degrees are in the three angles?

   Solve this problem just as you would an algebraic word problem, remembering that there are 180° in a triangle.

   Let x = the number of degrees in $\angle X$.

   Then $2x$ = the number of degrees in $\angle Y$

   and $2x + 40$ = the number of degrees in $\angle Z$.

   Thus,

   $$x + 2x + (2x + 40) = 180°$$
   $$5x + 40 = 180°$$
   $$5x = 140°$$
   $$x = 28°$$

   Therefore, the measure of $\angle X$ is 28°, the measure of $\angle Y$ is 56°, and the measure of $\angle Z$ is 96°.

2. In the figure below, the two lines are parallel. What is the value of *x*?

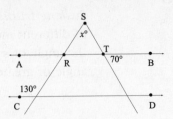

Corresponding angles are congruent, so m∠ARS is also 130°. ∠SRT is the supplement of ∠ARS and thus measures 50°. By the property of vertical angles, we have m∠STR = 70°. Finally, since the sum of the angles in triangle SRT is 180°, we have:

$$x + 50° + 70° = 180°$$
$$x + 120° = 180°$$
$$x = 60°$$

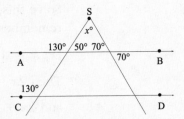

Right Triangles

Right triangles contain one right angle. Since the right angle measures 90°, the other two angles are complementary. They may or may not be congruent to each other. The side of a right triangle opposite the right angle is called the *hypotenuse.* The other two sides are called *legs.* The *Pythagorean Theorem* states that the square of the length of the hypotenuse is equal to the sum of the squares of the lengths of the legs.

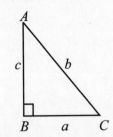

$\overline{AC}$ is the hypotenuse.
$\overline{AB}$ and $\overline{BC}$ are legs.
m∠B = 90°
m∠A + m∠C = 90°
$a^2 + c^2 = b^2$

Examples

1. If $\triangle ABC$ is a right triangle with right angle at B, and if $AB = 6$ and $BC = 8$, what is the length of $\overline{AC}$?

    $$AB^2 + BC^2 = AC^2$$
    $$6^2 + 8^2 = 36 + 64 = 100 = AC^2$$
    $$AC = 10$$

    If the measure of angle A is 30°, what is the measure of angle C?

    Since angles A and C are complementary:

    $$30° + C = 90°$$
    $$C = 60°$$

    If the lengths of the three sides of a triangle are a, b, and c and the relation $a^2 + b^2 = c^2$ holds, the triangle is a right triangle and side c is the hypotenuse.

2. Show that a triangle of sides 5, 12, and 13 is a right triangle. The triangle will be a right triangle if $a^2 + b^2 = c^2$.

    $$5^2 + 12^2 = 13^2$$
    $$25 + 144 = 169$$

    Therefore, the triangle is a right triangle and 13 is the length of the hypotenuse.

3. A plane takes off from the airport in Buffalo and flies 600 miles to the north and then flies 800 miles to the east to City C. What is the straight-line distance from Buffalo to City C?

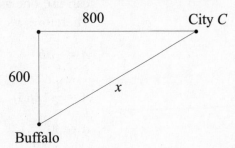

    As the diagram above shows, the required distance x is the hypotenuse of the triangle. Thus,

    $$(600)^2 + (800)^2 = x^2$$
    $$360{,}000 + 640{,}000 = x^2$$
    $$1{,}000{,}000 = x^2$$
    $$x = \sqrt{1{,}000{,}000} = 1{,}000$$

    Thus, the distance from Buffalo to City C is 1,000 miles.

Area of a Triangle

An *altitude* (or height) of a triangle is a line segment dropped as a perpendicular from any vertex to the opposite side. The area of a triangle is the product of one half the altitude and the base of the triangle. (The base is the side opposite the vertex from which the perpendicular was drawn.)

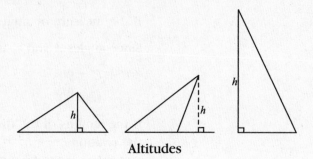

Altitudes

Examples

1. What is the area of a right triangle with sides 5, 12, and 13?

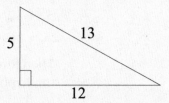

As the diagram above shows, the triangle has hypotenuse 13 and legs 5 and 12. Since the legs are perpendicular to each other, we can use one as the height and one as the base of the triangle. Therefore, we have:

$$A = \frac{1}{2}bh$$

$$A = \frac{1}{2}(12)(5)$$

$$A = 30$$

The area of the triangle is 30.

2. Find the area A of the following isosceles triangle.

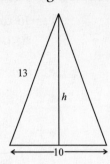

In an isosceles triangle, the altitude from the vertex angle bisects the base (cuts it in half).

The first step is to find the altitude. By the Pythagorean Theorem, $a^2 + b^2 = c^2$; $c = 13$, $a = b$, and $b = \frac{1}{2}(10) = 5$.

$$b^2 + 5^2 = 13^2$$
$$b^2 + 25 = 169$$
$$b^2 = 144$$
$$b = 12$$
$$A = \frac{1}{2} \cdot \text{base} \cdot \text{height}$$
$$= \frac{1}{2} \cdot 10 \cdot 12$$
$$= 60$$

Similarity

Two triangles are *similar* if all three pairs of corresponding angles are congruent. The sum of the measures of the three angles of a triangle is 180°; therefore, if the measures of two angles of triangle I are congruent to the measures of two corresponding angles of triangle II, the measure of the third angle of triangle I must be congruent to the measure of the third angle of triangle II and the triangles are similar. The lengths of the sides of similar triangles are in proportion to each other. A line drawn parallel to one side of a triangle divides the triangle into two portions, one of which is a triangle. The new triangle is similar to the original triangle.

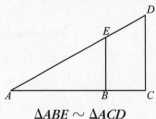

$$\triangle ABE \sim \triangle ACD$$

Examples

1. In the following figure, if $AC = 28$ feet, $AB = 35$ feet, $BC = 21$ feet, and $EC = 12$ feet, find the length of $\overline{DC}$ if $\overline{DE} \parallel \overline{AB}$.

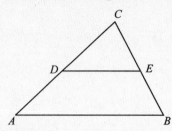

Because $\overline{DE} \parallel \overline{AB}$, $\triangle CDE \sim \triangle CAB$. Since the triangles are similar, their sides are in proportion:

$$\frac{DC}{AC} = \frac{EC}{BC}$$

$$\frac{DC}{28} = \frac{12}{21}$$

$$DC = \frac{12 \cdot 28}{21} = 16 \text{ feet}$$

2. A pole that is sticking out of the ground vertically is 10 feet tall and casts a shadow of 6 feet. At the same time, a tree next to the pole casts a shadow of 24 feet. How tall is the tree?

Below is a diagram of the tree and the pole. At the same time of the day, nearby objects and their shadows form similar triangles.

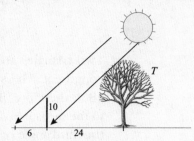

Call the height of the tree T. Then we can write a proportion between the corresponding sides of the triangles.

$$\frac{10}{T} = \frac{6}{24}$$

To solve this proportion, multiply by $24T$.

$$24 \times 10 = 6T$$
$$240 = 6T$$
$$T = 40$$

The tree is 40 feet tall.

QUADRILATERALS

A quadrilateral is a polygon of four sides. The sum of the measures of the angles of a quadrilateral is 360°. If the opposite sides of a quadrilateral are parallel, the quadrilateral is a *parallelogram*. Opposite sides of a parallelogram are congruent and so are opposite angles. Any two consecutive angles of a parallelogram are supplementary. A diagonal of a parallelogram divides the parallelogram into congruent triangles. The diagonals of a parallelogram bisect each other.

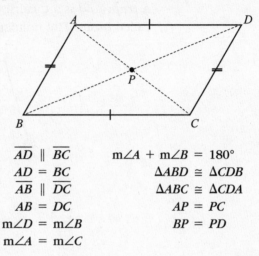

$\overline{AD} \parallel \overline{BC}$	$m\angle A + m\angle B = 180°$
$AD = BC$	$\triangle ABD \cong \triangle CDB$
$\overline{AB} \parallel \overline{DC}$	$\triangle ABC \cong \triangle CDA$
$AB = DC$	$AP = PC$
$m\angle D = m\angle B$	$BP = PD$
$m\angle A = m\angle C$	

Definitions

A *rhombus* is a parallelogram with four congruent sides. The diagonals of a rhombus are perpendicular to each other.

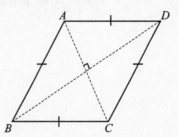

A *rectangle* is a parallelogram with four right angles. The diagonals of a rectangle are congruent and can be found using the Pythagorean Theorem if the sides of the rectangle are known.

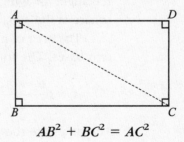

$$AB^2 + BC^2 = AC^2$$

253

A *square* is a rectangle with four congruent sides.

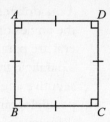

A *trapezoid* is a quadrilateral with only one pair of parallel sides, called *bases.* The nonparallel sides are called *legs.*

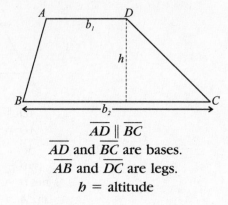

$$\overline{AD} \parallel \overline{BC}$$
$\overline{AD}$ and $\overline{BC}$ are bases.
$\overline{AB}$ and $\overline{DC}$ are legs.
$h = $ altitude

Finding Areas

The area of any *parallelogram* is the product of the base and the height, where the height is the length of an altitude, a line segment drawn from a vertex perpendicular to the base.

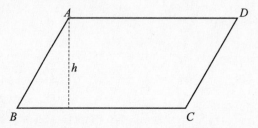

Since rectangles and squares are also parallelograms, their areas follow the same formula. For a *rectangle,* the altitude is one of the sides, and the formula is length times width. Since a *square* is a rectangle for which length and width are the same, the area of a square is the square of its side.

The area of a *trapezoid* is the height times the average of the two bases. The formula is:

$$A = h\frac{b_1 + b_2}{2}$$

The bases are the parallel sides, and the height is the length of an altitude to one of the bases.

Examples

1. Find the area of a square whose diagonal is 12 feet. Let $s =$ side of square. By the Pythagorean Theorem:

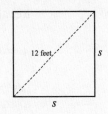

$$s^2 + s^2 = 12^2$$
$$2s^2 = 144$$
$$s^2 = 72$$
$$s = \sqrt{72}$$

Use only the positive value because this is the side of a square.

Since $A = s^2$,

$$A = 72 \text{ square feet}$$

2. Find the altitude of a rectangle if its area is 320 and its base is 5 times its altitude.

Let altitude $= h$. Then base $= 5h$. Since $A = bh$,

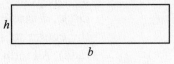

$$A = (5h)(h) = 320$$
$$5h^2 = 320$$
$$h^2 = 64$$
$$h = 8$$

If a quadrilateral is not a parallelogram or trapezoid but is irregularly shaped, its area can be found by dividing it into triangles, attempting to find the area of each, and adding the results.

3. The longer base of a trapezoid is four times the shorter base. If the height of the trapezoid is 6 and the area is 75, how long is the longer base?

    Recall that the area of a trapezoid is given by the formula:

    $$A = b\frac{b_1 + b_2}{2}$$

    Let b_1 represent the shorter base. Then the longer base is $b_2 = 4b_1$, and we have:

    $$A = 6\frac{b_1 + 4b_1}{2} = 6\frac{5b_1}{2} = 15b_1.$$

    Since the area is 75, we get:

    $$75 = 15b_1$$
    $$b_1 = 5.$$

    Thus, the short base is 5 and the long base is 20.

CIRCLES

Definitions

Circles are closed plane curves with all points on the curve equally distant from a fixed point called the *center*. The symbol ⊙ indicates a circle. A circle is usually named by its center. A line segment from the center to any point on the circle is called the *radius* (plural, radii). All radii of the same circle are congruent.

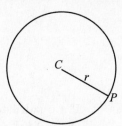

C = center
$\overline{CP}$ = radius = r

A *chord* is a line segment whose endpoints are on the circle. A *diameter* of a circle is a chord that passes through the center of the circle. A diameter, the longest distance between two points on the circle, is twice the length of the radius. A diameter perpendicular to a chord bisects that chord.

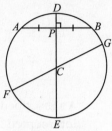

$\overline{AB}$ is a chord.

C is the center.

$\overline{DE}$ is a diameter.

$\overline{FG}$ is a diameter.

$\overline{AB} \perp \overline{DE}$ so $AP = PB$

A *central angle* is an angle whose vertex is the center of a circle and whose sides are radii of the circle. An *inscribed angle* is an angle whose vertex is on the circle and whose sides are chords of the circle.

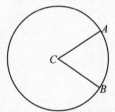 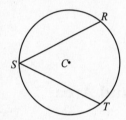

$\angle ACB$ is a central angle.

$\angle RST$ is an inscribed angle.

An *arc* is a portion of a circle. The symbol $\cap$ is used to indicate an arc. Arcs are usually measured in degrees. Since the entire circle is 360°, a semicircle (half a circle) is an arc of 180°, and a quarter of a circle is an arc of 90°.

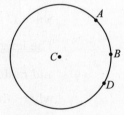

$\overset{\frown}{ABD}$ is an arc.

$\overset{\frown}{AB}$ is an arc.

$\overset{\frown}{BD}$ is an arc.

A central angle is equal in measure to the measure of its intercepted arc.

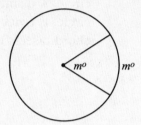

An inscribed angle is equal in measure to one half the measure of its intercepted arc. An angle inscribed in a semicircle is a right angle because the semicircle has a measure of 180°, and the measure of the inscribed angle is one half of that.

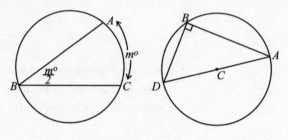

$$\text{m}\overset{\frown}{DA} = 180°; \text{ therefore,}$$
$$\text{m}\angle DBA = 90°.$$

Perimeter and Area

The perimeter of a circle is called the *circumference*. The length of the circumference is πd, where d is the diameter, or $2\pi r$, where r is the radius. The number π is irrational and can be approximated by 3.14159 . . . , but in problems dealing with circles, it is best to leave π in the answer. There is no fraction exactly equal to π.

Examples

1. If the circumference of a circle is 8π feet, what is the radius?

    Since $C = 2\pi r = 8\pi$, $r = 4$ feet.

    The length of an arc of a circle can be found if the central angle and radius are known. Then the length of the arc is $\dfrac{n°}{360°}(2\pi r)$, where the central angle of the arc is $n°$. This is true because of the proportion:

    $$\frac{\text{Arc}}{\text{Circumference}} = \frac{\text{Central Angle}}{360°}$$

2. If a circle of radius 3 feet has a central angle of 60°, find the length of the arc intercepted by this central angle.

$$\text{Arc} = \frac{60°}{360°}(2\pi 3) = \pi \text{ feet}$$

The area A of a circle is πr^2, where r is the radius. If the diameter is given instead of the radius,

$$A = \pi\left(\frac{d}{2}\right)^2 = \frac{\pi d^2}{4}.$$

3. Find the area of a circular ring formed by two concentric circles of radii 6 and 8 inches, respectively. (Concentric circles are circles with the same center.)

    The area of the ring will equal the area of the large circle minus the area of the small circle.

    $$\begin{aligned}\text{Area of ring} &= \pi 8^2 - \pi 6^2\\ &= \pi(64 - 36)\\ &= 28\pi \text{ square inches}\end{aligned}$$

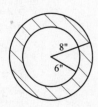

4. A square is inscribed in a circle whose diameter is 10 inches.
    Find the difference between the area of the circle and that of
    the square.

    If a square is inscribed in a circle, the diagonal of the square is
    the diameter of the circle. If the diagonal of the square is 10
    inches, then, by the Pythagorean theorem,

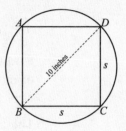

$$2s^2 = 100$$
$$s^2 = 50$$

The side of the square s is $\sqrt{50}$, and the area of the square is
50 square inches. If the diameter of the circle is 10, its radius is
5 and the area of the circle is $\pi 5^2 = 25\pi$ square inches. Then
the difference between the area of the circle and the area of the
square is:

$25\pi - 50$ square inches
$= 25\,(\pi - 2)$ square inches

Distance Formula

In the arithmetic section, we described the Cartesian coordinate
system when explaining how to draw graphs representing linear
equations. If two points are plotted in the Cartesian coordinate
system, it is useful to know how to find the distance between them.
If the two points have coordinates (a, b) and (p, q), the distance
between them is:

$$d = \sqrt{(a - p)^2 + (b - q)^2}$$

This formula makes use of the Pythagorean Theorem.

Examples

1. Find the distance between the two points $(-3, 2)$ and $(1, -1)$.

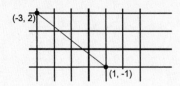

Let $(a, b) = (-3, 2)$ and $(p, q) = (1, -1)$. Then:

$$d = \sqrt{(-3-1)^2 + [2 - (-1)]^2}$$

$$= \sqrt{(-4)^2 + (2 + 1)^2}$$

$$= \sqrt{(-4)^2 + 3^2}$$

$$= \sqrt{16 + 9} = \sqrt{25} = 5$$

2. What is the area of the circle that passes through the point $(10, 8)$ and has its center at $(2, 2)$?

We can use the distance formula to find the radius of the circle.

$$r = \sqrt{(10 - 2)^2 + (8 - 2)^2} = \sqrt{8^2 + 6^2} = \sqrt{100} = 10$$

Thus, the radius of the circle is 10. The area would be $A = \pi r^2 = \pi(10)^2 = 100\pi$.

VOLUME

Definitions

The volume of any three-dimensional solid figure represents the amount of space contained within it. While area, as we have seen, is measured in square units, the volume of an object is measured in cubic units, such as cubic feet, cubic meters, and cubic centimeters. One cubic foot is defined as the amount of space contained within a cube that is 1 foot on each side.

There are several volume formulas for common solid figures that you should be familiar with.

A *rectangular solid* is a six-sided figure whose sides are rectangles. The volume of a rectangular solid is its length times its width times its height.

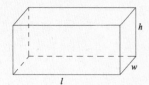

A *cube* is a rectangular solid whose sides are all the same length. The volume of a cube is the cube of its side.

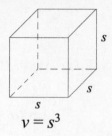

$$v = s^3$$

The volume of a *cylinder* is equal to the area of its base times its height. Since the base is a circle, the volume is $V = \pi r^2 h$.

A *pyramid* has a rectangular base and triangular sides. Its area is given by the formula $V = \frac{1}{3}lwh$.

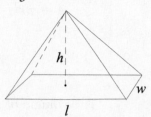

The volume of a *cone* is given by the formula $V = \frac{1}{3}\pi r^2 h$.

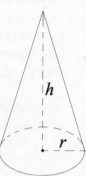

Finally, the formula for the volume of a *sphere* is given by the formula $V = \dfrac{4}{3}\pi r^3$.

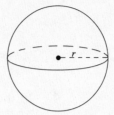

Examples

1. What is the surface area of a cube whose volume is 125 cubic centimeters?

    Since the formula for the volume of a cube is $V = s^3$, we have $V = s^3 = 125$. Thus, $s = \sqrt[3]{125} = 5$ centimeters.

    If the side of the cube is 5 centimeters, the area of one of its faces is $5^2 = 25$ square centimeters. Since the cube has 6 faces, its surface area is $6 \times 25 = 150$ square centimeters.

2. The volume of a cylinder having a height of 12 is 144π. What is the radius of its base?

    The formula for the volume of a cylinder is $V = \pi r^2 h$. Since $V = 144\pi$ and $h = 12$, we have

    $$144\pi = \pi r^2 (12).$$

    Divide both sides by π.

    $$144 = 12r^2$$
    $$12 = r^2$$
    $$r = \sqrt{12} = 2\sqrt{3}.$$

    Thus, the radius of the base is $2\sqrt{3}$.

Geometry Problems

1. In triangle QRS, $\mathrm{m}\angle Q = \mathrm{m}\angle R$ and $\mathrm{m}\angle S = 64°$. Find the measures of $\angle Q$ and $\angle R$.

2. In parallelogram $ABCD$, $\angle A$ and $\angle C$ are opposite angles. If $\mathrm{m}\angle A = 12x°$ and $\mathrm{m}\angle C = (10x + 12)°$, find the measures of $\angle A$ and $\angle C$.

3. What is the area of a trapezoid whose height is 5 feet and whose bases are 7 feet and 9 feet?

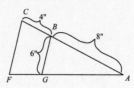

4. In the preceding figure, $\overline{CF} \parallel \overline{BG}$. Find the length of $\overline{CF}$.

5. The hypotenuse of a right triangle is 25 feet. If one leg is 15 feet, find the length of the other leg.

6. Find the area of a circle whose diameter is 16 inches.

7. Find the distance between the points $(-1, -2)$ and $(5, 7)$.

8. In the diagram below, $\overline{AB}$ is parallel to $\overline{CD}$. Find the measures of x and y.

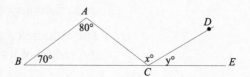

9. In the triangle below, find the measures of the angles.

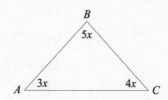

10. If the base of a parallelogram decreases by 20% and the height increases by 40%, by what percent does the area increase?

11. In the circle below, $AB = 9$ and $BC = 12$. If $\overline{AC}$ is the diameter of the circle, what is the radius?

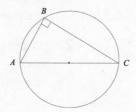

12. In the right triangle below, AB is twice BC. What is the length of BC?

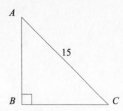

Solutions

1. $m\angle Q + m\angle R + m\angle S = 180°$

   $m\angle Q + m\angle R + 64° = 180°$

   $m\angle Q + m\angle R = 116°$

Since $m\angle Q = m\angle R$, they must each have measures of $58°$.

2. The opposite angles in a parallelogram are equal. Thus,

   $12x = 10x + 12$

   $2x = 12$

   $x = 6$

Thus, $12x = 12(6) = 72$.

$\angle A$ and $\angle C$ both measure $72°$.

3. $A = h\left(\dfrac{b_1 + b_2}{2}\right)$

   $= 5\left(\dfrac{7 + 9}{2}\right) = 5\left(\dfrac{16}{2}\right) = 5(8) = 40$

The area of the trapezoid is 40 square feet.

4. Since $\overline{CF} \parallel \overline{BG}$, $\triangle ACF \sim \triangle ABG$.

Therefore, $\dfrac{6}{CF} = \dfrac{8}{12}$

   $8\,CF = 72$

   $CF = 9$ inches

5. Using the Pythagorean Theorem,

   $a^2 + 15^2 = 25^2$

   $a^2 + 225 = 625$

   $a^2 = 400$

   $a = \sqrt{400} = 20$

The length of the other leg is 20 feet.

6. If $d = 16$, $r = 8$. $A = \pi r^2 = \pi(8)^2 = 64\pi$

The area of the circle is 64π square inches.

7. $d = \sqrt{(5 - (-1))^2 + (7 - (-2))^2}$

$ = \sqrt{6^2 + 9^2} = \sqrt{36 + 81} = \sqrt{117}$

The distance between the points is equal to $\sqrt{117}$.

8. Since $\overline{AB}$ and $\overline{CD}$ are parallel, $\angle BAC$ and $\angle ACD$ are alternate interior angles and are therefore congruent. Thus, $x = 80$. Similarly, $\angle ABC$ is a corresponding angle to $\angle DCE$, and so $y = 70$.

9. Since there are $180°$ in a triangle, we must have:

$3x + 4x + 5x = 180$

$12x = 180$

$x = 15$, and $3x = 45$, $4x = 60$, and $5x = 75$. Thus, the angles in the triangle measure $45°$, $60°$, and $75°$.

10. Let $b =$ the length of the base and $h =$ the height in the original parallelogram. Then the area of the original parallelogram is $A = bh$. If the base decreases by 20%, it becomes $.8b$. If the height increases by 40%, it becomes $1.4h$. The new area, then, is $A = (.8b)(1.4h) = 1.12bh$, which is 12% bigger than the original area.

11. Note that triangle ABC is a right triangle. Call the diameter d. Then we have:

$9^2 + 12^2 = d^2$, or

$81 + 144 = d^2$

$225 = d^2$

$d = 15$

If the diameter is 15, the radius is $7\dfrac{1}{2}$.

12. Let the length of $\overline{BC}$ be x. Then the length of $\overline{AB}$ is $2x$. By the Pythagorean Theorem, we have:

$x^2 + (2x)^2 = 15^2$

$x^2 + 4x^2 = 225$

$5x^2 = 225$

$x^2 = 45$

$x = \sqrt{45} = \sqrt{9 \times 5} = 3\sqrt{5}$

The length of BC is $3\sqrt{5}$.

TABLES AND GRAPHS

Tables and graphs give visual comparisons of amount. They show relationships between two or more sets of information. It is essential to be able to read tables and graphs correctly.

TABLES

Tables present data corresponding to classifications by row and column. Tables always state the units (thousands of people, years, or millions of dollars, for example) in which the numbers are expressed. Sometimes the units are percents. Both specific and general questions can be answered by using the information in the table.

Persons 5 Years Old and Over Speaking Various Languages at Home, by Age
(Numbers in thousands: civilian noninstitutional population)

Language spoken at home	Persons 5 years old and over	Total %	5 to 13 years	14 to 17 years	18 to 24 years	25 to 44 years	45 to 64 years	65 to 74 years	75 years and over
Total	200,812	*	30,414	15,955	27,988	59,385	43,498	15,053	8,519
Percent	*	100.0	15.1	7.9	13.9	29.6	21.7	7.5	4.2
Speaking									
English only	176,319	100.0	15.4	8.0	14.1	29.5	21.5	7.4	4.0
Speaking other									
language	17,985	100.0	14.4	6.9	12.6	30.8	21.8	7.5	6.0
Chinese	514	100.0	12.5	5.8	15.8	34.8	21.2	6.8	3.1
French	987	100.0	8.1	5.5	10.2	29.9	30.4	9.9	6.0
German	1,261	100.0	5.4	7.1	10.8	24.3	27.4	12.8	12.2
Greek	365	100.0	16.7	4.9	10.4	38.1	21.9	4.4	3.6
Italian	1,354	100.0	7.5	4.9	8.1	19.3	31.5	15.1	13.7
Japanese	265	100.0	7.9	6.8	7.9	27.2	36.6	9.4	3.8
Korean	191	100.0	16.2	5.8	17.8	35.6	19.9	3.7	1.0
Philippine languages	419	100.0	10.7	5.3	8.6	40.8	20.3	7.2	6.9
Polish	731	100.0	2.7	1.4	3.7	13.8	45.7	21.6	10.9
Portuguese	245	100.0	15.9	8.6	12.2	33.9	22.0	3.7	3.3
Spanish	8,768	100.0	20.2	8.8	15.4	34.6	15.8	3.1	2.2
Yiddish	234	100.0	8.5	0.4	3.0	15.8	20.9	29.1	21.8
Other	2,651	100.0	10.0	4.9	10.8	30.3	23.3	10.1	10.6
Not reported	6,508	100.0	11.1	8.4	13.5	26.9	25.1	9.5	5.6

(Notice that in this table, the numbers are given in thousands, so that the number speaking German at home, for example, is not 1,261 but 1,261,000.)

Examples

1. What language is spoken at home by almost one half of those not speaking English at home?

    Spanish; 8,768/17,985 is about 48%.

2. What language has the highest percent of its speakers in the 45- to 64-year-old age bracket?

    Polish, with 45.7%.

3. How many persons between the ages of 18 and 24 speak Korean at home?

    There are 191,000 of all ages speaking Korean, of whom 17.8% are between 18 and 24:

    $.178 \times 191,000 = 33,998$ persons

4. Of the people between the ages of 14 and 17, which is greater, the number who speak German at home or the number who speak Italian at home?

    The number of 14- to 17-year-olds speaking German at home is $1,261,000 \times .071 = 89,531$.

    The number of 14- to 17-year-olds speaking Italian at home is $1,354,000 \times .049 = 66,346$.

    Therefore, more people in the 14- to 17-year-old group speak German even though, overall, more people speak Italian.

GRAPHS

Bar Graphs

Bar graphs may be horizontal or vertical, but both axes are designed to give information. The height (or width) of the bar is proportional to the number or percent represented. Bar graphs are less accurate than tables but give a quick comparison of information. There may be only two variables, as in the following graph. One is the year and the other is the percentage of the labor force made up of women.

Women as a Percentage of the Labor Force

Examples

1. Between which 10 years does the chart show the greatest percent increase of women in the labor force?

    For each of the 10-year periods, there is some increase. Subtract each percent from the one to the right of it; four subtractions. The greatest increase, 4.6%, occurs between 1970 and 1980.

2. In 2000, what was the ratio of women in the labor force to men in the labor force?

    Since, in 2000, 42% of the labor force were women, it follows that 58% of the labor force were men. Therefore,

    $$\frac{Women}{Men} \rightarrow \frac{42}{58}$$

    This ratio can be simplified.

    $$\frac{42}{58} = \frac{21}{29}$$

    Thus, the ratio of women to men is 21 to 29. If we take the numerator and denominator of $\frac{21}{29}$ and divide by 21, we get $\frac{1}{1.38}$. Thus, another way to express this ratio is as 1 to 1.38. This means that, for every 1 woman in the labor force, there are 1.38 men.

In this bar graph, percents are written at the top of each bar. This is not always the case. If the numbers are not given, you must read across, using a ruler or card, to the relevant axis and estimate the height.

Bar graphs such as the following can compare two sets of data for varying years. This graph shows, for example, that 86.8% of the male population 16 years old and over was in the labor force in 1960. In that same year, 33.9% of the female population was in the labor force. It gives different information from the previous graph.

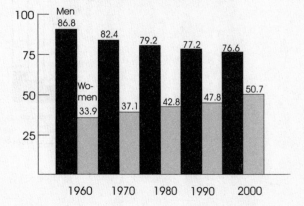

Percentage of Population 16 Years Old and Over in the Labor Force

Examples

1. Explain the apparent discrepancy for the year 1990 between the percentage for women in this graph (47.8%) and that in the previous graph (40.3%).

    This graph shows that 47.8% of all women were in the labor force in 1980—that is, 47.8 of 100 women were working. The previous graph showed that 40.3 of 100 *workers,* or 40.3%, were women. There is no discrepancy. The populations are different.

2. If, in 1990, there were 90,000,000 women 16 years old or older, approximately how many of these women were not in the labor force?

    In 1990, 47.8% of women 16 and over were in the labor force. Since there were 90,000,000 women in this age group, we have

    90,000,000 × .478 = 43,020,000 women in the labor force. Then the number of women not in the labor force was

    90,000,000 − 43,020,000 = 46,980,000.

Cumulative Bar Graphs

These graphs are similar to bar graphs, but each bar contains more than one kind of information and the total height is the sum of the various components. The following graph gives percentages of college graduates on the bottom and high school graduates on the top. There might well be other gradations, such as "some college" above the college section and "some high school" above the high school section.

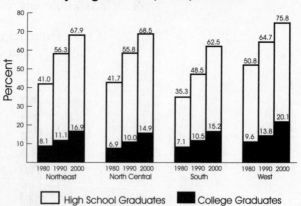

Percent of Persons 25 Years Old and Over Who Were High School and College Graduates, by Region: 1980, 1990, and 2000

270

Examples

1. For each of the 3 years, which region consistently has the lowest percentage of college graduates?

   North Central

2. Which region has the lowest *total* educational attainment for each of the 3 years?

   South

3. In 2000, which region had the highest percentage of high school graduates, and what was it?

   For 2000, subtract the percent of college graduates from the total percent; four subtractions. The highest is the West, with $75.8\% - 20.1\% = 55.7\%$.

4. Which region had the greatest increase in the percentage of college graduates between 1990 and 2000?

   West, with $20.1\% - 13.8\% = 6.3\%$.

5. In 2000, which of the four regions had the highest percentage of persons 25 years old and over who were neither high school nor college graduates?

   Since the South had the lowest percentage (62.5%) of persons 25 years old and over who were either high school or college graduates, then it must have the highest percentage of persons 25 years old and over who were neither high school nor college graduates. In fact, $100\% - 62.5\% = 37.5\%$ were neither high school nor college graduates in the South.

Circle Graphs

Circle graphs, also known as pie charts, show the breakdown of an entire quantity, such as a college budget, into its component parts. The circle representing 100% of the quantity is cut into pieces, each piece having a certain percentage value. The sum of the pieces is 100%. The size of the piece is proportional to the size of the percentage. To make a circle graph, you must have an instrument called a protractor, which measures degrees. Suppose the measured quantity is 10% of the whole. Because 10% of 360° is 36°, a central angle of 36° must be measured and radii drawn. This piece now has an area of 10% of the circle. When answering questions on circle graphs, compare percentages.

Percent Distribution of Voters in the Last Election by Years of School Completed and Family Income

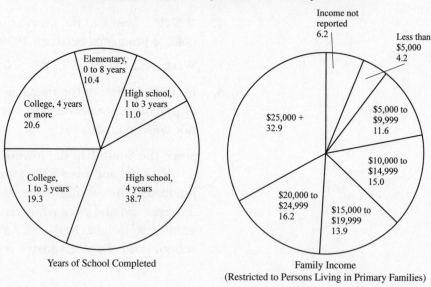

Years of School Completed

Family Income
(Restricted to Persons Living in Primary Families)

Examples

1. Of those who voted in the last election, what percentage attended college at some time?

   This information is in the first graph. Add 20.6% to 19.3% to get 39.9%.

2. Of those who voted in the last election and who reported their income levels, what percentage had a family income below $10,000?

   This information is in the second graph. Add 4.2% to 11.6% to get 15.8%.

3. If 36,000 people voted in the last election, how many of these people had family incomes of $20,000 or greater?

    To answer this question, we use the second circle graph. First note that 16.2% + 32.9% = 49.1% of the voters had family incomes of $20,000 or greater. Since there were 36,000 voters, we have

    $$36,000 \times .491 = 17,676.$$

    Therefore, 17,676 of the voters had family incomes of $20,000 or greater.

Line Graphs

Like bar graphs, line graphs follow vertical and horizontal information axes, but the line graph is continuous. There may be a single broken line or there may be several, comparing three or four stocks or incomes or, as in the case of this graph, numbers of workers in selected occupations. The line graph shows trends: increasing, decreasing, or not changing.

Number of Workers in Selected Occupations (In Millions)

In this graph, the actual number of people in an occupation in a given year must be estimated. For example, the number of social workers in 1985 seems to be 14 million, and the number of white-collar workers for the same year about 40 million.

Examples

1. In 1995, what was the total number of workers in all four occupations?

    Estimate each number by comparison with the values at the left. Then add the four. Estimates: farm workers, 3 million; social workers, 18 million; blue-collar workers, 33 million; and white-collar workers, 52 million; total 106 million.

2. In which year were the number of social workers and the number of farm workers approximately equal?

    The number of workers is equal at the point on the graph where the lines representing service and farm workers cross. Looking at the graph, the point where the lines cross appears to be approximately 1964. Prior to that, the number of social workers is fewer than the number of farm workers; after that, it is more.

Since the scale on graphs is usually marked in large increments, since the lines used are often thick, and since the estimates must often be made on the side of the graph far from the scale, use whole numbers as much as possible when estimating. Use only the fraction one half $\left(\dfrac{1}{2}\right)$ if your judgment tells you something less than a whole number should be used. Because all the information must be estimated, units less than one half will not significantly affect your answer. Do not spend time trying to figure the precise number on the scale. A reasonable estimate should let your answer be within 1 or 2 percent on either side of the correct answer choice. As part of your strategy for dealing with graphs, look at the answer choices to get an idea of the magnitude of your estimate before doing the estimating. Choose the answer choice closest to your estimate.

Example

If your estimate is 97 million and the answer choices are 3 million, 0.5 million, 90 million, 103 million, and 98 million, choose 98 million as your answer.

Tables and Graphs Problems

Use this bar graph to answer the following questions:

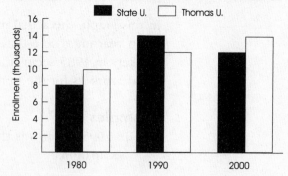

Student Enrollments: State U. vs. Thomas U.

1. What was the enrollment at State U. in 1980?

2. In 1990, how many more students were enrolled at State U. than at Thomas U.?

3. If the average tuition at State U. in 2000 was $6,500, what was the total revenue received in tuition at State U. that year?

4. In 1990, 74% of the students enrolled at State U. were males. How many males attended State U. in 1990?

5. Find the percent of increase in enrollment at Thomas U. from 1980 to 1990.

Use this circle graph to answer the following questions.

**Adult Education Courses
Based on 250,000 Courses Offered–1998**

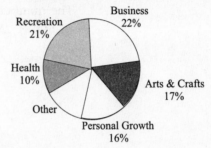

6. How many personal growth courses are offered?

7. How many health courses and business courses are offered?

8. How many courses offered are in the "other" category?

9. How many more business courses are offered than recreation courses?

10. If 20% of the arts & crafts courses offered are painting courses, how many painting courses are offered?

Solutions

1. 8,000 students

2. $14,000 - 12,000 = 2,000$ students

3. $12,000 \times \$6,500 = \$78,000,000$

4. $14,000 \times 74\% = 14,000 \times .74 = 10,360$ students

5. Increase in enrollment $= 12,000 - 10,000 = 2,000$

   Percent of increase in enrollment $= 2,000 \div 10,000 = \dfrac{1}{5} = 20\%$

6. $250,000 \times .16 = 40,000$ personal growth courses

7. Health and business together account for $10\% + 22\% = 32\%$ of the courses. Thus, $250,000 \times .32 = 80,000$ health and business courses.

8. Note that the percentage of courses for the "other" category is missing. To determine it, add the percentages for all of the other courses and subtract from 100%. The sum of all of the percentages shown is 86%, so 14% of the courses are in the "other" category. Thus, $250,000 \times .14 = 35,000$ courses are in the "other" category.

9. The easiest way to solve this problem is to subtract the percentage that represents business courses from the percentage that represents recreation courses. $22\% - 21\% = 1\%$. Thus, there is a 1% difference. $250,000 \times .01 = 2,500$.

10. The number of arts & crafts courses is $250,000 \times .17 = 42,500$. The number of painting courses is 20% of this number: $42,500 \times .20 = 8,500$.

STRATEGIES FOR READING COMPREHENSION

The Reading Comprehension portion of the ISEE is composed of nine passages with a total of 40 questions to be answered in 40 minutes. Each question has four choices (A–D). The SSAT Reading Comprehension section is 30 minutes long and also has 40 questions, each of which has five choices (A–E).

Reading Comprehension questions pertain to passages that fall into the following categories:

- Science—biology, general science, history of science

- Social studies—history, politics, current events

- Personal narrative—someone's story or opinion ("How camping taught me independence")

- Fiction or poetry—a short excerpt from a book or a short poem

As you can see, if you have to answer 40 questions in 30 or 40 minutes, you have a minute or less to answer each one, not even counting the time it will take to read each passage. Pacing yourself, therefore, is important. You need to move at a fairly steady pace; it is not necessary, however, that you answer the questions in the order in which they appear in the test. Just be sure when you skip a section that you put your answers in the proper location on your answer sheet. Answering more questions *correctly* is more important than merely answering questions. You do not need to have any special knowledge to answer any of these questions. Choose an answer based on the information provided in the passages.

The ISEE and the SSAT reading comprehension questions test your ability to handle the kinds of information you will meet in high school classes.

TYPES OF QUESTIONS

FACTUAL

These questions test whether you understood the information presented in the passage. The subject matter can deal with humanities (arts, biographies, and poetry), social studies (history, economics, and sociology), and science (medicine, astronomy, chemistry, physics, anthropology, and psychology). Remember, however, your answer is based solely on the information presented in the passage.

> *Example:* According to the passage, the kinds of relics located in the South American digs were . . .

VOCABULARY

These questions are designed to determine your grasp of key terms used in the selection. Typically these words are defined through examples, synonyms, or explanations.

Example: As used in the sentence, "infusion" most nearly means . . .

IMPLICATIONS OR INFERENCES

These questions test your ability to draw logical conclusions based on the material presented in the passage. Since the author of the passage tells us _____, then _____ must also be true.

Example: The passage implies that . . .

The reader can infer from the passage that . . .

Which of the following can be deduced from the passage? . . .

AUTHOR'S ATTITUDE

Questions of this type test your ability to recognize the author's judgment toward the subject matter. Is the attitude one of approval or disapproval? Is the attitude toward the subject matter humorous? Doubtful? Serious?

Example: Which of the following best describes the author's attitude toward the subject? . . .

BEST TITLE

These questions test your ability to recognize the difference between the main idea and supporting ideas in a passage.

Example: Which of these titles is the most appropriate for the passage? . . .

NARRATIVE

These are excerpts from novels, short stories, and essays.

Example: According to the passage, where does the action occur?

READING SKILLS: SQ3R

An important part of improving your reading skills is finding a dependable method or approach. The SQ3R method is one that many students have found to be beneficial. This approach gives you a logical way to boost your reading comprehension and maximize your time. The SQ3R study technique, developed in 1941 by Francis Robinson, can improve your reading comprehension in virtually all areas. Here are its components:

S = Survey	This first step, survey or preview, requires you to do a quick overview of what you're reading. Check the title of the passage (if there is one), read the first paragraph or introduction, and read the first sentence of each of the other paragraphs. Read the last paragraph or the conclusion. This approach gives you a glimpse of the material as well as an estimation of the time you'll need to complete the task.
Q = Question	Knowing the questions before you read a passage can give you a better sense of purpose as you read. You can quickly scan the questions that follow the selection to be a more actively involved reader. It's not necessary at this point to preview the choices of answers.
R = Read	This stage is definitely an important one. Don't rush! Completing the first two steps in this method should give you a clear sense of purpose. Read at a steady pace.
R = Recite	Although you cannot recite aloud the important ideas as you take a standardized test, you should make every effort to repeat them mentally. Studies have shown that reciting can increase your retention rate from 20% to 80%. Try to summarize the main idea in each paragraph.
R = Review	Although this step is more effective for remembering information over a long period of time, you can review the details mentally, thus reassuring yourself that you have read and understood the material.

USEFUL READING TECHNIQUES

As you read your test questions silently, keep these points in mind. *Vocalization* or moving your lips while you read can slow your reading rate. It takes too much time to say the words with your lips. To break this habit, try practicing reading with a pencil clenched between your teeth or chewing gum while you read. *Subvocalizing* is another problematic reading habit that is similar except that the reader isn't forming words with his or her lips; the reader forms words in his or her larynx. Practice reading rapidly under timed conditions to eliminate this habit. *Pointing* is also a problem that can slow a reader's progress. Keep your hands in your lap to break yet another habit that interferes with your development.

The movement of your eyes across the page is another important component in the way you read. Instead of reading in a straight line across the page and looking at each word separately, your eyes should move in arcs across the page in a sort of "bouncing" pattern. Your brain "sees" the words, but you are unaware of these arcs and fixations. Fast readers take in 2.5 to 3 words per fixation. Practicing speed and comprehension drills can also be beneficial in saving you time and helping you become a better reader. Try to read more rapidly by focusing on key words in each line.

Pre-reading a passage on a standardized test can provide a sense of purpose to your reading. You can have a clear sense of what kinds of details are important. Often reading the first and last sentences of the passage as well as the topic sentences in the body paragraphs can clarify the important points. Just taking a few minutes can be useful; however, you must preview rapidly. Even if you don't use the other steps in the SQ3R approach, previewing (or surveying) can help.

Skimming and *scanning* are two other reading methods that can be profitable. Both of these skills can help you become a better reader. In *scanning,* you glance at material, usually looking from the top to the bottom of the page, until you locate a particular piece of information. For instance, when you look up a number in a telephone book, you scan the entries until you find the number. *Skimming,* on the other hand, gives you an overview of the major points of a passage. You look over material quickly, just seeking main ideas. Of these two skills, skimming is probably more useful when you take a standardized reading comprehension test. In only a very few instances can you scan a passage to find as specific a detail as the answer to a question. Most questions, on the other hand, require inferences or conclusions that the reader must formulate after having read and understood the passage. The restrictions of time may be an important factor in deciding whether you can rely on skimming; a more deliberate pace is usually more suitable. In some instances, however, you'll need to read at a fast rate to finish the test.

Now it's time to put it all together. Following are three reading selections and accompanying questions. Using the reading skills and techniques we've given you, read the passages. Then, try to identify the types of questions that follow the passages. Answering the questions should now be an easy task.

SAMPLE PASSAGES AND QUESTIONS

> **Directions:** Each passage below is followed by questions. Answer the questions following each passage on the basis of what is stated or implied in that passage.

Passage 1

Line One of the attractions of a new car is its showroom shine. Eventually, however, exposure to light, water, air pollution, and other kinds of destructive factors begin to age the shine, and the gloss starts to fade. To restore the sheen, you can use an auto polish. Choices include
5 liquid, paste, and even spray forms of polish, also known as wax or sealants. Whichever form you choose, be sure to wash your car thoroughly beforehand. Rubbing tough road dirt into the surface will probably scratch the paint on your car.

Regardless of the type of polish you select, applying the polish
10 should be easy. Perhaps the easiest to apply are liquids because they spread better than paste polishes. Be careful not to get polish on any kind of vinyl because the polish may affect the appearance of the vinyl. Instructions for polishing also include explanation for burnishing the car once the polish has dried. Usually you can use a soft, dry
15 cotton cloth to restore that attractive showroom luster.

1. Types of car polish include
    (A) paste.
    (B) liquid.
    (C) spray-on.
    (D) All of the above

2. According to the passage, a car's showroom finish can be dulled because of
    (A) parking under trees.
    (B) exposure to pollution.
    (C) poor paint coverage.
    (D) hail.

3. The word "burnishing" (lines 13–14) in the passage is used to mean
    (A) degree of physical fitness needed to polish a car.
    (B) removing dirt before you polish the car.
    (C) washing the car.
    (D) rubbing the polish to restore the shine.

4. Which of the following is the best title for this passage?

(A) "Waxing and Waning Your Car"
(B) "Renewing the Sheen"
(C) "Washing Your Car"
(D) "How to Use a Sealant"

Passage 2

Line Historians believe that American science fiction movies popular in the 1950s were a manifestation of a general fear of invasion of the country. The Red Scare of the McCarthy era made American citizens aware of the possible presence of Communist spies who were
5 virtually impossible to detect. The original version of *Invasion of the Body Snatchers* depicted the ease with which outsiders could infiltrate our society. Besides this general fear of aliens, the movies also reflected concerns about the effects of radiation such as the aftermath of the atomic bomb dropped to end World War II. *Attack*
10 *of the Fifty-foot Woman* was a typical movie of this type. Even a film version of *War of the Worlds* generated anxiety not unlike the chaos Orson Welles created with his infamous radio broadcast on October 30, 1938, when thousands of New Jersey citizens were convinced that Martians were landing in their state. Space was still mysterious.
15 Who knew what or who was out there? Writers with vivid imaginations such as Isaac Asimov and Robert Heinlein offered thrilling possibilities. Readers envisioned little green men who might be real—or the "purple people eater" made famous by a popular song that attempted to poke fun at the obsession with aliens.

5. The writer of this passage implies that

(A) science fiction served as an outlet for fears in the fifties.
(B) science fiction was based on some real UFO sightings.
(C) it was easy for writers to fool Americans obsessed with invaders.
(D) all Americans feared invaders from space.

6. The term "infamous" (line 12) most nearly means

(A) not famous.
(B) notorious.
(C) well-known.
(D) unpopular.

7. It is possible to infer that science fiction experienced such popularity because

(A) the public was worried about invasion from Communist Russia.

(B) the public enjoyed being scared by outrageous sci-fi films.

(C) sci-fi literature appealed to a population tired of radio as entertainment but not quite ready for television.

(D) the sci-fi available played on obsessions with little green men.

8. The McCarthy "Red Scare" of the 1950s relates to the popularity of science fiction because

(A) the hearings revealed the truth about Joseph McCarthy.

(B) Americans learned of the existence of Communist spies in America.

(C) movies were made about the hearings.

(D) the hearings suggested a connection between Communist spies and invaders from space.

9. Which of the following was based directly on popular fears?

(A) *Invasion of the Body Snatchers*

(B) *War of the Worlds*

(C) *The Attack of the Fifty-foot Woman*

(D) All of the above

Passage 3

Line The earliest British settlers who came to what became the United States of America can be divided into two groups. First, there were those like Sir Walter Raleigh, who was intent on using the fertile soil of the area now known as Virginia to raise tobacco. Some of the men

5 who came with Raleigh were "second sons"; according to British law, the eldest son would inherit the bulk of the estate. Second and subsequent sons had to look elsewhere for livelihood. Some chose to enter the ministry; others came to Virginia, never intending to stay. Captain John Smith is a well-known figure from this era. These men

10 planned to turn tobacco into cash when they went back to Britain with their harvested crops. He and other entrepreneurs came to be known as "planters." Some even believed that they could easily turn the Native Americans into slaves. The fact, of course, is that none of this fledgling tobacco business was easy. While the area was remark-

15 ably arable, clearing the land required time and manpower. Many of the planters did not plan to do the manual labor themselves. They tended, however, to stake claims to huge acres of land. Eventually, a work force was brought in. Some of these workers were convicts; some were indentured servants; some were African natives. This

20 southern area of the New World would eventually become the American South; the beginning of slavery was already in kernel form.

The second group, the earliest arrivals in the North, were mostly British citizens who sought the freedom to practice religion as they wished. This religious group had fled Great Britain and moved to
25 Holland where they lived briefly, but they chose to move to the New World. They landed in the New England area, where the land was rocky and not very fertile. These settlers tended to form small communities because they shared religious beliefs and sought to establish a theocracy, a society in which civil law is the same as
30 religious law. They also feared the wilderness, which was believed to be the home of Satan. John Bradford, the first governor of this area, recorded much of the early history. These settlers came to America to stay; they worked together to create a community. Because of these qualities, their settlements thrived.
35 The basic differences in these two groups laid the foundation for the War Between the States, which did not occur until almost 200 years later.

10. The best title for this passage is

   (A) "Tobacco for Today."

   (B) "Early Settlers in America."

   (C) "Religion in Early America."

   (D) "Second Sons Settling the South."

   (E) "The First Slaves."

11. The word "arable" (line 15) most nearly means

   (A) fertile.

   (B) clear of trees.

   (C) dry, desert-like.

   (D) swampy.

   (E) unprofitable.

12. The writer implies that the group who came to Virginia

   (A) consisted entirely of members of the aristocracy.

   (B) was unwilling to do any physical labor.

   (C) was not as unified as the northern group.

   (D) planned to rely on tobacco for income.

   (E) tended to settle near the coast.

13. What was the writer's purpose in this passage?

   (A) To show how slavery began

   (B) To contrast the beginnings of two sections of America

   (C) To point out the stronger settlers

   (D) To explain why tobacco was such an important crop

   (E) To describe the religious roots of the North

ANSWERS AND EXPLANATIONS

Passage 1

1. **The correct answer is (D).** This is a factual question. All three types of car polish are mentioned in the passage.

2. **The correct answer is (B).** This is a factual question. Choice (A), though probably true, is incorrect because it is not included in the passage. Remember that you must answer the questions based solely on the information provided or implied in the passage. Choice (C) is incorrect; there is no mention of paint coverage. Choice (D) is incorrect. Although it may be a true statement, it is not mentioned in the passage.

3. **The correct answer is (D).** This is a vocabulary-in-context question. Choice (A) is incorrect; physical fitness is not mentioned in the passage. Choice (B) is incorrect; the sentence in which "burnishing" appears makes it clear that "burnishing" occurs after the polish has been applied. Choice (C) is incorrect; again, "burnishing" occurs after the polish has been applied. Logically, the car must be washed before the polish can be applied.

4. **The correct answer is (B).** This is a main idea question. Even if you were unsure of the meaning of "sheen," by process of elimination, you should select this answer because the other three are not appropriate. Choice (A) is incorrect; "waning" does not apply here. It means to reduce. For example, the moon "waxes" and "wanes" as it goes through its cycle. Choice (C) is incorrect because it is incomplete. Washing is only part of the process. Choice (D) is incorrect because there is only one mention of sealant.

Passage 2

5. **The correct answer is (A).** This is an implications question. Choice (B) is incorrect; there is no mention of UFOs. Choice (C) is incorrect; there is no evidence that writers were trying to "fool Americans." Choice (D) is incorrect; this sentence is an unsupported generalization.

6. **The correct answer is (B).** This is a vocabulary-in-context question. "Infamous" and "notorious" mean well-known for bad reasons. Choice (A) is incorrect; the "in-" prefix here does not mean "not." Choice (C) is incorrect; "well-known" has a positive connotation. Choice (D) is incorrect; "unpopular" is not relevant.

7. **The correct answer is (A).** This is an inference question. Choice (B) is incorrect because the passage offers no supporting evidence that the public enjoyed being scared. Choice (C) is incorrect; there is no mention of sci-fi as entertainment. Choice (D) is incorrect; there is no evidence of "obsessions with little green men."

8. **The correct answer is (B).** This is an inference question. Choice (A) is incorrect. Although probably true, this statement is not relevant. Choice (C) is incorrect; there is no mention of movies made about the hearings. Choice (D) is incorrect; no such connection was suggested.

9. **The correct answer is (D).** This is a factual question. All of these movies are cited in the passage.

Passage 3

10. **The correct answer is (B).** This is a main idea question. Choice (A) is incorrect because it is too narrow. Choice (C) is incorrect because it also is too narrow. Choice (D) is incorrect because it is not a main idea. Choice (E) is incorrect; it is another option that is too restricted.

11. **The correct answer is (A).** This is a vocabulary-in-context question. Choice (A), "arable," means that the land can be easily farmed because the soil is fertile. Choice (B) is incorrect because lack of trees does not necessarily mean the land can be plowed and planted. Choices (C), (D), and (E) are virtually the opposite in meaning.

12. **The correct answer is (D).** This is an implications question. Although several of the other options are included in the passage, the best answer is (D). Choice (A) is incorrect because only some were aristocratic. Choice (B) is incorrect; again, only some fell into this category. Choice (C) is incorrect. Although perhaps true, nothing in the passage offers compelling evidence to support this answer. Choice (E) is incorrect; the coast is not mentioned at all.

13. **The correct answer is (B).** This is a primary purpose question. Choice (A) is incorrect because the comments made about slavery are not the main focus of the passage. Choice (C) is incorrect; there is no mention of "stronger" settlers. Choice (D) is incorrect; there is no mention of the importance of the tobacco crop. Choice (E) is incorrect; this answer is too limited.

These passages and questions should give you a good idea of the types of questions that you will encounter on the actual exams. We have given you enough examples of question types so that you can recognize these on the exams. If you answered any reading comprehension questions incorrectly on the Diagnostic tests, go back to those again, reread the passages using your newly learned techniques, and try the questions again. You should now have improved scores, and these will also be evident when you take the practice tests at the end of this book.

STRATEGIES FOR WRITING THE ESSAY

HOW TO WRITE AN ESSAY—STRATEGIES FOR SUCCESS

An essay is a way to express your ideas in writing rather than by speaking. To do so effectively, you focus on a specific topic, roughly organize your ideas, and write as clearly and logically as possible in the time allotted. You will be provided with a "prompt" or topic about which to write. Be sure that you read the topic carefully, preferably twice. Then take a few minutes to organize your ideas and begin to write. Don't spend too much time organizing a rough outline; more ideas may occur to you as you write. While the readers at the schools to which you apply realize that you have a limited amount of time in which to write, you are expected to write logically and clearly.

Typically, an essay has three parts: an introduction, body, and conclusion. Writing the introduction is sometimes the most difficult part of the writing process. On the SSAT you usually will be asked to agree or disagree with a statement, and you have 25 minutes in which to write your essays. On the ISEE you will be given a broad topic about which to write, and you have 30 minutes in which to write your essay. Your opening sentence should be a response to this statement.

WRITING SAMPLE FOR THE SSAT

Here is a sample topic for the SSAT:

> **Topic:** Nothing can be gained without some loss. Do you agree or disagree with this topic sentence? Support your position with one or two specific examples from personal experience, the experience of others, current events, history, or literature.

INTRODUCTION

You must introduce your topic and establish your focus, that is, the point you want to prove about this topic. Strive to be concise and clear. Be sure that your first sentence responds *directly* to the topic. For the topic suggested, your opening sentence can be as simple as merely repeating the sentence; however, a paraphrasing of the statement, which means you summarize the statement in your own words, can show more clearly that you understand the question. If you disagree with the statement, your sentence can be as follows: "Some things can be gained without some loss." Check this opening sentence carefully to avoid making any errors. This first sentence will make a big impression on the admissions officers who read your essay. Be sure that this first sentence conveys a positive image of you. If you think you may be misspelling a word, choose another word that you know you can spell correctly.

BODY

This is the substance or main content of your essay. In this section of your essay, you will discuss the topic, offer supporting examples, and draw conclusions—in other words, prove your point. In this main part of your essay, you must be careful to develop your ideas as logically and smoothly as possible, trying to avoid major composition errors such as comma splices and sentence fragments. Typically, the body of an essay contains three paragraphs with one main idea per paragraph.

Fluency of expression and sentence variety are two areas the admissions officers or committee will evaluate when they read your essay. These skills, which refer to your ability to develop your ideas smoothly by using an array of types of sentences, are best produced by practicing; the more you write, the better you should become at expressing your ideas clearly and effectively. Another important quality necessary for a successful essay is sufficient evidence. Be sure that you have included enough evidence to prove your point. You will need at least two and possibly three pieces of evidence to support your view. Each of your supporting details also requires discussion to show its significance. While the admissions readers will read your essay to evaluate your writing skills to see how well you respond to the topic, they realize, of course, that your essay is a rough draft.

CONCLUSION

This is the final section of your essay, the place in which you remind your reader of the point you set out to prove. This last part may be only a sentence, or it could be several sentences. Just as there are a number of ways to write the opening paragraph or introduction, the conclusion can take many forms. Re-emphasizing your focus is the main purpose of this section. It is important, though, to offer some kind of conclusion to provide a sound essay.

SERIOUS GRAMMAR ERRORS TO AVOID

Comma splices occur when a writer attempts to connect two independent clauses with only a comma to join them. To connect these independent clauses correctly, a writer must use a coordinating conjunction, such as "and" or "but," and a comma, or the writer may use a semicolon instead of a comma, in which case the coordinating conjunction is unnecessary. Of course, a third choice is to treat the two independent clauses as two separate complete sentences.

Here is an example of a **comma splice:**

> Winning is something everyone wants to do, we all enjoy winning.

Two simple sentences (or independent clauses) are connected by a comma, which is not a strong enough mark of punctuation to join these constructions. To correct a comma splice, you have three options:

1. Change the comma to a semicolon (;), which is strong enough to connect independent clauses. Winning is something everyone wants *to do; we all* enjoy winning.

2. Add a conjunction such as "and," "but," "or," or "nor." These are known as coordinate conjunctions. Winning is something everyone wants to *do, and we all* enjoy winning.

3. Change the comma to a period and begin a new sentence with the second clause. Winning is something everyone wants *to do. We all* enjoy winning.

Next is another example of an error: a **sentence fragment.**

> Everyone has a chance. To win the contest.

This sentence fragment can be corrected in a number of ways. Here are some illustrations:

1. Make the fragment a sentence by completing the idea. To win the contest *will be exciting.* This sample has added a predicate, which the original construction lacked.

2. Attach the fragment to a nearby sentence. Everyone has a *chance to win the contest.* Here the fragment is attached to a simple sentence that already has a subject and a predicate.

STEP-BY-STEP EXAMPLE FOR THE WRITING SAMPLE

1. Read the topic or question "prompt." Be sure that you understand the topic. Do not write on any other topic.

2. Take a few minutes to generate some ideas. This process is sometimes called "brainstorming." Your goal here is to develop a sound approach to support your response to the topic.

Compose your thesis, which is a statement of the topic and your focus—that is, the point you are setting out to prove in your essay. For instance, if the topic is the one mentioned previously, you may choose to agree or to disagree with the statement. Your thesis, then, can be one of these: "Nothing can be gained without some loss" or "Some things can be gained without some loss." If you agree with the original statement, you are setting out to prove inevitably some loss occurs with every gain. Remember, however, you can choose to write an essay that supports the opposite position.

Let's continue the process and assume that you have decided to agree with the original statement. Begin writing the essay. Try to move into the body as quickly as possible.

3. Write the body of the essay. The actual number of paragraphs is not as important as the *content* in the body. Each of these body paragraphs should include a strong topic sentence that clearly establishes the main idea of the paragraph; each paragraph is designed to help you build an effective discussion of your topic and focus. You can choose to compose three body paragraphs, but you are not restricted to three. The admissions officers who read your essay will primarily evaluate it for content and logical development.

4. Write the conclusion or closing section of your essay. Remind the reader of what you set out to prove—your focus. Did you succeed in defending your approach?

5. Take a few minutes—if you have any time remaining—to review and proofread your essay.

Now, let's try part of this process with a sample topic.

Topic or Question Prompt

> **Nothing can be gained without some loss.** Do you agree or disagree with this topic sentence? Support your position with one or two specific examples from personal experience, the experience of others, current events, history, or literature. Develop your response into a well-written essay.

1. For our sample, let's assume that you decide to **agree** with the statement.

2. "Brainstorm" to come up with some ideas that will support or illustrate the statement. Make some notes, if you would like, in the test booklet, not on the page designated for the essay. Maybe you think of ideas like these:

   - Gaining years to become an adult means a loss of innocence

   - Gaining new friends sometimes means losing others

   - Gaining independence from your parents means losing dependence on them for money

   - Learning more about current events means losing some innocence

   - Huck Finn gains independence from Pap but loses his connection with the town.

   - The Allies won World War II but suffered many devastating losses of life and property.

   Notice that the last two in the list refer to a specific piece of literature and to history. Don't forget that you can write about literature or history—or even personal experience.

3. Assume you decide to write about World War II because you know some facts about it. After you devise an opening sentence or copy the topic sentence as your opening sentence, you can begin offering evidence or supporting details to illustrate the truth of the statement. You will offer examples to show that although the Allies did indeed win the war, they suffered great losses as well. Remember—you need three major pieces of evidence.

4. If time allows, try to proofread your essay. Remember that the admissions officers will read your essay, but it will not be scored. Write it as legibly as possible.

REVIEW

To recap the process of the writing sample, review these important steps:

1. Decide how you want to respond to the topic.

2. "Brainstorm" to generate some relevant details.

3. Write a topic sentence or thesis that clearly indicates your purpose. This sentence can be just a copy of the question prompt, or you may compose your own topic sentence. Just be sure that your response to the statement is clear. You will take a position and defend it.

4. Write the body of the essay, making sure to include enough evidence to prove your point.

5. If you have time left, proofread your essay and make any corrections as neatly as possible.

SAMPLE ESSAY TOPICS FOR THE SSAT

Choose one of these, agree or disagree with it, and write a practice essay:

1. We have become too dependent on technology in our lives today.

2. "Education means developing the mind, not stuffing the memory." (Anon.)

3. The most important qualities of a hero are bravery, compassion, and selflessness.

4. We can reduce the level of violence in society today by stronger gun control.

5. The event that most changed my life was _____. Explain why.

6. Sports in a school should be considered as important as academics.

WRITING SAMPLE FOR THE ISEE

Writing an essay for the ISEE is similar. You will have 30 minutes in which to write the essay. The topics, on the other hand, are different. For the ISEE, your choices are usually more personal. You will have the opportunity to write about yourself in most instances.

Here are some sample topics for the ISEE:

- My most important dream
- The most important change I have made in my life
- The person I admire most
- The word that describes me best
- The most important or significant book I have read

You may also have to respond to a statement similar to those on the SSAT; you have to agree or disagree with the statement and then offer evidence to support or prove your position.

This kind of statement may resemble the following:

Directions: Using the paper provided, write an essay in which you express your point of view on the topic presented in the following prompt:

Contrary to earlier times in American history, no true American role models exist today to serve as inspiration for teens. Most of what contemporary teens are exposed to is too violent, crime-related, and self-centered to provide a genuine hero that teens can admire and try to model their own lives after.

Your response will be evaluated for organization and development of ideas, appropriateness of examples and supporting details, and technique (spelling, punctuation, and usage).

The process for writing the essay is essentially the same for the ISEE. For the question prompt provided above, you will have to decide if you agree or disagree and what supporting details you can offer. Then you write your essay and strive to allow enough time to proofread the essay.

Another kind of ISEE question is an open-ended prompt in which you must decide how to complete the prompt. Instead of agreeing or disagreeing with a statement, you will be asked to complete a statement and explain your reasons. This kind of question will allow you to set up a more personal essay, writing that is based on your experience. After this beginning, the procedure for writing the essay is the same. Aim for developing your ideas logically and for including enough reasons to explain your response to the question.

HINTS FOR SUCCESS IN WRITING THE ESSAY

1.   Practice writing whenever you can. Success in writing is achieved just as success is in any other field—sports, art, games, scouting, music, community service, or spiritual life. You have to practice to improve your skills. Consider how long the members of a sports team train everyday after school to prepare for one game. And what about the cast members of a play as they rehearse for a production? Your skill as a writer is every bit as important—and not merely in anticipation of this standardized test. You will need to have strong writing skills throughout high school and college. The more you write, therefore, the better writer you can become.

2.   Try to simulate test conditions when you practice writing. Limit yourself to 30 minutes. Be sure that you will not be interrupted. Arrange to write at a desk that is clear of other materials.

3.   If you are unable to complete your essay by the end of 30 minutes, mark this point in your essay and then complete your writing. Afterward, look at the essay to see how you could have saved some time and finished within the 30-minute limit. Did you take too long to make up your mind about the topic? Did you try to offer too much evidence? Can you actually form the letters of the words more rapidly to write faster but still legibly?

4.   Now try to evaluate your writing. While we are all usually most critical of our own writing, try to make a fair assessment of what you have written. Check for grammatical errors, especially those noted earlier as particularly serious mistakes—the comma splice and the sentence fragment. It is also a good idea to put the essay away for a little while and then reread it to see if your evaluation has changed. Consider what you can do to improve your writing.

5.   Practice writing more often. One way to practice is to keep a daily journal. Of course, the contents of your journal are private, but for the purposes we are focusing on here, the contents are not actually the most important part of the journal. The journal is a way to drill and polish your writing skills in a nonthreatening way. After all, no one except you will see this journal. You can even choose to write about the sample topics in your journal. Aim to be as objective as possible when you evaluate your compositions.

Let's look at some additional sample topics for the SSAT and the ISEE and go through the steps needed to write a successful essay.

TOPICS

- Traveling is one way to learn about other cultures.
- Studying the past is one way to prepare for the future.
- I never felt better than when I . . . .
- If I could visit another city, I would choose . . . .
- Pets provide more for owners than owners provide for the animals.
- Students should wear uniforms to school.
- Everyone should be computer literate.

Assume that you decide to write about the topic "Students should wear uniforms to school."

1. Brainstorm to generate some ideas related to school uniforms. If you want to make a rough list, jot these points down in the test booklet, not on the paper provided for you to write the essay. Some sample ideas may be these:

eliminates distraction of clothes	minimizes competition about appearance
minimizes economic differences	makes student preparation for school fast
can be passed down for siblings	encourages students to behave with dignity

These are probably enough to get you started. Now, what about your opening sentence? You can use the sentence provided by the topic: Students should wear uniforms to school. You can, on the other hand, revise this sentence without changing its meaning. For instance, you can write, "In schools today, both public and private, students should wear uniforms." Be careful not to lapse into needless wordiness. Be concise. Develop an opening paragraph, which may be no more than a few sentences related to your topic sentence. Another sentence could be, "In schools today, student dress has sometimes become bizarre. Some students seem to be more concerned about their appearance than about academics. Uniforms can be a solution for some problems." Do not say something as blunt as "In this essay I will discuss school uniforms."

2. Next, you need to set up the body paragraphs. Looking at your rough list, you can select these points: economic differences, competition about appearance, and student behavior. In your opinion, these are the strongest choices you have. Decide in what order you wish to present these points. You can organize ideas from least to most important, from most to least important, or in chronological order (which is not an option with this topic), among other choices. Your decisions mean that you will

write the first body paragraph about competition about appearance or peer pressure to dress a certain way. The second body paragraph can deal with economic differences, because this point ties in well with the first one. Students sometimes feel pressure to wear certain labels, often expensive brands. Finally, you can discuss how student dress affects student behavior.

Remember, each paragraph must include explanation of the topic and supporting details or evidence to prove each of your ideas.

3. Finally, you should write a brief conclusion. Remind your reader of the most important points of your essay.

4. If you have any time remaining, try to proofread your essay. Look for the kinds of errors you know you are likely to make. For instance, check spelling, use of commas, or tense consistency.

Now let's repeat the process for a topic like those for the SSAT in which you agree or disagree with a statement. Let's assume that you select this topic:

Contrary to earlier times in American history, <u>no true American role models exist today to serve as inspiration for teens</u>. Most of what contemporary teens are exposed to is too violent, crime-related, and self-centered to provide a genuine hero that teens can admire and try to model their own lives after.

The underlined sentence is the key statement. Decide if you agree or disagree with it.

1. The first step, then, is deciding whether you agree or disagree with the statement. You choose to disagree.

2. Again, brainstorm to generate a rough list of possible ideas relevant to the position you have chosen.

Possible ideas include these:

Is there a difference between a hero and a role model? What differentiates the two?

Positive role models in a number of areas—sports, entertainment, education, family, church, government, family friends—name some

Volunteer work, community service, and other selfless actions performed by role models

List some well-known American figures, such as Christopher Reeve, Oprah Winfrey, Michael Jordan, and others.

Consider "ordinary" heroes, such as firefighters, police officers, soldiers, and teachers.

3. This topic is somewhat more involved than the previous one because you have to make more decisions before you begin to write. You can save some time by determining whether you want to focus on "ordinary" heroes or celebrity heroes. Let's assume you focus on "ordinary" heroes.

4. Establish three major ideas for the body paragraphs: (1) public servants, (2) elected officials, and (3) family members. Decide the order in which you want to present these ideas. Then write a paragraph about each, offering a few specific examples to illustrate each type. In the paragraph about public servants, for instance, you can discuss firefighters and police officers, who risk their lives daily to protect society.

5. The danger of a topic like this one is that it is easy to be tempted into writing more than you need and be unable to complete the essay in the time allotted. Be sure that you write concisely at a steady pace.

6. Finally, close your essay with a sentence or two that conclude your argument.

Now that we have gone over the process a few times, you should actually write a practice essay or two, following the suggestions offered. When you really take the SSAT or ISEE, you will feel more confident about this aspect of the test because you have practiced and you have a reliable strategy for success.

ENGLISH GRAMMAR REVIEW

USAGE REVIEW

PARTS OF SPEECH

Noun

A NOUN is the name of a person, place, or thing.

actor,   city,   lamp

There are three kinds of nouns, according to the type of person, place, or thing the noun names.

1. A *common* noun refers to a general type: girl, park, army.

2. A *proper* noun refers to a particular person, place, or thing, and always begins with a capital letter: Mary, Central Park, U.S. Army.

3. A *collective* noun signifies a number of individuals organized into one group: team, crowd, Congress.

Singular/Plural

Every noun has number. That means every noun is either singular or plural. The singular means only one; the plural means more than one. There are four ways to form the plurals of nouns:

1. by adding *-s* to the singular (horses, kites, rivers)

2. by adding *-es* to the singular (buses, churches, dishes, boxes, buzzes)

3. by changing the singular (*man* becomes *men*, *woman* becomes *women*, *child* becomes *children*, *baby* becomes *babies*, *alumnus* becomes *alumni*)

4. by leaving the singular as it is (moose, deer, and sheep are all plural as well as singular)

Note: When forming the plural of letters and numbers, add *'s*: A's, 150's. Otherwise, *'s* denotes possession.

Case

Nouns also have case, which indicates the function of the noun in the sentence. There are three cases—the nominative case, the objective case, and the possessive case.

1. **Nominative Case**

   A noun is in the nominative case when it is the subject of a sentence: The *book* fell off the table. The *boys* and *girls* ran outside.

   The subject of a sentence is the person, place, or thing that the sentence is about. Thus, the *book* fell off the table is about the book.

   A noun is in the nominative case when it is a predicate noun. This is a noun used after a linking verb. In such cases, the predicate noun means the same as the subject.

   > Einstein was a *scientist*. (Einstein = scientist)

   > Judith was a brilliant scholar and gifted teacher. (Judith = scholar and teacher)

   A noun is in the nominative case when it is used in direct address. A noun in direct address shows that someone or something is being spoken to directly. This noun is set off by commas.

   > *Claudel*, please answer the phone.

   > Go home, *Fido*, before you get hit by a car.

   A noun is in the nominative case when it is a nominative absolute. This is a noun with a participle (see verbs) that stands as an independent idea but is part of a sentence.

   > The *rain* having stopped, we went out to play.

   > The *bike* having crashed, the race was stopped.

   A noun is in the nominative case when it is a nominative in apposition. This is one of a pair of nouns. Both nouns are equal in meaning and are next to each other. The noun in apposition is set off from the rest of the sentence by commas.

   > Steve, *my son*, is going to college.

   > That man is Syd, *the musician*.

2. **Objective Case**

A noun is in the objective case when it is the direct object of a verb. A direct object is the receiver of the action of a verb. A verb that has a direct object is called a transitive verb.

> The team elected *David*.

> The team won the *game*.

A noun is in the objective case when it is the indirect object of a verb. This is a noun that shows *to* whom or *for* whom the action is taking place. The words *to* and *for* may not actually appear in the sentence, but they are understood. An indirect object *must* be accompanied by a direct object.

> Pedro threw *Mario* the ball. (Pedro threw the ball to Mario.)

> Anya bought her *mother* a gift. (Anya bought a gift for her mother.)

A noun is in the objective case when it is an objective complement. An objective complement is a noun that explains the direct object. The word *complement* indicates that this noun *completes* the meaning of the direct object.

> The team elected Terry *captain*.

A noun is in the objective case when it is an objective by apposition. An objective by apposition is very much like a nominative in apposition. Again we have a pair of nouns that are equal in meaning and are next to each other. The noun in apposition explains the other noun, but now the noun being explained is in the objective case. Therefore, the noun in apposition is called the objective by apposition. The objective by apposition is set off from the rest of the sentence by commas.

> The bully pushed Steve, the little *toddler*, into the sandbox.

> He gave the money to Sam, the *banker*.

A noun is in the objective case when it is an adverbial objective. This is a noun that denotes distance or time.

> The storm lasted an *hour*.

> The troops walked five *miles*.

A noun is in the objective case when it is an object of a preposition.

> The stick fell into the *well*. (*Into* is the preposition.)

> The picture fell on the *table*. (*On* is the preposition.)

See the section on prepositions.

3. **Possessive Case**

A noun is in the possessive case when it shows ownership. The correct use of the possessive case is often tested on the exam. The following rules will help you answer such questions correctly.

1. The possessive case of most nouns is formed by adding an apostrophe and *s* to the singular.

> The *boy's* book

> *Emile's* coat

2. If the singular ends in *s*, add an apostrophe, or apostrophe *s*.

> The *bus's* wheels

> > or

> The *bus'* wheels

> *Charles'* books

> > or

> *Charles's* books

3. The possessive case of plural nouns ending in *s* is formed by adding just an apostrophe.

> The *dogs'* bones

> Note: If *dog* was singular, the possessive case would be *dog's*.

4. If the plural noun does not end in *s*, then add an apostrophe and *s*.

> The *children's* toys

> The *men's* boots

5. The possessive case of compound nouns is formed by adding an apostrophe and *s* to the last word if it is singular, or by adding an *s* and an apostrophe if the word is plural.

> My *brother-in-law's* house
>
> My *two brothers'* house

6. To show individual ownership, add an apostrophe and *s* to each owner.

> *Joe's* and *Jim's* boats (They each own their own boat.)

7. To show joint ownership, add an apostrophe and *s* to the last name.

> Joe and *Jim's* boat (They both own the same boat.)

Pronouns

A pronoun is used in place of a noun. The noun for which a pronoun is used is called the *antecedent*. The use of pronouns, particularly the relationship between a pronoun and its antecedent, is one of the most common items found on the test. Always make sure a pronoun has a clear antecedent.

> John had a candy bar and a cookie. He ate *it* quickly. (Ambiguous) (What is the antecedent of *it*—*candy bar* or *cookie*?)
>
> The boy rode his bike through the hedge, *which* was very large. (Ambiguous) (What was very large—the *bike* or the *hedge*?)
>
> The captain was very popular. *They* all liked him. (Ambiguous) (Who liked him? *They* has no antecedent.)

Ten Pronouns

There are ten kinds of pronouns:

1. **Expletive Pronoun**
The words *it* and *there* followed by the subject of the sentence are expletive pronouns.

> *There* were only a few tickets left.
>
> *It* was a long list of chores.

When using an expletive, the verb agrees with the subject.

> There *remains* one *child* on the bus.
>
> There *remain* many *children* on the bus.

2. **Intensive Pronoun**

This is a pronoun, ending in *-self* or *-selves*, which follows its antecedent and emphasizes it.

He *himself* will go.

The package was delivered to the boys *themselves*.

3. **Reflexive Pronoun**

This is a pronoun, ending in *-self* or *-selves*, which is usually the object of a verb or preposition, or the complement of a verb.

I hate *myself*.

They always laugh at *themselves*.

Myself, yourself, himself, herself, and *itself* are all singular. *Ourselves, yourselves*, and *themselves* are all plural. There is no such pronoun as hisself or theirselves. Do not use *myself* instead of *I* or *me*.

4. **Demonstrative Pronoun**

This is used in place of a noun and points out the noun. Common demonstrative pronouns are *this, that, these*, and *those*.

I want *those*.

5. **Indefinite Pronoun**

This pronoun refers to any number of persons or objects. Following is a list of some singular and plural indefinite pronouns.

SINGULAR

anybody, anyone, each, everybody, everyone, no one, nobody, none, somebody, someone

PLURAL

all, any, many, several, some

If the singular form is used as a subject, the verb must be singular. *Every one* of *them* sings. (One person sings.)

If the singular form is used as an antecedent, its pronoun must be singular.

Did *anybody* on any of the teams lose *his* sneakers? (One person lost *his* sneakers.)

6. **Interrogative Pronoun**

This pronoun is used in asking a question. Such pronouns are *who, whose, whom, what*, and *which. Whose* shows possession. *Whom* is in the objective case. *Whom* is used only when an object pronoun is needed.

7. **Reciprocal Pronoun**

This pronoun is used when referring to mutual relations. The reciprocal pronouns are *each other* and *one another.*

> They love *one another.*

> They often visit *each other's* houses.

Note that the possessive is formed by an *'s* after the word *other.*

8. **Possessive Pronoun**

This pronoun refers to a noun that owns something. The possessive pronouns are as follows:

> SINGULAR
>
> > mine (my), yours, his, hers, its
>
> PLURAL
>
> > ours, yours, theirs

Notice that possessive pronouns do not use an *'s. It's* is a contraction meaning *it is; its* denotes possession.

9. **Relative Pronoun**

> Nominative case—who, that, which
>
> Objective case—whom, that, which
>
> Possessive case—whose

A relative pronoun used as the *subject* of a dependent clause is in the nominative case.

> I know *who* stole the car.
>
> Give the prize to *whoever* won it.

A relative pronoun used as the *object* of a dependent clause is in the objective case.

> He is the thief *whom* I know. (Object of verb *know*)

Note that the difficulty always comes when choosing *who* or *whom*. Remember that *who* is in the nominative case and is used for the appropriate situations discussed under nominative case in the section on nouns. *Whom* is in the objective case and is used for the appropriate situations discussed under objective case in the section on nouns.

Who is coming? (*Who* is the subject.)

Whom are you going with? (*Whom* is the object of the preposition *with*.)

The relative pronoun in the possessive case is *whose*. Notice there is no apostrophe in this word. The contraction *who's* means *who is*.

I know *whose* book it is. (Denotes possession)

I know *who's* on first base. (*who's* means *who is*)

10. **Personal Pronouns**

	SINGULAR	PLURAL
NOMINATIVE CASE		
First person	I	we
Second person	you	you
Third person	he, she, it	they
OBJECTIVE CASE		
First person	me	us
Second person	you	you
Third person	him, her, it	them
POSSESSIVE CASE		
First person	mine (my)	ours (our)
Second person	yours (your)	yours (your)
Third person	his, hers, its (his, her, its)	theirs (their)

Personal pronouns denote what is called *person*. First-person pronouns show the person or thing that is speaking.

I am going. (First person speaking)

Second-person pronouns show the person or thing being spoken to.

You are my friend. (Second person spoken to)

Third-person pronouns show the person or thing being spoken about.

Bea did not see *her*. (Third person spoken about)

Important for Exam

1. *Who* refers to persons only.

2. *Which* refers to animals or objects.

3. *That* refers to persons, animals, or objects.

> I don't know *who* the actor is. (Person)
>
> They missed their dog, *which* died. (Animal)
>
> I finished the book *which* (or *that*) you recommended. (Object)
>
> They are the people *who* started the fight. (Person)
>
> That is the tiger *that* ran loose. (Animal)
>
> The light *that* failed was broken. (Object)

Note that the singular indefinite antecedents always take a singular pronoun.

> *Every one* of the girls lost *her* hat.
>
> *None* of the boys lost *his*.
>
> *Someone* left *his* bike outside.

Note that collective singular nouns take singular pronouns; collective plural nouns take plural pronouns.

> The choir sang *its* part beautifully.
>
> The choirs sang *their* parts beautifully.

Note that two or more antecedents joined by *and* take a plural pronoun.

> Dave *and* Steve lost *their* way.

Note that two or more singular antecedents joined by *or* or *nor* take a singular pronoun.

> Tanya or Charita may use *her* ball.
>
> Neither Tanya nor Charita may use *her* ball.

If two antecedents are joined by *or* or *nor*, and if one is plural and the other is singular, the pronoun agrees in number with the nearer antecedent.

> Neither the *ball* nor the *rackets* were in *their* place.

Case

Remember that pronouns must also be in the correct case.

1. A pronoun must be in the nominative case when it is the subject of a sentence.

    James and *I* went to the airport.

    We freshmen helped the seniors.

    Peter calls her more than *I* do.

    Peter calls her more than *I.* (Here, the verb *do* is understood, and *I* is the subject of the understood verb *do.*)

2. A pronoun is in the objective case when it is a direct object of the verb.

    Leaving James and *me*, they ran away.

    John hit *them.*

    The freshman helped *us* seniors.

    A pronoun is in the objective case when it is the indirect object of a verb.

    Give *us* the ball.

3. A pronoun is in the objective case when it is an object of a preposition.

    To Ben and *me*

    With Sheila and *her*

    Between you and *them*

4. A pronoun is in the possessive case when it shows ownership.

    Her car broke down.

    Theirs did also.

    A pronoun is in the possessive case when it appears before a gerund (see verbals).

    His going was a sad event.

    For a more detailed analysis of the three cases, see the section on cases of nouns.

Adjectives

An adjective describes or modifies a noun or a pronoun. An adjective usually answers the question *which one*? Or *what kind*? Or *how many*? There are a number of types of adjectives you should know.

1. Articles (a, an, the)

   An article must agree in number with the noun or pronoun it modifies.

   > *A* boy

   > *An* apple

   > *The* girls

   If the noun or pronoun begins with a consonant, use *a*. If the noun or pronoun begins with a vowel, use *an*.

   > *A* pear

   > *An* orange

2. Limiting adjectives point out definite nouns or tell how many there are.

   > *Those* books belong to John.

   > The *three* boys didn't see *any* birds.

3. Descriptive adjectives describe or give a quality of the noun or pronoun they modify.

   > The *large* chair

   > The *sad* song

4. Possessive, demonstrative, and indefinite adjectives look like the pronouns of the same name. However, the adjective does not stand alone. It describes a noun or pronoun.

   > *This* is *mine*. (Demonstrative and possessive pronouns)

   > *This* book is *my* father's. (Demonstrative and possessive adjectives)

5. Interrogative and relative adjectives look the same, but they function differently. Interrogative adjectives ask questions.

   > *Which* way should I go?

   > *Whose* book is this?

   > *What* time is John coming?

   Relative adjectives join two clauses and modify some word in the dependent clause.

   > I don't know *whose* book it is.

Important for Exam

An adjective is used as a predicate adjective after a linking verb. If the modifier is describing the verb (a non-linking verb), we must use an adverb.

> The boy is *happy*. (Adjective)
> Joe appeared *angry*. (Adjective)
> The soup tasted *spicy*. (Adjective)
> Joe looked *angrily* at the dog. (Adverb—*angrily* modifies *looked*)

Positive, Comparative, and Superlative Adjectives

1. The positive degree states the quality of an object.

2. The comparative degree compares two things. It is formed by using *less* or *more* or adding *-er* to the positive.

3. The superlative degree compares three or more things. It is formed by using *least* or *most* or adding *-est* to the positive.

POSITIVE DEGREE	COMPARATIVE DEGREE	SUPERLATIVE DEGREE
Easy	easier; more easy; less easy	easiest; most easy; least easy
Pretty	prettier; more pretty; less pretty	prettiest; most pretty; least pretty

Do Not Use Two Forms Together

> She is the most prettiest. (Incorrect)
>
> She is the prettiest. (Correct)
>
> She is the most pretty. (Correct)

Verbs

A verb either denotes action or a state of being. There are four major types of verbs: transitive, intransitive, linking, and auxiliary.

1. Transitive verbs are action words that must take a direct object. The direct object, which receives the action of the verb, is in the objective case.

   > Joe *hit* the ball. (*Ball* is the direct object of *hit*.)

   > Joe *kicked* Bill. (*Bill* is the direct object of *kicked*.)

2. Intransitive verbs denote action but do not take a direct object.

   > The glass *broke*.

   > The boy *fell*.

Important for Exam

Set, lay, and *raise* are always transitive and take an object. *Sit, lie,* and *rise* are always intransitive and do not take a direct object.

> *Set* the book down, *lay* the pencil down, and *raise* your hands. (*Book, pencil*, and *hands* are direct objects of *set, lay*, and *raise.*)

> *Sit* in the chair.

> She *lies* in bed all day.

> The sun also *rises*.

The same verb can be transitive or intransitive, depending on the sentence.

> The pitcher *threw* wildly. (Intransitive)

> The pitcher *threw* the ball wildly. (Transitive)

3. Linking verbs have no action. They denote a state of being. Linking verbs mean "equal." Here are some examples: *is, are, was, were, be, been, am* (any form of the verb *to be*), *smell, taste, feel, look, seem, become, appear.*

    Sometimes, these verbs are confusing because they can be linking verbs in one sentence and action verbs in another. You can tell if the verb is a linking verb if it means equal in the sentence.

    > He felt nervous. (*He* equals *nervous.*)

    > He felt nervously for the door bell. (*He* does not equal *door bell.*)

    Linking verbs take a predicate nominative or predicate adjective. (See sections on nouns, pronouns, and adjectives.)

    > It *is I.*

    > It *is she.*

4. Auxiliary verbs are sometimes called "helping" verbs. These verbs are used with an infinitive verb (*to* plus the verb) or a participle to form a verb phrase.

    The common auxiliary verbs are:

    > All forms of *to be, to have, to do, to keep.*

    > The verbs *can, may, must, ought to, shall, will, would, should.*

    > He *has to go.* (Auxiliary *has* plus the infinitive *to go*)

    > He *was going.* (Auxiliary *was* plus the present participle *going*)

    > He *has gone.* (Auxiliary *has* plus the past participle *gone*)

There is no such form as *had ought*. Use *ought to have* or *should have*.

> He *ought to have gone*.

> He *should have gone*.

Every verb can change its form according to five categories. Each category adds meaning to the verb. The five categories are: *tense, mood, voice, number,* and *person.*

Tense

This indicates the *time*, or *when* the verb occurs. There are six tenses. They are:

present	past	future
present perfect	past perfect	future perfect

Three principal parts of the verb—the present, the past, and the past participle—are used to form all the tenses.

The *present tense* shows that the action is taking place in the present.

> The dog *sees* the car and *jumps* out of the way.

The present tense of a regular verb looks like this:

	SINGULAR	PLURAL
First person	I jump	We jump
Second person	You jump	You jump
Third person	He, she, it jumps	They jump

Notice that an *-s* is added to the third-person singular.

The *past tense* shows that the action took place in the past.

> The dog *saw* the car and *jumped* out of the way.

The past tense of a regular verb looks like this:

	SINGULAR	PLURAL
First person	I jumped	We jumped
Second person	You jumped	You jumped
Third person	He, she, it jumped	They jumped

Notice that *-ed* is added to the verb. Sometimes just *-d* is added, as in the verb *used*, for example. In regular verbs the past participle has the same form as the past tense, but it is used with an auxiliary verb.

> The dog *had jumped*.

The *future tense* shows that the action is going to take place in the future. The future tense needs the auxiliary verbs *will* or *shall.*

> The dog *will see* the car and *will jump* out of the way.

The future tense of a regular verb looks like this:

	SINGULAR	PLURAL
First person	I shall jump	We shall jump
Second person	You will jump	You will jump
Third person	He, she, it will jump	They will jump

Notice that *shall* is used in the first person of the future tense.

To form the *three perfect tenses,* the verb *to have* and the past participle are used.

- The present tense of *to have* is used to form the *present perfect.*

  The dog has seen the car and *has jumped* out of the way.

- The present perfect tense shows that the action has started in the past and is continuing or has just been implemented in the present.

- The past tense of *to have* is used to form the *past perfect.*

  The dog *had seen* the car and *jumped* out of the way.

- The past perfect tense shows that the action had been completed in the past.

- The future tense of *to have* is used to form the *future perfect.*

  The dog *will have seen* the car and *will have jumped* out of the way.

- The future perfect tense shows that an action will have been completed before a definite time in the future.

Following is a table that shows the present, past, and future tenses of *to have.*

PRESENT TENSE		
	SINGULAR	PLURAL
First person	I have	We have
Second person	You have	You have
Third person	He, she, it has	They have

PAST TENSE		
	SINGULAR	PLURAL
First person	I had	We had
Second person	You had	You had
Third person	He, she, it had	They had

FUTURE TENSE		
	SINGULAR	PLURAL
First person	I shall have	We shall have
Second person	You will have	You will have
Third person	He, she, it will have	They will have

The perfect tenses all use the past participle. Therefore, you must know the past participle of all the verbs. As we said, the past participle usually is formed by adding *-d* or *-ed* to the verb. However, there are many irregular verbs. Following is a table of the principal parts of some irregular verbs.

PRESENT	PAST	PAST PARTICIPLE
arise	arose	arisen
awake	awoke, awaked	awoke, awaked, awakened
awaken	awakened	awakened
be	was	been
bear	bore	borne
beat	beat	beaten
become	became	become
begin	began	begun
bend	bent	bent
bet	bet	bet
bid (command)	bade, bid	bidden, bid
bind	bound	bound
bite	bit	bitten
bleed	bled	bled
blow	blew	blown
break	broke	broken
bring	brought	brought
build	built	built
burn	burned	burned, burnt
burst	burst	burst
buy	bought	bought
catch	caught	caught
choose	chose	chosen
come	came	come
cost	cost	cost
dig	dug	dug
dive	dived, dove	dived
do	did	done
draw	drew	drawn
dream	dreamed	dreamed
drink	drank	drunk
drive	drove	driven
eat	ate	eaten
fall	fell	fallen
fight	fought	fought
fit	fitted	fitted
fly	flew	flown
forget	forgot	forgotten, forgot
freeze	froze	frozen
get	got	got, gotten
give	gave	given

PRESENT	PAST	PAST PARTICIPLE
go	went	gone
grow	grew	grown
hang (kill)	hanged	hanged
hang (suspended)	hung	hung
hide	hid	hidden
hold	held	held
know	knew	known
lay	laid	laid
lead	led	led
lend	lent	lent
lie (recline)	lay	lain
lie (untruth)	lied	lied
light	lit	lit
pay	paid	paid
raise (take up)	raised	raised
read	read	read
rid	rid	rid
ride	rode	ridden
ring	rang	rung
rise (go up)	rose	risen
run	ran	run
saw (cut)	sawed	sawed
say	said	said
see	saw	seen
set	set	set
shake	shook	shaken
shine (light)	shone	shone
shine (to polish)	shined	shined
show	showed	shown, showed
shrink	shrank	shrunk, shrunken
sing	sang	sung
sit	sat	sat
slay	slew	slain
speak	spoke	spoken
spend	spent	spent
spit	spat, spit	spat, spit
spring	sprang	sprung
stand	stood	stood
steal	stole	stolen
swear	swore	sworn
swim	swam	swum
swing	swung	swung
take	took	taken
teach	taught	taught
tear	tore	torn

PRESENT	PAST	PAST PARTICIPLE
throw	threw	thrown
wake	waked, woke	waked, woken
wear	wore	worn
weave	wove, weaved	woven, weaved
weep	wept	wept
win	won	won
write	wrote	written

Another aspect of tense that appears on the test is the *correct sequence* or *order of tenses. Be sure if you change tense you know why you are doing so. Following are some rules to help you.*

When using the perfect tenses, remember:

- The present perfect tense goes with the present tense.

  present
  As Dave *steps* up to the plate,

  present perfect
  the pitcher *has thrown* the ball to

  present perfect
  first and I *have caught* it.

- The past perfect tense goes with the past tense.

  past
  Before Dave *stepped* up to the

  past perfect
  plate, the pitcher *had thrown*

  past perfect
  the ball to first and I *had caught* it.

- The future perfect goes with the future tense.

  future
  Before Dave *will step* up to the plate, the pitcher

  future perfect
  will have thrown the ball to first

  future perfect
  and I *shall have caught* it.

- The present participle (verb + *ing*) is used when its action occurs at the same time as the action of the main verb.

  John, *answering* the bell, *knocked* over the plant.
  (*Answering* and *knocked* occur at the same time.)

- The past participle is used when its action occurs before the main verb.

> The elves, *dressed* in costumes, will *march* proudly to the shoemaker. (The elves dressed *before* they will march.)

Mood

The mood or mode of a verb shows the manner of the action. There are three moods.

1. The *indicative mood* shows the sentence is factual. Most of what we say is in the indicative mode.

2. The *subjunctive mood* is used for conditions contrary to fact or for strong desires. The use of the subjunctive mood for the verb *to be* is a test item.

Following is the conjugation (list of forms) of the verb *to be* in the subjunctive mood:

	PRESENT TENSE	
	SINGULAR	PLURAL
First person	I be	We be
Second person	You be	You be
Third person	He, she, it be	They be

	PAST TENSE	
	SINGULAR	PLURAL
First person	I were	We were
Second person	You were	You were
Third person	He, she, it were	They were

> If I *be* wrong, then punish me.

> If he *were* king, he would pardon me.

Also, *shall* and *should* are used for the subjunctive mood.

> If he *shall* fail, he will cry.

> If you *should* win, don't forget us.

3. The *imperative mood* is used for commands.

> Go at once!

If strong feelings are expressed, the command ends with an exclamation point. In commands, the subject *you* is not stated but is understood.

Voice

There are two voices of verbs. The *active voice* shows that the subject is acting upon something or doing something *to* something else. The active voice has a direct object.

> subject   object
> The *car* hit the *boy*.

The *passive* voice shows that the subject is acted upon *by* something. Something was done *to* the subject. The direct object becomes the subject. The verb *to be* plus the past participle is used in the passive voice.

> subject
> The *boy* was hit by the car.

Number

This, as before, means singular or plural. A verb must agree with its subject in number.

> The *list was* long. (Singular)

> The *lists were* long. (Plural)

Nouns appearing between subject and verb do not change subject/verb agreement.

> The *list* of chores *was* long. (Singular)

> The *lists* of chores *were* long. (Plural)

Subjects joined by *and* are singular if the subject is one person or unit.

> My *friend and colleague has* decided to leave. (Singular)

> *Five and five is* ten. (Singular)

> *Tea and milk is* my favorite drink. (Singular)

Singular subjects joined by *or, either-or,* and *neither-nor* take singular verbs.

> Either Alvin or Lynette *goes* to the movies.

If one subject is singular and one is plural, the verb agrees with the nearer subject.

> Either Alvin or the girls *go* to the movies.

The use of the expletive pronouns *there* and *it* do not change subject/verb agreement.

> There *is no one* here.

> There *are snakes* in the grass.

> Think: No one is there; snakes are in the grass.

A relative pronoun takes a verb that agrees in number with the pronoun's antecedent.

> It is the *electrician who suggests* new wiring. (Singular)
>
> It is the *electricians who suggest* new wiring. (Plural)

Singular indefinite pronouns take singular verbs.

> Everybody *buys* tickets.

It is hard to tell if some nouns are singular. Following is a list of tricky nouns that take singular verbs.

> Collective nouns—*army, class, committee, team*
>
> Singular nouns in plural form—*news, economics, mathematics, measles, mumps, news, politics*
>
> Titles, although plural in form, refer to a single work—*The New York Times*, Henry James's *The Ambassadors*
>
> The *army is* coming.
>
> *News travels* fast.
>
> *Jaws is* a good movie.

Don't (do not) is incorrect for third-person singular. *Doesn't (does not)* is correct.

> He *doesn't* agree.

Person

Person, as before, refers to first person (speaking), second person (spoken to), and third person (spoken about). A verb must agree with its subject in person.

> I study. (First person)
>
> He studies. (Third person)

Intervening nouns or pronouns do not change subject/verb agreement.

> *He* as well as I *is* going. (Third person)

If there are two or more subjects joined by *or* or *nor*, the verb agrees with the nearer subject.

> Either John or *we are* going. (First-person plural)

Adverbs

An adverb describes or modifies a verb, an adjective, or another adverb. Adverbs usually answer the questions *why?, where?, when?, how?*, and *to what degree?* Many adverbs end in *-ly*. There are two types of adverbs similar in use to the same type of adjective.

1. *Interrogative adverbs* ask questions.

   Where are you going?

   When will you be home?

2. *Relative adverbs* join two clauses and modify some word in the dependent clause.

   No liquor is sold *where* I live.

As with adjectives, there are three degrees of comparison for adverbs and a corresponding form for each.

1. The positive degree is often formed by adding *-ly* to the adjective.

   She was *angry*. (Adjective)

   She screamed *angrily*. (Adverb)

2. The *comparative* is formed by using *more* or *less* or adding *-er* to the positive.

3. The *superlative* is formed by using *most* or *least* or adding *-est* to the positive.

Here are two typical adverbs:

POSITIVE DEGREE	COMPARATIVE DEGREE	SUPERLATIVE DEGREE
easily	easier, more easily, less easily	easiest, most easily, least easily
happily	happier, more happily, less happily	happiest, most happily, least happily

Conjunctions

Conjunctions connect words, phrases, or clauses. Conjunctions can connect equal parts of speech.

and
but
for
or

Some conjunctions are used in pairs:

either . . . or
neither . . . nor
not only . . . but also

Here are some phrases and clauses using conjunctions:

John *or* Mary (Nouns are connected.)

On the wall *and* in the window (Phrases are connected.)

Mark had gone *but* I had not. (Clauses are connected)

Either you go *or* I will. (Clauses are connected.)

If the conjunction connects two long clauses, a comma is used in front of the coordinating conjunction:

Julio had gone to the game in the afternoon, but Pedro had not.

Some conjunctions are transitional:

therefore
however
moreover
finally
nevertheless

These conjunctions connect the meaning of two clauses or sentences.

Important for Exam

Be aware of *comma splices*. Comma splices occur when you connect two independent clauses with a comma, rather than with a semicolon or with a comma followed by a coordinating conjunction. An independent clause is a clause that can stand alone as a complete sentence.

His bike was broken; therefore, he could not ride. (Correct)

His bike was broken. Therefore, he could not ride. (Correct)

His bike was broken, and, therefore, he could not ride. (Correct)

His bike was broken, therefore, he could not ride. (Incorrect)

He found his wallet, however he still left the auction. (Incorrect)

The last two sentences are comma splices and are incorrect. *Remember, two independent clauses cannot be connected by a comma.*

Prepositions

A preposition shows the relationship between a noun or pronoun and some other word in the sentence.

The following are all prepositions:

about	for	through
above	in	to
across	inside	under
around	into	up
behind	of	upon
beneath	off	within
during	over	without

Sometimes groups of words are treated as single prepositions. Here are some examples:

> according to
>
> ahead of
>
> in front of
>
> in between

The preposition together with the noun or pronoun it introduces is called a prepositional phrase.

> *Under* the table
>
> *In front of* the oil painting
>
> *Behind* the glass jar
>
> *Along* the waterfront
>
> *Beside* the canal

Very often on the test, idiomatic expressions are given that depend upon prepositions to be correct. Following is a list of idioms showing the correct preposition to use:

Abhorrence of: He showed an *abhorrence of* violence.

Abound in (or *with*): The lake *abounded with* fish.

Accompanied by (a person): He was *accompanied by* his friend.

Accompanied with: He *accompanied* his visit *with* a house gift.

Accused by, of: He was *accused by* a person *of* a crime.

Adept in: He is *adept in* jogging.

Agree to (an offer): I *agree to* the terms of the contract.

Agree with (a person): I *agree with* my son.

Agree upon (or *on*) (a plan): I *agree upon* that approach to the problem.

Angry at (a situation): I was *angry at* the delay.

Available for (a purpose): I am *available for* tutoring.

Available to (a person): Those machines are *available to* the tenants.

Burden with: I won't *burden* you *with* my problems.

Centered on (or *in*): His efforts *centered on* winning.

Compare to (shows difference): An orange can't be *compared to* a desk.

Compare with (shows similarity): An orange can be *compared with* a grapefruit.

Conform to (or *with*): He does not *conform to* the rules.

Differ with (an opinion): I *differ with* his judgment.

Differ from (a thing): The boss's car *differs from* the worker's car.

Different from: His book is *different from* mine. (Use *different than* with a clause.)

Employed at (salary): He is *employed at* $25 a day.

Employed in (work): He is *employed in* building houses.

Envious of: She is *envious of* her sister.

Fearful of: She is *fearful of* thunder.

Free of: She will soon be *free of* her burden.

Hatred of: He has a *hatred of* violence.

Hint at: They *hinted at* a surprise.

Identical with: Your dress is *identical with* mine.

Independent of: I am *independent of* my parents.

In search of: He went *in search of* truth.

Interest in: He was not *interested in* his friends.

Jealous of: He was *jealous of* them.

Negligent of: He was *negligent of* his responsibilities.

Object to: I *object to* waiting so long.

Privilege of: He had the *privilege of* being born a millionaire.

Proficient in: You will be *proficient in* grammar.

Wait for: We will *wait for* them.

Wait on (service): The maid *waited on* them.

Like is used as a preposition. He wanted his dog to act *like* Lassie.

Verbals

Sometimes verbs can change their form and be used as nouns, adverbs, or adjectives. These forms are called verbals.

1. The infinitive is formed by adding *to* in front of the verb. The infinitive may act as a noun, adjective, or adverb.

> I love *to sing*. (Noun)
>
> Music *to sing* is my favorite kind. (Adjective)
>
> He went *to sing* in the choir. (Adverb)

An infinitive phrase is used as a noun, adjective, or adverb.

> I love *to sing songs*. (Noun)
> Music *to sing easily* is my favorite. (Adjective)
> He went *to sing very often*. (Adverb)

2. The participle can be either present or past. The present participle is usually formed by adding *-ing* to a verb. The past participle is usually formed by adding *-n, -en, -d,* or *-ed* to a verb. The participle is used as an adjective.

> The *swaying* crane struck the *fallen* boy.
>
> (*Swaying* is a present participle; *fallen* is a past participle.)
>
> A participle phrase is used as an adjective.
>
> *Blowing the crane fiercely*, the wind caused much danger.

Important for Exam

Beware of dangling participle phrases.

> *Blowing the crane fiercely*, the crowd ran.
>
> (The wind is blowing the crane, not the crowd.)

3. The gerund is formed by adding *-ing* to a verb. Although the gerund may look like a present participle, it is used only as a noun.

> *Seeing* clearly is important for good *driving*.
>
> (*Seeing* is the subject; *driving* is the object of the preposition *for*.)
>
> A participle phrase is used as a noun.
>
> *Seeing traffic signals* is important for good driving.

Phrases

A prepositional phrase begins with a preposition. A prepositional phrase can also be a noun phrase or an adjective phrase or an adverbial phrase.

> *"Over the hill"* was the slogan of the geriatric club. (Noun phrase)
>
> The top *of the statue* was broken. (Adjective phrase)
>
> The owl sat *in the nest*. (Adverbial phrase)

See the previous section on verbals for infinitive phrases, participle phrases, and gerund phrases.

Important for Exam

A dangling or misplaced modifier is a word or phrase acting as a modifier that does not refer clearly to the word or phrase it modifies.

> A bright light blinded his eyes *over the door*. (Misplaced modifier—his eyes were not over the door.)
>
> *Blowing the crane fiercely*, the crowd ran. (Misplaced participle phrase—the crowd was not blowing the crane.)
>
> *Watching television*, cookies were eaten. (Dangling gerund phrase—cookies were not watching television.)
>
> *Not able to stop*, the man jumped out of my way. (Dangling infinitive phrase—is it the man who could not stop?)

The following modifying phrases clearly show what they modify.

> A bright light over the door blinded his eyes.
>
> Because the wind was blowing the crane fiercely, the crowd ran.
>
> Watching television, Laura ate the cookies.
>
> Since I was not able to stop, the man jumped out of my way.

Clauses

Clauses are groups of words that contain a subject and a predicate (verb part of the sentence). There are two main kinds of clauses. One kind is the *independent clause*, which makes sense when it stands alone. Independent clauses are joined by coordinating conjunctions.

> I know how to clean silver, *but* I never learned how to clean copper.
>
> (The two independent clauses could stand alone as complete sentences.)
>
> I know how to clean silver. I never learned how to clean copper.

325

The other kind of clause is a *dependent or subordinate clause*. Although this type of clause has a subject and a predicate, it cannot stand alone.

When I learn to clean copper, I will keep my pots sparkling.

When I learn to clean copper, by itself, does not make sense. Dependent clauses are always used as a single part of speech in a sentence. They function as nouns or adjectives or adverbs. When they function as nouns, they are called *noun clauses*. When they function as adjectives, they are called *adjective clauses*. When they are adverbs, they are called *adverbial clauses*. Since a dependent or subordinate clause cannot stand alone, it must be joined with an independent clause to make a sentence. A *subordinating conjunction* does this job. A relative pronoun (*who, that, which, what, whose,* and *whom*) may act as the subordinating conjunction. For adjective and adverbial clauses, a relative adverb (*while, when*) may act as the subordinating conjunction.

I noticed *that he was very pale*.

That he was very pale is a noun clause—the object of the verb *noticed*. *That* is the subordinating conjunction.

Who was guilty is not known.

Who was guilty is a noun clause—subject of the verb *is*. *Who* is the subordinating conjunction.

She lost the belt *which was a present*.

Which was a present is an adjective clause—describing *belt*. *Which* is the subordinating conjunction.

She lost the belt *when she dropped the bag*.

When she dropped the bag is an adverbial clause answering the question *when* about the predicate. *When* is the subordinating conjunction.

Clauses should refer clearly and logically to the part of the sentence they modify.

We bought a dress at Bloomingdale's *which was expensive*.

(Misplaced adjective clause. Did the writer mean Bloomingdale's was expensive?)

Correct: We bought a dress *which was expensive* at Bloomingdale's.

When finally discovered, not a sound was heard.

(Misplaced adverbial clause. Who or what is discovered?)

Correct: *When finally discovered*, the boys didn't make a sound.

SENTENCES

A sentence is a group of words that expresses a complete thought. An independent clause can stand by itself and may or may not be a complete sentence.

Beth and Terry rode the Ferris wheel; they enjoyed the ride. (Two independent clauses connected by a semicolon)

Beth and Terry rode the Ferris wheel. They enjoyed the ride. (Two independent clauses—each is a sentence)

1. A simple sentence has one independent clause. A dependent clause is never a sentence by itself. Here are some simple sentences:

    John and Fred played.

    John laughed and sang.

    John and Fred ate hot dogs and drank soda.

    The following is not an independent clause:

    Fred said. (Incorrect—*said* is a transitive verb. It needs a direct object.)

    Fred said hello. (Correct)

2. A compound sentence has at least two independent clauses.

    Darryl bought the meat, and *Laverne bought the potatoes*.

3. A complex sentence has one independent clause and at least one dependent clause.

    Because she left early, she missed the end.

    (*Because she left early* is the dependent clause. *She missed the end* is an independent clause.)

4. A compound-complex sentence has two independent clauses and one or more dependent clauses.

    You prefer math and I prefer music, although I am the math major.

    (*You prefer math* and *I prefer music* are the independent clauses. The dependent clause is *although I am the math major*.)

Common Sentence Errors

Sentence Fragments

These are parts of sentences that are incorrectly written with the capitals and punctuation of a sentence.

Around the corner.

Because she left early.

Going to the movies.

A terrible tragedy.

Remember that sentences must have at least a subject and a verb.

Run-on Sentences

These are sentences that are linked incorrectly.

The rain was heavy, lightning was crackling he could not row the boat. (Incorrect)

Because the rain was heavy and lightning was crackling, he could not row the boat. (Correct)

The rain was heavy. Lightning was crackling. He could not row the boat. (Correct)

Faulty Parallelism

Elements of equal importance within a sentence should have parallel structure or similar form.

To sing, *dancing*, and to laugh make life happy. (Incorrect)

To sing, to dance, and to laugh make life happy. (Correct)

He wants health, wealth, and *to be happy*. (Incorrect)

He wants health, wealth, and happiness. (Correct)

Watch Arbitrary Tense Shifts

He *complained* while his father *listens*. (Incorrect)

He *complained* while his father *listened*. (Correct)

Watch Non-pronoun Agreements

A *person* may pass if *they* study. (Incorrect)

A *person* may pass if *he* studies. (Correct)

Watch These Don'ts

DON'T use *being that*; use *since* or *because*.

DON'T use *could of, should of, would of*; use *could have, should have, would have*.

DON'T use the preposition *of* in the following: off *of* the table, inside *of* the house.

DON'T use *this here* or *that there*; use just *this* or *that*.

DON'T misuse *then* as a coordinating conjunction; use *than* instead.

> He is better *then* he used to be. (Incorrect)

> He is better *than* he used to be. (Correct)

Capitalization

1. Capitalize all proper nouns.

    Capitalize names of specific people, places, things, peoples, and their languages: Americans, America, Spanish. Note: Henry takes Spanish three times a week. Henry takes math three times a week.

2. Capitalize religions and holy books: Islam, Koran, Bible

3. Capitalize calendar words: Monday, April

4. Capitalize historical periods and events: Renaissance, Civil War

5. Always capitalize the first word in a sentence: It is Henry.

6. Capitalize the first word in a letter salutation: Dear John, Dear Sir

7. Capitalize the first word of a letter closing: Very truly yours,

8. Capitalize the first word in a direct quote: He said, "Go away."

9. Capitalize the first, last, and important words in titles: *The Man Without a Country*

    Note: *A, an, and, the* are usually not capitalized unless they are the first word.

    Note also that conjunctions and prepositions with fewer than five letters are usually not capitalized.

10. Capitalize words used as part of a proper noun: Hudson Street, Uncle Fritz

11. Capitalize specific regions: I want to move to the South.

12. Capitalize abbreviations of capitalized words: D. B. Edelson

13. Capitalize acronyms formed from capitalized words: NASA, NATO

14. Capitalize the pronoun *I*: I beseech you to hear my prayer.

    Note that capitals are not used for seasons (summer, winter).

Note that capitals are not used for compass directions (east, northeast).

Note that capitals are not used for the second part of a quote: "I see," she said, "how smart Henry is."

Punctuation

The Period

1. Use the period to end full sentences.

   Harry loves candy.

   Although John knew the course was difficult, he did not expect to fail.

2. Use the period with abbreviations.

   Mr.

   Ph.D.

The Question Mark

1. Use the question mark to end a direct question.

   Are you going to the store?

2. Note that indirect questions end with a period.

   He asked how Sue knew the right answer.

The Exclamation Point

Use the exclamation point to denote strong feeling:

   Act now!

The Colon

1. The colon can introduce a series or an explanation, but it must always follow an independent clause.

   The following sciences are commonly taught in college: biology, chemistry, and physics. (Correct)

   The sciences are: biology, chemistry, and physics. (Incorrect)

   The sciences are is not an independent clause.

2. The colon is used after the salutation in a business letter.

   Dear Sir:

3. The colon is used to express the time.

   It is 1:45.

The Semicolon

1. The semicolon is used to link related independent clauses not linked by *and, but, or, nor, for, so,* or *yet*.

    No person is born prejudiced; prejudice must be taught.

2. The semicolon is used before conjunctive adverbs and transitional phrases placed between independent clauses.

    No person is born prejudiced; however, he has been taught well.

    No person is born prejudiced; nevertheless, he has always appeared bigoted.

3. The semicolon is used to separate a series that already contains commas.

    The team had John, the pitcher; Paul, the catcher; and Peter, the shortstop.

The Comma

1. The comma is used before long independent clauses linked by *and, but, or, nor, for, so,* or *yet*.

    No person is born prejudiced, but some people learn quickly.

2. The comma is used following clauses, phrases, or expressions that introduce a sentence.

    As I was eating, the waiter cleared the table.

    In a great country like ours, people enjoy traveling.

3. The comma is used with nonrestrictive, or parenthetical, expressions (not essential to the meaning of the main clause).

    He pulled the ice cream sundae, topped with whipped cream, toward him.

    John is afraid of all women who carry hand grenades. *Notice there is no comma.* John is not afraid of all women. He is afraid of all women who carry hand grenades (restrictive clauses).

4. Use commas between items in a series.

    Beth loves cake, candy, cookies, and ice cream.

5. Use the comma in direct address.

    Pearl, come here.

6. Use the comma before and after terms in apposition.

   Give it to Pearl, our good friend.

7. Use the comma in dates or addresses.

   June 3, 1996

   Freeport, Long Island

8. Use the comma after the salutation in a friendly letter.

   Dear Henry,

9. Use the comma after the closing in letters.

   Sincerely yours,

10. Use a comma between a direct quotation and the rest of the sentence.

    "Our fudge," the cook bragged, "is the best in town."

11. Be sure to use two commas when needed.

    A good dancer, generally speaking, loves to dance.

12. Do not separate subjects and verbs with a comma.

    Students and teachers, receive rewards. (Incorrect)

13. Do not separate verbs and their objects with a comma.

    He scolded and punished, the boys. (Incorrect)

The Apostrophe

1. Use the apostrophe to denote possession (see nouns).

   John's friend

2. Use the apostrophe in contractions.

   Didn't (did not)

   There's (there is)

3. Do not use an apostrophe with *his, hers, ours, yours, theirs,* or *whose*. Use an apostrophe with *its* if *its* is a contraction.

   The dog chewed *its* bone; *it's* hard for a little dog to chew such a big bone. (*It's* means it is; *its* is a pronoun that denotes possession.)

Quotation Marks

1. Use quotation marks in direct quotes.

   "Get up," she said.

2. Use single quotes for a quote within a quote.

   Mark said, "Denise keeps saying 'I love you' to Ralph."

Parentheses

Use parentheses to set off nonrestrictive or unnecessary parts of a sentence.

This book (an excellent review tool) will help students.

The Dash

1. Use the dash instead of parentheses.

   This book—an excellent review tool—will help students.

2. Use the dash to show interruption in thought.

   There are eight—remember, eight—parts of speech.

RHETORICAL REVIEW

STYLE

Good writing is clear and economical.

Avoid Ambiguous Pronoun References

Tom kicked Jerry. I feel sorry for *him*. (Who is *him*? Tom? Jerry?)

Burt is a nice man. I don't know why *they* insulted him. (Who does *they* refer to?)

Avoid Clichés

Betty is *sharp as a tack*.

The math exam was *easy as pie*.

It will be *a cold day in August* before I eat dinner with Louisa again.

Avoid Redundancy

Harry is a man who loves to gamble. (Redundant—we know that Harry is a man.)

Harry loves to gamble. (Correct)

Claire is a strange one. (Redundant—*one* is not necessary.)

Claire is strange. (Correct)

This July has been particularly hot in terms of weather. (Redundant—*in terms of weather* is not necessary.)

This July has been particularly hot. (Correct)

Avoid Wordiness

The phrases on the left are wordy. Use the word on the right.

WORDY	PREFERABLE
the reason why that is	because
the question as to whether	whether
in a hasty manner	hastily
be aware of the fact that	know
due to the fact that	because
in light of the fact that	since
regardless of the fact that	although
for the purpose of	to

Avoid Vague Words or Phrases

It is always preferable to use specific, concrete language rather than vague words and phrases.

The reality of the situation necessitated action. (Vague)

Bill shot the burglar before the burglar could shoot him. (Specific)

Be Articulate—Use the Appropriate Word or Phrase

The following are words or phrases that are commonly misused:

1. Accept: to receive or agree to (verb)

   I *accept* your offer.

   Except: preposition that means to leave out

   They all left *except* Dave.

2. Adapt: to change (verb)

   We must *adapt* to the new ways.

   Adopt: to take as one's own, to incorporate (verb)

   We will *adopt* a child.

3.   **Affect:**   to influence (verb)

Their attitude may well *affect* mine.

Effect: result (noun)

What is the *effect* of their attitude?

4.   **Allusion:**   a reference to something (noun)

The teacher made an *allusion* to Milton.

Illusion: a false idea (noun)

He had the *illusion* that he was king.

5.   **Among:**   use with more than two items (preposition)

They pushed *among* the soldiers.

Between: use with two items (preposition)

They pushed *between* both soldiers.

6.   **Amount:**   cannot be counted (noun)

Sue has a large *amount* of pride.

Number: can be counted (noun)

Sue bought a *number* of apples.

7.   **Apt:**   capable (adjective)

She is an *apt* student.

Likely: probably (adjective)

We are *likely* to receive the prize.

8.   **Beside:**   at the side of (preposition)

He sat *beside* me.

Besides: in addition to (preposition)

There were others there *besides* Joe.

9.   **Bring:**   toward the speaker (verb)

Bring that to me.

Take: away from the speaker (verb)

Take that to him.

10.   **Can:**   to be able to (verb)

I *can* ride a bike.

May: permission (verb)

May I ride my bike?

11. **Famous:** well known (adjective)

   He is a *famous* movie star.

   Infamous: well known but not for anything good (adjective)

   He is the *infamous* criminal.

12. **Fewer:** can be counted (adjective)

   I have *fewer* pennies than John.

   Less: cannot be counted (adjective)

   I have *less* pride than John.

13. **Imply:** the speaker or writer is making a hint or suggestion (verb)

   He *implied* in his book that women were inferior.

   Infer: to draw a conclusion from the speaker or writer (verb)

   The audience *inferred* that he was a woman-hater.

14. **In:** something is already there (preposition)

   He is *in* the kitchen.

   Into: something is going there (preposition)

   He is on his way *into* the kitchen.

15. **Irritate:** to annoy (verb)

   His whining *irritated* me.

   Aggravate: to make worse (verb)

   The soap *aggravated* his rash.

16. **Teach:** to provide knowledge (verb)

   She *taught* him how to swim.

   Learn: to acquire knowledge (verb)

   He *learned* how to swim from her.

17. **Uninterested:** bored (adjective)

   She is *uninterested* in everything.

   Disinterested: impartial (adjective)

   He wanted a *disinterested* jury at his trial.

ORGANIZATION

A paragraph, like an essay, must have some organization plan. Each paragraph should represent the development of some point the author is making. Learn to recognize topic sentences, which often come at the beginning or end of a paragraph. Topic sentences tell the reader the main point of the paragraph.

Here are some sample topic sentences:

- De Tocqueville is also concerned with the conflict between individual liberty and equality.

- Another of the social institutions that leads to disaster in *Candide* is the aristocracy.

- The Fortinbras subplot is the final subplot that points to Hamlet's procrastination.

Read the following paragraph and answer the appropriate questions.

(1) *Throughout history, writers and poets have created countless works of art.* (2) *The result is Paul's failure to pursue Clara and establish a meaningful relationship with her.* (3) *Paul's mother loves him, but the love is smothering and overprotective.* (4) *Although Paul feels free to tell his mother almost everything, he fails to tell her he is sexually attracted to Clara.* (5) *His feelings for Clara obviously make him feel he is betraying his mother.* (6) *Paul Morel's relationship with his mother in* Sons and Lovers *interferes with his relationship with Clara.*

1. Which sentence does not belong in the above paragraph?

   The correct answer is (1). The first sentence is inappropriate to the idea of the paragraph, which concerns Paul's relationship with his mother and with Clara. The first sentence is also vague and virtually meaningless. Obviously, many works of art have been created throughout history. So what?

2. Unscramble the above paragraph and put the sentences in the correct order.

   (A) 2, 4, 3, 6, 5
   (B) 6, 5, 2, 4, 3
   (C) 3, 4, 5, 6, 2
   (D) 6, 3, 4, 5, 2

   The correct answer is (D). Obviously, sentence 1 does not fit the paragraph. Sentence 6 mentions Paul by his full name, the name of the work, and his relationships with both women, all of which are covered in the paragraph. It is the topic sentence. Sentence 2 sums up the paragraph; the clue is in the phrase "the result is." Logically sentence 2 should end the paragraph. Since the paragraph concerns Paul's relationship with his mother and its effect on his relationship with Clara, the other sentences should fall in place.

This section has covered a lot of the basic rules of grammar. It is primarily a reference section and you will not be expected to know everything on the exam. However, we suggest you use this section as a handy guide to help you understand many of the answers that might involve certain grammar principles with which you may not be familiar. Feel free to highlight certain portions of these principles so you can go back to them from time to time, especially when confronted with more difficult explanations of some of the problems in the Strategy section and in any of the exams in the book.

MERRIAM-WEBSTER'S ROOTS TO WORD MASTERY

INTRODUCTION

If you're like many students today preparing for the SSAT or ISEE, you probably have never taken a course in Latin, which means you may never have learned how most English words came to be based on words from older languages. And you may never have realized how the study of word roots can lead to a much larger vocabulary than you now have. Studying and mastering vocabulary words will certainly improve your verbal score. So to maximize your chances of scoring high on your test, this chapter will set you on the path to learning a broad range of new vocabulary words.

You'll learn 50 of the Greek and Latin roots that form the foundation of most of the words in the English language as well as 150 English words based on those roots. Many of these 150 words will actually lead you to several more words each. By learning the word *credible,* you'll also understand *credibly* and *credibility* the next time you hear them; by learning *gratify,* you'll also learn *gratifying* and *gratification;* and by learning *theology,* you'll understand *theological, theologically,* and *theologian* when you run across them. So learning the roots and words in this chapter will help you to learn thousands of words!

Ancient Greek and Latin have been the sources of most words in the English language. (The third-biggest source is the family of Germanic languages.) And not just of the older words: Almost the entire English vocabulary was created long after the fall of the Roman empire, and it continues to expand to this day. Of the new words that are constantly being invented, the majority—especially those in the sciences, where most new words are introduced—are still based on Greek and Latin roots. Even new buzzwords that you think appear out of nowhere may be Greek or Latin in origin. For instance, *morph* is a short form of *metamorphose,* which comes almost straight from Latin; *def* is short for *definitely,* which is also based on Latin; *hype* is probably short for *hyperbole,* which comes straight from Greek; and *rad* is short for *radical,* which comes from the Latin *radix*—which actually means "root"!

Besides improved test scores, what can you expect to gain from expanding your vocabulary?

For more vocabulary-building exercises, visit Merriam-Webster's Web site at www.m-w.com.

A large vocabulary will allow you to read a wider range of writing than you had previously, and in the process, it will broaden your range of interests. If you've always limited your leisure reading to magazines about rock musicians and film stars, or cars and sports, or clothing and style, or fantasy and electronic games, you'll soon discover that newsweeklies, biographies, literary fiction, nature writing, or history can give you more pleasure and expand your mind at the same time.

Just as important, you'll find that a larger vocabulary will help you express your ideas more clearly. It will encourage you to describe, say, a film or a musician with more informative words than "really good" or "cool" or "awesome," and it will give you more precise ways to talk about, say, a news story, a mental state, a new building, or a person's face—in fact, almost any aspect of everyday life.

But it will also help make you more competent in your chosen career. According to research studies, people with large vocabularies are far more likely to be found in the most important and interesting and desirable jobs.

Let's suppose you want to become a doctor, nurse, or pharmacist. Doctors today prescribe thousands of drugs and treat thousands of identified medical conditions. Many of these drugs and conditions have long and complex names, almost all of which are derived from Greek and Latin. In your chosen career, you'd naturally want to have memorized as many of these names as possible. But since most of us don't have perfect memories, having a good grasp of Greek and Latin roots is the best way to be sure your memory is jogged whenever you come across a long medical or pharmaceutical term. Knowing a single Latin suffix or prefix (many short word endings are called suffixes, and many short word beginnings are called prefixes) or a root can prepare you to understand hundreds of words in which it appears. For instance, since the suffix *-itis* means "disease" or "inflammation," seeing a word with that ending (*gastroenteritis, nephritis, phlebitis,* etc.) will let you identify at once the class of words to which it belongs. *Hemo-* means "blood," so *hemophilia, hemoglobinopathy, hemorrhagic fever,* and *hemolytic anemia* are all conditions involving the blood. And let's not forget the middles of words. In *gastroenteritis,* the root *-enter-* refers to the intestines.

As you can see, many words contain more than one root. A single word may be a mix of Greek and Latin and even Germanic roots or elements, and a long scientific term may contain four or more elements. Such complex words are much less common in ordinary vocabulary, but even a conversation between elementary-school children will contain many words based on classical roots.

In a technical field, mastering a technical vocabulary may be a requirement for your job. But a broad nontechnical vocabulary can be highly valuable as well. Even in a narrowly focused field such as accounting or computer programming, a large vocabulary can prove to be of real practical value. And in a field such as law, which tends to get involved in many aspects of life, a large general vocabulary can turn out to be very advantageous.

While root study is very valuable, be cautious when you begin exploring it. A portion of a word may resemble a root only by coincidence. For example, the word *center* doesn't have anything to do with the root *cent* (meaning "hundred"), and the words *interest* and *interminable* don't have anything to do with the root *inter* (meaning "between"). It may take time to recognize which words actually contain the roots you think you see in them. Another problem is that not every root you think you've identified will necessarily be the right one. For example, *ped* may mean either "foot" or "child," and *liber* may mean either "book" or "free." A third problem is that many common roots are too short to recognize or change their spelling in a confusing way from word to word. So even though *perception, deceive, recipe, capture,* and *receipt* can all be traced to the same Latin root, the root changes form so much—*cip, cept, cap,* etc.—that root study probably won't help the student looking for a memory aid. Similarly, when the Latin word *ad* (meaning "to" or "toward") becomes a prefix, it usually changes to *ac-, ad-, af-, ag-, am-, an-,* or some other form, so the student can rarely recognize it. In addition, the meanings of some roots can change from word to word. So even though the *cip-cept-cap* root means "grasp," "seize," or "take," it may seem to change its meaning completely when combined with a prefix (*per-, de-,* etc.).

As long as you are aware of such difficulties, root study is an excellent way to learn English vocabulary (not to mention the vocabularies of Spanish, French, Italian, and Portuguese, all of which are based on Latin). In fact, it's the *only* method of vocabulary acquisition that relies on broadly useful memory aids. Without it, vocabulary study consists of nothing but trying to memorize unrelated words one by one by one.

So from here on, it's up to you. The more fun you can have learning your new vocabulary, the better you'll do. And it *can* be fun. For one thing, the results are instantaneous—you can show off your new knowledge any time you want. And you'll almost feel your mind expanding as your vocabulary expands. This is why people talk about the "power" of a large vocabulary; you'll soon realize your mental capacities are actually becoming more powerful with every new word.

Take every opportunity to use the words you're learning; the most effective way to keep a new word alive in your vocabulary is to use it regularly. Look and listen for the new words you've learned—you'll be surprised to find yourself running into them often, especially if you've also begun reading more demanding books and magazines in your leisure time. Challenge your friends with them, even if just in a joking way. Make up games to test yourself, maybe using homemade flash cards.

And don't stop acquiring new vocabulary words after you've mastered this chapter. Whenever you're reading, look for roots in the new words you keep encountering and try to guess each word's meaning before looking it up in a dictionary (which you should try to keep close at hand). Once you've acquired the habit, you'll be astonished at how quickly your vocabulary will grow.

INSTRUCTIONS

On the following pages, we introduce you to 50 of the most useful Greek and Latin roots (omitting the prefixes and suffixes that almost everyone knows—*anti-, co-, de-, -ism, mis-, non-, un-, vice-*, etc.). We call these roots useful because they are common and also because they nearly always keep their meaning in an obvious way when they appear in an English word. So if you encounter an unfamiliar word on your test, these roots may be the key to making an educated guess as to its meaning.

Each root is discussed in a short paragraph. Each paragraph is followed by three vocabulary words derived from the root. For each word, we provide the pronunciation, the definition, and a sentence showing how the word might actually be used in writing or conversation.

You'll be quizzed after every 15 words, and finally you'll be tested on every one of the 150 words. (All answers are given at the end of the chapter.) These tests will ensure that the words and roots become permanently fixed in your memory, just as if you'd been drilled on them in class.

For further study on your own, near the end of the chapter we list an additional 50 useful roots, along with three English words based on each one.

50 ROOTS TO SUCCESS

Pronunciation Guide: \ə\ abut \ər\ further \a\ ash \ā\ ace \ä\ mop, mar
\au̇\ out \ch\ chin \e\ bet \ē\ easy \g\ go \i\ hit \ī\ ice \j\ job \ŋ\ sing
\ō\ go \ȯ\ law \ȯi\ boy \th\ thin \<u>th</u>\ the \ü\ loot \u̇\ foot \y\ yet
\zh\ vision

agr Beginning Latin students traditionally learn the word *agricola*, meaning "farmer," in their very first class. Though most of us tend to think of the Romans as soldiers, senators, and citizens of the city of Rome, most inhabitants of the empire were actually farmers. We see the root today in words such as **agriculture**.

agronomy \ə-'grä-nə-mē\ A branch of agriculture dealing with field-crop production and soil management.

* The poor country was in dire need of an agronomy team to introduce its farmers to new crops and techniques.

agrochemical \ˌa-grō-'ke-mi-kəl\ An agricultural chemical (such as an herbicide or an insecticide).

* The river's pollution was easily traced to the runoff of agrochemicals from the cornfields.

agrarian \ə-'grer-ē-ən\ Of or relating to fields, lands, or farmers, or characteristic of farming life.

* The team of sharply dressed lawyers seemed nervous and awkward in this agrarian landscape of silos and feed stores.

ante *Ante* means "before"; its opposite, *post*, means "after." Both almost always appear as prefixes (that is, at the beginnings of words). *Ante* is easy to confuse with *anti*, meaning "against." **Antebellum** means "before the war," and we often speak of the antebellum South—that is, the South before the Civil War, not the "antiwar" South.

antedate \'an-ti-ˌdāt\ 1: To date as of a date prior to that of execution. 2: To precede in time.

* It appeared that Crowley had antedated his check to the contractors, helping them evade taxes for work done in the new year.

antecedent \ˌan-tə-'sē-dənt\ Prior, preceding.

* As Mrs. Perkins told it, the scuffle had started spontaneously, and any antecedent events involving her rowdy son had been forgotten.

anterior \an-'tir-ē-ər\ Situated before or toward the front.

* Dr. Singh was going on about anterior and posterior knee pain, but in her agony Karen could hardly remember a word.

anthro The Latin *anthro* means "man" or "mankind." Thus, in English we call the study of mankind **anthropology**. *Anthro* is very close to the Greek and Latin *andro*, which shows up in such words as **android**.

anthropoid \\'an-thrə-ˌpoid\\ Any of several large, tailless apes.
- The anthropoids—chimpanzees, bonobos, gorillas, orangutans, and gibbons—had diverged from the human evolutionary line by 5 million years ago.

misanthrope \\'mi-sən-ˌthrōp\\ A person who hates or distrusts mankind.
- Over the years she had retreated into an increasingly bitter solitude, and her former friends now dismissed her as a misanthrope.

philanthropy \\fə-'lan-thrə-pē\\ Active effort to promote human welfare.
- His philanthropy was so welcome that no one cared to inquire how he'd come by his fortune.

aqu The Greek and Latin root *aqu-* refers to water. The ancient world regarded all matter as made up of four elements—earth, air, fire, and water. Today, the root is found in such familiar words as **aquarium**, **aquatic**, and **aquamarine**.

aquaculture \\'ä-kwə-ˌkəl-chər\\ The cultivation of the natural produce of water, such as fish or shellfish.
- Having grown hugely, the aquaculture industry now produces 30 percent of the world's seafood.

aquifer \\'a-kwə-fər\\ A water-bearing stratum of rock, sand, or gravel.
- The vast Ogallala aquifer, which irrigates most of the Great Plains, is monitored constantly to ensure that it isn't dangerously depleted.

Aquarius \\ə-'kwar-ē-əs\\ 1: A constellation south of Pegasus pictured as a man pouring water. 2: The 11th sign of the zodiac in astrology.
- Many believe that the great Age of Aquarius began in 1962; others believe it commenced in 2000 or hasn't yet begun.

arti This root comes from the Latin word for "skill." *Art* could also mean simply "cleverness," and we still describe a clever solution as **artful**. Until recent centuries, almost no one made a real distinction between skilled craftsmanship and what we would now call **art**. So the words **artistic** and **artificial** turn out to be very closely related.

artifice \\'är-tə-fəs\\ 1: Clever skill. 2: A clever trick.
- She was stunned to find she'd been deceived by a masterpiece of artifice—the lifelike figure of a seated man talking on the phone, a lit cigarette in his right hand.

artifact \\'är-ti-ˌfakt\\ A usually simple object, such as a tool or ornament, made by human workmanship.
- Among the artifacts carried by the 5,000-year-old Iceman was a fur quiver with fourteen arrow shafts.

artisan \\'ar-tə-zən\\ A skilled worker or craftsperson.
- Ducking down an alley, he weaved quickly through the artisans hawking their wares of handworked brass and leather.

QUIZ 1

Answers appear at the end of this chapter.

1. Carnegie spread his _____ more widely than any previous American, building almost 1,700 libraries.

2. A long list of _____s—mainly herbicides and pesticides—were identified as health threats.

3. News of the cave's discovery soon leaked out, and local youths were soon plundering it of its Indian _____s.

4. Stalin moved swiftly to uproot Russia's _____ traditions and substitute his new vision of collectivized agriculture.

5. They had drilled down 85 feet before they struck the _____ and water bubbled to the surface.

6. The first X-ray image, labeled "_____," showed a frontal view of her heart.

7. George Washington Carver, a hero of American _____, transformed Southern agriculture through his research into the peanut.

8. The throne itself, its surface glittering with ornaments, was the most extravagant example of the sculptor's _____.

9. In his lecture on "The _____ Causes of the Irish Famine," he expressed wonder at rural Ireland's absolute dependency on the potato by 1840.

10. Before the development of _____, the Atlantic salmon was threatened by overfishing.

11. Her brother, always suspicious and unfriendly, was by now a genuine _____, who left his phone unplugged and refused all invitations.

12. Any contracts that _____ the new law by five years or more will remain in effect.

13. The man resembled an _____, with powerful sloping shoulders and arms that seemed to brush the ground.

14. A young boy pouring water into the basin below reminded her of the astrological symbol of _____.

15. All the handcrafts turned out to be the work of a large family of _____s.

bene In Latin, *bene* means "well"; its near-opposite, *mal*, means "bad" or "poorly." Both usually appear at the beginnings of words. We may hope to use this root often to list **benefits** and describe **beneficial** activities.

benediction \ˌbe-nə-'dik-shən\ The pronouncement of a blessing, especially at the close of a worship service.
- The restless children raced out to the church picnic immediately after the benediction.

beneficent \bə-'ne-fə-sənt\ Doing or producing good; especially performing acts of kindness or charity.
- Even the busy and poor willingly contribute to organizations recognized as beneficent.

benefactor \'be-nə-ˌfak-tər\ A person or group that confers aid, such as a charitable donation.
- Construction of the new playground had been funded by a generous benefactor.

bio *Bio* comes from the Greek word for "life." Thus, **biology** means the study of all living forms and life processes, and **biotechnology** uses the knowledge gained through biology. **Antibiotics** fight off bacteria, which are life forms, but not viruses, which may not be.

bionic \bī-'ä-nik\ Having normal biological ability enhanced by electronic or mechanical devices.
- A 1970s TV series featuring "the Bionic Woman" sparked interest in robotics.

biopsy \'bī-ˌäp-sē\ The removal and examination of tissue, cells, or fluids from the living body.
- Until the biopsy results came back, there was no way to tell if the lump was cancerous.

symbiosis \ˌsim-bē-'ō-səs\ The intimate living together of two dissimilar organisms, especially when mutually beneficial.
- In a display of symbiosis, the bird stands on the crocodile's teeth and pecks leeches off its gums.

chron This root comes from the Greek word for "time." A **chronicle** records the events of a particular time. **Chronometry** is the measuring of time, which can be done with a **chronometer**, a timepiece more accurate than an ordinary watch or clock.

chronic \'krä-nik\ Marked by long duration or frequent recurrence; habitual.
- Her roommate was a chronic complainer, who started off every day grumbling about something new.

anachronism \ə-'na-krə-ˌni-zəm\ 1: The error of placing a person or thing in the wrong period. 2: One that is out of its own time.
- After the collapse of the Soviet Union, some analysts felt that NATO was an anachronism.

chronology \krə-'nä-lə-jē\ An arrangement of events in the order of their occurrence.
- Keeping a journal throughout her trip gave Joan an accurate record of its chronology afterward.

circum *Circum* means "around" in Latin. So to **circumnavigate** is "to navigate around," often around the world, and **circumference** means the "distance around" a circle or other object. A **circumstance** is a fact or event accompanying ("standing around") another.

circumvent \ˌsər-kəm-'vent\ To evade or defeat, especially by trickery or deception.
- During Prohibition, many citizens found ways to circumvent the laws against alcohol.

circumspect \ˌsər-kəm-'spekt\ Careful to consider all circumstances and consequences; cautious; prudent.
- Unlike his impulsive twin brother, Claude was sober, circumspect, and thoughtful.

circumstantial \ˌsər-kəm-'stan-shəl\ 1: Describing evidence based on inference, not directly observed facts. 2: Incidental.
- The fact that he was gone all night was only circumstantial evidence, but still extremely important.

cosm *Cosm* comes from the Greek word meaning "order." Ultimate order, for the Greeks, related to the universe and the worlds within it, so **cosmos** for us means the universe. A **cosmonaut** was a space traveler from the former Soviet Union.

cosmopolitan \ˌkäz-mə-'pä-lə-tən\ International in outlook; sophisticated; worldly.
- The cosmopolitan actress Audrey Hepburn was born in Belgium and educated in England but won fame in America.

cosmology \käz-'mä-lə-jē\ 1: A branch of astronomy dealing with the origin and structure of the universe. 2: A theory that describes the nature of the universe.
- New Age philosophies and science fiction suggest a variety of possible cosmologies.

microcosm \'mī-krə-ˌkä-zəm\ An individual or community thought of as a miniature world or universe.
- Early thinkers saw the whole human world as a microcosm of the universe, which was considered the macrocosm.

QUIZ 2

Answers appear at the end of this chapter.

1. In ant–aphid _____, the aphids are protected by the ants, who "milk" them for their honeydew.

2. A _____ witch could end a drought by casting a spell to bring rain.

3. The diner's hours depended on such _____ factors as whether the cook's car had gotten repossessed.

4. Phenomena such as time warps and black holes made theoretical _____ the strangest subject in the curriculum.

5. Church members were surprised by the closing _____, "May God _deny_ you peace, but grant you love."

6. Neuroscientists believe they will soon have developed a complete _____ ear.

7. Identifying a suspicious tumor almost always calls for a _____ procedure.

8. The children's clinic was built soon after a significant gift by a single _____.

9. Both candidates had managed to _____ campaign finance laws through fraud.

10. Measles and flu are acute illnesses, while asthma and diabetes are _____ conditions.

11. Shakespeare's *Macbeth*, set in the eleventh century, contains such _____s as a reference to clocks.

12. A detailed _____ of the actions of company executives from April to July revealed some suspicious patterns.

13. Office life, with all its dramas and secrets, seemed to her a _____ of the world outside.

14. When we have only flimsy evidence, we should be _____ in our opinions.

15. With its international nightlife and a multitude of languages spoken on its beaches, Martinique is a _____ island.

cred This root comes from *credere*, the Latin verb meaning "to believe." Thus something **incredible** is almost unbelievable. We have a good **credit** rating when institutions believe in our ability to repay a loan, and we carry **credentials** so that others will believe we are who we say we are.

credence \'krē-dəns\ Mental acceptance as true or real; belief.
- Giving credence to gossip—or even to corporate financial reports these days—is risky.

credible \'kre-də-bəl\ Trustworthy; believable.
- The defense team doubted that the ex-convict would make a credible witness.

creed \'krēd\ A statement of the essential beliefs of a religious faith.
- The Nicene Creed of A.D. 381 excluded Christian beliefs considered incorrect.

dis In Latin, *dis* means "apart." In English, its meanings have increased to include "do the opposite of" (as in **disobey**), "deprive of" (as in **disillusion**), "exclude or expel from" (**disbar**), "the opposite or absence of" (**disaffection**), and "not" (**disagreeable**).

disarming \di-'sär-miŋ\ Reducing hostility or criticism; ingratiating.
- Their ambassador to the United Nations has a disarming manner but a cunning mind.

disburse \dis-'bərs\ To pay out; distribute.
- The World Bank agreed to disburse $20 million to Bolivia in recognition of its economic reforms.

discredit \dis-'kre-dət\ 1: To cause disbelief in the accuracy or authority of. 2: To disgrace.
- Lawyers with the states suing the tobacco company sought to discredit testimony of its chief witness.

dyna The Greek root *dyna* means "to be able" or "to have power." **Dynamite** has enough power to blow up the hardest granite bedrock. A **dynamic** person or group is powerful and energetic. A **dynamometer** measures mechanical force, which is measured in **dynes**.

dynamo \'dī-nə-ˌmō\ 1: A power generator. 2: A forceful, energetic person.
- The early dynamo was a mysterious mechanism for many, who saw no relation between steam and electric current.

dynasty \'dī-nə-stē\ 1: A line of rulers from the same family. 2: A powerful group or family that maintains its position for a long time.
- After the Mongols and before the Manchus, the Ming dynasty provided China a very stable era.

hydrodynamic \ˌhī-drō-dī-'na-mik\ Of or relating to the motion of fluids and the forces acting on moving bodies immersed in fluids.
- Water temperature, resistance, and depth are among the hydrodynamic aspects of rowing.

dys In Greek, *dys* means "bad" or "difficult." As a prefix in English, it has the additional meanings "abnormal" and "impaired." **Dyspnea** is difficult or labored breathing. **Dyspepsia** is indigestion (or ill humor). A **dysfunctional** family is one that functions badly.

dyslexia \dis-ˈlek-sē-ə\ A disturbance of the ability to read or use language.
- Dyslexia is regarded as the most widespread of the learning disabilities.

dysentery \ˈdi-sən-ˌter-ē\ An infectious intestinal disease with abdominal pain and severe diarrhea.
- Considering the poor sanitation, travelers were not surprised to find dysentery widespread.

dystrophy \ˈdis-trə-fē\ A disorder involving wasting away of muscular tissue.
- The telethon raises over $50 million a year to battle muscular dystrophy and related diseases.

epi Coming from the Greek, this root means various things, particularly "on" and "over." An **epicenter** is the part of the earth's surface directly over the focus of an earthquake. The **epidermis** is the outer layer of the skin, overlying the inner "dermis." An **epitaph** is an inscription upon a tomb in memory of the person buried there.

epithet \ˈe-pə-ˌthet\ A characterizing and often abusive word or phrase.
- Classic epithets used by Homer include "*rosy-fingered* dawn" and "Zeus, *the cloud-gatherer.*"

epigraph \ˈe-pə-ˌgraf\ 1: An engraved inscription. 2: A quotation set at the beginning of a literary work to suggest its theme.
- Chapter 5, describing the great battle, bears the Shakespearean epigraph "Let slip the dogs of war."

epilogue \ˈe-pə-ˌlȯg\ A concluding section, especially to a literary or musical work.
- Not until the novel's epilogue do we realize that all the characters were based on the author's family.

Quiz 3

Answers appear at the end of this chapter.

1. Most early Christian _____s developed around the act of baptism, where adult candidates proclaimed their faith.

2. With his _____ smile and quiet humor, he charms even the wariest clients.

3. Amoebic _____ is not just traveler's diarrhea—it is contracted by people who live in unclean conditions, too.

4. The dictator scornfully attempted to _____ the proceedings at his war crimes trial.

5. New reports lent _____ to the captive's story that the enemy had fled.

6. When students with undiagnosed _____ go on to higher education, their coping mechanisms often fall apart.

7. Henry Ford founded a _____; his great-grandson is now the company's chairman.

8. The listing of _____s included 40,000 reports of inscriptions found on Roman ruins.

9. Katie's research focused on the _____ drag of small sea kayaks.

10. Relief agencies explored how best to _____ funds and food to the disaster victims.

11. At the close of Shakespeare's *The Tempest*, Prospero speaks the wise _____.

12. Lou Gehrig's disease is one of about forty diseases in the area of muscular _____.

13. The shoplifter hurled obscene _____s at the guard conducting her to the office.

14. Her story is hardly _____, since she's already changed the facts twice.

15. Mayor Fiorello La Guardia of New York was considered a _____ in an already dynamic city.

extra This root, from Latin, places words "outside" or "beyond" their usual or routine territory. **Extraterrestrial** events take place "beyond" the Earth. Something **extravagant**, such as an **extravaganza**, goes beyond the limits of moderation. And **extra** is itself a word, a shortening of **extraordinary**, "beyond the ordinary."

extrapolate \ik-'stra-pə-ˌlāt\ To project (known data) into an unknown area to arrive at knowledge of the unknown area.
- Her department pored over export-import data endlessly in order to extrapolate present trade trends and predict the future.

extrovert \'ek-strə-ˌvərt\ An outgoing, sociable, unreserved person.
- Linda's boss is an extrovert, always happiest in a roomful of people.

extraneous \ek-'strā-nē-əs\ Not forming a vital part; irrelevant.
- Coaching in diving and dance often seeks to reduce extraneous movements.

fid *Fid* comes from *fides*, the Latin word for "faith." An **infidel** is someone who lacks a particular kind of religious faith. An **affidavit** is a sworn statement, a statement you can have faith in. Something that's **bona fide** is in "good faith"—absolutely genuine, the real deal.

fiduciary \fə-'dü-shē-ˌer-ē\ 1: Involving a confidence or trust. 2: Held or holding in trust for another.
- Corporate directors have often forgotten their fiduciary responsibility to their companies' stockholders.

confidante \'kän-fə-ˌdänt\ A person to whom secrets are entrusted, especially a woman.
- The famed advice columnist Ann Landers was in many ways America's confidante.

fidelity \fə-'de-lə-tē\ 1: The quality or state of being faithful. 2: Accuracy, as in sound reproduction.
- Harriet's comment left Lisa wondering about her husband's fidelity.

geo From the Greek word for "earth," *geo* almost always appears as a prefix. **Geography** describes the Earth's surface; **geology** deals with its history. We measure the Earth—and relationships of its points, lines, angles, surfaces, and solids—using **geometry**.

geopolitical \ˌjē-ō-pə-'li-ti-kəl\ Combining geographic and political factors such as economics and population spread, usually with reference to a state.
- Any invasion might trigger a series of geopolitical consequences, including the fall of other governments.

geosynchronous \ˌjē-ō-'siŋ-krə-nəs\ Having an orbit such that its position is fixed with respect to the Earth.
- Satellites in geosynchronous orbits are usually positioned over the equator.

geothermal \ˌjē-ō-'thər-məl\ Of, relating to, or using the heat of the Earth's interior.
- Geothermal energy technology is most developed in areas of volcanic activity.

graph This root is taken from the Greek word meaning "to write." Something **graphic** is "vividly described." **Graphology** is the study of handwriting. A **graph** is a diagram representing changes in something that varies. But *graph,* or *graphy,* actually most often appears at the end of a word.

spectrography \spek-'trä-grə-fē\ The dispersing of radiation (such as electromagnetic radiation or sound waves) into a spectrum to be photographed or mapped.

- Spectrography can determine what elements stars are made of and how fast they are moving.

seismograph \'sīz-mə-ˌgraf\ An apparatus for measuring and recording earthquake-related vibrations.

- Only recently have seismographs been enabling earthquake predictions that actually save lives.

topography \tə-'pä-grə-fē\ 1: The detailed mapping of geographical areas showing their elevations and natural and manmade features. 2: The contours of a geographical surface.

- Watching for the next El Niño, NASA monitors ocean surface topography from space for clues.

grat This root comes from *gratus,* the Latin word meaning "pleasing, welcome, or agreeable," or from *gratia,* meaning "grace, agreeableness, or pleasantness." A meal that is served **graciously** will be received with **gratitude** by **grateful** diners, unless they want to risk being called **ingrates.**

gratify \'gra-tə-ˌfī\ 1: To be a source of pleasure or satisfaction. 2: To give in to; indulge or satisfy.

- The victim's family was gratified by the guilty verdict in the murder trial.

ingratiate \in-'grā-shē-ˌāt\ To gain favor by deliberate effort.

- Backers of the proposed new mall sought to ingratiate themselves with community leaders.

gratuitous \grə-'tü-ə-təs\ Uncalled for; unwarranted.

- Luckily for Linda and all concerned, her gratuitous and offensive remark was not recorded.

QUIZ 4

Answers appear at the end of this chapter.

1. An _____ may assume that introverts are odd and antisocial.

2. To be named a child's guardian is to enter an important _____ relationship.

3. Broadcast journalists' microphones now reduce surrounding _____ noise to a whisper.

4. He kept the embarrassing details a secret from everyone but Kendra, his longtime _____.

5. The growth of telecommunications is causing a rapid increase in the number of _____ satellites.

6. Her scheme to _____ herself with the president began with freshly baked cookies.

7. _____ energy usually derives from the heat associated with young volcanic systems.

8. CAT scans and _____ are being used to analyze old bones from the Southwest.

9. After polling 840 well-chosen Americans, the firm _____s its results to the entire country.

10. The stock-market chart looked as if it had been produced by a _____ set on the San Andreas fault.

11. Chief Justice John Marshall called for an oath of _____ to the Constitution.

12. Haters of junk e-mail formed NAGS—Netizens Against _____ Spamming.

13. The map detailed the region's _____, indicating the approximate altitude of every square foot of land.

14. He hoped the award would _____ her without swelling her head.

15. Foster was devoted to national politics, but had no interest in wider _____ issues.

hydr *Hydr* flows from the Greek word for "water." **Hydrotherapy** uses water for healing physical infirmities. Water may spout from a **hydrant**. "Water" can also be found in the lovely flower called **hydrangea**: its seed capsules resemble ancient Greek water vessels.

hydraulic \hī-'drȯ-lik\ 1: Operated or moved by water. 2: Operated by the resistance offered or the pressure transmitted when a quantity of liquid is forced through a small opening or tube.
- The hydraulic brake system used in automobiles is a multiple piston system.

dehydrate \dē-'hī-ˌdrāt\ 1: To remove water from. 2: To lose liquid.
- To minimize weight on the challenging trail, the hikers packed dehydrated fruits and vegetables.

hydroelectric \ˌhī-drō-i-'lek-trik\ Of or relating to production of electricity by waterpower.
- Hydroelectric power sounded clean and renewable, but some asked about its social and environmental impact.

hyper This Greek prefix means "above and beyond it all." To be **hypercritical** or **hypersensitive** is to be critical or sensitive beyond what is normal. To **hyperextend** means to extend a joint (such as a knee or elbow) beyond its usual limits. Clicking on a **hyperlink** may take you beyond the Web site where you found it.

hyperbole \hī-'pər-bə-lē\ Extravagant exaggeration.
- The article called him the college's most popular professor, which even he thought was hyperbole.

hypertension \ˌhī-pər-'ten-shən\ The condition accompanying high blood pressure.
- Hypertension ran in Rachel's family and seemed to be linked to her relatives' heart attacks.

hyperventilate \ˌhī-pər-'ven-təl-ˌāt\ To breathe rapidly and deeply.
- Competitive short-distance runners hyperventilate briefly before running.

hypo Coming from Greek, *hypo* as a prefix can mean "under" or "below normal." A **hypocrite** says or does one thing while thinking or feeling something entirely different underneath. Many *hypo-* words are medical. A **hypodermic** needle injects medication under the skin. **Hypotension**, or low blood pressure, can be just as unhealthy as hypertension.

hypochondriac \ˌhī-pə-'kän-drē-'ak\ A person depressed in mind or spirits because of imaginary physical ailments.
- My grandmother is a hypochondriac; every time she hears about a new disease on the news, she thinks she has caught it.

hypothetical \ˌhī-pə-'the-ti-kəl\ Involving an assumption made for the sake of argument.
- The dating service provides hypothetical questions designed to predict success or failure.

hypothermia \ˌhī-pō-'thər-mē-ə\ Subnormal body temperature.
- Confusion and slurred speech are signs of hypothermia, a silent killer in all seasons.

inter This prefix is the Latin word meaning "between or among." Someone who **interferes** comes between two people; a player who **intercepts** a pass comes between the ball and its intended receiver. An **intermission** is a break between acts of a play. An **international** event takes place between or among nations.

intercede \ˌin-tər-'sēd\ 1: To act between parties as a mediator. 2: To plead on another's behalf.
- The bishop prayed, asking Mother Mary to intercede for us.

interdict \'in-tər-ˌdikt\ To destroy, cut off, or damage.
- U.S. Kosovo Force soldiers sought to interdict weapons at the Serbian and Albanian borders.

interface \'in-tər-ˌfās\ 1: A surface forming a common boundary between two bodies, spaces, or phases. 2: The place where independent systems meet and act on each other.
- Long before the computer age, the auto dashboard was designed as a man–machine interface.

jur *Jur* comes from the Latin verb *jurare*, "to swear or take an oath," and the noun *juris*, "right" or "law." A **jury**, made up of **jurors**, makes judgments based on the law. A personal **injury** caused by another person is "not right."

perjury \'pər-jə-rē\ Violation of an oath to tell the truth; lying under oath.
- Lying to a TV reporter is one thing; perjury before a Senate committee is another.

jurisprudence \ˌjùr-əs-'prü-dəns\ 1: A system of laws. 2: The science or philosophy of law.
- Juliana's heroes were the crusaders of 20th-century jurisprudence, especially Thurgood Marshall.

abjure \ab-'jùr\ 1: To give up, renounce, recant. 2: To abstain from.
- To the prison counselor, the three conspirators always solemnly abjured a future life of crime.

Merriam-Webster's Roots to Word Mastery

Quiz 5

Answers appear at the end of this chapter.

1. The novelist Lord Archer was found guilty of
_____ for lying during his libel suit.

2. "As a _____ example," she said, "let's suppose
it were the other way around."

3. Jared led the team up the river to visit the principal
_____ power plant in the region.

4. In the thinner air near the mountain top, the climbers
began to _____.

5. _____ technology uses fluid to give bulldoz-
ers and cranes their great power.

6. There are often no warning signs before
_____ triggers a stroke, heart attack, or heart
failure.

7. By 19 he was a _____, calling his mother
daily about some new ache or sniffle.

8. They urged the UN Secretary-General to
_____ in the bloody Middle East conflict.

9. By then her face was caked with ice and
_____ had caused her heart to stop.

10. In Web site design, a user-friendly _____ is
essential.

11. Accepting the peace prize, Hume again stressed the need
to _____ violence.

12. To preserve fruits, we learned how to can and freeze and even _____ them.

13. Feminist _____ is a philosophy of law based on the political, economic, and social equality of the sexes.

14. Jason's mom said he read thick books and took quantities of notes, but this was surely _____.

15. Once the enriched uranium left the lab, there would be no chance to _____ it.

mal *Mal*, from the Latin, means "bad." **Malodorous** things smell bad. A **malefactor** is someone guilty of bad deeds. A **malady** is a disease or disorder. **Malnutrition** is faulty or inadequate nutrition. **Dismal** means particularly bad.

malevolent \mə-'le-və-lənt\ Having, showing, or arising from intense ill will, spite, or hatred.
- Bookstores report that children still like stories with hairy beasts and malevolent aliens.

malign \mə-'līn\ To speak evil of; defame.
- Amanda didn't wish to malign her neighbors, but the late-night partying had to stop.

malpractice \ˌmal-'prak-təs\ An abandonment of professional duty or a failure of professional skill that results in injury, loss, or damage.
- The soaring cost of malpractice insurance forced many doctors into early retirement.

mar From the Latin word *mare*, meaning "sea," *mar* brings its salty tang to English in words like **marine**, "having to do with the sea," and **submarine**, "under the sea." It also forms part of such place names as Del Mar ("of the sea"), California. **Aquamarine** is the color of clear seawater in sunlight.

maritime \'mar-ə-ˌtīm\ Of or relating to the sea, navigation, or commerce of the sea.
- She achieved a national practice in maritime law, specializing in ship insurance.

marina \mə-'rē-nə\ A dock or basin providing secure moorings for pleasure boats.
- Florida has marinas all along its coast to meet the needs of watercraft from enormous yachts to flimsy sailboats.

mariner \'mar-ə-nər\ A sailor.
- Ann was haunted by some lines about the old mariner in Coleridge's famous poem.

morph This form comes from the Greek word for "shape." It appears in **anthropomorphic**, meaning "having human form." And **morph** is itself a new English word; by morphing, filmmakers can alter photographic images or shapes digitally, transforming them in astonishing ways.

amorphous \ə-'mȯr-fəs\ Shapeless; formless.
- The sculptor swiftly molded an amorphous lump of clay into a rough human shape.

metamorphosis \ˌme-tə-'mȯr-fə-səs\ 1: A change in physical form or substance. 2: A fundamental change in form and often habits of an animal as part of the transformation of a larva into an adult.
- Day by day we watched the gradual metamorphosis of the tadpoles into frogs.

morphology \mȯr-'fä-lə-jē\ A branch of biology dealing with the form and structure of organisms.
- As an example, she mentioned the morphology of whales, whose fins evolved from legs.

mort / mori These roots come from the Latin noun *mors* (and its related form *mortis*), meaning "death." A **mortuary** is a place where dead bodies are kept until burial, and a **mortician** prepares corpses for burial or cremation. **Memento mori**, a Latin phrase used in English, means "a reminder of death," such as a skull.

moribund \'mȯr-ə-bənd\ 1: Dying or approaching death. 2: Inactive or becoming outmoded.
- Evidence of the sagging industrial economy could be seen in the moribund factories and towns.

mortify \'mȯr-tə-ˌfī\ 1: To subdue or deaden (the body) with self-discipline or self-inflicted pain. 2: To embarrass greatly; humiliate.
- The parents' attempts to act youthful mortified their kids, who almost died of embarrassment when their friends were around.

mortality \mȯr-'ta-lə-tē\ 1: The state of being subject to death. 2: The proportion of deaths to population.
- The preacher takes every occasion to remind us of our mortality, as does the insurance agent.

mut *Mut* comes from the Latin *mutare*, "to change." Science-fiction movies often focus on weird mutations, changes in normal people or animals that lead to death, destruction, or comedy. A governor may **commute** or change a prison sentence; a person **commuting** between cities "exchanges" one location for another.

permutation \ˌpər-myu̇-'tā-shən\ 1: The changing of the order of a set of objects. 2: An ordering of a set of objects.
- The letters A, B, and C have six possible permutations: ABC, ACB, BAC, BCA, CAB, and CBA.

immutable \i-'myü-tə-bəl\ Unchangeable or unchanging.
- The physical world is governed by the immutable laws of nature.

transmute \trans-'myüt\ To change in shape, appearance, or nature, especially for the better; transform.
- A meek person may dream of being transmuted into a tyrant, or a poor person into a rich one.

QUIZ 6

Answers appear at the end of this chapter.

1. The _____ at Hyannis has over 180 slips for deep-draft sailboats, motorboats, and yachts.

2. _____ suits are being filed today against even fine doctors who have made no errors.

3. The monarch's transformation from caterpillar to butterfly represents a dramatic _____.

4. Computer users were warned about a _____ virus hiding in e-Christmas cards.

5. The fabled dream of the alchemist was to _____ lead into gold.

6. The store's nautical antiques and pond yachts should interest the armchair _____.

7. It would _____ her if she ever heard herself described as "middle-aged."

8. Al Capp's Shmoo was an _____ blob-like creature who sometimes helped his friends solve mysteries.

9. The moment he left the party, she started to _____ him mercilessly.

10. In terms of _____, bats' wings are skeletal hands with very long fingers, webbed with membranes.

11. The day the first CD appeared in the stores, the vinyl LP was _____.

12. The number of different ways eight people can line up in a row provides a nice illustration of _____s.

13. Detailed _____ records are kept by the National Center for Health Statistics.

14. The National _____ Museum was displaying personal possessions of the *Bounty* mutineers.

15. In an ever-changing world, people hunger for standards and qualities that are _____.

neo Old as its Greek source, *neo* means "new." **Neon** was a new gas when found in 1898. A **neoconservative** is a liberal who has become a conservative. A **neophyte** is a new convert, or a beginner. And a **neologism** is a new word.

neoclassical \ˌnē-ō-'kla-si-kəl\ Of or relating to a revival or adaptation of the style of classical antiquity.
- Neoclassical paintings are dignified and restrained, and they often radiate a noble spirit.

Neolithic \ˌnē-ə-'li-thik\ Of or relating to the latest period of the Stone Age, characterized by polished stone implements.
- Doctors have asked how the life spans of the Neolithic farmers compared with those of earlier hunter-gatherers.

neoplasm \'nē-ə-ˌpla-zəm\ A new growth of tissue serving no useful purpose in the body; tumor.
- Using digital X rays, the dentist examined Tom's gums for neoplasms and cysts.

omni This comes from the Latin prefix meaning "all." Thus an **omnidirectional** antenna will draw in stations from all directions. Something **omnipresent** is thought to be present at all places and at all times. An **omnivorous** animal might eat almost everything. Some companies apparently meaning to be everything to their customers name themselves simply "Omni."

omnibus \'äm-ni-bəs\ Of, relating to, or providing for many things at once.
- The Senate's omnibus bill includes money for everything from snail research to new bombers.

omnipotent \äm-'ni-pə-tənt\ Having unlimited authority or influence; almighty.
- The question arises, If God is good and omnipotent, why do bad things happen?

omniscient \äm-'ni-shənt\ Having infinite awareness, understanding, insight, or knowledge.
- His stories usually have an omniscient narrator, who reveals the thoughts of all the characters.

ortho *Ortho* comes from *orthos*, the Greek word for "straight," "right," or "true." **Orthotics** is a therapy that straightens out the stance or posture of the body by providing artificial support for weak joints or muscles. **Orthograde** animals, such as humans, walk with their bodies in an upright position. **Orthography** is correct spelling.

orthodox \'òr-thə-ˌdäks\ 1: Holding established beliefs, especially in religion. 2: Conforming to established rules or traditions; conventional.
- Gerald preferred orthodox, mainstream cancer treatments to untested alternative therapies.

orthopedist \ˌòr-thə-'pē-dist\ A medical specialist concerned with correcting or preventing skeletal deformities.
- A local orthopedist eventually managed to correct the child's spinal curvature.

orthodontic \ˌòr-thə-'dän-tik\ Pertaining to irregularities of the teeth and their correction.
- As much as she dreaded braces, Jennifer knew the time had come for orthodontic work.

pan Directly from Greek, *pan* means "all"; as a prefix in English it can also mean "completely," "whole," or "general." A **panoramic** view is a complete view in every direction. **Pantheism** is the worship of all gods. A **pandemic** outbreak of a disease will affect an exceptionally high proportion of the population, though probably not literally "all" people.

panacea \ˌpa-nə-ˈsē-ə\ A remedy for all ills or difficulties; a cure-all.
- Educational reform is sometimes seen as the panacea for society's problems.

panoply \ˈpa-nə-plē\ 1: A magnificent or impressive array. 2: A display of all appropriate accessory items.
- The full panoply of a royal wedding was a thrilling sight for millions.

pantheon \ˈpan-thē-ˌän\ 1: The gods of a people. 2: A group of illustrious people.
- Even during Dickens's lifetime, the critics had admitted him into the literary pantheon.

phon This Greek root means "sound" or "voice." It shows up in such words as **telephone** ("far sound"), **microphone** ("small sound"), and **xylophone** ("wood sound"). **Phonics** teaches reading by focusing on the sounds of letter groups. A **phonograph** is an instrument for reproducing sounds.

cacophony \ka-ˈkä-fə-nē\ Harsh or discordant sound.
- According to his grandfather, popular music since Bing Crosby had been nothing but cacophony.

phonetic \fə-ˈne-tik\ Relating to or representing the sounds of the spoken language.
- Some schools teach reading by the phonetic method, linking sounds with letters.

polyphonic \ˈpä-lē-ˈfä-nik\ Of or relating to music in which two or more independent melodies are sung or played against each other in harmony.
- Children singing "Three Blind Mice" are performing the simplest kind of polyphonic music.

MERRIAM-WEBSTER'S ROOTS TO WORD MASTERY

Quiz 7

Answers appear at the end of this chapter.

1. Some saw the antidepressant drug Prozac as a psychological _____.

2. Prehistory, the period of no written records, included the _____ and Bronze Ages.

3. Suzanne, age 16, said if she were _____ for a day, she would bring about world peace and save the rainforest.

4. Adventurous young people often challenge _____ religious belief systems.

5. The _____ Trade and Competitiveness Act touched on many aspects of labor, global commerce, and regulation.

6. The conductor chose a balanced program by composers from the musical _____.

7. A _____ alphabet was developed by NATO to be understandable by all allies in the heat of battle.

8. The checkup produced one cause for concern: a small _____ on the bile duct.

9. My _____ traces all our lower back problems to the time when the first humans stood erect.

10. Sandra's new sequencer could take complex _____ music and convert it into written notation.

11. Even several university degrees and eyes in the back of your head do not make you _____.

12. Looking down the long row of _____ buildings, we almost thought we were in ancient Rome.

13. His mouth was a disaster area, and his crooked rows of teeth had never had a minute of _____ attention.

14. Out over the ocean, the winter sky spread a brilliant _____ of stars.

15. The kids who liked producing the most outrageous music soon were styling themselves the "_____ Club."

photo Coming from the Greek word for "light," *photo* enlightens us in words like **photography**, which is the use of light to create an image on film or paper. A **photocopy** is a printed copy made by light on an electrically charged surface. A **photogenic** person is one highly suitable for being photographed.

photon \\'fō-ˌtän\\ A tiny particle or bundle of radiant energy.
* *Star Trek*'s photon torpedoes destroy their targets with intense radiation in the X-ray range.

photosynthesis \\ˌfō-tō-'sin-thə-səs\\ The process by which green plants use light to produce organic matter from carbon dioxide and water.
* Sagebrush is a hardy plant that can carry on photosynthesis at very low temperatures.

photoelectric \\ˌfō-tō-i-'lek-trik\\ Relating to an electrical effect from the interaction of light with matter.
* Photoelectric cells would trigger the yard lights when they sensed motion.

post *Post* comes from a Latin word meaning "after" or "behind." A **postscript** is a note that comes after an otherwise completed letter, usually as an after-thought. **Postpartum** refers to the period just after childbirth and all of its related concerns. To **postdate** a check is to give it a date after the date when it was written.

posterior \\pä-'stir-ē-ər\\ Situated behind or on the back; rear.
* A posterior view of the animal revealed unusual coloring and an extremely long tail.

posthumous \\'päs-chə-məs\\ Following or happening after one's death.
* The late singer achieved posthumous success when her film became a huge hit.

postmortem \\ˌpōst-'mȯr-təm\\ 1: Occurring after death. 2: Following the event.
* In 1999 the institute had issued a postmortem report on the Bosnian war, "NATO's Empty Victory."

pre One of the most common of all English **prefixes**, *pre* comes from *prae*, the Latin word meaning "before" or "in front of." A TV program **precedes** another by coming on before it. You **predict** an event by saying it will happen before it does. A person who **presumes** to know assumes something before having all the facts.

precocious \\pri-'kō-shəs\\ Showing mature qualities at an unusually early age.
* Some thought the sitcom's precocious child star was cute; others thought she was a show-off.

prerequisite \\prē-'re-kwə-zət\\ An action, event, or object required in advance to achieve a goal.
* Certain courses were prerequisites for majoring in engineering at the university.

predisposed \\ˌprē-di-'spōzd\\ Influenced in advance or made persuadable.
* The commissioner was predisposed to vote for the project since its developer had given his campaign a large contribution.

prim *Prim* comes from *primus*, the Latin word for "first." A **prime minister** is the chief minister of a ruler or state. Something **primary** is first in time, rank, or importance. Something **primitive** seems to be in an early stage of development.

primal \ˈprī-məl\ 1: Original or primitive. 2: First in importance.
- Much of civilization seems designed to disguise or soften the rawness of our primal urges.

primordial \prī-ˈmȯr-dē-əl\ Existing in or from the very beginning.
- He assumed his ancestors emerged from the primordial ooze, and not as gods.

primate \ˈprī-māt\ A member of an order of mammals that includes humans, apes, and monkeys.
- Do we have anything important to learn about human behavior from our cousins the primates?

rect This root comes **directly** from the Latin word *rectus*, meaning "straight" or "right." A **rectangle** is a four-sided figure whose straight sides meet at right angles. To **correct** something is to make it right. To stand **erect** is to stand straight.

rectitude \ˈrek-tə-ˌtüd\ Correctness in judgment; moral integrity.
- The school superintendent wasn't popular, but no one could question his fairness and rectitude.

rectify \ˈrek-tə-ˌfī\ To make or set right; correct.
- Problems with the Bowl Championship Series were rectified by a simple four-team playoff.

rectilinear \ˌrek-tə-ˈli-nē-ər\ Characterized by straight lines.
- In its rectilinear structure, the sculpture reflects the surrounding office buildings.

QUIZ 8

Answers appear at the end of this chapter.

1. Hamstrings, deltoids, and gluteus maximus are human muscles on the _____ side.

2. The lighting engineering firm offered _____ sensors for many uses.

3. The West Point students' reputation for _____ was badly damaged by the cheating scandal.

4. Average parents of specially gifted or _____ children face unusual challenges.

5. With the dead man now proven innocent, his relatives sought a _____ pardon.

6. The power of lasers results from a focused concentration of _____s.

7. For many, retreating to a rough-hewn home in the woods seems to satisfy a _____ urge.

8. Some children may be _____ to asthma by their genes.

9. Green plants don't graze, hunt, or shop; they make food by using sunlight through _____.

10. The association called on Congress to _____ the unfairness of health-care funding.

11. During the _____ exam, the medical examiner discovered a mysterious blackening of the liver tissue.

12. Her study of baboons earned Gloria a fellowship to the
_____ research center.

13. Over ten billion years ago, the Milky Way was just a giant
_____ gas cloud.

14. Simple _____ designs with bold vertical and
horizontal lines dominated the hotel's decor.

15. Detailed knowledge of psychology is not a
_____ for interviewing of job applicants.

retro *Retro* means "back," "behind," or "backward" in Latin. **Retro** itself is a fairly new word in English, meaning "nostalgically old-fashioned," usually when describing styles or fashions. To **retrogress** is to go back to an earlier and usually worse state. A **retrograde** action is a backward or reverse action.

retroactive \ˌre-trō-ˈak-tiv\ Intended to apply or take effect at a date in the past.
- The fact that the tax hike was retroactive was what annoyed the public the most.

retrofit \ˈre-trō-ˌfit\ To furnish something with new or modified parts or equipment.
- Owners were offered "fast-track" permits to retrofit their homes against earthquakes.

retrospective \ˌre-trə-ˈspek-tiv\ Of or relating to surveying the past.
- Excitement grew in anticipation of the rare retrospective exhibition of Avedon's photographs.

scrib / scrip This root comes from the Latin verb *scribere*, "to write." A **script** is written matter, such as lines for a play. **Scriptures** are sacred writings. **Scribble** means to write or draw carelessly. A written work that hasn't been published is a **manuscript**.

circumscribe \ˈsər-kəm-ˌskrīb\ To limit the range or activity of.
- Various laws have circumscribed the freedom of labor unions to strike and organize.

inscribe \in-ˈskrīb\ 1: To write, engrave, or print. 2: To dedicate (a book) to someone.
- As Mike turned to leave, the store clerk offered to inscribe the diamond ring for free.

proscribe \prō-ˈskrīb\ 1: To prohibit. 2: To condemn or forbid as harmful.
- If the doctor proscribes certain foods, you'd better not eat them.

sub *Sub* means "under," as in **subway**, **submarine**, and **substandard**. A **subject** is a person who is under the authority of another. **Subconscious** activity exists in the mind just under the level of awareness. To **subdue** is to bring under control.

subjugate \ˈsəb-ji-ˌgāt\ To bring under control; conquer; subdue.
- Bringing criminal charges against reporters seemed a government attempt to subjugate the media.

subliminal \sə-ˈbli-mə-nəl\ Not quite strong enough to be sensed or perceived consciously.
- Worried parents claimed that some songs contained disturbing subliminal messages.

subversive \səb-ˈvər-siv\ 1: Tending to overthrow or undermine by working secretly from within. 2: Tending to corrupt someone or something by weakening loyalty, morals, or faith.
- In the 1950s the nation became alarmed that subversive communists were lurking everywhere.

syn From the Greek word meaning "with" or "together with," *syn* as a prefix in English can also mean "at the same time." Thus **synesthesia** is the remarkable awareness of another sense (such as color) at the same time as the one being stimulated (such as sound). **Synergy** is the useful "working together" of distinct elements. **Syntax** is about how words are put together.

synthesis \ˈsin-thə-səs\ The combination of parts or elements into a whole.
- Chemical analysis separates a substance into its elements; chemical synthesis combines elements to produce something new.

synopsis \sə-ˈnäp-səs\ A condensed statement or outline.
- Having read the synopsis, Bill did not feel a need to read the full report.

syndrome \ˈsin-ˌdrōm\ A group of signs and symptoms that occur together and characterize a particular abnormality.
- Sufferers from chronic fatigue syndrome fought for a decade to have their symptoms recognized as a specific illness.

tele *Tele* comes from the Greek word for "far off"; in English its basic meaning is "distant" or "at a distance." A **telescope** looks at faraway objects. A **telephoto** lens on a camera magnifies distant objects for a photograph. A **television** allows us to watch things taking place far away (or sometimes not far enough away).

teleological \ˌte-lē-ə-ˈlä-ji-kəl\ Relating to design, purpose, or cause, especially in nature.
- The traditional teleological argument claims that humans are so remarkable that only God could have designed them.

telepathic \ˌte-lə-ˈpa-thik\ Communicating from one mind to another without known sensory means.
- Suzanne never considered herself telepathic, but she awoke with a start when her brother died at 2:00 a.m. 3,000 miles away.

telemetry \tə-ˈle-mə-trē\ The transmission, especially by radio, of measurements made by automatic instruments to a distant station.
- Satellite telemetry allowed the tracking of this year's great caribou migration.

Quiz 9

Answers appear at the end of this chapter.

1. Highly responsive to each other's actions, the twins at times seemed almost _____.

2. The catalog featuring vintage dinnerware of the 1940s through the 1970s was really a _____ display of modern design.

3. As a semi-invalid, she led a _____d life, rarely venturing beyond her garden.

4. Approval of the pay increase was confirmed, _____ to January 1st.

5. Did an early experiment in _____ advertising at a movie theater result in increased popcorn sales?

6. A cherub helped an angel _____ words so beautiful they fell like roses from her feather pen.

7. Her new album seemed to be a _____ of country and world music.

8. The scary part was when the _____ failed and the astronauts vanished from the screens.

9. Once in power, the mullahs proceeded to _____ the Westernized women of Tehran.

10. Smoking is now _____d in many U.S. medical and restaurant settings.

11. A Hollywood-based Web site offers a helpful _____ of the plots of hundreds of films.

12. The mayor hoped to _____ the vehicles to increase the mobility of the disabled.

13. The new special police unit was entrusted with intelligence gathering and monitoring _____ activities.

14. Schizophrenia is a _____ related to a variety of causative factors.

15. The claim that a gopher's cheek pouches are *intended* for carrying food is, to zoologists, a _____ statement.

terr This root was dug up from the Latin *terra*, "earth." **Terra firma** is a Latin phrase that means "firm ground," as opposed to the swaying seas. A **terrace** is a leveled area along a sloping hill; **territory** is a specific piece of land. A **terrier**, literally an "earth dog," was originally used by hunters to dig for small game.

subterranean \ˌsəb-tə-ˈrā-nē-ən\ Underground.
- The region, it was believed, was home to subterranean beings that emerged from their burrows only at night.

terrestrial \tə-ˈres-trē-əl\ 1: Having to do with the earth or its inhabitants. 2: Having to do with land as distinct from air or water.
- Unlike frogs, most toads are terrestrial, entering the water only to lay their eggs.

terrain \tə-ˈrān\ The surface features of an area of land.
- Mountain unicycling proved especially challenging over such rough terrain.

therm Still warm from centuries of use, *therm* comes from the Greek word meaning "heat." A **thermometer** measures heat; a **thermostat** makes sure it stays at the same level. A rising body of warm air, used by hawks and sailplanes, is called a **thermal**.

thermal \ˈthər-məl\ 1: Of, relating to, or caused by heat. 2: Designed to prevent loss of body heat.
- Thermal vents on the ocean floor release steam as hot as 600°.

thermodynamic \ˌthər-mō-dī-ˈna-mik\ Of or relating to the physics of heat.
- A chemical's thermodynamic properties indicate how it will behave at various temperatures.

thermonuclear \ˌthər-mō-ˈnü-klē-ər\ Of or relating to changes in the nucleus of atoms of low atomic weight brought about by very high temperatures.
- In those days thermonuclear devices were being proposed for such uses as excavating canals.

trans This root comes across from Latin to indicate movement "through, across, or beyond" something. A **translation** carries the meaning across languages. A TV signal is **transmitted** or "sent through" the air (or a cable) to your set. Public **transportation** carries you across a distance, though you may need to **transfer** from one bus or subway across to another.

transient \ˈtran-shənt\ 1: Passing through a place and staying only briefly. 2: Of brief duration.
- Tristan's inn in Vermont attracted transient tourists come to gaze at the autumn foliage.

transcendent \tran-ˈsen-dənt\ 1: Exceeding usual limits; surpassing. 2: Beyond comprehension.
- The symphony's hushed ending, with the solo violin melody trailing off into silence, is almost transcendent.

transfusion \trans-ˈfyü-zhən\ 1: The process of diffusing into or through. 2: The process of moving (as of blood) into a vein.
- Travelers needing blood transfusions have usually suffered severe accidents.

uni *Uni* comes from the Latin word for "one." A **uniform** is clothing of one design. A **united** group has one opinion or forms one **unit**. A **unitard** is a one-piece combination leotard and tights, very good for skating, skiing, dancing—or riding a one-wheeled **unicycle**.

unicameral \ˌyü-ni-ˈkam-rəl\ Having a single legislative house or chamber.
- Passing new laws was comparatively quick and easy in the unicameral government.

unilateral \ˌyü-ni-ˈla-tə-rəl\ Having, affecting, or done by one side only.
- Russia's unilateral withdrawal from Afghanistan, in return for nothing, astonished the world.

unison \ˈyü-nə-sən\ 1: Sameness of musical pitch. 2: A state of harmonious agreement; accord.
- Unable to read music well enough to harmonize, the village choir sang only in unison.

viv *Viv* comes from *vivere*, the Latin verb meaning "to live or be alive." A **vivid** memory is a lively one. A **survivor** has lived through something terrible. A **revival** brings something back to life—whether an old film, interest in a long-dead novelist, or the religious faith of a group.

vivacious \və-ˈvā-shəs\ Lively, sprightly.
- For the cheerleading squad, Sheri chose the most outgoing, energetic, and vivacious candidates.

vivisection \ˌvi-və-ˈsek-shən\ Experimental operation on a living animal.
- The firm reluctantly agreed to avoid research involving vivisection in favor of alternative methods.

convivial \kən-ˈviv-yəl\ 1: Enjoying companionship in feasting and drinking. 2: Festive.
- Alberta was known for hosting relaxed and convivial gatherings, where the wine flowed freely.

Quiz 10

Answers appear at the end of this chapter.

1. At the height of the Cold War, some Americans began digging _____ fallout shelters.

2. The _____ properties of metals affect technologies we don't think of as heat-related.

3. Forty-nine states have bicameral legislatures; only Nebraska's is _____.

4. Any chemical reaction that produces heat is a _____ reaction.

5. Over such rugged _____, mules were the only hope for transporting needed supplies.

6. It's a noisy, _____ crowd that gathers at McSorley's Restaurant after 5:00.

7. His bright idea turned out to be a _____ one, and he had soon moved on to something new.

8. He returned from the backpacking trip energized as if he'd been given a _____ of new blood.

9. Detonating a _____ bomb requires temperatures exceeding a million degrees Fahrenheit.

10. While singing in parts is difficult, singing modern compositions for _____ voices has challenges of its own.

11. Jessie was so _____ that she livened up every party she ever attended.

12. She emerged from the concert hall in a daze, feeling she had undergone a _____ experience.

13. Alabama has over 500 species of marine mollusks, and many _____ mollusks as well.

14. Animal lovers of every stripe wrote in, claiming that _____ had little scientific merit.

15. After failed negotiations with its neighbors, Iran announced a _____ decision to develop its own oil wells in the Caspian Sea.

REVIEW TEST

Fill in each blank in the sentences on the following pages with one of the following words. Answers appear at the end of this chapter.

abjure	discredit	marina	primate
agrarian	dynamo	mariner	primordial
agrochemical	dynasty	maritime	proscribe
agronomy	dysentery	metamorphosis	rectify
amorphous	dyslexia	microcosm	rectilinear
anachronism	dystrophy	misanthrope	rectitude
antecedent	epigraph	moribund	retroactive
antedate	epilogue	morphology	retrofit
anterior	epithet	mortality	retrospective
anthropoid	extraneous	mortify	seismograph
aquaculture	extrapolate	neoclassical	spectrography
Aquarius	extrovert	Neolithic	subjugate
aquifer	fidelity	neoplasm	subliminal
artifact	fiduciary	omnibus	subterranean
artifice	geopolitical	omnipotent	subversive
artisan	geosynchronous	omniscient	symbiosis
benediction	geothermal	orthodontic	syndrome
benefactor	gratify	orthodox	synopsis
beneficent	gratuitous	orthopedist	synthesis
bionic	hydraulic	panacea	telemetry
biopsy	hydrodynamic	panoply	teleological
cacophony	hydroelectric	pantheon	telepathic
chronic	hyperbole	perjury	terrain
chronology	hypertension	permutation	terrestrial
circumscribe	hyperventilate	philanthropy	thermal
circumspect	hypochondriac	phonetic	thermodynamic
circumstantial	hypothermia	photoelectric	thermonuclear
circumvent	hypothetical	photon	topography
confidante	immutable	photosynthesis	transcendent
convivial	ingratiate	polyphonic	transfusion
cosmology	inscribe	posterior	transient
cosmopolitan	intercede	posthumous	transmute
credence	interdict	postmortem	unicameral
credible	interface	precocious	unilateral
creed	jurisprudence	predisposed	unison
dehydrate	malevolent	prerequisite	vivacious
disarming	malign	primal	vivisection
disburse	malpractice		

1. Keith _____d the novel "To Melissa, my only muse and inspiration."

2. After the first trial, Collins was called to answer charges of _____ and evidence tampering.

3. Is it _____ to say that an eagle's wings were "designed" for soaring?

4. Rafael's clumsy attempt to _____ the contract led to his arrest for fraud.

5. Some interactive games let players achieve virtual destruction worse than that of a _____ bomb.

6. After his divorce, his legal practice shrank and a _____ suit almost bankrupted him.

7. _____ apes resemble humans in that they lack tails and walk semi-erect.

8. The "facts" on the "Astounding Facts" Web site turned out not to be very _____.

9. _____ runoff is blamed for creating a huge "dead zone" in the Gulf of Mexico.

10. Most people picture _____s as underground lakes rather than as expanses of soaked gravel.

11. The Water-Carrier, _____, is an old constellation carved in stones of the Babylonian Empire.

12. The formal gardens were showplaces of _____, with every tree and shrub shaped by human hands.

13. Aaron's fossil hunting in Alaska led to his unearthing of unusual ancient _____s.

14. The prison's star inmate, he had undergone a _____ from hardened criminal to contributing citizen.

15. The blonde Evita was seen by Argentina's poor as a _____ angel dispensing charity.

16. Paleolithic hunters, with their tools of chipped stone, gave way to _____ farmers, with their polished stone tools.

17. What anonymous _____ had contributed $500,000 to the medical fund?

18. Her aunt, previously blind, could now recognize faces with her new _____ eye.

19. For years Carol had managed her _____ heart condition through careful diet and exercise.

20. Using a telephone in a play set in 1765 is an obvious _____.

21. Veterinarians have often relied on _____ examinations in diagnosing disease.

22. A newly hired 22-year-old had easily managed to _____ the computer security system.

23. The sunny and _____ Doris Day started out as a jazz singer in the 1940s.

24. When asked about Russia's own success fighting corruption, the official quickly became _____.

25. The club was chic and _____, and everyone seemed to have a French or German accent.

26. Rural Maine is home to many _____s: woodworkers, potters, weavers, and the like.

27. The findings of Copernicus and Galileo proposed nothing less than a new _____.

28. Some building codes require _____ sensors, which are quick to detect smoky fires.

29. The _____ provided needed services after an exhausting day on choppy seas.

30. The game of Monopoly seems to present a
_____ of the world of real-estate dealing.

31. Scientists often refer to the ocean's surface as the
ocean-atmosphere _____.

32. A new find lends _____ to the claim that the
first Americans came from Europe.

33. She was skeptical about what lay behind his smooth and
_____ manner.

34. Society often depends on _____ to fill the
gaps left by government spending.

35. The new president turned out to be a ferociously energetic human _____.

36. Each winter, outdoor adventure groups often publicize
the best ways to avoid frostbite and _____.

37. She was always reading about alternative therapies, but
her doctor was as _____ as they come.

38. Muscular _____ is actually a family of
disorders that causes muscle degeneration.

39. A passage from *Othello* appeared as the
_____ of the long-awaited report.

40. The author's _____ listed the adventurers'
whereabouts five years after their rescue.

41. She told him his concerns were _____ and he
should stick to the subject at hand.

42. A data recorder and transmitters and receivers formed
part of the satellite's _____ system.

43. A prominent political _____, the Kennedy
family has seen many of its members elected to office.

44. He was a drifter, hardly the kind of person for a
_____ responsibility such as executor of
a will.

45. "Attack ads" attempt to _____ political candidates, often with half-truths and lies.

46. Whether the coup succeeded or failed depended on the _____ of the general's soldiers.

47. The clinic, in Canada's far north, serves a _____ Inuit population not likely to return for regular checkups.

48. Could _____ tensions in faraway Asia actually affect the national elections?

49. Study of the sun's magnetic fields requires _____ to reveal the solar spectrum.

50. For the America's Cup yachts, the keel by itself presents complex _____ problems.

51. Severe stomach distress ruined their trip, and it turned out they both had _____.

52. The Princeton Earth Physics Project tracks earthquakes using a network of _____s.

53. There were arguments about how best to _____ financial aid following the disaster.

54. Sandra knew it would _____ her husband if she wore the necklace he'd given her.

55. The fetus had gotten turned around into the _____ position, which can make the birthing process difficult.

56. Much modern _____ still is practiced in small mom-and-pop fishpond operations.

57. Those lurching virtual-reality thrill rides are powered by _____, pressurized-fluid technology.

58. Nick, the family _____, played touch football, organized reunions, and was his company's top salesman.

59. Astonishing examples of cooperative living between species appear as _____.

60. Having quit smoking, he was told he must now adopt a strict diet for his _____.

61. The meteorite, billions of years old, offered clues about the _____ solar system.

62. Best-selling novelists can sell a book idea to their publishers with nothing but a short _____.

63. The Garden of Eden is the biblical vision of a _____ paradise.

64. Melanie's problems with spelling and math were finally traced to _____.

65. Having entered the virtual body, the doctor may test a range of _____ drug interactions.

66. The response from the opposition was full of _____ insults and slurs.

67. A United Nations force was asked to _____ on behalf of both combatants and restore peace.

68. With public-relations help, the Nigerians hoped to _____ reports of genocide during the Biafran war.

69. As a context for discussion, Abu handed out a detailed _____ of Muslim history.

70. At halftime, the _____ mass of band musicians abruptly snapped into a tight formation.

71. The greatest Supreme Court justices could often be called philosophers of _____.

72. The awesome _____ of the procession made the hometown parade seem like a coronation.

73. Fascinated by plant breeding, Heather began to enroll in _____ courses.

74. After a terrible two-month binge, he solemnly

_____d alcohol forever.

75. That nasty remark was her first hint that her beloved Alex

had a _____ streak.

76. Two _____ power plants were being built

near the volcano's base.

77. Following the hijackings, the airline was forced to

_____ its jets with new cockpit doors.

78. To celebrate its seagoing history, the port city established

a _____ museum.

79. A specialist in vertebrate _____, he usually

explained skeleton structures in terms of evolution.

80. Looser laws in Canada may make it harder for the U.S. to

_____ drug trafficking.

81. Devout medieval Christians sought to "_____

the flesh"—to reduce their sensitivity to hunger, cold, and

discomfort.

82. Shuffling the deck ensures that the cards will be dealt in

almost infinite _____s.

83. The foes of freedom have tried to suppress books, films,

and songs, calling them _____.

84. The congregation then recites the _____, a

concise statement of Christian beliefs.

85. Many _____ sculptures from the 1780s could

be mistaken for works from ancient Rome.

86. It would take a heartfelt apology to _____ the

situation.

87. Before taking Tree Physiology, you must have completed

such _____s as Forest Botany.

88. The Senate finally threw everything together into a single

_____ bill.

89. Though there had been no eyewitnesses, the
_____ evidence was enough to convict him.

90. After a time, the supposed illnesses of a
_____ no longer attract the sympathy of
friends.

91. The investigation was focusing on a 48-year-old man—a
single, unemployed loner and _____.

92. One need not be _____ to write an encyclo-
pedia, but it would help.

93. The company produces a sports guard, dentures, braces,
and other _____ appliances.

94. Lawyers argued that the state constitution
_____d the legislature's power in cases like
this one.

95. Having failed to form a coalition, the president began to
consider taking _____ action.

96. Apollo and Dionysus were two of the most widely
worshiped gods in the Greek _____.

97. New to New York, Carol couldn't fall asleep with the
_____ of street sounds.

98. With her fortune declining, even Lady Armstrong could
see that the great estate was _____.

99. To prevent moisture-related spoilage, Gretchen said we
could _____ some foods.

100. The lawyers had argued that her injuries were actually
_____ to the accident.

101. With a liver _____, a small piece of tissue can
be examined for signs of disease.

102. Several simultaneous melodies combined to form a rich
texture of _____ sound.

103. The river's _____ dams block downstream movement of large wood, disturbing aquatic habitats.

104. The verdict awarded her complete survivor's benefits, _____ to the date of her husband's death.

105. She would later claim that she had _____d her grief into the songs that made her famous.

106. The university awarded _____ degrees to seniors killed in the crash.

107. Sandra tried using _____ motivational tapes while sleeping to improve her attitude.

108. _____ reading ability in children may not be matched by advanced writing skills.

109. Lottman's film was an odd _____ of ancient myth, film noir, and alternative comics.

110. Gazing into a campfire at night, we feel a _____ connection with our prehistoric ancestors.

111. Any system that turns heat into mechanical energy represents a _____ process.

112. A salty _____ may throw a tub of sea jargon at you to expose your ignorance.

113. It required all his charm to _____ himself with the power brokers.

114. Several Roman emperors, convinced that they were _____, declared themselves gods.

115. Sitting up straight at the table isn't necessarily an outward sign of moral _____.

116. The U.S. Geographic Survey has modeled and mapped the entire American _____.

117. The center compiled data on illness and _____ from blood diseases.

118. The region's _____ is dramatic, with sheer cliffs descending to parched plains.

119. Hilda's sleek, _____ designs featured sharp clean lines and squared corners.

120. His CAT scan revealed a large _____, but it turned out to be harmless.

121. With remarkable skill and patience, the _____ had restored Tyler's spine by surgical means.

122. The _____ exhibit on Project Apollo began with its birth in 1961.

123. Brett's doctors called on his close relatives to donate blood for the _____.

124. Even in war there are rules and norms of behavior that _____ the worst offenses.

125. The Founding Fathers rejected the idea of a _____ legislature, favoring a House and Senate to balance each other.

126. Wherever the great khan's army marched, it would conquer and _____ the local tribes.

127. From these incomplete statistics we can easily _____ the complete data.

128. People with this rare _____ are smart and mentally retarded at the same time.

129. Some groups argue that _____ is a barbaric and unjustified form of animal cruelty.

130. Audrey claims to have _____ communication with her pet ferrets while she's at the office.

131. Many have wondered if some murderers were biologically _____ to kill.

132. In 1880 a traveling salesman might have tried to sell you a single _____ for everything from mumps to arthritis.

133. Prehistoric peoples in harsh climates often lived in caves or even _____ dwellings.

134. He delivered his praise as solemnly as a priest's _____.

135. _____ orbits are ideal for maintaining contact with a specific location on Earth.

136. We distinguish between outright lies on the one hand and mere _____ on the other.

137. These get-togethers start out quietly but always become _____, and sometimes even rowdy.

138. She emitted the kind of radiant energy that isn't measured in _____s.

139. Giant tubeworms live on the ocean floor near _____ vents spouting scalding water.

140. The broken jawbone was clearly visible in the X-ray image that showed an _____ view of his skull.

141. The mob outside the _____ research center called for an end to tests on monkeys.

142. After awakening from her coma, she recounted a _____ experience of light and bliss.

143. Phyllis used the _____ approach with her first-graders, sounding out syllables one by one.

144. The student complaint involved the alleged yelling of racial _____s.

145. The new Web site, called "_____.com," is "for those who like to tell and those who like to listen."

146. It's common, but also dangerous, for freedivers to _____ in order to stay underwater longer.

147. The rebellious workers began chanting in _____, "No Contract, No Work!"

148. Economic growth in poor countries often depends on _____ reform and rural development.

149. In green plants, light energy is converted into chemical energy during _____.

150. Alicia kept a fixed and _____ order to her household, especially in the sock drawers.

50 MORE ROOTS

The roots and derived words in the table below are intended for further study. Learn the meanings of any of the words you are unfamiliar with (perhaps by drilling yourself with homemade flashcards), and try using each of them in sentences. Try to think of other terms that use each of the roots in the left-hand column.

aud ("hear")	auditor	audition	auditory
aut/auto ("same, self")	automaton	autonomy	autocratic
bell ("war")	bellicose	belligerent	antebellum
bi ("two")	bipartisan	binary	bipolar
carn ("flesh")	carnage	incarnation	carnal
cata ("down")	catalyst	catacomb	catatonic
cent ("hundred")	centenary	centigrade	centimeter
cid ("kill")	genocide	infanticide	fungicide
corp ("body")	corporal	corpulent	corporeal
crac/crat ("power")	bureaucrat	aristocracy	autocrat
crypt/cryph ("hidden")	cryptic	apocryphal	crypt
culp ("guilt")	culpable	exculpate	mea culpa
cur ("care")	curator	sinecure	curative
dec ("ten")	decathlon	decimate	decibel
demo ("people")	demotic	endemic	demographic
dict ("speak")	diction	edict	indict
domin ("lord")	domineer	predominant	dominion
duct ("lead")	abduct	duct	induct
ego ("I")	alter ego	egocentric	egoist
equi ("equal")	equivocal	equity	equilibrium
eu ("good")	euphemism	euphoria	euthanasia
flu ("flow")	influx	confluence	fluent
grad ("step")	degradation	gradient	gradation
grav ("heavy")	grave	gravitate	gravitas
hemi/demi/semi ("half")	hemiplegic	semiconductor	demigod
homo ("same")	homogeneous	homogenize	homologous
later ("side")	bilateral	collateral	unilateral
medi ("middle")	mediate	intermediary	median
mono ("single")	monotone	monologue	monotheism
neuro ("nerve")	neurology	neuron	neurotransmitter

50 MORE ROOTS (continued)

nom ("name")	misnomer	nomenclature	nominal
patr/pater ("father")	patriarch	patrimony	patrician
pun/pen ("punish")	punitive	impunity	penal
peri ("around")	peripheral	peripatetic	perimeter
phob ("fear")	agoraphobia	xenophobia	acrophobia
plac ("please")	placate	implacable	placebo
popul ("people")	populist	populace	depopulate
proto ("first")	protocol	protagonist	prototype
quadr ("four")	quadrennial	quadriplegic	quadruped
sacr/sanct ("holy")	sanctify	sacrosanct	sanctuary
simil/simul ("like")	simile	simulate	assimilate
son ("sound")	sonority	sonata	sonic
super/supra ("above")	superannuated	superimpose	superfluous
the/theo ("god")	theocracy	monotheism	theology
topo ("place")	topical	topographical	utopia
tri ("three")	trilogy	trinity	trimester
turb ("confused")	perturb	turbid	turbine
ver/veri ("true")	aver	veracity	veritable
verb ("word")	verbiage	verbose	proverb
vert ("turn")	subvert	revert	avert

ANSWER KEY

Quiz 1

1. philanthropy
2. agrochemical
3. artifact
4. agrarian
5. aquifer
6. anterior
7. agronomy
8. artifice
9. antecedent
10. aquaculture
11. misanthrope
12. antedate
13. anthropoid
14. Aquarius
15. artisan

Quiz 2

1. symbiosis
2. beneficent
3. circumstantial
4. cosmology
5. benediction
6. bionic
7. biopsy
8. benefactor
9. circumvent
10. chronic
11. anachronism
12. chronology
13. microcosm
14. circumspect
15. cosmopolitan

Quiz 3

1. creed
2. disarming
3. dysentery
4. discredit
5. credence
6. dyslexia
7. dynasty
8. epigraph
9. hydrodynamic
10. disburse
11. epilogue
12. dystrophy
13. epithet
14. credible
15. dynamo

Quiz 4

1. extrovert
2. fiduciary
3. extraneous
4. confidante
5. geosynchronous
6. ingratiate
7. geothermal
8. spectrography
9. extrapolate
10. seismograph
11. fidelity
12. gratuitous
13. topography
14. gratify
15. geopolitical

Quiz 5

1. perjury
2. hypothetical
3. hydroelectric
4. hyperventilate
5. hydraulic
6. hypertension
7. hypochondriac
8. intercede
9. hypothermia
10. interface
11. abjure
12. dehydrate
13. jurisprudence
14. hyperbole
15. interdict

Quiz 6

1. marina
2. malpractice
3. metamorphosis
4. malevolent
5. transmute
6. mariner
7. mortify
8. amorphous
9. malign
10. morphology
11. moribund
12. permutation
13. mortality
14. maritime
15. immutable

Quiz 7

1. panacea
2. Neolithic
3. omnipotent
4. orthodox
5. omnibus
6. pantheon
7. phonetic
8. neoplasm
9. orthopedist
10. polyphonic
11. omniscient
12. neoclassical
13. orthodontic
14. panoply
15. cacophony

Quiz 8

1. posterior
2. photoelectric
3. rectitude
4. precocious
5. posthumous
6. photon
7. primal
8. predisposed
9. photosynthesis
10. rectify
11. postmortem
12. primate
13. amorphous
14. rectilinear
15. prerequisite

Quiz 9

1. telepathic
2. retrospective
3. circumscribe
4. retroactive
5. subliminal
6. inscribe
7. synthesis
8. telemetry
9. subjugate
10. proscribe
11. synopsis
12. retrofit
13. subversive
14. syndrome
15. teleological

Quiz 10

1. subterranean
2. thermal
3. unicameral
4. thermodynamic
5. terrain
6. convivial
7. transient
8. transfusion
9. thermonuclear
10. unison
11. vivacious
12. transcendent
13. terrestrial
14. vivisection
15. unilateral

Review Test

1. inscribe
2. perjury
3. teleological
4. antedate
5. thermonuclear
6. malpractice
7. anthropoid
8. credible
9. agrochemical
10. aquifer
11. Aquarius
12. artifice
13. artifact
14. metamorphosis
15. beneficent
16. Neolithic
17. benefactor
18. bionic
19. chronic
20. anachronism
21. postmortem
22. circumvent
23. vivacious
24. circumspect
25. cosmopolitan
26. artisan
27. cosmology
28. photoelectric
29. marina
30. microcosm
31. interface
32. credence
33. disarming
34. philanthropy
35. dynamo
36. hypothermia
37. orthodox
38. dystrophy
39. epigraph
40. epilogue
41. extraneous
42. telemetry
43. dynasty
44. fiduciary
45. malign
46. fidelity
47. transient
48. geopolitical
49. spectrography
50. hydrodynamic
51. dysentery

52. seismograph
53. disburse
54. gratify
55. posterior
56. aquaculture
57. hydraulic
58. extrovert
59. symbiosis
60. hypertension
61. primordial
62. synopsis
63. terrestrial
64. dyslexia
65. hypothetical
66. gratuitous
67. intercede
68. discredit
69. chronology
70. amorphous
71. jurisprudence
72. panoply
73. agronomy
74. abjure
75. malevolent
76. geothermal
77. retrofit
78. maritime
79. morphology
80. interdict
81. mortify
82. permutation
83. subversive
84. creed

85. neoclassical
86. rectify
87. prerequisite
88. omnibus
89. circumstantial
90. hypochondriac
91. misanthrope
92. omniscient
93. orthodontic
94. circumscribe
95. unilateral
96. pantheon
97. cacophony
98. moribund
99. dehydrate
100. antecedent
101. biopsy
102. polyphonic
103. hydroelectric
104. retroactive
105. transmute
106. posthumous
107. subliminal
108. precocious
109. synthesis
110. primal
111. thermodynamic
112. mariner
113. ingratiate
114. omnipotent
115. rectitude
116. terrain
117. mortality

118. topography
119. rectilinear
120. neoplasm
121. orthopedist
122. retrospective
123. transfusion
124. proscribe
125. unicameral
126. subjugate
127. extrapolate
128. syndrome
129. vivisection
130. telepathic
131. predisposed
132. panacea
133. subterranean
134. benediction
135. geosynchronous
136. hyperbole
137. convivial
138. photon
139. thermal
140. anterior
141. primate
142. transcendent
143. phonetic
144. epithet
145. confidante
146. hyperventilate
147. unison
148. agrarian
149. photosynthesis
150. immutable

SSAT Practice Test 1

Part I

WRITING THE ESSAY

Directions: Using two sheets of lined theme paper, plan and write an essay on the topic assigned below. DO NOT WRITE ON ANOTHER TOPIC. AN ESSAY ON ANOTHER TOPIC IS NOT ACCEPTABLE.

Topic: Speech is great, but silence is greater.

Assignment: Do you agree or disagree with the topic statement? Support your position with one or two specific examples from personal experience, the experience of others, current events, history, or literature.

Name: _____

Write your essay here.

_____

_____

_____

_____

_____

_____

_____

_____

_____

_____

_____

_____

_____

_____

_____

_____

_____

_____

_____

_____

_____

(Continue, if necessary.)

Part II

MULTIPLE CHOICE

VERBAL	TIME: 30 MINUTES	60 QUESTIONS

Directions: Each of the following questions consists of one word followed by five words or phrases. You are to select the one word or phrase whose meaning is closest to the word in capital letters.

1. QUANDARY
   - (A) predicament
   - (B) decision
   - (C) requirement
   - (D) community
   - (E) information

2. PROTECT
   - (A) retain
   - (B) intend
   - (C) require
   - (D) defend
   - (E) secure

3. OVERDUE
   - (A) impending
   - (B) appointment
   - (C) including
   - (D) late
   - (E) library

4. VERBOSE
   - (A) wordy
   - (B) aloud
   - (C) orate
   - (D) speech
   - (E) complete

5. DIMINISH
   - (A) grow
   - (B) impede
   - (C) lessen
   - (D) forecast
   - (E) disappear

6. TRANSPARENT
   - (A) opaque
   - (B) filmy
   - (C) serene
   - (D) glass
   - (E) motivation

7. PLIABLE
   - (A) tool
   - (B) flexible
   - (C) useful
   - (D) rigid
   - (E) thrill

8. PROPHECY
   - (A) anticipation
   - (B) prediction
   - (C) fortune
   - (D) crystal
   - (E) seer

9. DEJECTED
   - (A) gifted
   - (B) rewarded
   - (C) concerned
   - (D) serious
   - (E) sad

405

10. BENEVOLENT

    (A) charitable
    (B) courageous
    (C) bravery
    (D) contest
    (E) seek

11. RECEDE

    (A) surrender
    (B) retreat
    (C) decline
    (D) lose
    (E) requite

12. FASTIDIOUS

    (A) chaos
    (B) unkempt
    (C) precise
    (D) classify
    (E) sanitary

13. SURLY

    (A) strong
    (B) wily
    (C) anticipate
    (D) rude
    (E) prodigal

14. FRUGAL

    (A) facility
    (B) careful
    (C) poverty
    (D) wealth
    (E) increase

15. DEPLETE

    (A) continue
    (B) guide
    (C) utilize
    (D) proceed
    (E) exhaust

16. FORCE

    (A) military
    (B) might
    (C) power
    (D) requirement
    (E) soldier

17. EXTINCT

    (A) brief
    (B) clear
    (C) inactive
    (D) imperfect
    (E) poor

18. THWART

    (A) love
    (B) frustrate
    (C) defend
    (D) grow
    (E) advance

19. STIPEND

    (A) plant
    (B) financier
    (C) fluid
    (D) bank
    (E) payment

20. REPUTABLE

    (A) star
    (B) capable
    (C) fame
    (D) honest
    (E) significant

21. LUCKY

    (A) happy
    (B) gleeful
    (C) hilarious
    (D) useful
    (E) fortunate

22. IRRESPONSIBLE

(A) inconclusive
(B) unsure
(C) unreliable
(D) incisive
(E) unrealistic

23. JEOPARDY

(A) entertaining
(B) endangerment
(C) vocabulary
(D) journey
(E) archival

24. MOIST

(A) swamp
(B) damp
(C) saturate
(D) sponge
(E) fresh

25. SHAMEFUL

(A) evil
(B) bewildering
(C) caustic
(D) willful
(E) humiliating

26. PRECLUDE

(A) prevent
(B) avoid
(C) promise
(D) listen
(E) imagine

27. FOIBLE

(A) story
(B) flaw
(C) strength
(D) tradition
(E) goodbye

28. MEDITATE

(A) compromise
(B) reject
(C) agree
(D) ponder
(E) repair

29. PARADOX

(A) occurrence
(B) heaven
(C) approval
(D) contradiction
(E) example

30. SURMISE

(A) guess
(B) daybreak
(C) provide
(D) shock
(E) govern

Directions: The following questions ask you to find relationships between words. For each question, select the answer that best completes the meaning of the sentence.

31. Astute is to acumen as

(A) indigent is to wealth.
(B) diplomatic is to tact.
(C) clumsy is to skill.
(D) vacuous is to intelligence.
(E) rainbow is to hue.

32. Judge is to adjudicate as

(A) lawyer is to propitiate.
(B) bodyguard is to guide.
(C) doctor is to sublimate.
(D) champion is to defend.
(E) suburb is to neighborhood.

33. Imperceptible is to notice as

(A) intangible is to touch.
(B) insoluble is to discern.
(C) invisible is to sense.
(D) enviable is to foresee.
(E) assuage is to repair.

34. Claustrophobic is to enclosure as

(A) miser is to money.
(B) narcissist is to sell.
(C) misogynist is to women.
(D) glutton is to food.
(E) myth is to tragedy.

35. Hammer is to carpenter as

(A) awl is to cobbler.
(B) computer is to printer.
(C) saw is to timber.
(D) author is to typewriter.
(E) scale is to musician.

36. Gullible is to bilk as

(A) valiant is to cow.
(B) confident is to perturb.
(C) docile is to lead.
(D) affluent is to impoverish.
(E) vanquish is to disappear.

37. Overblown is to exaggerated as

(A) warrant is to justify.
(B) anachronism is to timely.
(C) malapropism is to accurate.
(D) requirement is to optional.
(E) indefinite is to tomorrow.

38. Ruthless is to pity as

(A) merciful is to kindness.
(B) ingenious is to character.
(C) enamored is to love.
(D) bewildered is to comprehension.
(E) elderly is to longevity.

39. Clown is to zany as

(A) zealot is to patrician.
(B) showoff is to flamboyant.
(C) jester is to lugubrious.
(D) spy is to effusive.
(E) canvas is to paint.

40. Horn is to blow as harp is to

(A) democracy.
(B) play.
(C) denounce.
(D) pluck.
(E) pants.

41. Inveigle is to flattery as

(A) cozen is to encouragement.
(B) browbeat is to intimidation.
(C) reassure is to censure.
(D) cajole is to criticism.
(E) whine is to mourn.

42. Flammable is to inflammable as

(A) persistent is to important.
(B) opportune is to inopportune.
(C) relevant is to incoherent.
(D) truculent is to intrusion.
(E) impartial is to disinterested.

43. Devotee is to fervid as

(A) pundit is to apathetic.
(B) sycophant is to caustic.
(C) connoisseur is to discriminating.
(D) pessimist is to sanguine.
(E) optimist is to persuade.

44. Mule is to stubborn as

(A) pig is to idleness.
(B) horse is to iconoclastic.
(C) fox is to maladroit.
(D) elephant is to oblivious.
(E) turkey is to gullible.

45. Extortionist is to blackmail as

(A) kleptomaniac is to steal.
(B) criminal is to arrest.
(C) kidnapper is to crime.
(D) businessman is to profit.
(E) clerk is to stock.

46. Virtuoso is to éclat as

(A) gallant is to panache.
(B) proselyte is to untruth.
(C) harbinger is to conclusion.
(D) klutz is to tact.
(E) casual is to plan.

47. Bilious is to queasy as

(A) quizzical is to content.
(B) contumelious is to elated.
(C) dangerous is to alarm.
(D) ambivalent is to sleepy.
(E) adroit is to able.

48. Disorganized is to form as

(A) ineffable is to size.
(B) empty is to substance.
(C) epical is to scope.
(D) immediacy is to duration.
(E) idolize is to confound.

49. Midget is to minuscule as

(A) accomplished is to abortive.
(B) dictum is to risible.
(C) serious is to waggish.
(D) colossus is to gargantuan.
(E) enigma is to original.

50. Prude is to fastidious as

(A) puritan is to simple.
(B) prodigy is to lackluster.
(C) witness is to truth.
(D) hedonist is to malcontent.
(E) heathen is to adoration.

51. Waggish is to laughs as

(A) risible is to yawns.
(B) bilious is to smiles.
(C) sad is to tears.
(D) ribald is to sneers.
(E) morbid is to concern.

52. Diaphanous is to veils as

(A) noisome is to clouds.
(B) gossamer is to cobwebs.
(C) bulky is to showers.
(D) abortive is to breezes.
(E) fishing is to net.

53. Microcosm is to macrocosm as

(A) plenty is to lack.
(B) glutton is to craven.
(C) understand is to orbit.
(D) granite is to touchstone.
(E) diameter is to edge.

54. Homily is to church as

(A) sermon is to air show.
(B) diatribe is to game show.
(C) aria is to horse show.
(D) monologue is to talk show.
(E) eulogy is to celebrate.

55. Mnemonic is to memory as

(A) trousers are to speech.
(B) glasses are to vision.
(C) earmuffs are to movement.
(D) blinders are to hearing.
(E) denim are to jacket.

56. Healing is to health as

(A) pragmatic is to avidity.
(B) charity is to profit.
(C) biased is to justice.
(D) therapeutic is to recovery.
(E) mercury is to speed.

57. Arbitrate is to dispute as

 (A) solve is to mystery.
 (B) regard is to problem.
 (C) exacerbate is to problem.
 (D) organize is to labor.
 (E) management is to union.

58. Tearjerker is to maudlin as

 (A) opera is to prurient.
 (B) tragedy is to risible.
 (C) farce is to hilarious.
 (D) satire is to heartrending.
 (E) comedy is to wrenching.

59. Passion is to devotion as

 (A) liturgy is to ribald.
 (B) concern is to interest.
 (C) harangue is to restrained.
 (D) feisty is to mousy.
 (E) rapidity is to movement.

60. Klutz is to inept as

 (A) bigot is to intolerant.
 (B) dynamo is to supine.
 (C) aficionado is to blase.
 (D) pundit is to ignorant.
 (E) learned is to possess.

QUANTITATIVE (MATH) 1   QUESTIONS

Directions: Following each problem in [this] section, there are five suggested answ[ers]. Work each problem in your head or in [the] space provided (there will be space [for] scratchwork in your test booklet). Then l[ook] at the five suggested answers and de[cide] which is best.

[handwritten note: gave out 10/10/07]

... 88, what is

... integers ... greatest

1. A gas tank is $\frac{1}{3}$ empty. When full, the t[ank] holds 18 gallons. How many gallons ar[e in] the tank now?

    (A) 3
    (B) 6
    (C) 8
    (D) 12
    (E) 18

    (B) 9
    (C) 24
    (D) 33
    (E) 36

2. Which of the following is the least?

    (A) $\frac{1}{4} + \frac{2}{3}$

    (B) $\frac{3}{4} - \frac{1}{3}$

    (C) $\frac{1}{12} \div \frac{1}{3}$

    (D) $\frac{3}{4} \times \frac{1}{3}$

    (E) $\frac{1}{12} \times 2$

6. Which of the following is NOT a multiple of 4?

    (A) 20
    (B) 30
    (C) 36
    (D) 44
    (E) 96

Questions 7 and 8 refer to the following definition: For all real numbers m, $*m = 10m - 10$.

7. $*7 =$

    (A) 70
    (B) 60
    (C) 17
    (D) 7
    (E) 0

3. If the sum of x and $x + 3$ is greater than 20, which is a possible value for x?

    (A) -10
    (B) -8
    (C) -2
    (D) 8
    (E) 10

8. If $*m = 120$, then $m =$

    (A) 11
    (B) 12
    (C) 13
    (D) 120
    (E) 130

9. At Nifty Thrifty Buy 'N Sell, an item that usually sells for $9 is on sale for $6. What approximate discount does that represent?

(A) 10%
(B) 25%
(C) 33%
(D) 50%
(E) 66%

10. In Jackie's golf club, 8 of the 12 members are right-handed. What is the ratio of left-handed members to right-handed members?

(A) 1:2
(B) 2:1
(C) 2:3
(D) 3:4
(E) 4:3

11. The sum of five consecutive positive integers is 35. What is the square of the greatest of these integers?

(A) 5
(B) 9
(C) 25
(D) 81
(E) 100

12. $2^2 \times 2^3 \times 2^3 =$

(A) 24
(B) 64
(C) 2^8
(D) 2^{10}
(E) 2^{18}

13. If the area of a square is $100s^2$, what is the length of one side of the square?

(A) $100s^2$
(B) $10s^2$
(C) $100s$
(D) $10s$
(E) 10

14. If 10 books cost d dollars, how many books can be purchased for 4 dollars?

(A) $\dfrac{4d}{10}$
(B) $40d$
(C) $\dfrac{d}{40}$
(D) $\dfrac{40}{d}$
(E) $\dfrac{10d}{4}$

15. If g is an even integer, h is an odd integer, and j is the product of g and h, which of the following must be true?

(A) j is a fraction.
(B) j is an odd integer.
(C) j is divisible by 2.
(D) j is between g and h.
(E) j is greater than 0.

16. If a class of 6 students has an average grade of 78 before a seventh student joins, what must the seventh student get as a grade in order to raise the class average to 80?

(A) 80
(B) 84
(C) 88
(D) 92
(E) 96

17. If 6 is a factor of a certain number, what must also be factors of that number?

(A) 1, 2, 3, and 6
(B) 2 and 3 only
(C) 6 only
(D) 2 and 6 only
(E) 1, 2, and 3

18.

$x =$

(A) 8

(B) 30

(C) 50

(D) 65

(E) 70

19. For what priced item does 40% off equal a $2.00 discount?

(A) $5.00

(B) $4.00

(C) $10.00

(D) $80.00

(E) $40.00

20. On Monday, Gerri ate $\frac{1}{4}$ of an apple pie. On Tuesday, she ate $\frac{1}{2}$ of what was left of the pie. What fraction of the entire pie did Gerri eat on both days?

(A) $\frac{3}{8}$

(B) $\frac{1}{2}$

(C) $\frac{5}{8}$

(D) $\frac{3}{4}$

(E) $\frac{7}{8}$

21. If the area of a square is equal to its perimeter, what is the length of one side of that square?

(A) 1

(B) 2

(C) 4

(D) 8

(E) 10

22. If $6x - 4 = 38$, then $x - 5 =$

(A) 2

(B) 3

(C) 5

(D) 7

(E) 9

23. $3(x^2 y^{-4} z)^4 x^3 y =$

(A) $3x^{11} y^{-15} z^4$

(B) $81x^{-1} y z^4$

(C) $81x^{11} y^{-15} z^4$

(D) $3x^9 y z^4$

(E) $3x^3 y^{-5} z$

24. What is NOT a prime factor of 360?

(A) 2

(B) 3

(C) 4

(D) 5

(E) All of the above are prime factors of 360.

25. What is the area of an equilateral triangle whose altitude is 4?

(A) 16

(B) $4\sqrt{3}$

(C) $8\sqrt{3}$

(D) $\frac{16\sqrt{3}}{3}$

(E) 8

413

READING COMPREHENSION   TIME: 30 MINUTES   40 QUESTIONS

Directions: Read each passage carefully and then answer the questions about it. For each question, decide on the basis of the passage which one of the choices best answers the question.

Passage 1

Line In the spring of 1963, Martin Luther King Jr., a leader of the American civil rights movement, was invited by the Birmingham, Alabama, branch of the Southern Christian
5   Leadership Conference, an organization fighting for civil rights for African Americans, to lead a demonstration supporting their cause. King applied for a permit to hold a peaceful march through Birmingham, but
10   the city officials denied his request. Nevertheless, he scheduled the march. Because the marchers had no permit, their action was illegal, and the march was broken up by police. King and many of the marchers were
15   arrested. While King was in jail, eight clergymen signed a letter that was published in the local newspaper. The letter, while it asked the community to work to end racial problems, opposed marches and demonstra-
20   tions as the means of working toward a solution. After King read the letter, he wrote a response, replying to each point the clergymen raised. His response, published as "Letter from Birmingham Jail," includes an
25   analysis of when it is proper to act in violation of a law. He believed that if a law is unjust or unfair, people have not only a right but also a positive moral duty to oppose it, so long as their opposition

30   remains peaceful and nonviolent. Because of its balanced sentence structure, appropriate references to the Bible and historical fact, and its powerful wording, "Letter from Birmingham Jail" is considered to be a
35   masterpiece of rhetoric.

1. King went to Birmingham because he
    (A) wanted to lead a march.
    (B) believed desegregation was important.
    (C) could ask for a permit to demonstrate.
    (D) was asked to do so by an organization.
    (E) wanted to reply to the clergymen.

2. The march led by King was illegal because
    (A) the city officials did not favor civil rights.
    (B) the demonstrators did not have permission to march.
    (C) the letter from eight clergymen presented a case against it.
    (D) the marchers were arrested by the police.
    (E) the community was working to end racial problems.

3. King believed that breaking a law is
    (A) always wrong.
    (B) always the right thing to do.
    (C) one's duty if one dislikes the law.
    (D) a proper way to oppose an unjust law.
    (E) always proper if the opposition is not violent.

4. The clergymen who wrote the letter wanted to
    (A) stop the marches and demonstrations.
    (B) be sure King remained in jail.
    (C) oppose the ending of racial problems.
    (D) provide civil rights for African Americans.
    (E) help King get out of jail.

5. In the last sentence of the passage, "rhetoric" (line 35) means

(A) advertisement.
(B) excellent writing.
(C) an emotional speech.
(D) poetry.
(E) religious teaching.

Passage 2

Line When you buy a house plant, if the plant is healthy, it is likely to grow successfully in your home. How do you decide if a plant is sound? First, look at the leaves. If they are

5 brown at the edges, the plant has been given too much fertilizer or has been kept in temperatures that are too warm for its species. If the leaves are pale or yellow, the plant has been given too much or too little

10 water. If the leaves are very far apart from each other on the stem, this may mean the plant has been pushed to grow abnormally fast, and new leaves will not grow to fill in the gaps. You should look for a plant whose

15 foliage is dense.

After checking the leaves' general appearance, look carefully at the underside of the leaves and the places where the leaves join the stem for evidence of insects.

20 Because the insects that infest house plants are very tiny, it may be hard to see them. But they leave clues that they are living on the plant. Some secrete a shiny sticky substance called honeydew on the plant.

25 Others leave behind tiny fine white webs.

Finally, check to see if the plant's roots are growing out through the drainage hole in the bottom of the pot. If the roots are growing through the hole, the plant has

30 outgrown its pot, and it may not be the healthiest plant, even if you repot it in a larger container.

6. If a plant has been given too much fertilizer,

(A) its leaves may have brown edges.
(B) its leaves may be yellow.
(C) there will be tiny webs on the leaves.
(D) the foliage will be dense.
(E) the soil will appear dry.

7. To check a plant's health, examine

(A) leaf color.
(B) leaf density.
(C) the bottom of the pot.
(D) the stem.
(E) All of the above

8. In context, "infest" (line 20) most likely means

(A) infect.
(B) eat.
(C) grow from.
(D) live on.
(E) secrete.

9. Too much or too little water will cause

(A) dark-colored foliage.
(B) large gaps between the leaves.
(C) yellow or pale leaves.
(D) roots to grow out of the drainage hole.
(E) shiny spots on the stem.

10. Based on this passage, a reader can infer that

(A) all growers of plants for sale raise them in perfect conditions.
(B) some plants for sale have not been cared for properly.
(C) plants are forced to grow abnormally fast.
(D) it is difficult to care for a plant at home.
(E) a plant's health is based on its environment.

Passage 3

Line Some myths are stories told by early
civilizations to explain the origins of natural
phenomena. The Greek myth that explains
the origin of the seasons is about Demeter,
5 the goddess of the harvest. She had a
daughter, Persephone, whom she loved very
much. Hades, god of the underworld, fell in
love with Persephone, and he asked Zeus,
the ruler of the gods, to give Persephone to
10 him as his wife. Zeus did not want to offend
either Hades or Persephone, so he said he
would not agree to the marriage, but neither
would he forbid it. Hades, therefore, decided
to take the girl without permission. As she
15 was picking flowers in a meadow, he seized
her and took her to the underworld. When
Demeter found out what happened to
Persephone, she became so angry that she
caused all plants to stop growing. People
20 were in danger of starving. But Demeter
swore that no food would grow until
Persephone was returned to her. Zeus, still
not wanting to offend Hades, set a condition
for Persephone's return. She could go back
25 to her mother if she had not eaten anything
while she was in the underworld. Demeter
did not know it, but Persephone had eaten
several pomegranate seeds in the underworld. When Zeus discovered this, he
30 permitted a compromise. Persephone could
spend part of the year with her mother, but
because she had eaten the seeds, she must
spend part of the year in the underworld.
And when Persephone is in the underworld,
35 Demeter is sad, and therefore will not let the
crops grow. That is why we have winter,
when plants do not grow. When Persephone
returns, Demeter is happy, it is spring, and
plants begin to grow again.

11. Demeter is the goddess of
    (A) food plants.
    (B) the underworld.
    (C) marriage.
    (D) humanity.
    (E) the weather.

12. Myths are stories that
    (A) are always about gods and goddesses.
    (B) try to explain nature.
    (C) tell about mysteries.
    (D) have a religious purpose.
    (E) explain the origin of the seasons.

13. According to the story of Demeter, winter occurs because
    (A) Hades stole Persephone from her mother.
    (B) Zeus did not give Hades permission to marry Persephone.
    (C) Demeter is sad.
    (D) Persephone is unhappy.
    (E) Demeter disliked Hades.

14. Zeus did not give permission to Hades to marry Persephone because he
    (A) disliked him.
    (B) did not want to upset him.
    (C) wanted Persephone to be his wife.
    (D) thought this might make Demeter angry.
    (E) was the ruler of all the gods and goddesses.

15. Demeter stopped the growth of crops when
    (A) Zeus did not forbid the marriage.
    (B) Hades took Persephone to the under-world.
    (C) she discovered what Hades had done.
    (D) Persephone ate some pomegranate seeds.
    (E) Persephone was returned to her.

Passage 4

Line The Big Bang theory, an explanation of the
origins of our universe, is one of the greatest
intellectual achievements of the twentieth
century. According to this theory, about ten
5   to twenty million years ago, the matter of
which the universe is made was infinitely
tightly compressed. Something—called the
Big Bang—turned this matter into a gigantic
fireball. As the matter was set into motion
10   and flew away from its compressed state,
bits of it became glued together to create
galaxies and, later, stars and planets. The
motion of the matter that flew out of the
fireball continues today, and the universe
15   appears to be expanding. The theory grew
out of observations of the Doppler effect. It
explains that the frequency of radiation
given off by a moving body decreases as the
sources get farther from the observer. In
20   1965, scientists discovered that the radiation
bathing the earth is at the precise microwave frequency that would be expected if
the universe began with a big bang. Some
scientists think the expansion of the
25   universe will continue to infinity, while
others theorize that gravity will, at some
point in the far distant future, collapse back
onto itself in a "big crunch," returning it to a
state of compressed matter.

16. The best title for this passage is

  (A) "The Big Bang."
  (B) "The Big Crunch."
  (C) "Our Expanding Universe."
  (D) "The Doppler Effect."
  (E) "Scientific Discoveries."

17. As a moving object gets farther from its
source, its radiation frequency

  (A) stays the same.
  (B) grows larger.
  (C) grows smaller.
  (D) expands.
  (E) collapses.

18. The matter of which the universe is made
was originally

  (A) expanding.
  (B) loosely connected.
  (C) decreasing.
  (D) tightly packed.
  (E) growing.

19. According to the passage, which of the
following is true?

  (A) Scientists believe the universe will
expand infinitely.
  (B) The Doppler effect created the
universe.
  (C) Gravity will cause the universe to
collapse.
  (D) Stars and planets grew out of galaxies.
  (E) Scientists do not agree about the
universe's future.

20. The author of this passage thinks the Big
Bang theory

  (A) has not been proven.
  (B) does not explain the creation of the
universe.
  (C) is a very important contribution to
knowledge.
  (D) explains what happens when a moving
body gets farther from its source.
  (E) shows the frequency of radiation
bathing the earth.

Passage 5

Line Although the First World War had been
fought as the "war to make the world safe
for democracy," and the "war to end all
wars," the world's problems were not solved
5 when fighting was stopped by the cease-fire
agreement signed on November 11, 1918.
The world was not yet at peace. In Russia,
there was a civil war among various factions
wishing to replace the monarchy, which had
10 been lead by the Czar. Greece was fighting
Turkey over territory that had belonged to
the former Turkish Empire. In the Middle
East, the Jews were asking for the establish-
ment of a national homeland, and the Arabs
15 in the area were opposing them. In India, at
that time a colony of the British Empire,
educated Indians thought their contributions
to the war meant their nation was ready for
more self-rule and some independence from
20 Great Britain. And throughout the world,
populations had been reduced by the 1918
influenza epidemic, which, most public
health experts believe, killed more people
than were killed in the war's battles. When
25 the Paris Peace Conference began in January
1919, the defeated nations were not invited.
They would simply be notified of the terms
of the peace treaty and asked to sign it. In
the United States, Americans' disgust about
30 the huge human costs of the war lead to
isolationism, the desire to avoid international
political situations and focus only on
problems within the country. Thus, it is not
surprising that the League of Nations,
35 formed while the Peace Conference was in
session as an international organization to
create a better world, did not succeed in its
goals of achieving world disarmament and
preventing nations from invading one
40 another.

21. As used in the passage, the word "factions" (line 8) means

  (A) fractions.
  (B) international terrorists.
  (C) nationalists.
  (D) disagreeing groups.
  (E) followers of the king.

22. The influenza epidemic of 1918

  (A) was a result of the war.
  (B) increased the misery of the soldiers.
  (C) killed vast numbers of civilians.
  (D) surprised public health experts.
  (E) was localized in a few nations.

23. The conflict between Greece and Turkey and the conflict between Jews and Arabs were similar because both

  (A) were about control over land.
  (B) involved a new homeland.
  (C) arose from the terms of the peace treaty.
  (D) led to revolutions.
  (E) were settled by the League of Nations.

24. Wishing to withdraw from international politics is called

  (A) organization.
  (B) monarchy.
  (C) factionalism.
  (D) isolationism.
  (E) home rule.

25. The fighting of World War I ended

  (A) after the world was made safe for democracy.
  (B) in January 1919.
  (C) in November 1918.
  (D) when the League of Nations was founded.
  (E) by the terms of the peace treaty.

Passage 6

Line I was flying from Los Angeles to Tucson, Arizona, to celebrate New Year's weekend with some friends. Because of the holiday and winter weather delays, the airport was
5 crowded, and many flights were canceled or late. Boarding for my flight began at 1:15 P.M., the time originally scheduled for departure. The airline personnel appeared to be in a hurry. As passengers boarded, the
10 pilot announced on the public address system, "O.K., folks, we're cleared for departure at 1:35. If you'll all take your seats, we'll take off at that time." Cabin attendants guided people to their seats and
15 helped them stow baggage. "Are we all okay?" a cabin attendant asked.

Across the aisle from where I sat, a woman said, "Where are my son and grandson? They're supposed on be on the
20 plane with me. They came to the airport with me." She was an older woman with well-cut white hair. Her face, although lined, was carefully but not overly made up. She wore a stylish suit and small earrings. The
25 attendant leaned over and spoke to her, and then made an announcement. "Passengers Stuart and John Miller, please let me know where you are seated." There was no reply. She repeated her announcement. Again, no
30 one responded. She told Mrs. Miller that her son was not on the plane. "But they came with me," Mrs. Miller said. "They're supposed to be here."

The attendant went to the cockpit to
35 consult the flight officers. Returning to Mrs. Miller, she said, "Ma'am, I'm sorry. We need to have you deplane. I'm sure the airport personnel will be able to help you find your son." Then she guided Mrs. Miller to the
40 exit.

The doors closed; the engines fired; the plane began to taxi. A passenger seated next to me said, "Oh, dear! That woman was wrong. Her son left her with airline
45 personnel and told them to be sure to escort her onto the plane." My heart sank. Mrs. Miller probably suffered from confusion that sometimes affects older people. Someone, no doubt, would be waiting to meet her in
50 Tucson. Clearly, that person would be worried. And what of Mrs. Miller? Her son and grandson had probably left the airport by now. Would she remember their telephone number? And if she did, was it likely
55 they had already arrived home? Who would care for Mrs. Miller in a crowded, busy airport where passengers were trying to locate flights to replace canceled ones, and airline personnel were concerned about
60 sticking to a schedule? I thought I might weep.

26. As a result of bad weather,

(A) passengers were in a hurry.
(B) Mrs. Miller's son had not arrived home.
(C) flights were late or canceled.
(D) the flight attendant was rude to Mrs. Miller.
(E) Mrs. Miller was escorted onto the plane.

27. The reader can infer the plane took off

(A) on time.
(B) half an hour late.
(C) at some unknown time.
(D) in the morning.
(E) in the early afternoon.

28. The description of Mrs. Miller suggests that she

(A) cannot take care of herself.
(B) is a very wealthy woman.
(C) loves her son and grandson.
(D) has a sense of humor.
(E) cares about her appearance.

29. The airline people asked Mrs. Miller to leave the plane because

(A) she was confused.
(B) she didn't know her son's telephone number.
(C) they wanted to help her find her son.
(D) they wanted to take off as soon as possible.
(E) other passengers were in a hurry.

30. Which of the following word(s) describe the author of this passage?

(A) Observant
(B) Compassionate
(C) Sensitive
(D) None of the above
(E) (A), (B), and (C)

Passage 7

Line An intelligent and daring young woman who spoke many languages, Alexandrine Tinne seems to have been one of the more unusual explorers who ever lived. She was the
5 daughter of a wealthy Dutch merchant and a member of the Dutch aristocracy. Her father died when she was five, leaving her the richest heiress in the Netherlands at that time.
10   When she was grown up, after traveling throughout Europe, Tinne explored various parts of north central Africa. In 1863 and 1864, she charted the area around Bahr el Ghazal, a river system that flows into the
15 Nile. During this expedition, the group was struck with illness. One of the scientists died of fever in April of 1864, and Tinne's mother, who was also with the group, died in June. Tinne must have been a healthy
20 young woman to survive. Her expedition provided scientists with new and valuable information about the plants, animals, geology, and climate of this part of Africa. Later, traveling in Algeria and Tunisia, Tinne
25 became fascinated by the desert and the people who lived there. In 1869, she set out

on an expedition across the Sahara Desert. Unfortunately, this remarkable explorer was murdered by inhabitants of the desert during
30 these travels. It was reported that they believed that her iron water tanks were filled with gold.

31. As used in the passage, "charted" (line 13) means

(A) mapped.
(B) erased.
(C) invented.
(D) changed.
(E) carried.

32. The passage suggests Tinne's expeditions were important mainly because she

(A) could communicate in many languages.
(B) enjoyed the warmth of the desert and meeting interesting people.
(C) collected new scientific information.
(D) died before she could finish her work.
(E) took her mother along with her.

33. The Bahr el Ghazal river system is in

(A) Europe.
(B) South America.
(C) Asia.
(D) Antarctica.
(E) Africa.

34. The passage implies Tinne was murdered

(A) because the murderers did not like Europeans.
(B) because she was careless about guarding her group.
(C) because it was thought she had wealth that could be stolen.
(D) so that her scientific knowledge could be stolen.
(E) so that no one would ever explore the area again.

35. Which of the following best describes the author's attitude toward Tinne's actions?

    (A) Envy

    (B) Indifference

    (C) Sadness

    (D) Skepticism

    (E) Admiration

Passage 8

Line My father's family name being Pirrip, and my first being Philip, my infant tongue could make of both names nothing longer or more explicit than Pip. So, I called myself Pip, and
5 came to be called Pip.

    I give Pirrip as my father's family name, on the authority of his tombstone and my sister—Mrs. Joe Gargery, who married the blacksmith. As I never saw my father or my
10 mother and never saw any likeness of either of them (for their days were long before the days of photographs), my first fancies regarding what they were like were unreasonably derived from their tombstones. The
15 shape of the letters on my father's gave me an odd idea that he was a square, stout dark man, with curly black hair.

36. This passage was most probably written

    (A) last year.

    (B) about five years ago.

    (C) less than 25 years ago.

    (D) more than 100 years ago.

    (E) about 2,000 years ago.

37. In the passage, the word "fancies" (line 12) means

    (A) elaborate lettering.

    (B) hopes and dreams.

    (C) imagined ideas.

    (D) writing on tombstones.

    (E) grown-up thoughts.

38. Pip never saw any pictures of his birth parents because

    (A) he was adopted.

    (B) he ran away from home.

    (C) they died before cameras were invented.

    (D) they never wanted him to see any photographs of them.

    (E) his sister prevented him from seeing their photographs.

39 Pip's sister's name is

    (A) Mrs. Pirrip.

    (B) Mrs. Gargery.

    (C) Mrs. Philip.

    (D) Mrs. Pip.

    (E) Mrs. Stout.

40. Pip's sister's husband works as a

    (A) stonecutter.

    (B) gravedigger.

    (C) blacksmith.

    (D) photographer.

    (E) barber.

QUANTITATIVE (MATH) 2   TIME: 30 MINUTES   25 QUESTIONS

Directions: Following each problem in this section, there are five suggested answers. Work each problem in your head or in the space provided (there will be space for scratchwork in your test booklet). Then look at the five suggested answers and decide which is best.

1. At the start of the year, Terry invested $6,000 in South Bend Oil Corp. At the end of the year, his stock was worth $4,500. What was the percent decline in the value of his investment?

    (A) 25%

    (B) $33\frac{1}{3}$%

    (C) $66\frac{2}{3}$%

    (D) 75%

    (E) 125%

2. What is $\dfrac{a}{b} - \dfrac{b}{a}$?

    (A) $\dfrac{a - b}{ab}$

    (B) $\dfrac{a^2 - b^2}{ab}$

    (C) $\dfrac{(a - b)^2}{ab}$

    (D) $\dfrac{a^2 - b^2}{2ab}$

    (E) 1

3. Tracy has a test average of 90 after five tests. She only knows the scores of four of her tests: they are 80, 87, 94, and 89. What was the score on her other test?

    (A) 100

    (B) 98

    (C) 97

    (D) 90

    (E) 87

4. What is 4 percent expressed as a decimal?

    (A) 40

    (B) 4

    (C) .4

    (D) .04

    (E) .25

5. Express in simplest form the following ratio: 15 hours to 2 days.

    (A) $7\dfrac{1}{2}$

    (B) $\dfrac{16}{5}$

    (C) $\dfrac{5}{8}$

    (D) $\dfrac{15}{2}$

    (E) $\dfrac{5}{16}$

6. .58 × .14 =

    (A) 812

    (B) 8.12

    (C) 81.2

    (D) .812

    (E) .0812

7. If $3a - 5 = 7$, then $a =$

(A) -4

(B) 4

(C) $-\dfrac{2}{3}$

(D) $\dfrac{2}{3}$

(E) $\dfrac{5}{3}$

8. A gumball machine contains five red and three blue gumballs. If one gumball is removed, what is the probability that it will be red?

(A) $\dfrac{5}{3}$

(B) $\dfrac{3}{5}$

(C) $\dfrac{5}{8}$

(D) $\dfrac{3}{8}$

(E) $\dfrac{8}{3}$

9. How long is chord $\overline{AB}$ of circle O?

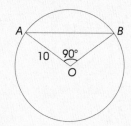

(A) $\sqrt{10}$

(B) $10\sqrt{2}$

(C) 100

(D) 10

(E) $\sqrt{50}$

10. $(2x^2 - 3x + 5) + (3x - 2) =$

(A) $2x^2 + 3$

(B) $2x^2 + 6x + 3$

(C) $2x^2 + 6x + 7$

(D) $2x + 3$

(E) $2x^2 - 6x + 3$

11. Using the formula $A = p + prt$, find A when $p = 500$, $r = .04$, and $t = 2\dfrac{1}{2}$.

(A) 700

(B) 600

(C) 550

(D) 500

(E) 450

12.

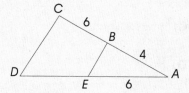

Triangles ABE and ACD are similar. Find the length of $\overline{DE}$.

(A) 9

(B) 15

(C) 4

(D) 11

(E) 8

13. The expression $(3K^2)^3$ is equivalent to

(A) $9K^6$

(B) $27K^6$

(C) $27K^5$

(D) $9K^5$

(E) $3K^5$

14. Find the value of y in the proportion $\dfrac{20}{12} = \dfrac{5}{y}$.

   (A) $\dfrac{3}{8}$

   (B) 3

   (C) 15

   (D) 8

   (E) $8\dfrac{1}{3}$

15. If $\dfrac{3}{x}$ is subtracted from $\dfrac{4}{x}$, the result is

   (A) 1

   (B) $\dfrac{7}{x}$

   (C) $-\dfrac{1}{x}$

   (D) $\dfrac{1}{x}$

   (E) $\dfrac{1}{x^2}$

16. The markdown price of a computer game was $36.75, which represented 75% of the original selling price. What was the original selling price?

   (A) $27.56

   (B) $42.35

   (C) $45.94

   (D) $49.00

   (E) $45.35

17. Use this chart to answer question 17.

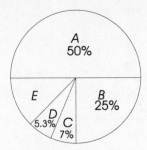

Freddie's Budget
Weekly net income = $350

A. Food
B. Rent and Utilities
C. Entertainment
D. Clothing
E. Miscellaneous

How much money does Freddie spend on miscellaneous items each week?

   (A) $43.05

   (B) $19.05

   (C) $130.95

   (D) $18.55

   (E) $44.45

18. What is the x-intercept of the line described by the equation $y = 3x + 7$?

   (A) 7

   (B) -7

   (C) $-\dfrac{3}{7}$

   (D) $-\dfrac{7}{3}$

   (E) 0

19. What is 60 expressed as the product of its prime factors?

   (A) (5)(13)

   (B) (5)(12)

   (C) (5)(3)(2)(2)

   (D) (4)(4)(3)

   (E) (15)(6)

20. If $|12a - 7| = 3$, what is a possible value of a?

    (A) 3

    (B) −3

    (C) 29

    (D) $-\dfrac{1}{3}$

    (E) $\dfrac{5}{6}$

21. What is the graph of the inequality $4 \le x \le 7$?

    (A)

    (B)

    (C)

    (D)

    (E)

22. $11^2 - 9^2 =$

    (A) 2

    (B) 4

    (C) −4

    (D) 40

    (E) 16

23. Eric's test scores were 98, 95, 84, 100, and 92. What would he need on his next test to have an average of 94?

    (A) 90

    (B) 92

    (C) 95

    (D) 100

    (E) It is not possible to get that average.

24. Where does the line $y = x - 3$ cross the y-axis?

    (A) $(0,3)$

    (B) $(0, -3)$

    (C) $(-3, 0)$

    (D) $(-3, 3)$

    (E) $(0,0)$

25.

If points A, B, C, and D are distinct collinear points, and $\overline{AC}$ is congruent to $\overline{BC}$, and B lies between A and D, and the length of $\overline{AC}$ is 7, what is the length of $\overline{CD}$?

    (A) 7

    (B) 14

    (C) 21

    (D) 28

    (E) It cannot be determined.

EXPLANATORY ANSWERS TO THE SSAT PRACTICE TEST 1

VERBAL

1. The correct answer is (A).
2. The correct answer is (D).
3. The correct answer is (D).
4. The correct answer is (A).
5. The correct answer is (C).
6. The correct answer is (B).
7. The correct answer is (B).
8. The correct answer is (B).
9. The correct answer is (E).
10. The correct answer is (A).
11. The correct answer is (B).
12. The correct answer is (C).
13. The correct answer is (D).
14. The correct answer is (B).
15. The correct answer is (E).
16. The correct answer is (C).
17. The correct answer is (C).
18. The correct answer is (B).
19. The correct answer is (E).
20. The correct answer is (D).
21. The correct answer is (E).
22. The correct answer is (C).
23. The correct answer is (B).
24. The correct answer is (B).
25. The correct answer is (E).
26. The correct answer is (A).
27. The correct answer is (B).
28. The correct answer is (D).
29. The correct answer is (D).
30. The correct answer is (A).
31. The correct answer is (B). The relationship is possession. Someone who is *astute* possesses *acumen*. Therefore, only choice (B) has the same relationship. Someone who is *diplomatic* possesses a great deal of *tact*.
32. The correct answer is (D). The relationship is one of object to its function: a *judge* would by definition *adjudicate*. A *champion* is a person who by definition would *defend* a matter.

426

33. **The correct answer is (A).** The relationship is word to antonym: if something is *imperceptible*, a person cannot *notice* it. The only answer that is an antonym is choice (A): if something is *intangible*, a person cannot *touch* it.

34. **The correct answer is (C).** The relationship is object to its function. A *claustrophobic* by definition hates *enclosure*. The only answer that is object to function is choice (C): a *misogynist* is a person who by definition dislikes *women*.

35. **The correct answer is (A).** A *hammer* is a tool used by a *carpenter*; an *awl* is a tool used by a *cobbler*. Choice (D) reverses the order of tool and user.

36. **The correct answer is (C).** The relationship is cause to effect. One who is *gullible* is easy to *bilk*. The only cause-to-effect relationship is choice (C): if you are *docile*, it would be easy to *lead* you.

37. **The correct answer is (A).** The relationship is word to definition. An *overblown* situation is *exaggerated*. Choice (A) has the same relationship: a *warrant* is by definition *justified*.

38. **The correct answer is (D).** Somebody *ruthless* has no *pity*, and somebody *bewildered* has no *comprehension*.

39. **The correct answer is (B).** The relationship is action of object. A *clown* acts *zany*. A *showoff* is a person whose actions could aptly be described as *flamboyant*.

40. **The correct answer is (D).** A horn is blown and a harp is plucked to make music.

41. **The correct answer is (B).** The relationship is cause to effect. You would *inveigle* someone by using *flattery*. Choice (B) has the same relationship: you would try to *browbeat* someone by using *intimidation*.

42. **The correct answer is (E).** *Flammable* and *inflammable* are synonyms; both mean easily inflamed. *Disinterested* means *impartial*.

43. **The correct answer is (C).** The relationship is action of object. A *devotee* is a person who by definition is *fervid*. Choice (C) has the same relationship: a *connoisseur* is a person who is by definition *discriminating*.

44. **The correct answer is (A).** The relationship is action of object. A *mule* is an animal that is proverbially *stubborn*. Choice (A) has the same relationship: a *pig* is an animal that is proverbially *idle*.

45. **The correct answer is (A).** The relationship is that of actor to action. An *extortionist blackmails*; a *kleptomaniac steals*.

46. **The correct answer is (A).** The relationship is action to object. A *virtuoso* is a person who would by definition perform with *éclat* (great brilliance). Choice (A) has the same relationship. A *gallant* is a person who would by definition perform with *panache* (dash).

47. **The correct answer is (C).** The relationship is cause to effect. Something that is *bilious* would by definition make a person feel *queasy*. Choice (C) has the same relationship: something that is *dangerous* would by definition make a person feel *alarmed*.

48. **The correct answer is (B).** The relationship is word to antonym. Something that is *disorganized* is lacking in *form*. Choice (B) has the same relationship: something that is *empty* is by definition lacking in *substance*.

49. **The correct answer is (D).** The relationship is word to synonym. A *midget,* by definition, is *minuscule.* Choice (D) has the same relationship: a *colossus* is by definition *gargantuan.*

50. **The correct answer is (A).** The relationship is object to its function. A *prude* is a person whose tastes could aptly be described as *fastidious.* Choice (A) has the same effect: a *puritan* is a person whose tastes could aptly be described as *simple.*

51. **The correct answer is (C).** The relationship is cause and effect. A remark that is *waggish* is designed to produce *laughs.* Choice (C) has the same effect: a remark that is *sad* is designed to produce *tears.*

52. **The correct answer is (B).** The relationship is word to synonym. Clothing that is *diaphanous* is reminiscent of *veils.* Choice (B) has the same relationship. Clothing that is *gossamer* is reminiscent of *cobwebs.*

53. **The correct answer is (A).** The relationship is word to antonym. A *microcosm* (small system) is the opposite of a *macrocosm* (universe). The same relationship is in choice (A): *plenty* means the opposite of *lack.*

54. **The correct answer is (D).** The relationship is object to its function. You would hear a *homily* at a *church.* The same relationship is in choice (D): you would be likely to hear a *monologue* in a *talk show.*

55. **The correct answer is (B).** The relationship is object to its function. A *mnemonic* is designed to help one's *memory.* The same relationship is in choice (B). *Glasses* are designed to help one's *vision.*

56. **The correct answer is (D).** The relationship is cause and effect. Something that is *healing* is conducive to one's *health.* Choice (D) has the same relationship: something that is *therapeutic* is conducive to one's *recovery.*

57. **The correct answer is (A).** This is a verb-to-noun relationship. *Arbitrate* is what one does to a *dispute. Solve* is what must be done to a *mystery.*

58. **The correct answer is (C).** The relationship is word to its synonym. A *tearjerker* is a literary form that is by definition *maudlin.* The same relationship is found in choice (C): a *farce* is a literary form that is by definition *hilarious.*

59. **The correct answer is (B).** The relationship is word to its synonym: one who has *passion* has *devotion.* The same relationship is in choice (B): one who has *concern* has *interest.*

60. **The correct answer is (A).** The relationship is object to its function. A *klutz* is a type of person who is *inept.* The same relationship is in choice (A): a *bigot* is a type of person who is *intolerant.*

QUANTITATIVE (MATH) 1

1. **The correct answer is (D).** If the tank is $\frac{1}{3}$ empty, it must be $\frac{2}{3}$ full. $\frac{2}{3}$ the total capacity of 18 gallons is 12.

2. **The correct answer is (E).** The value of choice (A) is $\frac{11}{12}$; the value of choice (B) is $\frac{5}{12}$; the value of choice (C) is $\frac{1}{4}$ or $\frac{3}{12}$; the value of choice (D) is $\frac{1}{4}$ or $\frac{3}{12}$; and the value of choice (E) is $\frac{1}{6}$ or $\frac{2}{12}$. Therefore, choice (E) has the least value.

3. **The correct answer is (E).** If $x + (x + 3) > 20$, then $2x > 17$. So $x > 8.5$. The only answer that is appropriate is 10.

4. **The correct answer is (C).** The perimeter of a square is found by summing the lengths of each side. Because the lengths are equal on a square, you can multiply one side by 4 to get the perimeter. Therefore, $4s = 88$, so $s = 22$.

5. **The correct answer is (D).** To find the greatest value of the four, assume the remaining three values are the least possible positive integer, 1. The average then is $\frac{1 + 1 + 1 + x}{4} = 9$.

   Solve for x. $3 + x = 36$, so $x = 33$.

6. **The correct answer is (B).** Multiples of 4 include: 4, 8, 12, 16, 20, 24, 28, 32, 36, 40, 44, etc. Comparing these with the answers provided, notice that the number 30 is not a multiple of 4.

7. **The correct answer is (B).** Substitute 7 for m. $*7 = 10(7) - 10 = 70 - 10 = 60$.

8. **The correct answer is (C).** If $*m = 10m - 10$ and $*m = 120$, then $10m - 10 = 120$.

   Solve for m: $10m = 130$, $m = 13$.

9. **The correct answer is (C).** The total discounted amount is $3 or ($9 − $6). The original amount × the discounted percent = the total discounted amount.

   $9 × discounted percent = $3.

   The discounted percent $= \frac{3}{9} = \frac{1}{3} \approx 33\%$.

10. **The correct answer is (A).** The number of left-handed members is equal to $12 - 8$, or 4. The ratio of left-handers to right-handers is 4:8, which simplifies to 1:2.

11. **The correct answer is (D).** Let the five consecutive integers be: x, $x + 1$, $x + 2$, $x + 3$, and $x + 4$.

    Then $x + x + 1 + x + 2 + x + 3 + x + 4 = 35$; $5x + 10 = 35$; $5x = 25$; $x = 5$

    Since the least of the five integers is 5, the greatest is $5 + 4$, or 9. $9^2 = 81$.

12. **The correct answer is (C).** When multiplying like values raised to a power, add the exponents.

    $$2^2 \times 2^3 \times 2^3 = 2^{2 + 3 + 3} = 2^8$$

13. **The correct answer is (D).** The area of a square is equal to the (length of the side)^2, or L^2.

    $$100s^2 = L^2$$
    $$\sqrt{100s^2} = \sqrt{L^2}$$
    $$10s = L$$

14. **The correct answer is (D).** Set up a ratio for this problem and solve:

    Let x represent the number of books purchased with 4 dollars.

    $$\frac{10}{d} = \frac{x}{4}$$

    $10 \times 4 = d \times x$ (using cross-multiplication)

    $$\frac{40}{d} = x$$

15. **The correct answer is (C).** Since integers can be both positive and negative, and the product of a positive and negative integer is always negative, choice (E) must be false. Looking further at the answers, notice that choices (B) and (C) are opposites of one another. Therefore, one of those must be true and the other false. Substitute two numbers for g and b and see which of the two is true. If $g = -4$ and $b = 5$, $g \times b = -4 \times 5 = -20$. Since -20 is even, choice (C) is correct.

16. **The correct answer is (D).** The sum of the first six grades is $78 \times 6 = 468$. (To find the average grade of 78, divide the sum of the six grades by 6.)

   The average with seven students is $468 + x = 80 \times 7$.

   $468 + x = 560$; $x = 92$

17. **The correct answer is (A).**

   All factors of 6 are factors of the number.

   The factors of 6 are:

   1×6

   2×3

18. **The correct answer is (C).** Since this is an isosceles triangle, the angles opposite the congruent sides are also congruent. The sum of the angles in a triangle equal $180°$. So $65° + 65° + x° = 180°$ and $x = 50°$.

19. **The correct answer is (A).**

   Let p equal the price of the item.

   Price $\times$ Discount Rate = Discount Amount

   So $\quad p \times 40\% = \$2.00$;

   $\qquad p \times .40 = 2.00$;

   $$p = \frac{2.00}{.40} = 5$$

20. **The correct answer is (C).** On Monday, $\frac{1}{4}$ of the pie was eaten. On Tuesday, there was $\frac{3}{4}$ of the pie left.

   $$\frac{1}{2} \times \frac{3}{4} = \frac{3}{8} \quad \text{and} \quad \frac{1}{4} + \frac{3}{8} = \frac{5}{8}$$

21. **The correct answer is (C).** The perimeter of a square equals $4s$. The area of a square equals s^2. Setting them equal will determine the length of one side, s.

   $$s^2 = 4s$$
   $$s^2 - 4s = 0$$
   $$s(s - 4) = 0$$
   $$s = 0 \text{ or } s = 4$$

   Since it would make no sense for the length to be 0, the correct answer is 4.

22. **The correct answer is (A).**

$$6x - 4 = 38$$
$$6x = 42$$
$$x = 7 \text{ so}$$
$$7 - 5 = 2$$

23. **The correct answer is (A).**

$$3(x^2y^{-4}z)^4x^3y =$$
$$3x^8y^{-16}z^4x^3y =$$
$$3x^{11}y^{-15}z^4$$

24. **The correct answer is (C).** They are all factors of 360, but 4 is not prime. (A prime number is a number that has exactly two factors, namely 1 and itself.)

25. **The correct answer is (D).** The altitude of an equilateral triangle bisects the vertex, forming a 30-60-90 triangle with sides in the ratios shown.

(This also comes from the Pythagorean Theorem, and the fact that the base of an equilateral triangle has been bisected to form this 30-60-90 triangle.)

The sides will be in the same ratio for the given triangle:

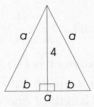

So, with the ratios $1:\sqrt{3}:2$ equaling the ratios $b:4:a$, we find $b = \dfrac{4}{\sqrt{3}}$ and $a = \dfrac{8}{\sqrt{3}}$.

Area = one half base times height, so

$$A = (4)\left(\frac{4}{\sqrt{3}}\right) = \frac{16}{\sqrt{3}} = \frac{16\sqrt{3}}{3}.$$

READING COMPREHENSION

Passage 1

1. **The correct answer is (D).** The word "invited" in the first sentence indicates he was asked to come to Birmingham. Choice (A) is incorrect because the passage does not say what King wanted to do. While choice (B) may be a true statement, the passage does not state that was his reason. Choices (C) and (E) refer to events after he had arrived, so they are incorrect.

2. **The correct answer is (B).** Choices (A), (C), and (E) are not related to any laws. Choice (D) is the result of an illegal action, not a reason that the action was illegal.

3. **The correct answer is (D).** Choice (A) is incorrect because the passage states he analyzes when a law can be broken. Choices (B) and (C) are incorrect because the passage states only unjust laws could be violated. Choice (E) is incorrect because according to King, if the law is not unfair, breaking the law is wrong even if the opposition is nonviolent.

4. **The correct answer is (A).** Choice (B) is incorrect because the letter did not discuss King's situation. Choice (C) is incorrect because it is contradicted by the passage. Choices (D) and (E) are incorrect because they name specific actions that are not in the letter.

5. **The correct answer is (B).** Choice (A) is incorrect because the letter does not try to sell a product, which is what an advertisement does. Choice (C) is incorrect because it is a letter, not a speech, and choice (D) is incorrect because the letter is not a poem. Choice (E) is incorrect because there is no mention of religion as part of the letter.

Passage 2

6. **The correct answer is (A).** Choice (B) applies to leaves that have not had the proper amount of water. Choice (C) applies to plants infested with insects. Choice (D) describes a healthy plant, and choice (E) is about the soil, not the leaves.

7. **The correct answer is (E).** All of the answers above it are discussed at some point in the passage.

8. **The correct answer is (D).** The sentence after the one in which "infest" appears gives the phrase "live on" to explain what infest means.

9. **The correct answer is (C).** Choice (A) is not mentioned in the passage. Choice (B) is a result of forcing the plant to grow too quickly. Choice (D) is a symptom of a plant that has outgrown its pot. Choice (E) is a sign of insects on the plant.

10. **The correct answer is (B).** If all plants were cared for properly, there would be no need to see if they were healthy before purchasing them. Choice (A) is incorrect because if all plants were raised perfectly, they all would be healthy. Choice (C) applies to some plants, not all of them. The passage does not discuss caring for plants at home or a plant's environment, so choices (D) and (E) are incorrect.

Passage 3

11. **The correct answer is (A).** Since Demeter is the goddess of the harvest, she oversees crops planted for food. Choices (B), (C), and (D) are contradicted by the passages because Hades is the god of the underworld, and the passage does not state who rules over marriage or humanity. Choice (E) is incorrect, because while the weather affects the growth of crops, Demeter rules the growth of plants, not what causes them to grow or not grow.

12. **The correct answer is (B).** The passage does not say myths always involved gods and goddesses, so choice (A) is incorrect. The passage does not indicate whether choices (C) and (D) are true or false statements. Choice (E) is true of the Demeter myth, but it would not be true of all myths.

13. **The correct answer is (C).** Choices (A) and (B) are true statements about the story, but they are not the reason Demeter causes winter to occur. Choices (D) and (E) might be inferred from the story, but they are not the reason given for winter.

14. **The correct answer is (D).** Choice (A) is incorrect because the passage does not state Zeus' feelings about Hades. Choice (B) is incorrect because if Zeus did not want to upset Hades, he would have given his permission. Choice (C) is incorrect because it was Hades, not Zeus, who wanted Persephone as his wife. Choice (E) is a true statement, but it is not the reason Zeus did not give permission to Hades.

15. **The correct answer is (C).** Although choices (A), (B), (D), and (E) state events that happened in the story, these events are not when, according to the story, Demeter first stopped the growth of crops.

Passage 4

16. **The correct answer is (A).** Choice (B) is a theory that only some scientists believe to be true. Choices (C) and (D) are about part of the passage's content, but they do not describe the whole passage. Choice (E) is too general; the passage deals with a specific scientific discovery.

17. **The correct answer is (C).** The passage states the radiation frequency "decreases," so choices (A), (B), and (D) are incorrect. Choice (E) is incorrect because "collapse" does not mean the same as "decrease."

18. **The correct answer is (D).** The passage states the matter was "tightly compressed." Choice (A) is incorrect, because while the matter may be expanding after the Big Bang, it was not expanding originally. Choice (B) means the opposite of "tightly compressed," so it is incorrect. Choices (C) and (E) refer to what may have happened after the Big Bang, so they are incorrect.

19. **The correct answer is (E).** The passage states some scientists think the universe will continue to expand, while others think it will collapse. Since both views are given, choices (A) and (C) are incorrect. Choices (B) and (D) are contradicted by the passage.

20. **The correct answer is (C).** This is indicated in the first sentence of the passage. That sentence also contradicts choice (B), and information in the passage about the 1965 discovery also suggests that the theory has been proven, so choice (A) is incorrect. Choice (D) is about the Doppler effect, not the Big Bang, so it is incorrect. Choice (E) is about evidence for the theory, not what the author thinks about the theory.

Passage 5

21. **The correct answer is (D).** Choice (A) is incorrect, because fractions means "parts," but it does not indicate they do not agree with each other. Choice (B) is incorrect because the factions are within a nation, so they cannot be "international." Choice (C) refers to people who believe in their nation, so it does not fit the passage. Choice (E) is contradicted because the factions wished to "replace" the monarchy.

22. **The correct answer is (C).** Choices (A) and (B) may or may not be true, but the passage does not state that they are true. Choice (D) is incorrect because the passage does not say how the experts felt about their discovery. Choice (E) is contradicted by the phrase "throughout the world."

23. **The correct answer is (A).** Choice (B) is incorrect because the conflict between Greece and Turkey did not involve a new land. Choice (C) is incorrect because it refers to events after the occurrence of these conflicts. Choices (D) and (E) are incorrect because the passage does not explain what these conflicts led to or how they were settled.

24. **The correct answer is (D).** The term is defined in the passage by the words occurring immediately after it.

25. **The correct answer is (C).** The passage gives November 1918 as the time when the "cease fire" was signed. Only after 1918 did the peace conference of January 1919 begin, choice (B), during which the League of Nations was founded, choice (D), and the peace treaty was not signed until the end of the conference, choice (E). Choice (A) is incorrect because while this was a slogan about the war, its hopes never came into existence.

Passage 6

26. **The correct answer is (C).** The passage does not say the passengers were hurrying, choice (A). Nor does it explain why Mrs. Miller's son had not arrived home, choice (B). Choice (D) is incorrect, because the flight attendant's words include "I'm sorry," so she is not being rude. Choice (E) is incorrect because the weather would not affect passengers inside the airport who were going to board a plane.

27. **The correct answer is (E).** Choice (A) is incorrect because the author was boarding the plane at the scheduled take-off time. Choice (B) is incorrect because the reader is not told exactly when the plane left. While this would make choice (C) a possibility, there is enough information in the passage to make it clear the plane took off some short time after 1:15 in the afternoon, so choice (D) would be incorrect.

28. **The correct answer is (E).** Choice (A) is contradicted by the description; she is well dressed and carefully made up. Choice (B) is incorrect, because the details of her appearance do not have examples of things that are very expensive. Choice (C) may be true about Mrs. Miller, but it is not suggested by what she looks like. Nothing in the passage reveals her sense of humor or lack of it, so choice (D) is incorrect.

29. **The correct answer is (D).** While choice (A) may be a correct statement about Mrs. Miller, and choice (E) might be inferred from the passage, neither explains the motives of the airline personnel. Choice (B) may or may not be true. The author asks if Mrs. Miller knows the number, but does not know if she does or does not. Choice (C) is incorrect because they take her off the plane so that they will not have to help her find her son.

30. **The correct answer is (E).** The author notices the details of Mrs. Miller's appearance, which is observant, choice (A). The author feels sorry for Mrs. Miller, which is compassionate, choice (B), and the author is moved to great sadness when considering the situation, which shows sensitive feelings, choice (C).

Passage 7

31. **The correct answer is (A).** None of the other answers makes sense in context because an area of land cannot be "erased," choice (B); "invented," choice (C); "changed," choice (D); or "carried," choice (E).

32. **The correct answer is (C).** Choices (A) and (B) may be true, but these reasons would not be important for anyone but Ms. Tinne. Choice (E) is also a personal statement. Choice (D) is incorrect because her death caused her work to end rather than make it important.

33. **The correct answer is (E).** The passage states in the sentence before Bahr el Gazal is mentioned that she explored "parts of north central Africa." Thus, the other answers are incorrect.

34. **The correct answer is (C).** Nothing in the passage suggests choices (A), (B), (D), or (E). Choice (C) may be inferred because the people who killed her believed she was carrying gold, according to the last sentence in the passage.

35. **The correct answer is (E).** Words like "intelligent," "daring," and "remarkable" and the statement that her information was valuable show the author's *admiration.* While the author calls her death "unfortunate," the overall tone of the passage is not sad, so choice (C) is incorrect.

Passage 8

36. **The correct answer is (D).** Since Pip's parents were alive "long before" photography was invented, choices (A), (B), and (C) are not probable. Choice (E) is incorrect because the reference to photography shows that the writer lived when the process was known.

37. **The correct answer is (C).** Choice (A) is incorrect because elaborate lettering would not indicate something in Pip's mind. Choice (B) is incorrect because since his parents are dead, he would have no "hopes" about them. Choice (D) is incorrect because it is the source of his fancies. Choice (E) is incorrect because Pip was a child when he had the fancies.

38. **The correct answer is (C).** In the passage, Pip says "their days were long before the days of photographs," lines 11–12.

39. **The correct answer is (B).** Since she is married, her name would not be Pirrip, so choice (A) is incorrect. Choices (C) and (D) refer to the speaker's first names, so they are not correct, and no Mrs. Stout appears in the passage, so choice (E) is incorrect.

40. **The correct answer is (C).** It is explicitly stated in the passage. While the passage talks about tombs and tombstones, neither stone-cutting nor grave digging is mentioned in connection with the husband, so choices (A) and (B) are incorrect. Choice (D) cannot be correct because the passage concerns a time before photography was invented. Choice (E) is incorrect because the passage does not mention a barber.

QUANTITATIVE (MATH) 2

1. **The correct answer is (A).** The stock declined in value by $1,500, from an initial value of $6,000. The fractional decline in value is

    $\dfrac{1500}{6000} = \dfrac{1}{4}$, which is 25%.

2. **The correct answer is (B).** Get common denominators to add fractions. Multiply $\dfrac{a}{b}$ by $\dfrac{a}{a}$ to get $\dfrac{a^2}{ab}$. Multiply $\dfrac{b}{a}$ by $\dfrac{b}{b}$ to get $\dfrac{b^2}{ab}$. Subtract the fractions by subtracting the numerators.

3. **The correct answer is (A).** To have an average of 90 after five tests, the total of all the scores must be $90 \times 5 = 450$. The known scores add up to $80 + 87 + 94 + 89 = 350$, so she needs 100 points on the last test.

4. **The correct answer is (D).** Percent means "per 100." 4 percent means $\dfrac{4}{100}$.

5. **The correct answer is (E).** Put time in like units. $\dfrac{15\ hours}{48\ hours}$

    Dividing the common factor of 3 results in $\dfrac{5}{16}$.

6. **The correct answer is (E).** When multiplying decimals, be sure the final decimal point is in the correct place.

.58	2 places
×.14	2 places
232	
58	
.0812	4 places

7. **The correct answer is (B).** To solve equations, use inverse operations. First add 5 to both sides.

$$3a - 5 = 7$$
$$\underline{+ 5 = +5}$$
$$3a \quad = 12$$

Then divide both sides by 3.

$$\frac{3a}{3} = \frac{12}{3}$$
$$a = 4$$

8. **The correct answer is (C).** There are eight outcomes (total gumballs), of which five are successes (red).

9. **The correct answer is (B).** $OA = OB$ because the radii in the same circle are equal. The triangle AOB is a right triangle. By the Pythagorean Theorem:

$$a^2 + b^2 = c^2$$
$$(\text{leg})^2 + (\text{leg})^2 = (\text{hypotenuse})^2$$
$$(10)^2 + (10)^2 = c^2$$
$$100 + 100 = c^2$$
$$200 = c^2$$
$$\sqrt{2 \times 100} = \sqrt{c^2}$$
$$10\sqrt{2} = c$$

10. **The correct answer is (A).** To add algebraic expressions, combine like terms.

$$2x^2 - 3x + 5$$
$$\underline{+ 3x - 2}$$
$$2x^2 + 0 + 3 = 2x^2 + 3$$

11. **The correct answer is (C).** Substitute values $p = 500$, $r = .04$, and $t = 2\frac{1}{2}$.

$$A = 500 + (500)(.04)2\frac{1}{2} = 500 + 50 = 550$$

12. **The correct answer is (A).** Corresponding parts of similar triangles are in proportion:

$$\frac{AB}{AC} = \frac{AE}{AD}$$

$$\frac{4}{4+6} = \frac{6}{6+x}$$

$$4(6+x) = 6(4+6)$$

$$24 + 4x = 60$$

$$\underline{-24 \qquad\quad = -24}$$

$$4x = 36$$

$$x = 9$$

13. **The correct answer is (B).**

$$(3K^2)^3 = (3K^2)\,(3K^2)\,(3K^2)$$

$$= (3)(3)(3)(K^2)\,(K^2)(K^2)$$

$$= 27K^{2+2+2} \quad \text{(multiply numbers)}$$

$$= 27K^6 \qquad\quad \text{(add exponents)}$$

14. **The correct answer is (B).**

$$\frac{20}{12} = \frac{5}{y}$$

$$20y = 12 \times 5 \text{ (cross-multiply)}$$

$$20y = 60$$

$$y = 3$$

15. **The correct answer is (D).**

$$\frac{4}{x} - \frac{3}{x} = \frac{1}{x}$$

The problem is written with all common denominators. Simply subtract the numerators.

16. **The correct answer is (D).**

$$75\% \text{ of } N = 36.75$$

$$75\% = \frac{75}{100} = .75 \qquad .75 \text{ of } N \text{ means } .75 \times N$$

$$.75 \times N = 36.75 \qquad \text{Divide both sides by .75 to isolate } N.$$

$$\frac{.75 \times N}{.75} = \frac{36.75}{.75}$$

$$N = \frac{36.75}{.75} = 49$$

17. **The correct answer is (E).** First find what percent of Freddie's income is spent on miscellaneous items.

$$50\% + 25\% + 7\% + 5.3\% = 87.3\%$$
$$100\% - 87.3\% = 12.7\%$$

Then find 12.7% of $350.

Amount = Weekly Net Income × Miscellaneous Percent
$$= 350 \times .127 = \$44.45$$

18. **The correct answer is (D).** The line described by the equation crosses the x-axis when $y = 0$.

$$0 = 3x + 7$$
$$-7 = 3x$$
$$-\frac{7}{3} = x$$

19. **The correct answer is (C).** To break a number into its prime factors, break it into factors, and break those factors into factors, until you cannot go any further. It doesn't matter what factors you begin with. You will reach the same prime factors.

$$60 = 10 \times 6 = 5 \times 2 \times 3 \times 2$$

5, 3, and 2 are prime numbers (they have no factors other than themselves and 1), and multiplication is commutative (can be performed in any order).

Another way to approach the problem is to rule out the answers that have composite (non-prime) numbers. This rules out choices (B), (D), and (E). Test the remaining answers by multiplying them out. Only choice (C) comes to 60.

20. **The correct answer is (E).**

$12a - 7$ can be 3 or -3.

In the first case:

$$12a - 7 = 3$$
$$12a = 10$$
$$a = \frac{5}{6}$$

In the second case:

$$12a - 7 = -3$$
$$12a = 4$$
$$a = \frac{1}{3}$$

The only solution that fits the given answers is $\frac{5}{6}$.

21. **The correct answer is (A).** x is less than or equal to 7, and at the same time, x is greater than or equal to 4. An open circle would indicate a "less than" or a "greater than" condition at the endpoint, while filled-in circles indicate a "less than or equal to" or a "greater than or equal to" condition at the endpoint.

22. **The correct answer is (D).**

$$11^2 = 121$$
$$9^2 = 81$$
$$121 - 81 = 40$$

23. **The correct answer is (C).** To have an average of 94 after six tests, Eric's total score would need to be $94 \times 6 = 564$. He already has a total score of $98 + 95 + 84 + 100 + 92$, which equals 469, so he needs $564 - 469$ points, which is 95.

24. **The correct answer is (B).** In the form $y = mx + b$, the slope is given by m and the y-intercept is given by b. The y-intercept is the value of y when $x = 0$.

25. **The correct answer is (E).**

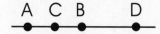

$\overline{AC}$ and $\overline{CB}$ are congruent, making C the midpoint of $\overline{AB}$. AC is 7 so BC is 7 and AB is 14. It is not given that B is the midpoint of $\overline{AD}$, just that it lies between A and D. Therefore, $\overline{AB}$ and $\overline{BD}$ are not necessarily congruent. There is no other relationship that will give the length of $\overline{BD}$ or of $\overline{CD}$.

SSAT Practice Test 2

Part I: Writing the Essay

Part II: Multiple Choice

Explanatory Answers to the

Part I

WRITING THE ESSAY

WRITING SAMPLE	TIME: 25 MINUTES

Directions: Using two sheets of lined theme paper, plan and write an essay on the topic assigned below. DO NOT WRITE ON ANOTHER TOPIC. AN ESSAY ON ANOTHER TOPIC IS NOT ACCEPTABLE.

Topic: Money is a good servant, but a dangerous master.

Assignment: Do you agree or disagree with the topic statement? Support your position with one or two specific examples from personal experience, the experience of others, current events, history, or literature.

Name: _____

Write your essay here.

_____

_____

_____

_____

_____

_____

_____

_____

_____

_____

_____

_____

_____

_____

_____

_____

_____

_____

_____

_____

_____

(Continue, if necessary.)

Part II

MULTIPLE CHOICE

Directions: Each of the following questions consists of one word followed by five words or phrases. You are to select the one word or phrase whose meaning is closest to the word in capital letters.

1. PREMONITION

   (A) payment
   (B) ghost
   (C) forewarning
   (D) reward
   (E) greeting

2. DECREE

   (A) quantity
   (B) loss
   (C) challenge
   (D) order
   (E) joke

3. RELINQUISH

   (A) release
   (B) conquer
   (C) discourage
   (D) excite
   (E) announce

4. IMMATERIAL

   (A) untidy
   (B) false
   (C) unimportant
   (D) wicked
   (E) substantial

5. CONTOUR

   (A) journey
   (B) outline
   (C) gathering
   (D) agency
   (E) photograph

6. THESIS

   (A) guess
   (B) hypothesis
   (C) debate
   (D) theme
   (E) definition

7. HABITAT

   (A) sleep
   (B) cushion
   (C) yarn
   (D) promise
   (E) home

8. INTERVENE

   (A) come between
   (B) withdraw
   (C) contact
   (D) construct
   (E) require

9. ASPHYXIATION

   (A) suffocation
   (B) extension
   (C) loss
   (D) delivery
   (E) breathing

447

10. ANTIDOTE

    (A) poison
    (B) story
    (C) opponent
    (D) cure
    (E) predecessor

11. BATTERY

    (A) ambush
    (B) corner
    (C) precarious
    (D) group
    (E) delirium

12. PATIENT

    (A) tolerant
    (B) irregular
    (C) leisure
    (D) multiple
    (E) military

13. PAINSTAKING

    (A) disease
    (B) scrupulous
    (C) delicate
    (D) medicine
    (E) generic

14. PRELUDE

    (A) symphony
    (B) soprano
    (C) postlude
    (D) beginning
    (E) drama

15. REVERENCE

    (A) nonfiction
    (B) simplicity
    (C) respect
    (D) love
    (E) glory

16. UNUSUAL

    (A) ordinary
    (B) rare
    (C) pedantic
    (D) sincere
    (E) common

17. NOISE

    (A) music
    (B) locomotive
    (C) sound
    (D) siren
    (E) crowd

18. EXPRESS

    (A) verbalize
    (B) quickly
    (C) overnight
    (D) careful
    (E) holster

19. KIND

    (A) significant
    (B) quality
    (C) equal
    (D) hermitage
    (E) good

20. CLANDESTINE

    (A) dated
    (B) secret
    (C) overt
    (D) exclusive
    (E) fortunate

21. HAPPY

    (A) wild
    (B) delighted
    (C) forthright
    (D) satisfied
    (E) scuttle

22. FRACTION

    (A) splinter
    (B) sect
    (C) piece
    (D) share
    (E) slice

23. GREAT

    (A) historical
    (B) famous
    (C) hearth
    (D) renown
    (E) immense

24. TALENTED

    (A) gifted
    (B) musical
    (C) artistic
    (D) dramatic
    (E) reputable

25. PSEUDONYM

    (A) falsehood
    (B) forgery
    (C) elephant
    (D) pen name
    (E) writer

26. ECCENTRIC

    (A) trustworthy
    (B) truthful
    (C) prompt
    (D) earnest
    (E) unusual

27. PRISONER

    (A) contain
    (B) penal
    (C) judge
    (D) captive
    (E) justice

28. LITTLE

    (A) periphery
    (B) minute
    (C) multiple
    (D) confection
    (E) gladden

29. ROBUST

    (A) florid
    (B) contained
    (C) healthy
    (D) considerable
    (E) weak

30. SPHERE

    (A) plane
    (B) balloon
    (C) orb
    (D) radial
    (E) horizon

Directions: The following questions ask you to find relationships between words. For each question, select the answer that best completes the meaning of the sentence.

31. Height is to mountain as

    (A) depth is to trench.
    (B) shade is to tree.
    (C) weight is to age.
    (D) speed is to highway.
    (E) mineral is to mine.

32. Oblivious is to awareness as

    (A) comatose is to consciousness.
    (B) serene is to composure.
    (C) erudite is to knowledge.
    (D) adroit is to skill.
    (E) invigorate is to energy.

33. Bellwether is to barometer as

    (A) proselyte is to spark plug.
    (B) panhandler is to kill.
    (C) embezzler is to abduct.
    (D) cynosure is to magnet.
    (E) morass is to catalyst.

34. Act is to action as

    (A) therapy is to thermometer.
    (B) oblivion is to obvious.
    (C) liturgy is to literature.
    (D) image is to imagine.
    (E) bowl is to bowdlerize.

35. Bibulous is to drink as

    (A) rapacious is to clothing.
    (B) gluttonous is to food.
    (C) altruistic is to money.
    (D) vegetarian is to meat.
    (E) controversy is to reconcile.

36. Venison is to deer as veal is to

    (A) calf.
    (B) cow.
    (C) steer.
    (D) sheep.
    (E) lamb.

37. Cursory is to superficial as

    (A) dismal is to cheerful.
    (B) approbation is to consecration.
    (C) death is to victory.
    (D) desultory is to aimless.
    (E) heroism is to reward.

38. Bacchus is to drink as

    (A) Orpheus is to Eurydice.
    (B) Amazon is to ruler.
    (C) Diana is to hunt.
    (D) Zeus is to Olympus.
    (E) Plato is to Aristotle.

39. Bald is to hairy as

    (A) small is to tiny.
    (B) broad is to fat.
    (C) anemic is to robust.
    (D) fatuous is to loud.
    (E) repetitive is to redundant.

40. Gold is to Midas as

    (A) bird is to eagle.
    (B) devil is to Satan.
    (C) hero is to conquest.
    (D) wisdom is to Athena.
    (E) genius is to Shakespeare.

41. Philanthropist is to generous as

    (A) dentist is to teeth.
    (B) iconoclast is to conformist.
    (C) rider is to horse.
    (D) teacher is to educated.
    (E) plagiarist is to robber.

42. Exhale is to lung as

    (A) exhume is to corpse.
    (B) pump is to heart.
    (C) think is to brain.
    (D) perspire is to skin.
    (E) taste is to tongue.

43. Nazis are to Nuremburg as

    (A) judge is to jury.
    (B) guard is to prison.
    (C) communist is to Marx.
    (D) persecute is to prosecution.
    (E) gun is to death.

44. Politics are to bribe as

    (A) parking is to meter.
    (B) business is to contract.
    (C) examinations are to cheat.
    (D) nesting is to leaving.
    (E) painting is to commission.

45. Fraud is to cheater as

    (A) infatuation is to love.
    (B) obsession is to interest.
    (C) impostor is to impersonator.
    (D) ignominy is to disloyalty.
    (E) castigation is to praise.

46. Bacon is to pound as

    (A) gun is to lead.
    (B) dime is to silver.
    (C) ceiling is to chandelier.
    (D) eggs are to dozen.
    (E) puppet show is to puppet maker.

47. Impeach is to dismiss as

    (A) arraign is to convict.
    (B) accuse is to charge.
    (C) imprison is to jail.
    (D) plant is to sow.
    (E) absent is to present.

48. Limousine is to car as

    (A) house is to cave.
    (B) railroad is to bus.
    (C) fur is to animal.
    (D) mansion is to house.
    (E) stone is to pebble.

49. Warts are to moles as mildew is to

    (A) dirt.
    (B) grass.
    (C) weeds.
    (D) alcohol.
    (E) gold.

50. Bass is to soprano as

    (A) art is to music.
    (B) light is to shading.
    (C) govern is to dictate.
    (D) low is to high.
    (E) chorus is to solo.

51. Braid is to hair as wind is to

    (A) run.
    (B) movie.
    (C) joke.
    (D) bow.
    (E) clock.

52. Blade is to grass as

    (A) air is to gas.
    (B) grain is to sand.
    (C) metal is to rod.
    (D) plant is to leaves.
    (E) roof is to house.

53. Athlete is to training as

    (A) mercenary is to money.
    (B) porpoise is to sea.
    (C) student is to studying.
    (D) child is to parent.
    (E) adult is to child.

54. Novel is to author as

    (A) rain is to flood.
    (B) form is to shape.
    (C) light is to switch.
    (D) opera is to composer.
    (E) song is to tape.

55. Miser is to gold as

    (A) engine is to caboose.
    (B) toastmaster is to dinner.
    (C) general is to victories.
    (D) prison is to criminal.
    (E) button is to zipper.

56. Horse is to centaur as

    (A) Pegasus is to fly.
    (B) cat is to lion.
    (C) unicorn is to tapestry.
    (D) worm is to snake.
    (E) fish is to mermaid.

57. Bat is to ball as

  (A) stove is to pan.
  (B) foot is to pedal.
  (C) theater is to seats.
  (D) glove is to hand.
  (E) fist is to mitt.

58. Ignition is to start as

  (A) radio is to antenna.
  (B) shut is to door.
  (C) brake is to stop.
  (D) air is to tire.
  (E) gas is to tank.

59. Touch is to push as

  (A) water is to milk.
  (B) angry is to choleric.
  (C) glass is to water.
  (D) translucent is to opaque.
  (E) sip is to gulp.

60. Bananas are to bunch as

  (A) capon is to rooster.
  (B) ram is to ewe.
  (C) chicken is to duck.
  (D) lettuce is to head.
  (E) surgeon is to operation.

QUANTITATIVE (MATH) 1   TIME: 30 MINUTES   25 QUESTIONS

Directions: Following each problem in this section, there are five suggested answers. Work each problem in your head or in the space provided (there will be space for scratchwork in your test booklet). Then look at the five suggested answers and decide which is best.

1. Which of the following is a multiple of both 4 and 5?

   (A) 10
   (B) 45
   (C) 50
   (D) 60
   (E) 90

2. Four less than a number is two thirds of that number. What is the number?

   (A) 12
   (B) 4
   (C) $\frac{12}{5}$
   (D) $\frac{5}{3}$
   (E) 6

3. On a test with 25 questions, Mark scored an 84%. How many questions did Mark answer correctly?

   (A) 22
   (B) 21
   (C) 16
   (D) 5
   (E) 4

4. $\frac{1}{2} + \frac{2}{3} + \frac{3}{4} - \frac{1}{2} - \frac{1}{3} + \frac{1}{4} - \frac{1}{3} =$

   (A) $\frac{1}{2}$
   (B) $\frac{2}{3}$
   (C) 1
   (D) 2
   (E) $\frac{3}{4}$

5. The perimeter of a square with a side length of 4 is how much less than the perimeter of a rectangle with sides of length 6 and width 4?

   (A) 8
   (B) 6
   (C) 4
   (D) 2
   (E) 0

6. Which of the following is most nearly 40% of $19.95?

   (A) $8.00
   (B) $4.00
   (C) $14.50
   (D) $12.00
   (E) $6.75

7. One fifth of a class chose electricity for the topic of a science project. If 2 students chose this topic, how many students are in the class?

   (A) 20
   (B) 10
   (C) 8
   (D) 5
   (E) 2

8. Don is 5 years older than Peter is. In 5 years, Don will be twice as old as Peter is now. How old is Peter now?

   (A) 5
   (B) 10
   (C) 15
   (D) 25
   (E) 35

9. If p pieces of candy cost c cents, 20 pieces of candy will cost

   (A) $\dfrac{pc}{20}$ cents.

   (B) $\dfrac{20c}{p}$ cents.

   (C) $20pc$ cents.

   (D) $\dfrac{20p}{c}$ cents.

   (E) $20 + p + c$ cents.

10. Durant's Trading Company earned profits of $750,000 in 1990. In 1998, their profit was $4,500,000. The profit from 1998 was how many times as great as it was in 1990?

    (A) 2
    (B) 4
    (C) 6
    (D) 10
    (E) 60

11.

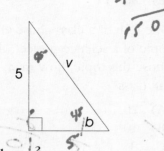

    If $b = 45°$, then $v^2 =$

    (A) 64
    (B) 50
    (C) 25
    (D) 10
    (E) It cannot be determined.

12. A pet goat eats 2 pounds of oats and 1 pound of grass each day. When the goat has eaten a total of 30 pounds, how many pounds of grass has been eaten?

    (A) 6
    (B) 8
    (C) 10
    (D) 30
    (E) 60

13. If $3x - 9 = 18$, what is $x \div 9$?

    (A) 6
    (B) 3
    (C) 0
    (D) 9
    (E) 1

14. One half the difference between the number of degrees in a rectangle and the number of degrees in a triangle is

    (A) 360
    (B) 240
    (C) 180
    (D) 90
    (E) 45

15. A zoo has 4 times as many gorillas as tigers. There are 4 more tigers than there are zebras at the zoo. If z represents the number of zebras, in terms of z, how many gorillas are in the zoo?

    (A) $4z$
    (B) $z + 4$
    (C) $z + 8$
    (D) $4z + 4$
    (E) $4z + 16$

16. If cats sleep $\frac{3}{4}$ of every day, how many full days would a cat sleep in a four-day period?

(A) $\frac{1}{4}$

(B) $\frac{3}{4}$

(C) 1

(D) 3

(E) 4

17. What is the least number that can be added to 2,042 to produce a result divisible by 9?

(A) 1

(B) 2

(C) 3

(D) 5

(E) 6

18. An art club of 5 boys and 4 girls makes craft projects. If the girls average 2 projects each and the boys average 3 projects each, what is the total number of projects produced by this group?

(A) 5

(B) 9

(C) 22

(D) 23

(E) 26

19. The area of a rectangle with width 3 and length 8 is equal to the area of a triangle with base 6 and height of

(A) 1

(B) 2

(C) 3

(D) 4

(E) 8

Questions 20 and 21 refer to the following definition: For all real numbers r and s, $r \clubsuit s = (r \times s) - (r + s)$.

20. $10 \clubsuit 2 =$

(A) 20

(B) 16

(C) 12

(D) 8

(E) 4

21. If $L(4 \clubsuit 3) = 30$, then $L =$

(A) 3

(B) 4

(C) 5

(D) 6

(E) 7

22. Jessie scores an 88, 86, and 90 on her first 3 exams. What must she score on her fourth exam to receive an average of 91?

(A) 92

(B) 95

(C) 98

(D) 99

(E) 100

23. Solve for x: $3x - 8 = 10x - 13$

(A) $\frac{5}{7}$

(B) $-\frac{5}{7}$

(C) -35

(D) -3

(E) 3

24. If the price of a handbag is $75.00 before a discount of 15%, what is the final discounted price?

   (A) $11.25
   (B) $60.00
   (C) $63.75
   (D) $75.00
   (E) $86.25

25. Find the height of a triangle whose base is 15 inches and whose area is 75 square inches.

   (A) 5 inches
   (B) 5 square inches
   (C) 10 inches
   (D) 10 square inches
   (E) 20 inches

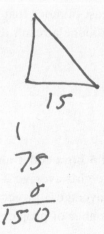

Directions: Read the passage carefully and then answer the questions about it. For each question, decide on the basis of the passage which one of the choices best answers the question.

Passage 1

Line Most people living between 1400 and 1600 lived in complete ignorance of science. They continued to accept superstitions and nonsensical beliefs and lived in a world in
5 which spirits, demons, and witches were very real for them. Even professional men were not noted for their use of reason. One French playwright, Molière, had so little faith in the knowledge of doctors that he
10 made one of the characters in a play say: "What will you do, sir, with four physicians? Is not one enough to kill any one body?"

Certainly the majority of men and women—educated or not—were not
15 constantly "scientific" in their attitudes. Talented individuals, rather than the mass of people, were responsible for the gains in the sciences. These individuals did outstanding work, not only in science and medicine but
20 also in the field of invention (the application of abstract scientific principles to produce something of concrete use). Johann Gutenberg (c. 1390–1468), a German, was one of several people who helped advance the art
25 of printing in a practical way. He constructed a workable press about the middle of the fifteenth century. By that date, paper and printer's ink were available for the printing process.
30 Gutenberg must not be called the "inventor" of the printing press. Printing developed too gradually for any one man to receive all of the credit. People living in

China and Korea had movable type as early
35 as the eleventh century A.D., and several Europeans in the Rhineland area of Germany experimented with printing during the early fifteenth century.

The invention of printing was one of
40 the greatest achievements in the history of civilization. Books could now be published in large numbers and sold at lower costs. Remember that in the Middle Ages each book was copied by hand on expensive
45 parchment (made from the stretched skin of a sheep or goat). A monk, illustrating and decorating the pages as he went, would take months or years on a single book. When paper was introduced to Europe, books
50 became cheaper, but they were still very scarce. Movable type meant that each letter or type was a tiny engraving. The letters could be arranged in words, then sentences, then a whole page. After ink had been
55 applied to the type and many impressions of the page made, the type was disassembled and could be used over and over. Hundreds or thousands of copies of each book or newspaper or sheet could easily be printed.
60 Books declined in price as a result, and the number of people who could afford to buy books increased greatly.

Statistics show the importance of the printing press. In 1400, when each book
65 was copied by hand and was very expensive, few men could afford to buy books. Yet by 1966 over 300 million paperback books were bought annually in the United States alone! The printed page became a
70 major bond in communication.

1. Which one of the following areas is NOT mentioned as a birthplace of printing?

   (A) The Rhineland
   (B) China
   (C) Korea
   (D) Germany
   (E) France

2. Which one of the following did most people living between 1400 and 1600 NOT believe in?

   (A) Science
   (B) Witches
   (C) Superstition
   (D) Spirits
   (E) Demons

3. Which invention allowed the creation of books in great number?

   (A) Parchment
   (B) Printing press
   (C) Typewriter
   (D) Movable type
   (E) Printer's ink

4. The best meaning of the word "disassembled" (line 56) is

   (A) taken apart.
   (B) put together.
   (C) a large gathering.
   (D) destroyed.
   (E) erased.

5. The best title for this passage is

   (A) "The Problems of the Dark Ages."
   (B) "Great Progress in Invention."
   (C) "The Story of Gutenberg."
   (D) "Inventions Across the Continents."
   (E) "The Ignorance of the Dark Ages."

Passage 2

Line Bananas ripe and green, and gingerroot,
      Cocoa in pods and alligator pears,
      And tangerines and mangoes and grapefruit,
      Fit for the highest prize at parish fairs.
5   Set in the window, bringing memories
      Of fruit trees laden by low-singing rills,
      And dewy dawns, and mystical blue skies
      In benediction over nunlike hills.
      My eyes grew dim, and I could no more gaze;
10   A wave of longing through my body swept,
      And, hungry for the old, familiar ways,
      I turned aside and bowed my head and wept.

6. The first three lines of the poem mention fruits grown in the tropics. Where exactly does the poet find himself?

   (A) At a church fair
   (B) In the West Indies
   (C) In a dream
   (D) On a city street
   (E) On a farm

7. In lines 7 and 8, the poet uses the words "mystical," "benediction," and "nunlike" to create which of the following images?

   (A) A collection of fruit in a store
   (B) A church fair
   (C) An almost religious experience
   (D) A forest
   (E) A stage set

8. Why does the poet weep at the end of the poem?

   (A) The fruits have been eaten.
   (B) He is cut off from the past.
   (C) He did not win the prize.
   (D) The future appears to be difficult.
   (E) He has become ill.

9. What is the best meaning of "rills" in line 6?

    (A) Singers

    (B) Trees

    (C) Winds

    (D) Streams

    (E) Birds

10. The tone of this poem can best be described as

    (A) humorous.

    (B) indifferent.

    (C) ironic.

    (D) sad.

    (E) happy.

Passage 3

Line   Is Earth flat or round? Until 1522, most people believed Earth was flat. In that year one of Magellan's ships completed the first trip all the way around Earth. Long before
5   the explorer Magellan, however, early scientists thought that Earth was shaped like a ball. In geometry the ball shape is called a sphere, so the earth scientists said that Earth is spherical.
10   The spherical model of Earth is based on such evidence as the following:
      The mast of a ship was the first part to appear over the horizon. It was the last part to disappear. The traditional cry of the
15   lookout in a sailing vessel is, "I see a mast."
      When ships sailed north or south, sailors observed that the nighttime sky changed in appearance. The North Star rose higher in the sky as they sailed northward. It
20   sank in the sky as they sailed southward. The position of the North Star changed so gradually and so evenly that it could only be explained in one way. The ship was sailing on a spherical surface. When ships sailed far
25   enough south, constellations such as the Big Dipper could no longer be seen, but new ones such as the Southern Cross appeared in the sky. Would this be true on a flat Earth?

      An eclipse of the moon occurs when
30   Earth's shadow falls on the moon. During an eclipse of the moon, the edge of Earth's shadow as it moves across the moon is always the arc of a circle. Only a sphere casts a circular shadow, no matter what
35   position it is in.
      The evidence listed above is, of course, still visible today, although a lookout is much more likely to see a smokestack than a mast. But now everyone can see the
40   evidence. Many photographs of Earth have been taken by orbiting spacecraft. Other photographs of Earth have been taken from the moon by the Apollo astronauts.

11. In the context of the passage, the word "constellation" (line 25) most likely means

    (A) a group of planets.

    (B) a number of spheres.

    (C) a pattern of stars.

    (D) the Big Dipper.

    (E) the North Star.

12. When a ship sails north, the North Star

    (A) stays in the same place in the sky.

    (B) rises higher in the sky.

    (C) sinks lower in the sky.

    (D) becomes the Southern Cross.

    (E) changes shape.

13. In the paragraph describing an eclipse of the moon, we can infer that the

    (A) earth is flat.

    (B) moon is closer to the earth than the sun.

    (C) earth is in shadow.

    (D) moon has an orbit.

    (E) earth is spherical.

14. The title that best expresses the idea of this passage is

(A) "Magellan's Trip Around the World."
(B) "What We Need from the Moon."
(C) "Science Has All the Answers."
(D) "The Earth Is Spherical."
(E) "The Meaning of a Lunar Eclipse."

15. The deduction that the earth is round is based on all of the following EXCEPT the

(A) observation of eclipse.
(B) observations of sailors.
(C) observation of constellations.
(D) observations of philosophers.
(E) observations of astronauts.

Passage 4

Line Each town is built in a given site and
situation. If the surrounding terrain is
mountainous, a town's accessibility and,
therefore, much of its potential growth are
5 limited. Most of our large cities have grown
on fairly flat land. Here they have ready
accessibility as well as the important
advantage of the low cost of developing and
servicing flat land. Thus, topographic
10 differences between towns, affecting
accessibility and cost, can help some
communities grow at the expense of others.
 Nevertheless, landforms are more often
important in determining how (that is, in
15 what shape) towns and cities grow than
why they grow. For example, Amsterdam, a
city virtually built on water, and San
Francisco, which is built on steep hills and
surrounded on three sides by water,
20 continue to grow and prosper. Each of these
has developed a unique character, partly
because of its physical setting. In the early
days of town building, when sites were
chosen for defense (for example, the island
25 location of Montreal), the landforms limited
the towns' outward growth. Although these
original limitations have ceased to affect any
but the downtown areas, some modern

communities must still adapt to their sites.
30 The outposts of western Newfoundland,
which are limited to a narrow strip of land
between the mountains and the ocean,
provide one picturesque example.
 It has often been observed by conserva-
35 tionists that cities such as Vancouver,
Toronto, and Los Angeles have grown at the
expense of some of our best farmland. This
phenomenon does not mean, however, that
good soils are a prerequisite for urban
40 growth. Many of these cities were originally
agricultural market towns and grew because
farming prospered. Only when transportation improvements enabled long-distance
shipping of food could the city afford to
45 "bite off the land that feeds it." The ease and
low cost of building on flat land were also
significant factors.
 An example of this conflict between
urban and agricultural land uses is found in
50 the Niagara Peninsula fruit belt of Ontario.
This district has both sandy, well-drained
soils and a moderate climate suited for
tender-fruit growing, a very rare combination
in Canada. However, the soils and climate,
55 combined with its proximity to the Toronto-
Hamilton urban industrial complex, make
this region ideal for urban growth. As a
result, some of the most valuable and
irreplaceable farmland in southern Ontario
60 has been taken out of production and
built on.
 A pleasant climate has played a
significant role in the growth of some towns
and cities. Many Florida cities have pros-
65 pered because of an almost year-round
tourist trade. Arizona's warm dry winters
attract many people, often with respiratory
diseases, to Tucson, Phoenix, and other
urban centers. The famous climate of
70 southern California has been one of the
major factors in its rapid urbanization and
general population growth. Much of the
California boom was also due to the fact that

the film and airplane industries located there
75 to take advantage of the sunshine and warm
winters. Thus, some urban growth can best
be explained by environmental factors.

16. The main idea of this passage is

(A) important cities are built by water.
(B) a town should be built on flat land.
(C) Los Angeles grew at the expense of farmland.
(D) climate is crucial to urban growth.
(E) town growth is affected by environmental factors.

17. From this passage one can assume that a "conservationist" (lines 34–35) is interested in

(A) the creation of cities.
(B) determining the growth of cities.
(C) the best use of land.
(D) transportation of goods and services.
(E) the creation of parks.

18. What is most unusual about the Niagara Peninsula?

(A) Its mountains and desert
(B) Its warm, dry winters
(C) Its location to cultural centers
(D) Its sandy soil and moderate climate
(E) Its abundance of flat land

19. In building a town today, which of the following can be inferred to be least important based on the passage?

(A) Accessibility
(B) Flat land
(C) Climate
(D) Transportation
(E) Defense

20. The best title of this passage is

(A) "Population Growth."
(B) "Great Cities of the World."
(C) "The Suburb Versus the Inner City."
(D) "Vancouver, Toronto, and Los Angeles: Great Cities."
(E) "Environment and Its Effects on City Growth."

Passage 5

Line A single flow'r he sent me, since we met.
All tenderly his messenger he chose;
Deep-hearted, pure, with scented dew still
wet—One perfect rose.

5 I knew the language of the floweret;
"My fragile leaves," it said, "his heart enclose."
Love long has taken for his amulet
One perfect rose

Why is it no one ever sent me yet
10 One perfect limousine, do you suppose?
Ah no, it's always just my luck to get
One perfect rose.

21. What is the tone of the first two stanzas?

(A) Sarcastic
(B) Ironic
(C) Angry
(D) Irritated
(E) Serious

22. Which word changes the meaning of the poem?

(A) Tenderly (line 2)
(B) Floweret (line 5)
(C) Scented (line 3)
(D) Language (line 5)
(E) Limousine (line 10)

23. The first two lines of stanza two use which of the following literary devices?

(A) Alliteration
(B) Realism
(C) Personification
(D) Dialect
(E) Hyperbole

24. The best meaning for "scented" (line 3) is

(A) attractive to the sense of smell.
(B) wet.
(C) rose colored.
(D) attractive to touch.
(E) pure.

25. What event is being described in the poem?

(A) A dream
(B) A mixed reaction to a gift
(C) A tale of miscommunication
(D) The story of all love affairs
(E) A tale of a flower-delivery service

Passage 6

Line The major intellectual change of the
eighteenth century was the widespread
acceptance among educated people of the
idea that reason could achieve solutions to
5 problems of many kinds, whether scientific
or social. It is easy to see the origins of this
attitude in the rationalism of Descartes, the
scientific method of Francis Bacon, the
achievements of Newton and other
10 seventeenth-century scientists, and the
writing of John Locke on psychology.

The Enlightenment thinkers applied
Newtonian methods to problems in such
areas as psychology and education, govern-
15 ment, religion, law codes, treatment of
criminals, the slave trade, and economic life.
They acted on the assumption that the
universe operated according to natural law,
similar to the all-embracing law of gravita-
20 tion, which Newton had discovered. They
believed that individuals, using a rational
approach, could discover these natural laws.

As in science, this would not necessarily be
easy, for these laws had been obscured by
25 an accumulation of centuries-old customs,
prejudices, and superstitions, which did not
accord with natural laws. However, with
education and a clear-headed approach,
people could rid themselves of their
30 superstitions and prejudices. Then reform in
many areas of human relations could bring
laws and customs into a harmonious
relationship in a naturally orderly universe.

What has just been said is a very broad
35 generalization. Not all thinkers in the
eighteenth century had unquestioning faith
in reason and natural law. There were limits
to human reasoning powers, as some
pointed out. Emotion, or feelings, also
40 played a great part in governing human
behavior. These thinkers were not in the
majority, but they were read and respected.

The majority attitude described above
was basically optimistic in the outlook
45 toward life. It saw people as moving
forward, making progress toward a better
life (and even toward perfection) through
use of reason. Some writers felt that
progress was almost inevitable under these
50 circumstances. Others thought it was
necessary to work for progress along many
different lines. Those who denied that the
use of reason was the answer to all problems were viewed as skeptics. The faith in
55 progress caused eighteenth-century individuals to undertake many crusades for reform—
the elimination of slavery, the end of
religious intolerance, the reform of criminal
codes, and the guarantee of permanent
60 world peace, for example.

26. Which of the following is NOT an element of "natural law"?

(A) Superstition
(B) Rationalism
(C) The scientific method
(D) Reason
(E) Observation and discovery

27. Someone who believes in "natural law" would suggest humans should NOT be guided by

(A) intellect.
(B) the wish for an orderly universe.
(C) a sense of optimism.
(D) science.
(E) emotions.

28. The best meaning of "inevitable" (line 49) is

(A) rational.
(B) reasonable.
(C) necessary.
(D) impossible.
(E) improbable.

29. The best title for this passage is

(A) "The Newtonian Age."
(B) "Reason Versus Emotion."
(C) "Descartes, Bacon, and Locke."
(D) "Faith in Progress."
(E) "Ideas in the Age of Enlightenment."

30. An "enlightened" approach to government would yield all of the following EXCEPT

(A) a constitution.
(B) separation of powers.
(C) the rule of law.
(D) totalitarianism.
(E) democracy.

Passage 7

Line Although land and soil are generally thought to be renewable, several problems limit their renewability. One problem is that the areas with the most fertile soil are often the areas
5 with the greatest population density. Few crops are grown in mountain areas, deserts, or polar regions; few people live in those same areas. Most crops are grown on level land in moderate climates. Most people live
10 on fairly level land in moderate climates. In some areas of the world, the conflict between land for housing and land for crops is a critical problem. In Japan, about 85 percent of the land surface is mountainous.
15 The amount of land suitable for farming is, therefore, quite limited. The bulk of the Japanese population, including farmers, lives in the same 15 percent of the country. As a result, the conflict between using land for
20 housing and for farming is a critical one.

A second problem in land and soil use is soil depletion. Crop plants use certain nutrients in the soil, as do natural grasses. When natural grasses die, the nutrients are
25 returned to the soil. When crops are harvested, however, the nutrients are removed from the soil. In time, the soil can become so lacking in nutrients that it will no longer grow a usable crop. The problem of
30 soil depletion can be managed through good farming practices. Fields can be left to rest. A crop can be allowed to return to the soil. Or, the kind of crop grown on a field can be changed from year to year. These
35 practices are not always followed, however, because they can be very expensive in the short term.

A third problem in soil use is desertification. This occurs in areas where plant
40 cover has been removed by farming or by farm animals. When this happens, the bare soil can be easily removed by wind or rain, like the soil in a desert. The lost soil is

difficult to replace. The land has become
45 nonrenewable.

Salinization is a problem in desert areas.
With water, some desert soils are very
fertile. However, water brought in to irrigate
a desert contains minerals. The dry air of the
50 desert causes water to evaporate rapidly.
When this happens, minerals in the water,
such as salt, are left behind on the soil
surface. In time, the soil surface has so
much mineral matter that crops can no
55 longer be grown. Such soil is difficult to
reclaim.

31. Which one of the following is NOT a
problem in land and soil use?

(A) Salinization
(B) Desertification
(C) Soil depletion
(D) Natural grasses
(E) Population density

32. From the passage we can infer which of the
following?

(A) Soil depletion is too difficult a problem
to control.
(B) Desertification only occurs in mountainous areas.
(C) In the future the Japanese may have
difficulty growing enough crops for
the people.
(D) Soil depletion increases nutrients in the
land.
(E) Salinization is good for crops.

33. The best meaning of salinization is

(A) an increase of water in the desert.
(B) detoxification.
(C) plant cover removed by farm animals.
(D) the loss of nutrients.
(E) an increase of minerals and soil due to
loss of water.

34. The best title for this passage is

(A) "Problems in Land and Soil Use."
(B) "Desertification and Salinization."
(C) "Japan and Its Land."
(D) "The Best Crops to Grow."
(E) "How to Renew the Land."

35. A solution to all the problems mentioned in
the passage would be

(A) good farming practices.
(B) developing a better import system.
(C) setting wind screens around farms.
(D) growing all food in moderate climates.
(E) changing one's diet.

Passage 8

Line Whose woods these are I think I know
His house is in the village, though;
He will not see me stopping here
To watch his woods fill up with snow.

5 My little horse must think it queer
To stop without a farmhouse near
Between the woods and frozen lake
The darkest evening of the year.

He gives his harness bells a shake
10 To ask if there is some mistake.
The only other sound's the sweep
Of easy wind and downy flake.

The woods are lovely, dark and deep.
But I have promises to keep,
15 And miles to go before I sleep,
And miles to go before I sleep.

36. The speaker's horse "must think it queer to
stop" because

(A) the horse is used to completing its
journey.
(B) it is late at night.
(C) it is too cold.
(D) they have run out of food.
(E) the horse is cold.

37. What is the author's purpose in repeating the last line twice?

    (A) To reinforce the rhyme

    (B) To catch the attention of the horse

    (C) To show the contrast between the village and the farm

    (D) To add meaning to the word "sleep"

    (E) To wake the reader

38. The woods seem to have a special meaning for the speaker. Which is most likely?

    (A) He is interested in buying them.

    (B) He wants to build a new house there.

    (C) They seem to pull him in.

    (D) He is thinking about their owner in the village.

    (E) He is interested in farming.

39. Which literary technique is used to define the relationship between the speaker and the horse?

    (A) Alliteration

    (B) Rhyme

    (C) Irony

    (D) Exaggeration

    (E) Contrast

40. The best meaning for "downy" in line 12 is

    (A) frozen.

    (B) soft.

    (C) clean.

    (D) wind-swept.

    (E) cold.

QUANTITATIVE (MATH) 2   TIME: 30 MINUTES   25 QUESTIONS

Directions: Following each problem in this section, there are five suggested answers. Work each problem in your head or in the space provided (there will be space for scratchwork in your test booklet). Then look at the five suggested answers and decide which is best.

1. What is .03 expressed as a percent?

   (A) 30%
   (B) 3%
   (C) .3%
   (D) .03%
   (E) .003%

2. What is 72 expressed as the product of prime factors?

   (A) $(2)(3)$
   (B) $(2)(3)(12)$
   (C) $(2)(2)(2)(3)(3)$
   (D) $(8)(9)$
   (E) $(6)(6)(2)$

3. Fred invested $4,000 at a simple interest rate of 5.75%. What is the total value of his investment after one year?

   (A) $200
   (B) $230
   (C) $4,200
   (D) $4,230
   (E) $4,400

4. The area of a circle is the same as the area of a square whose side is 5 centimeters. The radius of the circle is closest to

   (A) 25 centimeters.
   (B) 3 centimeters.
   (C) 3 square centimeters.
   (D) 8 centimeters.
   (E) 16 centimeters.

5. Solve for x: $7x - 3 = 4x + 6$

   (A) 3
   (B) -1
   (C) 4
   (D) 2
   (E) -4

6. The length of a side of a square is represented by $x + 2$, and the length of a side of an equilateral triangle is represented by $2x$. If the square and the equilateral triangle have equal perimeters, find x.

   (A) 24
   (B) 16
   (C) 12
   (D) 8
   (E) 4

7. A bag has five green marbles and four blue marbles. If one marble is drawn at random, what is the possibility that it is NOT green?

   (A) $\dfrac{1}{9}$
   (B) $\dfrac{4}{9}$
   (C) $\dfrac{5}{9}$
   (D) $\dfrac{5}{20}$
   (E) $\dfrac{4}{20}$

8. The expression $\sqrt{162}$ is equivalent to:

   (A) $4\sqrt{2}$
   (B) $4 + \sqrt{2}$
   (C) $9\sqrt{2}$
   (D) $3\sqrt{2}$
   (E) $9 + \sqrt{2}$

9.

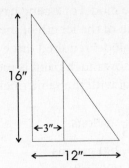

In the accompanying figure, the legs of a right triangle are 16 inches and 12 inches. Find the number of inches in the length of the line segment parallel to the 16-inch side and 3 inches from it.

(A) 16
(B) 12
(C) 9
(D) 15
(E) 10

10. On a map, 2 inches represent 15 miles. How many miles would 5 inches represent?

(A) 6
(B) 8
(C) 30
(D) $37\frac{1}{2}$
(E) 75

11.

Three congruent squares are arranged in a row. If the perimeter of $ABCD$ is 80, the area of $ABCD$ is

(A) 240
(B) 320
(C) 640
(D) 300
(E) 160

12. Express as a ratio in simplest form: 5 feet to 3 inches

(A) $\frac{5}{3}$
(B) $\frac{3}{5}$
(C) $\frac{60}{3}$
(D) $\frac{1}{20}$
(E) $\frac{20}{1}$

13. What is the slope of the line that passes through the point (2,6) and the point (7, −7)?

(A) $-\frac{13}{5}$
(B) $\frac{5}{13}$
(C) $-\frac{1}{5}$
(D) $\frac{13}{5}$
(E) $\frac{21}{7}$

14. 423,252 × 835,234 =

(A) 353,534,359,987
(B) 983,414,460,968
(C) 989,353,414,426
(D) 353,514,425,972
(E) 353,514,460,968

15. If points A, B, C, and D are collinear, and C is the midpoint of $\overline{AB}$, and B is the midpoint of $\overline{AD}$, and the length of $\overline{AD}$ is 24, what is the length of $\overline{CD}$?

(A) 12
(B) 24
(C) 18
(D) 6
(E) It cannot be determined.

16. If $x = 4$ on the graph of $y = -5x + 4$, what does y equal?

    (A) -1
    (B) 5
    (C) -5
    (D) 16
    (E) -16

17. What is the graph of the inequality $6 < x \leq 9$?

    (A)
    (B)
    (C)
    (D)
    (E)

18. What is $3x^5$ divided by $4x^7$?

    (A) $7x^{12}$
    (B) $12x^{12}$
    (C) $\dfrac{3}{4x^2}$
    (D) $12x^{35}$
    (E) $\dfrac{4x^2}{3}$

19. Express .075 as a percent.

    (A) 75%
    (B) 7.5%
    (C) .75%
    (D) .075%
    (E) 8%

20. A scale model of a cube has sides that are one fortieth of the length of the original. If the scale model required three gallons of paint to coat, how much paint is required to coat the original with the same thickness of paint?

    (A) $\dfrac{40}{3}$ gallons
    (B) 7,280 gallons
    (C) 4,800 gallons
    (D) 240 gallons
    (E) 120 gallons

21. Dinner (plus tax and tip) cost $93.60. The tax rate is 5% and Mr. Simmons left a 15% tip. Both tax and tip are calculated on the base amount of the check. What was the base amount of Mr. Simmons's bill?

    (A) $78.00
    (B) $113.32
    (C) $77.41
    (D) $112.00
    (E) $81.30

22. What is the area of a square whose diagonal is 6?

    (A) 36
    (B) 24
    (C) 18
    (D) 12
    (E) $6\sqrt{2}$

23. Which fraction lies between $\dfrac{2}{3}$ and $\dfrac{4}{5}$?

    (A) $\dfrac{5}{6}$
    (B) $\dfrac{17}{20}$
    (C) $\dfrac{7}{10}$
    (D) $\dfrac{13}{15}$
    (E) $\dfrac{9}{10}$

24. The circumference of a circle whose diameter is 7 inches is approximately

(A) 22 inches.
(B) 28 inches.
(C) 38 inches.
(D) 154 inches.
(E) 14 inches.

25.

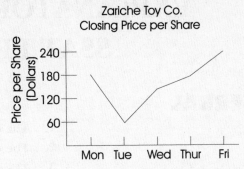

Zariche Toy Co.
Closing Price per Share

Josie bought 16 shares of Zariche stock at the closing price Monday and sold them at the closing price on Friday. What was Josie's profit on this investment?

(A) $60
(B) $96
(C) $600
(D) $960
(E) None of the above

EXPLANATORY ANSWERS TO THE
SSAT PRACTICE TEST 2

VERBAL

1. The correct answer is (C).
2. The correct answer is (D).
3. The correct answer is (A).
4. The correct answer is (C).
5. The correct answer is (B).
6. The correct answer is (D).
7. The correct answer is (E).
8. The correct answer is (A).
9. The correct answer is (A).
10. The correct answer is (D).
11. The correct answer is (D).
12. The correct answer is (A).
13. The correct answer is (B).
14. The correct answer is (D).
15. The correct answer is (C).
16. The correct answer is (B).
17. The correct answer is (C).
18. The correct answer is (A).
19. The correct answer is (E).
20. The correct answer is (B).
21. The correct answer is (B).
22. The correct answer is (C).
23. The correct answer is (E).
24. The correct answer is (A).
25. The correct answer is (D).
26. The correct answer is (E).
27. The correct answer is (D).
28. The correct answer is (B).
29. The correct answer is (C).
30. The correct answer is (C).

31. **The correct answer is (A).** One of the characteristics of a *mountain* is its *height*. One of the characteristics of a *trench* is its *depth*. Choice (B) will not work. While shade is often a characteristic of a tree, it is not a persistent characteristic, meaning that a tree does not always give shade. In addition, a mountain possesses height, but a tree GIVES shade. Choice (C) is incorrect: a characteristic of age is not always weight. The relationship is not the same as height and mountain. Choice (D) is incorrect: while we often associate speed with a highway, speed is not a characteristic of the highway. Choice (E) is incorrect: while a mineral comes from a mine, it is not a characteristic of the mine. It is a product of the mine. The relationship is not the same as height and mountain.

32. **The correct answer is (A).** Someone who is *oblivious* lacks *awareness*. The relationship is word to antonym or opposites. Choice (B) is incorrect. The relationship here is synonyms. One who is serene is composed. Choice (C) is incorrect. Again, the relationship is synonyms. One who is erudite possesses knowledge. Choice (D) is incorrect: one who is adroit possesses skill. The relationship is synonymous. Choice (E) is incorrect: the relationship is that of synonyms. One who is invigorated possesses energy.

33. **The correct answer is (D).** A *cynosure* functions as a *magnet*. A cynosure is the center of attention, or a magnet: a magnet attracts attention. The relationship is object to its function. A *bellwether* is a *barometer*. Choice (A) is incorrect: a proselyte does not function as a spark plug. Choice (B) is incorrect: a panhandler does not kill. Choice (C) is incorrect: an embezzler does not abduct. Choice (E) is incorrect: a morass (swamp) does not function as a catalyst (leavening).

34. **The correct answer is (D).** The relationship is word and derived form. The word "action" derives from the word "act." Choice (A) is incorrect: thermometer (temperature measure) does not derive from the word "therapy." There is no relationship. Choice (B) is incorrect: the relationship is antonyms or opposites. Oblivion means forgotten and obvious means apparent. The relationship is different. Choice (C) is incorrect: Liturgy (ritual) does not provide the root for the word "literature," which means a body of work. Choice (E) is incorrect: bowl (goblet) does not form the root for bowdlerize, which means to modify. There is no relationship.

35. **The correct answer is (B).** The relationship is object to its function. One who is *bibulous* consumes more *drink* than is advisable. Choice (B) is the correct answer because one who is *gluttonous* consumes more *food* than is advisable. Choice (A) is incorrect: rapacious (taken by force) has no relationship to clothing. Choice (C) is incorrect: one who is altruistic (concerned for the welfare of others) would not have more money than was advisable. The relationship is not the same. Choice (D) is incorrect. A vegetarian would not consume more meat than advisable. Choice (E) is incorrect: controversy and reconcile have the relationship of opposites.

36. **The correct answer is (A).** *Venison* is the meat of a *deer*. The relationship is part to whole. *Veal* is the meat of a *calf*. Choices (B), (C), (D), and (E) are incorrect because although they are animals from which we get meat, we do not get veal from any of them.

37. **The correct answer is (D).** *Cursory* and *superficial* are both adjectives and are synonyms—they have the same meaning. Choices (A), (B), and (C) are incorrect because the answers, while both adjectives, are antonyms—they have opposite meanings. Choice (E) is incorrect because the relationship is cause to effect.

38. **The correct answer is (C).** *Bacchus* is the god of *wine; Diana* is the goddess of the *hunt*. This is a worker and creation relationship. Choice (A) is incorrect because both Orpheus and Eurydice are mythological gods. Choices (B) and (D) are incorrect because the relationship is unclear. Choice (E) is incorrect because the relationship is item to category.

39. **The correct answer is (C).** *Bald* and *hairy* are antonyms. *Anemic* and *robust* are antonyms. Choices (A) and (E) are incorrect because the words are synonyms. Choices (B) and (D) are incorrect because the words are not related specifically.

40. **The correct answer is (D).** *Gold* was important to *Midas; wisdom* was important to *Athena*. The relationship is worker and creation. Choices (A) and (C) are incorrect because the relationship is item to category. Choice (B) is incorrect because the relationship is synonymous. Choice (E) is incorrect because the relationship is type to characteristic.

41. **The correct answer is (D).** A *philanthropist* is very *generous*. A *teacher* is usually very *educated*. The relationship is type to characteristic. Choice (A) is incorrect because the relationship is worker to workplace, a dentist works on teeth. Choice (B) is incorrect because the words are antonyms. Choice (C) is incorrect because the relationship is worker and workplace: a rider rides on a horse. Choice (E) is incorrect because the words are synonyms.

42. **The correct answer is (D).** All choices except (A) involve the activity of a bodily organ. Both *exhale* and *perspire* involve giving off something from within the body.

43. **The correct answer is (D).** The Nazis persecuted many during the Nuremburg trials, the place of prosecution. The relationship is object to its function. Choice (A) is incorrect because the judge and jury work together. Choice (B) is incorrect because the relationship is worker to workplace: a guard works in a prison. Choice (C) is incorrect because the relationship is type to characteristic. Marx was a communist. Choice (E) is incorrect because it is cause to effect. A gun causes death.

44. **The correct answer is (C).** A wrongdoing connected with politics is bribery, as cheating is a wrongdoing connected with examinations. The relationship is type to characteristic. Choices (A) and (B) are incorrect because the relationship is object to function: one parks at a meter; one may use contracts in a business. Choice (D) is incorrect because it is time sequence. Birds nest, then leave. Choice (E) is incorrect because the relationship is cause and effect: a painting earns a commission.

45. **The correct answer is (C).** A fraud, a cheater, an impostor, and an impersonator refer to people who are fakes. The relationship is synonymous. Choices (A), (B), and (D) are incorrect because while similar in many ways, the words are not synonyms. Choice (E) is incorrect because the words are antonyms.

46. **The correct answer is (D).** *Bacon* is sold by the *pound; eggs* are sold by the *dozen.* The relationship is part to whole. Choices (A) and (B) are incorrect because the relationship is item to category: a gun is made of lead; a dime is made of silver. Choice (C) is incorrect because the relationship is worker and workplace: a chandelier is located on the ceiling. Choice (E) is incorrect because the relationship is worker to creation. A puppet show is the work of the puppet maker.

47. **The correct answer is (A).** The relationship is sequential. *Impeachment* (accusation) comes before *dismissal. Arraignment* (accusation) comes before *conviction.*

48. **The correct answer is (D).** A *limousine* is a luxurious *car,* as a *mansion* is a luxurious *house.* The relationship is item to category. Choice (A) is incorrect because the relationship, while item to category, is not the same relationship. House and cave indicate lack of luxury. Choice (B) is incorrect because the relationship is modes of transportation. Choice (C) is incorrect because the relationship is object to material: an animal is covered with fur. Choice (E) is incorrect: stone and pebble are synonyms.

49. **The correct answer is (C).** Warts, moles, mildew, and weeds are all unwanted growths. This is a part-to-whole relationship.

50. **The correct answer is (D).** A *bass* sings in a *low* register; a *soprano* sings in a *high* register. The words are antonyms. Choice (A) is incorrect because art and music are forms of fine arts; they are a type of synonym. Choice (B) is incorrect: while light and shading are similar, they are not synonyms. Choice (C) is incorrect: while govern and dictate are both forms of government, they are not synonymous. Choice (E) is incorrect because a chorus is made up of many people, while a solo is performed by only one.

51. **The correct answer is (C).** We *braid hair,* as we *wind* a *clock.* To braid and to wind are actions applied to objects.

52. **The correct answer is (B).** *Blades* make up *grass* as *grains* make up *sand.* The relationship is that of part to whole. Choices (A), (D), and (E) are incorrect because the relationship is type to characteristic. Choice (C) has no obvious relationship other than rods may be made of metal.

53. **The correct answer is (C).** An *athlete* needs *training* to succeed: a *student* needs *studying* to succeed. The relationship is object to its function. Choice (A) is incorrect because the relationship is worker and creation. Choice (B) is incorrect because the relationship is worker to workplace. Choices (D) and (E) are incorrect because the relationship is that of antonyms.

54. **The correct answer is (D).** A *novel* is written by an *author.* An *opera* is written by a *composer.* The relationship is worker and creation. Choices (A) and (C) are incorrect because they show cause to effect. Choice (B) is incorrect because the relationship is that of synonyms. Choice (E) is incorrect because the relationship is part to whole. Several songs make up a tape.

55. **The correct answer is (C).** A *miser* desires *gold* as a *general* desires *victories.* The relationship is cause to effect. Choice (A) is incorrect because the relationship is item to category. Choice (B) is incorrect because it is worker and creation. Choice (D) is incorrect because it is worker to workplace. Choice (E) is incorrect because the relationship is that of synonyms.

56. **The correct answer is (E).** A *centaur* is a mythological *horse.* A *mermaid* is a mythological *fish.* The relationship is that of synonyms. Choice (A) is incorrect because it is the relationship of worker and creation. Choices (B) and (D) are incorrect because they are both item to category in relationship. Choice (C) is incorrect because there is no relationship.

57. **The correct answer is (B).** A *foot* moves against a *pedal,* as a *bat* hits against a *ball.* The relationship is action to object. Choices (A) and (C) are incorrect because the relationship is worker and workplace. Choices (D) and (E) are incorrect because the relationship is object to material.

58. **The correct answer is (C).** We *start* a car with the *ignition;* we *stop* a car with the *brake.* The relationship is action to object. Choices (A) and (B) are incorrect since the relationship is object to its function. Choices (D) and (E) are incorrect because the relationship is object to its material. A tire needs air; a tank needs gas.

59. **The correct answer is (E).** To *push* is an extreme *touch;* to *gulp* is an extreme *sip.* All four words are verbs. The relationship is type to characteristic. Choice (A) is incorrect. While the relationship is similar, the item to category relationship would better fit: both items are drinks. However, the words are nouns and therefore not a true analogy. Choice (B) is incorrect. The words are synonyms. Choice (C) is incorrect; one uses a glass to drink, therefore the relationship is item to function. Choice (D) is incorrect because the words are antonyms.

60. **The correct answer is (D).** *Bananas* are collected by the *bunch; lettuce* is collected by the *head.* The relationship is type to characteristic. Choice (A) is incorrect because the words are synonyms. Choice (B) is incorrect because the words are antonyms. Choice (C) is incorrect because the relationship is item to category—both words represent members of the fowl family. Choice (E) is incorrect because it is object to function: a surgeon performs an operation.

QUANTITATIVE (MATH) 1

1. **The correct answer is (D).**

    Factor out each of the given possibilities.

    The factors of 10 are 2×5.

    The factors of 45 are $3 \times 3 \times 5$.

    The factors of 50 are $2 \times 5 \times 5$.

    The factors of 60 are $2 \times 2 \times 3 \times 5$.

    The factors of 90 are $2 \times 3 \times 3 \times 5$.

    Since $4 = 2 \times 2$, 60 has factors of 4 and 5.

2. **The correct answer is (A).** Translate the sentence into a mathematical equation, then solve.

    $$x - 4 = \frac{2}{3}x$$

    $$x - \frac{2}{3}x = 4$$

    $$\frac{1}{3}x = 4$$

    $$x = 4\left(\frac{3}{1}\right) = 12$$

3. **The correct answer is (B).**

    $$score = \frac{\# \; correct}{\# \; questions}; \; 84\% = \frac{84}{100} = .84$$

    $$.84 = \frac{n}{25}$$

    $$n = .84 \times 25 = 21$$

4. **The correct answer is (C).** Rearrange the fractions to make it easier to solve by combining fractions with like denominators.

    $$\frac{1}{2} - \frac{1}{2} + \frac{2}{3} - \frac{1}{3} - \frac{1}{3} + \frac{3}{4} + \frac{1}{4}$$

    The first five fractions equal zero, leaving

    $$\frac{3}{4} + \frac{1}{4} = \frac{4}{4} = 1.$$

5. **The correct answer is (C).** The perimeter of a square is $4s$. With side length $= 4$, the perimeter is $4(4) = 16$.

    The perimeter of a rectangle is $2L + 2W$. With length $= 6$ and width $= 4$, the perimeter is $2(6) + 2(4) = 12 + 8 = 20$.

    The difference between the perimeters is $20 - 16 = 4$.

6. **The correct answer is (A).**

Round $19.95 to $20.00 and find 40% of 20.

$$40\% = \frac{40}{100} = .4$$
$$.4 \times 20 = 8$$

7. **The correct answer is (B).** Two students make up one fifth of a class.

Translating this into a mathematical equation, you get $\frac{1}{5}c = 2$.

$$c = 2\left(\frac{5}{1}\right) = 10$$

8. **The correct answer is (B).**

Let d represent Don's age now and $d + 5$ represent Don's age 5 years from now.

Let p represent Peter's age now and $p + 5$ represent Peter's age 5 years from now.

Set up mathematical equations for the problem.

$$d = p + 5$$
$$d + 5 = 2p$$

Substitute the value of d in the first equation into the second equation to find p.

$$(p + 5) + 5 = 2p$$
$$p + 10 = 2p$$
$$p = 10$$

9. **The correct answer is (B).** Set up a ratio for this problem and solve:

p represents the number of pieces of candy purchased with c cents $\left(\frac{p}{c}\right)$.

20 pieces of candy can be purchased for x cents $\left(\frac{20}{x}\right)$.

So,

$$\frac{p}{c} = \frac{20}{x}$$

$px = 20c$ (using cross-multiplication)

$$\frac{20c}{p} = x$$

10. **The correct answer is (C).**

$4,500,000 is t times greater than $750,000.

$$4,500,000 = 750,000t$$
$$t = \frac{4,500,000}{750,000} = 6$$

11. **The correct answer is (B).**

    This is a 45-45-90 triangle. Since this is true, the base is also 5 units long.

    By the Pythagorean Theorem, $v^2 = 5^2 + 5^2 = 25 + 25 = 50$.

12. **The correct answer is (C).**

    Let o represent the amount of oats eaten, and g the amount of grass eaten.

    Since twice as many pounds of oats are eaten as grass, $o = 2g$.

    $o + g = 30$

    Substituting the value for o into $o + g = 30$ gives $2g + g = 30$.

    So, $3g = 30$, and $g = 10$.

13. **The correct answer is (E).**

    $$3x - 9 = 18$$
    $$3x = 27$$
    $$x = 9$$
    $$9 \div 9 = 1$$

14. **The correct answer is (D).** There are 180° in a triangle and 360° in a rectangle (made up of four 90° angles).

    The difference is $360° - 180° = 180°$.

    One half of 180° is 90°.

15. **The correct answer is (E).**

    Let g represent the number of gorillas, and let t represent the number of tigers.

    If there are 4 times as many gorillas as tigers, then $g = 4t$.

    If there are 4 more tigers than zebras, then $t = z + 4$.

    To find the number of gorillas in terms of zebras, substitute the first equation into the second.

    Then, $g = 4(z + 4) = 4z + 16$.

16. **The correct answer is (D).** In four days, a cat sleeps $4\left(\dfrac{3}{4}\right) = 3$ full days.

17. **The correct answer is (A).** To determine if a number is divisible by 9, the sum of the digits in that number will equal a number divisible by 9. The sum of the digits in 2,042 is $2 + 0 + 4 + 2 = 8$. By adding 1 to this number, the sum of the digits will equal 9 and therefore be divisible by 9.

18. **The correct answer is (D).**

    4 girls make 2 projects each for a subtotal of $4 \times 2 = 8$.

    5 boys make 3 projects each for a subtotal of $5 \times 3 = 15$.

    The total number of projects made is $8 + 15 = 23$.

19. **The correct answer is (E).**

The area of the rectangle is $l \times w = 8 \times 3 = 24$.

The area of the triangle is $\frac{1}{2}bh = \frac{1}{2}6h$.

Since the areas are equal, set the equations equal to each other to determine the height of the triangle.

$$\frac{1}{2}6h = 24$$

$$3h = 24$$

$$h = 8$$

20. **The correct answer is (D).** Substitute 10 for r and 2 for s.

$$(10 \times 2) - (10 + 2) = 20 - 12 = 8$$

21. **The correct answer is (D).**

$$(4 \clubsuit 3) = \frac{30}{L}$$

$$(4 \clubsuit 3) = (4 \times 3) - (4 + 3) = 12 - 7 = 5$$

$$5 = \frac{30}{L}$$

$$L = \frac{30}{5} = 6$$

22. **The correct answer is (E).** To score an average of 91 on 4 exams, the total of the 4 exams added together must be $91 \times 4 = 364$. On her first 3 exams, Jesse has scored a total of $88 + 86 + 90 = 264$. Therefore, she needs 100 points on her last exam.

23. **The correct answer is (A).**

$$3x - 8 = 10x - 13$$

$$3x = 10x - 5$$

$$-7x = -5$$

$$x = \frac{-5}{-7} = \frac{5}{7}$$

24. **The correct answer is (C).** 15% expressed as a decimal is .15, so you can either calculate the discount $(.15)(75) = 11.25$ and subtract this from the original price of $75, getting $63.75, or you can calculate the final price directly. It will be 85% of the original price $(100\% - 15\% = 85\%)$, $(.85)(75) = 63.75$.

25. **The correct answer is (C).** Use the formula $A = \frac{1}{2}bh$.

$$75 = \frac{1}{2}(15)h$$

$$\frac{75}{7.5} = \frac{7.5h}{7.5}$$

$$10 \text{ inches} = h$$

READING COMPREHENSION

Passage 1

1. **The correct answer is (E).** France is mentioned in the passage but not in connection with the emergence of the printing press. Choice (A) is tricky since the Rhineland is part of Germany. Choices (B), (C), and (D) are all clearly mentioned in the passage.

2. **The correct answer is (A).** They believed in science, which is clearly stated in the first paragraph. Choices (B), (C), (D), and (E) are listed as beliefs in the same paragraph.

3. **The correct answer is (D).** Movable type allowed multiple copies to be made. Choices (B) and (E) are close—without them you could not have printing, but, by themselves, large amounts of books could not be made. Choices (A) and (C) are inappropriate.

4. **The correct answer is (A).** Choice (B) is an antonym, which is often used in the vocabulary question. Choices (D) and (E) are both close to choice (A) in meaning but are still incorrect. Choice (C) is used to trick the student who read half the word or just rushed through this too quickly.

5. **The correct answer is (B).** It is the main idea of the passage. Choice (A) is only a reference to the first paragraph. Choice (C) is close but not enough stress is placed on his role to warrant the title. Choice (D) is also close but is too specific. Choice (E) is inappropriate.

Passage 2

6. **The correct answer is (D).** These fruits are "set in a window." Choice (A) is a trick answer; these fruits could win a prize at a fair. Choice (B) is where the fruits come from; they are grown, perhaps, in choice (E). The experience makes him "dream," choice (C), but it was quite real.

7. **The correct answer is (C).** The poet's past is brought back to life for him. Choice (A) is the result of the first three lines, which could win at choice (B), but they are not an image of lines 7 and 8. Choices (D) and (E) are inappropriate.

8. **The correct answer is (B).** In his new town, the poet has lost his tropical past and it grieves him. We, perhaps, can infer choice (D), but the poem does not support this fully. Choices (A), (C), and (E) are all inappropriate.

9. **The correct answer is (D).** It refers to the babbling sounds water can make. Choice (E) is a trick answer; the birds can be in the trees. Choices (A) and (C) can both "sing" but are inappropriate, as is choice (B).

10. **The correct answer is (D).** The poet misses his life in the tropics. There is a touch of choice (E), which is overwhelmed by the wistfulness of the last 4 lines. Choices (A), (B), and (C) are inappropriate (although they are words you should know).

Passage 3

11. **The correct answer is (C).** Choice (D) is an example of the definition; therefore, it is not the same as the definition. Choices (A) and (B) describe groupings that are not constellations. Choice (E) refers to one star, not a group of stars.

12. **The correct answer is (B).** This tests your ability to read for detail. Choices (A) and (C) attempt to confuse the reader by giving the opposite seemingly logical but incorrect responses. Choice (D) refers to a constellation mentioned in the passage, which has little to do with the North Star. Choice (E) is not mentioned in the passage.

13. **The correct answer is (E).** This tests your ability to figure out what is suggested by a passage. Choice (A) is the opposite, and though choices (B) and (D) are correct ideas, they are not proved by the passage. Choice (C) misstates a fact.

14. **The correct answer is (D).** Choices (A) and (B) mentioned details from the passage, but they do not tell the whole story. Choice (C) is a false inference, and choice (E) refers to a possible proof of choice (D).

15. **The correct answer is (D).** Choices (A), (B), (C), and (E) are all details mentioned in the passage. Choice (D) may be true, but the passage deals only with scientific concepts.

Passage 4

16. **The correct answer is (E).** It covers the main points of the passage. Choices (A) and (C) are factual examples presented in the passage and thus do not deserve to be called the main ideas. Choices (B) and (D) can be inferred from the passage, but, again, these facts are not large enough to cover the whole passage.

17. **The correct answer is (C).** It covers the way cities use their resources. Choice (B) is very close and is one part of a conservationist's view, as is choice (E). Choices (A) and (D) are concepts interesting to conservationists, but they are not as central or as broad as choice (C).

18. **The correct answer is (D).** It is clearly stated in the fourth paragraph. Choices (B) and (E) are facts in the passage unconnected to the question, and choices (A) and (C) are inappropriate.

19. **The correct answer is (E).** This factor was most important in the "early days of town building," and other factors mentioned above have taken precedence.

20. **The correct answer is (E).** Every paragraph details examples of how the environment affects the growth of cities. Choice (A) is a general statement that affects city growth, but it is not the focus of this passage. Choice (D) mentions cities in the passage, but this detail does not make it worthy of becoming the title.

Passage 5

21. **The correct answer is (E).** You have to hear the author's voice to figure out his or her attitude. Given stanza three, one might think choice (B) is possible. Choices (A), (C), and (D) cannot be found in the poem.

22. **The correct answer is (E).** "Limousine" changes the poem from serious to amusing. Choices (A), (B), and (C) are words that signify love and its meaning, while choice (D) refers to what the flower means.

23. **The correct answer is (C).** The author has the rose speak. This is clearly not an example of choice (B). Choice (E), hyperbole (which means exaggeration), is the closest to the correct answer. Choices (A) and (D) are incorrect, but well worth looking up.

24. **The correct answer is (A).** The dew receives its smell from the rose. The dew may be rose-colored, but that is not the meaning of "scented." Choices (B), (D), and (E) are all inappropriate.

25. **The correct answer is (B).** One has to infer the positive response in lines 1–8 as a contrast to the wry response of lines 9–12. Choice (C) is close, but the receiver of the rose just has a different interpretation of what a rose can mean. Choice (A) is off base, and choices (D) and (E) are inappropriate.

Passage 6

26. **The correct answer is (A).** The concept of natural law is a reaction to superstition and contains aspects of choices (B), (C), (D), and (E).

27. **The correct answer is (E).** If you believe in natural law, emotions become secondary guides to truth. All the other responses are essential elements of the Age of Enlightenment discussed in the passage.

28. **The correct answer is (C).** It is closest to the exact meaning of inevitable (something must occur). The other words all "fit" in the sentence, but the larger context yields the best definition.

29. **The correct answer is (E).** This title is broad enough to cover all the subjects mentioned in the passage. Choices (A), (B), (C), and (D) are all aspects covered in the material, but they are not large enough to cover the concepts mentioned above.

30. **The correct answer is (D).** You must deduce from the Enlightenment concepts mentioned in the passage (rationalism, natural law, reason) that "totalitarianism" is least compatible. All the other answers can be defended by the ideas presented in the passage.

Passage 7

31. **The correct answer is (D).** Natural grasses help maintain land and soil use. The rest are examples of problems detailed in the passage.

32. **The correct answer is (C).** Only 10 percent of land in Japan is arable. Choice (A) is contradicted by the facts as are choices (D) and (E). Choice (B) is incorrect even though deserts could occur at high elevations.

33. **The correct answer is (E).** Choices (A), (C), and (D) are definitions of other terms in the passage. Choice (B) sounds like the word, but is far from defining it.

34. The correct answer is (A). Each paragraph deals with a specific issue of land and soil use. Choice (B) is close, but soil depletion is not mentioned. Choice (C) deals with the lead paragraph only. Choices (D) and (E) refer to topics connected to the passage but not mentioned here.

35. The correct answer is (A). It is mentioned in the second paragraph and implied in the other paragraphs. Choice (B) sounds good but is only a stopgap measure. Choice (C) may be helpful but is only worthwhile on a small scale. Choice (D) sounds correct but doesn't refer to how the food is grown. Choice (E) does not work at all.

Passage 8

36. The correct answer is (A). To complete its journey is to return or go to a farmhouse. Choices (B) and (C) refer to factual elements of the poem, but neither provides compelling reasons for the horse to "think it queer." Choice (D) is not supported by the poem, and neither is choice (E).

37. The correct answer is (D). "Sleep" is not only rest but eternal rest in this context. Choice (A) is a good answer about the poem's form but not nearly as strong as choice (D). Choices (B), (C), and (E) are not supported by the poem.

38. The correct answer is (C). The woods seem to pull him in because of their beauty and perhaps for a deeper, undisclosed reason. Even though he mentions the owner, choices (A) and (D) are not appropriate. Choices (B) and (E) are not supported by the poem.

39. The correct answer is (E). This best explains the difference between the horse and speaker. Choice (D) is the closest of the others, but it is used to point out the essential contrast. Choices (A), (B), and (C) are literary terms one should know, but they do not answer the question properly.

40. The correct answer is (B). Downy refers to the soft feathers of a swan, for example. Choice (D) is closest since the flakes are "wind-swept" but this does not refer to the feel of the flakes. Choices (A), (C), and (E) are elements in the poem but do not convey the meaning of downy.

QUANTITATIVE (MATH) 2

1. The correct answer is (B). To rename a decimal as a percent, multiply the decimal by 100.

$$.03 \times 100 = 3.00 = 3\%$$

2. The correct answer is (C). A prime number is a number that is divisible by itself and by 1. Hence, $72 = 8 \times 9 = 2 \times 2 \times 2 \times 3 \times 3$ → 2 and 3 are prime numbers

3. **The correct answer is (D).**

First find the amount of interest.

$I = P \times R \times T$

$ = \$4,000 \times .0575 \times 1 = \$230$

Add the amount of interest to the original amount to get the total amount after one year.

4. **The correct answer is (B).**

First find the area of the square.

$A = s^2$

$ = 5^2 = 25$ sq. cm.

Then, use the formula: $A = \pi r^2$

$25 \approx (3.14)r^2$

$7.96 \approx r^2$

$\sqrt{7.96} \approx r$

2.8 cm $\approx r$

5. **The correct answer is (A).**

Combine like terms by additive inverse:

$$\begin{array}{rl} 7x - 3 = & 4x + 6 \\ -4x + 3 = & -4x + 3 \\ \hline 3x = & 9 \end{array}$$

Divide 9 by 3.

$x = 3$

6. **The correct answer is (E).**

The perimeter of the square $= 4s$.

$P = 4s = 4(x + 2) = 4x + 8$

The perimeter of the equilateral triangle is $3s$.

$P = 3s = 3(2)\, x = 6x$

$ 4x + 8 = 6x$

$ 8 = 2x$

$ 4 = x$

7. **The correct answer is (B).** There are 4 marbles that are not green out of a total of 9 marbles, so $\dfrac{4}{9}$.

483

8. **The correct answer is (C).**

   Find two factors of 162, one of which is a perfect square.

   $$\sqrt{162} = \sqrt{81 \times 2}$$
   $$= \sqrt{81}\sqrt{2} \text{ (simplify perfect square)}$$
   $$\sqrt{81} = 9$$
   $$= 9\sqrt{2}$$

9. **The correct answer is (B).**

   If a line is parallel to one side of a triangle and intersects the other two sides, the line divides those sides proportionately.

   $$\frac{16}{12} = \frac{x}{9}$$
   $$12x = (16)(9)$$
   $$12x = 144 \text{ and } x = 12$$

10. **The correct answer is (D).**

    This problem can very easily be solved using a proportion:

    $$\frac{2 \text{ inches}}{15 \text{ miles}} = \frac{5 \text{ inches}}{x \text{ miles}}$$

    After cross-multiplication, this proportion becomes

    $$2x = 75$$
    $$x = 37\frac{1}{2}$$

11. **The correct answer is (D).** Count all the exterior sides of *ABCD;* 8 sides make up the perimeter, which is 80. So, 1 side = 10.

    area of rectangle = (length) × (width)

    length (*DC*) = 30

    width (*AD*) = 10

    Area = (30)(10) = 300

12. **The correct answer is (E).** Convert all measurements to the same units, such as inches. 5 feet is 60 inches. We now have the ratio 60 inches to 3 inches, expressed as $\frac{60}{3}$, and this simplifies to $\frac{20}{1}$.

    The ratio $\frac{60}{3}$, while correct, is not in simplest form.

13. **The correct answer is (A).** Slope is rise divided by run. Rise is the change in *y*-coordinate, run is the change in *x*-coordinate. Be sure you use the same point as the "first" point in both cases, or the algebraic sign will be wrong!

    $$\frac{rise}{run} = \frac{6 - (-7)}{2 - 7} = \frac{13}{-5} = -\frac{13}{5}$$

14. **The correct answer is (E).** No tedious multiplying is necessary. The last digit of each factor determines what the last digit of the product is; in this case it must be 8. There are only two answers that end in 8. A quick approximate multiplication (400,000 × 800,000) yields 320,000,000,000, ruling out choice (B).

15. **The correct answer is (C).**

A   C   B   D

C is the midpoint of $\overline{AB}$, so $\overline{AC}$ and $\overline{CB}$ are congruent and each is equal to half the measure of $\overline{AB}$. B is the midpoint of $\overline{AD}$ so $\overline{AB}$ and $\overline{BD}$ are congruent. This makes $\overline{AC}$ equal to one fourth the measure of $\overline{AD}$.

If AD is 24, then AC is 6, CB is 6, and BD is 12.

CD is $6 + 12 = 18$.

16. **The correct answer is (E).**

$$y = -5x + 4$$
$$y = -5(4) + 4$$
$$y = -20 + 4 = -16$$

17. **The correct answer is (A).** x is less than or equal to 9, and at the same time, x is greater than 6. The values between 6 and 9 satisfy this condition. The value 9 but not 6 also satisfies this condition. An open circle would indicate "less than" or "greater than" a condition at an endpoint, while a filled-in circle would indicate an endpoint is "less than or equal to" (or "greater than or equal to") a condition.

18. **The correct answer is (C).**

When dividing terms, subtract the exponents. You can see this by expanding. Remember x^5 is $x \times x \times x \times x \times x$ and x^7 is $x \times x \times x \times x \times x \times x \times x$. Then just divide. This is the basis for the rules of exponents.

$$\frac{3 \times x \times x \times x \times x \times x}{4 \times x \times x \times x \times x \times x \times x \times x} = \frac{3}{4x^2}$$

19. **The correct answer is (B).** To express a percent as a decimal, divide by 100. To express a decimal as a percent, multiply by 100. Literally, percent ("per cent") means "per hundred."

$.075 \times 100 = 7.5$

20. **The correct answer is (C).** The amount of paint needed depends on the area. The given ratios are ratios of length and the figures are similar. Therefore, the ratios of the areas are the squares of the ratios of the lengths.

1:40 in length

$1:40^2$ in area (that is, 1:1600 in area)

Since the model required three gallons, the original will require

$3 \times 1,600 = 4,800$ gallons.

21. **The correct answer is (A).** This one is easier to work backward. The total bill will be more than the base amount, thereby ruling out choices (B) and (D). Since both tax (5%) and tip (15%) are already included in the total, try adding 20% to each answer to see which results in a total of $93.60.

Or, work from the given $93.60, which represents 120% of the base amount. Divide 93.60 by 1.2 to get $78.00.

22. **The correct answer is (C).**

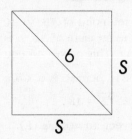

If the diagonal of a square is 6, then (by the Pythagorean Theorem), the sides of the square must be $\dfrac{6}{\sqrt{2}} = \dfrac{6\sqrt{2}}{2} = 3\sqrt{2}$. Square this to get the area of 18.

23. **The correct answer is (C).** Rename all fractions as decimal equivalents:

$$\frac{2}{3} = .6\overline{66} \qquad \frac{4}{5} = .800$$

$$\frac{5}{6} = .833\overline{3} \qquad \frac{17}{20} = .85$$

$$\frac{7}{10} = .7 \qquad \frac{13}{15} = .86\overline{66}$$

$$\frac{9}{10} = .9$$

$\dfrac{7}{10}$ is the only fraction between $\dfrac{2}{3}$ and $\dfrac{4}{5}$.

24. **The correct answer is (A).** Use the formula for circumference:
$C = \pi d$

$= (3.14)(7)$

$= 21.98$ inches

25. **The correct answer is (D).**

First find the amount Josie bought the shares for:
$180 \times 16 = \$2,880$

Then find the amount Josie sold the shares for:
$240 \times 16 = \$3,840$

Finally, subtract: $3,840 - \$2,880 = \$960$

ISEE Practice Test 1

Directions: Each question is made up of a word in capital letters followed by four choices. You are to circle the one word that is most nearly the same in meaning as the word in capital letters.

1. EXORBITANT
   - (A) essential
   - (B) lacking
   - (C) literal
   - (D) excessive

2. JARGON
   - (A) opposite
   - (B) decoy
   - (C) terminology
   - (D) membership

3. CHAGRIN
   - (A) disappointment
   - (B) fabrication
   - (C) acceptance
   - (D) exemption

4. STEALTHY
   - (A) small
   - (B) sly
   - (C) ashamed
   - (D) tardy

5. PONDEROUS
   - (A) amazed
   - (B) irregular
   - (C) trembling
   - (D) weighty

6. DAUNTLESS
   - (A) thoughtful
   - (B) believable
   - (C) brave
   - (D) pure

7. INCORRIGIBLE
   - (A) incredible
   - (B) immaterial
   - (C) shameless
   - (D) selective

8. FEINT
   - (A) fool
   - (B) proclaim
   - (C) penalize
   - (D) scavenge

9. CURT
   - (A) impending
   - (B) fair
   - (C) blunt
   - (D) meek

10. SPURN
    - (A) reject
    - (B) sew
    - (C) meddle
    - (D) warp

11. SUPPRESS
    - (A) subdue
    - (B) substitute
    - (C) liberate
    - (D) squander

12. INNOVATION
    - (A) balance
    - (B) certainty
    - (C) agreement
    - (D) change

13. SUBMISSIVE
    - (A) deceptive
    - (B) annoying
    - (C) compliant
    - (D) unflinching

14. CLIENTELE

   (A) militants
   (B) patrons
   (C) members
   (D) combatants

15. SUCCUMB

   (A) yield
   (B) irritate
   (C) echo
   (D) succeed

16. EULOGIZE

   (A) attack
   (B) disable
   (C) reduce
   (D) glorify

17. INFRINGE

   (A) equip
   (B) trespass
   (C) strike
   (D) shrink

18. PEER

   (A) equal
   (B) officer
   (C) beginner
   (D) patient

19. COWER

   (A) injure
   (B) insult
   (C) misrepresent
   (D) cringe

20. SLOTH

   (A) sadness
   (B) regret
   (C) laziness
   (D) forgetfulness

Directions: Each question below is made up of a sentence with one or two blanks. The sentences with one blank indicate that one word is missing. The sentences with two blanks indicate that two words are missing. Each sentence is followed by four choices. You are to circle the one word or pair of words that will best complete the meaning of the sentence as a whole.

21. The emotions of love and hate, though opposites, can be found even in the most _____ and _____ character in Shakespeare's plays.

   (A) virtuous..steadfast
   (B) wholesome..despicable
   (C) contemptible..decent
   (D) elderly..malicious

22. Some experts think that certain psychological conditions are the result of _____; others think it is _____.

   (A) contagion..communicability
   (B) milieu..surroundings
   (C) heredity..environment
   (D) coincidence..happenstance

23. Nutritionists say that when eating, it is important to _____ completely in order for proper _____ to occur.

   (A) inhale..respiration
   (B) absorb..rumination
   (C) repose..relaxation
   (D) masticate..digestion

24. After ruining her carpet when I spilled my dessert, I would have preferred her most sarcastic _____ to the _____ looks she cast in my direction.

   (A) invectives..disparaging
   (B) scurrilous..amiable
   (C) civilities..reproachful
   (D) amenities..agreeable

25. During the violent hurricane, the people in its path _____ God for divine _____.

   (A) entreated..intervention
   (B) disdained..interaction
   (C) importuned..wavering
   (D) ostracized..interference

26. The burglar was successful because he could move in a _____ and _____ manner.

   (A) flagrant..underhanded
   (B) stealthy..candid
   (C) furtive..evasive
   (D) inept..prominent

27. During commencement, the valedictorian delivered an inspiring _____, and it had a(n) _____ effect on the audience.

   (A) tribulation..debilitating
   (B) salutation..invigorating
   (C) oratory..incapacitating
   (D) defamation..heartening

28. According to the doctor, some medicines have side effects that can make people extremely _____ and _____.

   (A) dynamic..slumberous
   (B) vigorous..indolent
   (C) sluggish..vigorous
   (D) lethargic..impassive

29. The author found that her editor was very _____; he made many _____ in her work to make it as good as possible.

   (A) disorderly..avowals
   (B) fastidious..emendations
   (C) laggard..plaudits
   (D) militant..apparitions

30. The unpredictable nature of the student caused problems; his _____ _____ caused concern among the faculty.

   (A) periodic eruptions
   (B) invariable indiscretions
   (C) leisurely patrimony
   (D) immutable rebuttal

31. In a courtroom proceeding that was shown on television, the _____ heard the testimony and _____ the man to jail.

   (A) turncoat..committed
   (B) magistrate..pulverized
   (C) plebeian..dispatched
   (D) arbitrator..remanded

32. As a result of his recent accident, the _____ victim was _____ to a wheelchair.

   (A) inventive..cowered
   (B) auspicious..restrained
   (C) propitious..limited
   (D) hapless..confined

33. In Biology class we discussed animal families, and that farmers need to grow acres of grass because members of the _____ family are _____.

   (A) chivalrous..benevolent
   (B) porcine..carnivorous
   (C) bovine..herbivorous
   (D) patrician..wrathful

34. Anyone who is new at a job knows that novice _____ can lead to _____.

   (A) ineptitude..problems
   (B) facility..expertise
   (C) proficiency..deficiency
   (D) incapacity..aptness

35. One of the main concerns of the conservation movement is that we do not have a(n) _____ of energy sources; therefore, we must be _____ with what we do have.

   (A) abundance..excessive
   (B) paucity..intemperate
   (C) profusion..immoderate
   (D) deluge..frugal

36. In the principal's office, one can often see students _____ for their _____ behavior.

(A) castigated..antagonistic
(B) reprimanded..laudable
(C) chided..exemplary
(D) reverted..foreboding

37. Industrial waste products from the nearby factory made the once _____ lake into a _____ cesspool.

(A) pristine..contaminated
(B) tainted..unsullied
(C) portent..mutable
(D) sullen..untenable

38. In a tense situation, sometimes _____ remarks can _____ an argument.

(A) sarcastic..peruse
(B) facetious..precipitate
(C) deferential..yield
(D) acerbic..beleaguer

39. The political prisoner appealed for at least a _____ of his sentence, if not a total _____.

(A) filibuster..guffaw
(B) collusion..demurring
(C) vindication..diminishing
(D) reduction..acquittal

40. Although the judge is _____ to have taken bribes, no _____ evidence has been brought to the authorities.

(A) alleged..substantial
(B) supposed..deceptive
(C) desiccated..credible
(D) mandated..redolent

Directions: Any figures that accompany questions in this section may be assumed to be drawn as accurately as possible EXCEPT when it is stated that a particular figure is not drawn to scale. Letters such as x, y, and n stand for real numbers.

For Questions 1–18, work each in your head or on the space available on these pages. Then select the correct answer.

1. Which of the following fractions is greater than $\frac{3}{5}$?

   (A) $\frac{39}{50}$

   (B) $\frac{7}{25}$

   (C) $\frac{3}{10}$

   (D) $\frac{59}{100}$

2. What is .1% expressed as a decimal?

   (A) .001
   (B) .01
   (C) .1
   (D) 1

3. Five women had the following amounts of money in their wallets: $12.50, $11.83, $10.40, $0.74, and $0.00. What was the average amount of money carried by these women?

   (A) $7.09
   (B) $7.62
   (C) $9.88
   (D) $35.47

4. Solve for x: $7x - 3 = 4x + 6$

   (A) 2
   (B) 4
   (C) −1
   (D) 3

5. $2\frac{2}{3} + (-8) =$

   (A) $5\frac{1}{3}$

   (B) $-5\frac{1}{3}$

   (C) $10\frac{2}{3}$

   (D) $-10\frac{2}{3}$

6. Find the perimeter of a rectangle whose length is 7 centimeters and whose width is 5 centimeters.

   (A) 35 centimeters
   (B) 70 centimeters
   (C) 12 centimeters
   (D) 24 centimeters

7. The recipe for a cake calls for $\frac{2}{3}$ cup of sugar. How many cakes did Janet bake for a baked-goods sale if she used 4 cups of sugar?

   (A) 3
   (B) 4
   (C) 5
   (D) 6

8. Solve for x: $1.4x - 0.9 = 3.3$

   (A) 4.2
   (B) 3
   (C) 7.6
   (D) 4.7

9. Brian jogged $\frac{1}{2}$ of a mile, rested, then jogged $\frac{1}{3}$ of a mile. What fractional part of a mile must he jog to complete 1 mile?

(A) $\frac{2}{5}$

(B) $\frac{1}{6}$

(C) $\frac{5}{6}$

(D) $\frac{1}{12}$

10. $(-4)^2 - 3(-4) =$

(A) -4

(B) 52

(C) -52

(D) 28

11. The difference between the measures of two complementary angles is 50°. Find in degrees the measure of the smaller angle.

(A) 50°

(B) 70°

(C) 20°

(D) 10°

12. The expression $2(a + 1) - (1 + 2a)$ is equivalent to:

(A) 1

(B) -1

(C) 0

(D) $4a$

13. Each inch on a map corresponds to a distance of 110 miles. What distance corresponds to 5.5 inches on the map?

(A) 20 miles

(B) 550 miles

(C) 605 miles

(D) 1100 miles

14. Which of the following is a rational number?

(A) $\sqrt{2}$

(B) $\sqrt{3}$

(C) $\sqrt{5}$

(D) $\sqrt{9}$

15. An inheritance of $120,000 is divided among 3 people in a ratio of 3:4:5. How much is the greatest share?

(A) $40,000

(B) $45,000

(C) $50,000

(D) $55,000

16. If the price of an item triples, the increase is what percent of the new price?

(A) $33\frac{1}{3}\%$

(B) $66\frac{2}{3}\%$

(C) 200%

(D) 300%

17. Find the value of $-5S^2T$, when $S = -2$ and $T = -3$.

(A) -30

(B) 30

(C) -60

(D) 60

18.

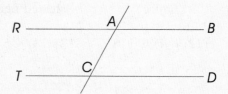

($\overline{RB}$ is parallel to $\overline{TD}$)

If m∠$BAC = (a + 30)°$, then m∠ACD expressed in terms of a is:

(A) $(a + 30)°$

(B) $(150 - a)°$

(C) $(60 - a)°$

(D) $(60 + a)°$

Directions: For Questions 19–35, note the given information, if any, and then compare the quantity in Column A to the quantity in Column B. Next to the number of each question, write

   A if the quantity in Column A is greater.
   B if the quantity in Column B is greater.
   C if the two quantities are equal.
   D if the relationship cannot be determined from the information given.

Column A	**Column B**
19. $12 \times 72 \times 250$	$10 \times 7 \times 200$
20. Least common denominator of $\frac{1}{4}$ and $\frac{3}{5}$	Least common denominator of $\frac{2}{3}$ and $\frac{5}{8}$
21. $4m - 3n - (3m + 2n)$	$m + 5n$

22.

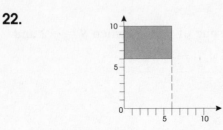

Area of the shaded figure	Perimeter of the shaded figure
23. $(12 + 4)\,5 + 8$	$12 + 4 \times 5 + 8$

24.

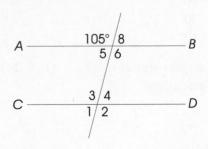

r	$180 - p$
25. $x - y$	$y - x$
26. $5\sqrt{2}$	$2\sqrt{5}$

Column A	**Column B**
27. $\left(1 \times \dfrac{1}{10}\right)$ $+ \left(8 \times \dfrac{1}{100}\right)$ $+ \left(3 \times \dfrac{1}{1000}\right)$	.183
28. $\left(-\dfrac{3}{5}\right)^{2}$	$\dfrac{6}{10}$
29. Price of 32 envelopes if purchased at a rate of two for 5 cents	Price of 1 lb. of coffee if a $3\frac{2}{3}$ lb. can costs \$3.30
30. Number of boxes in 12 rows of cartons with 16 cartons in a row and 9 boxes in each carton	1,728

Use this drawing for questions 31 and 32.

A ———— 105° / 8 ———— B
             5 / 6

C ———— 3 / 4 ———— D
             1 / 2

Column A	**Column B**
31. $m\angle 1$	$m\angle 6$
32. $m\angle 2$	$m\angle 8$
33. $\dfrac{1}{3}x + 3 < -6$ x	-18

	Column A	**Column B**

34.

$$\dfrac{7\frac{2}{3}}{\left(\frac{4}{5}\right)\left(\frac{5}{12}\right)} \qquad \dfrac{7\frac{1}{3}}{\left(\frac{5}{6}\right)\left(\frac{6}{15}\right)}$$

	Column A	**Column B**

35.

Area of Triangle   Area of Square

| READING COMPREHENSION | TIME: **40** MINUTES | **40 QUESTIONS** |

Directions: Each passage below is followed by questions based on its content. Answer the questions following a passage on the basis of what is *stated* or *implied* in that passage.

Passage 1

Line   Beneath the surface of Monterey Bay lies splendor seen only by a lucky few: Monterey Canyon. Hidden from view by thousands of feet of water, this submarine chasm pos-
5   sesses steep rocky cliffs and curving geography inhabited by strange and hard-to-find marine life. West of the Monterey Peninsula, the canyon walls gradually drop an incredible 7,360 feet—a quarter mile more than
10   the highest cliff of Arizona's Grand Canyon.

Monterey Canyon is part of a much larger geologic feature, the Monterey Canyon System, comparable in size to the 278-mile-long Grand Canyon. The 60-mile-long gorge
15   empties into the gently sloping Monterey Sea Valley. The valley continues out into the Pacific Ocean for an additional 180 miles until it reaches the flat Pacific Ocean plain.

Even at this size, Monterey Canyon is
20   not the world's largest undersea chasm. But to marine researchers, it is the most convenient. At the port of Moss Landing, the head of the canyon is within yards of the coast. From here, the floor of the canyon begins its
25   gradual descent to a depth of nearly 8,000 feet.

In the bay's sunless middle depths, otherworldly creatures drift through the darkness feeding on the blizzard of organic
30   material, or "marine snow," from above. In the canyon itself, dense colonies of clams, tube worms, and bacteria feed on chemical-rich fluids oozing from underwater springs.

Monterey Canyon's geology is a focus
35   of intense study. Although its geologic history is understood in its essentials, the details of how it was carved out of the continental shelf are not yet completely known. When submarine canyons were first
40   discovered, geologists assumed that they started out as canyons on dry land at a time when the sea level was lower. Then, according to this theory, the canyons were flooded by a rise in sea level. But there was
45   one problem: not all undersea canyons lie near a river old and powerful enough to have carved such canyons. A bigger, older knife was needed.

In the 1930s, geologists found a
50   mechanism that could, given enough time, carve even the grandest undersea canyons: turbidity currents. These are enormously powerful underwater debris flows, made up of a dense mixture of sea water, rock debris
55   of various sizes, and fine sediments. They flow down underwater slopes at high speed, tearing away rocks and sediments. Most geologists believe that turbidity currents carved undersea canyons as surely as the
60   Colorado River cut the Grand Canyon.

1. According to the passage, Monterey Canyon is convenient for marine researchers because it is

    (A) comparable in size to the Grand Canyon.
    (B) close to shore and easy to reach.
    (C) the world's largest undersea canyon.
    (D) the focus of intense study.

2. The main point of paragraph 5 is that the original theory of how undersea canyons were formed

(A) had to be abandoned.

(B) wasn't old enough.

(C) didn't explain flooding.

(D) didn't consider erosion.

3. According to the passage, turbidity currents contain all of the following EXCEPT

(A) fine sediments.

(B) rock debris.

(C) chemical rich fluids.

(D) sea water.

4. The "blizzard . . . of marine snow" (lines 29–30)

(A) is caused by weather conditions in the atmosphere.

(B) contains chemical-rich fluids from springs.

(C) falls from the bay's sunless middle depths.

(D) is made up of organic matter sea creatures eat.

5. According to the passage, how deep is the Monterey Canyon?

(A) 7,360 feet

(B) 60 miles

(C) 278 miles

(D) 180 miles

Passage 2

Line Shut it off, Steiner told himself, and the station wagon was silent. He had pulled into the driveway without the reality of any of it registering, and now he turned to his
5 9-year-old, James, in the seat beside him, and saw the boy's face take on the expression of odd imbalance that Steiner had noticed for the first time this afternoon.

Steiner got out and James bucked
10 against his seat belt, so Steiner eased back in, shoving the unruly hair off his forehead,

and took hold of the wheel. He was so used to James being out of the car and heading across the yard the second after he stopped
15 that he felt dazed. His 7-year-old twin daughters, who were in the rear of the car with his wife, Jen, were whispering, and Steiner turned to them with a look that meant "Silence!" Steiner got out again with a
20 heaviness that made him feel that his age, 45, was the beginning of old age, and that the remorse he'd recently been feeling had a focus: it was a remorse that he and Jen hadn't had more children.

25 As he was driving home, a twin had pulled herself forward from the backseat and whispered that James had reached over and honked the horn while Steiner was in the department store, where he had gone to
30 look for a shatterproof, full-length mirror and an exercise mat the physical therapist had recommended. And since James hadn't spoken for two weeks, the incident had set the twins to whispering hopefully about
35 James, for most of the long trip.

"I'm sorry," Steiner said, seeing that he was still the only one outside the car, as if he had to apologize for being on his feet. He slid back in, brushing aside his hair again,
40 and began to unbuckle James's seat belt. The boy stared out the windshield with a look Steiner couldn't translate, and, once free, tried to scoot over to the passenger door by bending his upper body forward and back.

45 "Take it easy, honey," Steiner said. Then, he added for the boy and the others, in the phrase that he'd used since James was an infant, "Here we are home." Silence. Steiner turned to Jen, who was leaning
50 close, and said, "Do you have his other belt?" She nodded.

Steiner got out and looked across the top of the station wagon at their aging house. He hadn't seen it in two weeks. He'd
55 spent that time at the hospital with James, first in intensive care, then in a private

room, where physical therapists came and
went. At the sight of the white siding that
he and James and Jen had scraped and
60 repainted at the beginning of the summer,
he had to swallow down the loss that he'd
started to feel when he realized he was
grieving for a son he might never see again.
    The boy's hair was as unruly as
65 Steiner's, and the curls at its edges needed
trimming. James's eyes were nearly covered
by it, Steiner saw, and then they rested on
his father with a dull love.

6. According to the passage, James is

   (A) Jen's stepson.
   (B) younger than the twins.
   (C) Steiner's son.
   (D) 45 years old.

7. Steiner had spent the past two weeks

   (A) scraping and repainting the house.
   (B) looking for an exercise mat.
   (C) in the hospital with James.
   (D) not speaking to anyone at all.

8. In the context of the passage, the statement
that Steiner is "grieving for a son he might never
see again" (line 63) most likely means that

   (A) his son, James, has died.
   (B) he fears James may never recover.
   (C) he knows he won't have more
       children.
   (D) his son is in the hospital.

9. It can be inferred from the passage that
Steiner says, "Here we are home" (line 48)
in order to

   (A) begin a conversation with Jen and the
       twins.
   (B) suggest that James needs help getting
       out of the car.
   (C) explain they have moved to a new
       house.
   (D) restore a feeling of normality to the
       situation.

10. James honked the horn while

   (A) Steiner was talking to the physical
       therapist.
   (B) the twins were whispering about him.
   (C) Steiner was looking for an exercise
       mat.
   (D) Jen was getting him out of the car.

11. When in the story does Steiner notice
James's hair needs cutting?

   (A) Before Steiner helps James out of the
       car
   (B) While the twins are whispering about
       him
   (C) When Jen asks him a question
   (D) As Steiner shuts off the car's engine

Passage 3

Line Carthage, a city on the Tunisian coast of
North Africa, originally settled by the
Phoenicians, was a major power of the
Mediterranean world in ancient times.
5 Bertold Brecht summed up seven centuries
of its history when he wrote "Great
Carthage made war three times. After the
first, she was powerful. After the second,
she was rich. After the third, no one knew
10 where Great Carthage had been." The last
sentence was a slight exaggeration. The
great general Hannibal, who used elephants
to cross the Alps in 281 B.C. to start the
Second Punic War with Rome ("Punic"
15 comes from the Roman word for "Phoenician"), was a well-known figure. Knowing
about him was part of Roman history; the
Romans had built a city of their own on the
site of Carthage after defeating it. Roman
20 Carthage was a center of industry, learning,
and luxury, arguably the second greatest city
of the Roman Empire, after Rome itself.
    In Carthage there had been great
libraries of books in the Punic language. Not
25 a page, not a line, remains. The works of a
Carthaginian named Magro, the greatest
writer on agriculture in antiquity, were

translated and studied by Roman landown-
ers, but now even the translations are lost.
30 What remains of the Punic language, a
variety of Phoenician, are mostly grave
inscriptions with the names of parents
offering children to a god or a goddess, and
some lines of comic dialogues put into the
35 mouths of Carthaginian merchants and slaves
in the work of a Roman playwright.

One consequence is that practically
everything we know about the Carthaginians
comes from the Greeks and Romans, who
40 made war on Carthage for centuries. Their
historians naturally tended to present a
biased picture of the enemy as cruel and
untrustworthy. But there is no reason to
think the people of ancient Carthage were
45 any more addicted to cruelty than the
Romans, who thought nothing of crucifying
prisoners along the public highways and
leaving them there till their bones were
picked clean by birds. Some scholars
50 challenge the whole idea that Carthaginians
practiced infant sacrifice, claiming that the
charred bones in the urns, when they are
not those of lambs and calves, are of infants
who died of natural causes.

12. The passage notes that our knowledge of
Carthage is incomplete because

   I.   none of the books written by
       Carthaginians has survived.
  II. the Roman portrayals of Carthage were
      inaccurate.
 III. Magro's book was only about
      agriculture.

(A) I only
(B) II only
(C) I and II
(D) I and III

13. In the context of the passage, what is the
purpose of the statement that the Romans
"thought nothing of crucifying prisoners
along the public highways" (lines 46–47)?

(A) The Romans did not practice infant
sacrifice.
(B) The Romans were as cruel as the
Carthaginians.
(C) The Romans treated the Carthaginians
cruelly.
(D) The Romans were even more cruel
than the Carthaginians.

14. The main idea of the second paragraph is
that

(A) the records of the Carthaginians were
almost totally destroyed.
(B) the city of Carthage was completely
destroyed.
(C) Punic was a form of the Phoenician
language.
(D) a Roman playwright preserved the
Punic language.

15. Although the author writes that the claim
"no one knew where great Carthage had
been" is a "slight exaggeration," which of
the following statements from the passage
best reveals how completely Carthage was
destroyed?

(A) The Phoenicians who had settled it no
longer lived there.
(B) Hannibal was not a well-known
general.
(C) The only remains of the Punic language are grave inscriptions.
(D) The Romans built a new city on the
site of Carthage.

Passage 4

Line   Twas in the merry month of May
When green leaves began swelling
Young William on his deathbed lay
For love of Barbara Allen.

5   He sent his men down through the town
To the place where she was dwelling
"O hurry to my master dear
If you are Barbara Allen."

  Slowly, slowly went she then
10 To the place where William was lying
And when she saw him to him said,
"Young man, I think you're dying."

  He turned his face unto the wall
And death with him was dealing
15 "Good-bye, good-bye, my dear friends all,
Be kind to Barbara Allen."

  Slowly, slowly rose she up,
And slowly, slowly left him,
And sighing said she could not stay
20 Since death from life had reft him.

  She had not gone a mile or two
When she heard the death bell tolling
And every stroke the death bell sang
"Oh woe to Barbara Allen."

25 "O mother, mother, make my bed!
O make it soft and narrow.
Since William died for me today;
I'll die for him tomorrow."

16. The story told by this poem takes place in

(A) winter.
(B) spring.
(C) summer.
(D) autumn.

17. Lines 7 and 8 of the poem are spoken by

(A) Young William.
(B) Barbara Allen.
(C) William's employee.
(D) Barbara's mother.

18. The stanza that best demonstrates Barbara Allen's cruelty is

(A) Stanza 3.
(B) Stanza 4.
(C) Stanza 5.
(D) Stanza 6.

19. Barbara Allen will die because she

(A) is extremely ill.
(B) realizes she truly loved William.
(C) recognizes her cruelty caused his death.
(D) hears the death bell ringing for William.

20. The word "reft" in line 20 most probably means

(A) torn.
(B) revived.
(C) freed.
(D) joined.

Passage 5

Line   I was on a visit to seven of Costa Rica's national parks and nature reserves. My first stop, Monteverde Cloud Forest Reserve, taught me a lesson. To see something
5   interesting in this naturalist's paradise of a country, all I had to do was sit down and wait. Something was sure to come by, and it was likely to be something new and wonderful. Names tell the story: quetzals, iguanas,
10 and howler monkeys; sloths; scarlet macaws, and green parrots; yellow toucans, anteaters, roseate spoonbills, giant turtles, and more. Endlessly more.
    Costa Rica is blessed with natural
15 beauty. It claims more than 830 species of birds living in a wide range of habitats, from volcanic summit to white-sand beach, from coral reef to rain forest. A large portion of its land, an amazing 25 percent, has been set
20 aside in one of the world's best systems of reserves and national parks, some 35 in all. And because the country averages only 150

miles across and 300 miles long, it's easy to get from one place to another.

25   For example, Monteverde is less than 100 miles from Costa Rica's capital, San Jose. I drove there in one morning, through the temperate central valley down into hot, dry country along the Pacific coast, and then up

30 to misty forest.

Monteverde is a prime sample of tropical cloud forest, named for its ability to derive moisture not only from rain but also from the misty touch of clouds, which

35 almost always blanket the area. Entering the trees felt like going underwater, sinking beneath the shimmering surface of a new and alien world. But gradually, I began to see a sort of order, an order defined by the

40 need for sunlight. Great trees had muscled their way skyward, blocking the sun from the forest floor. In their shade, ground-level plants had survived by growing huge leaves, often several feet in diameter, to collect

45 what light they could. I came to a single tree with a cluster of substantial trunks: a strangler fig. Starting as a seedling in the canopy, the fig had dropped shoots that took root in the forest floor and then

50 gradually enveloped and choked their host. The original tree, having served as a ladder to the soil, had long since disappeared.

The relationships of plants and animals weave into the complex fabric of the forest

55 like vines. I began to think of the forest as an organism itself, growing at a fantastic pace.

21. When the author states that "names tell the story" (line 9), it means that

(A) names of Monteverde's animals are unusual.

(B) there are more giant turtles than other animals in Monteverde.

(C) Monteverde is a cloud forest.

(D) Monteverde has many kinds of animals.

22. The author's purpose in paragraph 3 is to

(A) establish the fact that the capital is close to Monteverde.

(B) provide examples of climate differences in Costa Rica.

(C) provide an example supporting ease of getting from place to place.

(D) support the author's statement that there is a wide range of habitats.

23. What is the author's attitude toward Costa Rica's preserves?

(A) Strongly favorable

(B) Favorable with reservations

(C) Neutral

(D) Unimpressed

24. The author states that one sort of order in the Monteverde Cloud Forest occurs because of a need for

(A) sunlight.

(B) niches.

(C) tumult.

(D) recycling.

25. Which statement is NOT true of the strangler fig?

(A) It uses the host tree to reach the ground.

(B) It is a ladder to the soil.

(C) It has a cluster of trunks.

(D) It sends out shoots.

26. The best title for this selection is

(A) "Costa Rica: Biologist's Paradise."

(B) "Biological Diversity in Monteverde."

(C) "Monteverde Cloud Forest."

(D) "A Visit to Costa Rica."

Passage 6

Line   Although humans think of cockroaches as
bothersome, fewer than 1 percent of
cockroach species are pests. These annoying
bugs include the American cockroach and
5   the German cockroach, which live in
kitchens and bathrooms. They like the dark,
and it can be very unnerving to come home
at night, turn on a lamp, and see the roaches
scuttling across the floor to their homes in
10   cracks and behind the walls. However, most
cockroaches live out of doors, where
humans tend to ignore them.

   The roaches are one of the most successful species on our planet. Fossil records show
15   that cockroaches were around as long as 300
million years ago. By comparison, flowering
plants have only been around for 100 million
years, and humans for about two million
years. Interestingly, the differences between
20   the fossil cockroaches and today's roaches are
very slight; they mainly involve the position
of the veins on the wings.

   Why haven't the cockroaches changed?
They can live in a wide variety of habitats and
25   temperatures (they are even found in sub-
Arctic climates), and they are scavengers.
Their food includes plants, animal matter, and
debris. Their flat bodies are close to the
ground, so they can hide in any tiny space for
30   protection. When they hatch from their egg
cases, they are ready to move, although they
are very tiny and lack wings. Unlike some
other insects, they do not undergo a metamorphosis during which they might be vulner-
35   able. They shed their skins several times before they become adults, but they are always
speedy and mobile. While adults can fly, they
usually run.

   The cockroach's survival for many eons
40   in an unchanged form is a fact that, oddly,
supports the theory of natural selection. If
species succeed, there is no need for
evolutionary changes to help them survive.

27. Cockroaches have existed for about

   (A) 2 million years.
   (B) 100 million years.
   (C) 200 million years
   (D) 300 million years.

28. One reason for their success as a species is
that cockroaches

   (A) like the cold.
   (B) can hide easily.
   (C) don't have wings.
   (D) hatch from eggs.

29. The American and German cockroaches are
species that

   (A) are not pests.
   (B) live outdoors.
   (C) are ignored by humans.
   (D) dislike light.

30. As used in the passage, the word "vulnerable" (lines 34–35) means

   (A) valuable.
   (B) protected.
   (C) easy to attack.
   (D) confusing to predators.

Passage 7

Line   Biosphere 2 was a project designed as an
experiment to see if humans could live in a
totally self-sustaining sealed environment. A
huge glass greenhouse structure, it was
5   meant to duplicate Biosphere 1, our planet,
and to show that we could live on another
planet by creating such a project there.
Eight people lived in Biosphere 2 for two
years, and although they emerged in good
10   health, they were extremely thin. While they
lived in Biosphere 2, they had complained
frequently of hunger, fatigue, and weakness.

   One of the reasons for their feeling of
hunger was that the food-producing plants
15   and animals in the biosphere did not
develop as expected. The chickens laid very

502

few eggs. The pigs did not reproduce, and the goats provided little milk. Not all of the food plant species did well, and the biosphe-
20 rians' diet was composed mostly of beans and sweet potatoes.

The fatigue and weakness partially resulted from the hard physical labor the biospherians' performed many hours a day
25 so that there would be enough food to survive. But later research revealed a more significant problem. The atmosphere of Biosphere 2 was to be maintained by the plants and algae growing inside it and in its
30 simulated ocean; these, it was thought, would produce enough oxygen so the atmosphere would duplicate the 21 percent oxygen of Earth. In Biosphere 2, the oxygen levels sometimes dropped as low as 14.5
35 percent. In addition, the carbon dioxide level was about twice that of the area directly outside Biosphere 2.

But this problem in the original experiment has led to a new mission for the
40 Biosphere 2. According to a brochure given to tourists at the site, "researchers are working to understand how increased carbon dioxide in our atmosphere—such as that produced by cars, industry, and the
45 burning of forests—will affect us and the plant life we so depend on." So while the Biosphere 2 may not show how to survive on other planets, it may teach us how we can live in the increasingly polluted environ-
50 ment of Biosphere 1.

31. One cause of the biospherians' fatigue was

(A) a boring diet.
(B) too little oxygen.
(C) not enough to do.
(D) decreased carbon dioxide.

32. Food-producing animals in Biosphere 2

(A) did not develop normally.
(B) ate food meant for humans.
(C) provided variety in the biospherians' diet.
(D) died when they were young.

33. Oxygen in Biosphere 2 was to be produced by

(A) air from outside the sealed environment.
(B) the ocean inside it.
(C) chickens, pigs, and goats.
(D) land and water plants.

34. The carbon dioxide-rich atmosphere in Biosphere 2

(A) was a cause of the biospherians' weakness.
(B) provides the possibility of new experiments.
(C) is twice as high as that of the area surrounding it.
(D) All of the above

Passage 8

Line In the 1890s, Cuba was part of what remained of Spain's once huge empire in the New World. Several times Cuban insurgents had rebelled against Spanish rule, but they
5 had failed to free their country. As discontent with Spanish rule grew, in late February 1895, revolt again broke out.

Cuban insurgents established a military organization in New York City to raise
10 money, purchase weapons, and wage a propaganda war to sway American public opinion in their favor. Conditions in Cuba were grim. The insurgents engaged in a hit-and-run scorched-earth policy to force
15 the Spanish to leave, while the Spanish commander tried to corner the rebels in the eastern end of the island and destroy them.

After initial failures, Spain, in January 1896, sent General Weyler to Cuba. Relent-
20 less and brutal, Weyler gave the rebels ten

days to lay down their arms. He then put into effect a "reconcentration" policy designed to move the native population into camps and destroy the rebels' popular base.
25 Herded into fortified areas, Cubans died by the thousands—victims of unsanitary conditions, overcrowding, and disease.

There was a wave of sympathy for the insurgents, stimulated by the American
30 newspapers. The so-called yellow press printed gruesome stories of Spanish atrocities. But yellow journalism did not cause the war. It stemmed from larger conflicts in policy between Spain and the United States.

35. The word "insurgents" (line 3) as used in the passage means

   (A) natives.
   (B) rebels.
   (C) militia.
   (D) reconcentrationists.

36. The primary purpose of reconcentration was to

   (A) reduce the size of the rebel forces.
   (B) relocate the native Cubans.
   (C) cause disease among the rebels.
   (D) carry out the scorched-earth policy.

37. Yellow journalism refers to the newspapers'

   (A) cowardliness.
   (B) causing conflicts in policies.
   (C) sympathy.
   (D) use of sensationalism.

Passage 9

Line Cultural anthropologists are scientists who study how members of human societies experience events in their lives. They examine how people in a culture work, find
5 their food, build their shelters, marry, raise their children, care for the ill, and treat their dead. They may find that some cultures have practices unlike those of their own culture. For example, an American anthropologist
10 discovers that in some cultures it is normal to find insects as part of the human diet. The anthropologist also learns that in ancient cultures, human sacrifice was practiced. Most Americans would find these
15 practices abhorrent.

If anthropologists were to condemn such behaviors as "wrong," they would be assuming that their own culture is superior, since it does things the "right" way. But this
20 would lead to the conclusion they should not waste time studying other cultures. If their own way is "right," and others are "wrong," they would then merely be studying "mistakes." Instead, anthropologists
25 try to understand a culture on its own terms. What purpose or meaning do the behaviors have to the people who practice them? The ancient Aztec culture of Mexico believed that the universe was periodically destroyed
30 by the gods, and the only way to prevent this disaster was to sacrifice humans. While this does not mean anthropologists need to approve of human sacrifice, by understanding the role it played in a culture, they can
35 avoid judging it by their society's standards.

38. As used in the passage, "abhorrent" (line 15) means

   (A) illegal.
   (B) experimental.
   (C) disgusting.
   (D) unfamiliar.

39. Cultural anthropologists do not condemn behaviors that seem strange because they

   (A) know which behaviors are right and which are wrong.

   (B) want to understand how the culture views the behavior.

   (C) do not want to make mistakes.

   (D) do not think it is right to destroy the universe.

40. The best title for this passage is

   (A) "The Aztec Culture."

   (B) "What Is an Anthropologist."

   (C) "How Anthropologists Think."

   (D) "Judging Other Cultures."

MATH ACHIEVEMENT   TIME: 40 MINUTES   45 QUESTIONS

Directions: Each question is followed by four suggested answers. Read each question and then decide which of the four suggested answers is best.

1. Which of the following is equivalent to .00000072?

  (A) 7.2×10^{-5}
  (B) 7.2×10^{-6}
  (C) 7.2×10^{-7}
  (D) 7.2×10^{-8}

2. The three angles of a triangle are in the ratio 8:9:13. Find the number of degrees in the smallest angle.

  (A) $36°$
  (B) $48°$
  (C) $54°$
  (D) $60°$

3. $62\frac{1}{2}\% =$

  (A) $\frac{5}{8}$
  (B) $\frac{8}{5}$
  (C) $.62$
  (D) 62.5

4. Which of the following is the greatest?

  (A) $\frac{1}{4} + \frac{2}{3}$
  (B) $\frac{3}{4} - \frac{1}{3}$
  (C) $\frac{1}{12} \times \frac{1}{3}$
  (D) $\frac{3}{4} \times \frac{1}{3}$

5. If the sum of s and $s + 9$ is greater than 27, which is a possible value for s?

  (A) -10
  (B) -8
  (C) 8
  (D) 10

6. 21.49 is closest to

  (A) 22
  (B) 21
  (C) 21.5
  (D) 21.45

7.

The perimeter of $ABCD$ is 100. If $AB > AD$, AB may be equal to

  (A) 25
  (B) 35
  (C) 50
  (D) 55

8. $3\frac{1}{3} + (-6) =$

   (A) $2\frac{2}{3}$

   (B) $-2\frac{2}{3}$

   (C) $9\frac{1}{3}$

   (D) $-9\frac{1}{3}$

9. Find the value of $-5ST^2$ when $S = -2$ and $T = -3$.

   (A) -90
   (B) 90
   (C) -60
   (D) 60

10. If $ab + c = 2$ is solved for a, then a is equal to

    (A) $bc - 2$

    (B) $2 - c - b$

    (C) $\dfrac{c + 2}{b}$

    (D) $\dfrac{2 - c}{b}$

11. Find S using the formula $S = \dfrac{a(1 - r^n)}{1 - r}$ if $a = -2$, $r = 2$, and $n = 3$.

    (A) 14
    (B) -14
    (C) 2
    (D) -2

12. Find the length of the second leg of a right triangle whose hypotenuse is 30 feet and whose first leg is 18 feet.

    (A) 48 feet
    (B) 12 feet
    (C) 24 feet
    (D) 36 feet

13. If the length and the width of a rectangle are both tripled, the ratio of the area of the original rectangle to the area of the enlarged rectangle is

    (A) 1:3
    (B) 1:6
    (C) 1:9
    (D) 1:18

14. Which of the following is NOT a multiple of 8?

    (A) 24
    (B) 72
    (C) 100
    (D) 144

15. On Chuck's softball team, 8 of the 12 players are right-handed. What is the ratio of right-handed members to left-handed members?

    (A) 1:2
    (B) 2:1
    (C) 2:3
    (D) 3:4

16. If 5 books cost d dollars, how many books can be purchased for 2 dollars?

    (A) $\dfrac{10}{d}$

    (B) $10d$

    (C) $\dfrac{d}{10}$

    (D) $\dfrac{2d}{5}$

17. If 8 is a factor of a certain number, what numbers must be factors of that number?

   (A) 1, 2, 4, and 8
   (B) 2 and 4 only
   (C) 2, 4, and 8 only
   (D) 1, 2, and 4 only

18. $x =$

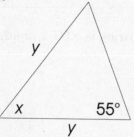

   (A) 80°
   (B) 70°
   (C) 55°
   (D) 50°

19. For what priced item does 40% off equal a $4.00 discount?

   (A) $16.00
   (B) $4.00
   (C) $8.00
   (D) $10.00

20. Sally has 3 skirts and 4 blouses ready for wear on a particular day. How many different outfits can Sally choose?

   (A) 12
   (B) 7
   (C) 9
   (D) 16

21. One day Tom completed $\frac{1}{4}$ of his tax returns. The next day he did $\frac{1}{2}$ of what was left. What fraction of his taxes did Tom complete over both days?

   (A) $\frac{3}{8}$
   (B) $\frac{5}{8}$
   (C) $\frac{3}{4}$
   (D) $\frac{7}{8}$

22. If $8x - 14 = 42$, then $x - 5 =$

   (A) 2
   (B) 3
   (C) 5
   (D) 7

23. $2\frac{2}{3} + (-7) =$

   (A) $4\frac{1}{3}$
   (B) $-4\frac{1}{3}$
   (C) $9\frac{2}{3}$
   (D) $-9\frac{2}{3}$

24. A carton of milk is $\frac{2}{3}$ empty. When full, the carton holds 60 ounces. How many ounces are in the carton now?

   (A) 40
   (B) 20
   (C) 30
   (D) 45

25. What is the area of an equilateral triangle whose altitude is 8?

(A) 16

(B) $\dfrac{64\sqrt{3}}{3}$

(C) $8\sqrt{3}$

(D) $\dfrac{16\sqrt{3}}{3}$

26.

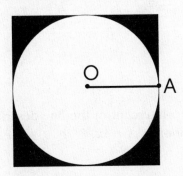

Radius $OA = 3$. Calculate the area of the shaded region.

(A) 9
(B) $36 - 36\pi$
(C) 36π
(D) $36 - 9\pi$

27. At the start of the year, Franklyn invested $11,000 in an Internet stock. At the end of the year, his stock was worth $9,500. What was the percent of decline in the value of his investment?

(A) 13.64%
(B) 15.79%
(C) 84.21%
(D) 86.36%

28. A radio has a list price of $350. There is a 10% discount sale, and the sales tax is 10%. What is the total paid, including tax?

(A) $350.00
(B) $346.50
(C) $315.00
(D) $365.00

29. What is the equation of a line with slope 8 that intersects the y-axis at $y = -3$?

(A) $y = 3x - 8$
(B) $y = 8x - 3$
(C) $y = 3x + 8$
(D) $y = 8x + 3$

30. Brittany has a test average of 80 after five tests. She only knows the scores of four of her tests: they are 70, 87, 94, and 69. What was the score on her other test?

(A) 90
(B) 96
(C) 80
(D) 82

31. What is $4\dfrac{1}{2}$ percent expressed as a decimal?

(A) 4.50
(B) .412
(C) .45
(D) .045

32. Express in simplest form the following ratio: 15 hours to 3 days.

(A) $\dfrac{5}{16}$

(B) $\dfrac{5}{1}$

(C) $\dfrac{5}{24}$

(D) $\dfrac{15}{72}$

33. Solve for x: $5x + 4 = 9x - 2$

(A) $-\dfrac{1}{2}$

(B) $\dfrac{1}{2}$

(C) $-\dfrac{3}{2}$

(D) $\dfrac{3}{2}$

34. A gumball machine contains five red, six white, and three blue gumballs. If one gumball is removed, what is the probability that it will be red?

(A) $\dfrac{1}{5}$

(B) $\dfrac{1}{14}$

(C) $\dfrac{5}{14}$

(D) $\dfrac{9}{14}$

35. $(2x^2 - 3x + 5) - (3x + 2) =$

(A) $2x^2 - 6x + 3$
(B) $2x^2 + 6x - 3$
(C) $2x^2 - 6x + 7$
(D) $2x^2 + 3$

36. Using the formula $A = p + prt$, find A when $p = 1,500$, $r = .04$, and $t = 2\dfrac{1}{2}$.

(A) 1,850
(B) 1,650
(C) 1,550
(D) 1,350

37. Find the value of y in the proportion:

$$\dfrac{30}{8} = \dfrac{12}{y}$$

(A) 20

(B) 6

(C) $3\dfrac{1}{5}$

(D) $4\dfrac{3}{4}$

38. If $\dfrac{9}{x}$ is subtracted from $\dfrac{12}{x}$, the result is

(A) $\dfrac{3}{x^0}$

(B) $\dfrac{21}{x}$

(C) $\dfrac{3}{x^2}$

(D) $\dfrac{3}{x}$

39. Evaluate $4^3 - 3^4$.

(A) 17
(B) −17
(C) 0
(D) 24

40. What is the x-intercept of the line described by the equation $y = -3x + 7$?

(A) $\dfrac{7}{3}$

(B) 7

(C) $-\dfrac{3}{7}$

(D) $-\dfrac{7}{3}$

41. What is 50 expressed as the product of its prime factors?

(A) (5)(10)
(B) (2)(25)
(C) (5)(2)(5)(2)
(D) (5)(5)(2)

42. Find the height of a triangle whose base is 40 and area is 320.

(A) 16
(B) 40
(C) 80
(D) 160

43. Lines *A* and *B* are parallel. The measure of ∠1 is 49°. What is the measure of ∠2?

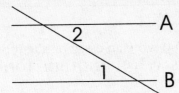

  (A) 49°
  (B) 41°
  (C) 131°
  (D) It cannot be determined.

44. How long of a shadow will a 120-foot pole cast if a foot-long ruler casts a three-inch shadow?

  (A) 25 feet
  (B) 30 feet
  (C) 350 inches
  (D) 90 feet

45. If points *A*, *B*, *C*, and *D* are distinct collinear points, and $\overline{AC}$ is congruent to $\overline{BC}$, and *B* lies between *A* and *D*, and the length of $\overline{AC}$ is 10, what is the length of $\overline{CD}$?

  (A) 10
  (B) 5
  (C) 20
  (D) It cannot be determined.

WRITING SAMPLE   TIME: 30 MINUTES

Directions: Using two sheets of lined theme paper, plan and write an essay on the topic assigned below. DO NOT WRITE ON ANOTHER TOPIC. AN ESSAY ON ANOTHER TOPIC IS NOT ACCEPTABLE.

Topic: Critics have said that rock bands rarely create any more, especially after becoming popular. They just recreate.

Assignment: Write an essay giving your view of this. Do you think that this is a true observation? Is money the key factor? Support your opinion with specific examples from history, current music, or personal observations.

Name: _____

Write your essay here.

_____

_____

_____

_____

_____

_____

_____

_____

_____

_____

_____

_____

_____

_____

_____

_____

_____

_____

(Continue, if necessary.)

EXPLANATORY ANSWERS TO THE ISEE PRACTICE TEST 1

VERBAL REASONING

1. The correct answer is (D).
2. The correct answer is (C).
3. The correct answer is (A).
4. The correct answer is (B).
5. The correct answer is (D).
6. The correct answer is (C).
7. The correct answer is (C).
8. The correct answer is (A).
9. The correct answer is (C).
10. The correct answer is (A).
11. The correct answer is (A).
12. The correct answer is (D).
13. The correct answer is (C).
14. The correct answer is (B).
15. The correct answer is (A).
16. The correct answer is (D).
17. The correct answer is (B).
18. The correct answer is (A).
19. The correct answer is (D).
20. The correct answer is (C).
21. **The correct answer is (A).** The clue is in the words *though opposites* and *even in the most*. This tells you that the opposite qualities of love and hate can reside in a character who is either very good or very bad. The trigger word is *and* because it shows that the words in the blanks will be synonymous (they will either demonstrate qualities of "goodness" or "badness"). Choices (B) and (C) can be eliminated because they are both good and bad qualities. Choice (D) can be eliminated because age has nothing to do with good or bad qualities.

22. **The correct answer is (C).** The clue can be found in the words *some experts think* and *others think* because it tells you that there is a difference of opinion. Therefore, the words that go in the blanks will be more opposite than alike. The trigger word is *psychological* because it tells you that the differing opinions are about the origins of mental illness. The debate is whether some of them are "genetic" or "behavioral." Choices (A), (B), and (D) can be eliminated because the two words are the same in each case, referring only to the environment, not genetics.

515

23. **The correct answer is (D).** The clue is the word *eating*. This lets you know that the words most likely have to do with the process of eating and getting nutrition ("chewing" and "digestion"). Therefore, choice (A) can be eliminated because it is about the breathing process. Similarly, choice (C) can be eliminated because it is about resting. The trigger words are *in order for*. This shows that the relationship between the first word and the second word is that of cause and effect.

24. **The correct answer is (A).** The clue is in the words *would have preferred*. The trigger word is *looks*. This tells you the first word is something other than looks, for instance, "harshly spoken words." Also, it shows that the looks were "angry." Choice (B) can be eliminated because the second word means friendly looks. Choice (C) can be eliminated because the first word means friendly words. Finally, choice (D) can be ruled out because both words are positive.

25. **The correct answer is (A).** The clue is in the words *violent hurricane*. They set up a cause-and-effect relationship between the storm and the action that the people take. The trigger words are *God* and *divine*. People pray to God in times of need. A prayer is a "request." The word "divine" modifies the second word as in divine help. Choices (B) and (D) can be eliminated because the first words are not related to a request. Choice (C) can be eliminated because the second word is not related to help.

26. **The correct answer is (C).** The clue in the words *successful* and *burglar* shows the blanks will contain words that are the "qualities of a successful burglar." The trigger word is *and*. That shows that the words will be synonyms that relate to those qualities. Choices (A) and (B) can be eliminated because the one word out of the two means to move in an obvious, observable manner. Choice (D) can be eliminated because the two words are not qualities of a successful burglar.

27. **The correct answer is (B).** The clue is *commencement*. At a graduation ceremony, the valedictorian would deliver a "speech." The trigger words are *inspiring* and *effect*. The second word will be a synonym for "inspiring." Choice (A) can be eliminated because both words are negative. Choice (C) can be eliminated because the second word means the speech was damaging. Also, choice (D) can be ruled out because the first word means to lie.

28. **The correct answer is (D).** The clue is in the words *medicines* and *side effects*. This shows that the words will be about the "effects" of medicines. The trigger word is *and*. This shows that the words will be synonyms. Choices (A), (B), and (C) can be eliminated because the pairs of words are antonyms (opposites).

29. **The correct answer is (B).** The clue is the word *editor*. The job requires a person to be "exacting" in order to correct errors. The trigger word is *many*. It is the work of an editor to make "corrections." So the word in the first blank will be a synonym for "exacting." The word in the second blank will be a synonym for "many." Choices (A) and (C) can be eliminated. The first word in each answer is an opposite of "exacting." Choice (D) can be eliminated. Neither of the words has any relationship to an "exacting" editor making many "corrections."

30. **The correct answer is (A).** The clue is in the words *unpredictable* and *problems.* The words in the blanks (an adjective and a noun because there is no comma between them) will relate to "unpredictability" and "problems." Choice (B) can be eliminated because the first word means constant, so it does not relate to "unpredictability." Choices (C) and (D) can be eliminated because neither of the words relates to the clue words.

31. **The correct answer is (D).** The clue word is *courtroom.* It tells you that a judge would be there to hear the testimony, so the first word will be a synonym for "judge." The trigger words are *to jail.* The second word will be a verb that is a synonym for "sending." Choices (A) and (C) can be eliminated because the first word in each answer is not a synonym for "judge." Choice (B) can be eliminated because the second word is not a synonym for "sending."

32. **The correct answer is (D).** The clue is in the words *As a result of,* and the trigger word is *accident.* The first word describes the "victim." The second word is a verb that relates to "being in a wheelchair." Choice (A) can be eliminated because neither of the words relates to a "victim" or "being confined in a wheelchair." Choices (B) and (C) can be eliminated because the first word in each answer is not a description suitable for a "victim."

33. **The correct answer is (C).** The clue words are *animal families.* A term for a "specific animal family" will be the first word. The trigger word is *grass.* The second word is a term for "eating grass." One animal that comes to mind readily is the cow. Choices (A) and (D) can be eliminated because they do not relate to "animal families" or "eating grass." Choice (B) can be eliminated because it describes a different animal family as eating meat.

34. **The correct answer is (A).** The clue is in the words *new at a job* and *novice.* Therefore, "novice" can be defined as being new on the job. Novice describes the noun that will be the first word. The trigger word is *lead.* Being new on an unfamiliar job would make one "unskilled." This could lead to problems. The second word would be a synonym for "problems." Choice (B) can be eliminated because they are the opposite qualities of a "novice." Choices (C) and (D) can be eliminated because the terms contradict each other.

35. **The correct answer is (D).** The clue is in the words *conservation movement, do not have,* and *energy sources.* It tells you that the movement is interested in "conserving" energy sources because we don't have many. The first word will be a synonym for "plenty" because it is preceded by "not." The trigger word is *therefore.* It establishes a cause-and-effect relationship between not having abundant energy sources and what we should do about it. The second word will be a synonym for "sparingly." Choices (A) and (C) can be eliminated because although they provide synonyms of "plenty," the second words are the opposite of "sparingly." Choice (B) can be eliminated because the first word is not a synonym for "plenty" but an opposite.

36. **The correct answer is (A).** The clue is in the words *principal's office* and *behavior*. The appearance of those words in the same sentence usually points toward "bad behavior." The trigger words are *for their*. They link a result of an action. The first word would be a synonym for "punishment." The second word would be a synonym for "bad." Choices (B) and (C) can be eliminated because the second word in each answer is the opposite of "bad" behavior. Choice (D) can be eliminated because the words have no relationship to "punishment" or "bad."

37. **The correct answer is (A).** The clue is in the words *industrial waste products*, and the trigger word is *once*. The first word will be an adjective that describes the lake before it was affected by the waste and would be a synonym for "pure." The second word would be a synonym for "polluted." Choice (B) can be eliminated because the order of "pure" and "polluted" synonyms is reversed. Choices (C) and (D) do not relate to the clue and trigger words.

38. **The correct answer is (B).** The clue is in the words *tense situation* and *an argument*. The trigger word is *remarks*. The first word would be an adjective that describes what kind of remarks would cause an argument. It would be a synonym for "sarcastic." The second word would be a synonym for "cause." Choice (A) can be eliminated because the second word in the answer is not a synonym for "cause." Choice (C) can be eliminated because the first word is an opposite of "sarcastic." The last answer can be eliminated because the second word in the answer is not a synonym for "cause."

39. **The correct answer is (D).** The clue is in the words *prisoner appealed*. That tells you the first word will be a synonym for "lessening." The trigger words are *if not* and *total*. That tells you the second word will be a synonym for "dismissal." Choices (A) and (B) can be eliminated because they do not relate to the clue words and the trigger words. Choice (C) can be eliminated because it reverses the order of the synonyms for "lessening" and "dismissal."

40. **The correct answer is (A).** The clue is in the words *although* and *taken bribes*. The first word would be a synonym for "suspected." The trigger words are *no* and *evidence*. The second word would be a synonym for "important." Choice (B) can be eliminated because the second word in the answer is not a synonym for "important." Choice (C) can be eliminated because the first word in the answer is not a synonym for "suspected." Choice (D) can be eliminated because the words in the answer do not relate to "suspected" and "important."

QUANTITATIVE REASONING

1. **The correct answer is (A).** Rename each fraction as an equivalent fraction with a denominator of 100.

   $$\frac{3}{5} \times \frac{20}{20} = \frac{60}{100}$$

   (A) $\frac{39}{50} \times \frac{2}{2} = \frac{78}{100}$

   (B) $\frac{7}{25} \times \frac{4}{4} = \frac{28}{100}$

   (C) $\frac{3}{10} \times \frac{10}{10} = \frac{30}{100}$

   (D) $\frac{59}{100} \times \frac{1}{1} = \frac{59}{100}$

   Thus, $\frac{39}{50} > \frac{3}{5}$.

2. **The correct answer is (A).** To rename percents as decimals, move the decimal point two places to the left:

   .1% = .001

3. **The correct answer is (A).** To find the average, divide the sum of the items by 5.

   $12.50 + 11.83 + 10.40 + 0.74 + 0.0 = 35.47$

   $\$35.47 \div 5 = \$7.09$

4. **The correct answer is (D).** $7x - 3 = 4x + 6$. Add 3 to both sides.

   $7x = 4x + 9$ Subtract $4x$ from both sides.
   $3x = 9$ Divide both sides by 3.
   $x = 3$

5. **The correct answer is (B).** To add signed numbers with different signs, subtract the numbers and use the sign of the number with the greater absolute value.

   $$8 - 2\frac{2}{3} = 5\frac{1}{3}$$

   Since 8 is greater than $2\frac{2}{3}$, the solution will be $-5\frac{1}{3}$.

6. **The correct answer is (D).** To find the perimeter, use the formula $P = 2l + 2w$.

   $P = 2(7) + 2(5) = 14 + 10 = 24$ cm

7. **The correct answer is (D).** Since 1 cake uses $\frac{2}{3}$ cup of sugar, let $x =$ the number of cakes for which you would need 4 cups of sugar. Now, set up a proportion:

$$\frac{1}{x} = \frac{\frac{2}{3}}{4} \qquad \text{Now, cross-multiply.}$$

$$(4)(1) = \frac{2}{3}x \qquad \text{Multiply both sides by } \frac{3}{2} \text{ to solve for } x.$$

$$4\left(\frac{3}{2}\right) = \left(\frac{3}{2}\right)\frac{2}{3}x$$
$$6 = x$$

8. **The correct answer is (B).**
$$1.4x - 0.9 = 3.3 \qquad \text{Add 0.9 to both sides.}$$
$$1.4x = 4.2 \qquad \text{Divide by 1.4.}$$
$$x = 3$$

9. **The correct answer is (B).** Begin by finding out how far Brian has jogged:

$$\frac{1}{2} + \frac{1}{3} = \frac{3}{6} + \frac{2}{6} = \frac{5}{6}$$

Subtract this result from 1 mile to determine how much is left to run.

$$1 - \frac{5}{6} = \frac{1}{6}$$

10. **The correct answer is (D).** Follow the order of operations.

$$(-4)^2 - 3\,(-4) = 16 - 3(-4) = 16 - (-12) = 16 + 12 = 28$$

11. **The correct answer is (C).** Let $x =$ the first angle.

Then, $90 - x =$ the second angle. We have:
$$x - (90 - x) = 50$$
$$x - 90 + x = 50$$
$$2x - 90 = 50$$
$$2x = 140$$
$$x = 70. \text{ Thus, the smaller angle must be } 20°.$$

12. **The correct answer is (A).** $2(a + 1) - (1 + 2a)$

Begin by distributing.

$$2a + 2 - 1 - 2a$$

Now, combine like terms.

$$2a - 2a + 2 - 1 = 1$$

13. **The correct answer is (C).** Set up a proportion:

$$\frac{1 \text{ inch}}{110 \text{ miles}} = \frac{5.5 \text{ inches}}{x \text{ miles}}$$

Now, cross-multiply.

$$x = 5.5 \times 110 = 605 \text{ miles}$$

14. **The correct answer is (D).** A rational number is a quotient of two integers x and y, $y \neq 0$. $\sqrt{2}, \sqrt{3}$, and $\sqrt{5}$ are all irrational numbers; they cannot be expressed as the quotient of two integers. However, $\sqrt{9} = 3 = \frac{3}{1}$, so it is rational.

15. **The correct answer is (C).** Picture the inheritance as being divided into $3 + 4 + 5 = 12$ portions, of which the greatest share consists of 5 of the 12 portions.

$$\frac{5}{12} \times 120{,}000 = 50{,}000$$

16. **The correct answer is (B).** The easiest way to solve this problem is to assume that the original price was some nice number, such as $100. Then, the price increases to $300, which is an increase of $200. Thus,

$$\frac{\text{increase}}{\text{new price}} = \frac{200}{300} = 66\frac{2}{3}\%$$

17. **The correct answer is (D).**

$$-5S^2T = -5(-2)^2(-3) = -5(4)(-3) = 60$$

18. **The correct answer is (B).** $\angle BAC$ and $\angle ACD$ are supplementary angles; hence, $m\angle BAC + m\angle ACD = 180$. Substituting, we obtain

$$(a + 30) + m\angle ACD = 180 \text{ or}$$

$$m\angle ACD = 180 - (a + 30) = 150 - a.$$

19. **The correct answer is (A).** Each factor in Column A is greater than the corresponding factor in Column B.

20. **The correct answer is (B).** The least common denominator is the least number divisible by both denominators.

The LCD of $\frac{1}{4}$ and $\frac{3}{5}$ is 20. The LCD of $\frac{2}{3}$ and $\frac{5}{8}$ is 24.

21. **The correct answer is (D).** $4m - 3n - (3m + 2n) = 4m - 3n - 3m - 2n = m - 5n$. Since we do not have numerical values for m and n, $m - 5n$ and $m + 5n$ cannot be compared.

22. **The correct answer is (A).** The rectangle depicted is 6 by 4. Since the area of a rectangle is length $\times$ width, the area is $6 \times 4 = 24$. The perimeter is given by the formula $2l + 2w = 2(6) + 2(4) = 12 + 8 = 20$.

23. **The correct answer is (A).** Follow the order of operations.

$$(12 + 4)5 + 8 = (16)5 + 8 = 80 + 8 = 88$$
$$12 + 4 \times 5 + 8 = 12 + 20 + 8 = 40$$

24. **The correct answer is (C).**

Since $r + p = 180$, we have $r = 180 - p$.

25. **The correct answer is (D).** Since we know nothing about the size of either x or y, we cannot determine whether $x - y$ or $y - x$ is greater.

26. **The correct answer is (A).**

$\sqrt{2} \approx 1.4$.

Thus, $5\sqrt{2} \approx 5 \times 1.4 = 7$.

$\sqrt{5} \approx 2.2$.

Thus, $2\sqrt{5} \approx 2 \times 2.2 = 4.4$.

27. **The correct answer is (C).**

$$\left(1 \times \frac{1}{10}\right) + \left(8 \times \frac{1}{100}\right) + \left(3 \times \frac{1}{1000}\right) = .1 + .08 + .003 = .183$$

28. **The correct answer is (B).** $\left(-\frac{3}{5}\right)^2 = \frac{9}{25}$

$$\frac{6}{10} = \frac{3}{5} = \frac{15}{25}$$

$$\frac{9}{25} < \frac{15}{25}$$

29. **The correct answer is (B).** For Column A, let x = the price of 32 envelopes. Then, set up a proportion and cross-multiply.

$$\frac{2}{32} = \frac{5}{x}$$

$$2x = 5 \times 32$$

$$2x = 160$$

$$x = 80 \text{ cents}$$

For Column B, divide 3.30 by $3\frac{2}{3}$.

$$\frac{3.30}{3\frac{2}{3}} = \frac{3.30}{\frac{11}{3}} = 3.30 \times \frac{3}{11} = \frac{9.90}{11} = 90 \text{ cents}$$

30. **The correct answer is (C).** 9 boxes $\times$ 16 cartons = 144 boxes in one row

144 $\times$ 12 rows = 1,728 boxes in 12 rows

31. **The correct answer is (B).** First, note that m$\angle 3 = 105°$ since corresponding angles are congruent.

Then, since $\angle 1$ is supplementary to $\angle 3$, we have m$\angle 1 = 75°$.

Also, m$\angle 6 = 105°$ since vertical angles are congruent. Thus, m$\angle 6 >$ m$\angle 1$.

32. **The correct answer is (A).** We have m∠2 = 105° since ∠2 and ∠3 are congruent.

    Then, since ∠8 is the supplement of a 105° angle, we have m∠8 = 75°.

33. **The correct answer is (B).** Solve the inequality for x.

    $$\frac{1}{3}x + 3 < -6$$

    Subtract 3 from both sides.

    $$\frac{1}{3}x < -9$$

    Multiply both sides by 3.

    $$x < -27.$$

    Since $-18 > -27$, the correct answer is (B).

34. **The correct answer is (A).**

    $$\frac{7\frac{2}{3}}{\left(\frac{4}{5}\right)\left(\frac{5}{12}\right)} = \frac{\frac{23}{3}}{\frac{1}{3}} = \frac{23}{3} \times 3 = 23$$

    $$\frac{7\frac{1}{3}}{\left(\frac{5}{6}\right)\left(\frac{6}{15}\right)} = \frac{\frac{22}{3}}{\frac{1}{3}} = \frac{22}{3} \times 3 = 22$$

35. **The correct answer is (C).** The area of a triangle is given by the formula $A = \frac{1}{2}bh$. Since the two legs labeled are perpendicular to each other, we can use one as the height and the other as the base:

    $$A = \frac{1}{2}(2s)(s) = s^2.$$

    The area of a square is given by the formula $A = s^2$.

READING COMPREHENSION

Passage 1

1. **The correct answer is (B).** Choice (C) is a poor answer since the passage notes that the canyon "is not the world's largest undersea chasm." Both choices (A) and (D) are possibilities, since they are mentioned in the passage; however, neither explains the convenience of the canyon.

2. **The correct answer is (A).** Choice (D) is the poorest answer since the subject of erosion is not mentioned in the passage. Choice (C) is incorrect because the paragraph explains that "the canyons were submerged by a rise in sea level." Choice (B) is a better possibility, since the passage mentions "a bigger, older knife," but the problem was not that the theory wasn't old enough; it was that the mechanism described wasn't old enough.

3. **The correct answer is (C).** Choices (A), (B), and (D) are listed in the passage. Since this is a negative question, the only item not on the list is the correct answer.

4. **The correct answer is (D).** Choice (A) is not mentioned in the passage. Choice (C) is not correct because the blizzard falls "from above" to the depths, not from the depths. Choice (B) is not correct because it describes another substance some of the creatures feed on.

5. **The correct answer is (A).** Choice (C) is the length of the Grand Canyon in Arizona. Choices (B) and (D) describe the length, not the depth, of the Monterey Canyon.

Passage 2

6. **The correct answer is (C).** Choice (A) is a poor answer because nothing in the story suggests that Jen is not James's mother. Choice (B) is contradicted because the passage says James is 9, and the twins are 7. Choice (D) is Steiner's age, not James's.

7. **The correct answer is (C).** Choice (D) is incorrect because it was James who has not spoken in two weeks, not Steiner. Choice (B) does not make sense since Steiner left the family in the car while he looked for the mat, so he could not have been looking for it for two weeks. Choice (A) refers to a time earlier than this part of the story.

8. **The correct answer is (B).** Choice (A) is impossible, since we are told of James's actions in the car. Choice (D) is incorrect because the passage states James is being driven home from the hospital. Choice (C) is possible since Steiner is described as feeling bad that he and Jen hadn't had more children; however, the wording of the question implies he is grieving for a son he has already had.

9. **The correct answer is (D).** Choice (C) is unlikely since it is clear they are returning to a home they have lived in before. Since he had used the phrase since James was an infant, it is unlikely it is meant to start a conversation, so choice (A) is incorrect. The phrase is general and does not suggest action is needed, so choice (B) is incorrect.

10. **The correct answer is (C).** Choice (A) is unlikely since any talks with a physical therapist happened before this story takes place. Choice (D) is incorrect because James honks the horn while he is still in the car. Choice (B) is incorrect since the twins start whispering about him because he honked the horn.

11. **The correct answer is (A).** Steiner notices James's long hair at the beginning of the last paragraph in the passage. Choices (B), (C), and (D) occur earlier in the passage, and they do not refer to Steiner's looking at James's hair.

Passage 3

12. **The correct answer is (C).** Since Magro's book has not survived, the limited subject of his work does not contribute to our lack of knowledge about the Carthaginians; thus choice (D) is not correct. Since I and II are both correct, neither choice (A) nor choice (B) is the right answer.

13. **The correct answer is (B).** Although choice (A) may be true, that is not the purpose of the statement about Roman crucifixion. Choice (C) is incorrect since the passage does not suggest that the Romans were cruel to any specific group. And since the passage states "there is no reason to think the people of ancient Carthage were any more addicted to cruelty than the Romans," the purpose of the description is not to show they were more cruel, but that they were equally cruel. Thus, choice (D) is incorrect.

14. **The correct answer is (A).** Choice (B) is described in the first paragraph. Choice (C) states a fact, but it is not broad enough to describe the entire paragraph, so it is incorrect. Choice (D) is inaccurate, since the language as a whole was not preserved; the playwright's lines are dialogues in his plays.

15. **The correct answer is (D).** Choice (A) is incorrect because the passage does not tell what happened to the Phoenicians. Choice (B) is contradicted by the content of the passage, and choice (C) omits the fact that the playwright uses dialogue in the Punic language, so these answers are incorrect.

Passage 4

16. **The correct answer is (B).** Since the month is May and the leaves are beginning to swell, it is spring. By summer, the leaves would be full grown, so choice (C) is incorrect, and leaves are not usually green in winter or autumn, making choices (A) and (D) incorrect.

17. **The correct answer is (C).** Since the person is talking to Barbara Allen, choice (B) cannot be correct, and since the person is talking about his master, choice (A) cannot be correct. Barbara's mother is not mentioned until the poem's last stanza, so choice (D) is incorrect.

18. **The correct answer is (A).** Her only words to William are to indicate what he already knows, that he is dying. Stanza 4 describes his death, not her behavior, so choice (B) is incorrect. Stanzas 5 and 6 occur after William dies, so he would not feel her cruelty. Thus, choices (C) and (D) are incorrect answers.

19. **The correct answer is (C).** There is no indication that she is ill, so choice (A) is incorrect. She does not express love for William, so choice (B) is incorrect. And while she has heard the death bell, it is not the cause of her death, choice (D). The last two lines of the poem imply she knows she caused William's death, making choice (C) the correct answer.

20. **The correct answer is (A).** Choice (B) would not make sense because William dies, so he is not revived. While death could be said to "free" a person from life, the word suggests something positive, which does not fit the context of the poem, so choice (C) is incorrect. Choice (D) is incorrect because William has been parted from life, not joined to it.

ISEE PRACTICE TEST 1

Passage 5

21. **The correct answer is (D).** The author states that "something was sure to come by." The paragraph ends by referring to endlessly more (wildlife). Choice (A) is incorrect because the story is the story of the animals, not of their names. Choice (B) is incorrect; there are not more turtles, but more animals. Choice (C) is a true statement, but it is unrelated to the names of the animals.

22. **The correct answer is (C).** The words "for example" send the reader to the previous sentence. The trip from Monteverde to San Jose is an example of how easy it is to get from one place to another. Choice (A) could not be correct because the words "for example" always send the reader to the previous text. Choice (B) is incorrect because the information about the climate is between dashes. Dashes indicate information is not the main part of the sentence. For the same reason, choice (D) is incorrect.

23. **The correct answer is (A).** Words such as "blessed," "naturalist's paradise," and "one of the world's best systems of reserves" demonstrate the author's attitude.

24. **The correct answer is (A).** The author states that the order is "defined by the need for sunlight." Choice (B) is incorrect; although the author mentions niches, there is no stated relationship between niches and order or need. Choice (C) means confusion. Choice (D) is addressed, but not in a context of order.

25. **The correct answer is (B).** The "original tree" was the ladder for the strangler fig. Choice (A) is true; the original tree disappears after having served as a ladder to the soil. Choice (C) is true; the strangler fig is a single tree with a cluster of trunks. Choice (D) is true; the strangler fig dropped shoots that took root in the forest floor.

26. **The correct answer is (C).** The author discusses the origin and size of Monteverde, as well as his personal observations. Choice (A) is too general, since only one aspect of Monteverde is mentioned. Choice (B) is too narrow to be a general title. Choice (D) is too general; the focus of the passage is Monteverde.

Passage 6

27. **The correct answer is (D).** The passage states humans have been around for two million years, choice (A), and flowering plants for 100 million years, choice (B). Choice (C) is not mentioned in the passage.

28. **The correct answer is (B).** Paragraph 3 states they can "hide in any tiny space." Although the passage states some cockroaches live in sub-Arctic climates, it does not imply all cockroaches like the cold, so choice (A) is incorrect. Choice (C) is incorrect because adult cockroaches have wings. While choice (D) is a true statement, the passage does not state this as a reason they have survived.

29. **The correct answer is (D).** The passage states that they "like the dark" and run to their homes when a light comes on. Choices (A), (B), and (C) refer to cockroaches that are not members of these species, according to the passage.

www.petersons.com

526

30. **The correct answer is (C).** The paragraph in which the word appears is about why cockroaches have survived without change. The sentence in which "vulnerable" appears says the cockroaches do "not" undergo metamorphosis, which might make them "vulnerable." Thus, to be vulnerable is undesirable. So choices (A), (B), and (D) would not be correct.

Passage 7

31. **The correct answer is (B).** Choice (A) is incorrect, because while the diet may have been boring, they did not starve. The passage notes they had a "feeling of hunger," but the fact that they "emerged in good health" means they were getting enough to eat. Choice (C) is contradicted by the fact they had to work hard, and choice (D) is the opposite of what the passage says about carbon dioxide.

32. **The correct answer is (A).** The passage does not say what the animals ate, so choice (B) is incorrect. Choice (C) is contradicted because while that may have been the intent of having the animals in Biosphere 2, they did not produce as expected. Choice (D) is incorrect because the passage does not say what happened to the animals.

33. **The correct answer is (D).** Since the environment was meant to be sealed, outside air could not be let in, so choice (A) is incorrect. Choice (B) is incorrect because it is plants in the ocean, not the ocean itself, that would provide oxygen. Choice (C) is incorrect because the passage states the animals were meant to be food producers, and animals consume oxygen rather than produce it.

34. **The correct answer is (D).** Each of the other answers is stated at some point in the passage.

Passage 8

35. **The correct answer is (B).** The insurgents had rebelled against Spanish rule, and the Spanish commander tried to corner "the rebels." Choice (A) would include the insurgents, but also many other Cubans not involved in a rebellion. Choice (C) suggests a fighting force. Insurgents based in New York, for example, were not directly involved in fighting. Choice (D) is a word that relates to reconcentration, which was a Spanish policy, so it would not describe Cubans rebelling against Spanish rule.

36. **The correct answer is (A).** The passage states the policy was "designed to move the native population into camps and destroy the rebel's popular base." That is, to remove the source of new rebel troops. Although native Cubans were relocated into camps, making choice (B) a possibility, the primary purpose of reconcentration was military. Choice (C) was a result of reconcentration, but not its purpose. Choice (D) refers to insurgent activity, not to the relocation carried out by Spaniards.

37. **The correct answer is (D).** This is supported by the statement about the press printing "gruesome" stories. Although "yellow" may mean cowardly in some contexts, it is incorrect in this passage, so choice (A) is incorrect. Choice (B) is a paraphrase of the sentence "it stemmed from larger conflicts in policy." "It" refers to the war, not to yellow journalism. Choice (C) refers to the sympathy of the American public, so it is incorrect.

Passage 9

38. **The correct answer is (C).** The word refers to the practices of normally eating insects and human sacrifice. While murder may be illegal, choice (A), there are no laws preventing Americans from eating what they choose to. Since the passage states eating insects is "normal," choice (B), "experimental," is not correct. Choice (D) is incorrect because it is a synonym for "unlike," in the passage's third sentence, so it would not add anything to the passage.

39. **The correct answer is (B).** Choice (A) is incorrect because it implies anthropologists do condemn some behaviors. Choice (C) is incorrect because the passage says that anthropologists do not condemn other behavior. Condemnation would imply that they were judging other cultures against their own—their own being "right" and others being "wrong," and therefore, wrong cultures were merely mistakes. After all, why waste time studying the mistakes of others. Choice (D) is incorrect because the destruction of the universe is part of an example about Aztec culture and is not about why anthropologists think as they do.

40. **The correct answer is (C).** Choice (A) only refers to one example in the passage, so it is too narrow. Choice (B) is possible, because the first sentence defines an anthropologist, but the passage's content has a broader purpose, showing how anthropologists go about their work. Choice (D) is incorrect because the focus of the passage is on anthropologists, not on judging other cultures.

MATH ACHIEVEMENT

1. **The correct answer is (C).**

$7.2 \times 10^{-7} = .00000072$

2. **The correct answer is (B).**

First find variable expressions to represent the three angles.

Let the three angles be $8x$, $9x$, and $13x$.

Since the sum of the angles of any triangle is 180°,

$8x + 9x + 13x = 180°$.

Now solve the equation.

$30x = 180$

$x = 6$

Since the smallest angle is $8x$, $8x = 8(6) = 48°$.

3. **The correct answer is (A).**

   To rename a percent as a fraction, divide by 100.

   $$62\frac{1}{2} \div 100 = \frac{125}{2} \div \frac{100}{1} = \frac{125}{2} \times \frac{1}{100} = \frac{125}{200} = \frac{5}{8}$$

4. **The correct answer is (A).**

   The value of choice (A) is $\frac{11}{12}$; the value of choice (B) is $\frac{5}{12}$; the value of choice (C) is $\frac{1}{36}$; and the value of choice (D) is $\frac{1}{4}$ or $\frac{3}{12}$. Therefore, choice (A) has the greatest value.

5. **The correct answer is (D).**

   If $s + (s + 9) > 27$, then $2s > 18$. So $s > 9$. The only answer that is appropriate is 10.

6. **The correct answer is (C).** To round a number to the tenths place, look at the digit in the hundreths place. If the digit is 5 or larger, increase the tenths digit by one.

   Since 9 is 5 or larger, 21.49 becomes 21.5.

7. **The correct answer is (B).** The perimeter of $ABCD = 2l + 2w = 100$. Divide by 2: $l + w = 50$. If the length $AB >$ the width AD, choice (A) would make $AB = AD$. Choices (C) and (D) are too great. Therefore, choice (B) is correct.

8. **The correct answer is (B).** To add signed numbers with different signs, subtract and use the sign of the number with the greater absolute value.

   $$3\frac{1}{3} + (-6) = 5\frac{3}{3} - \left(3\frac{1}{3}\right) = 2\frac{2}{3}$$

   Since -6 has the greater absolute value, $-2\frac{2}{3}$ is the answer.

9. **The correct answer is (B).**

   $$-5ST^2 = (-5)(-2)(-3)^2 = (-5)(-2)(-3)(-3) = 90$$

10. **The correct answer is (D).**

    $ab + c = 2$

    Subtract c: $ab + c - c = 2 - c$
    $$ab = 2 - c$$

    Divide by b to get a: $\dfrac{ab}{b} = \dfrac{2 - c}{b}$ $a = \dfrac{2 - c}{b}$

11. **The correct answer is (B).**

    Substitute the numerical values for a, r, and n and compute S.

    $$S = \frac{a(1 - r^n)}{1 - r} = \frac{(-2)(1 - 2^3)}{1 - 2} = \frac{(-2)(1 - 8)}{-1} = \frac{(-2)(-7)}{-1} = \frac{14}{-1} = -14$$

12.   The correct answer is (C).

Use the Pythagorean Theorem:

$$a^2 + b^2 = c^2$$
$$a^2 + (18)^2 = (30)^2$$
$$a^2 + 324 = 900$$
$$a^2 + 324 - 324 = 900 - 324$$
$$a^2 = 576$$
$$a = \sqrt{576}$$
$$a = 24$$

13.   The correct answer is (C).

Let the original rectangle be expressed as:

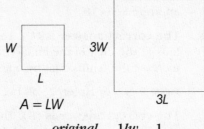

W   3W

L

A = LW   3L

$$ratio = \frac{original}{enlarged} = \frac{1lw}{9lw} = \frac{1}{9} = 1{:}9$$

14.   The correct answer is (C). Multiples of 8 include: 8, 16, 24, 32, 40, 48, 56, 64, 72, 80, 88, 104, etc. Comparing these with the answers provided, notice that the number 100 is not a multiple of 8. 144 is equal to 8×18.

15.   The correct answer is (B). The number of left-handed members is equal to $12 - 8$, or 4. The ratio of right-handers to left-handers is 8:4, which simplifies to 2:1.

16.   The correct answer is (A). Set up a ratio for this problem and solve.

Let x represent the number of books purchased with 2 dollars.

$$\frac{5}{d} = \frac{x}{2}$$

$5 \times 2 = d \times x$ (using cross-multiplication)

$$\frac{10}{d} = x$$

17.   The correct answer is (A).

All factors of 8 are factors of the number.

The factors of 8 are: $1 \times 82 \times 4$

18.   The correct answer is (B). Since this is an isosceles triangle, the angles opposite the congruent sides are also congruent. The sum of the measures of the angles in a triangle equal 180°. So $55° + 55° + x° = 180°$ and $x = 70°$.

19.   The correct answer is (D).

Let p equal the price of the item.

Price $\times$ Discount Rate = Discount Amount

So $p \times 40\% = \$4.00$;

$\quad p \times .40 = 4.00$;

$$p = \frac{4.00}{.40} = 10$$

20.   The correct answer is (A). There are 12 different outfits since for every skirt there is a choice of four different blouses.

$3 \times 4 = 12$

21.   The correct answer is (B).

The first day, $\frac{1}{4}$ of the taxes was done, so there were $\frac{3}{4}$ left.

$$\frac{1}{2} \times \frac{3}{4} = \frac{3}{8}$$

And

$$\frac{1}{4} + \frac{3}{8} = \frac{5}{8}$$

22.   The correct answer is (A).

$$8x - 14 = 42$$
$$8x = 56$$
$$x = 7, \text{ so}$$
$$7 - 5 = 2$$

23.   The correct answer is (B). To add signed numbers, if the signs are different, subtract and use the sign of the number with the greater absolute value.

$$2\frac{2}{3} + (-7) = 7 - 2\frac{2}{3} = 4\frac{1}{3}.$$

Because -7 has the greater absolute value, the solution is $-4\frac{1}{3}$.

24.   The correct answer is (B). If the carton is $\frac{2}{3}$ empty, it must be $\frac{1}{3}$ full.

$\frac{1}{3}$ the total capacity of 60 ounces is 20.

25. **The correct answer is (B).** The altitude of an equilateral triangle bisects the vertex, forming a 30-60-90 triangle with sides in the ratios shown.

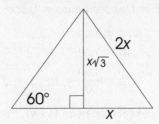

(This also comes from the Pythagorean Theorem, and the fact that the base of an equilateral triangle has been bisected to form this 30-60-90 triangle.)

The sides will be in the same ratio for the given triangle.

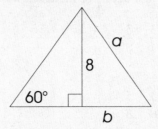

So, with the ratios $1:\sqrt{3}:2$ equaling the ratios $b:8:a$, we find

$$b = \frac{8}{\sqrt{3}} \text{ and } a = \frac{16}{\sqrt{3}}.$$

Area = one half base times height, so

$$A = (8)\left(\frac{8}{\sqrt{3}}\right) = \frac{64}{\sqrt{3}} = \frac{64\sqrt{3}}{3}.$$

26. **The correct answer is (D).** The area of the square minus the area of the circle equals the shaded area.

$OA = 3$

$2OA = 6 =$ diameter = side of square

area of square $= s^2$

area of circle $= \pi r^2$

$A = (6)^2 \qquad A = \pi(3)^2$
$= 36 \qquad\quad = 9\pi$

27. **The correct answer is (A).** The stock declined in value by $1,500, from an initial value of $11,000. The fractional decline in value is $\frac{1500}{11000} = .1364$, which is 13.64%.

28. **The correct answer is (B).** When you decrease a price by a given percentage, and then increase the (now lowered) price by that same percentage, the actual amount of increase is less than the actual amount of decrease.

    After a 10% discount, the sale price is 90% of the original amount. A 10% tax on this sale price means the final price is 110% of the taxable amount. (100% for the item, and 10% for the tax.)

    Expressing percents as decimals, we have:

    $(350 \times .9) \times 1.1 = 346.50$

    It doesn't matter what order the operations are performed in since multiplication is commutative and associative.

    $(350 \times 1.1) \times .9$ is still 346.50

29. **The correct answer is (B).** The equation of a line is given by $y = mx + b$ where m is the slope and b is the y-intercept. In this case, $y = 8x + (-3)$, which is the same as $y = 8x - 3$.

30. **The correct answer is (C).** To have an average of 80 after five tests, the total of all the scores must be $80 \times 5 = 400$. The known scores add up to $70 + 87 + 94 + 69 = 320$, so she needs $400 - 320 = 80$ points on the last test.

31. **The correct answer is (D).** Percent means "per 100."

    $4\frac{1}{2}$ percent means $\dfrac{4.5}{100} = .045$

32. **The correct answer is (C).**

    Put time in like units.

    $$\frac{15 \text{ hours}}{3 \text{ days}} = \frac{15 \text{ hours}}{3 \times 24 \text{ hours}} = \frac{15 \text{ hours}}{72 \text{ hours}}$$

    Divide the common factor of $3 = \dfrac{5}{24}$.

    Although choice (D) is correct, it is not expressed in simplest form.

33. **The correct answer is (D).**

    $$5x + 4 = 9x - 2$$
    $$5x + 4 - 4 = 9x - 2 - 4$$
    $$5x = 9x - 6$$
    $$5x - 9x = 9x - 6 - 9x$$
    $$-4x = -6$$
    $$x = \frac{-6}{-4} = \frac{6}{4} = \frac{3}{2}$$

34. **The correct answer is (C).** There are 14 outcomes (total gumballs), of which five are successes (red).

35. The correct answer is (A).

To add algebraic expressions, combine like terms.

$$\begin{aligned}2x^2 - 3x + 5 \\ \underline{-3x - 2} \\ 2x^2 - 6x + 3\end{aligned}$$

36. The correct answer is (B).

Substitute values $p = 1{,}500$, $r = .04$, and $t = 2\frac{1}{2}$.

$$A = 1{,}500 + (1{,}500)(.04)2\frac{1}{2} = 1{,}500 + 150 = 1{,}650$$

37. The correct answer is (C).

$$\frac{30}{8} = \frac{12}{y}$$
$$30y = 12 \times 8 \text{ (cross-multiply)}$$
$$30y = 96$$
$$y = \frac{96}{30} = 3\frac{1}{5}$$

38. The correct answer is (D).

$$\frac{12}{x} - \frac{9}{x} = \frac{3}{x}$$

The problem is written with all common denominators. Simply subtract the numerators.

39. The correct answer is (B).

$$4^3 - 3^4 = 64 - 81 = -17$$

40. The correct answer is (A). The line described by the equation crosses the x-axis when $y = 0$.

$$0 = -3x + 7$$
$$-7 = -3x$$
$$x = \frac{-7}{-3} = \frac{7}{3}$$

41. The correct answer is (D). To break a number into its prime factors, break it into factors, and break those factors into factors, until you cannot go any further. It doesn't matter what factors you begin with. You will reach the same prime factors.

$$50 = 10 \times 5 = 5 \times 2 \times 5$$

5 and 2 are prime numbers (they have no factors other than themselves and 1), and multiplication is commutative (it can be performed in any order).

Another way to approach the problem is to rule out the answers that have composite (non-prime) numbers. This rules out choices (A) and (B). Test the remaining answers by multiplying them out. Only choice (D) comes to 50.

42. **The correct answer is (A).**

$$A = \frac{bh}{2}$$

$$320 = \frac{40h}{2}$$

$$320 = 20h$$

$$16 = h$$

43. **The correct answer is (A).** If there are two parallel lines cut by a transversal, the alternate interior angles are congruent.

44. **The correct answer is (B).** Draw a diagram. They form similar triangles (m$\angle A$ = m$\angle B$). Therefore, corresponding sides are in the same ratio:

12 inches:3 inches = 120 feet:30 feet

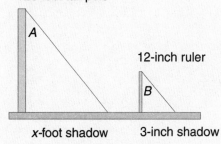

120-foot tall pole

A

12-inch ruler

B

x-foot shadow   3-inch shadow

45. **The correct answer is (D).**

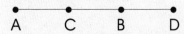

A   C   B   D

$\overline{AC}$ and $\overline{CB}$ are congruent, making *C* the midpoint of $\overline{AB}$. $\overline{AC}$ is 10 so $\overline{BC}$ is 10 and $\overline{AB}$ is 20. It is not given that *B* is the midpoint of $\overline{AD}$, just that it lies between *A* and *D*. Therefore, $\overline{AB}$ and $\overline{BD}$ are not necessarily congruent. There is no other relationship that will give the length of $\overline{BD}$ or of $\overline{CD}$.

ISEE Practice Test 2

Directions: Each question is made up of a word in capital letters followed by four choices. You are to circle the one word that is most nearly the same in meaning as the word in capital letters.

1. APPRAISE
   (A) search
   (B) estimate
   (C) prove
   (D) complain

2. AUGMENT
   (A) scatter
   (B) strike
   (C) honor
   (D) increase

3. TRITE
   (A) ignorant
   (B) unlikely
   (C) common
   (D) unskilled

4. SOLICIT
   (A) comfort
   (B) consent
   (C) help
   (D) request

5. VIGILANT
   (A) anxious
   (B) harmful
   (C) watchful
   (D) pleasant

6. BIZARRE
   (A) greedy
   (B) strange
   (C) brief
   (D) fortunate

7. ANALOGY
   (A) contract
   (B) contest
   (C) similarity
   (D) necessity

8. FRUGAL
   (A) showy
   (B) thrifty
   (C) abundant
   (D) grateful

9. DEFECTION
   (A) desertion
   (B) denial
   (C) reduction
   (D) obsession

10. DILEMMA
    (A) citation
    (B) scheme
    (C) difficulty
    (D) decree

11. EMINENT
    (A) profane
    (B) despicable
    (C) affluent
    (D) distinguished

12. PERCEIVE
    (A) reject
    (B) understand
    (C) persist
    (D) relinquish

13. COLLABORATE
    (A) work together
    (B) deny completely
    (C) walk briskly
    (D) leave alone

14. RUTHLESS

   (A) careless
   (B) useless
   (C) merciless
   (D) fearless

15. AGGRESSIVE

   (A) casual
   (B) lengthy
   (C) lenient
   (D) hostile

16. FIDELITY

   (A) timeliness
   (B) loyalty
   (C) hatred
   (D) spite

17. IRATE

   (A) enraged
   (B) dejected
   (C) economical
   (D) capable

18. ABDUCT

   (A) abbreviate
   (B) abdicate
   (C) kidnap
   (D) relieve

19. EGRESS

   (A) extreme
   (B) extra supply
   (C) exit
   (D) high price

20. REFUTE

   (A) disprove
   (B) assist
   (C) postpone
   (D) demolish

Directions: Each question below is made up of a sentence with one or two blanks. The sentences with one blank indicate that one word is missing. The sentences with two blanks indicate that two words are missing. Each sentence is followed by four choices. You are to circle the one word or pair of words that will best complete the meaning of the sentence as a whole.

21. After assessing the term of the elderly politician, one could conclude that as he neared _____, he became a(n) _____ leader, as shown by his forgetfulness on the floor of the Congress.

   (A) feebleness..competent
   (B) senility..unproductive
   (C) infirmity..capable
   (D) polarity..brackish

22. A refugee fleeing a country may have to _____ his allegiance to that country and _____ his family and friends.

   (A) anticipate..constitute
   (B) evaluate..abandon
   (C) renounce..forsake
   (D) relinquish..fluctuate

23. After taking a course in Home and Careers, she could conclude that _____ is a part of the study of _____.

   (A) anatomy..optometry
   (B) fatalism..etymology
   (C) ornithology..criminology
   (D) autism..agnosticism

24. Many great thinkers have observed that the lifetime of an individual is _____ when compared to _____, thereby making each of us seem less important in the big picture.

    (A) fatigued..energy
    (B) momentary..eternity
    (C) ephemeral..insignificance
    (D) juvenile..maturation

25. "When I am _____, I am also _____," explained the student with the downhearted look on her face.

    (A) blissful..sparkling
    (B) irrational..insightful
    (C) melancholy..lamentable
    (D) bellicose..affable

26. The psychologist could see that his patient suffered from _____ because he always thinks others _____ against him.

    (A) levity..crusade
    (B) paranoia..conspire
    (C) renown..falsify
    (D) finesse..rally

27. Historically, in witchcraft an evil witch when casting a _____ spell would use a small figurine as a _____.

    (A) malevolent..fetish
    (B) virtuous..charm
    (C) malignant..heretic
    (D) beneficent..amulet

28. Before the time of the internal combustion machine, during warfare it would not be unusual to see the _____ troops appear on the _____.

    (A) scapegoat..mercenary
    (B) shiftless..glut
    (C) sequestered..epoch
    (D) equestrian..mesa

29. People who live in large cities have to deal with the rushed pace of metropolitan life; as a relief from _____ pressures, many plan to vacation in _____ locales.

    (A) inert..kindred
    (B) urban..bucolic
    (C) rural..metropolitan
    (D) porous..ungainly

30. A male who has physically taken advantage of females should realize that his _____ has led him to _____.

    (A) whimsy..avowal
    (B) kindness..lechery
    (C) lust..carnality
    (D) lewdness..slothfulness

31. Although her natural abilities as an athlete are minimal, she has _____ them to the fullest; whereas her brother, who is a natural athlete, has _____ his.

    (A) maximized..squandered
    (B) subjugated..liberated
    (C) awed..slighted
    (D) breached..rectified

32. When trying to get the business owner to pay his fair share of taxes, the accountant often finds that _____ business owners are often mainly concerned only with the _____ aspects of life.

    (A) parsimonious..monetary
    (B) generous..charitable
    (C) dexterous..caustic
    (D) ample..estranged

33. During the summer cold snap, temperatures _____ to freezing, but the next week they _____ back into the nineties.

    (A) nullified..vied
    (B) evolved..maimed
    (C) skyrocketed..plunged
    (D) plummeted..soared

34. Even though the boxer had _____ a number of powerful punches, he refused to _____ to his opponent.

- **(A)** endured..submit
- **(B)** repelled..capitulate
- **(C)** engrossed..sustain
- **(D)** obstructed..infiltrate

35. The earthquake was so powerful that it _____ the entire city, leaving the once majestic skyscraper in piles of _____.

- **(A)** accorded..remains
- **(B)** rued..wreckage
- **(C)** enhanced..rubble
- **(D)** devastated..debris

36. The debater did not _____ many proofs to support his argument, but the ones that he did present were _____ enough to make him the winner.

- **(A)** summon..noisome
- **(B)** cite..cogent
- **(C)** enumerate..debilitating
- **(D)** reference..deleterious

37. Even though her happy birthday wish to me was _____, it was enough to _____ my hurt feelings.

- **(A)** churlish..pacify
- **(B)** verdant..bequeath
- **(C)** belated..assuage
- **(D)** punctual..damaged

38. The musician was _____ that most of the critics gave her concert complimentary reviews; however, she was still _____ by the negative ones.

- **(A)** elated..agitated
- **(B)** irate..contented
- **(C)** delighted..exhilarated
- **(D)** despondent..riled

39. In the medical malpractice lawsuit, the _____ was seeking _____ for the pain and suffering he experienced after a failed operation.

- **(A)** invalid..absolution
- **(B)** plaintiff..recompense
- **(C)** rustic..enlightenment
- **(D)** defrauder..compensation

40. The love story ended happily when the young husband returns to save his _____ bride from what surely would have been _____ death.

- **(A)** apex..flippant
- **(B)** surly..unavoidable
- **(C)** boorish..inevitable
- **(D)** cherished..inescapable

QUANTITATIVE REASONING   TIME: **35** MINUTES   **35 QUESTIONS**

Directions: Any figures that accompany questions in this section may be assumed to be drawn as accurately as possible EXCEPT when it is stated that a particular figure is not drawn to scale. Letters such as *x, y,* and *n* stand for real numbers.

For Questions 1–18, work each in your head or on the space available on these pages. Then select the correct answer.

1. 21.49 is closest to

(A) 22
(B) 21.4
(C) 21.5
(D) 21.45

2. Tom's bowling scores were 175, 155, and 210. What is his average score?

(A) 540
(B) 185
(C) 180
(D) 175

3. $62\frac{1}{2}\% =$

(A) $\frac{5}{8}$

(B) $\frac{8}{5}$

(C) 62.5

(D) $\frac{31}{50}$

4. Find the sum of
$2b + 5$, $4b - 4$, and $3b - 6$.

(A) $9b - 5$
(B) $9b - 10$
(C) $24b^2 + 120$
(D) $9b - 1$

5. $(-3)^2 - 4(-3) =$

(A) 3
(B) -15
(C) 108
(D) 21

6. At the Hoboken Gourmet Company, Karen is baking cookies. The recipe calls for 100 grams of flour per 40 ounces of water. How many ounces of water would be needed for 8,025 grams of flour?

(A) 2,006 ounces
(B) 1,284 ounces
(C) 3,210 ounces
(D) 3,325 ounces

7.

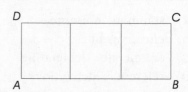

Three congruent squares are arranged in a row. If the perimeter of *ABCD* is 80, then the area of *ABCD* is

(A) 100
(B) 193
(C) 260
(D) 300

8. What is 72 expressed as the product of prime factors?

(A) (2)(3)
(B) (2)(3)(12)
(C) (6)(6)(2)
(D) (2)(2)(2)(3)(3)

9. Find the value of $\dfrac{8}{3-x}$ if $x = -1$.

   (A) $\dfrac{8}{5}$

   (B) 4

   (C) 2

   (D) $\dfrac{1}{2}$

10. The sum of two consecutive integers is 39. What is the value of the lesser of these integers?

   (A) 11

   (B) 12

   (C) 18

   (D) 19

11. The perimeter of a square is R meters. The area of the square is

   (A) $4R$

   (B) $\dfrac{R^2}{4}$

   (C) $\dfrac{R^2}{16}$

   (D) $2R^2$

12. Tom's weekly rent increased from \$125 to \$143.75. Find the percent of increase.

   (A) 1.15%

   (B) 1.5%

   (C) 8.7%

   (D) 15%

13. If $\dfrac{3}{x}$ is subtracted from $\dfrac{4}{x}$, the result is

   (A) 1

   (B) $\dfrac{7}{x}$

   (C) $\dfrac{-1}{x}$

   (D) $\dfrac{1}{x}$

14. Find the value of y in the proportion $\dfrac{20}{12} = \dfrac{5}{y}$.

   (A) $8\dfrac{1}{3}$

   (B) 3

   (C) 15

   (D) 8

15. Express as a trinomial: $(3a + 5)(2a - 3)$

   (A) $6a^2 + 15$

   (B) $6a^2 - 4a - 15$

   (C) $6a^2 + a - 15$

   (D) $6a^2 - a + 15$

16. If two fractions, each of which has a value between 0 and 1, are multiplied together, the product will be

   (A) always greater than both of the original fractions.

   (B) always less than both of the original fractions.

   (C) sometimes greater and sometimes less than both of the original fractions.

   (D) never less than both of the original fractions.

17. The expression $\sqrt{162}$ is equivalent to

   (A) $4\sqrt{2}$

   (B) $4 + \sqrt{2}$

   (C) $9\sqrt{2}$

   (D) $9 + \sqrt{2}$

18. If the length and the width of a rectangle are both tripled, the ratio of the area of the original rectangle to the area of the enlarged rectangle is

   (A) 1:3

   (B) 1:6

   (C) 1:9

   (D) 1:18

Directions: For Questions 19–35, note the given information, if any, and then compare the quantity in Column A to the quantity in Column B. Next to the number of each question, write

A   if the quantity in Column A is greater.
B   if the quantity in Column B is greater.
C   if the two quantities are equal.
D   if the relationship cannot be determined from the information given.

	Column A	Column B
19.	.01	.0099

20.

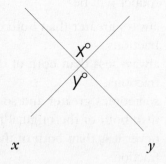

	x	y

	Column A	Column B
21.	$6 \times 5 + 3$	$(6 + 5)3$

22.

$$7y = 28$$

	Column A	Column B
	y	$(-2)^2$
23.	Ratio of $\dfrac{1}{4}$ to $\dfrac{3}{8}$	$66\dfrac{2}{3}\%$

Column A	Column B

24.

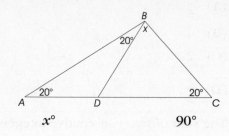

Column A	Column B
$x°$	$90°$

	Column A	Column B
25.	$\dfrac{1}{3}$ of $\dfrac{3}{5}$	.25

26.

$$r < 0$$

	Column A	Column B
	$\dfrac{1}{r}$	r^2
27.	8^2	2^8

28.

$$4{:}6 = m{:}15$$

	Column A	Column B
	m	10
29.	$\left(\dfrac{1}{10}\right)^2$	$\left(\dfrac{1}{10}\right)^3 \times 10$

| **Column A** | **Column B** | | **Column A** | **Column B** |

30.

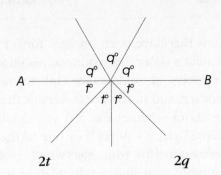

| 2t | 2q |

31. The average price per pound of a mixture of 3 lbs. of nuts at $1.89 per pound and 2 lbs. of pecans at $1.49 per pound | Average of $1.09, $2.19, and $4.75 |

32.

$$x = \frac{1}{2}$$

| $x^2 + x$ | $\left(\frac{\sqrt{3}}{2}\right)^2$ |

33. The area of a circle whose radius is 10 inches | The circumference of a circle whose diameter is 100 inches |

34. $\dfrac{\sqrt{7}}{3}$ | $\dfrac{3}{\sqrt{7}}$ |

35.

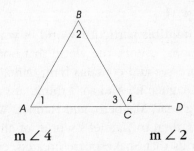

| m ∠ 4 | m ∠ 2 |

545

READING COMPREHENSION   TIME: 40 MINUTES   40 QUESTIONS

Directions: Each passage below is followed by questions based on its content. Answer the questions following a passage on the basis of what is *stated* or *implied* in that passage.

Passage 1

Line   Without his particular world of voices,
        persons, events, the world that both
        expresses and contains him, Othello is
        unimaginable. And so, I think, are Antony,
5   King Lear, Macbeth, and Hamlet. We come
        back then to Hamlet's world, of all the tragic
        worlds that Shakespeare created, easily the
        most various and brilliant, the most elusive.
        It is with no thought of doing justice to it
10   that I have singled out three of its attributes
        for comment. I know too well, if I may echo
        a sentiment of Mr. E. M. W. Tillyard's, that
        no one is likely to accept another man's
        reading of *Hamlet,* that anyone who tries to
15   throw light on one part of the play throws
        the rest into deeper shadow, and that what I
        have to say leaves many problems—to
        mention only one, the knotty problem of the
        text. All I would say in defense of the
20   materials I have chosen is that they seem to
        me interesting, close to the root of the
        matter even if we continue to differ about
        what the root of the matter is, and explana-
        tory, in a modest way, of this play's peculiar
25   hold on everyone's imagination, its almost
        mythic status, one might say, as a paradigm
        of the life of man.
            The first attribute that impresses us, I
        think, is mysteriousness. We often hear it
30   said, perhaps with truth, that every great
        work of art has a mystery at the heart; but
        the mystery of *Hamlet* is something else. We
        feel its presence in the numberless explana-

tions that have been brought forth for
35   Hamlet's delay, his madness, his ghost, his
        treatment of Polonius, or Ophelia, or his
        mother; and in the controversies that still go
        on about whether the play is "undoubtedly a
        failure" (Eliot's phrase) or one of the
40   greatest artistic triumphs; whether, if it is a
        triumph, it belongs to the highest order of
        tragedy; whether, if it is such a tragedy, its
        hero is to be taken as a man of exquisite
        moral sensibility (Bradley's view) or an
45   egomaniac (Madariaga's view).
            Doubtless there have been more of
        these controversies and explanations than
        the play requires; for in *Hamlet,* to para-
        phrase a remark of Falstaff's, we have a
50   character who is not only mad in himself
        but a cause that madness is in the rest of us.
        Still, the very existence of so many theories
        and counter-theories, many of them formu-
        lated by sober heads, gives food for thought.
55   *Hamlet* seems to lie closer to the illogical
        logic of life than Shakespeare's other
        tragedies. And while the causes of this
        situation may be sought by saying that
        Shakespeare revised the play so often that
60   eventually the motivations were smudged
        over, or that the original old play has been
        here and there imperfectly digested, or that
        the problems of Hamlet lay so close to
        Shakespeare's heart that he could not quite
65   distance them in formal terms of art, we
        have still as critics to deal with effects, not
        causes. If I may quote again from Mr.
        Tillyard, the play's very lack of a rigorous
        type of causal logic seems to be a part of
70   its point.

1. Which one of the names on the following list does NOT provide an opinion about *Hamlet?*

    (A) Tillyard
    (B) Eliot
    (C) Antony
    (D) Bradley

2. The best meaning of the word "paradigm" (line 26) is

    (A) example.
    (B) highlight.
    (C) opinion.
    (D) exalted view.

3. From this passage, we can infer that *Hamlet*

    (A) is open to many interpretations.
    (B) is best interpreted by Eliot.
    (C) cannot be interpreted.
    (D) can be explained only by logic.

4. This passage is written by which one of the following types of writers?

    (A) Journalist
    (B) Memoirist
    (C) Critic
    (D) Reviewer

Passage 2

Line Mechanical weathering happens in many
ways. Common mechanical weathering
processes are frost action, wetting and
drying, action of plant and animals, and the
5 loss of overlying rock and soil.

Water takes up about 10 percent more
space when it freezes. This expansion puts
great pressure on a container. For example,
think about a pail of water left outdoors in
10 freezing weather. The force of freezing water
may split the pail. In the same way, water
held in the cracks of rocks wedges the rocks
apart when it freezes. This process is called
ice wedging or frost action. Ice wedging oc-
15 curs in places where the temperature varies
from below the freezing point of water (32
degrees Fahrenheit) to above the freezing

point. In the northern United States and in
other places in which there are frequent
20 freezes and thaws, ice wedging is the most
damaging of all weathering processes.

Ice wedging occurs mostly in porous
rocks and in rocks with cracks in them. Bare
mountaintops, especially, are subject to ice
25 wedging. Vast fields of large, sharp-cornered
boulders are often found on such mountaintops. Ice wedging also causes potholes on
paved streets and highways. Here it is
helped by ice heaving. Ice heaving happens
30 when water in the ground freezes and lifts
the pavement above it. When the ice thaws,
the pavement collapses, leaving the pothole.

Repeated wetting and drying is especially effective at breaking up rocks that
35 contain clay. Clays swell up when wet and
shrink when dry. Constant swelling and
shrinking causes rock that contains clay,
such as shale, to fall apart.

Small plants, such as lichens and
40 mosses, grow on rocks. They wedge their
tiny roots into pores and crevices. When the
roots grow, the rock splits. Larger shrubs
and trees may grow through cracks in
boulders. Ants, earthworms, rabbits, wood-
45 chucks, and other animals dig holes in the
soil. These holes allow air and water to
reach the bedrock and weather it.

Granite is a rock formed far below
Earth's surface. It is exposed when the rocks
50 on top of it are worn away. The removal of
the rocks reduces the pressure on the
granite. When this happens, the relief from
the pressure lets the granite expand.
Upward expansion leads to long curved
55 breaks, or joints. The joints are parallel to
the surface and occur in exposed peaks or
outcrops. This process is sheet joining. From
time to time, large sheets of loosened rock
break away from the outcrop. This process
60 is called exfoliation—the peeling of surface
layers. Rounded mountain peaks called
exfoliated domes are formed in this way.

5. The best title of this passage is

   (A) "Some Geological Basics."
   (B) "How Rocks Change."
   (C) "Ice Wedging and Ice Heaving."
   (D) "Types of Mechanical Weathering."

6. The most damaging of all weathering processes is

   (A) ice wedging.
   (B) ice heaving.
   (C) wetting and drying.
   (D) exfoliation.

7. Which of the following combinations causes potholes?

   (A) Ice wetting and wetting and drying
   (B) Ice wedging and sheet joining
   (C) Sheet joining and exfoliation
   (D) Ice wedging and ice heaving

8. What is an "outcrop" (line 59)?

   (A) An exfoliated peak
   (B) An exposed peak
   (C) A granite peak
   (D) All exposed rock

9. Frost action is the same as

   (A) ice heaving.
   (B) ice wedging.
   (C) sheet joining.
   (D) exfoliation.

Passage 3

Line Unable to subdue Great Britain in the West,
Napoleon turned toward the East. In 1812,
he invaded Russia. At first, Napoleon's huge
army of about 600,000 men was successful.
5   It defeated Russian forces in several engage-
ments and pushed on toward Moscow.
However, the Russian emperor, Alexander I,
refused to risk the outcome of the war on a
single battle. His forces retreated deep into
10 Russia until, as the French General Caulaincourt said: "We (the French) were in the
heart of inhabited Russia and yet . . . we

were like a vessel without a compass in the
midst of a vast ocean, knowing nothing of
15 what was happening around us."

   Napoleon's army entered Moscow in
the middle of September and found a
deserted city. Napoleon waited for the
Russian emperor to surrender. He waited
20 while Russian peasants stole into Moscow at
night and set fire to parts of the city. He
waited while Russian Cossacks raided his
supply routes and cut his lines of communication. He waited while the winds of Russia
25 became colder and colder. He waited, but
Emperor Alexander I said nothing.

   With the approach of winter, his
supplies ran dangerously low. Napoleon
therefore decided to move his army out of
30 Russia. On October 19, he left Moscow.
Thus began one of the most disastrous
retreats. Soldiers starved or froze to death.
Horses, kept on the move for 14 and 15
hours a day, collapsed. The wounded fell off
35 carts only to have the drivers of other
vehicles ride over their bodies so as not to
lose their place in line. The Cossacks
waylaid stragglers and raided transport
wagons. Brotherhood was forgotten and,
40 according to General Caulaincourt, "every
man thought of himself, and himself alone."

   Napoleon, who rarely concerned
himself about the men who lost their lives,
issued this bulletin: "His Majesty (Napoleon)
45 has never been in better health." The
purpose of this was to end rumors in France
that he was dead or dying and to stifle any
plans to replace him. Then on December 5,
he abandoned his doomed army and hurried
50 to Paris to strengthen his position in France.
Only 40,000 of Napoleon's troops crossed
the border out of Russia.

10. The repetition of "He waited . . ." in paragraph 2 is intended to create which effect on the reader?

(A) Boredom

(B) Dread

(C) To provide images

(D) Suspense

11. The best title of this passage is

(A) "Napoleon's Greatest Battle."

(B) "Napoleon's Disastrous Invasion."

(C) "In the Middle of the Ocean."

(D) "The French and Russian War."

12. The passage illustrates which one of Napoleon's qualities best?

(A) His strategic brilliance

(B) His ability to negotiate

(C) His disdain for his own soldiers

(D) His ability to transform misfortune into victory

13. The best meaning of the word "stifle" (line 47) is

(A) suppress.

(B) encourage.

(C) delay.

(D) give voice to.

Passage 4

Line Imagine a steep valley high in the mountainous Alps of Switzerland. No river runs in this valley. Instead, the entire valley floor is covered by a mass of snow-covered ice,
5 hundreds of meters thick. This ice mass can be followed up the valley for many kilometers. It begins in huge fields of ice and snow just below the very highest peaks.

Careful study would show that the ice in
10 this valley has moved downhill at the rate of several meters a day. At the lower part of the valley, the thin ice runs out and suddenly ends. Milky-colored water runs from beneath the ice and flows down into the valley. This
15 long, slow-moving, wedge-shaped stream of ice is a valley glacier.

Imagine a great landmass in the polar latitudes of the far north or south. The climate is so cold that only snow falls. For
20 thousands of years snow has been falling, building up, and changing to ice. Almost the whole landmass is covered by the thick mass of ice. Only the highest mountain peaks reach above the ice.

25 The ice is thousands of meters thick, and it moves outward from its center in all directions toward the seacoasts. In some places it reaches the sea by traveling through low valleys. Here great chunks of ice break
30 off to float away as icebergs. This moving mass of ice, far larger than a valley glacier, is called an ice sheet.

Glaciers are born in areas always covered by snow. These are areas where
35 more snow falls than melts each year. Some snow is always left to add to the buildup of previous years. Climates cold enough to cause such conditions may be found in any part of the world. Air temperatures drop with greater
40 height above sea level and with greater distance from the equator.

Even in equatorial areas, then, permanent snows may be found on high mountains. Farther from the equator the mountains need
45 not be so high for snow to exist. In the polar areas, permanent snows may be found even at sea level. The lowest level that permanent snows reach in summer is called the snow line. A mountain that is completely covered
50 with snow in winter, but from which the snow is all melted by summer, has no snow line.

The snow line is highest near the equator and lowest near the poles. As climates become colder with greater latitude
55 (distance from the equator), less height is needed to reach a snow line. The position of the snow line also changes with the total yearly snowfall and the amount of exposure to the sun. Thus the height of a snow line is
60 not the same for all places in the same latitude.

14. From this passage, it is clear that a valley glacier

(A) is too heavy to move.
(B) runs swiftly like a river.
(C) can run downhill several yards a day.
(D) is stationary.

15. In which way does an "ice sheet" compare to a "valley glacier"?

(A) They both produce icebergs.
(B) An ice sheet is larger.
(C) A valley glacier is larger.
(D) They both are taller than mountains.

16. From this passage, we can infer that a snow line

(A) cannot exist near the equator.
(B) is always the same height.
(C) is lowest near the equator.
(D) is lowest near the poles.

17. From this passage, we can deduce that the latitude of a pole compared to the equator is

(A) greater.
(B) impossible to determine.
(C) constantly changing.
(D) equal.

Passage 5

Line Two roads diverged in a yellow wood,
And sorry I could not travel both
And be one traveler, long I stood
And looked down one as far as I could
5 To where it bent in the undergrowth;

Then took the other, as just as fair,
And having perhaps the better claim,
Because it was grassy and wanted wear;
Though as for that, the passing there
10 Had worn them really about the same.

And both that morning equally lay
In leaves no step had trodden black.
Oh, I kept the first for another day!
Yet knowing how way leads on to way,
15 I doubted if I should ever come back.

I shall be telling this with a sigh
Somewhere ages and ages hence;
Two roads diverged in a wood, and I—
I took the one less traveled by,
20 And that has made all the difference.

18. The best meaning of the word "diverged" in the last stanza is

(A) came together.
(B) became intertwined.
(C) became indistinct.
(D) branched off.

19. The poem is an extended metaphor that deals with which one of the following themes?

(A) Life's choices
(B) Building a roadway
(C) The battle between life and death
(D) The loss of the Garden of Eden

20. The choice the speaker makes in Stanza 2 suggests which quality of character?

(A) Conformity
(B) Adventurousness
(C) Indifference
(D) Fear

21. The line "Oh, I kept the first for another day!" (line 13) suggests which one of the following?

(A) The speaker will return tomorrow
(B) An arrogant disdain
(C) A need for people to maintain options as long as possible
(D) The speaker will return as an old person

22. The speaker says, "I shall be telling this with a sigh" (line 16). This suggests which possible emotion?

(A) Exasperation
(B) Glee
(C) Depression
(D) Weariness

Passage 6

Line North Dakota entered the United States as
the 39th state on November 2, 1889. South
Dakota, which is officially recognized as the
40th state, also became a state the same day.
5 Two other states, Montana and Washington,
were added later that same month. Colorado
had been named the 38th state 13 years
before North Dakota's admittance. North
Dakota is located at the geographical center
10 of North America in the great plains. North
Dakota is bordered on the north by Canada,
on the east by Minnesota, south by South
Dakota, and west by Montana.
　　　North Dakota can be divided into two
15 regions, east and west. The eastern part of
the state extends from the Red River Valley.
The Red River draws the North Dakota–
Minnesota border and is characterized as the
central lowlands. The central lowlands
20 consist of the Red River Valley and the
Young Drift Plains. These regions were
carved out by glaciers in the last ice age.
When these glaciers melted, a prehistoric
lake named Lake Agassiz was formed. With
25 time, Lake Agassiz dried up and left very
fertile soil in this region. The eastern part of
the state also gets an average rainfall of
about 30 inches. The combination of rich
soil and healthy rainfall during the growing
30 season results in farms that have among the
highest yield per acre in the world. Of
particular fame is the wheat and barley
grown in this region.

23. South Dakota

    (A) is east of North Dakota.
    (B) entered the United States after North
        Dakota.
    (C) is the geographical center of North
        America.
    (D) entered the United States before
        Colorado.

24. The Young Drift Plains and the Red River
    Valley were formed by

    (A) continental drift.
    (B) flooding of the Red River.
    (C) an earthquake.
    (D) glaciers from the last ice age.

25. Factors contributing to the high per-acre
    yield in eastern North Dakota include

    I. fertile soil.
    II. healthy rainfall during the growing
        season.
    III. a long growing season.

    (A) I and II only
    (B) II and III only
    (C) I and III only
    (D) I, II, and III

26. North Dakota is bordered on the east by

    (A) settlers.
    (B) Colorado.
    (C) Canada.
    (D) the Red River.

Passage 7

Line The word petroleum means "rock oil."
Petroleum, like coal, is a sedimentary
material of organic origin. It is a mixture
made mainly of liquid hydrocarbons, which
5 are compounds of hydrogen and carbon.
Gasoline and kerosene are hydrocarbons.
　　　Scientists think that petroleum was
formed by slow chemical changes in plant
and animal materials buried under sand and
10 clay in shallow coastal waters. Some of the
hydrocarbons formed were liquids and some
were gases. As the sediments became
compacted, the hydrocarbons were
squeezed into pores and cracks of nearby
15 sandstone or limestone. These rocks also
contained seawater. The lighter, mixed
hydrocarbon liquid (petroleum) rose above
the water, and the natural gas collected
above the petroleum.

20   Why haven't the petroleum and gas kept rising and escaped from the rock in the millions of years since they formed? Probably a good deal did. The petroleum found today was sealed in by an impermeable rock

25   layer, such as shale. Such rock structures are called oil traps.

     Wells were drilled into oil-bearing rock to release the oil. The pressure of the natural gas helps bring the oil to the surface.

30   Unless the drilling is carefully controlled, the high pressure causes wasteful oil gushers. Even with modern technology, only about 40 percent of the oil is pumped out of a given well.

35   Natural gas often occurs with petroleum. Yet it may also exist in great deposits of gas alone. It is a mixture of hydrocarbon gases, mostly methane. Natural gas is an efficient fuel for use in heating.

40   When petroleum is refined, it is separated into many different hydrocarbons. Gasoline is used in automobiles. Kerosene and fuel oil are used for heating. Other oils are used as lubricants. Both petroleum and

45   natural gas are used as raw material in making such substances as plastics, fertilizers, dyes, and medicines.

     At the present rate of use, United States reserves of petroleum are expected to last

50   between 30 and 50 years. United States reserves of natural gas are expected to last between 40 and 60 years. Other reserves may be found, but usage is likely to increase.

27. From this passage, we can assert that

(A) out of a given, well we can pump all its oil.

(B) the United States will never run out of oil reserves.

(C) petroleum is inorganic.

(D) natural gas can be used for heating.

28. The word "impermeable" (line 24) best means

(A) sedimentary.

(B) impassable.

(C) permanent.

(D) shale.

29. All of the following are examples of hydrocarbons EXCEPT

(A) seawater.

(B) petroleum.

(C) gasoline.

(D) kerosene.

30. From this passage, we can infer that petroleum has its origin in

(A) seawater.

(B) plant and animal material.

(C) crushed rock.

(D) gas.

Passage 8

Line   When I was 11 years old, my only brother, who had just graduated from Union College, came home to die. A young man of great talent and promise, he was the pride of my

5   father's heart.

     I recall going into the large darkened parlor and finding the casket, mirrors, and pictures all draped in white, and my father seated, pale and immovable. As he took no

10   notice of me, after standing a long while, I climbed upon his knee, when he mechanically put his arm about me, and, with my head resting against his beating heart, we both sat in silence, he thinking of the wreck

15   of all his hopes in the loss of a dear son, and I wondering what could be said or done to fill the void in his breast. At length he heaved a deep sigh and said: "Oh, my daughter, I wish you were a boy!"

20   Throwing my arms about his neck, I replied: "I will try to be all my brother was."

     All that day and far into the night I pondered the problem of boyhood. I

thought that the chief thing to be done in
25 order to equal boys was to be learned and
courageous. So I decided to study Greek and
learn to manage a horse. I learned to leap a
fence and ditch on horseback.

I began to study Latin, Greek, and
30 mathematics with a class of boys in the
academy, many of whom were older than I.
For three years one boy kept his place at the
head of the class, and I always stood next.
Two prizes were offered in Greek. I strove
35 for one and took the second. One thought
alone filled my mind. "Now," said I, "my
father will be satisfied with me."

I rushed breathless into his office, laid
down the new Greek Testament, which was
40 my prize, on his table and exclaimed:
"There, I got it!" He took up the book, asked
me some questions about the class, and,
evidently pleased, handed it back to me.
Then he kissed me on the forehead and
45 exclaimed with a sigh, "Ah, you should have
been a boy!"

31. The best title for this passage is

(A) "American Women of the 19th
Century."
(B) "The Struggle for Success."
(C) "The Prize."
(D) "You Should Have Been a Boy."

32. The tone of this passage is best stated as

(A) humorous.
(B) furious.
(C) sorrowful.
(D) indignant.

33. The best meaning of the word "void"
(line 17) is

(A) emptiness.
(B) vessel.
(C) blood.
(D) feeling.

34. We can infer that the speaker of this
passage will

(A) become angry, depressed, and with-
drawn.
(B) go to Greece to study its culture.
(C) go to Union College.
(D) continue to struggle to be seen as
equal to men.

35. Which word best describes the father's
feelings toward his daughter?

(A) Warm
(B) Scornful
(C) Reproachful
(D) Irritated

Passage 9

Line Between 1000 and 1750 A.D., few basic
changes were made in the way men lived in
England. Most of the people in 1750 were
still tilling the soil, and they were doing it
5 about the same way their ancestors had in
the year 1000. The "agricultural revolution"
was barely under way.

England's population was small, slightly
over six million. Her customs were deeply
10 rooted. Her pace of living, according to
British historian G. M. Trevelyan, was that of
"a slowly moving stream."

There were some industries, but most
of them were small. There was some
15 manufacturing, but much of this work was
done in private homes under the "domestic
system." Under this system a businessman
provided workers with equipment for
making finished products at home. There
20 were some important business centers, but
none of them had yet felt the frantic rush of
modern industrial life.

England was not a rural paradise. If the
villagers danced about the Maypole on
25 festival days, they also worked hard on other
days. If they breathed free air, they also
lacked some of the goods that came with
the smoke of factories. If they had sufficient

30 time to eat, they also rarely dined on rich meats and pastry. In short, life in England in 1750 was peaceful but rugged.

In the next hundred years, vast changes took place. By 1850, the English landscape was transformed in many places. There were
35 smoky factories, roaring machinery, crowded towns, and a new way of life. Similar changes were occurring or were about to take place in other parts of Europe and beyond. Our story is concerned with the
40 reasons for this remarkable change.

From about 1750 to 1860, new inventions, new techniques, and new sources of power helped to speed up tremendously the pace of life in England and
45 elsewhere. The many economic and social changes of this period make up what has been called the "Industrial Revolution."

The term "Industrial Revolution" is far from accurate. It suggests that there was a
50 sudden overthrowing of the past. Such was not the case. Actually, the economic and social changes of this so-called "revolution" grew out of the past and were to extend far into the future. One aspect of culture is
55 technology, defined as "the sum of the ways in which a social group provides its members with the material objects of their civilization." A study of articles, produced by men from ancient times on, shows high
60 levels of design, craftsmanship, and ingenuity in furniture, architecture, mechanical devices, and other fields. Industry had long been in existence, and many of its products were highly sophisticated. The new ele-
65 ments were the changes in methods of production and the resulting extension of the volume of production. Once these changes got underway, there was a tendency for one to bring about the next related
70 change. The Industrial Revolution fed on itself and spread within one industry and from one industry to another.

36. The image "a slowly moving stream" (line 12) conveys what message about England from 1000 to 1750 A.D.?

(A) It was a land dependent on fishing.
(B) There were major changes taking place.
(C) Change did not come quickly.
(D) The countryside was picturesque.

37. The sentences in the paragraph beginning "England was not a rural paradise" generally follow which pattern of construction?

(A) The combination of opposites
(B) The use of multiple examples
(C) General and particular
(D) Building to an ironic climax

38. The best meaning of the word "ingenuity" (lines 60–61) is

(A) clever talent.
(B) ability to make an engine.
(C) furniture design.
(D) industry.

39. We can infer from the passage that the Industrial Revolution

(A) only occurred in England.
(B) took place before the "agricultural revolution."
(C) was a sudden overthrow of the past.
(D) grew out of the past.

40. From this passage, we can assume that ancient people were

(A) slow-witted.
(B) incapable of chance.
(C) living in an agricultural paradise.
(D) sophisticated.

MATH ACHIEVEMENT	TIME: 40 MINUTES	45 QUESTIONS

Directions: Each question is followed by four suggested answers. Read each question and then decide which one of the four suggested answers is best.

1. Which of the following is a multiple of both 6 and 5?

    (A) 20
    (B) 45
    (C) 65
    (D) 90

2. Six less than a number is two thirds of that number. What is the number?

    (A) 18
    (B) 9
    (C) 4
    (D) $5\frac{1}{3}$

3. $(3a^3 - 6) - (2a^2 + 1) =$

    (A) $a - 5$
    (B) $3a^3 - 2a^2 - 5$
    (C) $3a^3 - 2a^2 - 7$
    (D) None of the above

4. On a test with 25 questions, Reyna scored 88%. How many questions did Reyna answer correctly?

    (A) 21
    (B) 22
    (C) 4
    (D) 5

5. The perimeter of a square with a side length of 5 is how much less than the perimeter of a rectangle with a side length of 6 and width of 5?

    (A) 6
    (B) 4
    (C) 2
    (D) 1

6. One fifth of a class voted to go to the science museum for a field trip. If 4 students chose this location, how many students are in the class?

    (A) 10
    (B) 20
    (C) 11
    (D) 24

7. If 35% of a number is 70, find the number.

    (A) 24.5
    (B) 200
    (C) 50
    (D) 140

8. The length of the side of an equilateral triangle is 10. Find the area of the triangle.

    (A) 25
    (B) 100
    (C) $25\sqrt{3}$
    (D) $20\sqrt{3}$

9. A father can do a job in a certain number of hours. His son takes twice as long to do the job. Working together, they can do the job in 6 hours. How many hours does it take the father to do the job alone?

    (A) 9
    (B) 18
    (C) 12
    (D) 10

10. How many 12.6-inch strips can be cut from a board 189 inches long?

    (A) 1.5

    (B) 15

    (C) 150

    (D) 176.4

11. David is 5 years older than Paul. In 5 years, David will be twice as old as Paul is now. How old is David now?

    (A) 15

    (B) 10

    (C) 25

    (D) 20

12. If $3x - 9 = 45$, what is $x \div 9$?

    (A) 6

    (B) 3

    (C) 2

    (D) 1

13. $\dfrac{1}{2} + \dfrac{2}{3} + \dfrac{3}{4} - \dfrac{1}{2} - \dfrac{1}{3} - \dfrac{1}{4} - \dfrac{1}{3} =$

    (A) $\dfrac{1}{2}$

    (B) $\dfrac{2}{3}$

    (C) 1

    (D) $\dfrac{3}{4}$

14. Which of the following is most nearly 60% of $19.95?

    (A) $8.00

    (B) $9.00

    (C) $14.50

    (D) $12.00

15. Find the sum of $2b + 5$, $4b - 4$, and $3b - 6$.

    (A) $9b - 5$

    (B) $7b - 10$

    (C) $6b - 1$

    (D) $9b + 5$

16.

Figure $ABCD$ is a parallelogram. $m\angle A = 105°$. $m\angle B = 75°$. Find the measurement of D.

    (A) 105°

    (B) 75°

    (C) 160°

    (D) 150°

17. If l laser discs cost d dollars, 10 laser discs will cost

    (A) $\dfrac{ld}{10}$ dollars.

    (B) $\dfrac{10d}{l}$ dollars.

    (C) $10ld$ dollars.

    (D) $\dfrac{10l}{d}$ dollars.

18. A salesman earns a commission of 8% of his total sales. How much must he sell to earn a commission of $124?

    (A) $9,920

    (B) $1,550

    (C) $992

    (D) $1,148.15

19. What is the least number that can be added to 42,042 to produce a result divisible by 9?

    (A) 6

    (B) 8

    (C) 5

    (D) 7

20. If $5x + 7 \geq x - 1$, then

    (A) $x \leq 2$.

    (B) $x \geq 8$.

    (C) $x \leq 8$.

    (D) $x \geq -2$.

21. The expression $\frac{1}{2}\sqrt{28}$ is equivalent to

    (A) $\sqrt{14}$

    (B) $2\sqrt{7}$

    (C) $\sqrt{7}$

    (D) $4\sqrt{7}$

22.

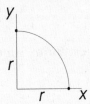

Determine the area between the curve and the x- and y-axes. Assume that $r = 10$.

    (A) 100π

    (B) 25π

    (C) 20π

    (D) 400π

23. Randi scores an 85, 81, and 95 on her first 3 exams. What must she score on her fourth exam to receive an average of 90?

    (A) 90

    (B) 94

    (C) 99

    (D) 100

24. Solve for x: $3x - 6 = 10x - 11$

    (A) $\frac{5}{7}$

    (B) $-\frac{5}{7}$

    (C) -3

    (D) 3

25. If $x < y$ and $y < z$, which statement about the integers x, y, and z must be true?

    (A) $x < z$

    (B) $x = z$

    (C) $x > z$

    (D) $y - x = z$

26. If $g(x) = 2x^2 - 4x + 5$, what is the value of $g(3)$?

    (A) 5

    (B) 11

    (C) 12

    (D) 18

27. Find the height of a triangle whose base is 25 inches and whose area is 75 square inches.

    (A) 3 inches

    (B) 3 square inches

    (C) 6 inches

    (D) 6 square inches

28. What is .09 expressed as a percent?

    (A) .009%

    (B) 9%

    (C) .9%

    (D) .09%

29. What is the equation of the line passing through the point (2,3) and parallel to the line $3x - 6y = 12$?

    (A) $x + 2y = 8$

    (B) $2x - y = 1$

    (C) $-x - 2y = 4$

    (D) $x - 2y = -4$

30. On level ground, a man 6 feet tall casts a shadow 8 feet long at the same time that a tree casts a shadow 20 feet long. Find the number of feet in the height of the tree.

    (A) $46\frac{2}{3}$

    (B) 15

    (C) 8

    (D) 120

31. The average of 2 and x is 7; find the value of x.

    (A) 9

    (B) 12

    (C) 14

    (D) 16

32. $\sqrt{16} - \sqrt[3]{27} =$

    (A) 1
    (B) 7
    (C) −1
    (D) −7

33. What is 64 expressed as the product of prime factors?

    (A) (2)(2)(2)(3)(3)
    (B) (2)(2)(2)(2)(2)(2)
    (C) (2)(2)(2)(2)(2)
    (D) (8)(8)

34. The area of a circle is the same as the area of a square whose side is 4 centimeters. The radius of the circle is closest to

    (A) 16 centimeters.
    (B) 5 centimeters.
    (C) 4 centimeters.
    (D) 2 centimeters.

35. The length of a side of a square is represented by $2x + 2$, and the length of a side of an equilateral triangle by $4x$. If the square and the equilateral triangle have equal perimeters, find x.

    (A) 6
    (B) 4
    (C) 1
    (D) 2

36. The expression $\sqrt{250}$ is equivalent to

    (A) $25\sqrt{10}$
    (B) $10\sqrt{2}$
    (C) $5\sqrt{10}$
    (D) $50\sqrt{2}$

37. On a map, 4 inches represent 15 miles. How many miles would 5 inches represent?

    (A) 12
    (B) $37\frac{1}{2}$
    (C) 60
    (D) $18\frac{3}{4}$

38. Express as a ratio in simplest form: 5 inches to 3 feet.

    (A) $\dfrac{5}{3}$
    (B) $\dfrac{3}{5}$
    (C) $\dfrac{5}{36}$
    (D) $\dfrac{36}{5}$

39. If $x = 1$ on the graph of $y = -5x + 4$, what does y equal?

    (A) −1
    (B) −5
    (C) 4
    (D) 9

40. $4x^5$ divided by $3x^7$ is

    (A) $12x^{12}$
    (B) $\dfrac{4}{3x^2}$
    (C) $\dfrac{4x^2}{3}$
    (D) $\dfrac{3x^2}{4}$

41. .0825 expressed as a percent is

    (A) 825%
    (B) 8.25%
    (C) .825%
    (D) .0825%

42. What is the area of a square whose diagonal is 12?

(A) 36
(B) 24
(C) $12\sqrt{2}$
(D) 72

43. Which fraction lies between $\frac{3}{5}$ and $\frac{4}{5}$?

(A) $\frac{5}{6}$
(B) $\frac{17}{20}$
(C) $\frac{7}{10}$
(D) $\frac{13}{15}$

44.

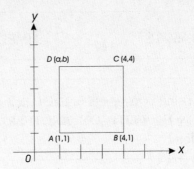

Find the coordinates of point *D*.

(A) (1,4)
(B) (4,1)
(C) (4,4)
(D) (1,1)

45. The circumference of a circle whose diameter is 9 inches is approximately

(A) 18 inches.
(B) 28 inches.
(C) 81 inches.
(D) 254 inches.

WRITING SAMPLE	TIME: 30 MINUTES

Directions: Using two sheets of lined theme paper, plan and write an essay on the topic assigned below. DO NOT WRITE ON ANOTHER TOPIC. AN ESSAY ON ANOTHER TOPIC IS NOT ACCEPTABLE.

Topic: The playwright George Bernard Shaw once said, "Youth is wasted on the young."

Assignment: Write an essay giving your view of this. Do you agree with this statement? Does the computer industry support this concept? Support your opinion with specific examples from history, current events, or personal observations.

Name: _____

Write your essay here.

_____

_____

_____

_____

_____

_____

_____

_____

_____

_____

_____

_____

_____

_____

_____

_____

_____

_____

_____

_____

_____

_____

(Continue, if necessary.)

EXPLANATORY ANSWERS TO THE ISEE PRACTICE TEST 2

VERBAL REASONING

1. The correct answer is (B).
2. The correct answer is (D).
3. The correct answer is (C).
4. The correct answer is (D).
5. The correct answer is (C).
6. The correct answer is (B).
7. The correct answer is (C).
8. The correct answer is (B).
9. The correct answer is (A).
10. The correct answer is (C).
11. The correct answer is (D).
12. The correct answer is (B).
13. The correct answer is (A).
14. The correct answer is (C).
15. The correct answer is (D).
16. The correct answer is (B).
17. The correct answer is (A).
18. The correct answer is (C).
19. The correct answer is (C).
20. The correct answer is (A).

21. The correct answer is (B). The clue is the word *elderly*. As people age, they can become physically and/or mentally impaired. The first word would be a synonym for "impairment." This eliminates choice (D) because the words have nothing to do with impairment. The trigger word is *forgetfulness*. The second word would be a synonym for "ineffective." This would eliminate choices (A) and (C).

22. The correct answer is (C). The clue is the word *refugee*. The trigger word is *fleeing*. Because the act is hasty and unplanned, both words in the blanks will be synonyms for "surrender" or "give up." That would eliminate choice (A). Choice (B) can be eliminated because the first word isn't a synonym for "surrender." Choice (D) can be eliminated because the second word is not a synonym for "surrender."

23. The correct answer is (A). The clue words are *part of*, and the trigger word is *study*. This shows that you are looking for a part of a whole. All other answers can be eliminated because they don't demonstrate that relationship.

24. **The correct answer is (B).** The clue is in the words *less important.* The trigger words are *when compared to.* The clue and the trigger tell you that the life of an individual seem less important in relationship to the big picture. The first word will be similar in meaning to the phrase "less important" as in not lasting forever. The second word will be similar to the concept of a "big picture," something larger and longer lasting than an individual. Choices (A) and (D) can be eliminated because the two words do not apply to the clue and trigger. Choice (C) can be eliminated because the second word is not similar to the concept of something larger.

25. **The correct answer is (C).** The clue is in the words *downhearted look.* This tells you that the person is "sad." The trigger word is *also.* That shows that the second word is related to the first word. Choice (A) can be eliminated because even though the words are related to one another, they do not correspond to the emotion of sadness. Choices (B) and (D) can be eliminated because the words in each answer do not relate to each another.

26. **The correct answer is (B).** The clue is in the word *psychologist.* That tells you the patient would be described using the terminology of psychology for the first word. The trigger word is *because.* That means the second part of the sentence, including the second word, defines the first word. Choices (A), (C), and (D) can be eliminated because even though the second word in each answer is a synonym for "conspire," the first words are not conditions from which a patient would suffer.

27. **The correct answer is (A).** The clue word is *evil.* The first word that describes "spell" would be an adjective that is a synonym for "evil." The trigger words are *small figurine.* The second word would represent a "small figurine." Choices (B), (C), and (D) can be eliminated because even though the second words in each answer are similar to "small figurine," the first words are opposites of "evil."

28. **The correct answer is (D).** The clue is in the words *Before the time of the internal combustion machine.* That would tell you that a means of transportation other than automotive is being used. The first would be a synonym for "horseback." The trigger word is *appear.* The second word would be a noun for "where riders could appear." Choices (A), (B), and (C) can be eliminated because the first words in each answer are not synonyms for "horseback."

29. **The correct answer is (B).** The clue is in the words *metropolitan life.* The first word would be a word that describes life in the big city, "city-like." The trigger words are *relief from.* The second word will be an adjective that describes settings that are the opposite of city. It would be a synonym for "country-like." Choices (A) and (D) can be eliminated because they don't relate to the clue or the trigger. Choice (C) reverses "city-like" and "country-like."

30. **The correct answer is (C).** The clue is in the words *physically taken advantage of.* This tells you that the first word will be a synonym for "desire." The trigger words are *has led.* This establishes a cause-and-effect relationship and tells you that the second word would be the result of his "desire." Choice (A) can be eliminated because neither word relates to "desire." Choices (B) and (D) can be eliminated because only one of the words relates to "desire."

31. **The correct answer is (A).** The clue is in the words *although* and *minimal.* That tells you the first word is a synonym for the phrase "made the most of." The trigger words are *whereas* and *natural athlete.* That tells you her brother is the opposite. The second word will be a synonym for "wasted." Choices (B), (C), and (D) can be eliminated because they do not relate to the clue and trigger.

32. **The correct answer is (A).** The clue is in the words *business owners.* They are often concerned with "money" as their profit. The first word would be related to "wanting to retain money." The trigger words are *mainly concerned.* The second word would be related to the "monetary" aspects of life. Choice (B) can be eliminated because it is the opposite of concern for personal wealth. Choices (C) and (D) can be eliminated because they have no relationship to "money."

33. **The correct answer is (D).** The clue is in the words *summer* and *freezing.* The first word would be a synonym for "dropped." The trigger words are *back* and *nineties.* The second word would be a synonym for "rising quickly." Choices (A) and (B) can be eliminated because the words do not relate to the clue and trigger. Choice (C) can be eliminated because the words are in reverse order of "rising" and "dropping."

34. **The correct answer is (A).** The clue is in the words *even though.* This tells you that the first word would refer to the boxer "taking punches." The trigger word is *refused.* The second word would refer to the boxer refusing to "give in." Choice (B) can be eliminated because the first word indicates that the boxer is doing well. Choices (C) and (D) can be eliminated because they do not relate to the clue and trigger words.

35. **The correct answer is (D).** The clue is in the words *powerful* and *earthquake.* That tells you the first word would be a synonym for "destruction." The triggers are the words *skyscraper* and *piles.* This means that the second word would be a synonym for "ruins." All other answers can be eliminated because the first word in each answer is not a synonym for "destruction."

36. **The correct answer is (B).** The clue is in the words *debater* and *proofs.* The first word would be a synonym for "present." The trigger words are *make him the winner.* The second word would be a synonym for "effective." All other choices can be eliminated because the second words in each answer are the opposites of "effective."

37. **The correct answer is (C).** The clue is in the words *even though*. The trigger words are *it was enough* and *hurt feelings*. The first word will be a synonym for "late," while the second word will be a synonym for "soothing." Choice (A) can be eliminated because the first word is not a synonym for "late." Choice (B) can be eliminated because the words do not relate to the clue and trigger words. Choice (D) can be eliminated because the words are the opposites of the clue and trigger words.

38. **The correct answer is (A).** The clue is in the words *complimentary reviews*. That tells you the first word is a synonym for "pleased." The trigger words are *however* and *negative ones*. That tells you the second word would be the opposite of pleased, a synonym for "angered." Choices (B) and (C) can be eliminated because the second word in the choice is the opposite of "angered." Choice (D) can be eliminated because the first word in the answer is the opposite of "pleased."

39. **The correct answer is (B).** The clue is in the words *medical malpractice lawsuit*. That tells you the first word will be a synonym for the "person who is suing the doctor." The trigger words are *was seeking*. The second word will be a synonym for "damages." Choice (A) can be eliminated because the first word in the answer is not a synonym for the "person suing." Choice (C) can be eliminated because the words have no relevance to the clue or trigger. Choice (D) can be eliminated because the first word in the answer misrepresents the person doing the suing.

40. **The correct answer is (D).** The clue is in the words *love* and *happily*. That tells you the first word that describes the bride would be a synonym for "beloved." The trigger words are *surely would have been*. The second word would be a synonym for "certain." Choice (A) can be eliminated because the words do not match the clue or trigger. Choices (B) and (C) can be eliminated because the first word in each choice is not a synonym for "beloved."

QUANTITATIVE REASONING

1. **The correct answer is (C).** To round a number to the tenth's place, look at the digit in the hundredth's place. If this digit is 5 or greater, increase the tenth's digit by one.

   Since 9 is greater than 5, 21.49 becomes 21.5.

2. **The correct answer is (C).** To find an average of a set of scores, add the scores and divide the sum by the number of scores.

   $$175 + 155 + 210 = 540$$
   $$540 \div 3 = 180$$

3. **The correct answer is (A).** To rename a percent as a fraction, divide by 100.

   $$62\frac{1}{2} \div 100 = \frac{125}{2} \div \frac{100}{1} = \frac{125}{2} \times \frac{1}{100} = \frac{125}{200} = \frac{5}{8}$$

4. **The correct answer is (A).** $(2b + 5) + (4b - 4) + (3b - 6) = 2b + 4b + 3b + 5 - 4 - 6 = 9b - 5$

5. **The correct answer is (D).** $(-3)^2 - 4(-3) = 9 - 4(-3) = 9 - (-12) = 9 + 12 = 21$

6. **The correct answer is (C).** To solve this problem, begin by setting up a proportion. Let x = the number of ounces of water we are looking for. Then,

$$\frac{\text{water} \rightarrow}{\text{flour} \rightarrow} \frac{40}{100} = \frac{x}{8,025} \qquad \text{Cross-multiply}$$

$$100x = 40 \times 8,025$$
$$100x = 321,000 \quad \text{Divide by 100}$$
$$x = 3,210$$

7. **The correct answer is (D).** The perimeter of the rectangle is equal in length to 8 sides of the squares. Since the perimeter is 80, each side of the square must be 10.

The area of a rectangle is equal to the length $\times$ width. Since the width is 10, and the length is $3(10) = 30$, we have $A = 10 \times 30 = 300$.

8. **The correct answer is (D).** A prime number is a number that is divisible by only itself and 1. Hence,

$72 = 2 \times 2 \times 2 \times 3 \times 3$; 2 and 3 are prime numbers.

9. **The correct answer is (C).** Replace the value of x with -1.

$$\frac{8}{3 - x} = \frac{8}{3 - (-1)} = \frac{8}{3 + 1} = \frac{8}{4} = 2$$

10. **The correct answer is (D).** Let the lesser of the integers equal x. Then, the greater integer is $x + 1$, and we have:

$$x + (x + 1) = 39$$
$$2x + 1 = 39 \quad \text{Subtract 1 from both sides.}$$
$$2x = 38$$
$$x = 19 \quad \text{The lesser integer is 19.}$$

11. **The correct answer is (C).** The perimeter of a square is $4s$. Thus,

$R = 4s$ or

$\dfrac{R}{4} = s$ The area of a square is s^2. Therefore,

$$A = s^2 = \left(\frac{R}{4}\right)^2 = \frac{R^2}{16}$$

12. **The correct answer is (D).** To find the percent of increase, divide the amount of increase by the original amount.

$$143.75 - 125 = 18.75$$

$$\frac{18.75}{125} = .15 = 15\%$$

13. **The correct answer is (D).** $\dfrac{4}{x} - \dfrac{3}{x} = \dfrac{1}{x}$. When the denominators are the same, subtract the numerators.

14. **The correct answer is (B).** Begin by cross-multiplying:

$$\frac{20}{12} = \frac{5}{y}$$
$$20y = 12 \times 5$$
$$20y = 60$$
$$y = 3$$

15. **The correct answer is (C).** $(3a + 5)(2a - 3)$

Multiply the two first terms: $(3a)(2a) = 6a^2$
Multiply the two outer terms: $(3a)(-3) = -9a$
Multiply the two inner terms: $(5)(2a) = 10a$
Multiply the two last terms: $(5)(-3) = -15$
The sum of the resulting products is

$$6a^2 - 9a + 10a - 15 = 6a^2 + a - 15$$

16. **The correct answer is (B).** The product of two fractions between 0 and 1 is always less than both of the original fractions. For example:

$$\frac{1}{2} \times \frac{3}{4} = \frac{3}{8}, \text{ and } \frac{3}{8} \text{ is less than both } \frac{1}{2} \text{ and } \frac{3}{4}.$$

Hence, only choice (B) can be true.

17. **The correct answer is (C).** Try to find two factors of 162, one of which is a perfect square:

$$\sqrt{162} = \sqrt{81 \times 2} = \sqrt{81}\sqrt{2} = 9\sqrt{2}$$

18. **The correct answer is (C).** Let the length of the original rectangle be L and the width be W. Then, the original rectangle has area $A = LW$.

The enlarged rectangle has length $3L$ and width $3W$. Its area is, thus, $(3L)(3W) = 9LW$. Then,

$$\frac{\text{original area}}{\text{enlarged area}} = \frac{LW}{9LW} = \frac{1}{9}.$$ The ratio is 1 to 9.

19. **The correct answer is (A).** Affix zeros to .01 = .0100. Now, compare to .0099.

.0100 > .0099

20. **The correct answer is (C).** All vertical angles are congruent.

21. **The correct answer is (C).** Follow the order of operations:

$$6 \times 5 + 3 = 30 + 3 = 33$$
$$(6 + 5)3 = (11)3 = 33$$

22. **The correct answer is (C).** Solving for y in the given information, we obtain $y = 4$. Similarly, $(-2)^2 = 4$.

23. **The correct answer is (C).** $\dfrac{\frac{1}{4}}{\frac{3}{8}} = \dfrac{1}{4} \div \dfrac{3}{8} = \dfrac{1}{4} \times \dfrac{8}{3} = \dfrac{8}{12} = \dfrac{2}{3}$

$$66\frac{2}{3}\% = \frac{66\frac{2}{3}}{100} = \frac{\frac{200}{3}}{100} = \frac{200}{3} \div \frac{100}{1} = \frac{200}{3} \times \frac{1}{100} = \frac{200}{300} = \frac{2}{3}$$

24. **The correct answer is (A).** The sum of the measures of the angles in a triangle is 180.

$$20 + 20 + (20 + x) = 180$$
$$60 + x = 180$$
$$x = 120$$

25. **The correct answer is (B).** $\dfrac{1}{3} \times \dfrac{3}{5} = \dfrac{3}{15} = \dfrac{1}{5}$

Since $.25 = \dfrac{1}{4}$, the entry in Column B is greater.

26. **The correct answer is (B).** We are given that r is negative. This means that $\dfrac{1}{r}$ is also negative. On the other hand, r^2 will be positive. Any positive number is greater than any negative number.

27. **The correct answer is (B).** $8^2 = 8 \times 8 = 64$

$2^8 = 2 \times 2 \times 2 \times 2 \times 2 \times 2 \times 2 \times 2 = 256$

28. **The correct answer is (C).** We are given that $\dfrac{4}{6} = \dfrac{m}{15}$. To solve for m, cross-multiply.

$$4 \times 15 = 6m$$
$$60 = 6m$$
$$10 = m$$

29. **The correct answer is (C).**

$$\left(\frac{1}{10}\right)^2 = \frac{1}{10} \times \frac{1}{10} = \frac{1}{100} \qquad \left(\frac{1}{10}\right)^3 \times 10 = \frac{1}{10} \times \frac{1}{10} \times \frac{1}{10} \times 10 = \frac{1}{100}$$

30. **The correct answer is (B).** $t° + t° + t° + t° = 180°$

$$4t° = 180°$$
$$t° = 45° \qquad \text{Similarly,}$$
$$q° + q° + q° = 180°$$
$$3q° = 180°$$
$$q° = 60°$$
$$2t° = 90° \qquad 2q° = 120°$$

31. **The correct answer is (B).** $1.89 \times 3 = \$5.67$

   $\$1.49 \times 2 = \$2.98$

   $\$5.67 + \$2.98 = \$8.65 = $ total price of the nuts and pecans. To find the average price per pound, divide by 5:

   $\$8.65 \div 5 = \$1.73$

   In Column B, $\$1.09 + \$2.19 + \$4.75 = \$8.03$. To find the average, divide by 3:

   $\$8.03 \div 3 = \$2.68$

32. **The correct answer is (C).** Given that $x = \dfrac{1}{2}$, we compute

   $$x^2 + x = \left(\frac{1}{2}\right)^2 + \frac{1}{2} = \frac{1}{4} + \frac{1}{2} = \frac{3}{4}$$

   $$\left(\frac{\sqrt{3}}{2}\right)^2 = \frac{(\sqrt{3})^2}{2^2} = \frac{3}{4}$$

33. **The correct answer is (C).** The formula for the area of a circle is $A = \pi r^2$. If the radius is 10, then the area is $A = \pi(10)^2 = 100\pi$.

   The formula for the circumference of a circle is $C = \pi D$. If the diameter is 100, we have $C = 100\pi$.

34. **The correct answer is (B).** If we multiply both sides by $3\sqrt{7}$, then Column A becomes:

   $$\frac{\sqrt{7}}{3} \times 3\sqrt{7} = \sqrt{7} \times \sqrt{7} = 7,$$

   while Column B becomes

   $$\frac{3}{\sqrt{7}} \times 3\sqrt{7} = 9.$$

35. **The correct answer is (A).** Since there are 180° in a triangle, $m\angle 1 + m\angle 2 + m\angle 3 = 180$.

   Since $\angle 3$ and $\angle 4$ are supplementary, $m\angle 3 + m\angle 4 = 180$. Overall, then, $m\angle 1 + m\angle 2 + m\angle 3 = m\angle 3 + m\angle 4$. Subtract $\angle 3$ from both sides. $m\angle 1 + m\angle 2 = m\angle 4$. Since $m\angle 1 > 0°$, we must have $m\angle 2 < m\angle 4$.

READING COMPREHENSION

Passage 1

1. **The correct answer is (C).** Antony is the name of a character from one of Shakespeare's plays. Choices (A), (B), and (D) are critics mentioned who provide opinions of Hamlet and his character.

2. **The correct answer is (A).** Choice (D) is the best of the wrong answers but it is not supported by the context. Choices (B) and (C) are inappropriate.

3. **The correct answer is (A).** The passage provides multiple responses to Hamlet's character. Choice (C) is contradicted at the beginning of the passage, and choices (B) and (D) are overridden by other details provided.

4. **The correct answer is (C).** In the last paragraph, he refers to "we . . . as critics." Choice (D) is the closest of the other responses, but the passage is not a review of the play. Choices (A) and (B) are inappropriate.

Passage 2

5. **The correct answer is (D).** The passage illustrates a number of ways mechanical weathering occurs. Choice (A) is too general to be the best title of this passage. Choice (B) is incorrect because there are other ways rocks can change. Choice (C) refers to only two of the four types of changes discussed.

6. **The correct answer is (A).** This specific detail is provided in paragraph 2. Choices (B), (C), and (D) are examples of weathering processes, but none are equal to choice (A) in damage production.

7. **The correct answer is (D).** The details are provided for us in paragraph 3. The other answers are all inappropriate.

8. **The correct answer is (B).** This is discussed in the final paragraph. Choice (A) is close, but it refers to only one type of outcrop. Choices (C) and (D) are both inappropriate.

9. **The correct answer is (B).** The synonym is provided in the paragraph discussing ice wedging. Choice (A) is often connected to frost action but it is not the same. Choices (C) and (D) are inappropriate.

Passage 3

10. **The correct answer is (D).** We wait with Napoleon for the Emperor to speak but he says nothing. Choice (C) is the closest of the other responses and is a secondary effect of what was occurring while Napoleon was waiting. Choices (A) and (B) are incorrect.

11. **The correct answer is (B).** The passage concentrates on the horrors of Napoleon's invasion of Russia. Choice (D) is the best of the wrong answers but it is not specific enough of a title. Choices (A) and (C) are incorrect.

12. **The correct answer is (C).** The final paragraph provides the necessary information to answer the question. Choices (A), (B), and (D) are all contradicted by details in the passage.

13. **The correct answer is (A).** Choices (B), (C), and (D) are incorrect.

Passage 4

14. **The correct answer is (C).** The answer is tricky—meters are converted to yards. Choice (D) means to stand still, and choices (A) and (B) are incorrect.

15. **The correct answer is (B).** This tests your ability to read for details. Choices (A), (C), and (D) are inappropriate.

16. **The correct answer is (D).** The answer is clearly stated in the last paragraph. Choices (A), (B), and (C) confuse the details.

17. **The correct answer is (A).** The information that gives us this answer is in the last paragraph. Choices (B), (C), and (D) are inappropriate.

Passage 5

18. **The correct answer is (D).** This reflects the theme of the entire poem. Choice (C) is inappropriate, while choices (A) and (B) are virtual synonyms.

19. **The correct answer is (A).** The roads are the "roads of life"—one can never return to the same time when one has made a choice. There are tinges of loss in this poem, and choice (D) is close to the right answer. Choices (B) and (C) are inappropriate.

20. **The correct answer is (B).** The speaker will take the road that "wanted wear"—in other words, was less traveled. Choices (A), (C), and (D) do not reflect the tone of the poem.

21. **The correct answer is (C).** The speaker wants to believe that the road is still available even though he knows he may never return. Choice (B) is closest to the correct answer; the speaker thinks he is special for going down a "less traveled" road. Choices (A) and (D) are inappropriate.

22. **The correct answer is (D).** The speaker laments having to make choices. Choices (A) and (C) are close but are not confirmed by the rest of the stanza. Choice (B) is inappropriate.

Passage 6

23. **The correct answer is (B).** The answer is provided in the first paragraph, which states that South Dakota became the 40th state after North Dakota became the 39th. Choice (A) is contradicted in the same paragraph, and choices (C) and (D) are incorrect.

24. **The correct answer is (D).** The detail is provided in paragraph 2. Choices (A), (B), and (C) are inappropriate.

25. **The correct answer is (A).** The question determines your ability to couple details to provide an answer. Choices (B), (C), and (D) are incorrect.

26. **The correct answer is (D).** This question demands an ability to seek a second level of response. In paragraph 1 we are told that Minnesota is east, but paragraph 2 tells us that the Red River is on the North Dakota-Minnesota border. Choices (A), (B), and (C) are incorrect.

Passage 7

27. **The correct answer is (D).** This question asks if you can read for the right detail. Choices (A), (B), and (C) are all contradicted by facts in the passage.

28. **The correct answer is (B).** In order for rock to contain the oil, it must be equivalent to a closed lid. Choices (A) and (D) refer to types of rock mentioned in the passage and choice (C) plays on the root of the word.

29. **The correct answer is (A).** Seawater and oil may be lodged in the same area, but they are not both hydrocarbons. Choices (B), (C), and (D) are listed in paragraph 1.

30. **The correct answer is (B).** This tests your ability to read for detail; this fact is mentioned in the second paragraph. Choices (A), (C), and (D) are inappropriate.

Passage 8

31. **The correct answer is (D).** The use of repetition underscores the power of this phrase. Choice (A) is too general; this is the tale of one woman. Choices (B) and (C) refer to elements in the passage only.

32. **The correct answer is (C).** The author is eager for her father to see her as more than just a girl and we infer that she is sad that he cannot recognize her efforts. Choices (B) and (D) are close—there is a touch of anger here but it is not the overriding tone of the passage. Choice (A) is inappropriate.

33. **The correct answer is (A).** The loss of his son creates an empty space in the father's heart. Choice (B) is the closest of the other answers—but a vessel is not always empty. Choices (C) and (D) are inappropriate.

34. **The correct answer is (D).** We can infer that she will continue to show the determination she showed in this passage. Choice (A) is a possible response that is not supported by the tone or details of the passage. Choices (B) and (C) refer to details in the passage but we would be wrong to assume they have such large importance.

35. **The correct answer is (A).** We must infer by the father's pleasure at his daughter's prize that there must be some warmth between them. There is nothing in the passage to suggest choices (B), (C), or (D).

Passage 9

36. **The correct answer is (C).** The "slowly moving stream" is England's pace of living. Choice (B) is its opposite, and choices (A) and (D) are inappropriate.

37. **The correct answer is (A).** You can see that most of the sentences start with an "If . . ." clause and end with a "they do . . ." clause with the opposite information. Choice (C) is incorrect but you should look up the words. Choice (B) is true about the entire paragraph but not individual sentences. Choice (D) is inappropriate.

38. **The correct answer is (A).** This refers to the high level of craftsmanship exhibited by the makers. Choice (D) is closest since "industry" also has the meaning of an individual who works hard (but who is not necessarily "ingenious"). Choices (B) and (C) are both inappropriate.

39. **The correct answer is (D).** This is discussed clearly in the last paragraph. Even though the passage concentrates on England, other parts of Europe are referred to. Choice (A) is wrong because the passage never refers to other countries. Choice (B) is wrong because it occurred before the Industrial Revolution, and choice (C) is never mentioned in the passage.

40. **The correct answer is (D).** This is suggested in the last paragraph. Choice (C) is contradicted in the passages, as are choices (A) and (B).

MATH ACHIEVEMENT

1. **The correct answer is (D).**

Factor out each of the given possibilities.

The factors of 20 are $2 \times 2 \times 5$.

The factors of 45 are $3 \times 3 \times 5$.

The factors of 65 are 5×13.

The factors of 90 are $2 \times 3 \times 3 \times 5$.

Since $6 = 2 \times 3$, 90 has factors of 6 and 5.

2. **The correct answer is (A).** Translate the sentence into a mathematical equation, then solve.

$$x - 6 = \frac{2}{3}x$$

$$x - \frac{2}{3}x = 6$$

$$\frac{1}{3}x = 6$$

$$x = 6\left(\frac{3}{1}\right) = 18$$

3. **The correct answer is (C).** To subtract algebraic expressions, change the signs of the subtrahend and use the rules for addition.

$$(3a^3 - 6) - (2a^2 + 1) = (3a^3 - 6) + (-2a^2 - 1) = 3a^3 - 2a^2 - 7$$

4. **The correct answer is (B).**

$$score = \frac{\# \, correct}{\# \, questions}; \quad 88\% = \frac{88}{100} = .88$$

$$.88 = \frac{n}{25}$$

$$n = .88 \times 25 = 22$$

5. **The correct answer is (C).** The perimeter of a square is $4s$. With side length $= 5$, the perimeter is $4(5) = 20$.

The perimeter of a rectangle is $2L + 2W$. With length $= 6$ and width $= 5$, the perimeter is $2(6) + 2(5) = 12 + 10 = 22$.

The difference between the perimeters is $22 - 20 = 2$.

6. **The correct answer is (B).** Four students make up one fifth of a class.

    Translating this into a mathematical equation, you get $\frac{1}{5}c = 4$.

    $$c = 4\left(\frac{5}{1}\right) = 20$$

7. **The correct answer is (B).**

    35% of $N = 70$. Divide the known part of the fractional equivalent of the percent.

    $$35\% = \frac{35}{100}$$

    $$70 \div \frac{35}{100}$$

    $$70 \times \frac{100}{35} \quad \text{Multiply by the reciprocal.}$$

    $$= 2 \times 100 = 200$$

8. **The correct answer is (C).**

    $$A = \frac{1}{2}bh$$

    $$b = \sqrt{10^2 - 5^2} = \sqrt{100 - 25} = \sqrt{75} = 5\sqrt{3}$$

    $$\frac{1}{2}(10)(5\sqrt{3}) = 25\sqrt{3}$$

9. **The correct answer is (A).**

    Let x = number of hours to complete a job (father).

    $\frac{1}{x}$ rate of work (father)

    Let $2x$ = number of hours to complete a job (son).

    $\frac{1}{2x}$ rate of work (son)

    (rate of work) $\times$ (time of work) = part of job done

    $$\frac{1}{x}(6) + \frac{1}{2x}(6) = 1 \text{ job (completed)}$$

    Multiply by $2x$: $2x\left(\dfrac{6}{x} + \dfrac{6}{2x} = 1\right)$

    $$\frac{12x}{x} + \frac{12x}{2x} = 2x$$

    Simplify: $12 + 6 = 2x$

    $$18 = 2x$$

    $$2x = 18$$

    Divide by 2: $x = 9$ (hours for father to complete the job alone)

    $2x = 18$ (hours for son to complete job alone)

10. **The correct answer is (B).** This is a problem in division.

$$\begin{array}{r} 15. \\ 12.6\overline{)189.0} \\ \underline{126} \\ 630 \\ \underline{630} \end{array}$$

11. **The correct answer is (A).**

Let d represent David's age now and $d + 5$ represent David's age 5 years from now.

Let p represent Paul's age now and $p + 5$ represent Paul's age 5 years from now.

Set up mathematical equations for the problem.

$d = p + 5$

$d + 5 = 2p$

Substitute the value of d in the first equation into the second equation to find p.

$$(p + 5) + 5 = 2p$$
$$p + 10 = 2p$$
$$p = 10$$

Therefore, $d = 10 + 5 = 15$.

12. **The correct answer is (C).**

$$3x - 9 = 45$$
$$3x = 54$$
$$x = 18$$
$$18 \div 9 = 2$$

13. **The correct answer is (A).**

Rearrange the fractions to make it easier to solve by combining fractions with like denominators.

$$\frac{1}{2} - \frac{1}{2} + \frac{2}{3} - \frac{1}{3} - \frac{1}{3} + \frac{3}{4} - \frac{1}{4}$$

The first five fractions subtract to zero, leaving:

$$\frac{3}{4} - \frac{1}{4} = \frac{2}{4} = \frac{1}{2}$$

14. **The correct answer is (D).**

Round $19.95 to $20.00 and find 60% of 20.

$$60\% = \frac{60}{100} = 0.6$$

$$0.6 \times 20 = 12$$

15. **The correct answer is (A).** Add like monomials and add coefficients.

$$
\begin{aligned}
2b &+ 5 \\
4b &- 4 \\
+3b &- 6 \\
\hline
9b &- 5
\end{aligned}
$$

16. **The correct answer is (B).** In a parallelogram, opposite angles are congruent; therefore, $m\angle B = m\angle D$, $m\angle D = 75°$.

17. **The correct answer is (B).** Set up a ratio for this problem and solve.

l represents the number of laser discs purchased with d dollars $\left(\dfrac{l}{d}\right)$.

10 laser discs can be purchased for x dollars $\left(\dfrac{10}{x}\right)$. So,

$$\frac{l}{d} = \frac{10}{x}$$

$$lx = 10d \quad \text{(using cross-multiplication)}$$

$$\frac{10d}{l} = x$$

18. **The correct answer is (B).**

Here, we must find the base. $B = \dfrac{P}{R} = \dfrac{124}{.08} = 1{,}550$

19. **The correct answer is (A).**

To determine if a number is divisible by 9, the sum of the digits in that number will equal a number divisible by 9. The sum of the digits in 42,042 is $4 + 2 + 0 + 4 + 2 = 12$. By adding 6 to this number, the sum of the digits will equal $18 = 1 + 8 = 9$ and therefore be divisible by 9.

20. **The correct answer is (D).**

Solving inequalities is very similar to solving equations.

$$5x + 7 - 7 \geq x - 1 - 7$$

$$5x - x \geq x - 8 - x$$

$$\frac{4x}{4} \geq \frac{-8}{4}$$

$$x \geq -2$$

21. **The correct answer is (C).**

Find two factors of 28, one of which is a perfect square. Then simplify the perfect square and multiply.

$$\frac{1}{2}\sqrt{4}\sqrt{7} = \frac{1}{2}\sqrt{2 \times 2}\sqrt{7} = \frac{1}{2}(2)\sqrt{7} = 1\sqrt{7} = \sqrt{7}$$

22. **The correct answer is (B).** A circle has a radius of 10 units. The area of the curve is $\frac{1}{4}$ that of the entire circle.

$$A = \pi r^2$$

$$A \text{ of } \frac{1}{4} \text{ circle} = \frac{1}{4}\pi(10)^2 = \frac{1}{4}\pi(100) = 25\pi$$

23. **The correct answer is (C).** To score an average of 90 on 4 exams, the total of the 4 exams added together must be $90 \times 4 = 360$. On her first 3 exams, Randi has scored a total of $85 + 81 + 95 = 261$. $360 - 261 = 99$. Therefore, she needs 99 points on her last exam.

24. **The correct answer is (A).**

$$3x - 6 = 10x - 11$$
$$3x = 10x - 5$$
$$-7x = -5$$
$$x = \frac{-5}{-7} = \frac{5}{7}$$

25. **The correct answer is (A).** If $x < y$ and $y < z$, then $x < z$. If one number is less than the second number, and the second number is less than the third number, then the first number is less than the third number.

26. **The correct answer is (B).**

If $g(x) = 2x^2 - 4x + 5$, then $g(3) = 2(3)^2 - 4(3) + 5 = 18 - 12 + 5 = 11$.

27. **The correct answer is (C).**

Use the formula: $A = \frac{1}{2}bh$

$$75 = \frac{1}{2}(25)h$$

$$\frac{75}{12.5} = \frac{12.5h}{12.5}$$

$6 \text{ inches} = h$

28. **The correct answer is (B).**

To rename a decimal as a percent, multiply the decimal by 100.

$.09 \times 100 = 9.00 = 9\%$

29. The correct answer is (D).

Begin by determining the slope of $3x - 6y = 12$ by writing it in slope-intercept form.

$$3x - 6y = 12$$
$$6y = 3x - 12$$
$$y = \frac{1}{2}x - 2$$

Thus, the slope of the equation is $\frac{1}{2}$. The line we are looking for must also have that slope because parallel lines have the same slopes.

Using the point-slope form, the line is:

$$m(x - x_1) = (y - y_1), \text{ or}$$
$$\frac{1}{2}(x - 2) = (y - 3)$$
$$(x - 2) = 2(y - 3)$$
$$x - 2 = 2y - 6$$
$$x - 2y = -4$$

30. The correct answer is (B).

Let $x =$ the height of the tree. The product of the means equals the product of the extremes.

$$\text{(objects)} \; \frac{6 \text{ ft.}}{x \text{ ft.}} = \frac{8 \text{ ft.}}{20 \text{ ft.}} \; \text{(shadows)}$$
$$8x = (6)(20) = 120$$

Divide by 8: $x = 15$ ft.

31. The correct answer is (B). To find the average of several numbers, find the sum and divide by the number of items.

$$\frac{2 + x}{2} = 7$$
$$2 + x = 14$$
$$x = 12$$

32. The correct answer is (A).

First calculate roots, then subtract.

$$\sqrt{16} = 4$$
$$\sqrt[3]{27} = 3$$
$$4 - 3 = 1$$

33. The correct answer is (B).

A prime number is a number that is divisible by itself and by 1. Hence, $64 = 8 \times 8 = 2 \times 2 \times 2 \times 2 \times 2 \times 2 \rightarrow 2$ is a prime number.

34. The correct answer is (D).

First find the area of the square.

$A = s^2$

$\quad = 4^2 = 16$ sq. cm.

Then, use the formula: $A = \pi r^2$

$\quad 16 \approx (3.14)r^2$

$\quad 5.10 \approx r^2$

$\quad \sqrt{5.10} \approx r$

$\quad 2.3$ cm. $\approx r$

35. The correct answer is (D).

The perimeter of the square $= 4s$.

$P = 4s = 4(2x + 2) = 8x + 8$

The perimeter of the equilateral triangle is $3s$.

$\quad P = 3s = 3(4x) = 12x$

$8x + 8 = 12x$

$\quad\quad 8 = 4x$

$\quad\quad 2 = x$

36. The correct answer is (C).

Find two factors of 250, one of which is a perfect square.

$\sqrt{250} = \sqrt{25 \times 10}$

$\quad\quad = \sqrt{25}\sqrt{10}$ Simplify the perfect square.

$\sqrt{25} = 5$

$\quad\quad = 5\sqrt{10}$

37. The correct answer is (D).

This problem can be solved very easily using a proportion.

$$\frac{4 \text{ inches}}{15 \text{ miles}} = \frac{5 \text{ inches}}{x \text{ miles}}$$

After cross-multiplication, this proportion becomes:

$\quad 4x = 75$

$\quad\quad x = 18\frac{3}{4}$

38. **The correct answer is (C).**

Convert all measurements to the same units, such as inches. 3 feet is 36 inches.

We now have the ratio 5 inches to 36 inches, expressed as $\frac{5}{36}$.

39. **The correct answer is (A).**

$y = -5x + 4$

$y = -5(1) + 4$

$y = -5 + 4 = -1$

40. **The correct answer is (B).** When dividing terms, subtract the exponents. You can see this by expanding:

Remember x^5 is $x \times x \times x \times x \times x$ and

x^7 is $x \times x \times x \times x \times x \times x \times x$. Then divide.

This is the basis for the rules of exponents.

$$\frac{4 \times x \times x \times x \times x \times x}{3 \times x \times x \times x \times x \times x \times x \times x} = \frac{4}{3x^2}$$

41. **The correct answer is (B).** To express a percent as a decimal, divide by 100. To express a decimal as a percent, multiply by 100. Literally, percent ("per cent") means "per hundred."

$.0825 \times 100 = 8.25$

42. **The correct answer is (D).**

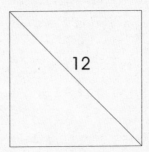

If the diagonal of a square is 12, then (by the Pythagorean Theorem), the sides of the square must be $\frac{12}{\sqrt{2}} = \frac{12\sqrt{2}}{2} = 6\sqrt{2}$. Square this to get the area of 72.

43. **The correct answer is (C).** Rename all fractions as decimal equivalents:

$$\frac{3}{5} = .6 \qquad \frac{4}{5} = .8$$

$$\frac{5}{6} = .8333 \qquad \frac{17}{20} = .85$$

$$\frac{7}{10} = .7 \qquad \frac{13}{15} = .8666$$

$\dfrac{7}{10}$ is the only fraction between $\dfrac{3}{5}$ and $\dfrac{4}{5}$.

44. **The correct answer is (A).** Point D is vertically aligned with A's x-coordinate, 1, and horizontally aligned with C's y-coordinate, 4.

45. **The correct answer is (B).**

Using the formula for circumference, $C = \pi d$

$= (3.14)(9)$

$= 28.26$ inches ≈ 28 inches

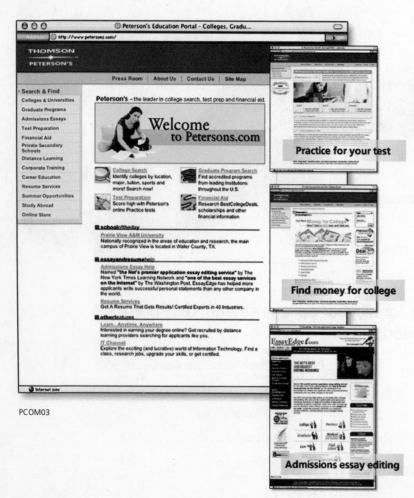